Resources and Regional Development in India

Resources and Regional Development in India

Festschrift in Honour of Professor Baleshwar Thakur

Edited by
RAMESHWAR THAKUR
INDER JEET
RAJESH KUMAR ABHAY
SWATI THAKUR

RAWAT PUBLICATIONS
Jaipur • New Delhi • Bangalore • Hyderabad • Guwahati • Kolkata

ISBN 978-81-316-0641-4

Published by
Prem Rawat for **Rawat Publications**
Satyam Apts, Sector 3, Jawahar Nagar, Jaipur 302 004 (India)
Phone: 0141 265 1748 / 7006 Fax: 0141 265 1748
E-mail: info@rawatbooks.com
Website: www.rawatbooks.com

New Delhi Office
4858/24, Ansari Road, Daryaganj, New Delhi 110 002
Phone: 011 2326 3290

Also at *Bangalore, Hyderabad, Guwahati* and *Kolkata*

Typeset by Rawat Computers, Jaipur
Printed at Chaman Enterprises, New Delhi

Contents

Preface

A while ago, teachers, research scholars and students of Delhi University approached us to edit a book in honour of Professor Baleshwar Thakur who has contributed and devoted 45 years of his scholarship and devotion to the field of urban and resource development. His contribution to the corpus of knowledge in these fields is well recognized. During this period he has taught us, inspired us and challenged us to be real and authentic geographers. We have, therefore, great pleasure in bringing out this book *Resources and Regional Development in India* to felicitate Professor Baleshwar Thakur.

It is a book that sums up a rich and eventful life of an academician who has made a place in the hearts and minds of all those who came in touch with him. We not only regard him for his dedicated service to his discipline, but above all, also admire him for the human qualities that endeavours him to one and all.

With the help of well-wishers, friends and his students, we are able to bring out this felicitation volume within the stipulated time frame. The book contains 26 articles on various aspects of resource and regional development which have been classified into two sections. The variety of scholars drawn from teachers, researchers, administrators and consultants who have contributed to this book, reflects the charismatic aura of Baleshwar Thakur. The book will be useful to academicians and researchers working in the fields of resource and regional development and different combinations of these disciplines. As his students, colleagues and authors, we feel great pleasure to see through the publication of this book to honour a scholar of eminence, a great teacher, and researcher and, above all, an excellent human being. He is a person committed to help build space for others. We wish Baleshwar Thakur a very happy, long, healthy and active life.

In the 21st century, geography is observed as a dynamic discipline with many roles in society. It is ushering in vitality and purpose. It is an interactive science that examines many ways. The changes in the tools and the methodologies of the discipline have positioned geography in the space age on a global scale. Geographers contribution to adjust their bases on the world through the use of both traditional methodologies and newly emerging technologies at global positions for the 21st century are also discussed in the chapters of the book. The chapters in this book are written by geographers and people engaged with geographic research and professional work. Each chapter is represented in a similar format with author's present research and focuses on the geographic topic of the 21st century. This is followed by a look at the future, with speculation and prediction regarding the further development of the discipline. Each author attempts to anticipate the future of this discipline. It takes intellectual courage to conjecture about the future, but each chapter provides a thoughtful consideration for the role of geography in the future.

Geography and its diversity that are produced through the content and methodologies within each topic by the authors are giving further evidence of the work of scholars and professionals. In each topic, author demonstrates the role of geography through the causes of that particular topic. The reader will be breath taken at the depth of scholarship that is characteristic of the discipline of geography.

Rameshwar Thakur
Inder Jeet
Rajesh Kumar Abhay
Swati Thakur

Professor Baleshwar Thakur (b. 16 July 1943)

Professor Baleshwar Thakur

A Biographical Profile

Baleshwar Thakur was born on 16 July 1943 at Sarabe village of Madhubani district in Bihar. He is the elder among two brothers. His father Late Shivanandan Thakur and mother Late Sanjha Devi took special care of young Baleshwar by providing good education in Madhubani and Patna. Married Chanda Thakur in 1962 and have two sons (Dr. Sudhir Thakur, Ph.D. (Ohio State), Dr. Rajiv Ranjan Thakur, Ph.D. (Indiana State). His understanding wife *Chanda* managed home front efficiently and provided congenial environment for academic work. Her continuous support proved worthy that he reached to greater heights in the academic aura.

Baleshwar, nicknamed as 'Bale', was brought up in an agricultural surroundings which ultimately paved his way to higher studies. He received his school education at Khajauli and intermediate education at R.K. College, Madhubani under Bihar University in 1960 and was placed in the top ten merit list in University and first position in the college. He obtained first class both in B.A. Hons. (1962) and M.A. (1964) in Geography from Patna University and got merit scholarships in Humanities. He obtained his second M.A. in Geography from University of Waterloo, Canada, where he was a Commonwealth Scholar and worked with Professor Lorne H. Russwurm on "The Changing Functional Makeup of Central Place Hierarchies in Southwestern Ontario: 1871–1971", during 1970–72. He obtained his Ph.D. from Patna University in 1978 on "Urban Settlements in Eastern India: Entropy Changes and Pattern Analysis", under the guidance of Professor P. Dayal, former Vice-Chancellor of Magadh University.

He retired as a Professor of Geography at Delhi School of Economics, University of Delhi, where he served as Head of the Department during 1996–99. He was also the Vice-Chancellor of L.N. Mithila University, Darbhanga (Bihar) during 2001–03. Before joining the University of Delhi as Reader in 1980, he taught at the Universities of Ranchi (1964–65) and Patna (1965–80). He was Visiting Fulbright Scholar at the University of Akron in USA (1992) and again Visiting Professor of Geography and Planning at the same university in 2000, where he had the privilege of working with an eminent Urban Geographer Professor Ashok K. Dutt on Urban Structure and Processes in India. Professor Thakur has behind him 45 years of teaching and research experience at the universities of Ranchi, Patna and Delhi, Waterloo, York (Canada), Akron and North Dakota (USA). He has successfully supervised 20 Ph.D. Thesis, 34 M. Phil. and 62 M.A. dissertations on resource management and urban development issues.

Professor Thakur's main research interest has been in areas of Resource Utilization, Natural Hazards and Resource Management, Political Economy and Ecology of Resource Depletion, Sustainable Development of Natural Resources, Urban Development Issues and Indian Geography. His significant research contribution lies in measuring hierarchical and functional stability and change of central places in southwestern Ontario. In this study, he found that the centralization of urban system as a whole appears to be more efficiently organized and on that basis, it could be predicted as well. He also identified the centre-periphery dichotomy in the evolution of urban pattern as well as in the development of regional urban systems in eastern India based on entropy analysis. In Natural Resource Management, he has worked on micro-scale water supply demand comparisons, decision making, institutional arrangements and watershed management. He has contributed over 110 research papers in both national and international journals and authored and co-edited numerous books.

Professor Thakur has been actively associated with and devoted to the cause of Earth System Sciences of the Indian Science Congress Association for over three decades and has served the Sectional Committee as its recorder (1990–92) and as Local Secretary (1997) in the ISCA held at Delhi. His name is familiar among geographers and geologists in India and abroad due to his decade-long association with the National Association of Geographers, India (NAGI) as Joint Secretary (1990–95), and Secretary General (1996–2002). Besides, he has been associated as Treasurer (1984–88), Editor (1988–94) and President (1994–98) of the Association for Geographical Studies, University of Delhi, President of Earth System Sciences Section, 88th India Science Congress Association (2000–01), National Association of Geographers, India (NAGI) (2003–04), Institute of Indian Geographers (IIG) (2012–13), Vice President of Indian Council of Geographers (1990–94), Institute of Indian Geographers (1995–97), Indian Regional Science Association (1997–98) and Indian Institute of Geomorphologists (1998–2000) and as Chairman of the Commission on Natural Hazards and Resource Management, NAGI (1993–98).

Professor Thakur's significant contribution in the field of Urban Geography earned him the position of a Member of the International Board of Directors of Asian Urban Research Association. He is also on the editorial board of *Indian Geographical Journal, Journal of Region, Health and Health Care, The East–West Geographer, The Social Profile, Aryabhatta Research Journal of Physical Sciences and Regional Symbiosis.* He has been member of the Governing Board of A.N. Sinha Institute of Social Studies (1994–96), Bhim Rao Ambedkar College (1992–95), Shivaji College (1997–99) and Rajdhani College (1999) of Delhi University, as also of the Board of Research Studies of Kurukshetra University; Banaras Hindu University; Maharshi Dayanand University; Chaudhary Charan Singh University; Himachal Pradesh University and Sri Sahuji Maharaj Kanpur University. He was also a member of Academic Council, University of Delhi for a three year term (1996–99). After the retirement in 2008, he has been engaged as a member of academic and executive council in the Central University of Ranchi and Kerala (2009–12) for their curriculum development.

He has worked extensively for the popularization of geography. He was the first Indian Geographer to be interviewed for a video talk on Indian Geographers (Geographers on Film) as part of a venture of 27th International Geographical Union (IGU) meet at Washington DC in August, 1992. He has presented papers at numerous workshops, refresher courses, seminars and conferences. He has also organized four national and international conferences.

Professor Thakur's Academic Journey

Assistant Professor	Ranchi University	1964–65
Assistant Professor	Patna University	1965–80
Commonwealth Research Scholar	University of Waterloo, Canada	1970–72
Associate Professor	University of Delhi	1980–90
Professor	University of Delhi	1990–2008
Fulbright Visiting Scholar	University of Akron, USA	1992
Head	Department of Geography Delhi School of Economics, University of Delhi	1996–99
Visiting Professor	Department of Geography and Planning University of Akron, Akron, Ohio, USA	2000
Vice-Chancellor	L.N. Mithila University, Darbhanga (Bihar)	2001–03
Shastri Indo–Canadian Fellow	Department of Geography York University, Toronto, Canada	2004

Books Published

1979 Thakur, B. *Urban Settlements in Eastern India: Entropy Changes and Pattern Analysis*, New Delhi: Concept.

1989 Thakur, B. (Editor) Dimensions of Geographical Research: Abstract of M.Phil. Dissertation and Ph.D. Theses submitted to the University of Delhi (1959–88), AGS Monograph No. 1, Department of Geography, University of Delhi.

2000 Noble, A.G., B. Thakur, A.B. Mukerji, F.J. Costa (Editors) *Geographic and Planning Research Themes for the New Millennium*, New Delhi: Vikas Publishing Pvt. Ltd.

2002 Tandon, S.K. and B. Thakur (Editors) *Recent Advances in Geomorphology, Quaternary Geology and Environmental Geosciences*, New Delhi: Manisha Publications.

2003 Jha, S., M. Thakur and B. Thakur (Editors) *Dimensions of Society and Culture of Bihar*, Allahabad: Academy Press.

2003 –14 Thakur, B. (Editor) *Perspectives in Resource Management in Developing Countries*, Vol. 1: Resource Management: Theory and Techniques; Vol. 2: Population, Resources and Development; Vol. 3: Ecological Degradation of Land; Vol. 4: Land Appraisal and Development; Vol. 5: Soil Deterioration and Conservation; Vol. 6: Water Supply and Quality; Vol. 7: Water Utilization and Management; Vol. 8: Groundwater Assessment and Development; Vol. 9: Bio-Resource Depletion and Conservation; Vol. 10: Environmental Hazards.

2004 Thakur, B., V.N.P. Sinha, M. Prasad, N. Sharma, R. Pratap, R.B. Mandal and R.B.P. Singh (Editors) *Urban and Regional Development in India*, 2 Vols, New Delhi: Concept.

2005 Thakur, B. (Editor) *Geography in Delhi: Research Themes and Perspectives*, AGS Publication No. 3, Department of Geography, University of Delhi, New Delhi: Manisha Publications.

2007 Thakur, B., G. Pomeroy, C. Cusak, and S.K. Thakur (Editors) *City, Society and Planning*, 3 Vols., New Delhi: Concept.

2009 Kumar, A., R.A. Kushwaha and B. Thakur (Editors) *Earth System Sciences*, 2 Vols., New Delhi: Concept.

2011 Thakur, B. *Depletion and Degradation of Land Resources in India*, Series Editor: L.R. Singh, Allahabad: R.N. Dubey Foundation.

2012 Dutt, A.K., V. Wadhwa, B. Thakur and Frank J. Costa (Editors) *Facets of Social Geography: International and Indian Perspectives*, New Delhi: Cambridge University Press of India.

2014 Thakur, B., H.S. Sharma, Suresh Misra, S.K. Chattopadhyay and Surendra Singh (Editors) *Regional Development Theory and Practice: Emerging Perspectives*, New Delhi: Concept.

2014 Ram, L.N. and B. Thakur (Editors) *Resources and Development in India*, 2 Vols, New Delhi: Concept. (Forthcoming)

Tribute to a Guru

Mentor, guide and a true teacher is what Professor Thakur professes. From examinations to appointments, class lectures to presidential and keynote addresses, seminars to workshops, occasional writings to scholarly books, Professor Thakur performed multiplicity of roles incumbent upon a committed academician. In the Department of Geography, paradigm shift and resource management were his pet concepts. His lectures in loud and clear voice have always impressed students. Abundance of material to write and study shows the reservoir of knowledge he possesses. A geographer even called him as 'bibliography', as he always quoted significant number of references for any particular topic. Huge amount of words written on blackboard explain the impression of knowledge that Professor Thakur has. The 'O my goodness' (*takiya kalam*) always support his long-long sentences explaining the difficult concepts of geography using simple words with stories. An avid admirer of the book *Explanation in Geography*, he would so often ask his students to go and at least touch this classic work by David Harvey. His liking for *Chholey Bhature* of Kamla Nagar and chowmein of D'School Cafeteria is well-known. He would so often tell us how harmful the coffee is by comparing that one coffee equals to twelve cups of tea.

He would always encourage, inspire and suggest the students to write a single book on the regional geography of their native place. Constantly press them to read the *AAAG* and *The Professional Geographer* journal or at least should go to Ratan Tata Library and read the title of the articles published in these journals. Always push Hindi medium students to write in English saying that it doesn't matter if they will write 'is' against 'are', because the meaning will be understood by the teachers.

Despite his retirement in 2008 from active service, he has been continuously contributing to this academic discipline through books and papers. His commitment to the subject, contributions to the area of knowledge and love for the students prompted us to pay our respect to him.

He is supremely balanced and soft-spoken, possessing a distinct nobility of his own. Even at the height of his academic and professional fame, he continues to be a dedicated teacher, devoted researcher, philosopher and guide to his students. He has yet to give much to the discipline. He continues to be the light of inspiration for the geographers of present time as well as of the future.

The present personality review of Professor Thakur's academic life and work indeed remains partial. It is indeed very difficult to reveal his multi-faceted genius and academic contribution in perspective.

Introduction and Overview

This book intends to explore the resource issues and regional development in India. Most geography texts and monographs address the role of natural resources in the development of country in much detail. It is evident that the environmental and allied problems faced by the developing countries are considerably different from those occurring in industrialized economies/countries. Mostly, rural population depends on the direct exploitation of natural resources for agriculture, livestock raising, fishing, basic materials and fuel, both to meet their own subsistence requirements as well as in the market for income. The lack of basic water supply, sanitation, land and other infrastructure services is highly valued by many households. Rapid change in land use has meant that many natural environments and habitats are disappearing quickly, with the result that critical ecological resources and functions are being disrupted or lost. Growing population has further increased the demand for use of natural resource for its livelihood. Mere numbers of people do not determine the extent and type of use of resources that occur. The impact depends upon demands for specific resources – how much, how they are extracted and where the impact occurs.

Natural resources include variety of tangible natural endowments including land, water, and minerals. Land on which to live and build one's cities, to farm, graze ones livestock, to mine and to recreate. As human population grows, the global land area, in effect, shrinks. In modern times it has been persuasively argued that perhaps the most important underlying cause of World War I was the pressure of population. Increase in population density has been the cause of substantive population displacement in India. India makes up 2.4 per cent of the world's land, while supporting 16 per cent of the world's population. The compounding result is a severely unsustainable use of natural resources for several generations. Currently, India is experiencing a rapid and widespread environmental degradation at alarming rates. Tremendous pressure is placed upon the country's land and natural resources to support the massive overpopulation. Natural resources (land, water, biodiversity and genetic resources, biomass resources, forests, livestock and fisheries)– the very foundation of human survival, progress and prosperity, have been degrading fast, and the unprecedented pace of their erosion is one of the root causes of the agrarian crisis that the country is facing. The demographic and socio-economic pressures notwithstanding, the unmindful agricultural intensification, over-use of marginal lands, imbalanced use of fertilizers, organic matter depletion and deteriorating soil health, extensive diversion of prime agricultural lands to non-agricultural uses, misuse and inefficient use of irrigation water, depleting aquifers, salanization of fertile lands and waterlogging, deforestation, biodiversity loss and genetic erosion, and climate change are the main underlying causes.

Of the country's total 142 m ha cultivated land, 57 m ha, 40 per cent of the total, is irrigated and the remaining 85 m ha is rainfed. Of the total geographical area of 329 m ha, about 146 m ha is classified as degraded, although varying estimates have been provided by different agencies. As generally agreed, the resources have been degrading fast. Land distribution is highly skewed, more than 80 per cent of the farmers are small, marginal and submarginal and together own about 40 per cent of the total cultivated land, and increasing proportions of the holdings are becoming uneconomical. The soil health has been deteriorating, especially in terms of widespread micro-nutrient deficiencies and fast depleting carbon content.

Aside from land, freshwater is also equally important for proper and uniform regional development. A number of recent international and national conflicts over scarce freshwater is growing in various regions of the world. The competition for limited supply of freshwater between India and neighbouring countries has led to severe political tension. At the heart of the numerous water related conflicts lies a competitive unsustainable demand for water. We are asking for water that does not exist. The availability from Bhakra Nangal project led to the paddy cultivation in Punjab and Haryana resulting in constant demand for more water. That kind of water intensive irrigation was then extended to Rajasthan, generating unsustainable demand for water. The stated water needs for Karnataka and Tamil Nadu would require two Cauverys. At inter-country level, the combined requirements of India/Pakistan and those of India/Bangladesh would need up to two Indus Rivers and two Ganga rivers, respectively.

Water availability at the national level is reaching close to 1,700 cubic metre (cu m) per capita – the threshold line, and if things do not improve, it will drop to water scarcity line by the year 2025. India annually receives about 350 million hectare metre (mhm) rainwater, but almost half of it finds its way back to the sea, whereas the per capita water storage in India is only 210 cu m per capita against 1,110 cu m in China and 3,145 cu m in Brazil. With nearly 60 m ha of net irrigated area and irrigation using over 80 per cent of all freshwater, India ranks first in the world in irrigated acreage. There is a huge gap of 14 m ha between irrigation potential created and utilized, and the irrigation intensity is only 135 per cent, which should be raised to 175 per cent or more. Besides low water use efficiency, there is high inequity in water use and irrigation development, let alone the fast receding aquifers and blocks after blocks turning 'dark' and 'grey' in certain parts of the country.

Today, minerals are often assumed to be the most likely cause leading to clashes. Despite the limited distribution of some important minerals, it is generally agreed that access to these natural resources is likely to be a primary cause of dispute in coming years. The world has become dependent upon continuing supplies of huge quantities of oil. Many nations depend upon imports to satisfy their demand for this commodity.

Rampant loss of biodiversity and agricultural genetic resources has greatly enhanced genetic vulnerability of our agricultural systems. Forests, the green cover, are the natural resource infrastructure for agriculture/primary production and rural economic growth. India, harbouring 16 major forest types – tropical, temperate, alpine, etc. is one of the 17 mega diversity centres and two biodiversity hotspots of the world. Per capita forest area in the country (0.064 ha) is one-tenth of that of the world's average, and 41 per cent of the country's forest cover is degraded.

The complex and dynamic links between natural resource and regional development have long been recognized by the research and development organizations and have generated voluminous literature. This literature has opened various dimensions of understanding of this intricate relationship. Nature can never be managed well unless the people closest to it are involved in its management and a healthy relationship is established between nature, society and culture. Common natural resources were earlier regulated through diverse, decentralized, community control systems. But the state's policy of converting common property resources into government property resources has put them under the control of centralized bureaucracies, who in turn have put them at the service of the more powerful. A lot of qualitative analysis on socio-economic and livelihood aspects of resource development is available. But very little research has been done to identify the issues of resources and regional development in India.

The present volume is envisaged with the following premises:

1. Human response to natural resources is process bound. These processes are interactions of the socio-economic structure of the region concerned and laws of development.
2. The problem of interaction between human society and the natural environment has become quite acute in the contemporary world. The depletion of non-renewable resources and decrease in the potential of renewable resources are quite evident at all levels – global, regional and local creating regional inequalities in the level of development.
3. While these problems can be properly studied in an interdisciplinary framework, geographers have to play a leading role in this field because they focus on men's interaction with nature and its spatial differentiations.
4. Resources for the regional development are identified as a theme due to the growing importance of these problems on the globe in general and in India in particular.

Following sets of questions and issues are of central interest in the present volume:

1. Is there a direct link between natural resource utilization and regional development?
2. Do natural resource regions differ from other regions with respect to development and economic growth?
3. Are institutional frameworks ensuring the uniform regional development through a system of policy-making?
4. How does the exploitation of natural resources create a pattern of regional development; given that it may lead to an unequal distribution of socio-economic benefits among different segments of population?

Scope and Organization of this Volume

In this book geography's dynamic nature is represented in two sections that comprise 27 chapters. The chapters in the book centre around the challenges coming out of the resource use and regional development of the country. The scope of the book does not extend to a specific treatment of resource use and development complexities that condition use and management, but involves various dimensions of confronting issues and challenges in the country during the 21st century. The selection and classification of topics in this book has inevitably depended upon the perceptions of subjects on which important research has been undertaken.

The sections are based largely on those used in research writing within the discipline. Section 1 concentrates on resource issues and includes 13 chapters. These chapters deal with the problems relating to land, water and agriculture. In the first chapter, Rameshwar Thakur tries to delimit 'Natural Resource Regions of Chotanagpur' on the basis of resource attributes and their exploitation. Accordingly, the region is divided into landform units considering structure, lithology and geomorphic character. Then, resource regions are carved out by superimposing maps of resource endowments and land use patterns. In delineating the regions, population distribution, crop-combinations, agricultural efficiency and possibility of agricultural expansion are specially considered. Some regions are industrial, i.e. mining and manufacturing and some are agro-economic in nature. But each of these regions has homogeneity from the resource potential viewpoint. It has been pointed out that there are regional inequalities in the distribution of resources throughout the region. The study reflects that resources should be managed for their sustainable supply. Mohammad Dilshad visualizes pattern of resource use and agricultural structure in medieval India. During medieval period, the peasants were engaged in both seasons rabi and kharif, for cultivating variety of food grains. The agriculture was characterized with favourable climate, fertile soil, availability of labourers and livestock. Besides the plenty of fertile land, lots of people worked as landless labourers. Rajiv Ranjan Kumar Sinha undertakes analysing various mechanism of land transformation in Bihar on the basis of land and cast dynamics. It is observed that caste is the important factor in land transformation, but political and market forces are also equally important. B.W. Pandey and Abhay Shankar Prasad discuss the change in land use pattern in the upper Beas Basin. It was found that there is considerable reduction in the area under forest cover. The major concerns in the study are on the ecological impacts of the land use changes in general and forest degradation in particular. Consequently, the ecological impact on the one hand centres around intensive cultivation and large scale use of fertilizer, insecticides, pesticides and urban wastes, etc. and, on the other hand, deforestation.

Surendra Singh Chawla highlights the major issues and challenges of water crises in India. Various challenges like infrastructure development and conservation of groundwater has been analysed. It has been suggested that there is a need to promote community initiatives with policy interventions from the government side. The role of water user associations has also been highlighted for water distribution management. Privatization of water has been examined as a solution to the water problem. The water use and its management in Damodar River Basin has been analysed by Rameshwar Thakur. The study reveals that water availability in the Damodar basin has been influenced by physiographic conditions. Geographically, the river lies in eastern Chotanagpur where the average rainfall is 1,400–1,600 mm. The basin is one of the dirtiest parts of the country and the deteriorating water quality has become a serious problem. Water supplies and environmental sanitation are vital for protecting the environment. Inder Jeet explores the scope of future water resources development in Haryana. It is argued that the expansion of irrigation from the mid-1960s provided the enabling environment for use of the new high-yielding varieties and fertilizer, pushing the production frontier to a new height and transforming the rural sector. The major gainers in terms of both productivity and area were wheat and rice. As a result, food grain production increased manyfold during this period. Paradoxically, Haryana is facing the threat of a declining water table because of the exploitation of resources in some areas and a rising water table caused by increased waterlogging and salinity in others. The decline in the water table is more marked in the semi-arid region than in the arid regions. Preeti Sachar found that the economy of study area is dependent upon the production and processing of agricultural products. The primary resources of land and water are not the limiting factors for the region's agricultural growth but overexploitation of groundwater resources and inefficient utilization of surface water resources may bring a fundamental change in value of both, land and water in the basin. It is suggested that there is urgent need to appraise the correct approach/latest concept of soil-water-plant-climate relationship, in order to avoid any layout of the faulty experiments, and to achieve economic and efficient utilization of the water resources.

Shweta Rani deals with the flood and flood forecasting techniques in Bihar. The paper tries to explore and unravel the changing scenario in the enigma of floods and associated constant threat to human civilizations. Flood is a hydrological event independently distributed in time and characterized by magnitude and recurrence interval. It has been assessed as a chronic and serious problem owing to the unabated population growth and high rate of developmental activities. Hence, the main thrust of the paper is to analyse the magnitude and frequency of floods using the method of flood forecasting techniques by Weibull's Plotting Positions. Sneh Gangwar notes that the plains of North Bihar have recorded the highest number of floods during the last 30 years. The total area affected by floods has also increased during these years. It has been concluded that conventional approach is not suitable to manage the flood menace in North Bihar.

D.P. Singh and R.B. Thakur take up the problems and prospects of interlinking of rivers in Bihar. It points out that in the region of North Bihar, floods are mostly caused by rainfall in catchments areas situated outside India, mainly in Nepal. All the rivers flowing through North Bihar originate in Nepal. The state of Bihar and even the Government of India does not have any control over this. Also, all the rivers of North Bihar deposit sand and silt resulting into destructive floods. In South Bihar, the situation is different from North Bihar. The absence of rain has aggravated the problems in South Bihar. Inter-basin water transfer link or interlinking of rivers is one of the solutions to this problem.

The water quality and water-borne diseases in Kanpur city has been analysed by Kanchan Gupta. It is found that currently, the rate of urbanization, industrialization and deterioration of water quality (both surface and groundwater) is of major concern in metropolitan cities and towns in India. Kanpur city receives water from the rivers Ganga and Pondu. These rivers are highly polluted because of the sewage disposal from more than a dozen of drains from the city itself. This chapter analyses the status of water quality in Kanpur city and tries to understand that water borne-diseases are due to the poor quality of water in the city. Aakash Upadhyay talks about impact of hydropower development on rural livelihood sustainability in Sikkim. It is argued that mountain economy is changing with the change of global economy. A fast transformation is taking place from agrarian to more industrial or service-oriented economies. Sikkim, a small state of India in the eastern Himalayas, has recently embarked on a programme of hydroelectricity project construction owing to its natural potential. This study examines the changes taking place on the basis of community response on the environmental and the socio-economic aspect, post-construction of hydropower projects and its implications for future sustainable livelihoods.

Section 2 deals with regions and regional perspective issues at different scales of investigation. Some issues are studied very well at the regional level, while others require a good deal of attention at the scale of state or local community. Many topics are studied within the region since region provides the framework for the investigation. Geographers often study both human and physical geography topics within regions. The human environment relationships of people within regions, both large and small in areas have been the subject of geographic research. At the beginning of the 21st century, geographic research on regions has gained insignificance as regional roles and territorial configurations emerge to meet the challenges of globalization. This section covers 14 chapters. The first paper by Guljit K. Arora briefly looks into the globalization process and its interconnecting dynamics of market integration and regional implications; reviews the nature and extent of inter-state variations in India; scans the regional development policies followed by Government of India during its different five-year plans and gives their failure to check regional inequalities; and highlights the impending dangers of the unarrested inter-regional inequalities in India. It goes on to demonstrate that the high order of the existing socio-economic inequalities, further induced by unchecked globalization, given our fragmented society in which people owe strong allegiances to region, religion, language, caste and culture, are likely to bring the economic disenchantment among the people living in excluded and marginalized regions. Such people are even more vulnerable to the growing politicization of the society in the period of coalition politics; if such regions continue to stagnate, the policy of balanced regional development will continue to be illusory and the central public sector investment will fail to make a dent in those regions. Thus, it is suggested that India needs a political class who could take the lead in finding a solution to the regional inequality problem, further compounded by the globalization forces, by rising above the negative politics in which peoples' feelings for development for regions and sub-regions are misused for petty political ends. The paper by Rajesh Kumar Abhay, has identified and suggested over 80 indicators to measure various type of development and can be combined together to measure the overall development of any region. It is suggested that the indicators for a region should be selected by taking the study area into consideration.

The paper by Monica Ahlawat finds the imbalances in the sex ratio in India. It is revealed that industrialization, urbanization, out-migration have greatly determined general sex ratio while economic development, literacy, personal attitude, modern way of life have disturbed child sex ratio in study area and, therefore, general sex ratios as well as child sex ratio differ from state to state. Furthermore, the Indian scenario of female discrimination is extremely complex in view of India's social and economic diversity. Om Jee Ranjan and Anjan Sen opine about the borrowing trend economy and its impact on education in the rural area of Aurangabad district, Bihar. It is an attempt to understand the relation between income time, borrowed money and average income capability of fulfilment of the demand of additional amount on education. The relationship between economic activity, its frequency and expenditure condition in an isolated rural area of Aurangabad, Bihar is estimated. Purposive stratified sampling has been used to select the respondents. The study reveals that the genetically engineered Bt crops' affect in an economy shows significant effect on expenditure for various development programmes. It is argued that when rural society of an isolated rural area depends only on subsistence agriculture, the borrowing trend has significant effect on the rural society. An important aspect of the caste system of Indian society has been covered by Vinod Kumar and Ajit Kumar. The paper concludes that Scheduled Caste (SC) population is socially and economically backward. The study also points out that root cause of these inequalities lies in poverty, caste-based discrimination, low enrolment ratio and higher drop rates at school level which result in low percentages of SC population in higher education and this further leads to minimal presence of SC professionals.

The paper by Mitrajit Chatterjee and Nageshwar Prasad explains the growth morphology and certain social problems of Chandannagar city of West Bengal. This work totally depends on the secondary sources in terms of data. In order to accommodate this huge mass of people, this city has experienced many restructuring in recent years. Restructuring in respect to residential pattern is most visible here. Due to lack of space, the city has grown vertically. The trend of restructuring old residential houses, open lands and orchards has started from 1990. As a result, the urban landscape of the city has changed and continues to change rapidly. Swati Thakur discusses the perception of climate change and its mitigation in Dehradun city. Study points out that nearly 28 per cent respondents misunderstood the description of climate change as global warming and generally people have negative perception about the climate change. The finding indicates that individuals alone will not voluntarily choose to alter their behaviour in the face of climate change unless they feel enabled to do so, in terms of government being a facilitator for the same and also perceive the rest of the society moving in the same direction. Delhi's Master Plan is critically reviewed by Priyanka Puri. This study highlights major challenges which Delhi is going to face in the coming years. The major challenges are that of unauthorized settlements and JJ (jhuggi jhonpari) clusters. These are suggested to be dealt in their present manifestation, future growth and proliferation.

Manjit Singh found that road transport and agricultural development have direct linkages in Himachal Pradesh. Here, most of the people are dependent on agriculture (over 93%). With the help of factor analysis, a strong relationship between road transport and agricultural development has been established. Krishna Kumar and Anjan Sen delimit the road transport regions and evaluate its impact on regional development of Gaya district in Bihar. It is explained that better the transport facilities in a region, the higher is the standard of living of its people. To demarcate road transport region, Graph Theory, buffering and normalization technique (Z-Square) has been used. It has been observed in the study area that road transport region has positive relation with regional development.

Sudeepta Adhikari traces the various stages of geopolitics in terms of classical, modern and post-modern geopolitics. It is suggested that to save the earth's future, India must have its own way by using *geosheeltics*. It is a combination of three different disciplinary ideas: geography, *sheel*, and politics. The term sheel, put between geography and politics signifies geopolitics mediated by sheel. Thus, the term geosheelitics means moralistic and ethical geopolitics. The objective of geosheelitics is to uncover the static approach of geopolitics, the one that dominated in the practices of states and is still prevailing in the contemporary world politics. According to the author, geosheelitics offers a continued examination of suppositions which underlie specific geopolitical constructions, that is, the production and usage of geographical knowledge to different political and spatial orders, so that conflictuality could be transformed into cooperation.

Swarnima Singh talks about the impact of climate change on South Asian forests. The study highlights the data, modelling and research gaps relevant to the Greenhouse Gas (GHG) inventory estimation, mitigation potential and vulnerability and impact assessments for the forest and biodiversity in South Asia. Further, her study observes the need for modelling the changes at regional level rather than relying on global level output. Krishnanand explains the vulnerability in mountain system to natural and anthropogenic hazards in Himachal Pradesh. Over the years, the forest wealth of the state is being destroyed by the incidences of fire attributed to both anthropogenic and other reasons. The destruction of rich flora and fauna in the state, due to forest fires will have serious repercussions on the ecological balance of the state. This study aims to present a conceptual framework for vulnerability and adaptation to climate variability and change in mountain systems, especially in case of Himachal Pradesh which may generally be applicable to a wide range of contexts, systems and hazards.

Barun Kumar deals with the rehabilitation effectiveness of Kutch earthquake, in Gujarat. This study is based on three objectives: first, rescue and rehabilitation measures adopted in the affected area. Second, lessons learned through these measures and third, mitigation strategies. According to the study, there is a need to examine the efficiency of rehabilitation programmes and assist communities in the exercise of their own role in such reviews. A greater emphasis on evaluative techniques will render all new programmes more accountable to real community needs. There should be fairness in the dealings of all types of rehabilitation programme.

Regional analysis of resources of a country is an amalgam of several disciplines especially economics, geography, political science, history and to a lesser degree sociology, anthropology and physical sciences like geology and climatology. Members of each discipline, when tackling regional issues, apply the broad methodology of their own discipline. Essentially, all these methods are scientific.

References

Aggarwal, S.K. (2009) *Regional Development in India*, New Delhi: Concept.

Baker, D. and D. McGregor (1995) *Environment and Development in Caribbean: A Geographical Perspective*, Mona (Jamaica): The Press of University of West Indies.

Carson, R. (1962) *Silent Spring*, New York: Houghton Mifflin.

Chand, M. and V.K. Puri (2010) *Regional Planning in India*, Mumbai: Allied Publishers.

Datt, G. and A. Mahajan (2013) *Indian Economy*, Delhi: S. Chand & Sons.

De Haan, Leo J. (2000) 'The Question of Development and Environment in Geography in the Era of Globalisation', *GeoJournal*, 50: 359–367.

Gore, C. (1984) *Regions in Question: Space, Development Theory and Regional Policy*, London: Methuen.

Gupta, A. and M.G. Asher (1998) *Environment and the Developing World: Principles, Policies and Management*, New York: John Wiley.

Gupta, K.R. and J.R. Gupta (2008) *Indian Economy*, New Delhi: Atlantic Publishers.

Jayasri, R.C. (2001) *An Introduction to Development and Regional Planning with Special Reference to India*, Hyderabad: Orient Longman.

Jeet, I. (2005) *Water Resource Management*, New Delhi: Manisha Publications.

Mitchell, B. (1979) *Geography and Resource Analysis*, London: Longman.

Simon, D. (ed.) (1990) *Third World Regional Development: A Reappraisal*, London: Paul Chapman.

Thakur, B. (ed.) (2000) *Resource Management in Developing Countries*, New Delhi: Concept.

Section – 1

Regional Resources

1

Identification and Delimitation of Natural Resource Regions in Chotanagpur

RAMESHWAR THAKUR

Overexploitation of resources with the thrust of rapid economic development in the recent past, has posed many themes of research in Chotanagpur region. It attracted attention of geographers after India's independence. Since then, geographers have paid their attention to different themes, viz., economic region, transport network, rural urban settlement and, geological and geomorphological history of Chotanagpur. Unfortunately, no attempt has been made to study the patterns, processes, delimitation and problems of resource development. This study fills the void in this field of research.

Geographers have contributed to the study of resources in a multivariate regional setting. In these studies, the approach is to treat the entire resource base of a micro- or macro-region and to suggest measures for its rational development. The National Resource Division of the Planning Commission has played pioneering role in conducting surveys to access resource base of a region for its planned development. Outside the planning commission, a number of social scientists, including geographers have adopted a similar approach to study spatial variations in resource endowment and disparities in levels of development in different regions of India.

An appraisal of research in geography of resources brings out lack of proper orientation to the spatial aspect. Studies on regional delineation are recent. There is a need for application of resource complex approach according to their local, regional and national importance. The lack of regional studies is reflected in the contribution. This has led to heavy reliance on the data available from survey of geology, hydrology, forest, etc. The data are of varying quality and unit area is not always comparable. Therefore, these studies lack geographical interpretation of available data.

The delimitation of Natural Resource Regions (NRRs) in Chotanagpur is based on resource attributes and their exploitation patterns. Physical conditions form an important basis for delimitation of the NRRs. Land is the basic resource and nature of terrain plays crucial role in framing the set-up on resources. The crops grown are a curious mixture of those cultivated in the drier regions towards west and those found in the wetter areas in the east. These differences are related to physical conditions. The change from one region to another is gradual and, even imperceptible. Each region divided is clearly defined by a distinctive feature of its resource geography and is unified by well-marked geographical features which provide the region its distinctive quality and mark it out from the rest. The resource development of this region is largely the result of transport development in different areas. The region is, therefore, classified on the basis of its physical conditions, because land resources, especially nature of terrain, plays important role in farming extra-territorial factors on resources.

Chotanagpur region was selected as a study area because it has the most fragile and sensitive ecosystem. Rapid changes in land use and emergent economy, coexisting with traditional economy have affected the region. Similarly, association between resource management and economic development shows linkage which provides opportunity to understand development processes. Secondly, Chotanagpur is poor in socio-economic development which is correlated with poor utilization of natural resources. The region with highland ecosystem has a tremendous potential for resource development. Thirdly, suitable measures and approaches to resource utilization can serve as an input for regional development. Lastly, the region has been chosen because of the deep familiarity with its resource distribution problems.

Review of Literature

Resource regionalization in India is recent. It helps in planning for balanced growth in the region with marked disparity in levels of development (Sengupta, 1967: 27). A survey of the efforts is presented by Sundaram (1980). A critical analysis of regionalization experiments is also presented by Pal and Learmonth (1964). In the evolution of this concept, a transition from physio-economic regionalization to resource, particularly energy resource regionalization is prominent (Sengupta and Sadasyuk, 1968: 15). Homogeneity in natures are used as criterion to identify physio-economic region. The first work of this nature is of Rao (1949), which stressed that regionalization is a dynamic concept which aims at the optimum utilization of regional resources. Report by Nath (1965) on Resource Development Region and Divisions of India is worth mentioning for the Planning Commission.

Investigation of Mysore State for planning is a geographical attempt (Learmonth et al., 1962). Bhat (1972), who has worked with various interdisciplinary teams in resource surveys of Mysore State and also micro-regional surveys of South India, has presented a pioneering effort. Bhat has stressed the need for recognizing resource region as a viable unit for planning and economic development purposes. Following the trend set by interdisciplinary team in survey of resource region, a number of individual scholars have adopted a similar approach in resource studies. Early attempt to study resource regionalization in India was made by Nath (1965), Sengupta (1967), Barthakur (1969), Muthoo (1969, 1970), Roy et al. (1971), Sundaram (1980), Bhat et al. (1982), Kayastha (1984), Sharma (1989, 1992), and Thakur (2003, 2007). Sengupta's (1967) work is pioneering in resource regionalization in India. The basic principle of planning is an effort to bring about fullest development of natural resources through production and specialization in regions for which they are suited. Evaluation of resource endowment of natural region is necessary to discover the region. The size of the unit varies according to the size and distributional pattern of natural resources.

Aims and Objectives

In this paper an attempt is made to: (i) demarcate the natural resource regions on the basis of formal regions, (ii) analyse and interpret the occurrence, distribution, accessibility, patterns of exploitation and utilization of resources in each natural resource region and (iii) highlight the problems and prospects of individual resource in perspective of development of the region.

The Study Area

Chotanagpur has irregular boundary from all sides, roughly coinciding the boundaries of Jharkhand State. Structurally, the region consists of Dharwar rocks, which include Archaean granites with some sedimentary deposits. It comprises 24 districts (Census of India, 2011) under the administrative boundary of the Jharkhand State (Figure 1). The region is one of the rainiest parts of Eastern India. It is drained by numerous rivers of which the South Koel, North Koel, Subarnarekha, Damodar and Barakar are prominent. The region produces 37.3 per cent of the mineral production of India. The Dharwarian rock is the source of many minerals. Around 63 per cent of the area is not suitable for cultivation due to rugged terrain and hilly topography. However, the major crops are rice, maize, millet, sugarcane, wheat, gram, ragi (marua) and pulses. On an average, 8 per cent of the crop area is irrigated. It is a home of 3,29,66,238 people comprising 2.72 per cent of India's total population. Population density is 413 persons per sq km (ibid.), which is marginally higher in

Figure 1

Jharkhand/Chotanagpur: Administrative Divisions, 2011

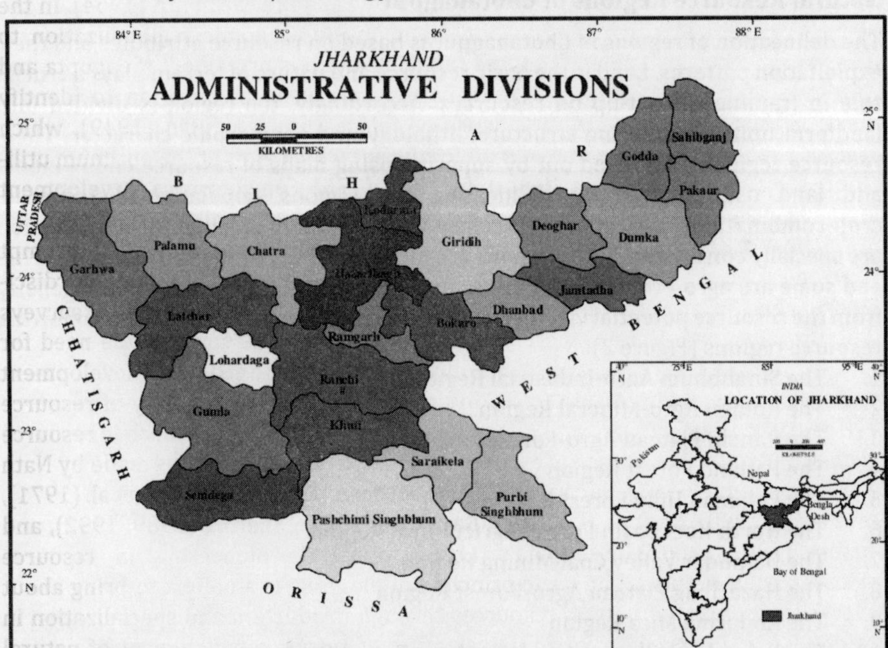

comparison to India (382 persons per sq km). The total number of towns are 152 in which 10 are Class I towns. Jamshedpur, Bokaro, Dhanbad and Ranchi are the metropolitan cities. The proportion of population living in urban areas is 20 per cent. Culturally, the region is well marked on the map of India for its tribal population. The principal tribes of this region are Munda, Oraon, Santhal, Bhumli, Bhuiya, and Kharia.

Chotanagpur forms a distinct geographical region defined by its varied morphology and man's activities ranging from primitive to modern. The anatomy, age, orography, resources, climate, forest cover, mineral resources, agricultural pattern and human resource, have produced a distinct resource region (Ahmad, 1965). However, within the region there are stark regional contrasts in natural resources and activities of man. The geological structure, relief, altitude and vegetation together with resources and associated economic developments distinguish one region from another. Nature has carved out its form but man has defined its significance by his attainment.

Physical conditions form an important basis for delimitation of the resource region. The crops grown are a curious mixture of those cultivated in drier regions towards west and those found in the wetter in the east. These differences are related to physical conditions. The change from one region to another is gradual and even imperceptible. Each region divided is clearly defined by distinctive features of its resource geography and is unified by well-marked geographical features which provide the region its distinctive quality and mark it out from the rest. The resource development of the region is largely the result of transport development in different areas. The region is, therefore, classified on the basis of its physical conditions because land resource, especially nature of terrain, plays an important role in framing extra-territorial factors on resources.

Natural Resource Regions of Chotanagpur

The delineation of regions in Chotanagpur is based on resource attributes and their exploitation patterns. Land is the basic resource and nature of terrain plays a crucial role in framing the set-up on resources. Accordingly, the region is divided into landform units considering structure, lithology and geomorphic character. Then, resource regions are carved out by superimposing maps of resource endowments and land use patterns. In delineating the regions population distribution, crop-combinations, agricultural efficiency and possibility of agricultural expansion are specially considered. Some regions are industrial, i.e., mining and manufacturing and some are agro-economic in nature. But each of these regions has homogeneity from the resource potential viewpoint. The region is, thus, divided into the following resource regions (Figure 2):

1. The Singhbhum Agro-Industrial Region
2. The Kolhan Agro-Mineral Region
3. The Ranchi Plateau Agro-Forest Region
4. The Patland Forest Region
5. The Palamau Hilly Forest Region
6. The North Koel Basin Forest-Agricultural Region
7. The Damodar Valley Coal Mining Region
8. The Hazaribag Plateau Agro-Forest Region
9. The Kodarma Mica Region
10. The Rajmahal Hills and Adjoining Agro-Forest Region

Figure 2

Chotanagpur: Natural Resource Regions

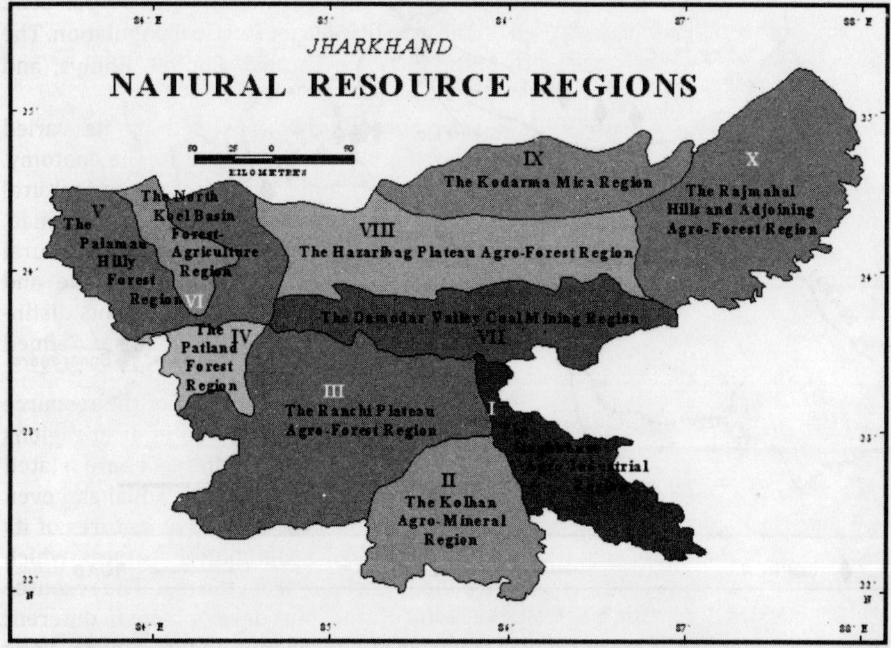

The Singhbhum Agro-Industrial Region/Subernrekha Valley

The rich resource-base region lies in the south-eastern portion of the state. It covers a limited narrow north south territory of Singhbhum district. It is a distinct natural unit lying mainly in the basin of the river Subernrekha. The region has a complex geological history which accounts for a great diversity in landforms as well as in natural resources. These resources have given rise to a large number of industries and have led to the growth of the giant industrial cities of Ranchi and Jamshedpur.

The area has a structural base of Dharwar rocks, which include the Archaean granites and gneisses of Ranchi and Singhbhum, separated by sedimentary and metamorphism and mineralization in a broad belt which runs roughly east-west and is known as the Singhbhum copper belt. The chief mining centres are concentrated in Mushabani, Ghatsila and Kharsawan in this belt (Figure 3). Workers of the region are engaged in manufacturing and mining, forestry and small industries. The distribution of these activities, however, is not uniform, rather they concentrate along the main transport arteries and in the copper belt.

The Singhbhum copper belt contains valuable deposits of 100 per cent copper. The most productive mine is Mosabani and other non-ferrous metals such as nickel, chromium, tungsten and uranium as well as minerals such as apatite, steatite, kyanite and asbestos are significant. In addition, there are also reserves of baryte, limestone, kaolin and vanadium. However, occurrence of such basic mineral resources has pushed up industrial development. There are iron and steel and engineering industries at Jamshedpur and Ranchi, copper industry at Ghatsila and aluminium industry at Muri. Other major industries are glass at Saraikela and cement at Jhinkpani. Among the forest-based industries lac industry is important.

Figure 3

The Copper Belt Showing Mines, Railways and Roads

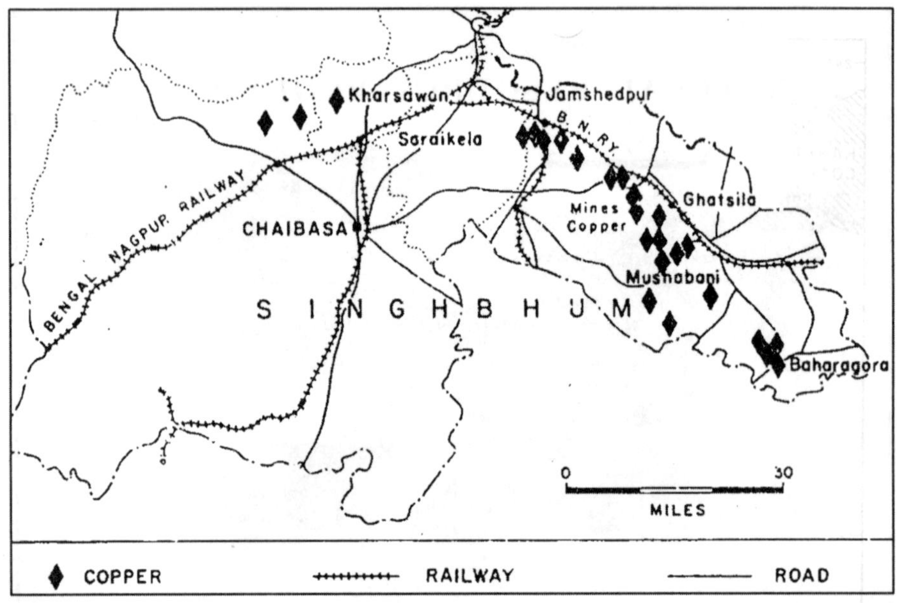

There are a number of other smaller factories at Jamshedpur and its suburb. They manufacture machine parts and tools, cement, concrete pipes, oxygen and acetylene gas, mineral wool, cranes, boilers, rubber goods, etc. Exploitation of minerals and development of industries have caused remarkable growth in transport. The National Highway No. 33 passes through the area and covers Chaibasa, Chakardharpur and Ranchi Road. There are several State Highways which connect Ranchi, Jamshedpur, Rajnagar, Chaibasa, Seraikela, etc.

The Kolhan Agro-Mineral Region/Chaibasa Plain and Adjoining Agro-Energy Region

This resource region covers the district of Chaibasa and the portion of Singhbhum. The region consists of plain/basin in the north-eastern part around Chaibasa town. The rest of the region on the north-west, west, south-west and south is a dissected and largely forested surface with scarps overlooking the Chaibasa plain as well as South Koel valley. The region has a complex geological history which accounts for the great diversity of landforms. It consists of granite-gneiss batholiths in the north and south and two geo-anticlines separated by geosynclines running through the region. The rocks are Dharwar in age and metamorphic deposits of the iron ore series in the middle. The Dalma and Dhanjore lavas are the most extensive which attain highest relief with diversified economy.

The region has emerged as a pocket of agro-mining production centre. To exploit the iron ore resource, railway line was laid in 1891 by the Bombay-Nagpur-Calcutta Railway. Iron ore and agricultural lands are significant natural resources. The important mines of the Kolhan region are Gua, Nuamundi, Kantoria, Barajamda, Bindu Buru and Pansira Buru. A branch railway from

Figure 4

Chotanagpur: The Iron and Steel works at Jamshedpur in Relation to the Raw Materials – Coal, Iron Ore, Manganese and Limestone

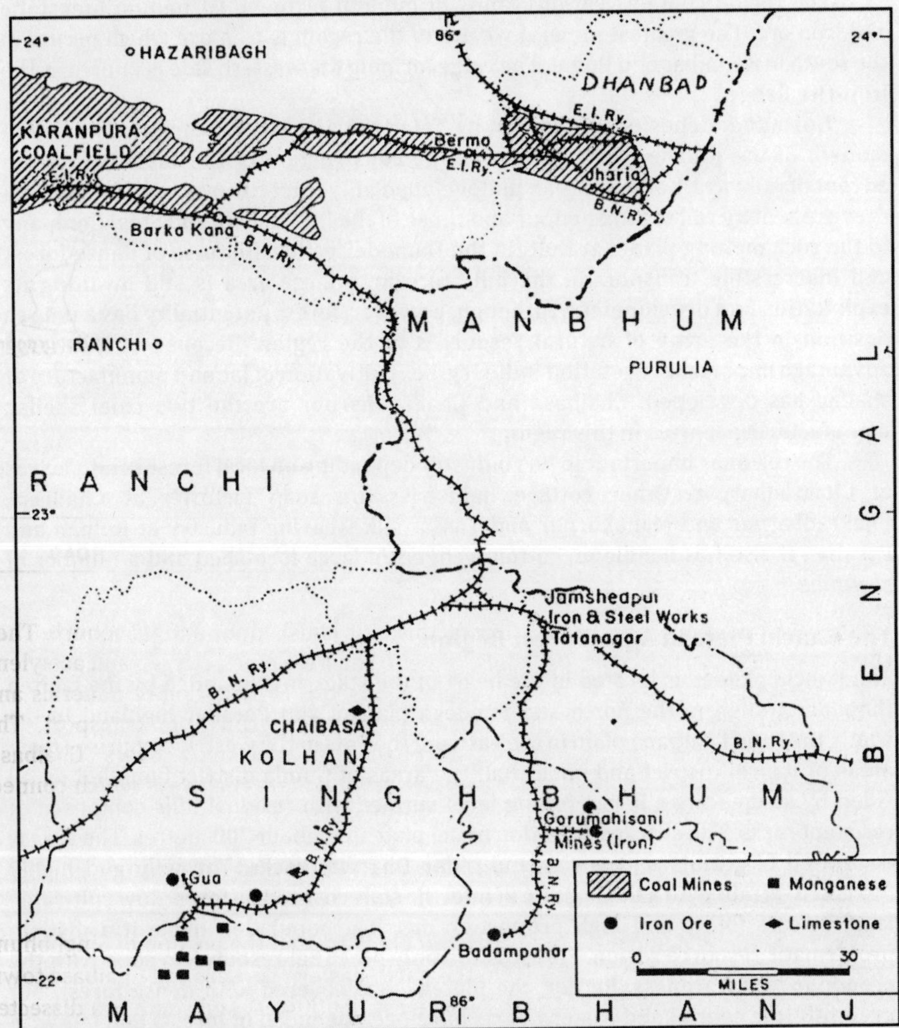

Rajkharsawan to Gua is the chief transport means of iron mines (Figure 4). The fast trains take the rich ore of the area to Tata Iron Steel Company and other steel areas. The opening of this railway branch accounts for the exploitation of the iron ore range at Gua, Nuamundi in the region and beyond the region.

This resource region is divided into three subregions: the Chaibasa plain, the Dalma range and the Kolhan iron ore mining region. It has mainly agricultural and forest product economy. Rice is the significant crop occupying more than 60 per cent of the cropped area. Other crops are maize, gram and arhar. Pulses and oil-seeds also occupy significant acerage. Gram is relatively important because of heavy soils. The human resource activities are concerned with mining and transport of minerals. The Chaibasa plain is served by a radial net of roads covering Chaibasa Road from Ranchi to Chaibasa and from Ranchi to Jamshedpur. A metalled highway connects the iron mines with Rourkela. Road from Chandil runs longitudinally below the Dalma Range till it winds through low schist hills to cross the Subernarekha.

The region contains various kinds of mineral pigment, corundum limestone and iron ore. The greatest mineral wealth of the region is iron ore which occurs in the south in Keonjhar and Bonai. The ridge forming the western side is known as the Iron-Ore Range.

Noamundi deposits are worked by Tata Iron and Steel Company. The development of the Kolhan iron ore follows the construction of railways. Before the advent of railways, Kolhan was an undeveloped hilly tract covered with forest. Iron ores are sent by rail to Jamshedpur and those of the Indian Iron and Steel Company to the rock melting plants at Kulti in the Damodar valley. Because of dense forest and inaccessible transport in the hilly terrain, a large area is still awaiting its exploitation and development. Although, however, forest potentiality has a unique position in the array of natural resources of the region. Because of locational advantage important vegetation industry, i.e., cultivation of lac and manufacture of shellac has developed. Chaibasa and Chakradharpur are the two chief shellac manufacturing centres in this region.

The region is important in biri industry depending on local forest kendu leaves at Chakradharpur. Other cottage industries are soap factories at Chaibasa, Chakradharpur and Manoharpur and Tassar silk weaving industry at Kolhan and Porahat. It also has handloom cotton weaving, a large loco-shed and a number of sawmills.

The Ranchi Plateau Agro-Forest Region

The Ranchi plateau is located in the heart of the state. It is bounded by the faulted Damodar trough in the north and Simdega plateau and Porahar highland in the south, the Panch Pargana plain in the east and the Pats in the west. It comprises most areas of Ranchi district and about half the areas of Gumla district bounded on all sided by steep scarps. It has rolling level surface with residual hills composed of resistant rocks. The average elevation of the plateau is about 700 metres. The area is composed of granite and gneiss and older Dharwar rocks. The hilly and highly dissected terrain with a thin mantle of infertile soils covered by forest, low cultivable land, inaccessibility and high proportion of tribal population make it a distinct problematic resource region. Forest is the only potential resource to cope with the economic backwardness. Earlier, the plateau was covered with dense forest, but presently, the central and eastern parts have been denuded of forests and left with only small jungles with very few big trees.

Some, of the minerals in the region are: near Itki, barite veins at Silwai, Bahea and Bongabera on the Mure Road, chromites in Hotag hill, galena near Silli and Silwai. Stealite and lac-schist red clay and Phyllites along the edge of Dalma lavas near Kubasa and Papirda.

Agricultural economy is predominant both on uplands and lowlands. The culturable land falls into two classes: terraced lowlands (dons) on which rice is the important crop and the uplands (tanr) which produce coarse rice, millet, pulses and oilseeds. The relative proportion of uplands and lowlands in villages in most cases is 40:60.

Water resources for irrigation are not resourceful. The hill streams remain dry except in the rainy season and do not offer much scope for irrigation. The ahars (reservoirs), wells and danaries (springs) are the traditional sources of irrigation. Some irrigation schemes have been developed by the government for conserving rainwater by controlling rivulets.

The region has recently registered development of heavy engineering works at Hatia, shellac industry and handloom weaving of cotton in the village, ball-bearing factory at Ratu, aluminum factory at Muri, cement industry at Khelari, high tension insulator factory at Namkum and electrical appliances at Tati Sibai, adding industrial landscape to the city. The heavy machine building plant, factory forge plant, machine tool plants and heavy machine tool plants are located at Hatia. Lac is produced at Ranchi, Bundu, Khunti and Gumla. The region is served by a radical pattern of excellent roads that converge from all directions on the metropolitan city of Ranchi, the best road nodes of India.

The Patland Forest Region

It is the extension of Deccan trap with an average elevation of 900 metres. It is comparatively one of the least developed regions of Chotanagpur. The region is cut off from a line of forest covered with steep hills which present difficulties for the development of transport system. There is only one metalled road up to Netarhat in the region. Neterhat flat-topped hills known as 'pat' is famous for its charm and beauty and also for health restoring sunrise on south-eastern face. The rainfall is high amounting to an annual fall of over 1,800 mm.

The region is covered with dry deciduous forest dominated with plentiful Sal, Bamboos, *Gamhar, Kusum, Shisham* and *Sabai* grass and *Palas* important species. Timber is transported from the forest to the market centre Daltonganj by means of motor trucks on the unmetalled hill roads. Forest product is the only potential resource to cope with economic wealth of the region. The region contains deposits of bauxite, mining of which has been recently developed at Bzgru, Pakhar and other parts. It is mined near Lohardaga and railed to Muri for processing. Cultivation is restricted on the descending slopes, but the valleys reflect paddy culture in lowland and dry crop culture on uplands.

The Palamau Hilly Forest Region

The region, lying in Palamau district, is characterized by distinctive divided terrain with broken and divided land. The North Koel separates the broken land into western and eastern segments. The resource region is further characterized by peaks and ranges, poor soils, forest and scrubs of dry deciduous vegetation and poor agriculture. The western upland is a table land with gently rolling relief and eastern upland has a highly dissected terrain.

Forests are the only potential resource to cope with economic backwardness. They cover two-thirds of the geographical area and are conspicuously dense. However, they cannot be utilized economically. The important forest products are timber and lac. The *sal* (shorea robusta) is the popular forest economy and is the mainstay of the poor people. The other trees are *khair, sida, pesar,* ebony. The manufacture of cutch (kath) from khair (Acacia Catecher) tree is also important. Khair, Kusum, Gamhar, Sabai grass and palas play their role in contributing to the economy of the region. The shallowness of the soils is a limiting factor to agricultural development. The soil is generally sandy and stony on the uplands but clayey in valleys. Rail and roads have given great incentive in exploiting the forest. Timber and bamboos are transported by carts and trucks to the nearest railway station and then by rail to its markets. The main market centres are Gharwa, Ranka, Satbarwa and Lesliganj. Gharwa is the main town and is an important collecting centre for forest products.

The North Koel Basin Forest-Agricultural Region

The region lies in the north-western part of Chotanagpur. Its area is approximately equal to the area of Palamau and Garhwa districts which is 1,21,749 sq km. The basin contains fertile alluvial soil covered with crops of rice, wheat, barley, maize and sugarcane. Agriculture is hazardous and precarious due to vagaries of the monsoon, therefore, it depends on irrigation. *Bandhs,* reservoirs and *ahars* are distributed throughout the basin which have provided inputs to agricultural development. Rice, maize, gram, wheat, barley and other pulses are grown throughout the basin.

The industrial activities include manufacture of lac and shellac, handloom industry weaving cotton cloth and coarse woolen blanket, biri industry, ghee-making, saw milling, etc. Rural areas are well served by electric transmission lines based on both hydropower as well as coalfields. Daltonganj, Hutar and Auranga are important coalfields of this region.

The Damodar Valley Coal Mining Region

The Damodar Valley covers large areas of Gondwana trough which lies in the middle of Chotanagpur. The region comprises of the drainage of Damodar and its tributaries. The Damodar River rises in the Khamar Pat in Palamau district and flows eastward. The length of the river is 538 km, out of which 290 km lie in Jharkhand State and is known as the Upper Damodar basin. The remaining length of 248 km lies in West Bengal and is called the Lower Damodar basin. The region includes the down faulted terrain with conspicuous Lugo and Jhumra Pahar of Hazaribag plateau marked by the Barakar Valley and the entire district of Bokaro. The Damodar Valley is characterized by narrow and steep hills and scarps on the south. The valley widens in the east and is marked by rice land interrupted with jungle-clad masses of hills. The hills are covered with forests. Rajrappa waterfall is a discordant junction below which imposing gorge and many juvenile features produce a classic segment of landscape. The region has complex geological history because of its relation with ancient landmass of the Gondwana land and prolonged denudation, igneous intrusion, tilting, warpings, upheaval, etc. The faulted basin of Damodar has rock formation of Gondwana period from the Hutter coal field in the west to Jharia and Raniganj coal fields in the east. The lower Gondwana made up of sandstones and shales contain storehouses of coal seams, the richest, largest and most productive coalfields of India. The Damodar Valley coal occuring in Damuda series of the lower Gondwana rocks is noted for exceptionally rich coal deposits. About 90 per cent of India's coal is mined from this valley. There are several coalfields, of which the Jharia, Bokaro, Ramgarh, Chandrapura and Karanpura are the premier producers (Figure 5). Table 1 shows the important coal mines of Damodar Valley region.

The Damodar multipurpose river valley project has transformed the region into a prosperous mining, industrial and commercial centre of Chotanagpur. The project was planned with a motive to control furious floods caused by the river Damodar especially in the lower parts, soil erosion, production of hydropower, afforestation, development of irrigation and industry. The project encompasses the entire basin of the Damodar and its tributaries, the Konar and Barakar with dams and powerhouses.

Figure 5

Damodar Valley Coal Fields: 1. Jharia, 2. Chandrapura, 3. Bokaro, 4. Ramgarh, 5. South Karanpura, 6. North Karanpura

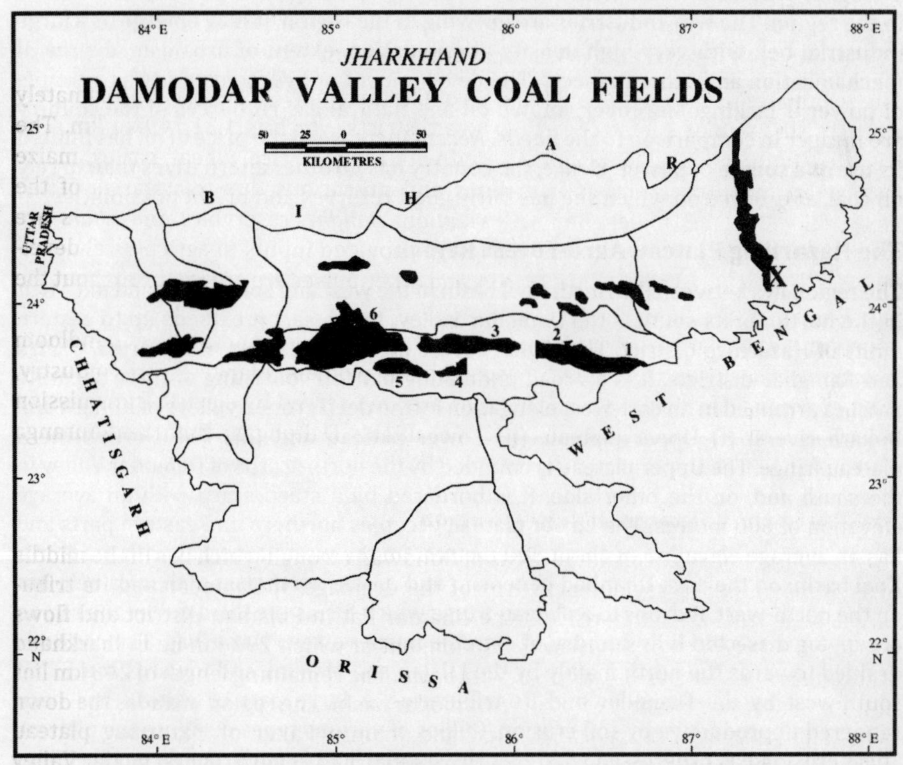

Table 1

Damodar Valley Coal Reserves: 2000–01 (million tonnes)

Coal Fields	*Known*	*Estimated*	*Total*	*Percentage*
Jharia	10,435.34	6,550.34	16,985.69	29.50
Bokaro	4,715.74	4,004.24	8,179.98	15.15
Ramgarh	434.54	624.66	1,059.20	1.84
North Karanpura	3,320.82	9,790.02	13,110.84	22.77
South Karanpura	1,807.34	3,950.51	5,757.85	10.00
Chotanagpur	22,168.29	35,402.61	57,570.90	89.26

Source: Indian Mineral Year Book, 2002.

Besides coal, the region also possesses fireclay, china clay, inferior quantity of iron ore, etc. Fireclay mineral helps the manufacture of firebricks and refractory materials. Other resources are graphite which are found in Dhanbad crystalline, limestone is found in Khalani, Hosir, Kurkuta, Bhurkunda and Bundu basins. Mineral waters are found in Karanpura, Bokaro coalfield areas and in eastern Dhanbad. Felspar used in making glass is found in Dhanbad district.

On the basis of coal resource, heavy metallurgy chemical and many other industrial groups came into existence. These coal fields have influenced considerably in the concentration of industries in the eastern states of India. The Sindri fertilizer factory, cement work at Sindri and Khelari, coal washeries, coke ovens, engineering works at Kumardhubi, refractory works in Dhanbad, glass factory, large steel plant at Bokaro, power plant at Chandrapura, Patratu, Bokaro, Sindri and Tenughat provide an industrial outlook about the development of natural resources in the region. The way industries are growing in the region, it may emerge as a large industrial belt with very high density of population, extent of urbanism, degree of mechanization and other respects. The development of hydroelectricity as a source of power is lacking. Moreover, known oil and natural gas resources of the country are meager in comparison to the needs. Recent increase in the price of oil has limited its use as a source of power. Hence, the country has no other alternatives than to rely on coal, a resource on which she has fairly good reserves and bright possibilities.

The Hazaribag Plateau Agro-Forest Region

The region lies between the North Koel basin in the west and south-west and mica belt in the north. On its south is the Damodar Valley. In the east it extends up to eastern limits of Hazaribag district. The region covers most of the parts of Kodarma, Chatra and Ramghar districts. It is a broad undulating plateau consisting of three separate patches arranged in an east-west elongation by the deep eroded valleys of Konark and Bokaro rivers: (i) Upper plateau, (ii) Lower plateau and (iii) The Northwestern plateau fringe. The Upper plateau is bounded by the north scarps of Damodar Valley in the south and, on the other side, it is bordered by a steep scarp with an average elevation of 600 metres. The Lower plateau occupies northern and eastern parts and has an average elevation of about 300 metres. On the west, it merges with the North Koel basin; on the east, Dhanbad peneplain and on the north-east with mica belt, but on the north-west, it drops to a plateau fringe which forms the third unit of the region occupying dissected hilly country of extreme northwestern Hazaribag. The region is drained towards the north mainly by the Lilajan and Mahani, and towards south and south-west by the Damodar and its tributaries. A large part of plateau has been rendered unproductive by soil erosion. Gullies of various types disfigure the plateau. Sheet erosion has progressed wherever the sloping land is not properly terraced into flat fields with proper embankments.

Important trees are *Sal, Khair, Semal, Mahua, Palas, Kusum, Kind, Ashor,* etc. The exploitation of forest is the most important activity. The hills and scarps are covered with deciduous trees. The principal tree, yielding good timber, is *sakhua* or *sal*. Other important resources are lac and shellac, *sabai* and other grasses and bamboos which form the greatest wealth of the region.

The region is served by electricity from Bokaro and Telaiya plants. The region is practically railless, but, Ramgarh on the Gomoh – Barkhakana and Hazaribagh road on Grand Chord eastern railway line serve the region. A new railway line is under construction from Koderma to Ranchi through Hazaribag, which will influence the economy of the region. Since the development of roads and railway, there has been a marked increase in the cultivated area and in the exploitation of forests. The main market centres Chatra, Simaria, Tandwa and Gidhaur are connected with Hazaribag by road communication.

Giridih coal field is the easternmost extension of the Lower Hazaribag plateau, an important resource potential region. Giridih has flourished as a colliery town where activities of the people are coal mining and mica industry. The surface is undulating and the scattered rocky ridge discloses the severity of the denudation to which this ancient land surface has been exposed. Soil of the area contains good proportion of sand while higher elevated areas have laterite soil. The area is suitable for agricultural purpose especially in the lower plateaus and the trough basin. Rice, maize, wheat and pulses are principal crops.

The region contains good quality coal. The important coal beds are Lower Karharbari seams varying between 3 to 11 metres in thickness. The Upper Karharbari seam varying from 1 to 3 metres is now exhausted and Bhadoah seam is 2 metres thick. The coal has a high colourific value and is used in the railways The region comprises 20 mining coal seams with an average thickness of 28 metres. Karharbari and Badua are important because of superior grade coking coal variety. Coal and mica resources have given rise to mica processing industries as well as coal mining activities. The district has considerable wasteland produced by mica mining after the exhaustion of mica.

The Kodarma Mica Region

On the northern fringe of the Chotanagpur plateau, the Kodarma mica resource region lies in south-west to north-east direction. The largest part of the mica belt falls within Kodarma district. The chief centres of mining are Dhorakhola, Domchanch, Masnodih, Dhad, Gawan and Tisri. The rocks exposed in the mica belt comprise of schists, gneisses, mica-bearing pegmatites and dolerites dykes. The excavated valleys have exposed the mica-bearing veins. The pegmatites, which are important in economic value, have been introduced into the schist in the form of sheets and lenses parallel to the foliation. Mica occurs as 'books' within the pegmatites. Mica-pegmatites are known to occur at least 360 metres thin, and less frequent, and mica obtained is of small size and inferior quality. Besides mica-pegmatite is remarkable for the large and varied assortment of minerals found therein of economic value. They are albite, tourmaline, beryl, garnet, quartz, columbite and fluorite. Mica is considered to be of pneumatolytic and hydrothermal origin. About 25 per cent of mica is obtained from surface mines and the rest is obtained from pits.

The mica industry of Chotanagpur is of enormous importance to India and the world. Nearly 70 per cent of the world's sheet mica comes from this belt. Chotanagpur's ruby mica is regarded as the best mica for electrical purposes. Mica is irreplaceable in its application, maintenance and development of the overgrowing electrical, radio, wireless and aeronautical industries. Railways and roads have given great support to its development. The diversified region with its numerous scarps, rapids and ravines has facilitated the direction of mica veins and has also directed the process of mining. Real development of mica belt started after the construction of the railway in 1916. The Grand Chord Line and the main line of Eastern Railway skirt the mica land on its western and eastern ends. Koderma, being the nearest railway station, receives mica mined in its vicinity. Metalled roads run through the belt. The Grand Trunk Road, Ranchi-Patna Road, Kodarma-Giridih Road and other roads form the network of roads. Railways and roads have added good deal in prospecting the mica resources.

The Rajmahal Hills and Adjoining Agro-Forest Region

The region lies at the north-eastern rim of Chotanagpur plateau or Peninsular India being bounded by the alluvial track of Ganga plains except in the south. It forms a part of Gondwana land consisting mainly of a series of hills and small plateaus intersected by a number of transverse river valleys. It contains most areas of Santhal Pargana except a narrow strip of alluvial plain of north and east. It comprises an area of 12,512 sq km. It is an upland track consisting of long spurs with alternating valleys. Agriculture is the dominant activity of the region.

The valleys lying between the undulating hills and ridges are full of fertile soils. The crest of the ridges is very poor made up of gravel of stiff clay lying on the hard subsoil, but, slopes contain good soil. Rice is cultivated on level terraces. Irrigation is used for paddy cultivation. Irrigation, generally, takes the form of embankment constructed across ravines, hollows or other natural depressions which impound drainage water. Paddy land is protected from drought by small irrigation works. The adjoining peneplain to the west and south is a land of good cultivation. Rice is grown mainly in the valleys and terraced slopes and accounts for about half of the total cropped area. The next important crops: maize, wheat, barley, linseed and gram are grown on uplands.

The region is thickly forested and is inhabited by Santhals and other primitive tribes. At places, *sabai* grass is grown wild on the hills and is used as raw material for the paper mills at Kolkata. On the uplands, forest cover is with Sal as the predominating species. Wood cutting, cattle rearing, poultry keeping and vegetable growing are the side occupations of the tribes of this region.

The region is not as rich as the Damodar and Subarnrekha basins, but, contains minerals of economic importance. Chief minerals are coal forming stones, limestone, pottery clays, iron ore, copper and lead ore. The coal is neither plentiful nor of good quality. China clay is another important mineral found on the western margin of Rajmahal. The region is ill-served by transportation lines. The population is sparse because of rocky surfaces, steep slopes and poor leteritic soil.

Conclusions

Thus, it can be concluded that Chotanagpur is a poverty-ridden land. There is regional inequality in the distribution of natural resources in the region. Exploitation of these resources has increased, but they have contributed less to the economic growth of the area. Resources are not available for utilization or for development of surrounding areas. State is responsible for safeguarding mineral resources but with no right to their beneficial use. Under the circumstances, growth in mineral output tells the story of expanding export of minerals. Thus, regional development through the growth of mining activities could not be fulfilled. The following conclusions are obtained from the above analysis: (1) due to planned efforts output of mineral resources has increased, (2) the outputs of minerals, power and forest resources are in high demand outside the region which yield large sum of revenue, (3) the rural areas are not directly benefited from the development of resources rather they suffer a deteriorating environment, (4) natural resources which are accessible to the common people could not be developed rapidly as in the case of revenue raising resources, (5) water has not been available to meet the needs of the people, in view of the requisition of yield-raising technology and the use of water for irrigation, (6) resources such as soil and livestock have not been paid attention, and (7) thus, the study reflects that resources should be managed rather than developed and the development should be planned in such a way that their sustainable supply can be maintained for a large section of the society with the least deterioration in the ecosystems.

References

Ahmad, E. (1965) *Bihar: A Physical, Economic and Regional Geography*, Ranchi: Ranchi University Press.

Anand, P.B. (2007) 'Semantics and Success or Pragmatics of Progress? An Assessment of India's Progress with Drinking Water Supply', *The Journal of Environment and Development*, 16(1): 32–57.

Auty, R.M. (2000) 'How Natural Resources Affect Economic Development', *Development Policy Review*, 18: 347–364.

Barthakur, M. (1969) 'Regional Approach to Resource Planning and Development of Assam', *Journal of the Northeast Indian Geographical Society*, 1(1–2): 32–40.

Bhat, L.S. et al. (1982) *Regional Inequalities in India*, New Delhi: Society for the Study of Regional Disparities.

Bhat, L.S. (1972) *Regional Planning in India*, Calcutta: Statistical Publishing Society.

Gensburg, N. (1957) 'Natural Resources and Economic Development', *Annals of the Association of American Geographers*, 47: 196–212.

Hodder, B.W. (1971) 'Natural Resources and Tropical Development', in A.B. Mukherjee (ed.), *Developing the Underdeveloped Countries*, London: Macmillan, 69–75.

Kayastha, S.L. (1984) 'Resource Geography', in *ICSSR: A Survey of Research in Geography*, New Delhi: Concept, 51–63.

Learmonth, A.T.A. and L.S. Bhat (eds) (1960) *Mysore State: Atlas of Resources*, Vol. I, Calcutta: Indian Statistical Institute.

Learmonth, A.T.A. et al. (1962) *Mysore State: Regional Synthesis*, Vol. 2, Mumbai: Asia Publishing House.

Muthoo, M.K. (1969) 'The Renewable Resource Planning Problem with Special Reference to Kashmir', *The Indian Geographical Journal*, 44(3–4): 64–80.

— (1970) 'The Concept of Renewable Resources', *The Geographer*, 18(1): 4–20.

Nath, V. (1965) *Resource Development Regions and Divisions of India*, New Delhi: Planning Commission, Government of India.

Pal, M.N. and Learmonth, A.T.A. (1964) quoted in Bhargava, A. (1991) *Resources and Regional Planning for Economic Development: A Case Study of Sagar Division, 'M.P.*, Delhi: Northern Book Centre, p. 130.

Prasad, M. (2008) 'Impact of New Mining Technology on Land Degradation in Coal Fields of Chotanagpur', in B. Thakur (ed.), *Perspectives in Resource Management in Developing Countries, Vol. 3: Ecological Degradation of Land*, New Delhi: Concept, 212–231.

Rao, V.L.S. Prakasa (1949) quoted in Bhargava, A. (1991) *Resources and Regional Planning for Economic Development: A Case Study of Sagar Division, M.P.*, Delhi: Northern Book Centre, p.130.

Roy, B.B., R.K. Gupta and L.S. Bhal (1971) 'Integrated Approach for Development of Natural Resources in Santhalpur Block', *Annals of Arid Zone*, 10(1): 15–28.

Schultz, T.W. (1965) 'Connection between Natural Resource and Economic Growth', in I. Burton and R.W. Kates (eds), *Readings in Resource Management and Conservation*, Chicago: University of Chicago Press, 397–403.

Sengupta, P. (1967) 'The Principles and Techniques of Regional Planning', *The Geographer*, 12: 29–36.

Sengupta, P. and G. Sadasyuk (1968) *Economic Regionalization of India: Problems and Approaches*, Monograph No. 8, New Delhi: Census of India.

Sharma, S.K. (1989) *Resource Development in Tribal India*, New Delhi: Northern Book Centre.

—— (1992) *Resource Utilisation and Development*, New Delhi: Northern Book Centre.

Smith, D.M. (1977) *Human Geography: A Welfare Approach*, London: Edward Arnold.

Sundaram, K.V. (1980) 'Techniques and Methods of Resource-Based Regionalization', Paper Presented at the Indo-Soviet Symposium on Rational Utilisation and Conservation of Renewable Resources for Regional Development, New Delhi, 10–15 December.

Thakur, B. (2003) 'Introduction', in B. Thakur (ed.), *Perspectives in Resource Management in Developing Countries, Vol. I: Resource Management: Theory and Techniques*, New Delhi: Concept, 1–45.

—— (2007) 'Emerging Trends in India's Resource Development: Implications for Sustainable Management in Developing Countries', in B. Thakur (ed.), *Perspectives in Resource Management in Developing Countries, Vol. 2: Population, Resources and Development*, New Delhi: Concept, 3–87.

Thakur, R. (2009) 'Development of Natural Resources in Chotanagpur Region', in A. Kumar, R.S. Kushwaha and B. Thakur (eds), *Earth System Sciences: Felicitation Volume in Honour of Professor V.K. Verma*, New Delhi: Concept, 415–437.

Tosi, J.A. and R.F. Voertman (1964) 'Some Environmental Factors in the Economic Development of the Tropics', *Economic Geography*, 40(3): 189.

White, G.F. (1965) 'The Special Problem of the Underdeveloped Countries with Respect to Natural Resources', in I. Burton and R.W. Kates (eds), *Readings in Resource Management and Conservation*, Chicago: University of Chicago Press, 422–426.

2

Resource Use and Agricultural Structure in Medieval India

MOHAMMAD DILSHAD

Agriculture is closely related to environment and these are interdependent. In medieval economy, the environment had played a significant role in the production process. It is a very fundamental question considering that Indian economy was largely dominated by agriculture throughout its history. It has been found that during the pre-colonial period in spite of colonization and wars resulting in deforestation, to a certain extent, there was 'harmony' and 'equilibrium' between man and environment. Cutting of forests and export of timber was sustainable because of the low population pressure. On the other side, the cutting was limited largely to the extent nature was ready to replenish. But during the colonial period, this balance got disturbed. However, recent studies emphasizes that even earlier the picture does not seem to be as ideal as it is projected. For fuel and building material, timber from neighbouring forests was regularly supplied and forests were cut. Advancing armies brought no less harm to the existing forest line apart from clearances for agriculture. Thus, the aim of this paper is to understand relationship of environment and man by analysing the resource use pattern and the agriculture structure during the medieval period of Indian history.

Pattern of Resource Use

In the context of agriculture, the term resources imply the 'means' that were instrumental in the process of agricultural production. Land occupied the important place in this context. Besides land, capital was another important component of it. Working capital represents ploughs, bullocks, etc. The other factors were the capacity and capability of the peasants to organize the cultivation. The peasant himself alongwith his family members occupied foremost place in the production process, particularly in the medieval period context when the cultivation was largely based on individual peasant farming. Further, the role of hired labour and tenants-at-will was also equally significant.

Land Resource

Land was available in abundance throughout the medieval period. Therefore, the high land-man ratio was an important characteristic of the medieval agrarian structure. Though it is very difficult to assess the actual size of landholdings per household during the Sultanate period, some regional studies pertaining to the Mughal period do throw some light. Singh (1990) has calculated the size of landholdings per *alami* for eastern Rajasthan as high as approximately 90 bighas.

Since land was in abundance, it was the state's concern to keep the peasant tied to the land. Another important aspect relating to resource use was the capacity of the peasant to possess the ploughs. The more the ploughs in his possession, the more the *jots* (ability to cultivate) he could manage and the higher would be his status in the village hierarchy. Gupta (1986) has mentioned as much as 9 ploughs in the possession of a *patel* (village headman) of *pargana* Mauzabad in eastern Rajasthan as against the maximum of one or two by the poor peasants.

The availability of animal power was another important factor instrumental in the extension of cultivation. Abul Fazl, court chronicler of Akbar, records the number of cattle allowed tax free for each plough was 4 bullocks, two cows and one buffalo. While in 1924–25 in Uttar Pradesh average number of cattle per yoke was 2 bullocks, 1.1 cows and 1 buffalo suggests the availability of higher stock of cattle in circa 1595. It also suggests the greater capacity of peasants to plough (Habib, 1982).

Soil Resource

Depending on the nature of soil and local conditions, the Mughal rulers adopted the indigenous methods of land classification. In *suba* (province) Bihar, the lands were classified under the heads *kahelfi* (irrigated) and *kanhel* (tank irrigated lands; also known as *talabi* in certain areas). *Bhoor* was sandy soil generally yielded *kharif* crops. The other two major land classifications were *bangur* (upland) *khadir* (low land). *Khadir* crop was generally uncertain. Similarly, as compared to arid regions alluvial soil does not require deep ploughing.

Under the Mughals, land was divided into *polaj, parauti, chachar and banjar. Polaj* never allowed to remain fallow and less labour was required for cultivation. *Parouti* was left out of cultivation for sometime to recover its strength for cultivation. *Chachar* lay fallow for three of four year. *Banjar* remained largely uncultivated for five or more years. Even some of the *banjar* tracts remained barren permanently particularly in a desert and hilly tracts.

Forest

The medieval period was commonly characterized with clearing of forest line for the purpose of agrarian expansion. The history of agriculture development is same as the history of forest depletion. The growth of one from that of sustenance (agriculture) resulted in depletion of another form of sustenance (pastoral/forest economy). The beginning of modern period has seen large expanse of forest cover in the Indo-Gangetic plains. The forest cover drastically changed by the close of the 17th century. Armed power went hand in hand in the process of extension of cultivation by clearing forest. Armed band accompanying woodcutters was a common feature in North India during the medieval period. In the Ganga-Yamuna doab we get frequent references to peasants/rebels taking refuge in the forest. Balban harshly dealt with such uprisings of the Mewatis and the Kateharias (Katehr region, modern Rohilkhand) and cleared the jungles of the nearby areas where they took refuge and established forts with Afghan garrisons.

Nurul Hasan has brought to notice with regard to *suba* (province) Bihar that during the reign of Shahjahan most of the *zamindaris* originated in Bankati or land populated after clearing forests. From the time of Shahjahan, it was customary that woodcutters and plough men used to accompany his troops, so that forests may be cleared and land cultivated. Ploughs used to be donated by the government. Short-term *pattas* (documents stating revenue demand) were given, and government demand at the rate of 1 *anna* per *bigha* during the first year. *Chaudhuries* (intermediaries) were appointed to keep the *riaya* (peasants) happy with their considerate behaviour and to populate the country. They were to ensure that the *pattas* were issued in accordance with imperial orders and pledged word was kept. There was the great order that whosoever cleared a forest and brought land under cultivation, such land would be his *zamidari*.

Agriculture Structure

Extent of Agriculture

Delhi Sultans, particularly Alauddin Khilji and later Muhammad Tughluq experimented with measurement of the agricultural land. Abul Fzal provides great details with regard to the extent of cultivation. It is interesting to note that both crops *kharif* and *rabi,* were separately measured. Suppose, in a village both *rabi* and *kharif* crops are harvested then that village land was calculated, twice.

Abul Fazl's *arazi* (measured area) figures probably comprised not only the gross cropped area as more land has pointed out, but also included current fallows, cultivable waste and parts of uncultivated waste as rightly pointed out by Irfan Habib (1963) and Shireen Moosvi (1987). Moosvi has calculated that Ain's *arazi* figures included around 10 per cent of the uncultivable waste. Singh (1990) and Gupta (1986) calculated for eastern Rajasthan show that the range of wastelands varied from 7–20 per cent. This could be *basti* (habitation), forest, nallah, nadi, tank, garden land or hills. Moosvi for Akbar's period and Gupta for eastern Rajasthan have pointed out that the total cultivated area was around area 50–65 per cent of the measured area.

Moosvi (1987) has calculated the average rate of extension of cultivation at 0.23 per cent as against 0.21 per cent rate of growth of population during 1600–1871. She has compared the gross cultivation in 1595 with that of 1910 agricultural statistics and concluded that the average extent of cultivation comes out to be 47.35 per cent, i.e., it was almost half of what it was in 1910. Habib (1982) found that average yields per head under the Mughals were probably much higher than what it was in 1900. Trivedi study on *suba* Agra also points out that in case of food crops the yields were 20 per cent higher in 1595 as compared to 1892 statistics. Moosvi, however, argues that yields per acre between 1540 to 1870 for major food crops remained practically the same, while in case of cash crops there was relative decline in their output. South India also records high level of productivity during this period. But there occurred sharp decline in the productivity during the 19th century in the region.

High yields for various crops entered in the *Ain-i Akbari* (1595) led Trivedi (1998) to conclude that in *suba* Agra "the cultivation was normally confined to fertile land". Singh (1991) also points out that in Punjab the extension of cultivation has largely occurred only in agriculturally developed areas during the 17th century. One reason for the large-scale expansion of cultivation was distribution of secular (*jagir*) and religious (*madad-I maash*) grants. Each Madad–I Maash grant normally consisted of 50 per cent *banjar* (waste) or *liak ufrada* (cultivable waste) under the Mughals.

Cropping Pattern

In North India, there were two crop seasons – *kharif* and *rabi*. In Rajasthan, they were known as *siyalu* (autumn) and *unhalu* (spring) while in South India on the basis of specific variety of rice cultivation there existed two crop seasons *kuddapah-kar* and *samb-perhanam*. Otherwise, in the case of other crops there was complete absence of crop seasons.

Sujan Rai Bhandari (1695) found that in certain areas of Punjab even three or more crops were cultivated. But some areas like western Rajasthan on account of aridity even the areas containing sweet water wells were not enough for double cropping. In Rajasthan, double cropping was possible only in clayey soils; in lighter soils it was rather rare. Crops grown on rainfed tracts fetched low prices as compared to the crops which required artificial means of irrigation (Bhadani, 1999). For Maratha region, Kulkarni (1969) found only in the *Des* area, where black soil could be found, rotation of crops was possible. Along the coastal regions where soil largely contained marine deposits was favoured for garden crops. Where irrigation facilities were available second crop was possible otherwise in the Maratha region usually one crop was raised.

During the medieval period there was a tendency to encourage cultivation of high grade crops replacing the inferior ones. Muhammad Tughluq asked the peasants to grow high grade crops like wheat replacing barley, sugarcane replacing wheat, and cultivation of dates and grapes in place of sugarcane. Aurangzeb also clearly emphasized in his *farman* to Rasikdas (1665–66) that attempt should be to replace from inferior *(jins-i adana)* to high grade crops *(jins-i ala)*.

Crops

Cropping pattern still continued to be the same in the Gangetic plains. Largely wheat, barley, pulses, sugarcane, cotton oil seeds (sesame, mustard, etc.) were grown in the tract. Barley was the major crop of Rajasthan. However, it was not the favoured crop in the region of Bengal, Bihar and Assam. In southern parts of India, rice was the major crop on irrigated lands (*nancai*). Other crops were cholam, ragi, varagu, sesame, flax, groundnut, cotton, etc. In medieval Orissa, Kashmir, and Assam also, rice was the staple crop, though wheat, barley, pulses, gram, etc., were also produced in the region. In Kashmir almost 2/3rds of the land was covered under paddy cultivation grown on *abi* (irrigated) land. Bihar was also known for its rice production. However, in Rajasthan rice was not at all produced. Chilli was introduced in India during the 17th century, but its spread became more common during the mid-18th century only.

Among the garden crops, Ibn Battuta (1377) speaks a lot of mangoes in Bengal, Golconda and Delhi. The entire Konkan coastal belt produced mangoes, coconuts, betel-nuts, betel-vine, areca-nut, palm, pineapple, jack-fruit, sweet potatoes, etc. *Des* gardens in Maharashtra with irrigation facilities were famous for production of grapes, betel leaves, etc. Al-Breuni found the use of betel-leaf (*pan*) fairly widespread in India. Amir Khusrau (13th century) in his *Aijaz-i Khusrawi* mentions as much as 42 varieties of it. Bihar was known for the production of *maghi pan*. Hajipur (Bihar) was acclaimed for the production of jackfruit. In *sarkar* Tirhut, *suba* Bihar, orange grooves extended as far as 30 miles.

During the 13th century production of grapes was not as widespread as at the turn of the century. Muhammad Tughluq encouraged peasant to shift to production of grapes. Production of fruits and vegetables was largely confined to the vicinity of the urban centres. In North India, Mali caste specialized in its production. In medieval period, there developed the tradition of maintaining orchards. But they were largely maintained in the Deccan during the late 17th century.

Agricultural Productivity

Productivity of an area is related with soil fertility. The soil quality depends upon rainfall pattern, availability of irrigation facilities, organic material and mineral deposits in the soil. The pattern of productivity on irrigated and dryland varied from region-to-region. In Kashmir, the average output of *abi* (irrigated) land was six times higher than yields of the *Khushki* (unirrigated) land. In Maharashtra, cultivable land available was very little. Kulkarni (1969) found out in village Menoli (Vai *taluka*) cultivated land was just 16 per cent the total village land while availability of irrigated land was even much less. It constituted only 1 per cent in village Nayagav, *pargana* Sirval (modern Bhor *taluka*).

Besides, during the medieval period, Indian agriculture was quite dynamic and new techniques were constantly being innovated and adopted. In agriculture sector drastic changes took place not only in terms of techniques but also in the patterns of crops grown.

Techniques of Irrigation

In north India, *kharif* crops were largely depended upon the monsoons rains while *rabi* crops heavily relied on the availability of the artificial irrigation. There were the absence of running waters. There are frequent references that bad monsoon or excessive rains resulted in migration of the peasants. In contrast to Babur Zainuddin Khawaf (*Tuzuk-i-Babri*) highlighs the presence of rivulets from the rivers for irrigation purposes. *Ain* records a number of *mahals* (smallest unit for revenue assessment) and villages located on river/stream banks largely using water from them for irrigation. As compared to the north, rainfall pattern in southern India was much more evenly distributed on account of south-western and south-eastern monsoons. Further, in southern India, dry cultivation (based on artificial means of irrigation) was more common as compared to northern parts of India. Though extensive irrigation ventures were undertaken by the rulers, elites as well as villagers, hardly much care was taken for its maintenance.

Wells

In medieval period, the most common means for irrigation was from wells. Muhammad Tughlaq granted loans to the peasants for digging up wells. Babur notes the prevalence of both the Persian wheel in Lahore and Dipalpur and indigenous *charas* in the region east of Yamuna. The *charas* (in Gujarat called *kasa*) could work both on the well and on the river banks. *Rabi* crop largely depended upon artificial means of irrigation. In his *farman* to rasikdas karori (revenue collector) (1665–66) Aurangzeb also emphasized that the old wells fallen out of use should be repaired and that new wells be dug at different places for extension of cultivation and production of *jisns-i kamil* (high grade crops). The *baoris* (step-wells) were also used for irrigation purposes. Muhnot nainsi, *diwan* of Raja Jaswant Singh (AD 1638–78) in his *Marwar ra Pargana ri Vigat* mentions two types of wells used for irrigation – *kisita* (shallow; largely *kachcha* wells) and *kohar* (deep; largely brick lined wells). *Kachcha* wells generally outnumbered *pucca* wells.

Tanks, Dams and Reservoirs

Use of dams for irrigation purposes was widespread during the medieval period. Babur equally acknowledged the use of lakes, tanks, ponds, and reservoirs for irrigation purposes. Zainuddin khawaf refers to *jalhas*, i.e., lakes and ponds in some cases extending from 1–3 *kuroh* (2.5–7.5 miles). These were particularly useful for irrigating vegetable fields and orchards. Babur records that where proper cannels were not available, people themselves used to carry water in pitchers to irrigate plants. However, such cumbersome method could possibly be used to irrigate only small plots.

Dams were used efficiently to utilize the flood waters. Chandelle dam of Muzaffarpur village, tehsil Chakiya, district Varanasi, Uttar Pradesh that survived till 1954–56, utilized efficiently the floodwater flowing into river Chandeaprabha used for irrigating vast tract of Chandraprabha-Karmanara *Doab*.

Raja Bahroz Singh of Kharagpur (1631–76) erected a dam, Bhimbandh (south-west of Kharagpur). It utilized the rainwater from the hills. He chalked out an interesting plan of distributing rainwater. Large channels on raised platform were erected to carry out water from the dam. Such was the distribution that water was made available throughout the year.

The most popular forms of artificial means of irrigation in southern India were reservoirs, tanks and dams. However, its construction involved huge amount of money that made individual efforts impossible. Invariably, one finds largely the involvement of either the entire village or group of villages or else of the elite or the state. Vijayanagara rulers took special interest to lay vast network of tanks in their territory (Figure 1). The earliest record of tank construction by the Vijayanagara ruler is in 1369, when Bukka I's son Bhaskara Buvafura (Prince Bukka) brought the water of Maldevi river for irrigation. The tank is still used for irrigating fields. The tank is seven miles long and two and half miles broad. He also endured the water supply at Penukonda by digging a channel and connecting it to a tank.

Figure 1

Terraced Tank in Vijaynagara

Canal

In South India, rivers are largely rainfed and water level often fluctuates. On account of this, canal irrigation was hardly favoured as means of irrigation. In contrast, in North India from the beginning of the 14th century our period saw the establishment of huge canal networks for irrigation purposes. Though, the beginning was done by Ghiyasuddin Tughluq (1320–25), it was Firuz (1351–86) who established a huge network of canals for irrigation purposes. To obtain continuous water supply to his newly built town of Hissar, Firuza Firuz dug two canals from Yamuna – the Rajabwah and the Ulughkhani. It greatly helped in the extension of cultivation in the region. During Shahjahan's reign another important canal was excavated in the Upper Bari *Doab* region (Punjab) on river Ravi that carried the water up to Lahore.

To a large extent in the northern region, agriculture was rainfed. Digging up of wells was the result of individual efforts. In the Deccan and southern plains we do find creation of artificial lakes by constructing dams across the streams. However, in spite of the great concern of the state to provide irrigation facilities, approximately total irrigated land in South India constituted 3–7 per cent, at the turn of the 19th century (except Tanjure where the percentage was as high as 50).

Commercialization of Agriculture

Habib (1963) argues that the state's insistence to collect revenue in cash and also to gain profit was the major factor behind the commercialization of agriculture during the medieval period. An alternative opinion is that there is plenty of evidence of prevalence of money and exchange in the rural economy prior to the state's demand of revenue in cash. However, this action of the state would certainly push commercialization in the agricultural sector. At any rate the cultivator also benefited from it either by selling his produce in the market or by producing high value crops. The peasants responded to the needs of the market. Cotton was one of the crops produced keeping in view the demand of its final product, the textile, outside the local market. Sugar, both, candy and powdered was produced of the market. Indigo was one of the most important of the commercial crops in demand. Indigo cultivators from Sehwan in Sindh who used to export their produced to the Middle East had to face a lot of difficulty when the demand declined sharply in 1640s. Tobacco, though a 17th century incorporation, also got commercialized very fast. Thus considerable amount of agricultural production was actually 'commodity production'. Habib (1982) argues that the cultivation of cash crops required larger investments and it was beyond the affordability of an ordinary peasant. Thus, he links the commercialization of superior agriculture to *khwud-kashta* cultivation. He says that *khwud-kashta,* organized for commodity production, comes closest to capitalist farming.'

Summary and Conclusions

Based on the above discussion on resource use and agriculture structure during the medieval period, various conclusions can be drawn. It is clear that during medieval period, the peasants were engaged in both seasons – rabi and kharif, for cultivating variety of food grains. The agriculture was characterized with favourable climate, fertile soil, availability of labourers and livestock. Besides the plenty of fertile land, lots of people still worked as landless labourers. To provide the irrigation facilities, deforestation took place at a large scale. Major sources of water for irrigating the field were wells, ponds, tanks and canal system. Discovery of the new route opened up new channels of contacts that brought in knowledge of new crops, particularly from the new world, resulting in the variety of crops that were sown during the medieval period in India.

References

Bhadani, B.L. (1999) *Peasants, Artisans and Entrepreneurs: Economy of Marwar in 17th Century*, Jaipur: Rawat Publications.

Gupta, S.P. (1986) *The Agrarian System of Eastern Rajasthan*, New Delhi: Manohar Publications.

Habib, I. (1982) 'The Peasant in Indian History', Presidential Address, Proceedings of the Indian History Congress, Kurukshetra.

—— (1963) *The Agrarian System of Mughal India, 1556–1707*, Delhi: Oxford University Press.

—— (1980) 'Changes in Technology in Medieval India', *Studies in History*, 2(1).

Hasan, S.N. (1971) *Thoughts on Agrarian Relations in Mughal India*, New Delhi: People's Publishing House.

Kulkarni, A.R. (1969) *Marathas in the Age of Shivaji*, Pune: Deshmukh.

Moosvi, S. (1987) *The Economy of Mughal Empire, c: 1596: The Statistical Study*, Delhi: Oxford University Press.

Mukhiya, H. (1968) 'Agricultural Technology in Medieval North India', in H. Mukhiya (ed.), *Perspectives on Medieval History*, New Delhi: Vikas Publishing.

Singh, C. (1991) *Region and Empire: Punjab in the 17th Century*, Delhi: Oxford University Press.

Singh, D. (1990) *The State, Landlords and Peasants: Rajasthan in the 18th Century*, Delhi: Manohar Publications.

Trivedi, K.K. (1998) *Agra: Economy and Political Profile of a Mughal Soba, 1580–1707*, Pune: Ravish Publishers.

3

Mechanism of Land Transfer in Bihar

A Case Study of Six Villages

RAJEEV RANJAN KUMAR SINHA

Land is the most important natural resource and is the principal means of production upon which the whole superstructure of social and political power rests. That is why the struggle for control over land is endemic in an agrarian society. It provides *raison d'etre* for the struggle and the shifting pattern of control over land and the resultant changes in land use management practices (Thakur and Vir, 2003). Ownership of land defines the prestige, power and status in agrarian societies (Chakravarti, 2001). Control over land, however, depends upon and is influenced by the pattern of agrarian structure, which is, defined by the segregating aspect of the caste system and the hegemony of the dominant caste (Beteille, 1971a). Therefore, this study probes into questions, such as does the same phenomenon exist in all the selected regions? Are there any inter-regional variations? Has any change taken place during the last three decades in the above characteristic features? That is why the main focus of the study is to analyse the quantitative relationship between caste and transfer of land.

The Study Area

The study area comprises three distinct ecological regions of Bihar with having distinct socio-cultural set-ups. To understand the dynamism of transfer of land in these distinct socio-cultural set-ups, two sample villages from each ecological region have been selected. The three ecological regions are:

1. *The Adhwara Plain*: It has riverine ecology with very gentle slope towards south and south-east and is drained by the Adhwara system of rivers, namely, Kamla and Balan, which join and divide several times, creating several rivers of the same name. This region is subject to frequent floods. As a result, settlement in this region is found on the uplands or *bhit* and is of compact type. The region covers the districts of Sitamarhi, Madhubani, Darbhanga, Khagaria, eastern Samastipur and northern Begusarai (Prasad, 1983). Rainfall ranges between 1,200–1,400 mm. The soils are calcareous and alluvial with rice, wheat and maize as the principal crops.
2. *The Western North Bihar Plain or the Gandak Plain*: It covers the entire area from the western boundary of the State to the river Burhi Gandak in the east. It includes the districts of Gopalganj, Siwan, Saran, Vaishali, Samastipur,

Muzaffarpur, Purbi Champaran and Pashchim Champaran (Dayal, 1968). The entire region is a level alluvial plain and is covered by light loamy *'bhit'* uplands (levees) where there is usually high proportion of lime. Rain occurs during the monsoon whose amount is around 1,200 mm. The predominant agricultural crops are paddy, barley and maize, and sugarcane is the most important cash crop. The region has highest population density. The settlements are of clustered type.

3. *The Central South Bihar Plain*: It spreads over the districts lying between the Sone and the Kiul River, namely, Patna, Jehanabad, Aurangabad, Gaya, Nawada, Nalanda, Munger and Jamui. It is characterized by vast plain traversed by narrow and long quartzite ridges of Rajgir and Kharagpur (Ahmad, 1965). The slope of this region is from south to north and from west to east. The region enjoys the moist subhumid type of climate with an average rainfall of 1,200 mm. The area of lowest rainfall in the State lies here. The region is drained by small rivers of Punpun, Phalgu, Sakri, Kiul, etc., largely consisting of older alluvium, which is heavy textured with greater clay proportion. Wheat is the dominant crop of this region with rice, khesari and masoor. The settlement is compact in the plain area, while dispersal is seen in the fringe near the foothills.

Methodology

The study is dynamic in nature and the period selected for study was 1971 to 2001. The total enumeration method was adopted by taking the household and individual plot as a unit. Base maps were collected for each village from the Patwari or from the District Collectorate. Village *Khasra, Khatauni* or *Khatiyan* with Demand or Register II were helpful in collecting data related to name and caste of household, amount and plot number of land possessed by each household, money value of the plot, types of crop grown for the period 1971–2001, sale and purchase of land among different caste groups and their patterns. The Chakbandi Officer and the Circle Officer were consulted for unravelling the occasional change brought by the government in restructuring the village *Khatiyan.* The District Census Handbook and the Gazetteer were consulted for the basic characteristics and history of the district. Literatures with general observation and discussion in the field with the old and the knowledgeable persons helped in understanding the factors responsible for transfer of land in rural society of Bihar. Further, on the basis of data collected from Khatiyan and other sources, a comparative table for the years, 1971–2001 has been prepared for each villages that helped in analysing the dynamism of transfer of land in rural Bihar from one caste to another, over a period of 30 years and more.

Theme

The transfer of land conceptually involves broader areas of transfer of land across different castes and classes through any means, via any ways and in any form. This encapsulates many factors such as natural fragmentation under population pressure through the generations, structural changes and social factors. The most recent factor that contributes to this phenomenon is out-migration. The stipulated time of the empirical analysis falls in between 71 to 2001; the coverage of the present study is altogether six villages located in four districts of three ecological regions. The quantitative data arranged into six exhaustive tables is obtained from the official records. And, the qualitative analysis is based on our understanding of the theme, which is obtained through diverse interaction and conceptual studies available on the subject. The reasons for land transfer and the factors responsible for the same interact with each other. For simplicity and clarity the 'factor' aspects is made the key point in the following sub-part. This also explains as how and why land transfer has taken place in the purview of this study area.

Factors Responsible for Transfer of Land

Demographic

Demographic factors include natural fragmentation and consolidation of land that takes place under demographic pressure. Land resource normally happens to be joint property and it is divided among those sons, who stay at home in the village and look after farming activities. This, however, does not mean that those who stay away from home are deprived of their rights (to land). In fact, locational situation decides land resource management. In whatever way it takes place, the important factor is ongoing transfer of land through the mechanism of natural fragmentation generation after generation. Over the last three decades, two generations have come up to accelerate this process. The quantitative data utilized in this chapter though does not throw light on this factor of transfer, yet this process must have taken place – this fact cannot be denied.

Structural Factors

The main mechanism of land transfer during 1960s and thereafter was land ceiling legislations, which accelerated the process of land redistribution and the process of 'desperate' market in land, simultaneously. In North Bihar, then the huge land consolidation and control of land by the big landowners, had to face serious jolt under the land reforms legislations. To save their holdings, as much as possible, the big landowners adopted four-pronged strategies; first, settlement of land through its transfer in the name of religious places like Mandir, Maszid, Math, etc., second, through transfer of land in the name of distant relatives, kiths and kins; third, desperate sale of those plots, which were already leased out to *bataidars;* and fourth, eviction of petty bataidars as they were not capable of becoming buyers of the plots they were cultivating since long. The upper caste landowners were cultivating their huge farms via layers of big and small bataidars and bataidari was the main mode of land resource management before the land reforms measures were adopted in Bihar. It was this 'desperate' sale of land to this big bataidar class, which led to the emergence of 'rich peasant' as a dominant class in rural Bihar after the first phase of land reforms was over. The phenomenon of emergence of rich and middle peasant and decline of huge landowning 'zamindari' system, therefore, may be treated as the dominant mechanism of land transfer since 1960s onwards.

The second important phenomenon was introduction of new technology since late 1960s and thereafter. The newly emerged 'rich peasant' class was its vanguard. The new technology substantially increased production cost in farming. This led to eviction of small and petty farmers, as they were incapable of bearing increased production cost and therefore, were left with no option but to lease-out their small plots to rich peasants in return for some money. This process, known as 'reverse tenancy' gradually led to the process of 'reconsolidation' of land in favour of rich peasants. This is why our quantitative data (see tables in following pages) reflects very little change in the landowning status of the dominant castes in respective villages. The period between 1971–2001 is a volatile period in the history of rural

Bihar, which has witnessed the above stated important processes of land transfer and its different mechanisms, but the available official land records fail to explain these processes. Here lies the importance of qualitative data, which supplemented with quantitative data may produce a picture close to the reality.

The ensuing process of land transfer after introduction of new technology, twice eviction of petty landholders from their tiny plots (this process is conceptually established as the proletarianization of peasantry, which became the prime mover for labour out-migration from Bihar), 'reverse tenancy' and 'land reconsolidation' continued through intensification of food and cash-cropping via growing mechanization in farming. This made farming even more cost-intensive. Further, land-contracting based on cash payment also came into existence after 1980s. These factors have contributed to land transfer process from weaker section of peasantry to stronger sections. We may sum up these processes as 'structural' nature of land transfer mechanism, because these processes are a direct outcome of the overall process of structural change in agrarian Bihar.

Social Factors

The social factors include those transfers, which have taken place not as a part of structural changes but as a part of changing life conditions of the people concerned. It is an established fact that land resource serves as the dominant 'asset' as well, for the landed people. Their life conditions are directly/indirectly associated with this 'asset'. They have to bank upon this asset in critical times, and for more than one reasons land is sold, mortgaged or gifted on many occasions. Right from the survival, the health, education, marriage of son and daughter, occasional ceremonies such as festivals, birth, death, etc., in the family – all depends on the income generated from the land, farming and associated works. Even for securing job opportunities at local or distant places, farmers have to provide their sons (and now, in some cases daughters too) with money. For meeting all these usual and unusual needs, the landed people have to rely on their land resource. They have to sell land to meet dowry demands and other expenses of marriage; have to gift part of land to daughter in her marriage; they have to sell part of land to meet educational needs for children. Normally, in an upper caste upwardly mobile families, sons are encouraged to go for higher or technical studies. This involves heavy expenditure. Transfer of land resource takes place on all such occasions in different ways and via different means.

Out-migration

In a village, located in Bihar, rootedness aspect associated with landownership is a normal feature. This is in contrast to the other face of rural society of Bihar, which is characterized by huge scale of 'out-migration'. The phenomenon of 'out-migration, in the context of Bihar, usually refers to labour out-migration. While labour out-migration is one reason for transfer of land, the migration of students across the country for study purpose is a reason that is much more important for transfer of land. For the landed class, it is their single resource or asset that is sold or mortgaged for enabling their sons to pursue their studies in distant academic locations.

The small farmers and labour class with tiny plots usually sell or mortgage or lease-out (to big farmers) their land for migration arrangements as well as for securing their family's looking after in their absence. They help the transfer process through reinvestment in land. Here, the rootedness aspect holds value.

Now the question arises: What about migrant service-holders or professionals or those engaged in off-farm sector jobs? There is another aspect in this context that exists. The landed people (big landowners also) who are involved in service sector or professionals or those engaged in off-farm sector jobs adopt two kinds of approach. Firstly, they either get settled in their place of job and manage their property in the village with the help of a manager, bataidar, etc., or secondly, due to increase in their status and also development of an urban mindset, they slowly but steadily sell out their land in the village. Here one important thing that has been identified through the qualitative survey of the villages is that the main buyers of those lands are usually the families of the migrated people, because they annually used to send big amount of their savings to their natives/relatives. As a result, they start improving their hold in the rural power structure by owning large amount of land. We will see this phenomenon in the coming analysis of the tables.

Data Interpretation

The interpretation of the data given below in six different tables one each for a village, is to verify and help the above mentioned qualitative analysis through the land transfer mechanism.

The Adhwara Plain

Kokri Village

Kokri is a medium-sized village in Madhubani district. Villages of North Bihar are normally much bigger in area and also more densely populated as compared to South Bihar. This village had altogether 2,108 plots accommodated in altogether 613.13 acres in 1971. This figure continues till 2001 with a difference in total number of plots, which increased from 2,108 to 2,841 during 1992–1993. A simple conclusion is that disproportionate distribution of plots during 1992–1993 reduces the average plot-size since then. How does this relate to transfer of land mechanism? It might be under the population pressure that facilitated natural fragmentation of land. Or, it might be market in land that compelled big landowners to sell their plots and fragment some others in this process. We do not have comparative population figures to corroborate these facts. However, above factors associated with transfer of land can hardly be denied.

Table 1 reveals that the dominating land occupant caste in this village is Brahmin that occupies a little more than 320 acres (54.21% of the total) distributed over 1,207 plots in 2001. It was 227.62 acres (46.94%) distributed over 619 plots in 1971 and almost similar figures appear in 1981. Remarkably, a hike is registered in 1992–1993 with 321.02 acres (54.40%) distributed over as many as 1,210 plots occupied by Brahmin caste! There must be some important explanation for this. Another observable fact is the decline in plot-size since 1992–1993 because, the percentage of plots and acres is increased by about 10.5 and close to 8 (as compared to 1971 and 1981) but the number of plots has almost doubled (from 619 to 1,210). This clearly suggests natural fragmentation and transfer of land, under the population pressure. Big joint families are common features in North Bihar villages and nature of migration in landed class is different from the landless class, who migrate for their survival. The landed castes (classes also), normally diversify in other occupations, but, the landed families retain their hold over land resources simultaneously. Kokri village appears to be such a standard village in this respect.

Table 1

Kokri: Pattern of Land Transfer Among Different Castes, 1971–2001

Caste	1971		1981		1992–3		2001	
	No. of plots occupied (%) to the total	*Area occupied (in acres) (%) to the total*	*No. of plots occupied (%) to the total*	*Area occupied (in acres) (%) to the total*	*No. of plots occupied (%) to the total*	*Area occupied (in acres) (%) to the total*	*No. of plots occupied (%) to the total*	*Area occupied (in acres) (%) to the total*
Brahmin	619 (36.37)	227.62 (46.94)	618 (36.31)	220.65 (45.52)	1210 (46.88)	321.02 (54.40)	1,207 (46.76)	320.07 (54.21)
Sonar	191 (11.22)	42.78 (8.82)	191 (11.22)	42.78 (8.27)	133 (5.15)	21.09 (3.57)	130 (5.04)	20.83 (3.53)
Barai	144 (8.46)	21.42 (4.42)	144 (8.47)	21.42 (4.14)	180 (6.97)	20.5 (3.39)	178 (6.89)	19.85 (3.36)
Mallah	121 (7.10)	24.70 (5.10)	123 (7.23)	24.70 (5.10)	116 (4.49)	15.14 (2.56)	117 (4.53)	16.60 (2.81)
Kewat	119 (6.99)	22.60 (4.67)	119 (6.99)	22.60 (4.37)	80 (3.10)	12.74 (2.16)	83 (3.21)	13.97 (2.36)
Dusadh	102 (5.99)	26.84 (5.53)	96 (5.64)	26.61 (5.48)	59 (2.28)	5.71 (0.96)	49 (1.90)	4.47 (0.76)
Barhai	92 (5.40)	21.36 (4.40)	91 (5.34)	21.26 (4.38)	87 (3.37)	13.73 (2.32)	87 (3.37)	13.73 (2.32)
Teli	85 (4.99)	33.92 (6.99)	85 (4.99)	33.92 (6.55)	289 (11.19)	76.93 (13.03)	294 (11.39)	77.12 (13.10)
Dhanuk	66 (3.88)	14.52 (2.99)	65 (3.82)	14.49 (2.98)	31 (1.20)	4.44 (0.75)	31 (1.20)	4.44 (0.75)
Hajjam	33 (1.94)	09.24 (1.91)	33 (1.94)	9.24 (1.79)	38 (1.47)	4.85 (0.82)	38 (1.47)	4.85 (0.82)
Chamar	33 (1.94)	07.96 (1.66)	33 (1.94)	7.96 (1.54)	40 (1.55)	3.90 (0.66)	40 (1.55)	3.90 (0.66)
Khatwe	22 (1.29)	03.46 (0.71)	21 (1.23)	3.44 (0.70)	05 (0.20)	0.36 (0.06)	05 (0.19)	0.36 (0.06)
Kayastha	16 (0.94)	08.57 (1.77)	16 (0.94)	8.57 (1.66)	—	—	—	—
Kalwar	14 (0.83)	02.04 (0.43)	14 (0.82)	2.04 (0.39)	02 (0.08)	0.77 (0.13)	02 (0.08	0.77 (0.13)
Ahir	10 (0.59)	02.71 (0.56)	10 (0.59)	2.71 (0.52)	04 (0.16)	2.44 (0.41)	04 (0.15)	1.28 (0.22)
Luhar	07 (0.42)	01.70 (0.35)	07 (0.41)	1.70 (0.33)	—	—	—	—
Amat	07 (0.42)	01.36 (0.28)	06 (0.35)	1.33 (0.27)	60 (2.32)	6.34 (1.07)	61 (2.36)	6.42 (1.09)
Kumhar	07 (0.42)	01.46 (0.30)	07 (0.42)	1.46 (0.28)	37 (1.43)	6.10 (1.03)	37 (1.43)	6.10 (1.03)
Halwai	04 (0.23)	7.82 (1.62)	04 (0.23)	7.82 (1.51)	151 (5.85)	57.13 (9.67)	151 (5.85)	57.13 (9.67)

Cont'd...

Cont'd...

Dhobi	04 (0.23)	01.59 (0.32)	04 (0.23)	1.59 (0.31)	12 (0.46)	1.99 (0.34)	12 (0.48)	1.99 (0.34)
Thathera	03 (0.17)	0.37 (0.07)	03 (0.17)	0.37 (0.07)	—	—	—	—
Mali	02 (0.12)	0.27 (0.05)	02 (0.12)	0.27 (0.05)	—	—	—	—
Kasera	01 (0.06)	0.55 (0.11)	01 (0.06)	0.55 (0.11)	—	—	—	—
Bania			09 (0.53)	7.38 (1.52)	04 (0.16)	4.41 (0.75)	10 (0.40)	4.90 (0.83)
Muslim			—	—	34 (1.33)	5.60 (0.95)	34 (1.33)	5.60 (0.95)
Nunia			—	—	01 (0.04)	0.32 (0.05)	01 (0.04)	0.32 (0.05)
Suri			—	—	07 (0.28)	5.17 (0.88)	07 (0.28)	5.17 (0.88)
Rajput			—	—	01 (0.04)	0.21 (0.04)	—	—
Tatma			—	—	—	—	01 (0.04)	0.38 (0.06)
Koiri			—	—			02 (0.08)	0.19 (0.03)
Total	1702 (100.00)	484.86 (100.00)	1702 (100.00)	484.86 (100.00)	2581 (100.00)	590.44 (100.00)	2581 (100.00)	590.44 (100.00)
Gair mazarua	279	67.24	279	67.24	260	22.69	260	22.69
Bkashta land	127	61.03	127	61.03	—	—	—	—
Grand Total	2108	613.13	2108	613.13	2841	613.13	2841	613.13

Source: Khatiyan, 1971, Register II, 1971–81, 1992–93, 1991–2001.

Now, the table reveals that *Sonar, Barai, Kewat, Mallah* and *Dusadh,* these five castes occupy land within the range of 45–25 acres (200–100 plots) in 1971. Interestingly, Sonar caste loses more than half of its occupied acres in 1992–93 and in 2001 the figures come down to 20.83 acres (130 plots). It was 42.78 acres (191 plots) in 1971 and 1981. Clearly, the plot size is also reduced compared to 1971 and 1981. Does it suggest that Brahmins have bought large share from Sonar caste? Though no qualitative data is available, this fact holds validity.

The trends about transfer of land mechanism in relation to four other castes of this segment also reveal similar characteristics. While occupation in acres has declined since 1992–93 the plot numbers have not declined in the same pace. This reflects reduction in plot-size since 1992–93, which is indicative of natural fragmentation of land over one decade and more. For instance, in case of *Barai* and *Mallah* the total plot number is 144 (21.42 acres) and 121 (24.70 acres) in 1971 and 1981, respectively, it is 178 (19.85 acres) and 117 (16.60 acres), respectively in 2001. The decline is registered in 1992–93.

Barhai and Dhanuk castes occupy 92 plots (21.36 acres) and 66 plots (14.52 acres) in 1971 and almost similar in 1981. Their plots and acres both register a sharp decline by more than half and three-fourths in 1992–1993 and 2001, respectively. Obviously, they have sold out their plots for some reasons. The case of Teli caste, however, appears to be distinguished as this caste has augmented its land occupancy in 1992–1993 by more than double. In 1971 and 1981 Teli caste occupied 33.92 acres (85 plots), which is augmented in 1992–1993 and 2001 to the tune of 76.93 (289 plots) and 77.12 acres (294 plots), respectively. It may be inferred that Barhai and Dhanuk have lost land while Teli caste has considerably gained. The former have sold and the latter have bought. In absence of qualitative data, this inference cannot be denied though accurate picture would emerge with the help of relative quantitative and qualitative data as who bought what and who sold how much and for what reasons and when, etc. But, the transfer of land has definitely taken place before 1992–1993 (and over 1980s), this fact cannot be denied.

The table also reveals appearance of some castes on the scene at some other points of time and also disappearance of some other at other points of time. For instance, Bania has appeared in 1981; Muslim, Tatma, Suri, Rajput, Koeri and Nunia castes have appeared on the scene in 1992–93 and Luhar, Kayastha, Thathera and Mali castes have disappeared in 1991 and onwards. Rajput caste has again disappeared in 2001. All these castes have small acres to lose or to gain via market mechanism of land transfer.

In Kokri, it may also be observed that Bakashta land is available to the tune of 61.03 acres (127) in 1971 and 1981. This category is absent since 1992–1993. The interesting fact, however, is still existence of 22.69 acres (260 plots) 'gair mazarua' category of land since 1992–93 and onwards. Both facts must have some convincing explanation. In absence of this explanation, here it may be simply and safely concluded that while bakashta category has been transferred through different mechanism among different castes, the gair mazarua category is still undistributed among landless and thus, untransferred to landless castes (people). This also reflects that how callous has been the attitude of the government machinery in transfer of land to the landless under the land ceiling legislations.

Naulakkha Village

Village Naulakkha shows a very interesting feature related to the transfer of land among different castes. Table 2 reveals the dominating land occupant caste in the village Naulakkha is Koiri who occupy about 34.86 acres of land (39.96% of the total) distributed over 81 plots in 2001. It was 20.50 acres (24.10%) distributed over 66 plots in 1971. That time, this was the second dominating caste in the village and Bhumihars were on the top of the hierarchy with 43.93 acres of land (51.61% of the total) and distributed over 93 plots (47.70%) in the village. Presently, they are on second on the ladder with 28.73 acres (32.92%) distributed on 74 plots (37.39%) in the village. During the study period (1971–2001), Bhumihar after 1971 show a continuous decline in their occupancy of land in the village, while at the same time Koiri the second dominating caste of the village shows an increasing trend. During the period of three decades, i.e., from 1971–2001, Bhumihar loses about 18 per cent of land while Koiri shows a gain of 15 per cent of land of the village. Therefore, it can easily be said that the large portion of loss of land occupancy among Bhumihar has been converted into a gain for Koiri. This, therefore, led to the emergence of Koiri as the dominant caste in the village.

Table 2

Naulakkha: Pattern of Land Transfer Among Different Castes, 1971–2001

	1971		1981		1991		2001	
Castes	*No. of plots occupied (%) to the total*	*Area occupied (in acres) (%) to the total*	*No. of plots occupied (%) to the total*	*Area occupied (in acres) (%) to the total*	*No. of plots occupied (%) to the total*	*Area occupied (in acres) (%) to the total*	*No. of plots occupied (% to the total*	*Area occupied (in acres) (%) to the total*
Bhumihar	93 (47.70)	43.93 (51.61)	87 (44.38)	36.26 (42.28)	79 (39.90)	30.84 (35.34)	74 (37.39)	28.73 (32.92)
Koiri	66 (33.85)	20.50 (24.10)	71 (36.22)	27.71 (32.31)	78 (39.39)	33.62 (38.53)	81 (40.90)	34.86 (39.96)
Ahir	13 (6.67)	5.54 (6.51)	15 (7.65)	6.27 (7.31)	18 (9.10)	8.32 (9.53)	20 (10.10)	8.92 (10.22)
Brahmin	08 (4.10)	5.13 (6.03)	07 (3.60)	4.84 (5.64)	05 (2.52)	3.61 (4.14)	04 (2.02)	3.37 (3.86)
Dhanuk	05 (2.56)	5.77 (6.78)	05 (2.54)	5.77 (6.73)	06 (3.03)	5.89 (6.75)	06 (3.03)	5.89 (6.75)
Kanu	03 (1.54)	2.25 (2.64)	03 (1.53)	2.25 (2.62)	04 (2.02)	2.46 (2.82)	05 (2.52)	2.97 (3.40)
Hajjam	01 (0.51)	0.57 (0.67)	02 (1.02)	1.23 (1.41)	02 (1.01)	1.23 (1.41)	02 (1.01)	1.23 (1.41)
Barai	04 (2.05)	0.57 (0.67)	04 (2.04)	0.57 (0.70)	04 (2.02)	0.57 (0.66)	04 (2.02)	0.57 (0.66)
Julaha	01 (0.51)	0.33 (0.38)	01 (0.51)	0.33 (0.38)	—	—	—	—
Kayastha	01 (0.51)	0.52 (0.61)	01 (0.51)	0.52 (0.60)	02 (1.01)	0.72 (0.82	02 (1.01)	0.72 (0.82)
Total	195	85.11	196	85.75	198	87.26	198	87.26
Gairmaza rua	11	6.71	10	6.07	08	4.56	08	4.56
Grand Total	206	91.82	206	91.82	206	91.82	206	91.82

Source: Khatiyan, 1971, Register II, 1971–81, 1981–91, 1991–2001.

While going through the status for the other residing or non-residing land-occupant castes in the village, it is found clear that except Ahir, the third ranked land-occupant caste in the village, all have either just maintained their status or improved it insignificantly during the last three decades. Even Brahmin, the other upper caste in the village, has lost half of their land while, Julaha disappeared from the list after 1981. So, the plots lost by them have been taken by the other occupant castes in the village. Ahir has consistently increased his occupancy by either from Bhumihar or from the other castes like, Brahmin and Julaha.

Now, further about the *gair mazarua* land in the village, it is clear that after 1971, a distribution of that land appears in the village. However, it is very less till 1981 as only 1 plot of 0.64 acre has been distributed. Nevertheless, after this a better decline appears in this category (6.07 to 4.56 acres) in 1991, it means that land has further been distributed to the marginal section of the society, i.e., landless people. The figure for gair mazarua land is again constant for 2001. So, it could be said that the distribution of those lands is not showing a consistent trend in this village.

The Gandak Plain

Asadnagar Bataraul Village

This is a small village with 123.85 acres distributed over 590 plots among different residing or non-residing castes of the village as per 2001 land records (Table 3). This means the average plot size is little more than 0.20 acres. The plot size varies by castes. For instance, the average plot size under possession of Bhumihar caste, which occupies 46.54 acres (37.64% of the total) distributed over 202 plots as per 2001 land records is little more than 0.25 acres. Next dominating caste is, Ahir, who occupies 33.54 acres (27.12%) distributed over 139 plots as per 2001 land records. Muslim community occupies third place with 12.15 acres (9.83%) distributed over 89 plots as per 2001 records. It is obvious that plot-size in this community is very small compared to the above two Hindu castes. Though plot-size does not have any direct relationship with transfer of land mechanism, yet this may determine transaction or gift of land factors. For instance, it is easier to sell or gift smaller plots rather than bigger ones, which are more suitable for cultivation.

Table 3

Asadnagar Bataraul: Pattern of Land Transfer Among Different Castes, 1971–2001

	1971		*1981*		*1991*		*2001*	
Caste	*No. of plots occupied (%) to the total*	*Area occupied (in acres) (%) to the total*	*No. of plots occupied (%) to the total*	*Area occupied (in acres) (%) to the total*	*No. of plots occupied (%) to the total*	*Area occupied(in acres) (%) to the total*	*No. of Plots occupied (% to the total*	*Area occupied (in acres) (%) to the total*
Bhumihar	252 (42.70)	53.42 (43.13)	247 (42.03)	52.77 (42.60)	229 (38.80)	48.17 (38.89)	202 (34.24)	46.54 (37.58)
Ahir	101 (17.10)	26.43 (21.34)	104 (17.80)	26.73 (21.60)	125 (21.18)	30.79 (24.86)	139 (23.56)	33.54 (27.08)
Muslim	81 (13.70)	11.30 (9.12)	84 (14.23)	11.93 (9.63)	89 (15.08)	13.18 (10.64)	89 (15.08)	12.15 (9.81)
Koiri	35 (5.90)	5.12 (4.13)	37 (6.27)	5.40 (4.36)	37 (6.27)	5.99 (4.84)	45 (7.63)	6.98 (5.63)
Dusadh	31 (5.25)	3.05 (2.46)	28 (4.75)	2.48 (2.00)	22 (3.72)	2.08 (1.68)	28 (4.74)	2.48 (2.00)
Suri	17 (2.90)	8.26 (6.70)	14 (2.35)	7.94 (6.42)	13 (2.20)	7.90 (6.39)	13 (2.20)	6.79 (5.48)
Nunia	2 (0.33)	1.44 (1.16)	02 (0.34)	1.44 (1.16)	01 (0.17)	0.73 (0.59)	02 (0.34)	0.57 (0.46)
Halwai	2 (0.33)	0.30 (0.24)	02 (0.34)	0.30 (0.24)	02 (0.34)	0.30 (0.24)	02 (0.34)	0.30 (0.24)

Cont'd...

Cont'd...

Brahmin	6 (1.01)	2.21 (1.78)	06 (1.02)	2.21 (1.79)	04 (0.68)	1.91 (1.54)	05 (0.84)	1.97 (1.60)
Rajput	17 (2.90)	1.50 (1.21)	17 (2.90)	1.50 (1.21)	30 (5.10)	4.48 (3.62)	33 (5.60)	4.63 (3.74)
Kalwar	7 (1.19)	1.35 (1.09)	07 (1.19)	1.35 (1.09)	07 (1.19)	1.35 (1.09)	07 (1.20)	1.35 (1.09)
Teli	17 (2.90)	4.71 (3.81)	17 (2.90)	4.71 (3.81)	06 (1.02)	1.46 (1.18)	02 (0.34)	0.86 (0.70)
Kahar	3 (0.51)	0.50 (0.40)	03 (0.51)	0.50 (0.40)	03 (0.51)	0.50 (0.40)	03 (0.51)	0.50 (0.40)
Dhobi	6 (1.02)	2.31 (1.87)	06 (1.02)	2.31 (1.87)	06 (1.02)	2.31 (1.87)	06 (1.02)	2.31 (1.87)
Chamar	8 (1.35)	17 (0.13)	08 (1.36)	0.17 (0.14)	08 (1.36)	0.17 (0.14)	08 (1.36)	0.17 (0.14)
Dhanuk	3 (0.51)	1.78 (1.44)	03 (0.51)	1.78 (1.44)	03 (0.51)	1.78 (1.44)	03 (0.51)	1.78 (1.44)
Kurmi	—	—	03 (0.51)	0.33 (0.27)	03 (0.51)	0.33 (0.27)	03 (0.51)	0.38 (0.30)
Luhar	—	—	—	—	01 (0.17)	0.07 (0.05)	01 (0.17)	0.07 (0.05)
Baniya	—	—	—	—	01 (0.17)	0.35 (0.28)	02 (0.34)	0.35 (0.28)
Total	590 (100.00)	123.85 (100.00)	590 (100.00)	123.65 (100.00)	590 (100.00)	123.65 (100.00)	590 (100.00)	123.65 (100.00)

Source: Khatiyan, 1971, Register II, 1971–81, 1981–91, 1991–2001.

It is interesting to locate that this small village dominated by Bhumihar caste has undergone change from a transfer of land viewpoint over the last three decades in a different way. While Bhumihar caste consistently dominates with a successive decline in occupation of land by each decade, the next dominant segment, i.e., Ahir caste register a gradual increase of its possession of land by each decade. The average decline percentage for Bhumihar is 7, the average increase in case of Ahir caste is interestingly the same, i.e., 7 per cent. It appears that the former has been the seller of their plots and the latter is the buyer, though this may not be such a simple equation in practice.

Further, the third dominant segment, the Muslim community also registers increasing trends with moderate rate. Koiri and Dusadh, these two Hindu lower castes reveal almost similar landholding status, though the former emerges as the gainer in 2001 (by about 2 acres) while the latter ends up as the loser approximately by half acre.

It is further interesting to observe that Kurmi has emerged on the land occupancy scenario in 1981. This caste was absent in 1971. Again, it is startling that Luhar and Baniya castes have emerged on this scene in 1991.

Pakri Kanth Village

Table 4 reveals that Pakri Kanth is a medium size village with 330.30 acres occupied by different caste people residing in the village as per 2001 land records. The total number of plots is 1,047. This means the average plot size is less than 0.33 acres. The average plot size, however, varies by castes.

The single dominating caste in this village is Rajput followed by Bhumihar. These two castes together occupy 41.07 per cent of the total acres. *Koiri* caste, i.e., the most efficient vegetable farmers in Bihar, also occupies more than 10 per cent of the total acres and third position in the occupancy ladder. And, Brahmin caste with about 7.57 per cent of acres occupies fourth position in the occupancy hierarchy. It is interesting to observe that land occupancy (by caste) structure in this village is less skewed and moderate. This could be observed in Table 4, which reveals that Luhar, Dusash, Muslim, Kumhar, Tatma, Teli and Kurmi all have between 3–6 per cent of acres under their occupation. This segment of the village society constitutes lower middle peasant status. This occupancy pattern also suggests more democratic market behaviour that facilitates transaction and transfer of land in favour (against) without much caste bias.

Table 4

Pakri Kanth: Pattern of Land Transfer Among Different Castes, 1971–2001

Caste	*1971*		*1981*		*1991*		*2001*	
	No. of plots occupied (%) to the total	*Area occupied (in acres) (%) to the total*	*No. of plots occupied (%) to the total*	*Area occupied (in acres) (%) to the total*	*No. of plots occupied (%) to the total*	*Area occupied (in acres) (%) to the total*	*No. of plots occupied (% to the total*	*Area occupied (in acres) (%) to the total*
Rajput	252 (24.06)	84.95 (25.72)	260 (24.86)	88.58 (26.82)	241 (23.02)	75.99 (23.00)	234 (22.35)	74.23 (22.47)
Bhumihar	137 (13.08)	57.49 (17.40)	133 (12.70)	52.85 (16.00)	136 (12.00)	54.81 (16.59)	152 (14.51)	61.44 (18.60)
Koiri	101 (9.64)	30.11 (9.11)	105 (10.02)	32.66 (9.90)	103 (9.85)	30.25 (9.16)	105 (10.02)	34.65 (10.28)
Brahmin	63 (6.02)	20.64 (6.250	57 (5.44)	18.74 (5.67)	78 (7.45)	25.29 (8.26)	75 (7.16)	25.02 (7.57)
Luhar	91 (8.70)	15.23 (4.61)	95 (9.07)	14.91 (4.81)	91 (8.69)	13.65 (4.13)	82 (7.84)	12.71 (3.85)
Dusadh	64 (6.11)	10.51 (3.18)	61 (5.82)	9.87 (2.99)	57 (5.44)	9.51 (2.90)	60 (5.74)	10.90 (3.30)
Muslims	53 (5.06)	18.45 (5.60)	55 (5.25)	18.69 (5.66)	59 (5.63)	17.97 (5.44)	58 (5.53)	17.78 (5.40)
Kumhar	49 (4.68)	10.56 (3.19)	49 (4.68)	11.35 (3.43)	51 (4.87)	12.89 (3.90)	55 (5.25)	11.90 (3.60)
Tatma	47 (4.49)	06.91 (2.10)	43 (4.11)	6.47 (1.95)	45 (4.30)	7.76 (2.35)	41 (3.02)	7.28 (2.20)
Teli	47 (4.49)	18.99 (5.75)	44 (4.20)	18.29 (5.53)	44 (4.20)	17.43 (5.28)	39 (3.72)	16.85 (5.10)
Ahir	25 (2.40)	10.79 (3.27)	28 (2.68)	11.18 (3.37)	30 (2.86)	13.82 (4.18)	31 (2.96)	15.37 (4.65)
Kurmi	20 (1.91)	07.56 (2.30)	33 (3.15)	12.15 (3.67)	42 (4.01)	16.22 (4.91)	47 (4.50)	10.71 (3.24)

Cont'd...

Cont'd...

Chamar	11 (1.05)	01.17 (0.35)	04 (0.38)	0.48 (0.14)	04 (0.38)	0.48 (0.14)	04 (0.38)	0.48 (0.14)
Hajjam	06 (0.57)	6.14 (1.85)	07 (0.67)	6.14 (1.86)	07 (0.67)	6.14 (1.86)	07 (0.67)	6.14 (1.86)
Others	81 (7.74)	30.80 (9.32)	73 (6.97)	28.10 (8.50)	59 (5.65)	26.09 (7.90)	57 (5.44)	25.55 (7.74)
Total	1047 (100.00)	330.30 (100.00)	1047 (100.00)	330.30 (100.00)	1047 (100.00)	330.30 (100.00)	1047 (100.00)	330.30 (100.00)

Source: Khatiyan, 1971, Register II, 1971–81, 1981–91, 1991–2001.

Now, the movement of land transfer from 1971 to 2001 may be seen clearly in Table 4 above. While Rajput caste had occupied 84.95 acres (252 plots) in 1969, it has further elevated its position in 1981 with 88.58 acres (26.82%) under its possession. This trend, however, is reversed in 1991 and 2001 with a reduction of 12.5 acres in land occupancy, which has come down to about 76 acres (23%) in 1991 and 74.23 (22.47%) in 2001. It is obvious that this caste had bought (gained) about 4 acres over the period 1971–1980 and lost about 14 acres between 1981–2000, i.e., over two decades. Where had this land gone? It must be seen in the elevated occupancy status of other castes. The transfer of land appears to have taken place within different caste people residing in the village. This is obvious from Table 4, which reveals some castes as 'gainers' over the stipulated period, while some other as 'losers'. The Koiri caste appears to be the largest gainer, who had 30.11 acres under its possession in 1971 occupied 34.65 acres in 2001 – a gain of 4.54 acres. Brahmin caste is also another gainer with about 4.5 acres (20.64 acres in 1971 and 25.02 acres in 2001). Bhumihar caste is the next gainer with about 4 acres (57.49 acres in 1971 and 61.44 acres in 2001). While, these four castes are the main players in land transfer mechanism, other middle and lower castes may also be seen as 'loser' and 'gainer' over three decades. The 'other' caste segment also emerges as 'loser' in 2001.

The Central South Bihar Plain

Bharathua Village

Table 5 reveals important facts about transfer of land in Bharathua village of Jehanabad district over the last three decades. It is well reflected in columns two, four, six and eight (2, 4, 6, 8) that the highest number of plots occupied by Ahir caste people has recorded consistent decline from 1971 to 2001; however, the hegemony of the same caste continues with occupation of as many as 1,246 (83.51% of the total) plots even in 2001. This figure is 1,318 (88.34%) for 1971. The total area occupied by this caste is also highest with 323.22 acres (87.47% of the total) in 1971 to 292.86 acres (79.24% of the total) in 2001. It is further interesting to note that while a consistent decline in the acres occupied takes place till 1991, it has increased in 2001. This reflects a process of reconsolidation of some area, though the number of plots record consistent decline over successive decades. It may be safely concluded that some plots must have expanded in terms of area though their number has declined. The overall situation reflects a reconsolidation process in 2001 with about 0.40 per cent increase in the area occupied compared to 1991.

Table 5

Bharathua: Pattern of Land Transfer Among Different Castes, 1971–2001

	1971		*1981*		*1991*		*2001*	
Caste	*No. of plots occupied (%) to the total*	*Area occupied (in acres) (%) to the total*	*No. of plots occupied (%) to the total*	*Area occupied (in acres) (%) to the total*	*No. of plots occupied (%) to the total*	*Area occupied (in acres) (%) to the total*	*No. of plots occupied (% to the total*	*Area occupied (in acres) (%) to the total*
Ahir	1,318 (88.34)	323.22 (87.47)	1,267 (84.19)	300.04 (81.91)	1,249 (83.71)	291.40 (78.85)	1246 (83.51)	292.86 (79.24)
Dusadh	113 (7.58)	20.00 (5.41)	127 (8.51)	25.45 (6.88)	135 (9.05)	29.94 (8.10)	138 (9.25)	30.15 (8.15)
Gareri	31 (2.08)	05.08 (1.375)	29 (1.94)	4.91 (1.32)	30 (2.01)	5.62 (1.52)	29 (1.94)	5.27 (1.43)
Kumhar	15 (1.00)	02.69 (0.73)	26 (1.74)	6.75 (1.82)	29 (1.94)	7.28 (1.97)	32 (2.14)	7.36 (1.99)
Muslims	14 (0.94)	18.53 (5.01)	20 (1.34)	21.64 (5.85)	21 (1.41)	22.06 (5.96)	16 (1.07)	19.49 (5.27)
Barhai	01 (0.06)	0.02 (0.005)	09 (0.60)	3.75 (1.05)	11 (0.74)	4.21 (1.15)	19 (1.27)	4.66 (1.26)
Kahar	—	—	02 (0.16)	0.62 (0.17)	02 (0.14)	0.62 (0.17)	01 (0.07)	0.43 (0.14)
Koiri	—	—	07 (0.47)	3.67 (0.99)	07 (0.47)	3.74 (1.01)	04 (0.27)	4.80 (1.30)
Bhumihar	—	—	05 (0.33)	2.71 (0.73)	05 (0.33)	2.91 (0.79)	04 (0.27)	2.88 (0.78)
Kurmi	—	—	—	—	03 (0.20)	1.76 (0.48)	03 (0.21)	1.64 (0.44)
Total	1492 (100.00)	369.54 (100.00)	1492 (100.00)	369.54 (100.00)	1492 (100.00)	369.54 (100.00)	1492 (100.00)	369.54 (100.00)

Source: Khatiyan, 1971, Register II, 1971–81, 1981–91, 1991–2001.

Now, which castes stand next on these ladder of number of plots and acres occupied? The same table reveals that Dusadh caste occupies a second place followed by Gareri, Kumhar and Muslim community who occupy the next ladder. Dusadh caste has consistently elevated its position with 113 plots occupied in 1971 to 138 plots in 2001. Further, while Gareri caste has retained its 1971 position (31 plots, 5.08 acres) with slight decline (of 2 plots) in 2001 (with 29 plots but 5.27 acres), Kumhar caste has doubled its number of plots from 15 (2.69 acres) in 1969 to 32 (7.36 acres) in 2001. It is obvious that the plot size has recorded an increase of more than double over three decades. This further confirms a reconsolidation process of land. Even more interesting is the case of Muslim community, which occupied just 14 plots expanded over 18.53 acres in 1969. The strength of this community increases in 1981 (with 20 plots and 21.64 acres) and 1991 (with 21 plots and 22.06 acres) and declines in 2001 with 16 plots expanded over 19.49 acres. The average plot size occupied by this community is always more than one acre, which is a unique feature as it is well reflected in the Table that in all castes the average plot size is normally below one acre with another exception of Barhai caste, which occupied just one (1) plot of 2 acres in 1971. This records sharp decline in 1981, 1991 and 2001. It appears that natural fragmentation under population pressure has taken place with this community.

Another significant indicator of transfer of land in this village is inclusion of some other castes during 1970s as it is revealed in the 1981 land records. Kahar, Koiri and Bhumihar castes have recorded their presence on the scene in the 1981 land records and Kurmi has entered the scene, probably, during 1980s as their presence is recorded in the 1991 land records. These new entrants are petty sharers of the plots and acres.

Makhdumpur Pali Village

Table 6 reveals that Makhdumpur Pali is a Muslim caste dominated village where upper caste Muslim (Sayyad) had occupied as much as 41.56 per cent of the total acres in 1971. This percentage has declined to 33.06 as per 2001 land records. Eight-and-a-half per cent decline is noticeable yet not enough to alter the hegemonic position of this ruling caste and community. Interestingly, Yadav caste ranks second in this hierarchy with 21.83 per cent of the total acres in 1971, which records a two-and-a-half per cent decline (19.23) in 2001. Hajjam is another Hindu caste, which occupied 6.61 per cent of the total acres in 1971 and has almost maintained its level of occupancy (6.19%) in 2001, with a slight decline of less than half per cent. Kahar is another Hindu caste, which has maintained its level of occupancy. Sheikh and Ansari, two other Muslim castes have also made their presence felt, over three decades.

The question is – those castes, who have lost their acres over three decades must have transferred them to other castes. Who must have emerged as the 'gainers'? While slight ups and downs may be noticed in acres of more than one caste people listed in Table 6.

Table 6

Makhdumpur Pali: Pattern of Land Transfer Among Different Castes, 1971–2001

	1971		*1981*		*1991*		*2001*	
Caste	*No. of plots occupied (%) to the total*	*Area occupied (in acres) (%) to the total*	*No. of plots occupied (%) to the total*	*Area occupied (in acres) (%) to the total*	*No. of plots occupied (%) to the total*	*Area occupied (in acres) (%) to the total*	*No. of plots occupied (% to the total*	*Area occupied (in acres) (%) to the total*
Sayyad	270 (38.13)	33.54 (41.56)	251 (35.47)	29.63 (36.71)	247 (34.89)	28.73 (35.60)	234 (33.05)	26.68 (33.06)
Ahir	124 (17.51)	17.62 (21.83)	119 (16.80)	15.41 (19.09)	116 (16.40)	15.21 (18.84)	119 (16.80)	15.52 (19.23)
Hajjam	67 (9.46)	5.34 (6.61)	67 (9.46)	5.34 (6.61)	67 (9.46)	5.34 (6.61)	65 (9.17)	5.00 (6.19)
Shiekh	58 (8.20)	5.03 (6.23)	68 (9.60)	7.46 (9.24)	77 (10.87)	8.54 (10.60)	79 (11.16)	8.60 (10.65)
Kahar	44 (6.21)	5.17 (6.40)	44 (6.21)	5.17 (6.40)	44 (6.21)	5.17 (6.40)	44 (6.21)	5.17 (6.40)

Cont'd...

Cont'd...

Pasi	25 (3.53)	1.93 (2.39)	29 (4.10)	2.50 (3.10)	29 (4.10)	2.50 (3.10)	36 (5.08)	4.02 (4.96)
Julaha	22 (3.10)	2.25 (2.80)	22 (3.10)	2.25 (2.79)	21 (2.97)	2.28 (2.82)	21 (2.97)	2.54 (3.15)
Teli	20 (2.82)	2.34 (2.90)	20 (2.82)	2.34 (2.90)	20 (2.84)	2.34 (2.90)	20 (2.82)	2.34 (2.90)
Dusadh	13 (1.84)	1.09 (1.35)	15 (2.11)	1.76 (2.18)	14 (1.98)	1.63 (2.02)	13 (1.84)	1.54 (1.91)
Bhumihar	13 (1.84)	2.88 (3.59)	17 (2.40)	3.81 (4.72)	16 (2.26)	4.11 (5.10)	21 (2.97)	4.35 (5.40)
Ansari	13 (1.84)	0.65 (0.80)	13 (1.84)	0.65 (0.80)	13 (1.84)	0.65 (0.80)	13 (1.84)	0.65 (0.80)
Musahar	13 (1.84)	0.34 (0.43)	13 (1.84)	0.34 (0.43)	15 (2.11)	0.34 (0.43)	13 (1.84)	0.34 (0.43)
Barhai	10 (1.41)	0.91 (1.13)	13 (1.84)	1.78 (2.20)	12 (1.70)	1.60 (1.96)	13 (1.84)	1.69 (2.10)
Kasai	04 (0.56)	0.27 (0.33)	04 (0.56)	0.27 (0.36)	04 (0.56)	0.27 (0.33)	04 (0.56)	0.27 (0.33)
Kumhar	03 (0.42)	0.35 (0.43)	04 (0.56)	1.0 (1.24)	04 (0.56)	1.00 (1.24)	04 (0.56)	1.00 (1.24)
Nat	02 (0.29)	0.09 (0.11)	02 (0.29)	0.09 (0.11)	02 (0.29)	0.09 (0.11)	02 (0.29)	0.09 (0.11)
Darji	02 (0.29)	0.27 (0.33)	02 (0.29)	0.27 (0.33)	02 (0.29)	0.27 (0.33)	02 (0.29)	0.27 (0.33)
Others	05 (0.71)	0.63 (0.78)	05 (0.71)	0.63 (0.78)	05 (0.71)	0.63 (0.78)	05 (0.71)	0.63 (0.78)
Total	708+ 128 836	80.70+ 20.53 101.23	708 (100.00)	80.70 (100.00)	708 (100.00)	80.70 (100.00)	708 (100.00)	80.70 (100.00)

Source: Khatiyan, 1971, Register II, 1971–81, 1981–91, 1991–2001.

It is Pasi and Bhumihar castes, who have elevated their occupancy level. While Pasi caste occupied 1.93 acres in 1971, it occupied 4.02 acres in 2001. Similarly, Bhumihar caste occupied 2.88 acres in 1971, it raised its occupancy level to 4.35 acres in 2001.

Analysis

On account of above interpretation of data it may be safely analysed that in Kokri village of Madhubani from Adhwara Plain the phenomenon of land transfer has been more dynamic than other villages falling under the purview of this study. Fragmentation of land and reduction in the average plot size is another feature that could be observed in the village. In the southern Adhwara Plain, the Gandak Plain and the Central South Bihar Plain though such dynamism is not observed yet all mechanism of transfer must have taken place in different degrees. Local conditions in transaction may also have some impacts in different districts.

Since the thrust of this study has been basically on quantitative data, therefore, it is difficult to explain the qualitative factors and features of land transfer mechanism. For instance, it cannot be explained as to which caste has sold and bought what quantity of land and when? How many plots or acres have been sold (and bought) to meet dowry demands, to meet the expenses of study of the next generation and other such family needs, etc. Similarly, it is not possible to explain as to how many plots and acres were transferred to bataidars (and also later sold to them) to evade land-ceiling acts.

In fact, natural fragmentation of land under population pressure, structural change, out-migration and social factors appear to have operated as important mechanisms of land transfer in all villages. Sale or purchase of land due to dowry, customary needs or under pressure of market in factors of production, etc., has vibrantly taken place. As stated above, we must not forget the fact that farming activities have acquired market orientation due to cash farming and heavy investment, even in food farming sector over the last three decades. The growing size of investment, reduction in farm subsidies and rental provisions in irrigation, ploughing and other production activities – all have contributed to the economic pressure of the farming classes across all castes. These factors have led to sale of small farming units in the hands of big farmers, who can afford high costs involved in production. The tiny plot-holders have also rented out their plots to big landholders on rent or on traditional batai terms. The rich farmers with joint families have captured income-generating opportunities in off-farm sectors also and they have invested back in land. This is reflected in those dominating castes in all villages, where they have either retained their huge land-occupancy status or augmented it over the last three decades. This process is known as established concept of 'land-reconsolidation' process in agrarian and rural studies area of research. But, at the same time there is an important phenomenon of purchase of land by migrated population from the upper and dominant castes also found.

The redistribution of land under the provisions of land-ceiling act is another factor to accelerate land transfer. Therefore, this may be treated here as one of the important mechanisms of land transfer. This process has taken place from late sixties onwards and has been accelerated during seventies and eighties under the pressure of poor-peasant movements launched by the Communist Party of India during seventies and by the Communist Party of India (Marxist-Leninist) during eighties. It is revealing that in few villages bakashta land and gair mazarua land category is significantly present before 1981 and consistent decline after 1980s and thereafter.

Conclusions

The preceding parts suggest that land ceiling legislations and the market may be treated as the prime movers of land transfer in rural Bihar. Though market in land was introduced with the Permanent Settlement during British rule, market mechanism was accelerated during 1960s onwards with the implementation of the Land Ceiling Act in Bihar. Desperate market in land to evade the land-ceiling legislation has been a glaring feature in the state. Other factors are family needs, which generate constant pressure upon the upwardly mobile farming families as they have opted for educating their children to enable their future generation secure jobs at the urban centres. While some of them have come up to expectations, there always have been some, who had to stay back in the village to run the farming activities. Those, who go for urban jobs, often invest back into the village to secure their lost 'land asset'.

Caste traits are also important. While, some upper caste people do not hesitate to be uprooted after they get settled at the urban centres, some other never like it. Backward caste people such as Kurmi, Yadav (Ahir) are, however, very much rooted. The greatest aspiration of the landless is how to get a tiny piece of land. Migrant labour class usually invest their income into land. This is in sharp contrast to the old economic conceptualization, which holds that migrant labour class squander away hard earned money back home. The overall situation suggests that transfer of land usually takes place within the village or within panchayat or within close proximity. And, may be predominantly within the same caste people. This is well reflected in continuation of hegemony dominance of the same caste over a three-decade long, time span. The incidence of transfer of land, through any mechanism, within different castes is very low compared to the transfer within the same caste.

Acknowledgement: The present paper is a part of my M.Phil. Thesis, supervised by Professor B. Thakur, the person who taught me the A.B.C. of Research.

References

Ahmad, E. (1965) *Bihar: A Physical, Economic and Regional Geography*, Ranchi: Ranchi University Press.

Aziz, A. (1982) 'Man-Land Relations in India', *The Geographer*, 29(2): 12–20.

Bailey, F.G. (1958) *Caste and the Economic Frontier*, Bombay: Oxford University Press.

Beteille, A. (1971) 'The Causes of Agrarian Unrest', *The Citizen*, 1(23): 16–18.

—— (1971a) *Caste, Class and Power*, California: University of California Press.

—— (1974) *Studies in Agrarian Social Structure*, London: Oxford University Press.

Bhagwati, A.C. (1990) 'Social Structure and Agricultural Performance in Dolabari Irrigated Area of Sonitpur District, Assam', *Geographical Review of India*, 52(4): 71–79.

Bharti, I. (1988) 'Farce of Land Reforms in Jehanabad', *Economic and Political Weekly*, 23(47): 2519–2520.

—— (1990) 'Farce of Farm Wages Hike', *Economic and Political Weekly*, 25(27): 1677–1678.

—— (1990a) 'Mobilisation of Agricultural Labour: Jehanabad Experience', *Economic and Political Weekly*, 25(22): 1481–1482.

Bichel, U. (1983) 'The Dominant Caste and its Landscape Expression in Indian Village', *Geographical Review of India*, 43: 9–26.

Brass, T. (1993) 'Migration, Tenancy and Bondage Labour in Purnea District, Bihar', in B.N. Yugandhar and K. Gopal Iyer (eds), *Land Reforms in India, Vol. 1: Bihar: Institutional Constraints*, New Delhi: Sage Publications, 283–296.

Chakravarti, A. (2001) *Social Power and Everyday Class Relations: Agrarian Transformation in North Bihar*, New Delhi: Sage Publications.

Choudhary, P.K. (1993) 'Land Reforms in Bihar: Need for a Fresh Appraisal', in B.N. Yugandhar and K. Gopal Iyer (eds), *Land Reforms in India, Vol. 1: Bihar: Institutional Constraints*, New Delhi: Sage Publications, 24–33.

Das, A. (2001) 'Dynamic Analysis of Land and Caste Relations in a Madhubani Village: 1960–1999', MPhil Dissertation, Department of Geography, University of Delhi, Delhi.

Das, A.N. (1983) *Agrarian Unrest and Socio-Economic Change in Bihar, 1900–1980*, New Delhi: Manohar Publications.

Dayal, P. (1968) 'The Bihar Plain: A Regional Study', *Transactions of the Indian Council of Geographers*, 5: 1–30.

Diwakar, D.M. (2000) *Emerging Agrarian Relations in India: Micro Realities*, New Delhi: Manak Publications.

Economic Commission for Africa (2004) *Land Tenure Systems and Their Impacts on Food Security and Sustainable Development in Africa*, Addis Ababa.

Frykenberg, R.E. (1969) *Land Control and Social Structure in Indian History*, Wisconsin: University of Wisconsin Press.

Geddes, A. (1960) 'The Alluvial Morphology of the Indian Gangetic Plain: Its Mapping and Geographical Significance', *Transactions of the Institute of British Geographers*, 28: 253–276.

Griffin, K., A.R. Khan and A. Ickowitz (2002) 'Poverty and the Distribution of Land', in V.K. Ramachandran and M. Swaminathan (eds), *Agrarian Studies: Essays on Agrarian Relations in Less-Developed Countries*, New Delhi: Tulika.

Gupta, R. (1982) *Bihar Peasantry and the Kisan Sabha*, New Delhi: People's Publishing House.

Held, R.B. and D.W. Visser (1984) *Rural Land Uses and Planning: A Comparative Study of the Netherlands and the United States*, Oxford: Elsevier.

Louis, P. (2002) *People Power: The Naxalite Movement in Central Bihar*, Delhi: Wordsmiths.

Mitra, C. and G. Sarkar (1987) *Some Social Aspects of Agricultural Development in India*, New Delhi: Concept.

Mohammad, N. (1988) *Caste and Primary Occupations: A Geographical Analysis*, New Delhi: Concept.

Mukherji, K. and M. Kala (1979) 'Bhojpur: The Long Struggle', in A.N. Das and V. Nilkant (eds), *Agrarian Relations in India*, Delhi: Manohar Publications.

Mutatkar, R.K. (1978) *Caste Dimensions in a Village*, Pune: Subhada-Saraswat.

Neele, W.C. (1969) 'Land is to Rule', in R.E. Frykenberg (ed.), *Land Control and Social Structure in Indian History*, Wisconsin: University of Wisconsin Press, 112–123.

Prasad, P.H. (1991) 'Rise of Kulak Power and Caste Struggle in North India', *Economic and Political Weekly*, 26(33): 1923–1926.

Prasad, R.C. (1983) *Bihar*, Delhi: National Book Trust.

Prasad, Shankar (1993) 'Implementation of Land Reforms Legislations in Bihar', in B.N. Yugandhar and K. Gopal Iyer (eds), *Land Reforms in India, Vol. 1: Bihar: Institutional Constraints*, New Delhi: Sage Publications, 34–49.

Pratap, R. (2001) 'Land-Based Social Conflicts in South Bihar Plain Region', *Annals of the National Association of Geographers, India*, 21(1): 62–73.

Ram, B. (1997) *Land and Society in India: Agrarian Relations in Colonial North Bihar*, Chennai: Orient Longman Ltd.

Rao, V.M. (1972) 'Land Transfer in Rural Communities: Some Findings in the Ryotwari Region', *Economic and Political Weekly*, 45(3): 168–172.

Sastry, G.S. (2000) 'Land Resource System: Problems, Patterns and Policy', *Indian Journal of Regional Science*, 32(2): 49–60.

Sengupta, N. (1979) 'Caste as an Agrarian Phenomenon in Twentieth Century Bihar', in A.N. Das and V. Nilkant (eds), *Agrarian Relations in India*, Delhi: Manohar Publications.

Shivmaggi, H.B. (1968) 'Trends in Purchase and Sale of Farmland: Caste for Lower Ceiling', *Economic and Political Weekly*, Annual Number Issue, 78–83.

Singh, A. and A.S. Kahlon (1976) 'The Impact of New Technology on Farm-Size, Terminal Relations and Land Rents in Punjab', *Indian Journal of Agricultural Economics*, 31(3): 36–44.

Singh, B.N. and Kalindi Sinha (2000) 'Agro-Climatic Zones of Bihar and Their Characteristics', *National Geographical Journal of India*, 46(1–4): 191–196.

Singh, H.N. (1960) 'Caste, Land and Power: A Case Study of Dhobi Block in Jaunpur District, UP', in K.L. Sharma (ed.), *Social Stratification in India*, Jaipur: Rawat Publications, 1–46.

Singh, K.K. (1967) *Pattern of Caste Tension: A Study of Inter-Caste Tension and Conflict*, Bombay: Asia Publishing House.

Singh, R.D. (1982) 'Spatial Aspects of Rural Modernization Process: A Comparative Study in Bhabhua and Bikramganj Blocks', *National Geographer*, 19(2): 12–20.

Singh, R.L. (1955) 'Evolution of Settlement in the Middle Ganga Valley', *National Geographical Journal of India*, 1(2): 69–114.

—— (1960) 'Geographical Concepts and Methods in Research Work', *National Geographical Journal of India*, 6(3): 127–136.

Singh, R.L. (ed.) (1971) *India: A Regional Geography*, Varanasi: National Geographical Society of India, Silver Jubilee Publications.

Singh, S.C. (1965) 'Delimitation of the Middle Ganga Plain', *National Geographical Journal of India*, 11(2): 74–83.

Sinha, I.B. (1998) 'Enforcement of Distributive Justice in Central Bihar', in D.M. Diwakar (ed.), *Distributive Justice Through Social Mobilization*, New Delhi: Manak Publications, 112–124.

Srinivas, M.N. (1959) 'The Dominant Caste in Rampura', *American Anthropologist*, 61(1): 1–16.

—— (1972) *Social Change in Modern India*, New Delhi: Orient Longman Ltd.

Thakur, B. and P.S. Bhushan (1991) 'Land-Man Relationship and Distribution of Agricultural Land in East Sikkim', *Transactions of Institute of Indian Geographers*, 14(1): 13–32.

Thakur, B. and P. Vir (2003) 'Caste Structure, Patterns of Land Ownership and Crop Security in Ramgarh Block, Bhabhua District', in S. Jha, M.M. Thakur and B. Thakur (eds), *Dimensions of Society and Culture of Bihar*, Dr M. Mishra Felicitation Volume, Allahabad: Academy Press, 288–303.

4

Globalization, Land Use Changes and Marginality of Livelihood in Western Himalayas

B.W. PANDEY AND ABHAY SHANKAR PRASAD

Changes in the land use pattern, application of scientific methods of cultivation, commercial exploitation of the forest cover, illicit felling of trees and uncontrolled growth of tourism are important factors affecting geoecology of the valley. Most of the changes that have taken place over the last 50 years in the land use pattern include: (i) bringing of the larger part of the cropped area under the network of modern methods of cultivation namely, double cropping, high yielding varieties and multi-cropping patterns, (ii) large increase in the area under orchards (iii) large increase in the area under hotels and guest houses for tourism and (iv) considerable reduction in the area under forest cover. Consequently, the ecological impact on the one hand centres around intensive cultivation and large scale use of fertilizer insecticides, pesticides and urban wastes, etc., and on the other hand deforestation. A constant loosening of the soil and consequent exposure to hazards of soil erosion and soil exhaustion become a common feature in the Upper Beas Basin.

The Issue

In the Himalayan goesystem, changing relationship between man and environment have brought about irreversible changes in the ecosystem – those of fast depleting forest cover, of the dismantling soil layer and the sediment-laden stream, of increasing numbers of landslips, of changing glacier behaviour and increasing number of avalanches, and overflowing of river and streams. Most research efforts are directed towards analysing man and livestock numbers and resultant pressures on the ever-shrinking resource base. Hence, frequent occurrence of hazards have been correlated with the above facts.

Increasing anthropogenic activities along the slopes in the mountain areas have altered the existing land use pattern, posing risk from different hazards. The hazards are the risk to people encountered in the physical environment. However, for all practical purposes natural hazards are perceived as events having abrupt modifying capabilities such as earthquakes, landslides, floods, snow avalanche, fire and others. Hazards are also caused by human factors and exceeds the tolerable magnitude, makes imbalance and leads in catastrophic losses of property, resources and lives. The complexity of land in Upper Beas Basin has

Figure 1

The Study Area

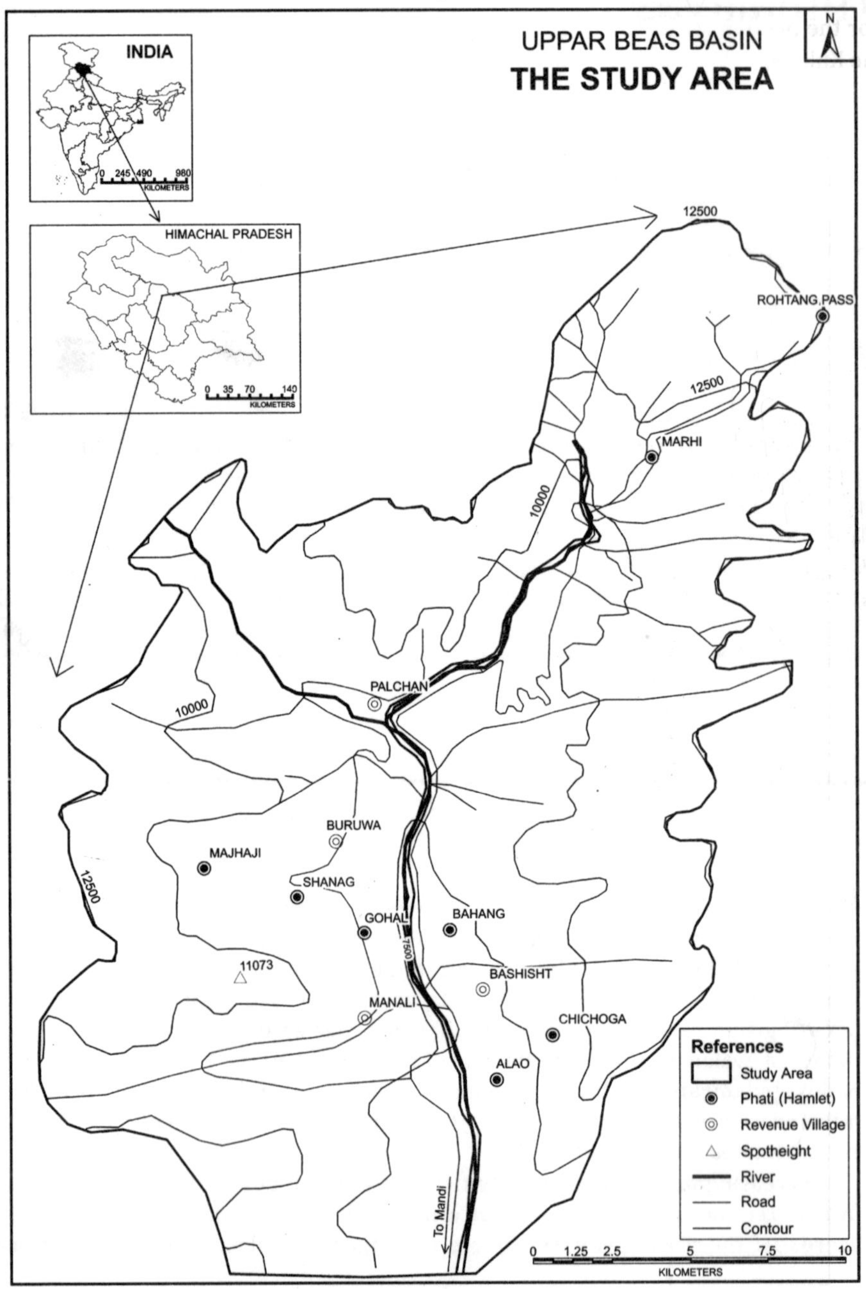

arisen due to the declining land-man ratio, non-availability of additional arable land, compulsion of increasing intensity of land uses and careless application of technology leading to further land loss through soil erosion and other land degradation. Frequent occurrences of hazards are becoming a common feature in Upper Beas Basin. These hazards and the changing bio-physical set-up have a great impact on mountain geosystem.

The Study Area and Research Methodology

For the present research, it covers the Upper Beas Basin, the northernmost part of the Kullu Valley (Himachal Pradesh). Spreading over an area of 120 sq km it extends

Figure 2

Upper Beas Basin

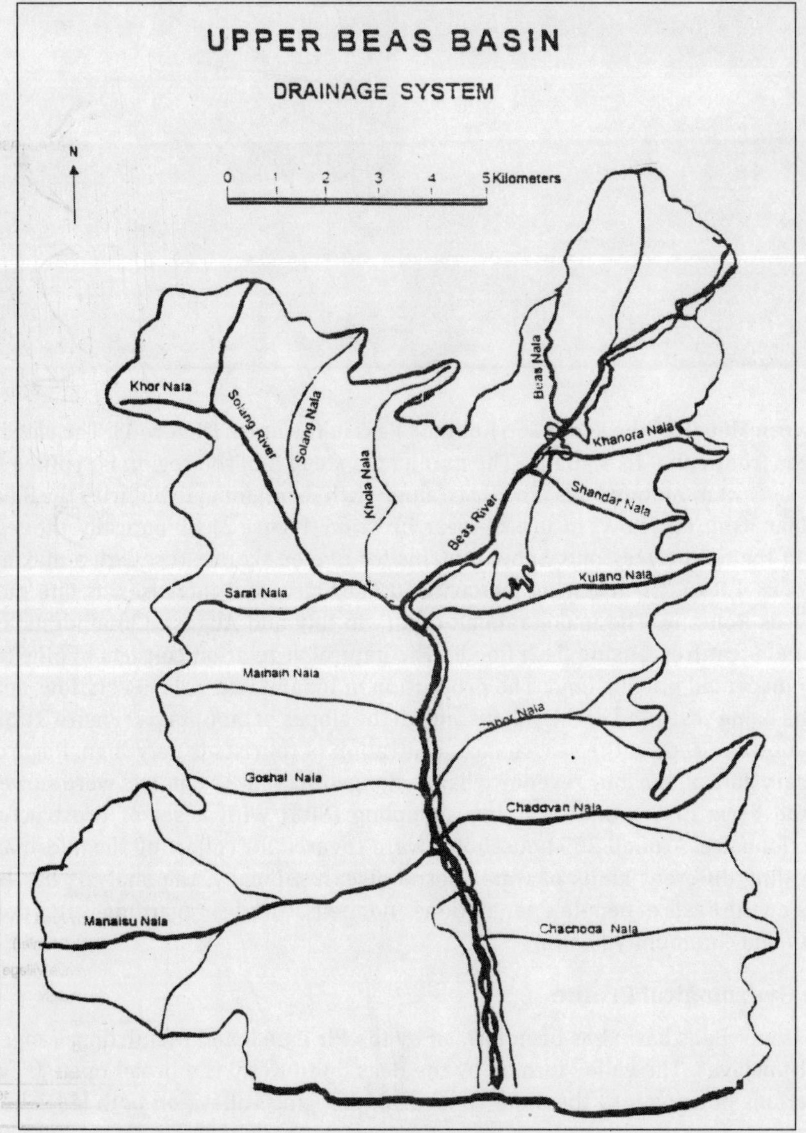

Figure 3

(1) The extensive deforestation in Western Himalaya. (2) The fruit package industry is the main factor for deforestation. (3) Change in land use by encroaching agricultural over grazing land. (4) Unchecked haphazard growth of hotels due to tourism and urbanization.

between Manali in the south and Rohtang Pass in the north (Figure 1). The elevation ranges from 2,000 to 4,000 m. The gradient is steep and the region is typified by a thin layer of mountain soils. The Beas, along with its regional tributaries the Solang, the Manalshu, etc., flows in an east-west direction (Figure 2). Climatically, the region lies in the temperate zone. Snow remains for five or six months, with a maximum depth of 1.8 to 2.1 m during January and February, and increases as one moves towards Rohtang. The major rainfall occurs in July and August. Cloudbursts are a common feature, causing flash floods. The natural vegetation consists of pine trees with dispersed grazing land. The proportion of inhabitable area is very low, settlements being scattered in the valleys and on the slopes of mountains (Figure 3). Since it is a tourist centre, the seasonal concentration of tourists is very high. Regarding primary data all the four revenue villages alongwith their 22 hamlets were surveyed on the basis of Stratified Random Sampling (SRS) with a set of prestructured questionnaire. Around 200 households were covered for collecting the information regarding different kinds of water-borne diseases. Finally, the analysis has been done on the basis of people's perceptions and their attitudes regarding water potentiality and community health.

The Hydrological Profile

The Upper Beas basin has been formed by the Pir Panjal and Dhauladhar ranges of the Himalayas. The valley formed by the Beas up to Kothi is a broad open 'U', with waterfalls pouring into the main valley from hanging valleys on both sides below

Kothi. The river plunges into a deep gorge, hardly ten metres wide, descending 300 m, and after tumbling down it flows out into a very broad valley.

The Beas is one of the five rivers of Punjab, and the only one among them which lies entirely in India. The Beas River rises from the western slopes of the Beas Rikhi, a peak 4,600 m high, one kilometre west of Rohtang Pass. It is a small stream at the source and takes its first water from a spring on Beas Rikhi. A large quantity of water is added in the river by the melting of the glacier and snow. As soon as it comes down from its source, two tributaries, the Serinal and Khanernal, join it at Palchan. The water in the river goes on increasing, and at Largi it cuts the Dhauladhar Range. It maintains an average slope of 2.4 per cent up to Largi. In the catchment areas, the chief tributaries on the right are Solang, Manalshu, Phojal and Sarvani, while on the left are Parbati, Malana, Hurla, Sainj, and Tirthan. Apart from these, there are various other small streams which contribute considerable amounts of water to the Ravi River. Among them the important ones are the Rahni Nala, Sahu Nala, Chhor Nala, Shikar Nala and Prini Nala. During winter, the flow of these nala(s) becomes very low, but during summer and the rainy season they provide a great deal of water to the river Beas.

The general trend of the research in hydrology is concerned more especially with the assessment of water resources in terms of water availability and potential, water generating capacity of the land, water flow and discharge, geohydrological balance, anthropogenic impact on water resources, and also the prediction of extreme events such as drought and floods (Tiwari, 1995). So far as the water potential of the Kullu Valley is concerned, the main source of surface water is precipitation. In general, the whole of Kullu Valley lies in a rainshadow zone and experiences very low annual precipitation. Average rainfall is 11 and 125 mm for the months of November and July, the driest and wettest ones, respectively. November is followed by October (15mm), December (23mm), and August (48mm), on the one hand, and the highest rainfall distribution bearing months after July on the other. In a descending order are March, February, and January. Precipitation in these three months takes place in the form of snow. The depth of snow around Rohtang Pass is recorded from 3 to 4.5 m, while in the lower areas this depth decreases to 0.3 to 0.9m (in and around Manali). The Beas Rikhi Glacier and other smaller glaciers are the sources of about 20 perennial streams, both big and small and about 18 springs which discharge into the river Beas.

The hydrological potential of any place depends on the complexity of various factors operating in combination in a watershed, such as precipitation, evapotranspiration, overland flow, infiltration, percolation, and subsurface flow. Since no comprehensive arid scientific investigations have been carried out in the region so far as part of a complete hydrological appraisal of the Upper Beas Basin watershed, information on baseline hydrological charactetistics and also on spatio-temporal aspects of water resources is not available. Even the very general information available on hydrological aspects of the region is not based on proper scientific observations. Nalas and springs are the main sources of water which can be utilized directly for agricultural and domestic purposes. The springs are the only ultimate source of drinking water in the area. Till the end of the 1990s, these sources were used primarily by villagers for their domestic needs. But since the mushrooming of new hotels and guest houses, most of these sources are being used heavily by the private owners of the hotels, and this has led to acute shortages of water in the villages. Since the consumption of water is greater in hotels than in homes, most of the spring water is supplied through pipes to the hotels. Villages in remote locations fetch their water directly from small streams.

In the agricultural sector, the consumption of water is also very low. Since apple cultivation is increasing by leaps and bounds, the demand for irrigation water is decreasing gradually as agricultural land is transformed into orchards. However, there are about 30 lift irrigation schemes in the Kullu Valley covering the area between the northernmost village, Kothi, and Largi village in the lower part. The general trend of stream water utilization shows that the small streams (nala) are more useful than the main river because of their location nearer to agricultural fields.

Status of Natural Resources and their Utilization

The concepts of land utilization is basically related to man's physical environment in the region. It is essential for human survival and man has a definite role in managing and transforming his physical environment. In the Himalayan region, land resources is the backbone of the economy because agriculture is the main occupation of the people. Land use pattern is a better index for indicating the level of agricultural development in the Upper Beas Basin. It is also a function of the interaction of various physio-environmental, socio-economic and techno-institutional parametres of the region (Singh and Mishra, 1995). It is dynamic in nature which emphasizes the process of spatial change rather than the functioning of land use systems in the temporal context.

Man's dynamic relationships with the physical environment have induced several ecological changes like degradation of the agricultural lands due to excessive and faulty cultivation practices, large scale deforestation due to extension of agriculture lands towards the forest fringes, extraction of excessive fuelwood and increasing demand of timber and other forest products. A faulty land use pattern in the hills affects the human life through frequent occurrences of environmental hazards.

An attempt has been made to study and analyse the land use changes in Upper Beas Basin over the period between 1919 and 1998 in this chapter. The study of land use of the past several years is very important not only in studying the land use pattern obtaining hitherto but also to project its future trend. Such a study would enable to reach a suitable land use policy for a particular region. Physiographic, socio-economic and technological development of the area primarily govern the use of land resources.

Mixed topography determines the wide range of land use patterns in the basin. This aspect in turn has resulted in rapid bio-climatic gradient to aridity. The agricultural activities is reduced during the winter season ranging from December to April since the land remains covered by snow during this period. Hence, the study of changing scenario of the land use pattern in Upper Beas basin over several decades has revealed many anthropogenic, ecological problems and their implications over the natural environment and the living habitat in the region.

There are four revenue villages, namely Palchan, Buruwa, Bashist and Manali. The land use system has changed gradually from 1945 to 1995. During 1945, there were 166 ha land in Palchan village which increased to 176 ha in 1994–95 (Table 1) In the same way the entire villages follow almost the same pattern of agricultural activities. In all the villages of Upper Beas Basin forest recession is a common phenomenon.

Table 1

Land Use Pattern (Revenue Villagewise)

(Area in ha)

S. No.	*Land use*	*Palchan*		*Buruwa*		*Bashisth*		*Manali*	
		1945	*1995*	*1945*	*1995*	*1945*	*1995*	*1945*	*1995*
1	Total Geographical Area	166.4	176.0	567.0	612.0	206.0	262.0	112.0	176.0
2.	Cultivated area	145.2	152.0	383.0	511.0	152.0	207.0	97.0	147.0
3.	Orchard	NA	6.0	NA	85.0	3.2	37.0	0.8	6.0
4.	Housing	4.0	4.0	5.0	5.0	3.2	4.0	4.0	4.09
5.	Road	N.A	1.0	14.0	16.0	4.0	6.0	0.9	1.0
6.	Wasteland	20.6	19.0	165.0	80.0	43.6	9.8	12.0	NA
7.	Landholdings	293	413	436	81.8	672	1075	144	413
8.	No. of plots	1,808	1,927	5,100	6,000	3,032	3,619	1,228	1,927

Source: Lal Kitab, Patwari Office, 2001.

Massive decline of forest resources and disruption of traditional management system, due to ill-conceived public policy and side effects of development strategies has been observed. The major impact of such changes are exploitation and is manifested in degradation of resources threatening sustainable livelihood. Among all the common property resources, the grazing lands have been reduced in size due to "Nature Land Act" (1986), in which common grazing lands have been privatized as people shifted to garden farming. Also the Forest Department has closed the thatches in the forests in order to check the over exploitation of the forests (Pandey and Singh, 1984).

The development policies and activities of the government, particularly growth of tourism, is mainly responsible for the degradation of common resources. Roads have been actively damaging the slopes. Explosive blasts have opened new fissures in the fractural-slopes and have weakened by the vibrations caused by movements of heavy vehicles. Study reveals that the developmental activities such as road development, forest clearing, timber extraction, tourism, urbanization, cultivation on steep slopes and horticulture indicates the land uses with negative implications in the geo-ecology of Upper Beas Basin.

Globalization, Land Use Changes in Urbanization and Tourism

The high degree of tourist influx and the high rate of urbanization has changed the traditional attitude of the inhabitants and has made them more materialistic. Hence, the burgeoning population and (Bandyopadhyay, 1992) the changes in the age-gold developed eco-friendly habits have created various environmental problems which now threaten the livelihood security of the area The influx of tourist to the Kullu Valley has resulted in disturbance to the environment.

The number of vehicles increased from 82 in 1969 to 20,585 in 1994. The number of vehicles increases during the tourist season breaking the security and peace of the area. The development of tourist activities in the valley has resulted in a marked increase in urbanization. Until the 1970s the proportion of urban settlement was very low. With the increase in tourism, urbanization increased simultaneously. The total area under urban settlements increased from 212 sq km in 1981 to 300 sq km in 1991. The process of urbanization in the region has brought a significant change in the trend of consumption, supply and management of mountain water resources in the area Among the positive indicators, distribution of pipelines, storage tanks, and, in some places, sewerage lines are important, while pollution, open garbage dumped into streams, and the privatization of water storage are important negative impacts of the urbanization process. The rapid increase of hotels and guests houses has led to water crises in the region which now make serious impact for the villagers at critical times of year (Chadha, 1991).

Land Use Dynamics, Changing Cropping System and Sustainability

Human and livestock population pressure on the limited land resources have increased in recent years. This has resulted from the construction of roads, encroachment into forest and conversion of land for horticulture and agricultural expansion. Increased pressure on the remaining forest has brought tremendous changes in the pattern of land use including a reduction in forest cover. Present research provides empirical evidence about the changes in land use, the cropping system and encroachment of common land in the Upper Kullu Valley. The 1970–1994 period has been used as the standard time span over which the impact of changes in the land use system of the village can be measured. Five-year intervals have been taken as standard units for comparison of data. Finally, research has provided guidelines for optimum use of land and has suggested preventive measures to avoid misuse and over-exploitation and to promote conservation of common resources for sustainable livelihood.

The expansion of agricultural land can mainly be attributed to population growth and fragmentation of farm-owning families and results in agricultural encroachment into forest areas and wastelands. The majority of settled agriculture fields in the region are on sloping terraces along the foot of steep hill sides. Some agricultural land has a slope, which exceeds 40 although most of them fall between 20–35. The present paper also evaluates the environmental transformation of the Upper Kullu Valley over the last two decades. Agriculture has changed drastically due to the changing nature of crops, cropping intensity, agricultural productivity and additional income generated through agro-horticultural activities (Table 2). The nutrient content of the soil is poor and fertility is difficult to sustain. Even so, higher yields of wheat have been achieved by the use of chemical fertilizers. No consideration has been given to the impact of chemical fertilizers on the fragile characteristics of the mountain area (Pandey, 2002).

Table 2

Changes in Cropping Pattern in the Upper Kullu Valley (Area in ha)

	Crops							
Years	*Saruyara*	*Kodra*	*Maize*	*Potato*	*Rice*	*Wheat*	*Barley*	*Mustard*
1969–70	83	46	79	66	72	61	180	8
1974–75	89	41	86	62	60	159	154	5
1979–80	74	16	110	158	54	77	166	19
1984–85	38	9	66	96	54	93	52	8
1989–90	13	5	213	36	79	211	131	60
1994–95	3	3	268	21	110	93	93	71

Source: Lal Kitab, Patwari House, Kullu (2001).

The changes in the biophysical system of the valley have had a direct bearing on the hydrological set-up of the watershed. The two major factors responsible for this have been the effects of deforestation and changes in the land use pattern associated with increased cropping intensity. The mass felling of trees during the 1950s and 1960s have made the ecosystem more vulnerable by reducing the biodiversity of the region. The decrease in the amount of snowfall and increase in the average temperature for the last few decades has reduced the water resource potential. Similarly, the introduction of irrigation due to changes in cropping patterns has increased the consumption of water, thereby affecting the hydrological set-up of the entire valley (Singh and Pandey, 1995; Singh, 1998).

Environmental Implications of Land Use Changes

The degradation of the natural environment is intrinsically linked with the development process. It is true that in the past, industrial and agricultural development have created many environmental problems largely due to the mismanagement and improper use of technology. But environmental problems are also caused by a lack of adequate development. Such environment is directly related to the living environment of the people, though forced by the natural environment. Environmental issues which emerge due to various factors vary widely from place of place, basically determined by the environmental status of the place and the degree of human interference with the natural environment for the development activities (Sharma and Minhas, 1993).

Man's dynamic relationship with the physical environment has induced several ecological changes in the face of numerous anthropogenic activities like degradation of agricultural lands due to excessive and faulty cultivation practices, large-scale deforestation resulting from extension of agricultural lands towards timber and other minor forest products. The degradation of the hills is bound to affect the human life in plains too, through frequent occurrence of droughts. Upper Beas Basin which has a mixed topography of river bed and high hill zones, owing to its contrasting topography, soil depth and agroecological differences has given rise to almost uneven distributional pattern of land use. Although the statistical figures do not reveal any major changes in the land use pattern over the last four decades, certain alarming changes have been highlighted with respect to specific categories of land use at different levels of the Upper Beas (Pandey, 2002).

Hence, the major concern in the study are on highlighting the ecological impacts of the land use changes in general and forest degradation in particular. Thereafter, the environmental sensitivity of the area would be discussed which is the result of gradual degradation of the natural environment. In fact, the identification of the environmental sensitive zones in the area would be of invaluable help in suggesting the measures for the sustainable development of the Upper Beas Basin in all the major sectors of development, i.e., agriculture, forestry, horticulture and infrastructure, etc.

Critical Issues

An analytical observation of changes in the land utilization reveals that attention needs to be focused over changes particularly under unculturable wastelands, cultivable wastelands, permanent pastures and grazing lands and forest lands. The land area under cultivation though has not shown any significant changes probably due to the physiographic constraints, the mounting pressure on the limited available lands undoubtedly is a significant environmental concern in some areas of the Upper

Beas Basin (Singh, 1992) Hence, the assessment of environmental impacts of these changes need to be analysed separately for suggesting ecologically compatible programmes to combat the degradation ecology in the Basin (Table 3).

Table 3

Environment Issues in Land Use

	Issues	*Causes*	*Remedies*
1.	Deforestation	• Increase in human population • Unauthorized forest removal • Lacks of regeneration • Inappropriate forest policy	• Awareness to control child birth • Planned management • Peoples voluntary cooperation • Effective legislation • Increased investments in afforstation
2.	Uncontrolled and unsustainable grazing	• Excessive livestock • Nomadic grazing • Lack of grassland management • Non-availability of data on grassland	• Reduction of scrub cattle • Encouraging stall feeding practices. • Setting nomdic grazes • Assessment of carrying capacity of pastures • Introduction of improved varieties of grass
3.	Soil erosion	• Deforestation • Faulty agricultural practices • Extension of agriculture on marginal slopes. Excessive road and buildings activities. • Landslides, storms	• Increased in trees cover • Improved agricultural practices • Planned construction activity
4.	Waste disposal	• Urban sprawl • Non-existent sewage disposal	• Public awareness • Environmental education • Planned water supply & sewage disposal • Effective legislation

Source: Pandey (2002).

Tourism and Urbanization

Manali, situated in the beautiful Kulu Valley, has been an important tourist spot since the era of British rule. Till the 1970s, the valley showed a rational distribution of population in terms of carrying capacity. The rise of tourism in Kullu Valley is the result of disturbances in other hill stations of the Himalayas. The major tourist growth started in 1986, when the number of tourists doubled. This brought about a change in the economy and community development. Settlements that included hotels started springing up over the steep slopes, and thus the green 'jungles' were replaced by building construction. This exposure of the surface led to soil erosion. The debris intermingled and flowed into the river water. During 1985–86 there were only about ten hotels, and these have increased to monumental 1500 or so at present. The number of tourists arriving in the valley rose from 11,062 to 67,132 between 1975 and 1991 (Table 4 and Figure 4). The influx of tourists to the Kullu Valley has disturbed its splendid environment. The number of vehicles increased from 80 in 1970 to 205,185 in 1994 (Table 5 and Figure 5).

Table 4

Tourist Flow in Kullu Valley

Year	Total	Domestic No.	%	Foreign No.	0/0
1975	11,062	10,497	94.9	565	5.1
1976	14,477	13,779	95.0	698	5.0
1977	15,792	14,718	93.2	1,074	6.8
1978	11,003	10,239	93.0	764	7.0
1979	13,310	12,519	94.0	791	6.0
1980	15,306	14,235	93.0	1,071	7.0
1985	22,959	19,974	87.0	2,985	13.0
1987	48,744	41,366	84.9	7,378	15.1
1988	52,745	44,261	83.9	8,484	16.1
1989	57,116	47,359	82.9	9,757	17.1
1990	61,596	50.675	82.3	10,921	17.7
1991	67,132	54,222	80.8	12,910	19.2
2001	1,58,867	1,06,663	—	52,204	—

Table 5

Number of Vehicles Coming to Manali

Years	Vehicles	Years	Vehicles
1970	80	1975	93
1980	98	1985	189
1986	814	1987	10,259
1988	10,321	1989	24,117
1990	80,999	1991	1,37,304
1992	1,87,364	1993	1,99,026
1994	2,05,185	1995	2,15,800
1996	2,60,320	1997	2,98,300

Figure 4

No. of Tourists

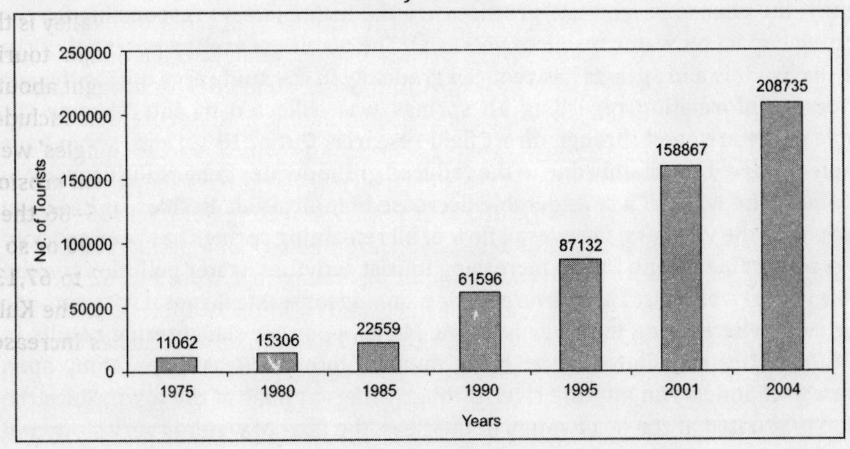

Figure 5

No. of Hotels

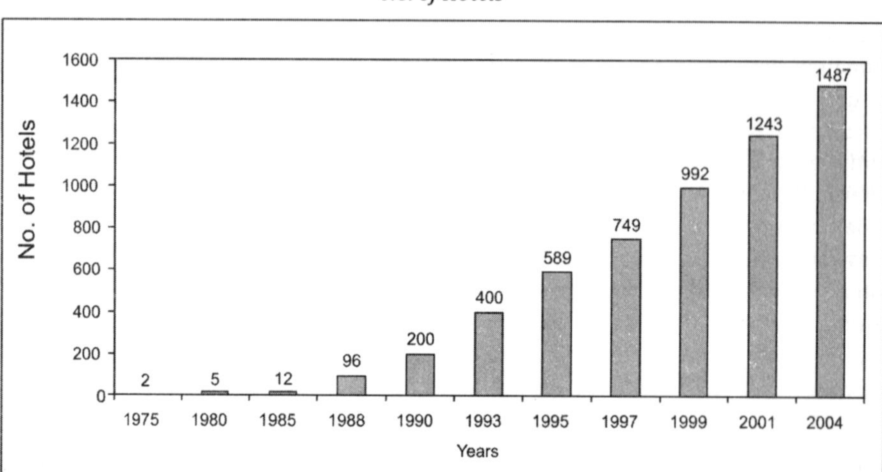

Source: Department of Tourism, Shimla 1998.

The number of vehicles increases during the tourist season, shattering the serenity and calm of the area. The developmental activities related to urbanization are the outcome of tourism. The urban settlements in the valley were once very few. With the increase in tourism, urbanization has also increased simultaneously.

Tourism and Ecohydrology

It is important to understand anthropogenic interference in the ecohydrology of a region. Apart from the knowledge of water resource potential, it is necessary to know the magnitude of impact that human transformation processes, such as deforestation, agriculture, and the construction of roads, have on the geographical balance (Singh and Haigh, 1995). Large-scale deforestation, mainly for fuel and fodder, and poorly and unscientifically managed agricultural practices are some of the major human transformation processes that have been causing reduced groundwater recharge through increased overland flow and declining rates of infiltration. So far as the Upper Beas Basin is concerned, the growth of tourism and, consequently, the change in land use practices are the major factors responsible for the negative impact on water resource potential. The water generating potential of the land in channels and springs has reduced gradually in the study area during the last ten years. Information regarding 18 springs was collected by interviewing the people of the area and through direct field research. Out of 18 springs, seven have completely dried up, mainly due to the reduced groundwater generating capacity of the land in the wake of a considerable decrease in infiltration. Besides, as has been reported by the villagers, the overall flow of all remaining springs has been reduced to a considerable extent. Due to increasing tourist activities, water pollution is quite visible in the river Beas. There is no proper planning for waste disposal with garbage lying everywhere along the river bank. At Manal, open air slaughtering results in large quantities of polluted water being dumped into the Beas River. Many open sewerage channels run into the river through different pans of the town. Since the region is situated at the headwaters of the Beas, the flow of water is very slow, and thus even a small amount of pollutants has a serious effect on the stream. Due to the increase in apple farming, the consumption of chemicals, pesticides, fungicides and other chemical and toxic materials is on the rise. They intermingle and are ultimately flushed by rain from the fields into the river contaminating the water. Though there is not enough quantitative evidence of water pollution from this source, it may be said that if the spread of orchards and the use of chemicals continue, the time is not far off when the entire region will suffer a severe crisis from water pollution. Also, in this tourist dominated area, with a highly seasonal concentration of people, the use of polythene bags is very common. The ultimate result of throwing away these bags is seen in the river Beas on both the banks. Finally, the water resources of the entire area are affected. A few positive initiatives relating to tourism and other development processes which may be considered for the study area are sanitation and sewerage facilities in the towns of Manali, Kullu and Bhuntar and water treatment plants in private hotels to create awareness among the rural masses regarding sanitation and hygiene.

Water-borne Diseases in Upper Kullu Valley

Since tap water is not available for dinking purposes, hence, number of water-borne diseases get spread over in the area. Local people are bound to drink open water or running water directly, as spring water has dried up in the area. During summer, due to water crisis, people store the rainwater (rainwater harvesting) and also they dig small wells to store the water for lean period. After the questionnaire of 200 local people, the following diseases and their perceptions have been listed below:

Name of diseases	*Yes*	*Percentage*	*No*	*Percentage*	*Don't know*	*Percentage*
Viral encephalitis	30	15	90	45	80	40
Typhoid	190	95	10	5	00	00
Cholera	170	85	20	10	10	5
Jaundice	200	100	00	00	00	00
Diarrhoeal	134	67	48	24	18	9
Poliomyelitis	42	21	34	17	124	62
Amaebiasis	34	17	26	13	160	80
Hapatities	24	12	36	18	140	70
Gastroenteritis	86	43	76	38	38	19

Source: Personnel Survey, 2001.

Concluding Remarks

The Himalayan geosystem had a congenial relationship in the past with abundant natural resources for life support system of the local communities. The land use pattern was more or less similar up to early eighties. The basic changes occurred due to large scale and unplanned tourism and development. Owing to terrorist activities in the Kashmir region, the mass movement of the tourists was channelized to the Upper Beas Basin making Manali as epicentre. Hence, to support the tourism infrastructures' development a heavy congestion of buildings and roads took place. A large-scale immigration from different parts of the country is still going on altering the land ownership pattern of the valley. Once an agrarian landscape, it has now changed to a concrete urbanized landscape. No doubt, the tourism is a lucrative cash incentive in nature, but, without agricultural development, livelihood security of the local community is at stake, Not only the agricultural land use changes, but also grazing land uses have also been transformed. There were a large number of 'thatches' (grazing land) in the temperate region of the Kullu Valley and the dry cold region of Patan, Lahul and Spiti valleys. Due to climatic extremity and weather anomalies, the transhumance is very common across the valley. The Guddies communities have developed a winter camp in the Bilaspur and in the lower region of Mandi district and of the Lahul and Spiti districts due to shortage of grazing land in the Upper Beas Basin.

The present anthropogenic activities with unrestful economic growth and unplanned haphazard growth of the tourism and urban agglomerations have degraded not only the local environment but also have reduced the natural resources base of the transhumance communities.

Apart from above, the anti-ecological approaches of the government particularly, "Nature Land Act 1986" (distribution of land to the landless people) in which the forest land (thatches) were redistributed to the landless communities of Himachal Pradesh. Since, the Kullu Valley is more fertile with green lush forests which attracted maximum number of the new settlers from Lahul, Spiti and other peripheral areas. The concentration of migrated population led to deforestation for agriculture, later to horticulture and now to tourism and recreation. Consequently, a large number of thatches have now disappeared leaving behind the livelihood crisis to the local communities of the transhumance. Hence, new dimensions have emerged between economy and ecology, dependency and self-reliance. An urgent and immediate action and remedies have become the need of the time to save the livelihood resource base of the local community and to save the geoecology of the Upper Beas Valley.

References

Aggarwal, A., R. Chopra and K. Sharma (1982) *The State of India's Environment 1982: A Citizen's Report*, New Delhi: Centre for Science and Environment.

Bandyopadhyay, J. (1992) 'From Environmental Conflicts to Sustainable Mountain Transformation: Ecological Action in the Garhwal Himalaya', in D. Ghai and J.M. Vivian (eds), *Grassroots Environmental Action*, London: Routledge, 259–278.

Berkes, F. (ed.) (1989) *Common Property Resource: Ecology and Community-Based Sustainable Development*, London: Belhaven Press.

Chadha, S.K. (ed) (1989) *Environmental Holocaust in Himalayas*, New Delhi: Ashish Publisher.

Chanha, S.K (ed.) (1992) *Environmental Holocaust in Himalaya*, New Delhi: Concept.

CIDC-SICI Project (1995) *On Sustainable Development of Mountain Environments in India and Canada*, Technical Report No. 1.

Geist, H.J. and E.F. Lambin (2002) 'Proximate Causes and Underlying Driving Forces in Tropical Deforestation', *BioScience*, 52(2): 143–150.

Jodha, N.S. (ed.) (1992) *Sustainable Mountain Agriculture Perspectives and Issues, Vol. I: Community Forestry*, New Delhi: IBH Publications.

Pandey, V. and J.S. Singh (1984) 'Energetics of Hill Agro-Ecosystems: A Case Study from Central Himalaya', *Agricultural Systems*, 13: 83–95.

Pandey, B.W. (2002) *Geo-Environmental Hazards in Himalaya: Assessment and Mapping*, New Delhi: Mittal Publications.

Pandey, B.W. (ed.) (2005) *Natural Resource Management*, New Delhi: Mittal Publications.

Sharma, P.D. and R.S. Minhas (1993) 'Land Use and Biophysical Environment of Kinnaur District, Himachal Pradesh', *Mountain Research and Developments*, 13: 41–60.

Singh, N. and V. Titi (1993) 'Empowerment for Sustainable Development', Working Paper, International Institute for Sustainable Development, Winnipeg (USD).

Singh, R.B. (ed) (1992) *Dynamics of Mountain Geosystems*, New Delhi: Ashish Publishing House.

Singh, R.B. (1998) 'Land Use/Cover Changes, Extreme Events and Ecohydrological Responses in the Himalayan Region', *Hydrological Process*, 12: 2043–2055.

Singh, R.B. and Haigh, M.J. (eds) (1995) *Sustainable Reconstruction of Highland and Headwater Regions*, New Delhi: Oxford and IBH Publisher.

Singh, R.B. and Mishra, D.K (1995) 'Dynamics of Landuse and Cropping Pattern: Historical Prognostications in Upper Beas Basin', in R.B. Singh, and M.J. Haigh, (eds) *Sustainable Reconstruction of Highland and Headwater Regions*, New Delhi: Oxford and IBH Publisher, 649–662.

Tilman, D. (1999) 'Global Environmental Impacts of Agriculture Expansion: The Need for Sustainable and Efficient Practices', *Proc. Natl. Acad. Sci. USA*, 96(11): 5995–6000.

Tiwari, P.C. (1995) *Natural Resources and Sustainable Development in Himalaya*, Almora: Shree Almora Book Dept.

5

Water Crisis in India

Issues and Challenges

SURENDRA SINGH CHAWLA

The water crisis in India has become an important issue of concern for the planners, policy makers and development experts. At the time of independence, water was taken for granted as an abundant renewable resource (Narasimhan and Gaur, 2010). But the post-independence era saw the crisis emerging and evolving at various levels in the context of prevailing socio-political environment. India has been facing water crisis in varied degrees for long in different parts of the country. Falling water table due to excessive extraction of groundwater – for irrigation, industrial use and for drinking purposes – has reached an alarming situation in a number of regions. Growing population and urbanization, increasing needs of industry and agriculture, along with poor and unsustainable water development and management system, have posed a serious threat to India's water future. The scarcity of water has acquired such a dimension that water riots have been reported from time to time from different parts of the country. Not only this, the involvement of different countries on the issue of sharing river waters has the potential to cause water wars among the nations. The situation may further worsen due to the uncertainties and variability in terms of spatial and temporal availability of water due to climatic changes. Besides the availability, the quality of water has also become a major issue of concern. The present paper has highlighted various issues relating to water crisis in India. Important determinants leading to water crisis have been highlighted. Some emerging issues like lack of effective legislation and its enforcement, privatization of water have also been presented. The paper has also forwarded various recommendations to mitigate the challenges of water crisis in India as well as options for policy formulation with regard to proper use, maintenance and conservation of water resources in globalizing India.

Water Crisis in India: Alarming Concerns

The issue of water security has become one of the major challenges to India's economic and social development. The long held perception that water is an unlimited resource capable of being automatically replenished every year has been the main reason of the too-liberal and even wasteful use. India's need to become self-reliant in food prompted it to take steps towards Green Revolution strategy in mid-1960s, which resulted in manyfold increase in food production in some selected states. However, besides the use of inputs like High Yielding Variety seeds, fertilizers, pesticides, the success of green revolution in those states was based on unrestricted and excessive use of water. It required augmentation of irrigation facilities. Initially, the farmers depended on the canal irrigation facilities developed during the colonial period. However, with the surface water facilities for irrigation on vast and dispersed lands gradually becoming inadequate and the shortage getting further aggravated by the inefficiencies of the system, farmers progressively resorted to the use of groundwater. Since 1970s groundwater irrigation has been expanding at a very rapid pace (UNICEF, 2013), while tank irrigation almost disappeared and surface water irrigation grew much more slowly (World Bank, 2005). The net irrigated area tripled from 21 million hectares in 1950–1951 to 63 million hectares in 2008–2009; the share of groundwater irrigation through wells rose substantially from 28 per cent to 61 per cent. The main contribution in this came from rapid growth in tubewell irrigation, the share of which rose from zero in 1950–51 to over 41 per cent by 2008–2009. This shows that groundwater irrigation, and within that tube-well irrigation technology, has made a huge contribution to irrigation growth in India (Gandhi and Bhamoriya, 2011). Over the last two decades, 84 per cent of the total addition to net irrigated area came from groundwater, and only 16 per cent from canals (World Bank, 2005). A number of factors such as subsidies on electricity, lack of metering, credit availability and commercialization of agriculture provided extra boost for rapid water extraction. It is found that an increase in village electrification by one percentage point may result, on the average, in an increase of half to two-thirds of a percentage point in the rate of utilization of groundwater potential (Kazmi, 1978).

The benefits of using the groundwater were quite high, but over a period of time it led to the depletion of the groundwater causing sharp decline in water table as the replenishment could not match with the limitless extraction. As per an assessment by NASA, during 2002–2008 three states (Punjab, Haryana and Rajasthan) together lost about 109 cu km of water leading to a decline in the water table to the extent of 0.33m per annum (Rodell et al., 2009; quoted in UNICEF, 2013). According to the Central Groundwater Board's latest assessment (MoWR, 2011) at the all-India level, the stage of groundwater development has increased from 58 per cent in 2004 to 61 per cent in 2009. The overexploited areas are mostly concentrated on three parts of the country: in north-western part in Punjab, Haryana, Delhi and Western Uttar Pradesh; in western part, particularly in Rajasthan; and in peninsular India like Karnataka and Tamil Nadu. Number of overexploited and critical administrative units are significantly higher in Delhi, Gujarat, Haryana, Himachal Pradesh, Karnataka, Punjab, Rajasthan and Tamil Nadu and also the UTs of Daman & Diu and Pondicherry (Puducherry).

Surface water bodies in India – not only the small, but also the big ones – are under threat. A number of rivers and lakes in different parts of the country are in bad shape due to overexploitation and pollution. River water pollution has increased over the years and more stretches of rivers are getting polluted due to millions of litres of sewage, industrial and agricultural wastes they receive every day. As much as 33 per cent of the stretches out of the total 45,019 km of length of rivers in India are polluted (GOI, 2011). Discharge of untreated sewage is a singlemost important cause for pollution of surface and groundwater since there is a large gap between generation and treatment of domestic wastewater in India (MoEF, 2007). Industrial waste discharge, the other major source of water pollution, has become a great health hazard in a number of regions. High incidence of harmful chemical constituents and heavy metals like fluoride, arsenic, nitrate, iron, chromium, lead, nickel, etc., in groundwater has been reported from various parts of the country mainly due to unplanned disposal of industrial effluents. Excessive extraction has also caused groundwater salinity in various parts of the country. Besides these, the growing construction of the septic tanks for want of sewer lines in the countryside has become another possible source of subsoil contamination (GOI, 2011).

A number of lakes in different parts of the country are progressively degenerating by the growing pollution and many of them are losing their depths and also gradually shrinking in size due to encroachments. A joint study by the Water Mission, FICCI and the Earthwatch Institute India (2013) has given significant information in this regard. A study conducted by Alternate Hydro Energy Centre, University of Roorkee (quoted in the above-mentioned study) states 15 major drains disposing their wastes in the Dal; thereby impacting the water quality and aquatic life. The area of the water body which was 1,538 ha in 1971 shrunk to 1,305 ha in 2008. The Hussain Sagar Lake in Hyderabad is threatened by the disposal of industrial effluents and domestic sewage to the tune of an estimated 150 million litres per day (CSE, 2012, cited in WM-EII, 2013) and as a result of growing encroachment the lake has shrunk in size by 40 per cent in the last four decades (WM-EII, 2013). The depth of Naini Lake which was 29 m in 1871 has reduced to 13 m in 2007 (CSE, 2012). A number of water bodies have been killed by human greed. The Bhadkal and Surajkund lakes on the outskirts of New Delhi are the classic examples which have gone dry due to illegal mining in the surrounding Aravali hills.

High degree of pollution and lack of proper sanitation and sewerage have raised severe water quality problems causing drinking water vulnerability in many parts of the country. The National Water Policy, 2002 has accorded priority to domestic use, followed by irrigation, industries, and other uses. The UN has recognized the 'right to safe and clean drinking water and sanitation' as a human right (UN Resolution, July 2010). However, the development of an efficient sanitation system remains one major challenge before India's water and sanitation sector. A very large proportion of the population in India still does not have basic facilities of sanitation. While in urban India an estimated 18.6 per cent households do not have latrines within the premises, in rural areas the situation is highly grave where as high as 67.3 per cent population defecates in the open (Census of India, 2011). The lack of safe drinking water has serious health implications, especially for the vulnerable sections of society. It is estimated that around 37.7 million Indians are affected by waterborne diseases annually, 1.5 million children are estimated to die of diarrhea alone and 73 million working days are lost due to waterborne diseases each year (Khurana and Sen, 2007). Inadequate sanitation causes India 'considerable economic losses' each year, equivalent to 6.4 per cent of its Gross Domestic Product (GDP) in 2006 (US$53.8 billion) (WSP, 2010; cited in UNICEF, 2013). Though the National Urban Sanitation Policy, 2008 seeks to generate awareness, eliminate open defecation, promote integrated citywide sanitation (Plannning Commission, 2012), the real targets can be achieved only if these measures are accompanied by adequate water availability.

The water situation is progressively becoming more and more grave in the face of growing population, industrialization and urbanization. While between 2001 and 2011, the population in India increased from 1,029 million to 1,210 million, the per capita annual water availability during the same period declined from 1,816 cubic metre to 1,545 cubic metre, suggesting that we are already in a 'water stressed' situation. The future projections for per capita annual water availability are more disturbing (UNICEF, 2013). The growing industrialization and urbanization have resulted in substantial changes in the population composition of the country in the last two decades. Not only the number of urban population, but also the number of towns has increased significantly. As per the UNICEF report (2013), during 1991–2011, the overall population of the country increased by 43 per cent – the rural population increased by 32 per cent while urban population increased by 75 per cent. The share of urban population was 25.49 per cent in 1991, which has increased to 31.16 per cent in 2011. The number of towns (urban centres) has increased from 5,161 to 7,935, an addition of 2,774 towns during 2001–11. In the coming decades a rapid growth in demand for water from non-irrigation sectors such as industry, power, etc., has been projected. The demand for water in the domestic sector will grow 2.6 times, energy 3.7 times, and industry 2.2 times during 2010–50 (Thatte et al., 2009; cited in Gaur and Amerasinghe, 2011). The Water Resources Group estimates that if the current pattern of demand continues, about half of the demand for water will be unmet by 2030 (WRG, 2009; cited in Tiwari and Pandey, 2011).

Managing Water Crisis: Initiatives and Way Forward

Water scarcity is fundamentally dynamic, which intensifies with increasing demand or decreasing availability in terms of quantity and/or quality of the resource; therefore, it is possible to bring about a change in the situation by taking appropriate measures. In view of the future projections of growing demand it is clear that the current water development and management system in India is not sustainable. Therefore, to avert the crisis new approaches to long-term water planning and management that incorporate principles of sustainability and equity are required (Gleick, 1998). The supply-side approach rather than improving the efficiency of existing systems is no longer suitable in view of the increasing demand of water. An integrated approach to water planning and management is required at two levels of functioning: first, at the level of conservation and development of water resource, which requires infrastructure development; and second, at the level of distribution which relates to the water distribution management and is highly crucial in view of the growing and competing demands of different sectors.

Infrastructure Development

Though massive storage structures to store surface water have been constructed after independence, yet water storage infrastructure in India remains one of the lowest in the world. Even with 4,525 large and small dams, the per capita storage of 213 cu m in the country is relatively very low (UNICEF, 2013). Need for storage will further grow because global climate change is going to have major impacts in India. Increased uncertainty in terms of spatial and temporal availability of water resulting from the rapid glacial melting in coming decades in the western Himalayas and the increased variability of rainfall in large parts of the subcontinent can further aggravate the already skewed situation of water availability. If the long-term sustainability is to be achieved, the development of new water infrastructure is indispensible, besides maintenance and rehabilitation of the already existing infrastructure.

The issue of infrastructure development raises some important concerns. After independence, construction of major water infrastructure received high priority. However, the cost-benefit analysis of large dams has given rise to serious controversy especially after the 'Narbada Bachaao Aandolan' (Save Narmada Movement) of 1980s (Jensen, 2004). The economic benefits of large dams are being evaluated against the social and environmental costs. Added to this is the threat they pose due to lack of proper maintenance. The increased siltation of large dams, time and cost over-runs, and tail-ender deprivation have also raised questions on the efficacy of large dams in India (Oza, 2007). Maintenance and rehabilitation of these ageing structures require huge sums of money to be allocated in the budget. However, major proportion of this money gets absorbed by the salary payments of the bureaucratic structures responsible for their operation and maintenance, resulting in an 'enormous backlog of deferred maintenance' (World Bank, 2005). Even the financial assistance received from the international agencies such as the World Bank is used for the rehabilitation of poorly maintained systems, rather than financing new infrastructure for augmenting irrigation and water supply. This 'build-neglect-rebuild' syndrome (Mohanty, 2005; quoted in World Bank, 2005), though serious in its own right, also means the lack of public financing for the development of water infrastructure in a big way. In such a scenario efforts in augmentation of surface water sources should include building of smaller-scale, community-level water storage infrastructure such as tanks, check dams and local water recharge systems. Large dams should be considered only when other options are not available and after the thorough study of ecological impact. Also, while constructing dams it has to be kept in mind that those structures do not affect the minimum flow of the stream, which is essential to maintain the self-purification quality of the rivers. Encroachments on the areas of the water bodies including the flood plains and the high flood plains of the rivers should be checked through stringent legislation. Notifying the River Regulating Zone (RRZ) under the Environment Protection Act will help in regulating activities in the flood plains of rivers across India (*Hindustan Times,* 2013a). This will also give the rivers the space in times of their excessive behaviour due to probable impacts of climatic change and reduce the impact of any such disasters.

Conservation of Groundwater

Over 80 per cent of India's rural water and about 50 per cent of its urban and industrial water requirements are being met from groundwater sources. Further, about 45 per cent of created irrigation potential in the country is through exploitation of groundwater sources (GoI, 2011). Heavy dependence of agriculture on groundwater due to country's failure to develop its ultimate irrigation potential and inadequacy of surface water sources in terms of quantity and quality to meet the domestic and other needs of population have been responsible in a major way for the depletion of groundwater. However, if the steps are not taken to minimize the overdrawl of groundwater and it is allowed at the existing rate, people will not have water even for self-provisioning. Promoting water saving infrastructure and agricultural practices can reduce groundwater extraction rates (Sekhri, 2012). Improving tank irrigation systems through technical and management interventions can save water and extend the surface irrigation or increase recharge and conjunctive use of groundwater or both (Palanisami et al., 2010). Using micro-irrigation techniques including drip and sprinkle technologies can improve the water efficiency in agriculture and can lead to 30–70 per cent water savings relative to flood irrigation

(Oza, 2007). It is a general belief that subsidies promote bad practices. Therefore, metering and charging of electricity at differential rates with an objective of reducing subsidy, and thus the inefficient use of water in irrigation, will help in checking overexploitation of groundwater. Restricting the number of tubewells through licensing would also be useful.

There has been a conscious effort on the part of the government to regulate groundwater use as well as its development. Water is a state subject and therefore, the central government prepared model bills from time to time in the past few decades, especially in the post-liberalization era to provide a model bill for the states. The first groundwater model bill was formulated in 1970 to regulate and control the development and management of groundwater for adoption by the states. This model bill has been revised several times (1992, 1996 and 2005), but the basic scheme adopted in 1970 has been retained (Cullet, 2012). Several states have passed groundwater related legislation based on the Model Bill. The basic scheme of the model bill is to provide for the establishment of the groundwater authority at state level under the direct control of the government. The authority is invested with powers to regulate and control the development and management of groundwater. However, the bill with no specific provision for public participation in the scheme has several other shortcomings including its failure to prioritize domestic use of water over other uses, to differentiate between the commercial and non-commercial uses of groundwater and between the small and big users; and its focus on the right of use of land owners whereas the non-land owners/occupiers by and large continued to be excluded. These weaknesses along with the growing over-dependence on the groundwater in the changing times made this model bill inappropriate. The Model Bill for the Conservation, Protection and Regulation of Groundwater, 2011 is a step forward: it clearly differentiates between the commercial and non-commercial uses of groundwater, prioritizes the use of water by different sectors with first priority to basic water for rural and urban domestic needs and applies decentralization principles to groundwater regulation (Plannning Commission, 2012). However, a more effective legislation is required to control groundwater exploitation, and a constitutional amendment separating the right to groundwater from the right to land would help provide the necessary foundation for stronger laws and institutional controls (Gandhi and Bhamoriya, 2011).

Water Conservation: Community Initiatives

Community efforts in the revival of the traditional water harvesting systems would be of great help in augmenting the water availability in dry areas. This has proved to be quite a successful strategy in water scarce district Alwar in Rajasthan, where seven rivers which had completely dried up were revived by using the earthen check dam technique, and now they are having the perennial flow (Singh, 2012). Comprehensive plans need to be made to capture the rainwater for groundwater recharging, storage and recycling. In urban areas, particularly the metros, the rapid urbanization has resulted in increasing concretization of space, thus blockading the possibilities of natural percolation of water into the ground and thus the precious commodity goes down the drain. Though it is not possible to do away with the concrete structures, but the same structures can be used for rainwater harvesting. Rainwater harvesting systems at institutional, colony and even at individual residence levels can help recharge groundwater significantly over a period of time. The Badarpur flyover in Delhi which has proved to be a good example of water conservation where rainwater harvesting system was clubbed with water reuse and recycling methodology including recharging the groundwater table using the storm water flowing from the elevated highways (*Hindustan Times,* 2013b). Similarly, government buildings can be used for rainwater harvesting. A calculation shows that approximately 80 million litres of water can be saved in Delhi every year by using the metro rail structures for harvesting rainwater (*Hindustan Times,* 2013c). Besides augmenting the efforts to increase conservation, some preventive measures in urban areas are also needed. Dewatering of large tracts of areas by the rapidly growing construction industry in the metros and other cities should be prevented. In order to prevent further depletion of groundwater in Gurgaon, the Punjab and Haryana High Court in August 2012 asked Haryana to ban groundwater extraction for construction work, which is a welcome step.

Water Distribution Management: Government Initiatives

The scope of water development is not infinite and therefore an efficient use of water enforced through regulated distribution is the key to the solution of water crisis in the present scenario. The growing realization of inadequacy of water legislation and policy framework necessitated coordinated effort for changing water law. In the post-liberalization era, this change is being effected in the 'form of reforms' (Cullet, 2007) incorporating in its scope various aspects of water use as well as governance. The reforms seek to emphasize direct contributions of individuals in their water needs, reduction of the role of public sector and involving private sector in water services.

Water sector reforms reflect a conscious effort by the government to change its role from provider to regulator and make for it to divest from its responsibilities of managing water services. The underlying idea is that since water services are being provided by the government at subsidized rates, people do not treat water as a valuable commodity and hence are inclined to use it inefficiently. The present water reforms seek to treat water as an economic good which entails that all water services must be based on the principle of cost-recovery and the water users should pay for the services they want to get. In a situation where the water services have been substantially subsidized, this implies a significant policy reversal. These changes are to be accompanied with decentralization ensuring the participation of water users. Creation of Water User Associations (WUAs) in villages for irrigation services and starting of a new scheme named 'Swajaldhara' to ensure better drinking water in villages manifest these policy changes. The urban water distribution system is proposed to be put under private control.

Water User Associations

The creation of WUAs, is meant to ensure community participation by putting control of local resources in the hands of local people and introducing decentralization of decision-making to the lowest level. It makes for farmers' direct involvement in irrigation system management. The WUAs have been entrusted with the task of managing of irrigation services including distribution of water to the people, upkeep of irrigation systems as well as the financial costs involved. It is believed that where the state had failed in the past the farmers will not, and that operation and management of the irrigation system by the farmers themselves can change things around (Upadhyay, 2011). However, the provisions of the proposed scheme are questioned on many counts. The intended participation of people is deceptive as only the landowners have been granted the right to participate in decision-making. It is also expected that such associations will be dominated by local landlords and therefore the responsibilities of making equitable distribution will not be performed in true spirit.

'Swajaldhara'

A new initiative 'Swajaldhara' (2002) was launched to open up the reform initiatives in the rural drinking water supply sector throughout the country. It is a community participatory scheme. It derived its policy framework from the World Bank sponsored pilot project called 'Swajal' (1996–2002) and proposes the progressive withdrawal of the State from its responsibility to make provision of safe drinking water in the rural areas. It aims to work at achieving household level drinking water security with an objective to ensure universal access. The scheme can be implemented by the States/UTs at various levels such as Gram Panchayats, Blocks, Beneficiary Groups who, on adopting the reforms principles, will be eligible for Swajaldhara Projects. It empowers the panchayats/communities to plan, implement, operate, maintain and manage all drinking water schemes. The full ownership of drinking water assets lies with Gram Panchayats; and full operation and maintenance will be managed by the users/Panchayats.

Under the scheme only individuals or households that make the stipulated first ten per cent contribution towards the capital cost will benefit from its implementation. The basic economic rationale of 'Swajaldhara' is that people should be made to pay for part of the capital cost (intended to be progressively raised to full) of drinking water project and for the whole cost of operation and maintenance. The argument forwarded by the government is that providing water free to the users leads to uneconomic consumption of this scarce resource. Therefore, it is proposed to shift from what is seen as a supply-driven approach to one which focuses on the need of the end users, i.e., demand focused approach. Thus, those who do not pay will remain excluded, implying that the poor can only postpone paying up of their share, but cannot avoid it altogether. On the other hand the landlords can purchase water rights of the poor by paying their share at the beginning of the scheme. In this way the reforms fail to address existing inequalities in access to water, as access to water through new schemes has been kept restricted to 'users' (who pay). Cullet (2008) also raises a fundamental issue that the drinking water priority needs to be anchored in law, not policy.

Privatization of Water

One of the major issues of concern with regard to water crisis and the changing role of the government relating to water issues in India is privatization of water services. Water crisis in India is largely seen as resulting from the failure of the public sector as service provider. The public sector was projected, and widely perceived, as inefficient, cash-strapped, corrupt, unaccountable and lacking modern technology and management skills (Dwivedi and Dharmadhikary, 2007). The proponents of privatization, i.e., the global institutions like World Bank (WB, 1993), WHO/UNICEF (Planning Commission, Government of India, 2002), systematically highlighted the ills of public sector and brought up the need for privatization. It was proclaimed that privatization would bring in finances needed to build water services infrastructure; cheaper tariffs for users as competition and free-market forces take over operations; new technology and improve service extension to low-income and poor regions in urban areas.

The agenda of water privatization was incorporated in the National Water Policy of 2002, which proclaims that "Private sector participation should be encouraged in planning, development and management of water resources projects for diverse uses, wherever feasible. Private sector participation may help in introducing innovative ideas, generating financial resources and introducing corporate management and improving service efficiency and accountability to users. Depending upon the specific situations, various combinations of private sector participation, in building, owning, operating, leasing and transferring of water resources facilities, may be considered" (MoWR, 2002). The National Water Policy 2012 also envisages the minimization of the government's role in water services and promotes the involvement of private parties through Public Private Partnership (PPP) model, encouraging commercialization of water services (MoWR, 2012).

Regarding privatization of water, several theoretical questions have been raised and the commodification and commercialization of water resources and services have been opposed by many the world over including India (Barlow and Clarke, 2002; Dwivedi and Dharmadhikary, 2007). It has been argued that water is the common property of all and must be protected and used as such, and should not be monopolized by a few. Right to safe and clean drinking water is a human right, and the State has the obligation to ensure that its policies guarantee water to all, on equitable and a non-profit basis. Designating water as a 'need' by the proponents of privatization divests the state of its role and also paves the way for making valid the pricing practices of the private companies. However, the supporters of the policy suggest that privatization does not mean paying a price for water but rather for the purification and supply of water, and therefore it does not imply that the status of water as a human right is taken away (Bhattacharya, 2004). Still, the perception that the only motive of the private companies is profit making and that they are not interested in providing service to the underprivileged at affordable price persists strongly. There has been substantial increase in water charges at all those places where a private company has taken over. While making a detailed report on privatization in India, Dwivedi and Dharmadhikary (2007) observe, "the experiences of water sector privatization from all over the world ... not only illustrate that the privatization in water has failed to meet its promises, but also challenge the very rationale provided in support of privatization – more investment, cheaper tariffs, better service, improved reliability, latest technology, increased efficiency and others. They show that privatization cannot address the fundamental issues of the sector – including resource conservation and augmentation, equity, and environmental sustainability". Experts have questioned the PPP model in the water sector on a number of grounds. Serious issues of concern, including its constitutionality, have been raised with regard to rationale for the PPP model being implemented in a number of cities in the country as part of water supply reforms (Koonan and Sampat, 2012; *The Hindu,* 2013).

Conclusions

The growing water crisis in India is the result of several factors ranging from our callous attitude towards water use and conservation to poor management of water development and distribution. The subsidized water services of early decades of post-colonial era probably emanating from the socialistic ideals of the government and the general perception that water is unlimited and easily available resulted in the overexploitation of the resource by different sectors. Health hazard created by the pollution of water bodies is a serious issue and needs to be addressed at the earliest. There is an urgent need on the part of the state governments and local authorities to give priority to build and maintain proper sewerage and sewage treatment systems without which abatement of pollution and preservation of rivers and other water bodies is not possible. Responsibility for managing water issues is fragmented among a number of Ministries and departments without any coordination. Sustained and integrated efforts are required on the part of different Ministries such as Water Resources, Agriculture, Environment and Forests and others so that there is greater interaction and sharing of knowledge and data among these Ministries and other concerned departments. A system of accountability has to be developed so that, unlike in the majority of cases in the past, the action plans to clean rivers and other water bodies yield results. Strong political will is required to enforce the existing water laws and formulate new ones appropriate for different regions. Privatization of water as a policy in India requires a critical examination before it is implemented on a large scale.

An integrated and holistic approach to water resource development and management based on the principle of decentralization and community participation, a top-down planning based on bottom-to-top feedback by different stakeholders, a balanced approach towards demand and supply solutions along with essential legislation on water governance, profiling the water bodies and their revival and restoration, reclamation and restoration of catchment areas, combination of traditional wisdom with scientific knowledge; and above all, creating awareness among the users and a change in the attitude can help us to save ourselves from the imminent water crisis.

References

Barlow, M. and T. Clarke (2002) *Blue Gold: The Fight to Stop the Corporate Theft of the World's Water*, New York: The New Press.

Bhattacharya, S. (2004) 'Globalization and Stress on Water Resources', *Economic and Political Weekly*, 28 August: 3901–3903.

Census of India (2011) Houselisting and Housing Census Data Highlights, Houses, Household Amenities and Assets.

Centre for Science and Environment (2012) *Churning Still Water*, New Delhi.

Cullet, P. (2007) 'Water Law in India: Overview of Existing Framework and Proposed Reforms', IELRC Working Paper 2007–01, Geneva: International Environmental Law Research Centre.

—— (2008) 'Water Sector Reforms and Water Law Reforms in India: The Case of Drinking Water', International Conference on the Right to Water and Sanitation in Theory and Practice, Oslo, 26–27 November.

—— (2012) 'The Groundwater Model Bill: Rethinking Regulation for the Primary Source of Water', *Economic and Political Weekly*, XLVII(45): 40–47.

Dwivedi, G. Rehmat and S. Dharmadhikary (2007) *Water: Private Limited – Issues in Privatisation, Corporatisation and Commercialisation of Water Sector in India*, Bhopal: Aadarsh Printers & Publishers.

Gandhi, V. and V. Bhamoriya (2011) 'Groundwater Irrigation in India: Growth, Challenges and Risks', in P. Tiwari and A. Pandey (eds), *Water: Policy and Performance for Sustainable Development*, India Infrastructure Report, New Delhi: Oxford University Press, 90–117.

Gaur, A. and P. Amerasinghe (2011) 'A River Basin Perspective of Water Resources and Challenges', in *Water: Policy and Performance for Sustainable Development*, India Infrastructure Report, New Delhi: Oxford University Press.

Gleick, P.H. (1998) 'Water in Crisis: Paths to Sustainable Water Use', *Ecological Applications*, 8(3): 571–579.

Government of India (2011) 'Augmentation of Depleted Groundwater Level, Sustainable Development, Conservation, Management, Use of Ground Water and Prevention of Water Pollution', Lok Sabha Standing Committee on Water Resources Report on Groundwater (Accessed on 1 December 2013).

Jensen, R. (2004) 'Large Dams in India: Temples or Burial Grounds?', *Counterpunch*, 21 September.

Kazmi, N.A. (1978) 'Utilization of Groundwater Resources', *Economic and Political Weekly*, 13(17): 738–739.

Khurana, I. and R. Sen (2007) *Drinking Water Quality in Rural India: Issues and Approaches*, Water Aid.

Koonan, S. and P. Sampat (2012) 'Delhi Water Supply Reforms', *Economic and Political Weekly*, 47(17): 32–39.

Ministry of Environment and Forests (2007) Evaluation of Operation and Maintenance of Sewage Treatment Plants in India 2007, Central Pollution Control Board, Government of India, New Delhi.

Ministry of Water Resources (2002) National Water Policy 2002, Government of India, New Delhi.

—— (2011) Dynamic Groundwater Resources of India (Accessed on 31 March 2009), Central Groundwater Board, Government of India, Faridabad.

—— (2012) National Water Policy 2012, Government of India, New Delhi.

Narasimhan, T.N. and V.K. Gaur (2010) 'A Framework for India's Water Policy', *Economic and Political Weekly*, 45(30): 20–23.

Oza, A. (2007) 'Irrigation: Achievements and Challenges', in *India Infrastructure Report*, New Delhi: Oxford University Press, 178–196.

Palanisami, K. et al. (2010) 'Climate Change and Water Supplies: Options for Sustaining Tank Irrigation Potential in India', *Economic and Political Weekly*, XLV(26–27): 183–190.

Planning Commission (2002) India: Assessment 2002, Water Supply and Sanitation, WHO-UNICEF Sponsored Study, Government of India, New Delhi.

—— (2012) Report of the Steering Committee on Water Resources and Sanitation for Twelfth Five Year Plan (2012–2017), Government of India, New Delhi.

—— (2013) Twelfth Five Year Plan (2012–2017): Faster, More Inclusive and Sustainable Growth, Vol. 1, Government of India, New Delhi.

Sekhri, S. (2012) *Sustaining Groundwater: Role of Policy Reforms in Promoting Conservation in India*, New Delhi: National Council of Applied Economic Research.

Singh, R. (2012) *Mewat Ke Johad* (in Hindi), Delhi: Rajkamal Prakashan.

The Hindu (2013) 'Water Privatization is Not for India', Delhi Edition, 20 March.

The Hindustan Times (2013a) 'Lack of River Zone Angers Activists', 21 June, 3.

—— (2013b) 'Badarpur Flyover: An Example of Conservation', Delhi Edition, 10 June.

—— (2013c) 'Only Rain God Can Quench City's Thirst', Delhi Edition, 18 April, 4.

Tiwari, P. and A. Pandey (2011) *Water: Policy and Performance for Sustainable Development*, India Infrastructure Report, New Delhi: Oxford University Press.

UNICEF (2013) *Water in India: Situation and Prospects*, New Delhi: UNICEF, FAO and SaciWATERs.

United Nations Resolution (2010) General Assembly Adopts Resolution Recognizing Access to Clean Water, Sanitation as Human Right, UN General Assembly, GA/10967.

Upadhyay, V. (2011) 'Water Rights and the New Water Laws in India', in P. Tiwari and A. Pandey (eds), *Water: Policy and Performance for Sustainable Development*, India Infrastructure Report, New Delhi: Oxford University Press.

Water and Sanitation Program (WSP) (2010) *Economic Impact of Inadequate Sanitation in India*, New Delhi: World Bank.

Water Mission, FICCI and Earthwatch Institute India (WM-EIT) (2013) *Safeguarding Urban Fresh Water Bodies*, New Delhi. Last retrieved from www.ficci.com/...guarding-Urban-FreshWater-Bodies.pdf on 4 December 2013.

World Bank (WB) (1993) *Water Resources Management*, Washington, DC.

—— (2005) *India's Water Economy: Bracing for a Turbulent Future*, Report No. 34750-IN, India.

6

Water Use and Its Management in Damodar River Basin

RAMESHWAR THAKUR

Water is an important natural resource. It is vital for increasing the agricultural production. It is also in great demand for domestic as well as industrial use. It is an important medium for generating cheap hydroelectric power. Water is a precious and scarce resource which is indivisible and, therefore, its utilization has to be planned for the river basin as a whole. Water, as a resource, is not evenly distributed over space and time. Sometimes, in the year, it is in plenty and sometimes it becomes scarce. Looking at the importance of water as a resource, the National Resources Council adopted the National Water Policy on 9 September 1987.

A concerted effort has been made to utilize the water resources for agricultural purposes by developing the irrigation facilities since 1951 under different Plan periods. There are many sources of irrigation in the basin: canals, tanks and wells including tubewells are important. The supply of drinking water to rural and urban population is another important aspect of utilization of water resources. Accelerated Rural Water Supply Programme (ARWSP) and National Mission on Drinking Water (NSDW) have been launched to achieve the goal of supplying drinking water to all the villages of the basin.

In several parts of India, utilization of both surface and groundwater has reached or even exceeds the limit of sustainable use. Wasteful and efficient uses of harnessed water increase the gap between effective supply and demand at the users end. As a result, supply has not kept pace with demand and the gap has grown. This has led to intensified competition over access to and allocation of available supplies between use and users. The efforts indicate how to bridge some of the gap between the developed advanced technologies of water resources planning, designing and management and their applications. Water is also one of the most manageable of the natural resources as it is capable of diversion, transport, storage and recycling. All these properties impart to water its great utility for human beings.

There is a pressing need for conservation of water resources. The major task is to reduce the run-off and evaporation losses. Over irrigation leads to the deterioration of soils. Salinity and alkalinity are the outcomes of misuse of water. The sprinkler and drip irrigation may prove to be better techniques of applying water to crops. The affluents from settlements and industrial establishments form major pollutants of the water bodies. Recycling is essential to economize the water use. Flooding causes damage to life and property of people in about half area of the basin which has been declared flood-prone. The basin should be treated as one unit for planning the water utilization.

Objectives

The major objectives of this paper are: (1) to examine the use of water; (2) to analyse the problems of water utilization; and (3) to suggest management of water in the study area.

Study Area

Geographically, the Damodar river basin lies between 22°10'N to 24°50'N latitudes and 84°30'E to 88°10'E longitudes (Figure 1). The Tropic of Cancer traverses to the south of the region or a little to the north of Ranchi city. The Damodar river is a tributary of the Hooghly and flows across Jharkhand and West Bengal for about 541

Figure 1

Catchments: Damodar Basin

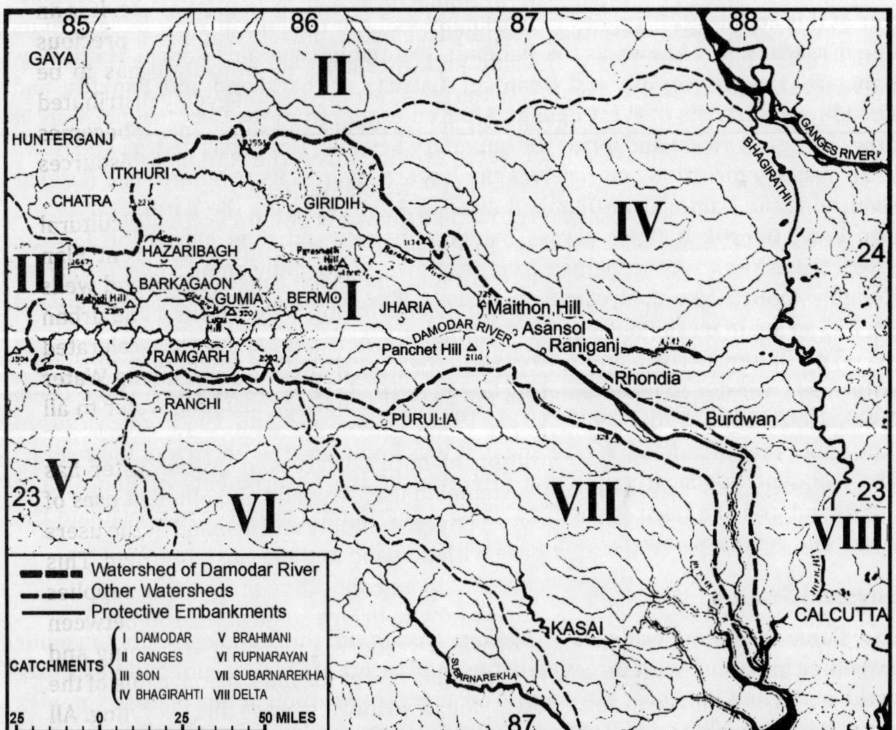

Catchment basin of the Damodar in relation to the general drainage of the Chota Nagpur Plateau. The Brahmani and Subarnatekha Rivers drain to the Orissa coast, the rest to the Ganges. Note the contrast in stream pattern between the plateau, the alluvial fans that skirt it to the east and north, and the delta. Land over 1000 feet in the basin is shaded.

Source: Kirk (1950: 422).

Figure 2

Physiographic Block Diagram of Upper Damodar Basin

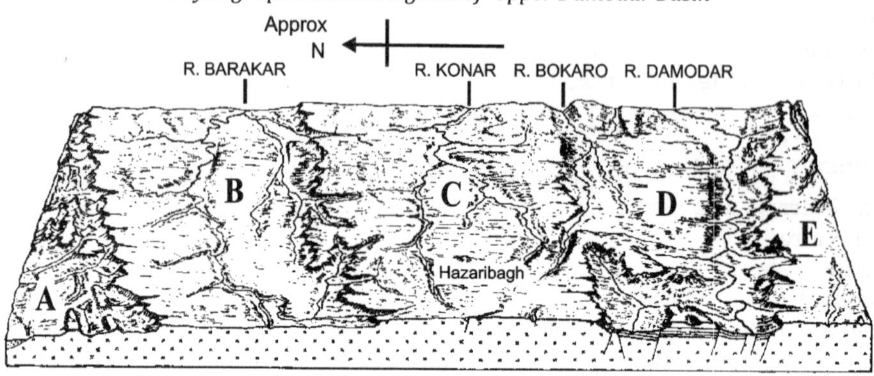

Physiographic block diagram of the upper Damodar Basin, showing the broken country of nortern "ghats" with skirt of alluvial and detrital fans (A), the 1250-foot (B) and 2000-foot (C and E) surfaces, and the trough-faulted Gondwana sedimentary basins (D)

Source: Kirk (1950: 422).

km from its origin in the hills of the Chotanagpur to its confluence with the Hooghly. Out of this course, 270 km lies in Jharkhand and the rest lies in West Bengal. In its upper reaches, it is known as the Deonadi. The Damodar drains Ranchi, Hazaribag, Ramgarh, Bokaro, Giridih and Dhanbad districts of Jharkhand and Bankura and Burddhwan districts of West Bengal. After emerging from the Chotanagpur hills, it flows for about 40 km and forms the boundary between Hazaribag district and flows in an easterly direction and receives the Bokaro river as its tributary. The Barakar river joins the Damodar in Dhanbad district. After receiving the Barakar, it enters into West Bengal. It flows across Bankura district and then enters Burddhwan district. It takes a southerly turn from the town of Burddhwan and falls into river Hooghly about 50 km upstream from Kolkata. The Damodar basin covers an area of 24, 235 sq km in Jharkhand and West Bengal.

The Damodar river flows across the major coal belt of India. It used to be a notorious river due to its devastating floods in 1823, 1848, 1856, 1859, 1863, 1882, 1890, 1898, 1901, 1905, 1907, 1913, 1916, 1923, 1933 and 1943 which caused damage to Jharkhand and West Bengal. It was known as the 'sorrow of the region'. The frequent floods attracted the attention of the governments of Bengal and Jharkhand and the need was felt to control the floods, conserve and regulate the water and generate power.

Physical Setting

The Damodar basin occupies a sunken trough in the middle of Chotanagpur extending in an east-west direction between plateaus of Chotanagpur and Hazaribag in the north and Ranchi in the south. The average elevation of this plateau complex varies between 300 and 600 metres above the mean sea level. The river originates at an altitude of 610 metres above the mean sea level and discharges its water in Hooghly at an altitude of less than 30 metres above mean sea level. This difference in elevation gives an idea of its gradient and also about its erosive power. The river leaves the plateau at a height of about 150 metres and reaches the plains in Burddhwan district. The topography in its course is varied and undulating. Figure 2 shows block diagram of part of the upper Damodar basin with different forms. Its descent from one surface level of the plateau to the other is sudden. Most of its major tributaries joining the mainstream have provided break points which are suitable sites for locating hydropower stations. The undulating nature of the topography and the faulted nature of the strata have not only favoured the extraction of coal but also provided suitable sites for damming the river (Qureshi, 1990).

Climatic Characteristics and Water Power Development

The average annual rainfall experienced in the region is about 1,250 mm which is concentrated between June and September. Sometimes, the region experiences cyclonic storms accompanied by heavy rainfall. The source region of the river receives higher rainfall than the lower reaches. The incidence of flooding is higher during the stormy rainfall when the channel is unable to accommodate the rush of water. The weathered rocks and the erosive power of the river add to the load of debris which often chokes the channel and, thus, the flood situation is aggravated. The deforestation in the upper hills has further accentuated the erosion. As soon as the river emerges through a narrow passage near Asansol its flow is burst open. The plains below Burddhwan get submerged under floodwaters, sometimes to a depth of 2 to 2.5 m and the crops and settlements are devastated. While major floods occur at intervals, minor floods are experienced almost every year. The sediments brought by the Damodar create the problem of sedimentation in the Hooghly which, in turn, endangers the Kolkata port.

In order to control floods and other related problems, the Central Government in consultation with the governments of Jharkhand and West Bengal worked out a unified development project for Damodar basin on the basis of the Tennessee Valley Authority (TVA). The Damodar Valley Corporation (DVC) became a reality on 18 February 1948, when the draft of its constitution was passed by the parliament.

The original memorandum envisaged the construction of seven major dams: Aiyar and Panchet Hill on the Damodar river; Maithon, Belpahari and Tilaiya on the Barakar river; Konar on the Konar river; and Bokaro on the Bokaro river. The statutory functions of the DVC are: promotion and operation of schemes of irrigation; water supply and drainage; generation, transmission and distribution of electrical energy and flood control; production and control of navigation in the Damodar river, its tributaries and channels; promotion of afforestation and control of soil erosion in the Damodar basin and promotion of public health, agricultural, industrial, and general well-being of the Damodar basin. Thus, it became a multipurpose project with major objectives of flood control, irrigation, generation, and transmission of HIP, and promotion of year-round navigation. The DVC has implemented the construction of four multipurpose dams, Tilaiya, Maithon, Konar and Panchet out of seven dams. Rest three, i.e., Aiyer, Balpahari, and Bokaro Dams were not constructed. The details of the reservoir construction and design have been adequately summarized by Bhattacharyya (1973). He concludes that deforestation and soil erosion in the upper basin have increased the floods with bigger peak flows. Three thermal power stations at Chandrapura, Bokaro and Durgapur with a network of transmission and distribution lines have also been completed.

The Durgapur barrage located at about 23 km from Raniganj has been created for the storage of irrigation water. It is 831 metres long and about 12 metres high. It stores the water from Konar, Tilaiya, Maithon and Panchet Hill dams. The bulk of the water for storage is provided by Maithon and Panchet hill dams. This irrigation water is regulated through a network of canals extending over an area of about 5,000 sq km in Bankura, Burddhwan, Hooghly and Howrah districts in West Bengal. The barrage was completed in 1955. About 4 lakh ha will be irrigated mainly along the left bank in Burddhwan and Hooghly districts. The hilly nature of the terrain in Jharkhand has restricted the irrigated area. The left bank of Damodar canal is navigation-cum-irrigation canal connecting Kolkata with the Damodar basin coalfields.

Soil Conservation and Afforestation

Soils in the Damodar Basin are heavy clays and loams. They are deep and heavy on flat coal layers of low-lying tracts and light, coarse and thin in the uplands. Most of the land in the upper part of the basin in Jharkhand is of relatively low fertility. The terrain is undulating and lacks irrigation facilities. The population is not very high but limited nature of arable land available to the peasants has brought down the land-man ratio. The coal-mining activity, heaps of removed overburden, mining settlements, dense network of transportation lines, thick forest cover and obliterated local drainage have constrained the agriculture in the region. There are rich *Sal* forests. The hill slopes are covered with poorer vegetation like palm, bersabai, grass, bamboo and thorny plants.

The DVC has also been entrusted with the responsibility of soil conservation and afforestation. The main objective of soil conservation and afforestation in the catchment area is to reduce the soil erosion and save the reservoirs from heavy siltation. The problems of soil erosion is being tackled on watershed basis. The measures adopted for soil conservation are survey of soils taking into account the various physio-chemical properties of the soils, degree of slope, extent of erosion, present land use and suitability of irrigation, demonstration of better methods of land management and assessing the soil fertility. Afforestation within the catchment of Damodar basin is being carried out by the Forest Division of the Corporation as well as the forest departments of the state governments of Jharkhand and West Bengal.

Mineral Resource Base

The Damodar basin is a highly mineralized region in India. The Gondwana sedimentary rocks in the basin contain rich coal deposits. The richest, largest and most productive coalfields lie in this region. Jharia and Chandrapura coalfieds are located in Dhanbad. Jharia is the most important coalfield with a reserve of about 1,862 crore tonnes of good grade bituminous coal. It spreads over an area of about 440 sq km. Chandrapura is the second important coalfield in Dhanbad district. Its coal is used in the Chandrapura thermal power station. East and West Bokaro, Giridih, North and South Karanpura and Ramgarh coalfields also lie in the basin. The Kargali seam of East Bokaro coalfields spreads over 1,560 sq km and in production they rank next to Jharia and Raniganj coalfields.

Raniganj coalfields are spread over 1,067 sq km across Burddhwan, Purulia and Bankura in West Bengal. A large quantity of coal from Raniganj is used for producing thermal power at Bandel, Durgapur, and New Kashipore. Fireclay, graphite, limestone, quartz, bauxite, copper, and manganese are other minerals which are found in the Damodar basin. Besides, the surrounding regions also have rich mineral deposits. The Damodar basin itself has abundant forest resources, from where lac and grasses for manufacturing paper are extracted. The richness of the region in mineral and forest resources coupled with the hydro-thermal power development has been the basis of the economic development of the Damodar river basin (Figure 3).

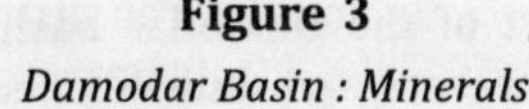

Figure 3

Damodar Basin : Minerals

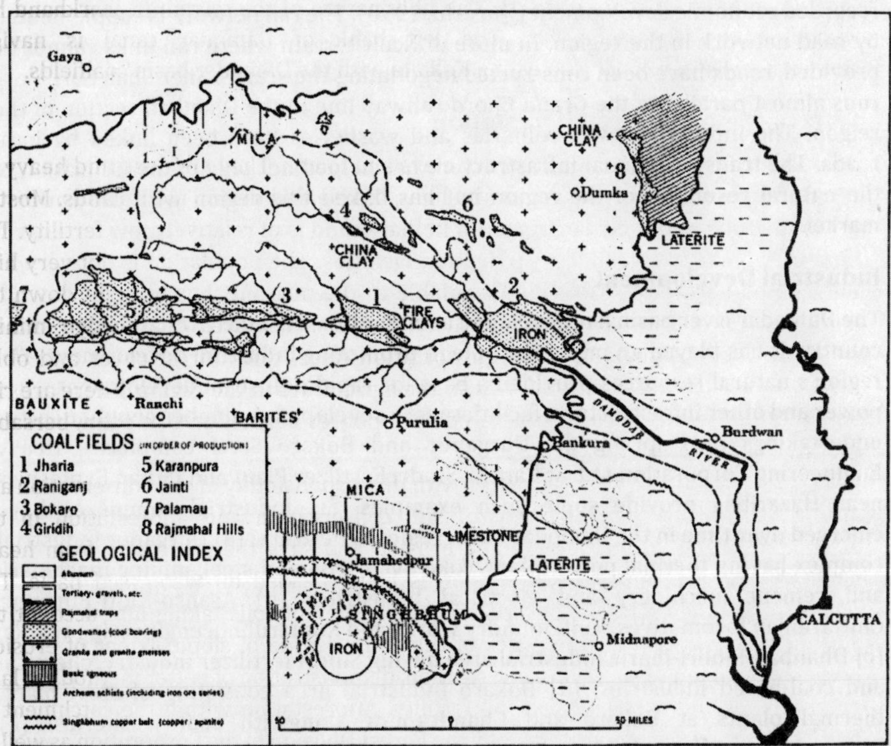

Mineral deposits, showing the five important coal fields. the rich mineral zone of eastern Singhbhum is also shown, including the copper belt where ores of copper and apatite veins occur in soda-granites associated with thrust zone. Circled "iron" represents ore of Gorumahisani; "iron" in Raniganj coal basin represents weathered ores of ironstone shales. In addition to minerals shown, asbestos, chromite, steatite, vanadium, and mineral pigments occur in workable quantities.

Source: Kirk (1950: 424).

Development of Transport Infrastructure

Transport is vital for basin development as it provides outlet for flows of both human beings and goods. The lower basin of the Damodar has dense rail network where railways from north, north-west, west, south-west and east converge. It has the locational advantage of lying near Kolkata, one of the prominent port towns of the country. Dhanbad has become the foci of convergence of road and rail networks. The Grand Chord line joining Delhi and Kolkata passes through the northern part of the Damodar basin. This line is now fully electrified. Besides this, many short railway lines criss-cross this area. A number of routes diverge towards west of Asansol. The watershed between the Ajai and the Damodar rivers is not very prominent; hence, the railway links Giridih. The railway line linking Kolkata-Asansol to Gaya-Patna passes through the upper Barakar river basin.

A railway line from Dehri-on-Son, via, Daltonganj runs along the coalfields belt. A branch line of this links Jamshedpur, via, Muri. The scarp-slope of Ranchi plateau has receded and this has provided gap through which the routes to Jamshedpur have been laid. The western part of the Damodar basin is hilly, forested and thinly populated. Therefore, it represents an undeveloped side while eastern part has recorded economic development (Qureshi, 1990). The rail network is supplemented by road network in the region. In more difficult terrain where rail links cannot be provided, roads have been constructed negotiating the scarps. Sher Shah Suri Marg runs almost parallel to the Grand Chord railway line in the Dhanbad section of the reigon. The industrial town, collieries and washeries have been linked by local roads. The transportational infrastructure has helped not only in the utilization of the natural resources of the region but has linked this region with the national market.

Industrial Development

The Damodar river basin has developed a mineral-based industrial landscape in the country. It has played an important role in promoting industrial development. The region's natural resources provided a base for rapid industrial development, once power and other infrastructural facilities were developed. A number of public sector undertakings also sprang up. Durgapur and Bokaro Steel complexes, Heavy Engineering Corporation Ltd. at Ranchi, Sindri Fertilzer Plant and Indian Explosives near Hazaribag provide some such examples. Six industrial complexes have emerged over time in the Damodar basin region. These are: (a) Durgapur industrial complex having thermal power plant, coke oven, iron and steel, mining machinery and cement machinery and electrical industries; (b) Asanso-Kulti-Burnpur, Chittaranjan locomotives, Kulti foundry works and Kumardhubi engineering works; (c) Dhanbad-Sindri-Jharia industrial area having Sindri fertilizer industry, chemical and coal-based industries; (d) Bokaro industrial area consisting of steel plant, thermal plants at Bokaro and Chandrapura alongwith coal washeries; (e) Ramgarh-Patratu area with Indian explosives and thermal power plants; and (f) Ranchi Industrial township with HEC, HMT and foundry plants.

The preponderance of mining and industry can be seen from the structure of the workforce in various districts in the basin. About 8.7 per cent of the main workers in Giridih, 4.8 per cent in Dhanbad, 9.8 per cent in Hazaribag and 6.3 per cent in Santhal Parganas are engaged in mining. About 16 per cent of the main workers in Dhanbad are engaged in other than household industries. With the availability of hydroelectric power aided by thermal power plants, more power intensive industries may emerge. Steel plants, coal washeries, industries based on coal by-products and forest-based industries will ensure a large size industrial zone in this basin.

The People

There is large variation in the population density in the Damodar basin. The upper catchment, which is hilly and forested, has low density, whereas the lower part of the basin is thickly populated and more urbanized. Since, the process of urbanization and industrialization are closely interlinked, the districts having concentration of industries witnessed rapid urbanization. The figures of 2001 census showing proportion of urban population to total population clearly depict this trend. Around 52.9 per cent of the total population in Purbi Singhbhum has been recorded as urban, followed by Dhanbad, 51.3 per cent, and Burddhwan, 35.4 per cent, Garhwa and Dumka have low proportion of urban population, which have recorded 2.8 and 6.1 per cent urban population, respectively.

A major part of the Damodar basin, especially lying in the Chotanagpur plateau, has higher proportion of tribal population. Development has its own course. It does not help all the classes uniformly. This has caused social tensions, and one often reads reports about the operations of the anti-social elements and mafia gangs. The benefits of development will have to be given social protection by developing their own organizations.

Water Availability

Geographical location, physical conditions like orography and monsoon climate affect the surface water availability in the basin. The availability is relatively more in the upper part due to the presence of seasonal rivers during the rainy season. The important rivers are the Barakar, Konar, Ajay, Dwarakeswar, Mundeswari, Rupnarayan, Saraswati, etc. (Figure 1). The important source of water is the surface flow through rivers and water contained in lakes, tanks and reservoirs. Rivers and river basins have always attracted human habitations. Rivers are fed by rainfall as well as snowmelt. This water is harnessed by damming the rivers and a number of multipurpose projects have been launched since the independence of the country. Agriculture is a major claimant of water, as the assured supply of water through irrigation reduces its dependence on rainfall which is highly variable and unreliable. Groundwater is another important source of water and is more ubiquitously available. This water is available through dug-wells, tubewells and other devices of lifting water. It is estimated that about 3,33,000 mcm (million cubic metres) of groundwater is available in India. About 90 per cent of it is associated with the unconsolidated rock formations of North Indian plains. It shows that the peninsular part of it is not well placed as far as groundwater resources are concerned.

Rainfall

The basin is rich in water resource potential because of heavy rainfall in its source region. Rainfall is associated with the north-east monsoon or shallow cyclonic depressions and disturbances and local storms from the Bay of Bengal and the presence of depression over land. This is supported by Kirk (1950) who refers to high intensity monsoon thunderstorms of 1911 and 1917 in the upper catchment and suggests that run-off coefficients of 80 per cent have been calculated after the storm. However, Kirk (1950) suggests that the Damodar river during the dry period is a more of a string of dry spots with zero discharge but becomes swollen during the wet period. Moderate to heavy rainfall occurs due to such depressions. The deep depressions mostly travel in the months of late August and September and sometimes in early October. Hence, the month of September records usual rainfall.

The mean monthly rainfall recorded over the upper and middle part of the basin is nearly 1,200 mm, whereas the lower part receives more than 1,650 mm of rainfall. Comparatively, higher rainfall (1,400–1,600 mm) is recorded in the south and south-western parts of Ranchi plateau. Such higher rainfall is related to the relief of the land as well as depressions. On the other hand, the extreme northern leeward part of the Kodarma hills receives lower rainfall (less than 1,200 mm). Broadly, the basin has been identified into four rainfall zones (Figure 4). They are as follows:

1. Low rainfall zone (less than 1,200 mm).
2. Moderate rainfall zone (1,201–1,400 mm).

Figure 4

Damodar River Basin: Rainfall Zones

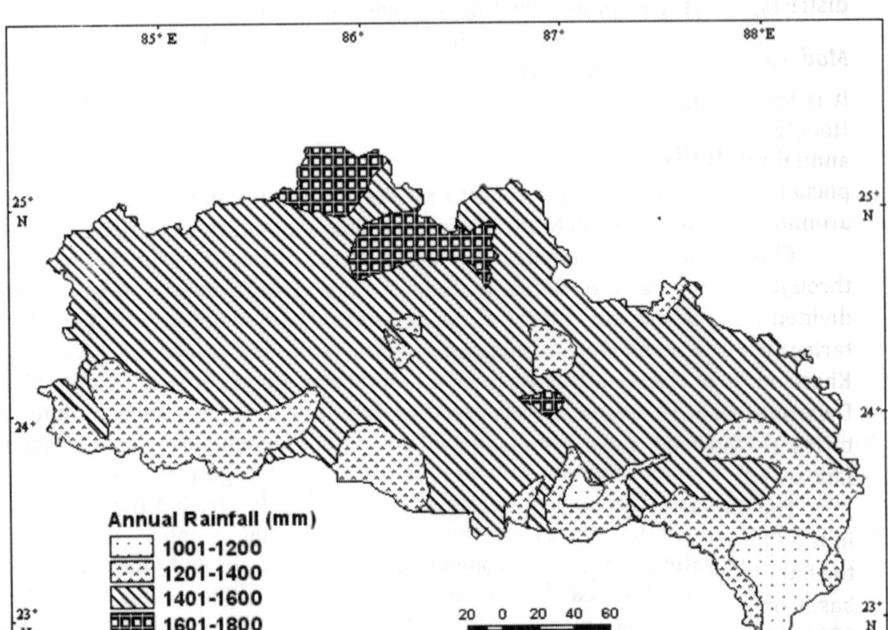

3. High rainfall zone (1,401–1,600 mm).
4. Moderately high rainfall zone (more than 1,600 mm).

Low Rainfall Zone

The low rainfall zone is confined to the northern part of the upper and middle parts of the basin. The rainfall ranges between 1,001 to 1,200 mm. It lies near the Sakri basin on the leeward side of Kodarma hills. Another zone also lies on the eastern Kodarma plateau of the middle basin region. It records lowest rainfall of 1,030 mm in the basin region.

Moderate Rainfall Zone

The region of moderate rainfall extends from extreme west to the east covering all parts of the basin, i.e., upper, middle and lower. This region is extensive and covers whole of the basin region (about 75%). Even the northern and central part of the lower basin region in Bakura, Birbhum and Burddhwan districts in West Bengal record moderate rainfall.

High Rainfall Zone

High rainfall zones are located in a few pockets of the upper and middle basin to the south of Ranchi metropolis where rainfall increases to about 1,550 mm on the plateau escarpment at Chutupalu Ghat. The Khomarpal hill bounded by Lohardaga Ghat is south-western part of the basin region which records high rainfall. It also occurs at Baghmundi-Ajodhya hills in the middle basin region. High rainfall zone also extends to the lower part of the basin which lies partly in Hoogly and Bankura districts of West Bengal intervening the moderately high rainfall zone.

Moderately High Rainfall Zone

It is located mostly in the lower part of the lower basin region lying within the Hoogly-Rupnarayan 'doab' in Hoogly and Howrah districts of West Bengal. The annual rainfall of 1,778 mm is recorded at Chanditala in Hoogly district. Another pocket of moderately high rainfall is found in the Kasi plain of Bankura district around Taldangra where annual rainfall is recorded at about 1,831 mm.

Chotanagpur is gifted with a number of river systems which drain into the sea through different directions. On the basis of size of catchment, the river basin is divided into five basins: (a) Cultural basin of the Damodar-Barakar and its tributaries. (b) Old data having old distributaries like the Kunti, the Behula, the Banka, the Khari, etc. (c) Southern basin with the South Koel, the Subrnarekha and the Dwarakeshwar and its tributaries. (d) Northern basin with the Ajay and its tributaries. (e) Western basin traversed by several smaller streams like the Sakri , the Lilajan, etc.

The Damodar and the Barakar rivers have developed extensive drainage basins in the Chotanagpur region. They are characterized by wide shallow channels over the flat plateaus and exhibit youthful characteristics marked by steep-sided, narrow basin or gorges, the courses being interrupted by rapids and waterfalls (Singh, 1997). The river regime is highly fluctuating with continuous flow during the monsoon season and is either completely dry or forms disconnected pools of water during the rest of the year. The rivers rise suddenly after the monsoon downpour but after a few hours they quickly subside to fordable level. The Damodar and its principal tributaries, the Barakar, form the core area of the Damodar basin region covering nearly 40 per cent. Other river systems lie in the southern, northern and western basins covering nearly 23 per cent, 19 per cent and 8 per cent, respectively.

Surface Water Availability

In addition to rainwater, which is the main source of water to the river, the other inflow comes from surface and groundwater. The Damodar basin (DB) comprises of the Damodar and the Barakar river as major sources of surface water. The basin receives an average rainfall of 1,200 mm.

The Damodar Valley Corporation (DVC) constructed five reservoirs at different stretches to store the rainwater and protect the lower basin from floods. Out of the five reservoirs, Tenughat and Panchet are located on Damodar river, Tilaiya and Maithon on Barakar river and one on Konar river, a tributary of Damodar. Tenughat reservoir is mainly constructed to meet the water requirements of Bokaro steel plant, while Durgapur barrage was constructed on Damodar to meet the irrigation water requirements of West Bengal. Some important lakes also exist to provide surface water for drinking and industrial purposes, out of which Topchanchi and Nalkari lakes are important. Topchanchi lake serves as source of drinking water for Jharia coalfields, whereas water from Nalkari is used for Patratu thermal power plant. Surface water availability is summed up as given in Table 1.

Table 1

Surface Water Availability in Damodar River Basin

Source	*Amount (MCM)*
Damodar basin reservoirs dependability (Konar, Tilaiya, Maithon, Panchet and Durgapur)	4,855
Reduced availability due to decrease in water holding capacity of reservoirs	1,030
Net available	3,825
Presently available otherwise	223
Total Water Availability	4,048

Source: Office of the Damodar Valley Corporation. From the Centre for Study of Man and Environment (CSME), Final Study Report, 1998.

Groundwater Availability

In Chotanagpur's total water resources, groundwater is most valuable and dependable. It is gaining importance once as a vital source for making our requirements. Its occurrence depends on the regional and local topographic and climatic conditions. The basin contains diversified hydrological settings. The hard rock terrain of Chotanagpur plateau bears limited quantities of groundwater and the water table is deep. Unfortunately, there is no accurate survey of groundwater resources in the basin but at present it is being exploited mainly through open dug-wells. The dug-wells are 10–15 m deep below groundwater level is fissured formations. The field from borewells in fissured formation varies from 2 to 36 m^3/h. The yield of tubewells constructed in sandstones up to 200 m depth varies from less than 50 to 150 m^3/h. The alluvial deposits occurring in West Bengal vary in thickness from 50 to more than 300 m. The yield prospect of tubewells constructed to depths of 60 to 150 m below ground level ranges from 100–180 m^3/h. In the eastern, central, and southern parts of the basin or command area, groundwater resources are available in aquifers of 50–80 m thickness. Tubewells dug upto 120–150 m depth yield about 200 m^3/h of water for economic drawdown. Large-scale groundwater withdrawal through deep tubewells has gained momentum in the lowermost reaches of the basin. The groundwater potential of the river basin is presented in Table 2 based on CGBW observation.

Table 2

Groundwater Resources in Damodar River Basin

District	*Utilizable groundwater resources for irrigation (MCM*)*	*Net groundwater draft (MCM/year)*	*Groundwater balance (MCM/year)*	*Status of groundwater development (%)*
Hazaribag	615.09	8.93	606.16	1.45
Ranchi	27.67	0.72	26.95	2.60
Giridih	476.57	5.83	470.74	1.20
Palamu	38.96	0.23	38.73	0.59

Cont'd...

Cont'd...

Dhanbad	180.28	2.77	177.51	1.53
Bankura	108.04	42.48	65.56	39.23
Burddhwan	2,269.45	444.52	1,824.93	19.58
Hoogly	907.61	224.15	683.46	24.69
Howrah	142.37	26.77	115.60	18.80
Purulia	134.18	15.87	118.37	11.83

* MCM = Millon Cubic Metre

Source: Office of the Damodar Basin Corporation. From the CSME Final Study Report, 1998.

Water Flow in the Damodar River

In addition to rainwater, other flow comes from the drainage of mines, or the water pumped out of coal mines in the process of mining operations. The mine drainage is significant not because of its total volume, which is small in comparison to the total volume of flow, but because of the quantity of water drained out of mines. Although it is generally agreed that the volume of water pumped out of mines is substantial (in absolute term), no reliable estimates are available. Hence, only the figures pertaining to rainwater are given here. The data on available water in the river are presented in Table 3 and Figure 5.

Table 3

Total Water Flow in the Damodar River (MCM/Year)

Basin	*Annual volume of rainwater*	*Volume of water loss by evaporation*	*Volume of water loss by seepage annually*	*Available water after evaporation and seepage*
Upper Damodar	15,484.1	10,021.8	2,291.7	3,110.6
Lower Damodar	7,058.0	4,105.5	1,009.3	1,943.2
Barakar	9,295.5	5,830.3	1,357.1	2,108.1
Total	31,837.6	19,957.6	4,658.1	7,221.9

Source: Office of the Damodar Basin Corporation. From the CSME, Final Study Report, 1998.

Figure 5

Waters of the Damodar River

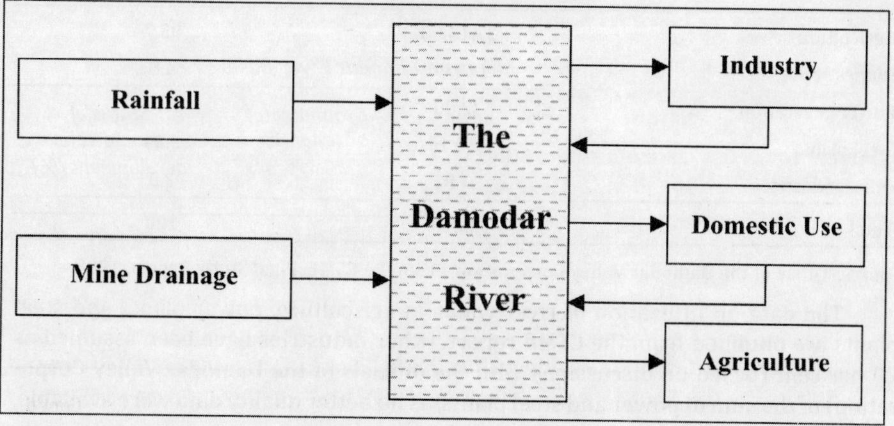

Utilization of River Water

Water is not equitably distributed in nature, but man has made adjustment with nature by developing different practices regarding use of water as per its availability. Multipurpose use of water is made due to its scarcity. Utilization of water for different purposes in urban and rural areas depends upon the nature of requirements. Damodar river water used in urban areas is largely for domestic consumption, sewage disposal, and industrial and recreational purposes. Both surface and groundwater are pumped out after purification and are supplied at suitable pressure to individual homes. The pattern of domestic water use is according to the type of dwellings, type of waste disposal, metred or non-metred supply, lot size, number of persons per dwelling and water rates; similarly lawn sprinkling system and overhead irrigation makes secondary demands upon the domestic water supply system. Hazaribag town is facing the problem of domestic water due to wrong and myopic management strategy. There is a need for rational management of drinking water resource for plateau region (Thakur, 2007a). Most of the industrial establishments are generally located in towns and cities and the water supply to these places is made by municipalities or corporations. Most of the towns and cities have their sources of water supply from rivers, lakes and tubewells.

Government has made progress in harnessing rivers and constructing canals systems through dams and reservoirs to distribute water to the land. In Chotanagpur, the dams are mostly multipurpose, that is for irrigation, flood control, generation of hydroelectricity, navigation, recreation, fisheries and erosion control. Among the most noteworthy multipurpose projects are the Damodar Valley Corporation in Jharkhand and West Bengal.

Both the supply and demand of water vary locally and regionally in Chotanagpur and so is the contrasting patterns of utilization. It is the modernization of cultures which increase water utilization. The basin has made increasing use of its water resources. Agriculture, domestic, industrial and hydro-generation are major uses. A concerted effort has been made to utilize the water resources for agricultural purposes by developing the irrigation facilities. As per the estimates available, the utilization of waters of the basin is shown in Table 4.

Table 4

Water Utilization of Damodar River

Sectors	*Quantity used (MCM/year)*	*Quantity used (%)*
Agriculture	2,416.00	83.7
Domestic use	140.00	4.8
Power generation	32.00	1.11
Steel plants	242.19	8.39
Other industries	54.81	2.0
Total	2,885.0	100

Source: Office of the Damodar Valley Corporation. From the CSME, Final Study Report, 1998.

The data on utilization of river water in agriculture, power plants and steel plants are obtained from the CSME report. Other industries have been assumed as 20 per cent (based on discussions with the officials of the Damodar Valley Corporation) of the sum of power and steel plants, as no better quality data were available.

Domestic use is assumed to be 10 cubic metres per capita per year (based on the estimates presented in the CSME report). Domestic use also includes consumption by small establishments such as the ubiquitous tea-stalls.

As can be seen from Table 4, the largest use of water is for agriculture (84%). Hence, if any assessment has to be made of the industrial metabolism of the region, impact of agriculture on river waters and, conversely, impact of river waters (often polluted) on the agricultural operations need to be examined thoroughly. To study the impact of each of the human activities, it is necessary to understand how water is used in each of these operations.

Agricultural Water Use

Agriculture in the Damodar basin is not different from the prevailing patterns in other parts of the Chotanagpur region. Generally, one crop is produced in one agricultural year. Having irrigation facilities helped the agriculture of the basin not only by augmenting the crop outturn but also by offering a vast intensive agricultural practice followed by a wide range of crop rotation (Basu, 1990). The Damodar basin irrigation system have enhanced the crop production to a large extent during the last three decades.

Mostly small and marginal farmers, who use the irrigation facilities available through the Damodar Valley Corporation (DVC) carrying out the agriculture in the basin, has grown rapidly in the recent past. An attempt was made to understand the sources and uses of water by the agriculturists. The estimate represented in Figure 6 indicates that the patterns of usage of water in the agriculture sector are significant from many points of view.

A study of the pattern of usage of water in agriculture sector is significant from many points of view:

1. The bulk of the industrial activity in upstream of river and the agricultural operations are carried out almost uniformly in the entire basin. Much of the agriculture consists of food crops such as paddy. The river is also a major source of fish, which forms a predominant part of diet of the local population.

Figure 6

Utilization of Water in Damodar Basin, Agricultural Operations

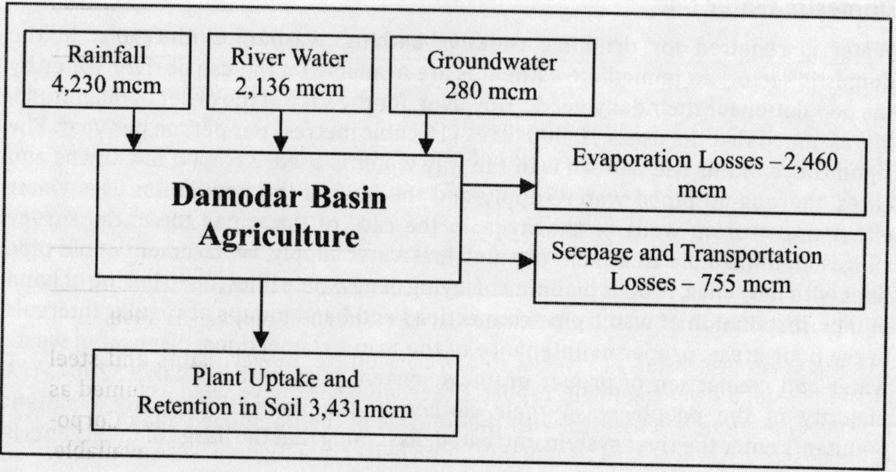

2. While industrial wastes are discharged into the river, river water is used in agriculture. The danger of toxic pollutions, particularly heavy metals, moving up the food chain needs to be studied in detail (Rao and Rao, 1991).
3. Conversely, run-offs from agriculture, which are normally ignored in any discussion on pollution in India, which may include contamination from chemical fertilizers and pesticides, by them, could be a serious threat to the health of the flora and fauna.
4. As can be seen from Figure 5, there is a substantial loss of water through seepage. This seepage carries pollution into the aquifers, which are used untreated by the population.

Industrial Water Use

Around 23 per cent of pure water is utilized by industries. That is why most of the industries are established near water sources (bank of river or lakes). Many industrial units have their own water purifying plants so as to have regular supply of water. Water is used in industries in many respects. Presently, the increasing number of industries has reduced the quantity of water due to which scarcity of water is felt in spite of its availability. The present water use in industrial sector is estimated to be about 19 km^3. In view of shortage of water, industries are expected to switch over to water efficient technologies.

The industrial activity in the basin draws about 329 MCM water per year. At least 92.81 MCM of the water is returned to the river as an untreated affluent. This figure is the sum of the discharge from the power generation and steel sectors; data on the discharge by other industries is not available. The estimated quantities of selected pollutants that are reportedly a result of industrial activity in the basin suggests that the thousands of tonnes of pollutants through the ecosystem decrease a thorough investigation.

Water is also required for generating cheap hydroelectric power and also as an input in various industries, e.g., iron and steel industry requires large quantities of water for cooling purposes and textile industries require it for bleaching and washing. Food processing and pulp making, jute industry, chemical industry and atomic power plant require huge quantities of water. Hence, all these industries are located at such places where water supply is sufficient.

Domestic Water Use

Water is required for drinking, cooking, bathing, washing clothes, etc. In the domestic sector, no immediate estimates are available on the use of river water by the population for their daily needs. However, for the sake of the order of magnitude, it is assumed that the use is 10,000 litres (10 cubic metres) per person per year. The significance of this use pattern is in the way water is used. Except a few towns and cities, there is no piped water supply and the bulk of the population uses water either drawn from wells or the river. In the case of Hazaribag town, the survey suggested immediate treatment of municipal water supply, replacement of old pipe lines with new ones, proper planning of laying of new pipe lines, deep boring of hand pumps, installation of water pipe connections and hand pumps at regular intervals in the poor areas, proper maintenance of the water connections, disposal of waste water and connection of proper drainage system is essential (Thakur, 2007a). A majority of the people wash their clothes in the river. Hence, any resultant pollutants enter the river system untreated. Assuming that the usage of detergents is half kilogram per capita per year, the total use of detergents by the estimated population of 14 million is likely to be 7,000 tonnes. This impact on the river system may need to be looked at. Even in cities located on river banks, the problems have arisen in spite of availability of water, because cities have contaminated water resources. All cities drain domestic wastewater into rivers.

Problems of Water Utilization

There is vast potential resource of water which can be utilized. It is a tragic irony that Jharkhand with a large and well-distributed river system should suffer from water shortage. The rapid growth of agriculture, industry and urban centres has imposed pressure on the basin in terms of both quantity and quality of water. The growing population has gradually declined per capita availability of water. Floods and droughts are the annual ordeals in the country but the problems of water utilization in the Damodar basin are different. The region is confined to the wettest part of the country, where an average rainfall occurs between 1,400–1,600 mm, but the basin does not hold water which it receives. It is because of deforestation, a large portion of monsoon water disappears into the sea as surface run-off. Community resources as ponds, tanks and rivers are misused and continuously neglected. The Damodar river is shallow, wide, seasonal and flashy. During the rains, its flow is torrential. It erodes the land of Jharkhand and floods West Bengal with water and silt. It causes much distress and loss in both the states. The river Damodar is polluted with minerals, mine rejects and toxic effluents. Both, its water and its sand are infested by coal dust and waste from industries that have sprung up in its basin. The major problems of the Damodar river are flood control, water quality, groundwater withdrawal, water pollution, fly ash and industrial sewage.

The disastrous flood of 1900 revived deliberations on the issue and the government decided to take measures to construct dams. The consequent high flood of 1907, 1909 and 1911 were apparently dealt within an adhoc manner. Once again, 1913 flood caused wide breaches in embankments and serious damage to the region, which aroused public outcry and demands for revised scheme for the construction of reservoirs. The Government of India investigated the possibility of flood control by means of reservoirs in the upper reaches of the Damadar river. To control the flood water in lower basin from different reservoirs located at Tenughat, Panchet, Tilaiya, Maithon, and Barakar for various purposes, i.e., power, irrigation, navigation, industry and domestic uses, the DVC was set up. Between 1823 and 1943, sixteen major floods were recorded in the lower basin. The highest floods were in 1913 and 1935. Both these floods brought down a peak discharge of 18,500 cumecs (cubic metres per second) at Durgapur (DVC, 1978). Thus, the problems of Damadar basin stem from the extreme fluctuations in seasonal discharge of water.

All the reservoirs are almost over-silted. It cannot make its exaggerated claims. Thus, the catchment of flood-prone river as well as of reservoirs are vulnerable to premature siltation which should be given top priority for better use of water. Apart from that, waterlogging in lower part of the basin is a problem caused by large irrigation projects. Interstate water dispute also creates problems in water utilization. Water is shared among the states (Jharkhand and West Bengal) through which the river flows. Several such issues have emerged in India and Bangladesh dispute (Bandyopadhyay and Gyawali, 1994). There is also a notorious wastage of water throughout from linking pipe, hasty urbanization, and industrial development.

Deteriorating water quality is another problem. Both, surface and groundwater are seriously contaminated. This deterioration is a consequence of a range of human activities including intensive use of mineral fertilizer and pesticides; aiso discharge of heavy metal and hazardous chemicals into rivers, release of water effluents either directly into the streams or into drains that eventually join the streams. The Damodar is, perhaps, the most polluted river in India (Thakur, 2007). Discharge of sewage from towns and industries located near the rivers are the important sources of pollution of water (Khoshoo, 1983; Roy, 1991; Bobba, Singh and Bengtsson, 1997).

Since groundwater withdrawal is greater than the recharge, groundwater table declines rapidly. This problem assumes serious proportions in many parts of the country, e.g., eastern Haryana (Inderjeet, 2001) and Punjab (Dhawan, 1993). Overexploitation of groundwater also leads to the intrusion of saline water, making the water unfit for drinking or irrigation. There is another danger to groundwater resource. Normally groundwater cannot be polluted, however, in recent years, cases of dangerous groundwater pollution have been reported from different parts of the basin.

Many coal-based industries and thermal power projects use water from the Damodar river and its tributaries and daily produce 9,000 tonnes of fly ash which pollutes water. The impact of polluted water can be seen in the form of disease, neurological disorder and liver-related problems. Apart from that, the wastewater discharge by industries find ways into the rivers and pollutes water which directly affect the flora and fauna. The public sector (Coal India Ltd, Central Coalfield Ltd., Bharat Coking Coal Ltd. and Eastern Coalfields Ltd.) extract coal in the basin and in the underground mining, huge volume of polluted water is pumped into the rivers and users of water are the main culprits for the industrial pollution.

The State Pollution Control Board's of Jharkhand and West Bengal resolved to fight against pollution of Damodar under the banner of "Damodar Bachao Abhiyan". Some of the people present at the meeting had been displaced from their ancestral land due to the construction of various dams and power projects in the basin. They made efforts to save their sacred river in the area by 'Damodar Bachao Abhiyan' in the long run.

Water Management Strategies

In view of the existing status of water resources and increasing demand of water for meeting the requirements of growing population as well as problems that are likely to rise in future, a holistic well-planned long-term strategy is required for sustainable water management in the basin. The water management practices may be based on providing water of the right quality, right quantity, at the right place, at the right time and at the right prices to meet the demands. Having too much, too little or poor quality of water is poor management (Mather, 1984: 23) because either there is too much for the particular use and it is wasted or there is not enough for the purpose at hand.

The way in which water is found in nature, the volume of water is available for use, of discussion. It has led to the belief that water per se is not in short supply but due to poor distribution of precipitation or concentration of people and industry in certain areas is needed short supply. The problem then, is not one of insufficient water resources but rather one of resource management (ibid.).

Water resource management involves both quantity and quality. We generally think in terms of only one use of water. If it is polluted through use, it should be discharged or return to the river. But, in practice, water is cleansed by natural and human processes and reused several times in its passage towards downstream. This is one of the fundamental parts of water management. Water quantity management involves rational planning as well as planning for ways to conserve valuable supply of water.

The harmonization of water development with environment quality is a principal challenge to water management. The proper use of water for its continuous availability to the present and future generations is essential. Therefore, measures should be taken to protect water from its misuse and pollution. It should be managed in a manner so as to free us from the impact of floods and droughts, and water conflicts.

Many problems in water management have statements from our thinking and planning. Water in all aspects is interrelated with modern technology, it cannot separate the influence of water situation in one section of the country now to another part of the country. Thus, the recent trend towards water management is to understand the interrelation of water to land, to politics, to economics, to human and cultural factors that are keys to proper development of water management.

The latest thinking on water management in India by the Ministry of Irrigation and Central Water Commission is to build up storage and smaller dams to store water for use as well as to reduce flood and provide benefits to drought-prone areas. In the 21st century there is a need to meet challenges of water management in concept, approaches, and institutional and technological modernization (Chaturvedi, 1985) (Figure 7). Finally, the National Water Policy of 1988 and 2002, stresses treating river basin as the basic unit for water resources planning (Government of India, 1995).

Figure 7

Damodar Valley: Water Management Project

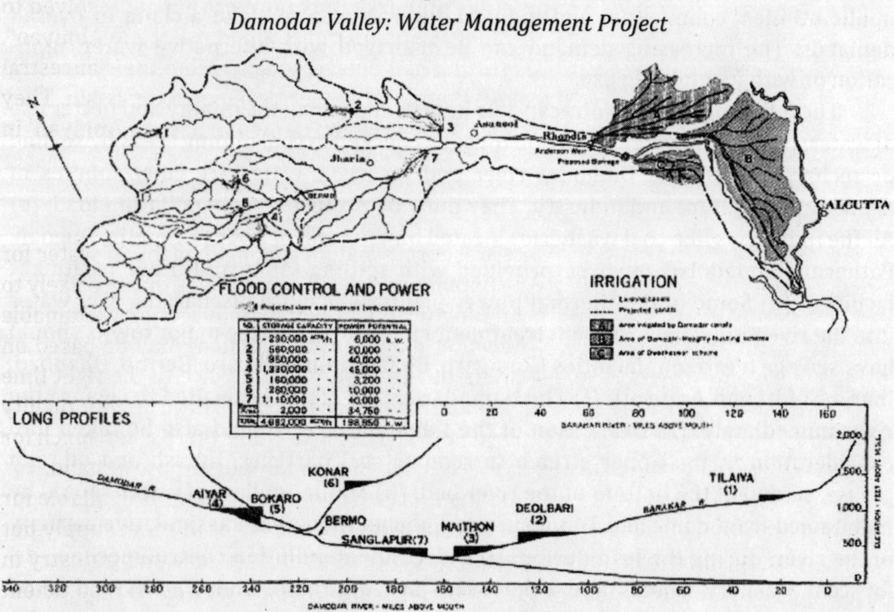

The Damodar Valley Project. When the seven proposed dams are completed, 175 square miles of land will be submerged, but nearly 10,000 square miles will benefit.

Source: Kirk (1950: 440).

Keeping in view the demand on water resources and the present state of our water resources, alternatives must be devised to supplement the present reserves of freshwater and reduce overexploitation. Micro-watershed development is a viable method of harnessing water by cheaper and quicker means. In order to sustain the available water resources, key factors and technological options for groundwater recharge must also be explored.

Today, the problem seems to be the paucity of drinking water in urban centres. To supplement the domestic water requirements, rainwater harvesting is a wise option. The use of traditional system of water harvesting to catch and store water is a feasible option. The rooftop harvesting is a good supplementary source of water for domestic purpose which also enhances recharging potentials of aquifers by allowing water to percolate into the ground through the new borewells and through the use of defunct borewells as well. However, effectiveness of the options is subject to eccentricities of climatic conditions; but, whenever rain takes place, water should be harvested through various suggested methods and judiciously utilized during lean period.

Efficiency and equity in water management can also be achieved if different water sources are utilized simultaneously. Conjunctive use of surface and ground-water resources can help in a better way. It will, firstly, fulfil the needs; secondly, will allow the resources to be replenished and kept sustainable. The combined use of water sources is an important step to integrated water management and, whenever feasible, needs to be adopted to meet the crop water requirements.

Every drop of water should be used and reused judiciously both at off-farm and on-farm activities. Domestic water, instead of being allowed into storm-water drains or rivers, should be collected into community or dam water treatment plants for cleaning and recycling. Non-domestic water supplies for parks, recreation places, public utilities, commercial and industrial purposes also stake a claim in overall demands. The increasing demand can be managed with alternative water application or with its multiple use.

The following suggestions can also help in improving the quality and better use of water: (a) Groundwater depletion must be checked in coal mining areas by sealing or recharging; (b) The Damodar river and reservoir water are chief sources of drinking, agriculture and industry. They must be protected from pollution load; (c) All the industries like coal washeries located on the bank of river (Sumadih, Dugdah, Patherdih, Jamadoba) must be provided with settling tanks and other treatment facilities; (d) Some of the thermal power plants, which are discharging raw water into the river, must have effluent treatment facilities; (e) All the major towns should have sewage treatment facilities (Ramgarh, Chandrapura, Phusro, Bermo, Dhanbad, Jharia, Suidri and Asansol); (f) The Damodar Action Plan be executed to cleanse the river immediately; (g) Desiltation of the Damodar river should also be taken into consideration in the upper stretch to remove coal particles, fly ash and oil, and grease, settled at the bottom of the river bed; (h) Minimum flow of water should be maintained from dams like Tenughat and Panchet to increase assimilative capacity of the river, during the lean period; (i) Independent pollution control mechanisms for coal washery rejects and coke overs are desirable; and (j) Physical flood protection works like embankment and dykes will continue to be necessary, increased emphasis should be laid on non-structural measures for losses and to reduce the recurring expenditure on flood relief.

Conclusions

The study has revealed that water availability in the Damodar basin has been influenced by physiographic conditions. Geographically, the river lies in eastern Chotanagpur where average rainfall that occurs is 1,400–1,600 mm. The source of water is mainly rainfall in the form of river that flows in a hit and miss fashion. The Damodar passes through an important industrial and mining areas of the country and as it was causing floods frequently, a comprehensive plan of flood control was formulated and dams and canals were constructed for irrigation and power. The analysis has highlighted that water is mainly used in agriculture (84%), domestic (5%) and industry, power and plants (11.1%). But the basin is one of the dirtiest parts of the country. The deteriorating water quality has become a serious problem and water supplies and environmental sanitation are vital for protecting the environment. There is a need to frame legislation to arrest groundwater depletion in the basin. Thus, a distinct discourse on political ecology of water management emerges as a fruitful research agenda.

References

Ahmad, E. (1965) *Bihar: A Physical, Economic and Regional Geography*, Ranchi: Ranchi University Press.

Ajwani, H.J. (1952) 'Notes on the Water Control and Water Management of the Damodar River Basin', Proceedings of Regional Technical Conflict, Flood Control in Asia and Far East, UN, Bangkok.

Bandyopadhyay, J. and D. Gyawali (1994) 'Himalayan Water Resources: Ecological and Political Aspects of Management', *Mountain Research and Development*, 14(1): 1–24.

Basu, S. (1990) 'The Lower Damodar Basin in the Economic Spectrum', *Geographical Review of India*, 52: 27–35.

Bhattacharjee, D.K. (1984) 'Flood Control and Utilization of Water Resources in Damodar Basin Area', *Journal of the Institute of Engineers of India*, 64.

Bhattacharyya, A.K. (1973) 'Flood Control in Damodar Valley', *Geographical Review of India*, 35(2): 134–146.

Bobba, A.G., V.P. Singh and L. Bengtsson (1997) 'Sustainable Development of Water Resources in India', *Environmental Management*, 21(3): 367–393.

Chatterjee, S.P. (1968) *The Planning Atlas of the Damodar Basin*, Kolkata: Joint Committee for Diagnostic Survey of the Damodar Valley Region.

Chaturvedi, M.C. (1985) 'Water in India's Development: Issues, Development Policy, Programmes and Planning Approach', in M.C. Chaturvedi and P. Rogers (eds), *Water Resources System Planning: Some Case Studies for India*, Bangalore: Indian Academy of Sciences, 39–72.

Damodar Valley Corporation (1978) *DVC: Statistical Handbook*, Information Department, Kolkata, 889.

Dayal, P. (1953) *Bihar in Maps with Explanatory Text*, Patna: Kusum Prakashan, 80–82.

Dhawan, B.D. (1993) 'Groundwater Depletion in Punjab', *Economic and Political Weekly*, 30 October: 2397–2401.

Fannoon, A.I. (1973) 'Some Aspects of Water Resources and Development in the Damodar Basin Region: A Study in Runoff', Unpublished PhD Dissertation, Department of Geography, University of Delhi, 401.

Government of India (1988 and 2002) National Water Policy, Ministry of Water Resources, New Delhi.

Inderjeet (2001) *Groundwater Depletion and its Management in Haryana*, New Delhi: Manisha Publications.

Karan, P.P. (1958) 'The Bihar Mica Belt of India', *National Geographical Journal of India*, 4(1): 16–34.

Kayastha, S.L. (1981) 'An Appraisal of Water Resources of India: Needs for National Water Policy', *GeoJournal*, 5(6): 563–572.

Khoshoo, T.N. (1983) 'Water Quality Management in India: Retrospect and Prospect', Keynote Address, Seminar on Strategy and Technology for Water Policy Management, Bombay: Indian Institute of Technology, 10.

Kirk, W. (1950) 'The Damodar Valley – "Valles Opima"', *The Geographical Review*, 40(3): 415–443.

Kumar, A. and R. Pandey (1981) 'Morphometric Analysis of Some Drainage Basins of Hazaribag Plateau Region', *National Geographical Journal of India*, 27(1–2): 50–59.

Mahamaya, M. (1970) 'Aspects of Recent Industrialization in Chotanagpur', *National Geographical Journal of India*, 16(2): 101–109.

Mather, J.R. (1984) *Water Resources: Distribution, Use and Management*, New York: John Wiley.

Pathak, C.R. (2002) 'Damodar Basin Region: A Case Study in Regional Development', in R.P Misra (ed.), *Regional Planning: Concept, Techniques, Policies and Case Studies*, New Delhi: Concept, 705–716.

Prasad, P. (2003) 'Water Quality in Jharia Coalfield', *National Geographical Journal of India*, 49(4): 31–36.

Prasad, R.K. (1995) 'Groundwater Development: Problems and Prospects', *Yojana*, 39(1–2): 29–34.

Prasad, S.N. (1991) 'Water Resources', in L.N. Ram (ed.), *A Systematic Geography of Bihar*, Patna: Patna University, 60–70.

Qureshi, M.H. (1990) *India: Resources and Regional Development*, Delhi: National Council of Educational Research and Training, 88–92.

Rao, K.L. (1975) *India's Water Wealth: Its Assessment, Uses and Projections*, New Delhi: Orient Longman.

Rao, N.S.L. and M.N. Rao (1991) 'Pollution in Selected Rivers of India: Three Case Studies', in J. Rose (ed.), *Water and the Environment*, Philadelphia: Gordon and Breach Science Publishers, 17–26.

Roy, B.K. (1991) 'Water Availability in India: An Analysis of Current Setting and Future Needs', *Water Resources Development*, 7(2): 107–716.

Sharan, A. (1958) 'Evolution of Drainage System in the Damodar Basin', *National Geographical Journal of India*, 4(3): 130–136.

Sharma, V.K. (1976) 'Some Hydrologic Characteristics of the Damodar River', *Geographical Review of India*, 38(4): 330–343.

Singh, J. (1997) 'Chotanagpur Region', in R.L. Singh (ed.), *India: A Regional Geography*, Varanasi: National Geographical Society of India, 649–675.

Singh, R.P. (1957) 'Landscape of South-East Chotanagpur', *National Geographical Journal of India*, 3(3–4): 137–138.

—— (1961) 'Bokaro: The Future Steel Town', *National Geographical Journal of India*, 7(4): 245–256.

—— (1969) *Geomorphological Evolution of Chotanagpur Highlands, India*, Varanasi: National Geographical Society, 64–72.

Singh, R.P. and A. Kumar (1970) *Monograph of Bihar: A Geographical Study*, Patna: Bharti Bhawan, 180–183.

Sinha, R.L.P. (1962) 'Dhanbad: A Study in Urban Geography', *National Geographical Journal of India*, 8(3–4): 284–300.

Sinha, V.N.P. (1988) *Chotanagpur Plateau: A Study in Settlement Geography*, New Delhi: Rajesh Publications.

Sinha, V.N.P. and L.K.P. Singh (2003) *Jharkhand: Land and People*, Delhi: Rajesh Publications.

Thakur, B. (2007) 'Emerging Trends in India's Resource Development: Implications for Sustainable Management in Developing Countries', in B. Thakur (ed.), *Perspectives in Resource Management in Developing Countries, Vol. 2: Population, Resources and Development*, New Delhi: Concept, 3–87.

Thakur, R. (2007a) 'Domestic Water Supply in Hazaribag Town', in B. Thakur (ed.), *City, Society and Planning: Essays in Honour of Professor A.K. Dutt, Vol. 1: City*, New Delhi: Concept, 336–356.

Vaidyanathan, A. (1999) *Water Resource Management: Institution and Irrigation Development in India*, New Delhi: Oxford University Press.

7

Irrigation Expansion and Water Resources Development in Haryana

INDER JEET

In most parts of the overexploited areas, the prime cause of overexploitation is the rising demand for groundwater from agriculture. (In some parts, it is growing urbanization and industrialization.) Further, in many groundwater irrigated areas, decisions on cropping pattern and cropping intensity, which are the predominant determinants of agricultural demand for groundwater, are being taken largely independent of the ease of groundwater availability. Thus, water intensive crops have tended to be grown even in the face of scarcity of groundwater, if these crops are perceived to be relatively remunerative. Such distortions occur partly due to the legal/regulatory regime governing groundwater and partly due to the minimum support price policy and agricultural trade policy currently being followed.

Haryana is mostly arid or semi-arid with limited rainfall ranging from 300 mm in the south-west to 1,100 mm in the north-east. There are no perennial rivers running through the State, and about two-thirds of the area is underlain in brackish water with rising water table and inadequate natural drainage. The State lies in the basins of the Indus and Yamuna rivers and receives water from the Sutlej and Yamuna rivers and its share of surplus water from the Ravi and Beas rivers. According to Government of Haryana (GOH) estimates, the water resources available in the State is about 24.5 billion cubic metres (BCM). This estimate includes: (i) about 11.2 billion cubic metres (BCM) from externally sourced surface water, which may increase up to 15.9 million BCM after Haryana gets its full share of the Sutlej, Ravi, Beas and Yamuna waters; (ii) about 2.05 BCM from internal surface water resources; and, (iii) 11.2 BCM of groundwater resources (4.55 BCM from normalized monsoon recharge and 6.7 BCM from annual groundwater recharge). The GOH places high priority on surface irrigation and drainage. As a result, about 75 per cent of the State's arable land are served by irrigation canals. Present average surface irrigation intensity is about 70 per cent reflecting the limited availability of water supplies in the system.

Haryana is not fully covered by canal network and in some parts, surface water is not supplied and all the demands are met from groundwater only. Hence, groundwater availability is classified into two types: inside a surface irrigation command area (conjunctive use) and outsidethe surface irrigation command area (direct use). Estimates indicate that the groundwater depth in the state varies considerably. During the pre-monsoon period it ranges from 1m to 60 m below ground level (bgl). Deeper water levels are observed (20 to 60 m bgl) in the south-western part of the State, especially in the Mahendragarh district. It ranges between 20 to 30 m bgl in the north and north-western boundary area of the State in the Ambala and Panchkula districts. Pockets of deep water levels of around 20 m bgl exists in the Kurukshetra, Kaithal, Sirsa, Hissar, Panipat, Gurgaon, etc. Shallow water level conditions exists in Rohtak and Jind districts, i.e., central parts of the State in general. Pockets of shallow water levels are spread over almost all the districts from Ambala in the north, through Yamunanagar, Panipat, and Sonepat in the east, to Faridabad in the South, to Bhiwani, Hissar and Sirsa in the south-west and west. The water table has registered a fall in fresh water belts and a rise in saline groundwater areas. Water levels have thus declined in most parts of Panchkula, Ambala, Yamunanagar, Kaithal, Kurukshetra, Karnal, Panipat, Sonepat, Faridabad, Gurgaon, Rewari, Hissar, Rohtak, Jind and Sirsa districts. Overexploitation of groundwater resources is occurring in many parts of the State as evidenced by the decline in groundwater levels, particularly in the north-eastern and southern districts. On the other hand, in the central-western part of the state, the water table has risen causing waterlogging. Public tubewells, which are mostly deep, supply water for irrigation, drinking, and industrial needs or to augment canal supply in certain parts of the State. Private tubewells, which are mostly shallow, are also used for the same purposes. Groundwater exploitation in the State is mainly from the shallow aquifer, which reached a volume of 8,830 million cubic metre (MCM) in Financial Year 95. Groundwater exploitation through deeper wells amounted to 1,406 MCM during the same year (1,544 MCM for direct irrigation and 1,643 MCM for augmentation/conjunctive use of tubewells). Various analyses of the role of irrigation in Haryana's agriculture have shown that irrigation has played a core role in agricultural production and growth. In a monsoon-dependent farming system, with unreliable rains and large areas with rainfall less than 1,000 mm per annum, irrigation has been a crucial input for agricultural production in this part of the country. Irrigation enables a higher productive potential from the land, and significant production response from associated use of high yielding varieties, fertilizer and other inputs. Both, at the national and regional levels, agricultural growth and rural development have closely followed the growth and regional pattern of irrigation expansion. The production impact of Indian irrigation has occurred through four routes: (i) cultivated area expansion; (ii) cropping pattern shifts; (iii) productivity enhancement; and (iv) increase in reliability.

Ascertaining irrigation's precise contribution is, however, difficult. Nevertheless, various estimates point to a contribution from irrigated agriculture to overall agricultural production of about two-thirds, and under some estimates an even higher contribution. Even more difficult is the assessment of irrigated agriculture's contribution to agricultural growth. It is probable, however, that irrigated agriculture has contributed the bulk of past agricultural growth. Today, the average aggregate productivity of irrigated agriculture per unit of land would seem to be seven times that of rainfed agriculture (Saleth, 1997). While estimates of impact of irrigation vary, all point to its significance in Indian agriculture; and its importance to past agricultural growth (Dhawan, 1989).

The most important contribution of irrigation to State agriculture was in facilitating the spread of the Green Revolution. The expansion of irrigation from the mid–1960s provided the enabling environment for use of the new high-yielding varieties and fertilizer, pushing the production frontier to a new height and transforming the rural sector. The major gainers in terms of both productivity and area share were wheat and rice. As a result, food-grain production increased manyfold during this period. Irrigation expansion has also imparted a greater degree of stability to farm production (Dhawan, 1989; Rao et al., 1988).

Haryana is one of India's major irrigating states, with approximately 2.9 mha under surface irrigation (Hellegers et al., 2007). Haryana, from being a food deficit state in 1966 at the time of its inception, has now emerged as a major contributor to the national pool of food grains. Agriculture accounts for 31 per cent of the state GDP and, along with Punjab, Haryana led India's Green Revolution. Grain yields are some 30–40 per cent above the national average and with just 1.4 per cent of India's area, this small state provides 30 per cent of the national procurement of wheat and 10 per cent of its rice (ibid.). Development of water for irrigation can be cited as one of the major contributor to Haryana's agricultural success. Western Yamuna Canal (WYC) with majority of its command area falling in Haryana and a liberal use of groundwater can be considered to be the most significant influences on the agricultural turn-around in the state of Haryana. Haryana is mostly arid or semi-arid with limited rainfall ranging from 300 mm in the south-west to 1,100 mm in the north-east. There are no perennial rivers running through the State, and about two-thirds of the area is underlain in brackish water with rising water table and inadequate natural drainage. The State lies in the basins of the Indus and Yamuna rivers and receives water from the Sutlej and Yamuna rivers and its share of surplus water from the Ravi and Beas rivers. According to Government of Haryana (GOH) estimates, the water resources available in the State is about 24.5 billion cubic metres (BCM). This estimate includes: (i) about 11.2 billion cubic metres (BCM) from externally sourced surface water, which may increase up to 15.9 BCM after Haryana gets its full share of the Sutlej, Ravi, Beas and Yamuna waters; (ii) about 2.05 BCM from internal surface water resources; and, (iii) 11.2 BCM of groundwater resources (4.55 BCM from normalized monsoon recharge and 6.7 BCM from annual groundwater recharge). The GOH places high priority on surface irrigation and drainage. As a result, about 75 per cent of the State's arable land are served by irrigation canals. Present average surface irrigation intensity is about 70 per cent reflecting the limited availability of water supplies in the system.

Groundwater Depletion

Paradoxically, Haryana is facing the threat of a declining water table because of the exploitation of resources in some areas and a rising water table caused by increased waterlogging and soil salinity in others. The decline in the water table is more marked in the semi-arid region than in the arid region. The semi-arid region, which has good groundwater quality, derives approximately 80 per cent of water for irrigation and drinking purposes from subsurface sources. The arid region, by contrast, consists of desert and drought-prone areas and has poor groundwater quality. Approximately, 76 per cent of the water used for irrigation in the arid region is obtained from surface water canals.

Over the last two and a half decades a shift has been observed in the cropping pattern for irrigated crops in Haryana. The area devoted to wheat cultivation has increased by more than 150 per cent, and the area used for the cultivation of paddy, a highly water-intensive crop, has increased threefold (Gangwar and van den Toorn,

1987). After remunerative price policies for paddy rice were initiated in the late 1970s, the area devoted to rice cultivation expanded, resulting in exploitation of groundwater resources. Subsidies for the use of electricity in the rural sector and the lack of regulatory measures for the use of groundwater only exacerbated the exploitation and encouraged inefficient use of groundwater. As a result, the water table declined rapidly, especially in the semi-arid region.

At the state level, more groundwater could be harnessed, because only 68 per cent of the resources are being utilized. The semi-arid region, however, is experiencing an average fall in the water table of 0.3–0.6 metres annually, indicating that groundwater utilization is exceeding recharge. The districts of Yamunanagar, Karnal, Kurukshetra, and Ambala have shown signs of overextraction, and in other districts the rate of decline of the water table is alarming. In Kurukshetra, the water table declined from 8.2 metres in 1974 to 17.8 metres in 1994. The phenomenon of a declining water table is not confined to the semi-arid region. In Mahendragarh, in the arid region, the water table declined from 19.7 metres in 1974 to 30.4 metres in 1994. The cost of replenishing groundwater in these locations will be enormous if the trend continues. For example, according to the Tata Energy Research Institute (TERI), the cost of replenishing groundwater in districts like Karnal and Panipat is likely to be ₹ 371 million ($8.5 million) and ₹ 169 million ($3.9 million), respectively.

Objectives

The primary objective of the paper is to examine the patterns of irrigation expansion and its impact on water resources development in the State. The paper will review the current status of existing irrigation development for future development.

Methodology

The study is based on secondary data collected from various government agencies. Number of minor irrigation structures obtained from groundwater cell of agriculture department and data about behaviour of water table from Groundwater Cell of Agriculture Department of Haryana State. Following techniques are adopted to analyse the data and to infer the result.

Estimation of Groundwater Draft

The gross yearly groundwater extraction for irrigation from shallow tubewells during monsoon and non-monsoon period is considered for the present investigation. The computation of groundwater draft is based on the number of minor irrigation structures in a unit area in a particular year and average unit draft from these structures, which is based on well-yield capacity in a command area and techno-economic viability of a groundwater structure. Draft norms as approved by Groundwater Resource Estimation Committee, 1984 have been adopted.

Levels of Groundwater Development

The level of groundwater development in an area is taken as ratio of net yearly draft to total utilizable resource in a unit for irrigation. It can be expressed as:

Level of groundwater development = net yearly draft/utilizable resource for irrigation x 100

70 per cent of gross annual draft is taken as net yearly draft. The 30 per cent is presumed to go as return seepage to groundwater regime.

Accordingly, analysis emphasis to find out the degree to which groundwater draft (independent variable) and groundwater development (dependent variable) vary together and it is tried to measure the direction of co-variation with the help of regression technique.

Result and Discussion

The region has made impressive development of groundwater resource through private (shallow tubewells) and government (direct irrigation tubwells and augmentation tubewells) tubewells in and outside canal commands. The groundwater draft by these structures has increased manyfold during 1974–2011. In 1974, the total annual groundwater draft was 2,573.4 million cubic metre/year (MCM), which increased to 6,433 million cubic metre/year during 2011 (Table 1).

Table 1

Eastern Haryana: Groundwater Draft and its Volumetric Increase (1974–2011)

S. No	*District*	*Groundwater draft (1974)*	*Groundwater draft (2011)*	*Volumetric increase (1974–2011)*
1.	Ambala	150.8	473.1	323.0
2.	Yamunanagar	289.6	488.1	198.5
3.	Kurukshetra	437.3	677.1	239.2
4.	Karnal	716.3	1,361.4	645.1
5.	Panipat	311.9	708.8	390.9
6.	Sonipat	84.07	503.6	419.5
7.	Gurgaon	160.0	465.1	305.1
8.	Faridabad	181.9	262.2	80.1
9.	Rewari	137.7	305.2	167.5
10.	Mahendragarh	99.2	188.0	1,088.8
	Total	2,573.4	6,433.0	3,860.0

Source: Column 3 and 4 from Agriculture Department and Column 5 computed by author.

Table 1 demonstrates a comparative picture of groundwater draft in different districts during 1974 and 2011. Groundwater draft varies from 84.07 million cubic metre in the Sonipat district to 716.3 million cubic metres (mcm) in Karnal district in 1974. In 2011, it ranges from 188 mcm in Mahendragarh district to 262.2 mcm in Faridabad district and 1,361 mcm in Karnal district. In the study area as a whole it increased approximately two times during the span of three decades. The foregoing values of groundwater draft are giving substantial indication about the large-scale groundwater tapping by farmers.

In the Ambala , and Yamunanagar districts due to unfavourable physiographic conditions, agricultural developments are low, despite fresh groundwater quality. But in Faridabad district, seepage recharge from the Yamuna river compensates the gap created by groundwater draft. Therefore, per cent increase in groundwater development is also very low (50, 25.9 and 15.2 respectively) (Table 2). In the districts like Sonipat, Gurgaon and Rewari groundwater development is comparatively high due to insufficient surface water availability. It is noted that a large area of these districts comes under saline groundwater quality, which does not encourage a great deal of groundwater draft except those along the Yamuna river.

Table 2

Eastern Haryana: Groundwater Development and Per cent Increase (1974–2011)

S. No.	*District*	*Available groundwater resource (MCM/Yr)*	*Groundwater development during 1974 (%)*	*Groundwater development during 2011(%)*	*Per cent increase (1974–2011)*
1.	Ambala	32.39	51.0	101.0	50.0
2.	Yamunanagar	491.55	84.0	92.2	15.2
3.	Kurukshetra	264.88	165.0	255.6	90.6
4.	Karnal	748.85	95.0	181.9	172.3
5.	Panipat	340.62	91.5	208.1	116.3
6.	Sonipat	454.30	18.5	110.8	92.3
7.	Gurgaon	400.05	40.0	116.2	76.2
8.	Faridabad	308.91	58.9	84.8	25.9
9.	Rewari	163.68	84.1	186.5	102.4
10.	Mahendragarh	139.44	71.1	461.4	390.3

Source: Column 3 from Central Groundwater Board and Column 4, 5 and 6 are based on computed values.

Other remaining districts, namely, Karnal, Kurukshetra, Panipat and Mahendragarh exhibit tremendous increase in the level of groundwater development. These districts excluding Mahendragarh are growing high water consumptive crops like sugarcane, paddy and wheat, which require more quantity in the form of irrigation. Therefore, in the absence of sufficient network of canals, groundwater is the only source to meet the irrigation demands.

It may also be noted that from 1969–70 onwards, the demand on groundwater has been enhanced. With the inception of HYV seeds, the State farmers were encouraged by the government to instal their own shallow tubewells by giving subsidies on equipments and electricity charges. Therefore, the large-scale installation of shallow tubewells is causing enormous burden on the groundwater reservoir in the study area. Consequently, the area is experiencing heavy water table fluctuations since since 1974 (the year when scientific groundwater monitoring started in the State) onwards.

Figure 1 presents a contrasting picture of spatial distribution of water table fluctuations in the region. In the north and south of the sub-alluvial ridge particularly in the district of Ambala, Yamunanagar, Kurukshetra, Karnal, Panipat, Sonipat and Faridabad, water table fluctuations vary less than zero metre in to more than 7 metres. The fluctuation are less than zero metre in north-eastern Ambala, north-western Yamunanagar and extreme southern Ambala and western Yamunanagar. In the remaining parts, fluctuations vary from less than one metre to more than 5 metres.

Various factors are responsible for low water table fluctuations in these districts of the study area. The hilly and piedmont plain of the Ambala (Naraingarh and Raipurani blocks) and Yamunanagar districts (Bilaspur and Sadoura) is cut by seasonal streams producing extreme unevenness that is not suitable for minor irrigation structures. Hence, groundwater withdrawal is quite low. Annual precipitation is more than 1,000 mm in these parts, which provides ample quantity of water in the seasonal streams and rivers to recharge the groundwater. The Yamuna river, which is a perennial river, provides seepage recharge throughout the year in the adjoining areas.

Figure 1

Haryana: Water Table Fluctuation (June 1974–2011)

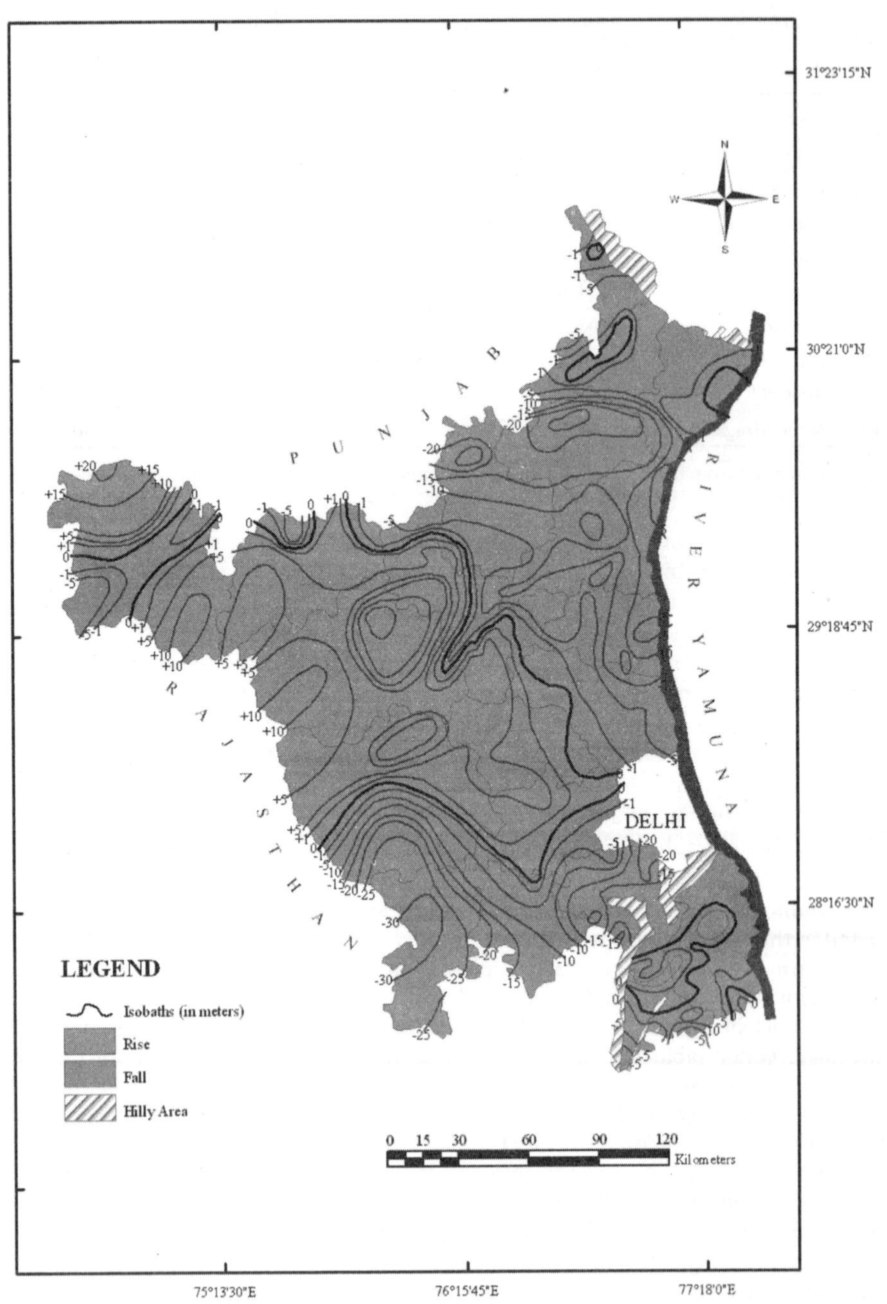

The major part of the study area lying in the south spreading over the Gurgaon, Rewari and Mahendragarh districts is characterized by steep water table fluctuations exhibiting close spacing of water table contours, particularly, in the

Mahendragarh district. Annual precipitation is less than 300 mm , surface irrigation is almost nil in the absence of any perennial river, the surface drainage system is poor. Therefore, these factors are responsible for low groundwater recharge. Contrary to it, farmers are continuously extracting groundwater through tubewells to meet the irrigation demands, and this extraction has created overdraft in the groundwater reservoir by disturbing the natural balance. The foregoing is the manifestation of the fact that increase in groundwater draft is the main influencing factor of water table depth, which is responsible for large-scale groundwater development in this area.

Again, to keep in mind the purpose of the study, the result of the degree to which groundwater draft and groundwater development vary together is given in Table 3. We note from the Table 3 that one unit increase in the groundwater draft results in a .242 units increase in the groundwater development. The next observation is about the standard error of *'b (SEB)'*. This value is being used to establish the confidence interval for *'b'*. Two standard errors (the reported standard error multiplied by 2) establish the 95 per cent confidence interval for *'b'*. The next reported statistics is standardized partial slope *(BETA)* for increase in groundwater development, reported as .933. This value tells that how much 1 standard deviation change in the independent variable will affect the dependent variable also in standard deviation units.

Table 3

Bivariate Regression for the Effect of Groundwater Draft on Groundwater Development

Variable	*ß*	*SE B*	*Beta*	*T*	*Sig. T*	*R*	R^2
Per cent Increase in Groundwater Draft	.242	.032	.933	7.342	.0001	.933	.871
Constant	8.818	15.679		.562	.589		

'Y' intercept *(Constant)* is 8.818 points. This value has its importance for prediction about the increase in the groundwater draft. The slope of regression line is statistically significant, as it has been shown that coefficient of correlation is significantly different from zero.

Conclusions

The study establishes that there is immense increase in groundwater draft since 1974, causing enormous burden on groundwater reservoir in the study area. Private owned shallow tubewells has increased manyfolds during the last three decades, which are extracting huge quantity of groundwater in an injudicious and unplanned manner. It is observed that majority of districts have experienced more than 90 per cent increase in the groundwater development in this span of time. Therefore, according to Groundwater Estimation Committee (1997), these districts are overexploited and need thorough managerial attention from government agencies. Furthermore, these districts require exhaustive monitoring and evaluation for future groundwater development.

References

Chattopadhayay, S. and R.A. Carpenter (1991) 'Sustainable Development: Scientific Jargon or a Practical Management', *Annals of the National Association of Geographers, India*, 11(2): 1–12.

Dhawan, B.D. (1989) *Studies in Irrigation and Water Management*, New Delhi: Commonwealth Publishers.

Gangwar, A.C. and W.H. van den Toorn (1987) 'The Economics of Adverse Groundwater Conditions in Haryana State', *Indian Journal of Agricultural Economics*, 42(April–June).

Groundwater Estimation Committee (1997) Ministry of Water Resources, Government of India, New Delhi.

Hellegers, P.J.G.J., Perry, C.J. and Berkoff, J. (2007) 'Water Pricing in Haryana, India', in F. Molle and J. Berkoff (eds) *Irrigation Water Pricing*, CAB International.

Jeet, I. (1997) 'Spatio-Temporal Analysis of Groundwater Balance in Eastern Haryana', *Transactions, Institute of Indian Geographers*, 19(1): 7–16.

Mathews, J.A. (1981) *Quantitative and Statistical Approaches to Geographers*, Oxford: Pergamon Press.

Mitchell, B. (1989) *Geography and Resource Analysis*, London: Longman.

Omara-Ojungu, P.H. (1992) *Resource Management in Developing Countries*, Harlow: Longman Scientific and Technical Group.

Rao, C.H.H., Ray, S.K. and Subbarao, A. (1988) *Unstable Agriculture and Droughts*, New Delhi: Vikas Publications.

Saleth, R.M. (1997) *Farm Technologies and Rural Poverty: An Evaluation of Linkages at the Macro Level*, Delhi: Institute of Economic Growth.

Tanwar, B.S. (1994) 'Environmental Impact of Groundwater Development', Paper Presented at the Regional Workshop on Environmental Aspects of Groundwater Development, Kurukshetra, Haryana, 17–19 October.

Wash, A. (1989) *Statistics for the Social Sciences*, New York: Harper and Row Publishers.

8

Irrigation Water Demand for the Hindon Basin

PREETI SACHAR

Water is an environmental resource and the principles of sound natural resource utilization and its management necessitate the understanding of the relationship between supply of water and the demand that exists. The efficient and optimal use of our global natural resource base, including air, land and water has emerged as an area of universal concern during recent decades. In water sector, resources are needed to restore degraded environments, to clean up water systems and polluted land, to replant forests, to regulate water flows and to recreate damaged habitats. To create an economic system that is environmentally friendly and non-polluting will require a significant mobilization of resources. In many current social systems that are based on the concept of continuous growth, a shift to a more sustainable development path will involve profound changes in the social structure. The wise utilization, availability of water resources along with equity questions are critical since sustainable development in water and other sectors involves, in essence, a shift of resource allocation from current generations to those of the future. However, the major issues vary widely over the space and time but, here, for the purpose of analysis the irrigated water demands, as per the available water resource potential, needs specifications.

Water has played a critical role in every facet of human activity. In more recent times, water has emerged as a key natural resource to be efficiently managed for environmentally sustainable development. Water is vital in a modern economy, not only in urban-industrial context, but also in rural areas through its more widespread use in productive activities and its potential to improve living conditions.

The micro-basin irrigation water demand for Hindon here refers to both theoretical as well as empirical demands. In this study, the micro-basin irrigation water demand refers to water requirements for different crops during different seasons. This article highlights the basic water requirements of important crops grown in the basin in different agriculture seasons, namely, kharif, rabi, zaid, etc. In other words, the aim is to assess the micro-basin water demand in terms of total water required in order to grow the crops in the basin.

Water is one of the most important inputs for assured crop production in an area, specially where production suffers due to its scarcity or irregular rainfall distribution. Water is required in large quantities and also needs to be supplied at regular intervals to meet the crop demands. Thus, adequate and timely water supply is one of the basic inputs for obtaining desired crop yields. Very often, it is also a limiting factor in the crop production because of three reasons: first, water is required in huge quantity; second, it needs to be supplied several times at interval throughout the crop growth because of evapotranspiration and limited water holding capacity of soil; and third, it affects yields not only directly, but, also indirectly by influencing sowing time, responses to fertilizers and other management factors.

In tropical country like India, with erratic, inadequate and unevenly distributed rainfall, assured irrigation is the only way for permanent and profitable farming. It is here that most of the natural water harnessed by man is used in agriculture, but, it is seldom realized that irrigation water is the most costly input which farmers are using. However, this costly input can be used judiciously and economically for producing optimum crop yield per unit of irrigated land or per unit of water used in irrigation by working out the precise water management technique. The economic and efficient utilization of water, therefore, becomes essential in water use for which the knowledge on water requirements for crops and its relations with other input factors is imperative.

The Hindon basin, in spite of being in a favourable position in respect of water potential, continues to import colossal quantities of food. The basin's miserable food output results from a wasteful system of irrigation, due to lack of proper technical guidance and inefficient administrative control. Irrigation water supply along with efficient utilization of available irrigation water is an important factor for an assured crop production. It permits better utilization of other production factors and leads to increased yield per unit of land. The integrated development of water resources, judicious method of water application, proper soil and crop management practices and scientific scheduling of irrigation according to the developmental rhythm of plant, form important aspects of comprehensive irrigation development programme. The present paper attempts to assess the requirement of irrigation water in the Hindon basin and also to make the future projection of water demand.

The Study Area

The delimitation of the study area, namely, the Hindon basin is done on the basis of the existing Hindon river system falling in north-western portion of Uttar Pradesh. The Hindon river flows in an interfluvial area falling between the two great canal systems, namely, the Eastern Yamuna Canal and the Upper Ganga Canal. These two canal systems are taken as the western and eastern boundary, respectively, for the Hindon basin. The Hindon river in its upper reaches and that of the lower reaches forms the meeting point of the northern and southern part of the basin, respectively. The area, thus, selected for the study is Hindon basin which forms part of Upper Ganga-Yamuna Doab. It lies between 28°N and 31°N Latitude and 77° 10'E and 79° 10'E Longitude. The Hindon basin, on the whole contains 16 tehsils and 48 blocks and 4 districts, i.e. Saharanpur, Muzaffarnagar, Meerut and Ghaziabad each having 4 tehsils (Figure 1). Nature has endowed the basin with plentiful supply of both the surface and sub-surface water. The area is drained by the river Hindon, which is 258

Figure 1

The Hindon Basin: Administrative Devisions

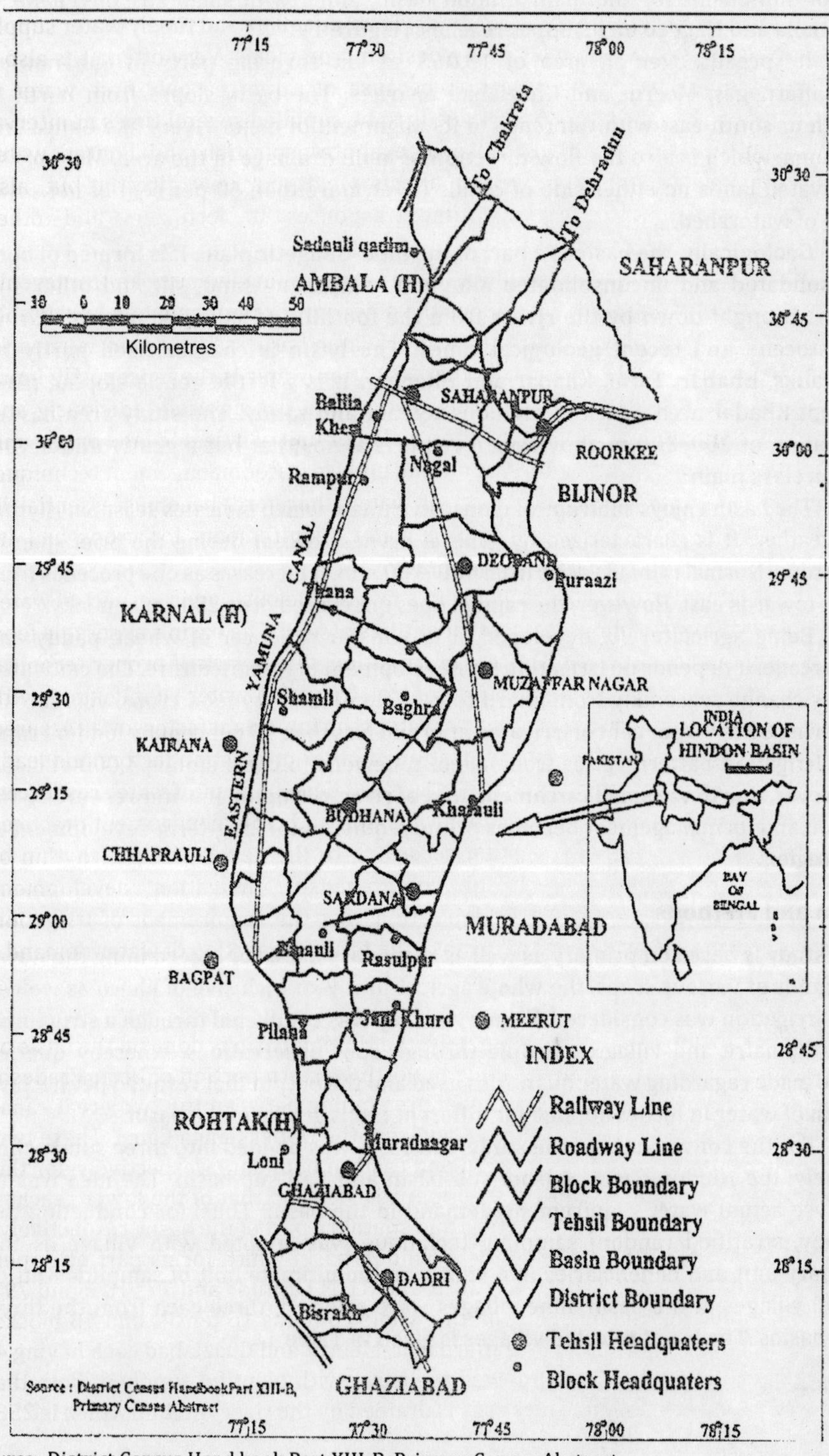

Source: District Census Hand book Part XIII-B, Primary Census Abstract.

km in length. It is an important perennial tributary to Yamuna river that originates from Shiwalik foothills. Its major tributaries are Krishni and Kali, which form two major sub-basins for the main Hindon basin, along with small streams, namely, Dhamola and Nagdeo on its upper reaches. (Figure 1).

It spreads over an area of 13,065 sq km covering parts of Saharanpur, Muzaffarnagar, Meerut and Ghaziabad districts. The basin slopes from north to south or south-east with reference to its alignment of major rivers like Ganga and Yamuna, which is also the flow direction of main drainage in the area. Most of the cultivated lands on either side of canals cover more than 60 per cent of net sown area of watershed.

Geologically, the basin is a part of the Indo-Gangetic plain. It is formed of both consolidated and unconsolidated alluvium comprising sand, silt and other soil forms brought down by the rivers from the foothills of Shiwalik, formed during Pleistocene and recent geological times. The basin is characterized partly by Shivaliks, Bhabar, Tarai, Khadar and Bhangar. It is a fertile gentle sloping plain except Khadar area which is ravinous terrain and sandy. The study area has an elevation of 200–300 m above sea level. It is almost flat but a gently undulating featureless plain.

The basin enjoys subtropical monsoon climate which indicates seasonal rhythm of weather. It is characterized by general dryness except during the brief span of monsoon. Normal rainfall varies from 400–700 mm. It increases as one proceeds from west towards east. However, the rainfall does not exceed over 250 cm annually.

Being agriculturally developed, it is a major producer of wheat, paddy and sugarcane. It depends on irrigation for development of its agriculture. The cultivated crops change seasonally from kharif to rabi, dominated by food crops, viz., cereals covering 80 to 90 per cent of irrigated area and less than 10 per cent by fodder crops. The irrigation pattern varies from use of tubewells to canal among 4,000 villages. However, due to the small catchment area of river, the optimal water resource utilization and its management becomes prime requisites for long-term development of the region.

Data and Methods

The study is based on primary as well as secondary data. For ascertaining the water demands of various crops, the whole agricultural year inclusive of kharif as well as rabi irrigation was considered. Primary survey was conducted through a structured questionnaire and village schedule through spot observations, whereby queries were made regarding water quantities used and the output that resulted per hectare depth of water in inches applied for different crops grown in the basin.

For the convenience of the study, the basin was divided into three sub-basins, namely, the Hindon basin, Krishni sub-basin and Kali sub-basin. The idea was to analyse actual water requirement/demand in the basin. Thus, for conducting the survey, stratified random sampling technique was adopted with village as the primary unit and beneficiaries in a village as the ultimate unit of sampling. Out of 4,000 villages in the basin, nine villages were selected, three each from the three sub-basins. The list of selected villages is given in Table 1.

Table 1

List of Selected Villages

Ghaziabad	Ghaziabad	1	Hindon	Bikhanpur
Meerut	Baghpat	1	Krishini	Mansoorpur
Meerut	Sardana	1	Kali	Chandana
Muzaffarnagar	Muzaffarnagar	1	Hindon	Dholra
Muzaffarnagar	Muzaffarnagar	1	Kali	Saidpur Khurd
Muzaffarnagar	Kairana	1	Krishini	Sainta
Saharanpur	Roorkee	1	Kali	Saidpura
Saharanpur	Saharanpur	1	Hindon	Sona
Saharanpur	Saharanpur	1	Krishini	Ismailpur

Review of Methods

The basic concepts of water requirements are confusing. Proper techniques are not employed to determine water needs of crops, which results in obtaining little information, causing enormous misuse of water and earning poor returns from the major irrigation projects. Major irrigation research stations in India for carrying out water use researches are Pusa, Roorkee, Shajahanapur, Banaras, Coimbatore and New Delhi, where work has been carried out on water requirements for rice, wheat, cotton and sugarcane. Several individuals and agencies have also worked on this problem. The approaches employed in determining water requirements for different crops are broadly grouped into the following four categories: (1) Transpiration ratio, (2) Depth-interval yield, (3) Soil-moisture deficit and (4) Climatiological.

Initially, water requirement was taken as transpiration ratio, i.e., the quantity of water transpired by a crop to produce a unit amount of dry matter. Plants were grown in a pot culture house, evaporation was minimized by sealing the soil surface. Water was added at intervals on the basis of periodic weighings of the pots. Records were maintained on the quantity of water added and dry matter produced by plants. Later, effect of different species, durations, manures and fertilizers applied were also studied on transpiration ratio. The values, however, reported were far from those obtained under field conditions and, thus, had limited practical utility so far as irrigation scheduling for field crops was concerned. The values of transpiration ratio varied from one place to another and for one crop to another. For example, wheat transpiration ratio varied for water requirement from 200 to 1,000 mm and sugarcane from 250 to 1,500 mm. It was observed that addition of manures, etc., reduced the ratio. Based on first two approaches, lot of work that commenced, as early as 1910, were at Pusa, Cuttack, etc., were of Leather, Singh et al., Ganguli, Choudhary and Mahapatra along with Institute of agriculture research at Varanasi. Based on the same approach, Penman also established theorem that the water requirements for all crops must be the same, if they are grown on the same soil and in the same growing season. It was based on the law of physics that inside the plants, functions performed by water are innumerable, but the quantity of water directly required by plants is limited. It is now recognized that for a given growth of dry matter, the amount of water transpired may vary greatly according to climatic conditions. The above approach was found to be of no use as less attention was paid to different components of water requirements, namely consumptive use, effective rainfall, irrigation efficiency, percolation loss, contribution from water table, etc.

It was followed by field experiments known as depth-interval yield approach. In this, the delta (depth of irrigation), interval of irrigation were tried for scheduling irrigation and to find out the optimum water requirements of crops. Different depths of irrigation such as 150, 225, 300 mm were applied at intervals of 2–4 weeks. Irrigation treatment which gave the maximum yield with the minimum delta of water was taken as the optimum water requirement of that particular crop. Bulk of work conducted in this field are anonymous like Rao (1951), Pandey (1963), Malik and Das (1968), Ramiah and Vachhani (1951), Hiranandani (1953) etc.

A real breakthrough was made when field experiments based on soil-water regime concept were conducted for various crops. It is the usage of above depth-interval yield approach by fixing the treatment of depth of irrigation on the basis of soil-moisture deficit. In this concept, water content at field capacity, (upper limit of regime) was considered as 100 per cent available for crop growth and that at the permanent wilting point as 0 per cent. The safe limit of allowable soil water depletion (lower limit of regime) for a crop was determined by experimentation and was taken as a criteria for scheduling of irrigation. The formula used under this is:

$$d = \frac{FC - A}{100} \times ASG \times D \qquad \text{(Dastane et al., 1970)}$$

Where: d = Moisture deficit in soil layer
FC = Field capacity in per cent
A = Actual moisture content in per cent
ASG = Apparent specific gravity of soil
D = Depth of soil layer

The net deficit in the root zone, thus, worked out was corrected by the value of irrigation efficiency which gave the depth of water to be applied at each irrigation. Experiments of this nature have been in progress since 1956 at IARI, New Delhi and many other agricultural colleges. This technique is found satisfactory for all practical purposes for working out precise scheduling, depth of irrigation and water requirements for various crops.

According to the recent concept, consumptive use of water by a crop, which is the main part of water requirement in most field crops, is governed primarily by meteorological parameters. The climatic parameters play a predominant role in governing the water needs of crops and the criteria of soil water availability for scheduling of irrigations. In this approach, consumptive use of water by a crop is first worked out by recording soil moisture losses throughout the growth, correlating it with the values of meteorological parameters and thus deriving quantitative relationships. It has been concluded that this technique of climatological approach is simple, rapid, reliable and has high extension value. Using this approach, work has been carried out in India mainly at IARI, New Delhi.

The latest approach developed and found more widely adopted for scheduling of irrigation is the plant water status itself. It is considered an ideal criterion as the plant is a good integrator of soil, water and climate factors.

Estimation of Water Requirement of Crops

Estimation of water requirement of crops is one of the basic needs for crop planning on a farm. Water requirement may be defined as the quantity of water, regardless of its source, required by a crop or diversified pattern of crops in a given period of time for its normal growth under field condition at a place.

Evapotranspiration refers to the total water loss due to evaporation from the soil and transpiration from a crop for a particular area during a specified time, whereas effective rainfall is total precipitation or a fraction thereof which forms part of the water requirement. The soil moisture deficit in the rooting depth of a crop before precipitation mostly decided the value of effective rainfall. According to the climatological concept of water requirements of crops, even light showers come under it. Only that rainfall which is lost by run-off and deep percolation is ineffective. Thus, the role of evapotranspiration and effective rainfall for estimating water requirement of crops in the basin becomes important.

For the proper development of agriculture, the quantum of irrigation supply is important. The Hindon basin, in spite of being in a favourable position in respect of water potential, continues to import colossal quantities of food. The basin's miserable food output results from a wasteful system of irrigation, due to lack of proper technical guidance and inefficient administrative control.

Irrigation water supply along with efficient utilization of available irrigation water is an important factor for assured crop production. It permits better utilization of other production factors and leads to increased yield per unit of land. The integrated development of water resources, judicious method of water application, proper soil and crop management practices and scientific scheduling of irrigation according to the developmental rhythm of plants, form important aspects of comprehensive irrigation development programme. The efficient water management requires thorough study of not only soil properties but also plant-water relationship, climate, agronomic practices and economic assessment. An effort, thus, has been made here to highlight the importance of soil-water-plant relationship in the crop production through the demand factor in terms of water requirements.

Irrigation water is thus needed mainly to meet the demands of evapotranspiration and metabolic activities of plants, together known as consumptive use (cu or u). Since water used in the later part is negligible, evapotranspiration is practically considered equal to Cu. Water requirement, thus, includes losses due to ET (Cu) + losses during application of irrigation water (unavoidable), and quantity of water required for special operations like preparation, transplanting, leaching, etc. It is formulated as:

WR = ET or Cu + Application losses + special needs.

Water requirement is, therefore, demand and supply and would consist of contribution from any source of water, major source being irrigation water (IR), effective rainfall (ER), and soil profile contribution (s) including that from shallow water table.

To assess the relation between irrigation supply and the yields, various experiments were tested at Varanasi for different crops. Yields for different crops were obtained and plotted against amount of water consumed by them. The result showed a linear relationship or proportion between the yields and the amount of water consumed, provided additional manure is used. Further, length of life cycle of plants has great influence over its water requirements. Again, a linear correlation exists between them, provided plants are irrigated in periods which ensure maximum possibilities of their growth and yield. It is only, then, we have reliable information about exact number of times when plants need maximum water, that any scientific irrigation of crops is possible. The optimum yield, namely, highest yield with most economic use of water was obtained by a supply of three inches depth of irrigation provided at the intervals of two to four week. The Irrigation Research Institute at Roorkee (UP) has conducted such experiments for different crops grown in Hindon basin (Table 2).

Table 2

Water Requirements of Different Crops Grown in the Hindon Basin

Crop	*Dry matter produced/ AC in labs*	*Water transpired by crop in inches gallon*	*Depth in inches AC*	*Water evaporated from soil gallons/ AC*	*Inches depth*	*Et water required by crops in inches depth*	*Total requirements of crops in inches depth*	*Duration of crops in days*	*Daily water requirements of crop in inches depth*
Cotton	4,025	1,69,590	7.5	4,73,772	20.9	28.4	44.0	230	0.19
Rice	4,932	2,56,346	11.3	3,65,904	16.1	27.4	45	105	0.43
Potato	8,014	4,35,969	19.2	27,583	1.2	20.4	27	88	0.30
Sugarcane	20,594	4,44,009	19.6	5,82,146	25.7	45.3	88	310	0.28
Wheat	4,079	1,66,645	7.4	2,7,582	1.2	8.6	16	168	0.10
Barley	2,664	1,50,161	6.6	27,582	1.2	7.8	14	88	0.16
Maize	1,150	86,162	3.8	93,638	4.2	8.0	20	105	0.19
Mustard	1,358	71,063	3.1	27,582	1.2	4.3	11	88	0.12
Linseed	1,260	1,18,798	5.2	27,582	1.2	6.4	13	88	0.14

Source: Irrigation Research Institute (1993), Roorkee, Uttar Pradesh.

Major Cropwise Requirements of Water

While reviewing the work on different techniques adopted for water requirements for different crops, it was found that each of the techniques is relevant in itself. Though some of the essential details are required in order to utilize the above-mentioned methods, water requirements for different crops as assessed are summarized below:

Cereals and Millets

Rice: It occupies 20–30 per cent of irrigated area in the basin. Its water requirements are many times more than other food crops. Being a semi-aquatic plant, it is a major consumer of water and needs careful water management in order to increase efficiency of water use. It is grown under varied soil and climatic conditions and one to three crops per annum are taken in the basin. Irrigation depth of as high as 300 mm and interval as long as 28 days were selected in UP by Public Works Department. Values of water requirements vary from 750 to 2,500 mm as obtained by different workers. Rice offers the maximum scope and challenge for economizing water resource. The percolation loss within the field can be reduced by following various practices, such as selection of heavy soils and shallow depths, land levelling, puddling to permeability, intermittent drying of field at proper stage, etc. (Table 2).

Wheat: It occupies a considerable area in the basin and nearly 50 per cent of this is irrigated. It constitutes one of the best wheat producing regions where cool and dry climate prevail during the growing season (rabi). Studies on water requirements of wheat are easier on account of its short duration and medium rooting depth. The number of times the irrigation required for this crop are lower than the other crops. Using the empirical depth interval yield, application in fixing depth and frequency of irrigation, trials had been conducted by Singh (1945), Singh and Nijhawan (1951), Gupta and Bhattacharya (1963), Singh et al. (1985) etc. The work in general shows that for tall Indian wheat varieties, 3 to 4 irrigations are required for obtaining maximum yield in low rabi rainfall tracts (50–100 mm) on medium textured soils. The consumptive use of water is about 250–300 mm during the growth. The yield of wheat increased with the number of irrigations, but the response per irrigation decreased gradually. For deciding the policy of intensive vs. extensive irrigation in the command area, the assessment is provided in (Table 3).

Table 3

Intensive Vs. Extensive Irrigation in Wheat

Number of irrigations/ha	*Irrigated crops*		*Unnirigated*		*Total irrigations (AxB)*	*Total yield (g/100 ha) (BxC) + (DxE)*
	Area (ha)	*Yield (a/ha)*	*Area left unirrigated*	*Yield (q/ha)*		
5	20	47	80	9.3	100	1,700
4	25	42	75	9.3	100	1,768
3	33	35	66	9.3	100	1,799
2	50	34	50	9.3	140	2,175
1	100	30	—	—	100	3,040

Source: Dastane et al. (1970).

Review of Work Done on water requirement of crops in India. Navbharat Prakshan: Pune, p. 45

Maize: The work reported on water requirements of maize is meagre. In the Hindon basin, maize is grown mostly in kharif (June – October) as rainfed or irrigated, and on smaller scale during summer season (February/March/May/June) under irrigated conditions. The improved varieties of maize require 100–120 days to mature, except in hilly tract of the basin where they take 10–20 days more to mature (Table 4).

Table 4

Effect of Soil Moisture Regime on Grain Yield of Maize on Sandy Loam Soil of Hindon Basin

Treatment	*Yield q/ha*	*Irrigation requirement*		*Seasonal consumptive use (mm)*	*Water use efficiency kg/ha – mm of consumptive use*
		Number	*Amount*		
25% ASM	305	4	300	531	5.74
50% ASM CD at 5%	37.6	6	450	573	6.56

ASM: Available soil moisture as measured in 15–30 cm depth of soil layer.

Source: Indian Agricultural Research Institute (1977), *Water Requirement and Irrigation Management of Crops in India*, New Delhi: Caxton Press Private Limited, p. 198.

The irrigation requirements of maize vary with the type of soil and the season it is grown. Maize is normally sown in the basin after a pre-sowing irrigation as the monsoon arrives late, and crop requires two to three irrigation during pre-monsoon period (Table 5).

Table 5

Irrigation Requirements of Major Crops in the Hindon Basin

Crop	*Soil type*	*Season*	*Irrigation number*	*Requirements amount (mm.)*
Maize	Sandy loam	Kharif	4	225–275
Sorghum	Sandy loam	Kharif	4	250
Barley	Sandy loam	Rabi	4	300
Ragi	Loam	Kharif	2–3	150
Gram	Sandy loam	Rabi	1–2	150–180
Mustard	Sandy loam	Kharif	1–3	75–80
Sugarcane	Sandy loam	Kharif/Rabi	11	660

Source: Sharma and Upadhyay (1973) 220–21.

Jowar (Sorghum): It is found next in area and importance to rice and wheat in the basin. It is grown best in semi-arid areas with well-distributed rainfall of about 300 to 1,000 mm. Temperature is found favourable within the range of 16–40°C. Crop is grown mostly in the kharif (June – November) season and is also cultivated in rabi season (October – March) on the moisture retentive deep soils. According to Patil et al., irrigation at 25 per cent soil water availability in surface 30 cm layer on heavy clay soil was adequate for sorghum grown for grains in kharif season (Table 5).

Bajra: It is well suited to warm areas of low rainfall (250–500 mm.). It is mostly grown in the kharif season under rainfed conditions and takes 85 to 90 days to mature. Bajra is preferred when the rainfall is inadequate for maize and jowar, as it is more tolerant to drought. Regarding soil moisture requirements, bajra tolerated 75 per cent depletion of available water from 0–30 cm depth of soil on heavy clay soil and on the sandy loam soil; best yields are obtained with irrigation at 50 per cent depletion level. The irrigation requirement of bajra is given in Table 5 above. It shows that the irrgation requirement during kharif varies from 150–200 mm in most parts.

Barely: Next to wheat, barley is an important rabi cereal (October – March) under irrigation. It is harder than wheat and can tolerate saline soil/water. It has wide ecological adaptation. It needs less water than wheat or oat for growth. It is, however, grown as a rainfed crop in areas having rainfall of 400–500 mm in the growing season. In dry areas crop needs irrigation for good growth. It is generally grown on sandy loam soils of medium fertility level. It is found suitable on saline and alkaline soils. Yield of this crop is lower under drier than irrigated conditions. The crop is taken after rice and with a pre-sowing common irrigation. Regarding soil moisture requirement, barley is grown on sandy loam soil with irrigation at 50 per cent available soil moisture. The treatments of one irrigation at 30 days or at pre-flowering were at par, but, both the treatments were superior to no irrigation in yield responses (Table 5).

Ragi: It is grown on small areas and is one of the drought-tolerant crops suited only to dry-farming areas. The crop is grown as rainfed in the rainy season (June-October), and is irrigated all the year round. It can be grown on variety of soils including saline and alkali soils. The soil moisture and irrigation requirements on heavy clay soils, as observed by Patil et al. (1963), refer that irrigation at 50 per cent available moisture depletion in the top 30 cm soil layer was necessary to obtain higher yields of ragi sown in summer season, while, that sown in the kharif season did not require any irrigation. Irrigation at 50 per cent depletion of available soil moisture on sandy loam soil was found adequate for ragi grown in rabi season.

Pulses: Work on pulses is scanty since they are grown during kharif as mixed crop with cereals. They utilize soil moisture very efficiently by virtue of deep root system and, hence, require less irrigation as compared to cereals. Legumes in kharif season are normally grown without any irrigation in most parts unless rain is unfavourable. Most of legumes grown in rabi and summer seasons depend on irrigation.

Gram (Chana): It is grown extensively in rabi season on alluvial sandy loam to loam soils. It is best suited in low rainfall areas, as it has been found to respond to irrigation in the absence of winter rains especially on the lighter soils. One irrigation of 6 cm was found adequate after planting which may, however, be required if no winter rains are received till flowering. Frequent irrigation did not benefit the crop except for the vegetative growth.

Red Gram (Arhar, Tur): It is mostly grown on alluvial sandy loam soil in the basin. The crop benefits from irrigation, if dry spells prevail for longer period. Two irrigatioins, one at flower initiation (75 days after sowing) and the other at pod filling (100 days after sowing), were found adequate for short duration red gram. It will give higher yield of red gram. This involved irrigation at 40 per cent available soil moisture.

Mustard (Edible Oilseed or Yellor Sarson): It is grown in rabi season (September/October – February/March) on sandy loam to clay loam soils. These crops benefit from irrigation, if there are no or low winter rains. Regarding irrigation requirement of crop at Roorkee on sandy loam soil, one irrigation of 60 mm use was found best as compared with rainfed mustard (Table 5).

Fibre Crops

Cotton: It is a subtropical crop grown in area with 750 to 2,500 mm rainfall. It tolerates temperature high up to 45–46°C, but, below 28°C is not conducive. Being a deep-rooted crop, it requires less irrigation water for its growth after establishment as compared to many grain crops having shallow roots. It is grown on a variety of soils, but, in the Hindon basin it is grown on sandy loam to loam soils, where it requires irrigation water for its good growth. The most optimum time of sowing cotton is May. Work on water requirements of cotton shows wide range of results, as there are several species with different life durations and growing seasons. Also, cotton being a kharif crop and can grow on light as well as heavy soils, therefore, frequency and depth vary considerably with the soil type. During rainy season normally, no irrigation is required if rainfall is well distributed. The water requirement varies from 250–260 mm. More irrigations are required on light soil and in low-rainfall areas than on medium soil and moderate rainfall areas like the Hindon basin.

Sugarcane: Nearly 70 per cent of the area under sugarcane is irrigated. It occupies the land for about 10 to 18 months and, thus, necessitates adequate irrigation for realizing its yield potential. On account of its commercial importance, considerable works exist on water requirements of this crop. It grows best on clay loam to loam soil and irrigation requirement is more on sandy loam. Heavy clay soil is also suited, provided it is well drained. It acquires warm-humid climate for its good growth with temperature ranging from 20 to 45°C. In the basin, planting is mostly done with the commencement of spring season. For soil moisture requirement, the sugarcane crop tolerated 50 per cent of depletion of available soil layer on clay loam soils. It was found that 5 irrigations during pre-monsoon period at one to two irrigations during post-monsoon period was conducive to good growth. However, pre-monsoon irrigations from February to June are important. The rainfall is about 700–800 mm during the growth (Table 5).

Sugarbeet: It is grown in rabi season under cool temperatures (upto 18–22°C) which favour its rapid growth and better sugar accumulation. For irrigation requirement sugarbeet required irrigation at 0.20 bar tension measured at 25 cm depth of soil. The moisture loss by sugarbeet varies from 950 to 1,010 mm during the entire growth period.

Projected Water Requirements

The total water requirement up to the year AD 2025 for three districts of Uttar Pradesh, namely, Meerut, Muzaffarnagar and Saharanpur comprising the Hindon basin, on the whole, is provided in Table 6. These studies were carried out by the Central Groundwater Board.

Table 6

Estimated Water Use and Projected Requirement for Hindon Basin (million ham/year)

Place	*1980–81*	*1990–91*	*2000–2001*	*2011–2021*
Hindon Basin	0.942	1.128	1.229	1.330

Source: Central Groundwater Board (1984: 37–38).

Thus, it can be seen from the above table that the demand as estimated is showing continuous increase from 0.942 million ham/year in 1980–81 to 1.330 million ham/year in the projected year 2011–2021 for the basin. However, among various demands, irrigation constitutes the major component as the basin is agriculturally developed. A major part of demand for water is made for the variety of crops that are grown in the basin. Table 7 presents total irrigation water requirements for the entire basin. Along with the requirement, cropping intensity, total cropped area and the average consumptive use is also shown. It is, thus, inferred that all the parameters show continuous increase except that of net sown area which remains constant throughout. The total water requirement for irrigation has grown from 0.857 million ham/year in 1980–81 to 1.194 for the projected year 2021, indicate an intensive land and water utilization practice as the demand is on continuous increase (Figure 2).

Figure 2

Total Irrigation Water Requirement for Hindon Basin

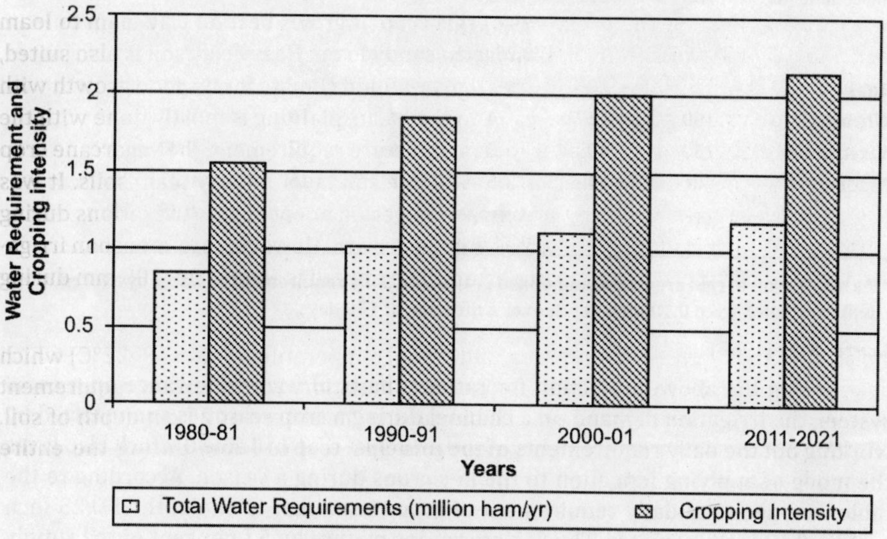

Table 7

Total Irrigation Water Requirement for the Hindon Basin

Year	*Net sown area*	*Cropping intensity*	*Total cropped area (million ha)*	*Average consumptive use (mm)*	*Total requirement (million ham/year)*
1980–81	1.387	1.55	2.143	400	0.857
1990–91	1.387	1.85	2.566	400	1.026
2000–01	1.387	2.00	2.774	400	1.110
2011–21	1.387	2.15	2.982	400	1.194

Source: Central Groundwater Board (1984: 37–38).

Table 8

Daily Water Requirements of Principal Crops for Designing Water Allowance on a Canal System

Crop	*Life of crop in days*	*Frequency in days*	*Number*	*Inches depth each time*	*Total depth in inches*	*Daily requirement in inches depth*	*Total in inches acre*
Kharif							
Rice	105	7	15	3	45	0.42	25.8
Sugarcane	310	14	22	4	88	0.28	14.0
Cotton	230	21	11	4	44	0.19	1701
Maize	105	21	5	4	20	0.19	9.5
Fodders	100	14	7	3	21	8.21	6.3

Cont'd...

Cont'd...

Miscellaneous	100	21	5	4	20	0.20	4.0
			Average: 0.25 inch				
Rabi							
Wheat	160	42	4	4	16	0.10	
Mixed grains	150	49	3	4	12	0.08	
Fodders	70	14	5	3	15	0.21	
			Average: 0.13 inch			0.39	

* As major crop in rabi are wheat and mixed grains, the daily requirement of water by average crop will vary much from 0.10 inch depth over a life span of 150 days.

Source: Sally (1968).

Seeing the above projection for rational basis of water allowance on a canal system, the irrigation demand on a channel during a crop season is summarized by working out the daily requirements of the principal crop in Table 8 which also gives the mode of applying irrigation to the key crops during a season. According to the table, average total daily requirement of crop in summer is on depth of 0.25 inch against 0.13 inch in winter. Thus, winter crops mature on 52 per cent of the supply required by crops in summer. Due to lower winter discharges in canals, the per cent of losses are higher. The actual winter supply at head of the canal is only 66 per cent of its designed supply. Actually, the capacity factor, which is the ratio of mean supply in a canal during period to its designed full capacity, varies from 0.60 to 0.70 inch depth in winter and from 0.90 to 0.95 inch depth in summer.

The peak of water requirement curve could be seen, as maximum demand on one day on the canal supply being 67.7 inch acre. This is equivalent to 5.64 ac ft/daily or 5.64/1.98 = 2.87 cusecs in the fields. This corresponds to a water allowance of 3.60cu per thousand acres at outlet head, allowing 20 per cent loss in water courses. The ratio of average water requirement or average discharge utilized to the capacity of canal is capacity factor for the season. If the channels are run in rotation during winter so that every channel is used for a week after a run of 2 weeks, the capacity factor for rabi will be 0.66. This will allow an average discharge of 3.60 x 0.66 = 2.40 cusecs at the outlet head for rabi crops. This quantity of water available per day in fields will be varying, as given in Table 8 as 0.25 for kharif with the average daily water requirement of rabi crops accepted as 0.13 inch depth/day.

The water requirement of crops during kharif of Indian summer is plotted graphically to have water requirement curve for last column of Table 8. The demand for water starts from nil on first date and becomes full on second date as indicated from watering period mentioned in the table. All these requirements are plotted in Figure 3 and are added up, to obtain a water requirement curve for the season in inch acres in the fields. The peak of water requirement curve could be seen as maximum demand on one day on the canal supply being 67.7 inch acre; this is equivalent to 5.64 ac ft daily or 5.64/1.98 = 2.87 cusecs in the fields. This corresponds to a water allowance of 3.60cu per thousand acres at the outlet head, allowing 20 per cent loss in water courses. The ratio of average water requirement or average discharge utilized to the capacity of canal is the capacity factor for the season. It will be given by ratio of areas ABDE to ABCDEF. If the channel are run in rotation during winter so that every channel is used for week after a run of 2 weeks, the capacity factor for rabi will be 0.66. This will allow an average discharge of 3.60 x 0.66 = 2.40

Figure 3

Daily Water Requirement of Crops During Kharif Crop Season of Indian Summer (inches)

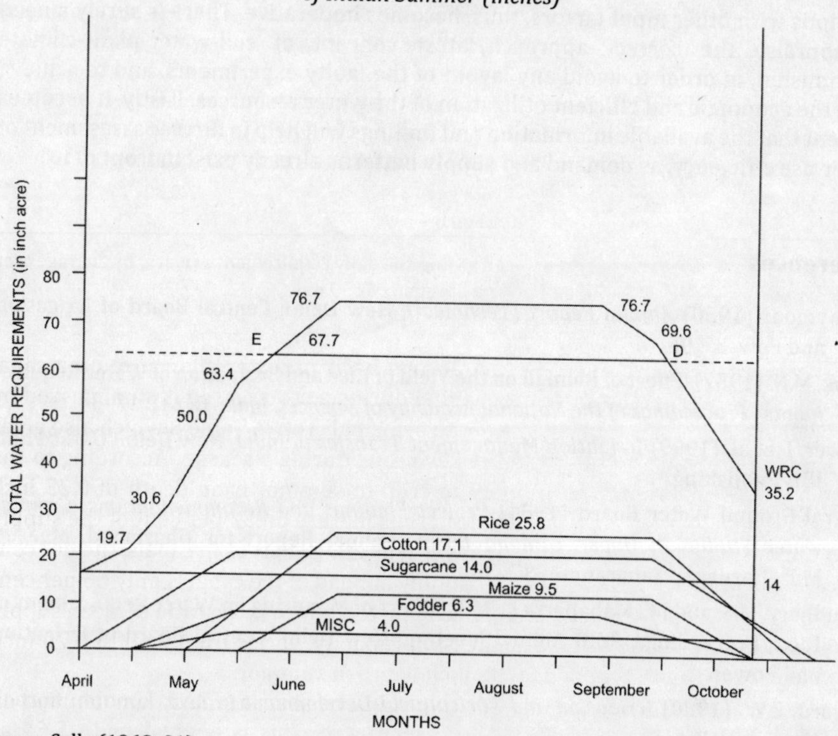

Source: Sally (1968: 91).

cusecs at outlet head for rabi crops. This quantity of water available per day in fields will be varying, as given in Table 8 as 0.25 for kharif with the average daily water requirement of rabi crops accepted as 0.13 inch depth/day.

Thus, water allowances from available canal system in the Hindon basin form a vital portion, in order to meet the specific total requirements of principal crops, for which the existing cropping pattern and required water frequencies for the same are needed to be looked into. This will further help to meet the inefficiencies existing in irrigation water scheduling, and subsequently, the reduction in the crop yields. Thus, it can be concluded that with the very fact of water allowances made in the basin, it will be quite possible to double the production in the irrigated areas, specially with the present availability of the water resources.

Conclusion

The economy of study area is based much on the production and processing of agricultural products. The primary resources, land and water are not the limiting factors for the region's agricultural growth but overexploitation of groundwater resources and inefficient utilization of surface water resources may bring fundamental change in value of both land and water in the basin. As far as the micro-basin water demand in terms of water requirement for different crops that are grown in basin is concerned, it is evident that the demand varies throughout the basin area. Even though considerable and commendable work has been done in the country on various dimensions of water requirements of crops, it has a limited value since, some of the basic data on experimental conditions were not either fully reported or recorded. The precise knowledge of water requirements of different crops, and its relations with other input factors, thus, becomes imperative. There is surely a need to appraise the correct approach/latest concept of soil-water-plant-climate relationship, in order to avoid any layout of the faulty experiments, and to achieve both the economic and efficient utilization of the water resources. Lastly, it becomes evident that the available information and findings will help in further assessment of water use efficiency, as demand and supply patterns already exist in front of us.

References

Anonymous (1950) *Annual Report (Technical)*, New Delhi: Central Board of Irrigation and Power, 406.

Basak, M.N. (1957) 'Effect of Rainfall on the Yield of Rice and Evaluation of Water Requirements', *Proceedings of the National Academy of Sciences, India*, B(23): 17–34.

Brewer, J. et al. (1999) *Irrigation Management Transfer in India*, New Delhi: Oxford and IBH Publishing.

Central Ground Water Board (1984) *Project Findings and Recommendations: Groundwater Studies in Upper Yamuna Basin*, Annual Report for Ghaziabad, Meerut, Muzaffarnagar, Saharanpur, 37–38.

Chaudhary, M.S. and I.C. Mahapatra (1963) 'Effect of Manuring on Water Requirement of Rice', Proceedings, 36th Annual Meeting, New Delhi: Central Board of Irrigation and Power.

Coward, E.W. (1980) *Irrigation and Agricultural Development in Asia*, London: Cornell University Press.

Dastane, N.G. (1970) 'New Concepts in Irrigation: Necessary Changes for New Strategy', *Economic and Political Weekly*, 4(13): 27–30.

Dastane, N.G., M. Singh, S.B. Hukkeri and V.K. Vamadevan (1970) *Review of Work Done on Water Requirements of Crops in India*, Pune: Navbharat Prakashan, 1–2.

Dhawan, B.D. (1989) *Studies in Irrigation and Water Management*, New Delhi: Commonwealth Publishers.

Doddiah, D. (1957) *Studies on Water Requirements of Crops as an Aid to Economic and Optimum Utilisation of Irrigation Supplies of Water with Special Reference to the Studies Carried out in Mysore Engineering Research Station*, New Delhi: Central Board of Irrigation and Power.

Ganguli, P.N. (1952) 'Water Requirement of Rice Plant', Proceedings, 9th Meeting, Crop Soils, Central Board of Agriculture, India.

Gupta, S.N. and A.P. Bhattacharya (1963) 'Water Requirement of Rice: A Principal Crop of Uttar Pradesh', Proceedings, 36th Annual Meeting, New Delhi: Central Board of Irrigation and Power.

Hiranandani, M.G. (1953) *Duty of Irrigation Water Proposed to be Adopted for Various Crops in Delta Area of Mahanadi River*, New Delhi: Central Board of Irrigation and Power.

Hooja, Rakesh (2006) *Management of Water for Agriculture*, Jaipur and New Delhi: Rawat Publications.

Iyer, R.R. (2003) *Water: Perspectives, Issues and Concerns*, New Delhi: Sage Publications.

Kumar, P. (1977) *Economies of Water Management*, New Delhi: Heritage Publishers.

Leather, J.W. (1911) 'Water Requirements of Crops in India', *Memoirs of the Department of Agriculture in India*, 1: 133–134 and 205–281.

Malik, S.N. and K.L. Das (1968) 'Preliminary Study on Water Requirement of Crops in Hirakund Irrigated Area', Proceedings of Symposium on Water Management, Udaipur, 107–109.

Merrett, Stephen (2002) *Water for Agriculture*, London: Spon Press.

Mukherjee, B.K. and S.C. Chatterjee (1957) *Review of Work Done on Water Requirements of Crops in India*, New Delhi: ICAR.

Nagarajan, R. (2006) *Water: Conservation, Use and Management for Semi-Arid Region*, New Delhi: Capital Publishing Company.

Pandey, H.N. (1963) 'A Study of Effect of Light Irrigation on the Grain and Straw Yield of Late "Aman" Paddy', Proceedings, 36th Annual Meeting, New Delhi: Central Board of Irrigation and Power.

Patil, N.P. (1963) 'Optimum Utilisation of Water for Irrigated Crops in Red Soil Areas of Bangalore District, Mysore State', Proceedings of Symposium, New Delhi: Central Board of Irrigation and Power.

Penman, H.L. (1948) 'Natural Evaporation from Open Water, Bare Soil and Grass Proceedings', *Proceedings of the Royal Society of London*, 193A: 12–45.

Ramiah, K. and M.N. Vachhani (1951) 'Farming Under Irrigation', *Indian Journal of Power and River Valley Development*, 1: 5–8.

Rao, N.M.B.V. (1951) 'Water Requirements of Crops with Special Reference to Rice', *Agriculture Journal*, 38: 539–549.

Rege, R.D. (1937) 'Review Work on Water Requirement of Crops in India with Suggestions for Future', Proceedings, 2nd Meeting, Crops and Soiling Board, Agriculture and Animal Husbandry, India, 30.

Sally, H.L. (1968) *Irrigation Planning for Intensive Cultivation*, New Delhi: Asia Publishing House.

Sharma, H.C. and S.C. Upadhyay (1973) 'A Note on Irrigation Requirement of Maize', *Indian Journal of Agronomics*, 18: 220–221.

Singh, B.N., B.R. Singh and K. Singh (1985) 'Investigations into the Water Requirements of Crops Plants', *Proceedings of Indian Academy of Science*, B(1): 471–495.

Singh, D. (1945) 'Water Requirement of Crops', Proceedings, Crops and Soil Wing, Board of Agriculture and Animal Husbandry, India, 166–168.

Singh, D. and S.D. Nijhawan (1951) *Water Requirement of Crops*, Technical Annual Report, New Delhi: Central Board of Irrigation and Power, 976–977.

Talathi, R.P. and D.D. Gopani (1963) 'Optimum Requirement and Utilisation of Water for Irrigated Crops in Gujarat State', Proceedings of Symposium on Optimum Requirement and Utilisation of Water for Irrigated Crops, New Delhi: Central Board of Irrigation and Power.

Thornthwaite, W. (1948) 'An Approach Towards a Rational Classification of Climate', *Geographical Review*, 38(1): 55–94.

Yadav, R.N. (2007) 'Consequences of Groundwater Depletion in Southwest Haryana: A Study of Bhankri Village', *Geographical Review of India*, 69(1): 88–94.

9

The Enigma of Flood and Flood Forecasting Techniques

A Saga of Bihar

SHWETA RANI

This study will examine and unravel the magnitude and frequency of floods for the major river basins in Bihar. In particular, the study intends to make a comparative analysis of the changes in hydrologic regime in terms of trends and severity of floods in the Gandak and Kosi river systems from 1990–2002. Flooding represents a major risk to riverside populations and floodplains, in addition to causing substantial impacts on the environment, including aquatic fauna and flora, bank erosion and other aspects. Although it is a natural phenomenon, flooding is often exacerbated by the presence of riverside infrastructures – such as dams, piers, and landing wharves and by poor development practices including riverside "development", excessive clearing, encroachment upon waterways, dredging, which may cause changes in the hydrological balance of the waterways involved (Brookes, 1985; Nolan and Marron, 1995). A number of researchers have studied the physical, sedimentological and biological impact of flooding on the receiving environment (Irvine and Drake, 1987; Kochel, 1988; Friedman et al., 1996; Asselman and Middelkoop, 1998; Palik et al., 1999). Meanwhile, other researchers have investigated anthropogenic factors and the impact of urban development on changes to the river system and increased flooding (Hollis, 1975; Roberts, 1989; Costa and O'Connor, 1995; Awadallah et al., 1999).

Influenced by the precipitation pattern and orography, water resources in India show a high spatial variability. About 62 per cent (1,202 km^3) of annual water availability in India is generated in the Ganges, Brahmaputra and Meghna river systems, which accounts for 33 per cent of the geographical area of the country. With an approximate length of 2,510 km, the Ganga river system drains a total area of 9,07,000 square km in India. The high annual peak discharge (in cumecs)[1] and the load of heavy silt carried by the tributaries of river Ganga causes flooding during the monsoons, especially in the North Bihar plains.

The State of Bihar, in India is blessed with the two Hindu mythological holy rivers, viz., Alaknanda and Bhagirathi. They unite at Devprayag and the combined river is known as the mighty Ganges (see Figure 1). As many as 17 tributaries join it, both on the left and right bank. Being the master drain of Ganga basin, this river

Figure 1

River Basins of Bihar

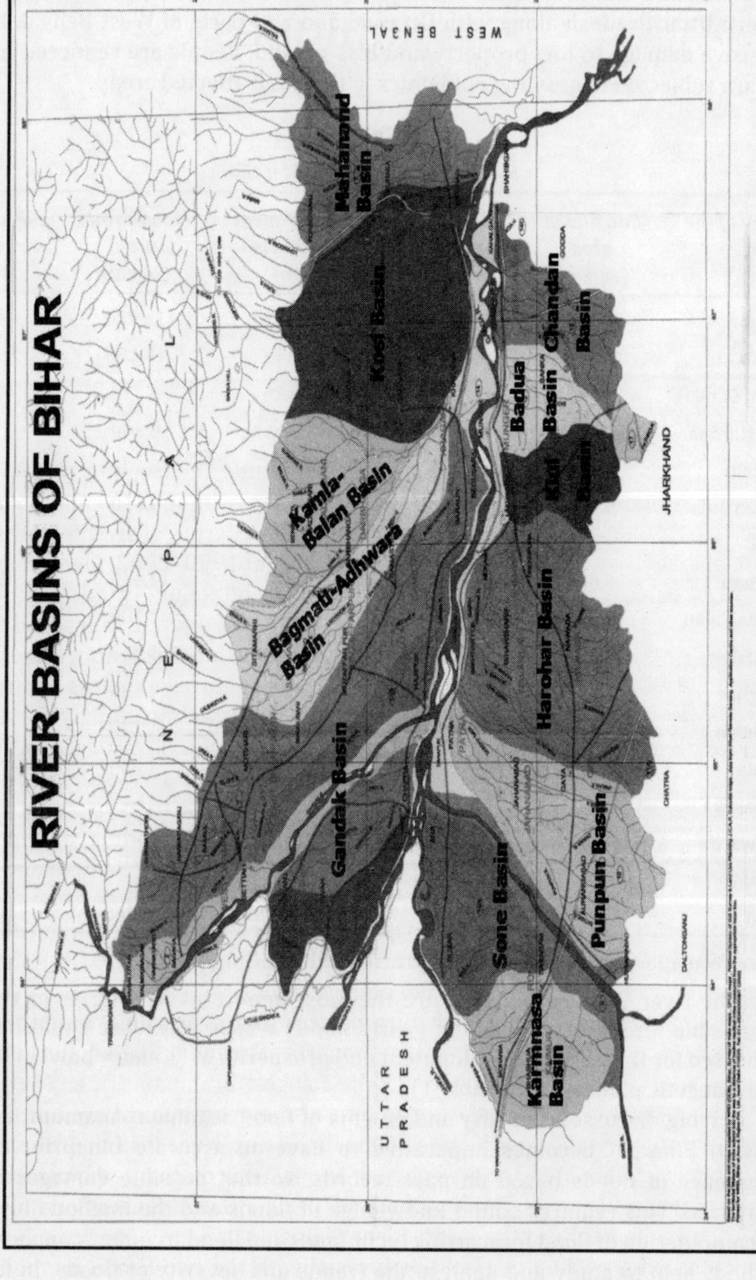

Source: Water Resource Department, Government of Bihar.

drains 26 per cent of area in India and is divided into 23 river systems (Ganga Flood Control Commission (Patna), Annual Report 2010–11). The left bank tributaries of Ganga originate in the high peaks of Himalayas flowing at a very high velocity with deep undercutting. In the process they carry with them huge amount of silts, loads and sediments and are chiefly responsible for floods in northern plains of Bihar, eastern Uttar Pradesh along with Uttarakhand and parts of West Bengal. It causes extensive damage to life, property and loss of land. People are rendered homeless and are subjected to growing epidemics in the flood affected areas.

Table 1

River Basins in Bihar: At a Glance

Name of the basin	*Catchment area (sq km)*	*Length of river in Bihar (km)*	*Embankment constructed (km)*	*Flood-prone area (sq km)*	*Protected area (sq km)*
Ganga	19,322	445	596.92	12,920	4,300
Kosi	11,410	260	387.51	10,150	9,300
Burhi Gandak	9,601	320	704.26	8,210	4,010
Kiul Harohar	17,225	—	14	6,340	NIL
Punpun	9,026	235	37.62	6,130	260
Mahananda	6,150	376	225.33	5,150	1,210
Sone	15,820	202	59.54	3,700	210
Bagmati	6,500	394	400.79	4,440	3,170
Kamla Balan	4,488	120	184.9	3,700	2,810
Gandak	4,188	260	511.66	3,350	3,350
Ghaghra	2,995	83	132.9	2,530	790
Chandan	4,093	118	83.18	1,130	80
Badua	2,215	130	NIL	1,050	NIL
Lalbakeya	—	—	54.35	—	—
Adhwara	—	—	181.5	—	—
Bhuthi	—	—	54.7	—	—
Total	—	—	3629.16	68,800	29,490

Source: Water Resource Department, Government of Bihar.

The river Gandak and Kosi are the most important tributaries of the Ganga responsible for the recurrence of yearly floods which otherwise could have been harnessed for the growth, development and prosperity of 'granary bowl of India' i.e., Indo-Gangetic plains (refer Table 1).

Having discussed, the fury and enigma of flood, leading to mammoth devastations in Bihar, it becomes imperative to have an accurate blueprint of future occurrence of floods based on past records; so that possible damages could be minimized. This requires sound knowledge of floods and the methods involved in the computation of flood forecasting techniques and flood frequency analysis. These methods help to study and analyse the trends and severity of floods. In fact, such non-structural measures are a must to minimize the impacts of short-term and long-term damages to human life, crop, public and private property, animals and the community as a whole.

A flood frequency analysis[2] using flood forecasting techniques has been attempted for the tributaries of river Ganga in the plains of Bihar on the basis of gauge/discharge data available from Central Water Commission, Government of India for the periods between 1990 and 2002. The technique of dealing with the run-off data measured at a particular site across a river is known as flood frequency analysis. This revered technique helps to measure only the peak discharge for a particular frequency or return period rather than the hydrograph. Out of the 32 flood forecasting and guage/discharge sites in Bihar, the major discharge sites listed are Birpur, Barahshetra, Basua, Kurshella and Baltara on river Kosi; and Dumariyaghat, Lalganj, Triveni and Rewaghat on river Gandak. Out of these important sites, 4 sites have been chosen, 2 each on river Gandak and Kosi to study and analyse the frequency of floods be facing the state.

History of Flood Forecasting and Warning Techniques

Flood Forecasting activities in India made a beginning in a scientific manner in 1958 when the erstwhile Central Water and Power Commission (CW&PC) set up a Flood Forecasting Unit (FFU) for issuing flood warnings for the river Yamuna at the National Capital, Delhi. Since then, it has extended to cover almost all major flood prone inter-State river basins of India with 175 flood forecasting stations across 9 major river systems spread over 15 states (CWC, Ministry of Water Resources, 2009–10).

Objectives of the Study

In the light of preceding discussion, the main objective of the research paper is:

1. To explore and unravel the magnitude and frequency of floods for 13 years (1990–2002) through techniques of Weibull's Plotting Positions.
2. To make a comparative analysis of the trend and severity of floods for the Gandak and Kosi river systems.

Database

Having determined the purpose and objectives of the study, information is sought on various sources of database within the research framework. The present research is solely based on information sought from secondary database. The hydro-meteorological data of annual peak rainfall discharge for 13 years from 1990–2002 has been collected from three important sources namely,

- Water Resources Department, Government of Bihar.
- Central Water Commission, Patna.
- Ganga Flood Control Commission, Patna.

In fact, the peak discharge data has been collected at two sites each on river Gandak and river Kosi in Bihar. The chosen sites are Dumariaghat and Triveni, i.e., Valmikinagar on river Gandak and Baltara and Birpur on river Kosi respectively. While Dumariaghat and Baltara are downstream sites, Triveni and Birpur are identified as upstream sites.

Techniques of Analysis

Based on preceding sources of data, a comparative hydrological analysis has been done for the two high intensity flood causing rivers in Bihar, i.e., river Gandak and river Kosi respectively. In fact, the induced flood related damage associated with these two rivers is assessed to be severe and devastating. For the purpose of study, 13 years annual peak rainfall discharge data has been collected at four discharge sites and analysed for the calculation of flood frequency and return period (5years, 7 years, 10 years and 17 years) to estimate the past flood occurrence and their intensity.

Flood forecasting method is treated and recognized as one of the most important, reliable and cost-effective non-structural measures for flood management initiated by Central Water Commission (CWC) in 1958. Further insight into flood frequency analysis is provided by the computation of 'return period' that provides the most efficient formula for computing plotting positions for unspecified distributions. The method involved in the plotting of distribution is to rank the data in descending order of their magnitude. It is commonly referred to as Weibull's plotting positions and is illustrated by the equation:

$$P = m/n+1$$

Where, m is data ranked from lowest to highest (ascending order), P is an estimate of the probability of values being equal to or less the ranked value. For the probabilities expressed in percentages, the value of P becomes:

$$P = (m/n+1) \times 100$$

For analysis of flood frequency, the population is taken as the annual maximum flood occurring at a location on a river (called the site). In fact, the recorded flood peak values observed for a period of 13 years are only a sample of the total population. Since, we assume that the sample is representative of the population, therefore it is expected that recurrent flood of similar nature and intensity is likely to continue and return in the coming years. Thus, the average number of years during which a flood of a given magnitude (m) is likely to return is referred to as 'recurrence interval' or 'return period' and is denoted as,

$$T = (N+1)/m$$

T is N+1 year for the highest flood and T is 1-year for the lowest flood. In fact, the flood frequencies in terms of return years T for every mth rank in the data is scaled and plotted along the abscissa of a semi-logarithmic graph paper (starting with common logarithmic value 1) with the discharge along the ordinate. On the horizontal axis on the top of this graph the corresponding precent probability values, p in per cent are plotted. Thus, the interpolation of the relative frequency with discharge done on probability graph paper, and based on this graph prediction can also be made with reasonable accuracy.

Hence, the analysis of flood frequency and the flood forecasting techniques becomes imperative and thus, provides a blueprint to minimize the devastations caused by flood in the future. At the same time, it should be noted that the data for annual peak discharge at a particular site is independent of each other and random in nature.

Spatio-Temporal Analysis of Flood Frequency: Kosi and Gandak River Systems

The headwaters of the Kosi and Gandak river lie in the Tethyan Sedimentary Series of the Tibetan Plateau, which lies within the rain shadow of the Higher Himalaya (Singh et al., 2008). With regard to the peak discharge, data obtained from Central Water Commission proves to be significant from year to year for the two major rivers of Bihar, i.e., Kosi and Gandak.

Table 2

Catchment Area Sites on at River Kosi and River Gandak

Name of sites	*River systems*	*Area (square km)*
Baltara	Kosi	88,480
Birpur		50,710
Dumariaghat	Gandak	42,981
Triveni		37,845

Source: Central Water Commission, Patna and Water Resource Department, Government of Bihar.

Flooding in Kosi River

The river Kosi originates at an altitude of over 7,000 m above MSL in the Himalayas. The upper catchment of the river system lies in Nepal and Tibet. In fact, two of the highest peaks in the world namely, the Mount Everest (8,848 m) and the Kanchenjunga (8,598 m) lies in the Kosi catchment area. With a total length of about 260 kms in the state, the river drains about 11,410 sq km area in Bihar which is 15.4 per cent of the total drainage area of Kosi basin in India. In plains of Bihar, the river has two important right bank tributaries; these are the Bagmati and the Kamla Balan. The other tributaries worth mentioning on the right bank are the Trijuga and the Butahi Balan. It is the lower catchment area of the river along with its tributaries (mostly lying in the state of Bihar) that is severely affected by floods every year.

The Kosi river is known as the "Sorrow of Bihar" as the annual floods affect about 21,000 km^2 (8,100 sq mi) of fertile agricultural lands thereby disturbing the rural economy of Bihar (Sharma, 1996; Wells and Dorr, 1987). The Kosi has an average water flow (*discharge*) of 2,166 cubic metres per second (76,500 cu ft/s) with the greatest recorded flood recorded of the order being 24,200 m^3/s (8,50,000 cu ft/s) on 24 August 1954. In lieu to flood control measure Kosi barrage has been constructed to overcome the maximum peak discharge of 27,014 m^3/s (9,54,000 cu ft/s).

Geographically speaking, the bed slopes and nature of sandy rocks of the river course are crucial factors responsible for land degradation and heavy silt concentration in the run-off. The river bed slope of the Kosi ranges from 5 to 1 foot per mile up to its middle reaches, and less than one foot per mile in its tail end near its confluence with the Ganga at Kursella (Das, 1967). There are undulations and innumerable depressions called "Chaurs", where water remains accumulated for most part of the year.

Shifting Regime of the Kosi River

The river Kosi is well known for profuse branching into many interlacing channels in its course. It does not remain static in a fixed channel for a long time. Since ancient times, it has been oscillating over a vast tract of North Bihar. Due to extensive soil erosion and landslides mostly induced in the high rainfall regions of upper Himalayan ranges and Shiwalik ranges, the river carries one of the highest silt load in the entire Indian subcontinent (i.e., 95 MCM/year). Such a heavy silt load with chocked river mouth causes the river to take acute sharp bends thereby depositing silt at every turn of meander[3] and thus, laterally shifts. In fact, river Kosi is known for its highly meandering course and excessive lateral shift.

With regard to the oscillating character of river Kosi, the most common and widely accepted explanation given by Das (1968) deserves special attention. According to these authors, siltation, rapid water discharge, and bed slopes of the

Kosi flood plain, are responsible for ever shifting nature of the river. In addition to these, some of the geomorphic characters of the Kosi catchment basin, viz., smallest width of the valley, steep sides, absence of wide basins (pockets), anticlinal cracks, fissures and joints in the rocks, and above all, the excessive deforestation and rainfall have a cumulative impact on heavy sediment loads (boulders, pebbles, shingles, sands, silt, big trees, etc.) in the flood waters (Singh, 1986).

Hydrological Analysis and Observations on Kosi River (1995–2002)

High discharge of the rivers is a regular and ongoing phenomenon chiefly responsible for the recurring threat of flood devastations in Bihar. Such a high discharge of the rivers exceeding the carrying capacity of the embankments results due to reduction in the velocity of rivers as they enter the plains in Bihar. A reduction in the velocity also reduces the carrying capacity of silt, load and sediments by the rivers. Hence, silt starts depositing on the river beds causing a rise in the river bed and ultimately leading to bank erosion. Even at times, due to heavy silt deposition, the mouth of the river gets blocked and chocked finding alternate routes thereby flooding new areas. This phenomenon is aggravated by the rise in water level due to high intensity rainfall during monsoonal season in the Terai regions of Himalayas. The excessive water in the river due to the two phenomenons discussed above, thus, overtops the existing banks, embankments and barrages to engulf the surrounding basin area causing floods. It leads to inundation of villages situated within the flood plains of the rivers.

With regard to the recurrent and ongoing floods in Kosi river, the CWC has maintained five hydrological observation sites namely Birpur, Barahkshetra, Basua, Kursela and Baltara. While, Birpur is an upstream site of the river; Baltara lies very far down the main channel belt, a few kilometres above the confluence with the Ganga. In between the two sites, at Kursela, river Kosi takes an eastward direction and has a single defined channel which joins the river Ganga in Katihar district of Bihar.

Data pertaining to annual peak discharge of river Kosi at Birpur and Baltara has been collected. However, it should be noted that out of the 13 years, the peak discharge data is available only for 10 Years (1993–2002) for Baltara station and 11 years (1982–1992) for Birpur site. Hence, the trend, magnitude and frequency of floods are analysed for these 8 years for Baltara and Birpur sites respectively in Kosi river and the results are both discussed and tabulated below.

Figure 2 depicts the variations observed in the peak discharge data for Baltara and Birpur. However, it should be noticed that there is a data gap between 1990 and 1992 for Baltara. From 1993 onwards, the trend in the peak discharge of river Gandak is discernible by means of line graph (see Figure 2a). The highest peak discharge of 10,350 cumecs is recorded in 1998.

Figure 2(b) represents the trend for flood hazard during 1982–2002[4] for the upstream site of Birpur. Differing with the preceding peak discharge recorded for Baltara, the maximum discharge observed for the upstream site of Birpur is as high as 14,833 cumecs (recognized as the annual maximum discharge till date). In fact, the study area has been challenged three times with high flood hazard during the years 1986, 1992 and 1982 in order of flood magnitudes recorded.

Table 3 reveals that the highest discharge for Baltara has a recurrent interval of 11 years with 9 per cent probability. Maximum peak discharge for Birpur is 8.33 per cent probable to return in the next 12 years. Contrary to this, the low intensity floods have very quick and successive return period; almost once every year with more than 90 per cent probability. A low peak discharge well below 7,755 cumecs for Baltara and those below 8,150 cumecs in Birpur presents the classis case to this.

Figure 2

Variations in Peak Discharge Through the Years in Kosi River

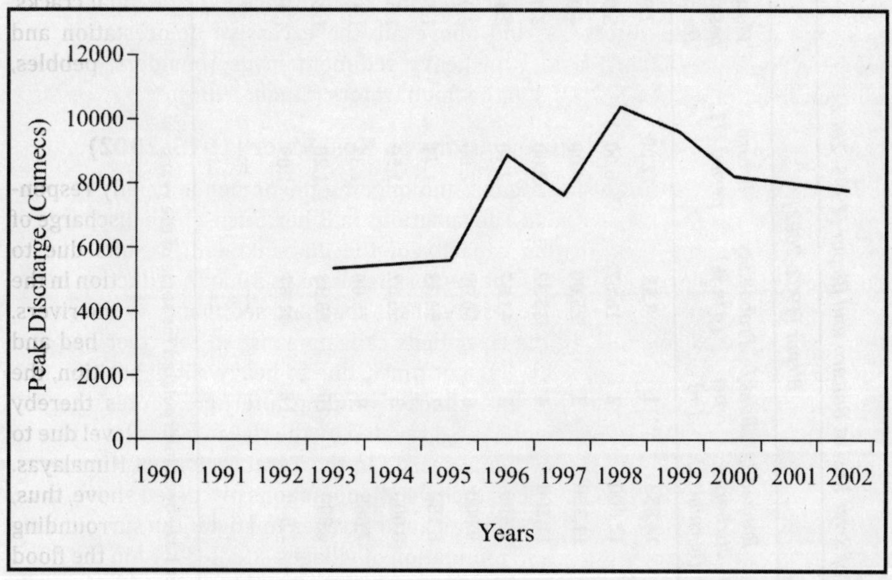

(a) Baltara (Downstream): 1990–2002.

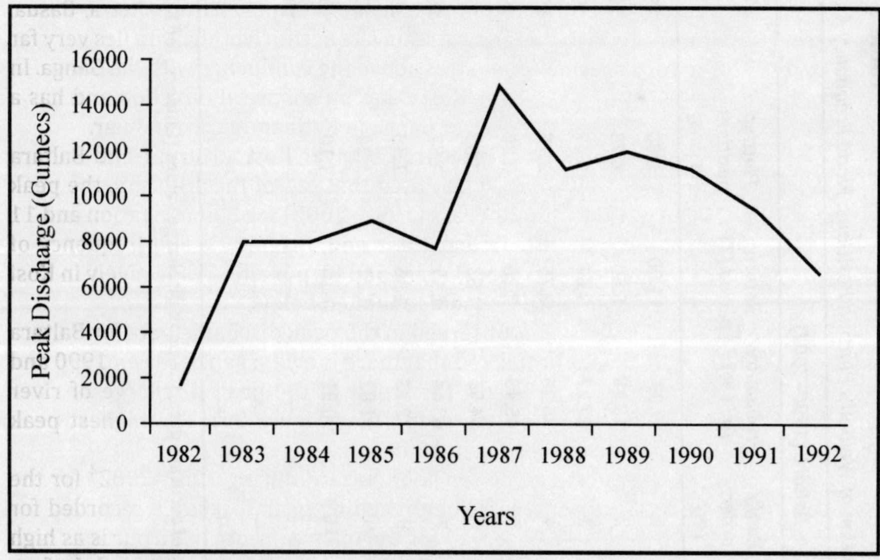

(b) Birpur (Upstream): 1982–1992.

The results derived in Table 3 is represented through the method of scatter diagram (see Figure 3) with the peak discharge data plotted on ordinates (y-axis) and the corresponding return years on the abscissa (x-axis). Semi-log graph has been purposely used to depict return period to achieve a new linear pattern in trends. It is an observed fact that flood of a given magnitude occurred after a definite interval. Majority of the low intensity floods have a higher probability to return with low

Table 3

Computation of Weibull's Plotting Positions: Flood Frequency Analysis of River Kosi at Baltara and Birpur (1995–2002)

Baltara (1990–2002)						Birpur (1982–2002)					
Year	*Ranked discharge (in cumecs)*	*Rank/ order (m)*	*Probability (p in %)*	*Return period (T)*	*Plotting positions (in cms)*	*Year*	*Ranked discharge (in cumecs)*	*Rank/ order (m)*	*Probability (p in %)*	*Return period (T)*	*Plotting positions (in cms)*
1998	10,350	1	9.09	11.00	6.80	1987	14,833	1	8.33	12.00	7.00
1999	9,600	2	18.18	5.50	4.75	1989	12,000	2	16.67	6.00	5.00
1996	8,865	3	27.27	3.67	3.67	1988	11,350	3	25.00	4.00	4.00
2000	8,200	4	36.36	2.75	2.75	1990	11,200	4	33.33	3.00	3.00
2001	7,900	5	45.45	2.20	2.20	1991	9,400	5	41.67	2.40	2.40
2002	7,755	6	54.55	1.83	1.83	1985	9,000	6	50.00	2.00	2.00
1997	7,600	7	63.64	1.57	1.57	1984	8,150	7	58.33	1.71	1.71
1995	5,560	8	72.73	1.38	1.38	1983	8,000	8	66.67	1.50	1.50
1994	5,430	9	81.82	1.22	1.22	1986	7,865	9	75.00	1.33	1.33
1993	5,300	10	90.91	1.10	1.10	1992	6,800	10	83.33	1.20	1.20
1990	N.A.	—	—	—	—	1982	1,800	11	91.67	1.09	1.09
1991	N.A.	—	—	—	—	—	—	—	—	—	—
1992	N.A.	—	—	—	—	—	—	—	—	—	—

Note: Due to non-availability of accurate data, the peak discharge values (Cumecs) for Kosi river have been interpolated for some of the years.

Figure 3

Flood Frequency Analysis (peak discharge values plotted against return period) on Probability Scale in Kosi River (1995–2002)

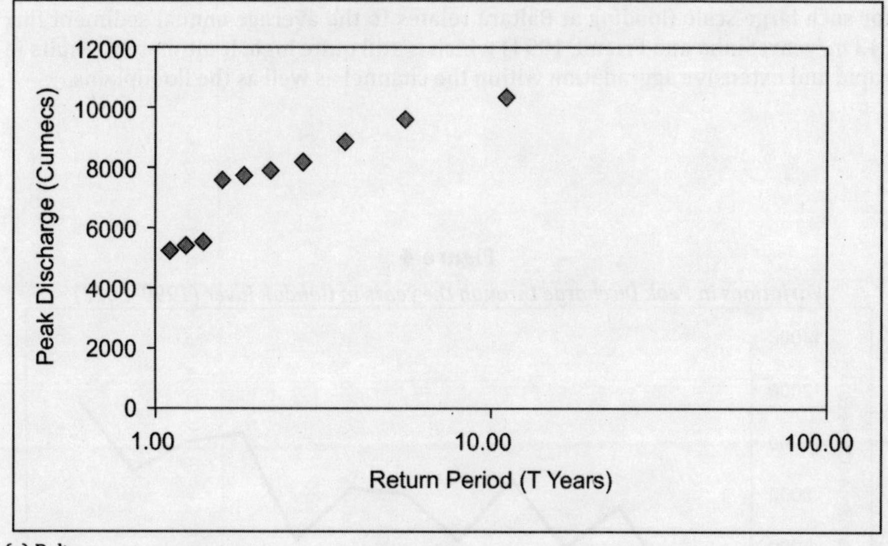

(a) Baltara.

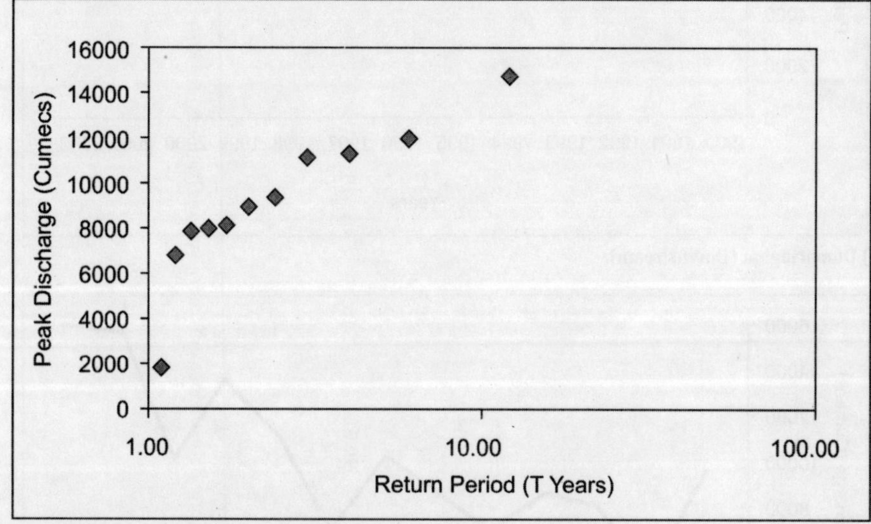

(b) Birpur.

recurrence interval. Hence, it is inferred that there exists a reciprocal relationship between the probability of occurrence of floods (in %) and the return period (T).

Based on preceding discussions on the hydraulic regime of river Kosi, it is established that floods are a natural phenomenon and they play a vital role in maintaining the river form. It is observed that the upstream stations of Birpur (along with Barahkshetra) show higher peak discharges than that at the downstream station (Baltara) for the approximately similar return period. The possible reasons for this are the diversion of water for irrigation (East Kosi Canal System and Chatra Canal System) and also the embanking of the river, which prevents the tributaries from joining the Kosi (Development Research on Bihar, 2000–2010). It is observed that during the periods while Birpur station has not seen any major floods; Baltara has recorded two significantly large floods in 1998 and 1999. The main reason cited for such large scale flooding at Baltara relates to the average annual sediment flux (43 m/year; Sinha and Friend, 1994) which is still quite high. It ultimately results in rapid and extensive aggradation within the channel as well as the floodplains.

Figure 4

Variations in Peak Discharge through the years in Gandak River (1990–2012)

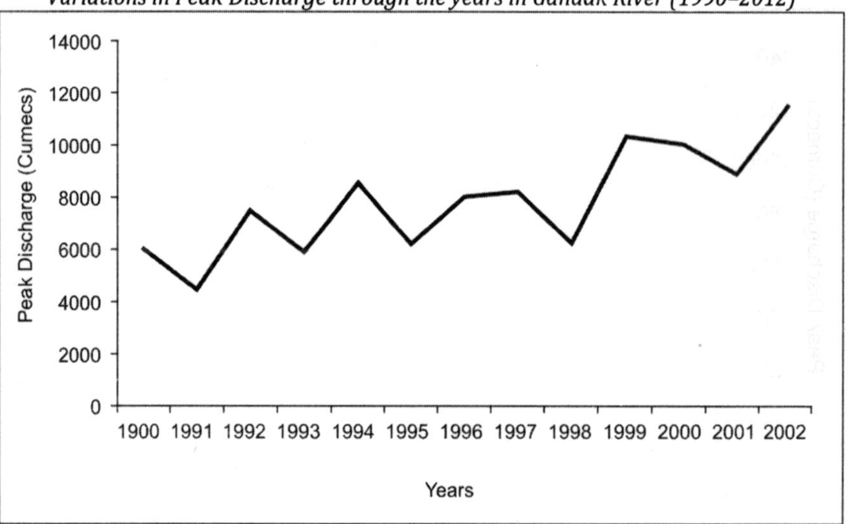

(a) Dumariaghat (Downstream).

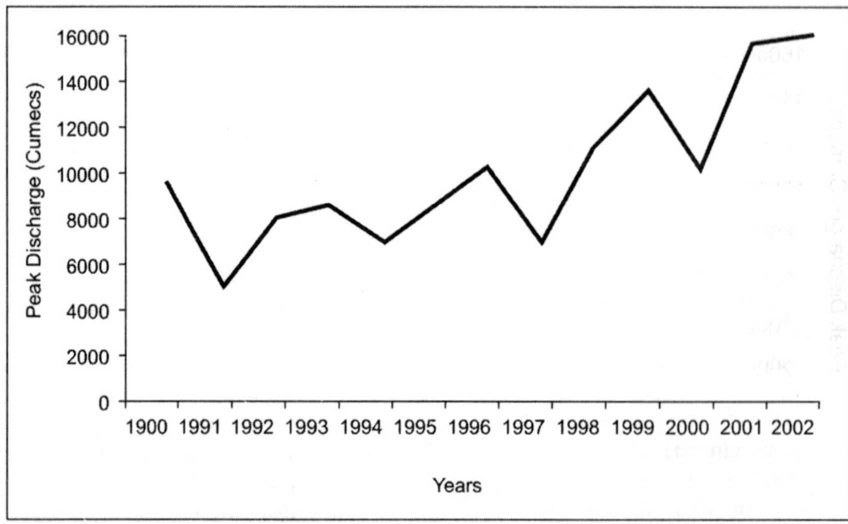

(b) Triveni (Upstream).

Hydrological Analysis and Observations on Gandak River (1990–2002)

The Gandak river originates from the Nhumbine Himal Glacier at the Tibet border, and is fed by seven Himalayan tributaries (Daraudi, Seti, Madi, Kali, Marsyandi, Budhi and Trisuli). The Gandak then flows south eventually to its confluence with the river Ganga at Triveni.

Compared to Kosi, Gandak is less migratory and avulsive. It is supposed to be more stable than Kosi with a significantly slower rate of migration. Mohindra et al. (1992) used aerial photography and soil chronoassociation to determine a net 80

Figure 5

Flood Frequency Analysis (peak discharge values plotted against return period) on Probability Scale in Gandak River (1992–2012)

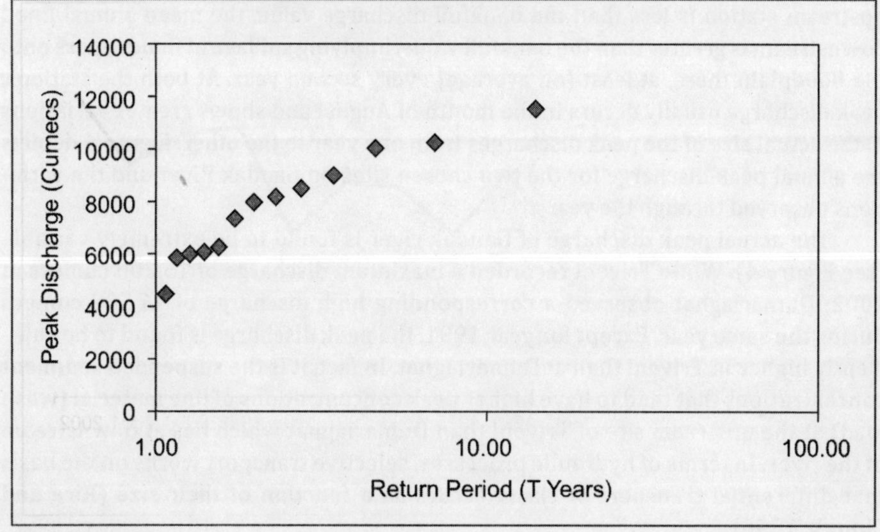

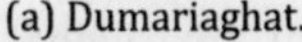

(a) Dumariaghat.

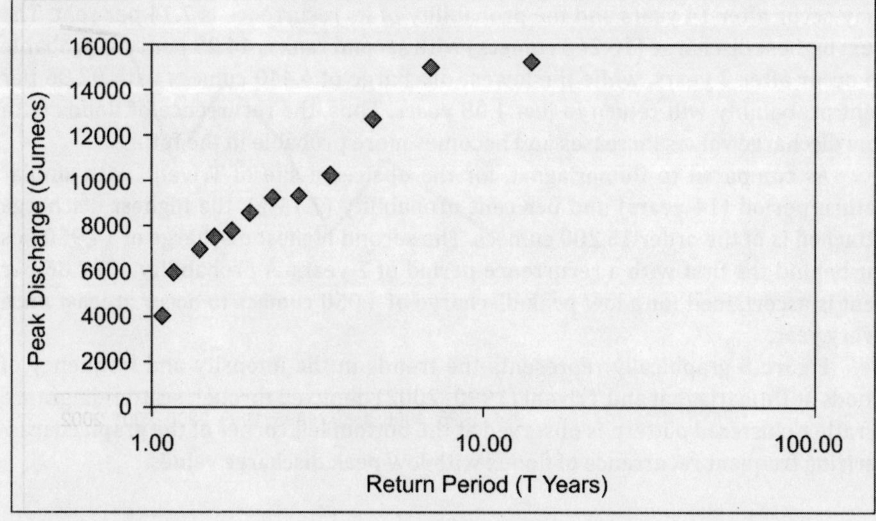

(b) Triveni.

km eastward migration of the Gandak river over its mega fan surface in the last 5,000 years.

There are seven hydrological observation sites maintained by CWC on the Gandak. All these sites are located on the main-stem river. Out of the seven sites, discharge observation and silt analysis are being observed at three sites, namely Triveni, Durmariaghat and Lalganj. In fact, Triveni (Valmikinagar) is the first site located in India near Indo-Nepal border. The word Triveni derived its name from the confluence of three major tributaries of Kosi river, viz., Tamur, Arun and Sun Kosi, from where they are called Sapta Kosi meaning seven rivers. After flowing through the 'Chatra Gorge', the Sapta Kosi is controlled by the Koshi barrage before it drains into the Gangetic plain (Nepal, 2012).

And it is also interesting to note that, whereas the mean annual flood at the upstream station is less than the bankfull discharge value, the mean annual flood downstream is greater than the bankfull value, implying spillage of floodwaters onto the floodplain there, at least (on average) every second year. At both the stations, peak discharge usually occurs in the month of August and shows greater variations in the actual size of the peak discharges from one year to the other. Figure 4 depicts the annual peak discharge for the two chosen sites on Gandak River and the variations observed through the years.

The actual peak discharge of Gandak river is found to be extremely variable (see Figure 4). While Triveni recorded a maximum discharge of 15,200 cumecs in 2002; Dumariaghat observed a corresponding high discharge of 11,500 cumecs during the same year. Except for year 1991, the peak discharge is found to be sufficiently higher in Triveni than at Dumariaghat. In fact, it is the suspended sediment concentrations that tend to have higher peak concentrations of fine material (wash load) at the upstream site of Triveni than Dumariaghat which lies at downstream of the river. In terms of hydraulic processes, selective transport works on the basis that differential transport of clasts occurs as a function of their size (Rice and Church, 1996).

Table 4 reveals that the maximum discharge of 11,500 cumecs for Dumariaghat may occur after 14 years and the probability of its recurrence is 7.14 per cent. The next highest discharge (10,260 cumecs) with second rank is 14.29 per cent probable to occur after 7 years, while the lowest discharge of 4,440 cumecs with 92.86 per cent probability will return in just 1.08 years. Thus, the recurrence of floods with low discharge values increases and becomes more probable in the future.

As compared to Dumariaghat, for the upstream site of Triveni, with similar return period (14 years) and per cent probability (7.14%), the highest discharge attached is of the order 15,200 cumecs. The second highest discharge of 14,950 lies far behind the first with a recurrence period of 7 years. A probability of 92.86 per cent is ascertained for a low peak discharge of 4,050 cumecs to occur at least once every year.

Figure 5 graphically represents the trends in the intensity and frequency of floods at Dumariaghat and Triveni (1990–2002) depicted through scatter diagrams. A rather clustered pattern is observed at the bottom left corner of the graph characterizing frequent recurrence of floods with low peak discharge values.

Table 4

Computation of Weibull's Plotting Positions: Flood Frequency Analysis of River Gandak at Dumariaghat and Triveni (1990–2002)

Dumariyaghat						Triveni					
Year	Ranked Discharge (in Cumecs)	Rank/ Order (m)	Probability (p in %)	Return Period (T)	Plotting Positions (in cms)	Year	Ranked Discharge (in Cumecs)	Rank/ Order (m)	Probability (p in %)	Return Period (T)	Plotting Positions (in cms)
2002	11,500	1	7.14	14.00	7.50	2002	15,200	1	7.14	14.00	7.50
1999	10,260	2	14.29	7.00	5.50	2001	14,950	2	14.29	7.00	5.50
2000	10,000	3	21.43	4.67	4.35	1999	12,700	3	21.43	4.67	4.35
2001	9,000	4	28.57	3.50	3.50	1998	10,220	4	28.57	3.50	3.50
1994	8,500	5	35.71	2.80	2.80	2000	9,290	5	35.71	2.80	2.80
1997	8,200	6	42.86	2.33	2.33	1996	9,200	6	42.86	2.33	2.33
1996	8,000	7	50.00	2.00	2.00	1990	8,550	7	50.00	2.00	2.00
1992	7,350	8	57.14	1.75	1.75	1995	7,750	8	57.14	1.75	1.75
1995	6,250	9	64.29	1.56	1.56	1993	7,500	9	64.29	1.56	1.56
1998	6,000	10	71.43	1.40	1.40	1992	6,950	10	71.43	1.40	1.40
1990	5,965	11	78.57	1.27	1.27	1997	5,960	12	85.71	1.17	1.27
1993	5,850	12	85.71	1.17	1.17	1994	5,913	12	85.71	1.17	1.17
1991	4,440	13	92.86	1.08	1.08	1991	4,050	13	92.86	1.08	1.08

Figure 6

Flood Situation in Bihar (as on 11th September, 2013)

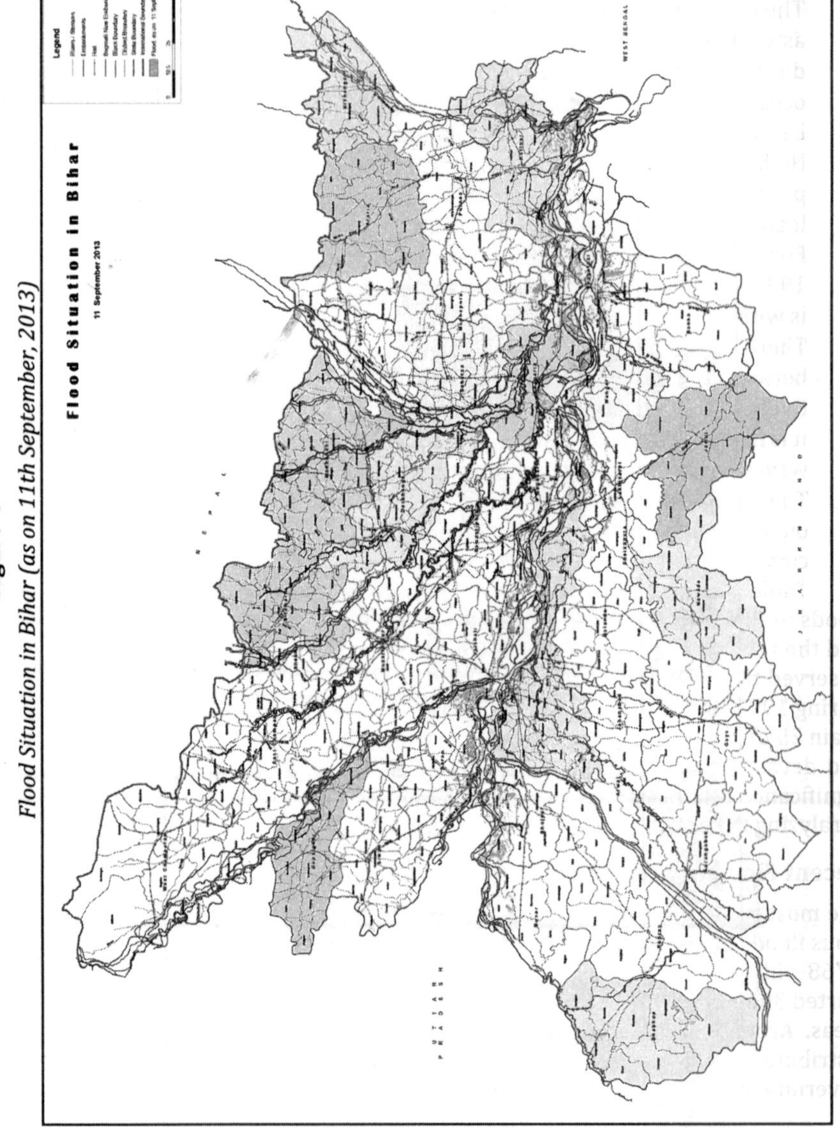

Source: Flood Management Information System, Water Resource Department, Bihar.

Flooding in Gandak River System Versus Kosi River System

Flood frequency analysis of Gandak and Kosi river systems yield seven important observations. The findings are illustrated as:

1. The actual size of peak discharge is extremely variable from year to year both at the Batara and Birpur sites on Kosi River and Dumarighat and Triveni sites on Gandak River.
2. The maximum peak discharge of 15,200 cumecs is recorded at Triveni in 2002 as compared to Dumariaghat (11,500 cumecs) during the same period. High discharges in the range of 10,000–15,500 cumecs were recorded on four occasions, i.e., in 1998, 1999, 2001 and 2002 at Triveni and on two occasions, i.e., in 1999 and 2002 at Dumariaghat respectively.
3. High peak discharge is a function of both hydraulic and sediment supply processes which induce higher peak concentrations of fine material (wash load) at the upstream sites of Triveni on Gandak river.
4. For Kosi river system, a maximum discharge of 10,350 cumecs is recorded in 1998 for Baltara and the highest annual discharge of 14,833 cumecs for Birpur is witnessed in 1987.
5. There seems to be no distinct relationship in pattern or range of variations between the upstream and downstream stations of Birpur and Baltara, respectively, due to variations in the period of analysis.
6. It is inferred that peak discharge at a particular station is a function of local flood waves created by tributaries apart from the monsoonal rains in the plains.
7. The plotting of return-years or the probability values against the discharge data on the semi-log graph for both Gandak and Kosi river does not give a straight line curve; rather the line bends off towards the tails of the data given as a skew curve.

Table 5 depicts and elucidates a synoptic and furious briefing of the recurrent floods in Bihar during the last 20 years (1992–2012). The total figure of death toll and the related catastrophe speaks for themselves. Over the 20 years analysis, it is observed that as many as 26 out of 38 districts in Bihar were reeling under floods during 1995 which increased to 29 districts in the adjacent year, i.e., 1996. In 2012, again 25 districts were found to be inundated with flood waters. In terms of fatality and devastations, however, the floods of 2007, 2008 and 2013 holds prominent significance rendering lacs of people homeless and at the mercy of nature, thus, paralyzing the entire economic fabric of the society.

Recent Flood in Bihar (2013): Through Facts and Figures

The most recent flood in Bihar, i.e., in 2013 is believed to be one of the most disastrous floods in the state after the '2008 Bihar flood'. More than 5.9 million people in 3,768 villages in 20 districts have been affected. The State Health Department started 306 Health Check-up Camps and 128 Veterinary Camps in the flood-affected areas. Around 22,623 tonnes of solid food items and ₹ 25 crores of cash was distributed among the victims of the flood, according to a statement released by the Government of Bihar.

Measures and Concluding Remarks

Based on earlier discussions and the results obtained for rivers Kosi and Gandak, it is established that flood forecasting techniques and flood frequency analysis proves to be extremely useful and fruitful and acts as a boon in planning and flood management strategies. These are inferred to be the most efficient, cost effective and non-structural measures of 'flood risk reduction'. The detailed geomorphological investigation must

Table 5

The Havoc of Floods in Bihar (Through figures): 1992–2012

	Number of Affected									
Years	*Districts*	*Blocks*	*Panchayats*	*Village*	*Humans (Lacs)*	*Area (Lac Hectares)*	*Crop Damage (₹ Lac)*	*House Damage*	*Public Property Damaged (₹ Lac)*	*Deaths (Humans + Animals)*
2012	11	28	152	277	2.4	1.1	300.0	473	162.2	15+0
2011	25	166	1296	3,577	71.4	38.2	10,295.7	851	153.7	249+183
2010	9	44	277	679	7.2	2.0	311.9	6,868	169.2	32+0
2009	16	91	602	1546	22.0	11.1	2,182.6	7,674	530.1	97+2
2008	18	116	924	2585	50.0	8.8	3,420.3	2,97,916	9772.0	258+878
2007	22	269	3,816	18,832	244.4	18.8	76,83,782.0	7,84,328	64241.5	1287+2423
2006	14	63	375	959	10.9	1.8	706.6	18,637	8456.2	36+31
2005	12	81	562	1464	21.0	4.6	1164.5	5,538	305.0	58+4
2004	20	211	2,788	9,346	213.0	27.00	52,205.6	9,29,773	103049.6	885+3272
2003	24	172	1,496	5,077	76.02	15.08	6,266.1	45,262	1035.2	251+108
2002	25	6	2,504	8,318	160.2	19.69	51,149.6	4,19,014	40892.2	489+1450
2001	22	194	1,992	6,405	90.9	12.0	26,721.8	2,22,074	18353.8	231+565
2000	33	213	2,327	12,351	90.2	8.1	8,303.7	3,43,091	3780.7	336+2568
1999	24	150	1,604	5,057	65.7	8.5	24,203.9	91,813	5410.0	243+136
1998	28	260	2,739	8,347	134.7	25.1	36,696.7	1,99,611	9284.0	381+187
1997	26	169	1,902	7,043	69.7	14.7	5,737.7	1,74,379	2038.1	163+151
1996	29	195	2,049	6,417	67.3	11.9	7,169.3	1,16,194	1035.7	222+171
1995	26	177	1,901	8,233	66.3	9.3	19,514.3	2,97,765	2183.6	291+3742
1994	21	112	1,045	2,755	40.1	6.3	5,616.3	33,876	151.7	91+35
1993	18	124	1,263	3,422	53.5	15.6	13,950.2	2,19,826	3040.9	105+420
1992	8	19	170	414	5.6	0.8	58.1	1,281	0.8	4+0

Source: Water Resources Department, Government of Bihar (http://disastermgmt.bih.nic.in/Statitics/Statistics.htm).

be coupled with long-term hydrological data to develop a better understanding of the causative factors of floods in the concerned river basins.

Any negligence on the part of the government in coping with floods is a threat to the economy of Bihar, thereby undermining poverty alleviation efforts. The need of the hour is to develop long-term goal-oriented and sustainable flood control strategies. The flood mitigation procedure must take into account the geomorphological factors to derive long-term benefits. In fact, some of the Government of Bihar documents on floods like the Second Bihar Irrigation Commission Report (1994), Sanyal Committee Report (2008), etc., presents the case of excellence in mitigating floods using the combination of both structural and non-structural measures.

With the sole mission to mitigate and manage floods in the Ganga Basin states, the Ganga Flood Control Commission (GFCC), a subordinate office of Ministry of Water Resources, with its headquarters at Patna, was created in the year 1972. Headed by Hon'ble Union Minister of Water Resources, Chief Ministers of Basin states or their representative and Members of, Planning Commission, are the members of the Board. Chairman, GFCC acts as the Member-Secretary of the Board. The chief objective of the commission is underlined as:

- Formulation of comprehensive plans for flood control in the Ganga Basin.
- Regular monitoring and maintenance of formulated plans.
- Evaluation of the major flood control measures executed within the state.

Quick and timely response of flood warning system and automation of flood control devices can minimize the risk of vulnerability and possible occurrence of high intensity floods in the near future. Although 90–95 per cent accuracy has been achieved in flood forecasting techniques in the recent years, the enigma of flood continues to be a recurrent feature and a nightmare for the people of Bihar. It calls for mass mobilization of people who are largely affected by flood. These local people in the flood-prone areas should be well trained and equipped with latest flood coping strategies with the active involvement of NGOs.

A participatory approach with voluntarily joint efforts of people from every nook and corner of the society is sought; be it the government officials, academicians, policy makers, NGOs, scholars, or the local people. Only then, can we together join hands in giving a checkmate to this natural fury.

In the concluding paragraph, it is proposed that the surplus water resources available to the state especially during the monsoon seasons should be rationally utilized and harnessed for the fertile agricultural tracts in Bihar and other future needs. The abundance in water should be treated as a 'blessing in disguise' for agricultural prosperity and the overall development of the state.

Notes

1. Cumecs refers to the unit of discharge of rivers measured at a particular site and is expressed as cubic metre per second (m3s–1).
2. Frequency of floods represents the number of times an area is inundated during a particular time interval.
3. Meander refers to the deviations in the channel of stream maintaining, however, a general deviation of the channel on the whole (Ganga Flood Control Commission, Patna).
4. Due to paucity and inaccuracy of peak discharge data for Birpur the period of analysis has been shifted from 1990–2002 to 1982–2002.

References

Agarwal, A. and S. Narain (eds) (1991) *State of India's Environment: The Third Citizens' Report, Floods, Floodplains and Environmental Myths*, New Delhi: Centre for Science and Environment.

Asselman, N.E.M. and Middelkoop, H. (1998) 'Temporal Variability of Contemporary Floodplain Sedimentation in the Rhine-Meuse Delta, The Netherlands', 23: 595–609.

Awadallah, A.G., Rousselle, J. and Leconte, R. (1999) 'Evolution du hydrologique sur la Chateauguay', *Canadian Journal of Civil Engineering*, 26: 510–523.

Brookes, A. (1985) 'River: Traditional Engineering Methods, Physical Consequences and Alternative Practices', *Progress in Physical Geography*, 9: 44–73.

Central Water Commission (1989) *Manual on Flood Forecasting*, River Management Wing, New Delhi.

—— (2004) *Water and Related Statistics*, New Delhi, India.

Central Water Commission Diary (2010) *Details of Hydrological Observation Stations: Basin-Wise*, New Delhi, India.

Chander, S. and T. Prasad (1981) 'Forecasting and Prediction of Floods', Indo-US Workshop on Flood Mitigation, New Delhi.

Chander, S., S.K. Spolia and A. Kumar (1980) 'Flood Stage Forecasting in Rivers', in M.J. Lighthill (ed.), *Monsoon Dynamics*, London: Cambridge University Press.

Costa, J.E. and O'Connor, J.E. (1995) 'Geomorphologically Effective Floods', in J.E. Costa, A.J. Miller, K.W. Potter and P. R. Wilcok (eds) *Natural and Anthropogenic Influences in Fluvial Geomorphology*, American Geophysical Union, Washington, DC, Geophysical Monograph, 89: 45–56.

Das, K.N. (1967) 'The Kosi Drainage and Its Geographical Significance', *Trans. of the ICG*, 4: 27–28.

—— (1968) 'Soil Erosion and the Problem of Silting in the Kosi Catchment', *JSWCI*, 16(3–4): 62–64.

—— (1968) 'Westward Shifts in the Course of the Kosi', *The National Geographical Journal of India*, 14(1):23–32.

Friedman, J.M., Osterkamp, W.R. and Lewis Jr., W.M. (1996) 'Channel Narrowing and Vegetation Development Following a Great Plains Flood', *Ecology*, 77: 2167–2181.

Hollis, G. (1975) 'The Effect of Urbanization on Floods of Different Recurrence Intervals', *Water Resources Research*, 11: 431–435.

Hydrological Observation Stations in India Under CWC (2004) Central Water Commission, New Delhi, India.

India Floods (1993) *DHA-Geneva Information Report*, No. 223.

India WRIS Hydro Observation Info System (2011).

IPCC (2007) *Climate Change, Synthesis Report: An Assessment of the Intergovernmental Panel on Climate Change*, IPCC Secretariat, Geneva, Switzerland: World Meteorological Organization.

Irvine, K.N. and Drake, J.J. (1987) 'Spatial Analysis of Snow- and Rain-Generated Highflows in Southern Ontario', *The Canadian Geographer*, 31: 140–149.

Knighton, D. (1989) *Fluvial Forms and Processes*, London: Edward Arnold.

Kochel, R.C. (1988) 'Impact of Large Floods: Review and New Perspectives on Magnitude and Frequency', in V.R. Baker, R.C. Kochel and P.C Patton (eds) *Flood Geomorphology*, New York: Wiley-Interscience, 169–187.

Meteorological Data Year Book (2005) Central Water Commission, Narmada Basin Organisation.

Mohindra, R. et al. (1992) 'Historical Geomorphology and Pedology of the Gandak Megafan, Middle Gangetic Plains, India', *Earth Surface Process, Landf.*, 17: 643–662.

Nepal, S. (2012) 'Evaluating Upstream Downstream Linkages of Hydrological Dynamics in the Himalayan Region', Dissertation, Faculty of Chemical and Earth Sciences of the Friedrich-Schiller-University Jena.

Nolan, K.M. and Marron, D.C. (1995) History, Causes, and Significance of Changes in the Channel Geometry of Redwood Creek, Northwestern California, 1936 to 1982, Professional, Paper 1454N.

Palik, B.J., Michener, W.K., Mitchell, R.J. and Jones, J. W. (1999) 'The Effects of and Plant Size on Mortality and Recovery Longleaf Pine During a 100-year Flood', *Ecoscience*, 6: 255–263.

Rice, S. and M. Church (1996) 'Sampling Surficial Fluvial Gravels: The Precision of Size Distribution Percentile Estimates', *Journal of Sedimentary Research*, 66(3): 654–665.

Roberts, C.R. (1989) 'Flood Frequency and Urban-Induced Channel Change: Some British Examples', in K.J. Beven and P.A Carling (eds) *Floods: Hydrological, Sedimentological and Geomorphological Implications*, Chichester: Wiley & Sons, 57–82.

Sharma, U.P. (1996) 'Ecology of the Kosi River in Nepal-India: A Typical River Ecosystem', in P.K. Jha, G.P.S. Ghimire, S.B. Karmacharya, S.R. Baral and P. Lacoul (eds), *Environment and Biodiversity in the Context of South Asia*, Proceedings of the Regional Conference on Environment and Biodiversity, Kathmandu: Ecological Society, 7–9 March, 92–99.

Singh, S.K., Rai, S.K., and Krishnaswami, S. (2008) 'Sr and Nd isotopes in River Sediments from the Ganga Basin: Sediment Provenance and Hotspots of Physical Erosion', *Journal of Geophysical Research-Earth Surface*, 113(F3).

Sinha, R. and P.F. Friend (1994) 'River Systems and Their Sediment Flux, Indo-Gangetic Plains, Northern Bihar, India', *Sedimentology*, 41: 825–845.

Sinha, R. and V. Jain (1998) 'Flood Hazards of North Bihar Rivers, Indo-Gangetic Plains', in V.S. Kale (ed.), *Flood Studies in India*, Bangalore: Geological Society of India, Memoir 41: 27–52.

Sinha, R., G.V. Bapalu, L.K. Singh and B. Rath (2008) 'Flood Risk Analysis in the Kosi River Basin, North Bihar Using Multi-Parametric Approach of AHP', *Indian Journal of Remote Sensing*, 36: 293–307.

Sinha, R., V. Jain, G. Prasad Babu and S. Ghosh (2005) 'Geomorphic Characterization and Diversity of the Fluvial Systems of the Gangetic Plains', *Geomorphology*, 70(3–4): 207–225.

Users Manual, SWDES Version 3.0, Central Water Commission, New Delhi, India.

Wells, N.A. and J.A. Dorr, Jr. (1987) 'Shifting of the Kosi River, Northern India', *Geology*, 15(3): 204–207.

10

Sustainable Management of Floods in North Bihar

SNEH GANGWAR

In a developing country like India where an overwhelming majority of the population lives in rural areas and is oppressed by chronic poverty, disaster plays a vital role. Disasters are shared reality spanning individuals, villages, blocks, districts, states, nations and even regions and have to be responded to with a multipronged approach. About 211 million people are affected by disasters every year. According to World Disaster Report, two-thirds of the people affected are from countries with low human development index (International Federation of Red Cross and Red Crescent, 2001). India is one of the world's major theatres of disasters, both human made and natural. Floods, droughts, cyclones and earth-quakes pound it end-to-end every year. Floods are the most recurring, widespread and disastrous calamity in India. The Central Water Commission, a nodal government agency, has noted that 11.2 per cent of India is flood prone. Floods in the eastern part of India (Orissa, Bengal, Andhra Pradesh, Bihar) in the recent past, are striking examples. In which, Bihar is the worst flood-affected state in India. Its geographical area and population are, respectively, 2.85 per cent and about 8 per cent of those of the country, but about 17 per cent of the flood-prone areas and 36 per cent of the flood-affected population of the country belong to this state. The state's share in total average annual flood damage in the country is about 23 per cent. Of all the river basins in the state, the ratio of flood-prone to catchment area within the state is maximum in the Kosi basin (89%). Floods have been a chronic and a serious problem for the state, particularly for North Bihar. As per the information published by different government agencies, flood-prone area in North Bihar has been increasing dramatically. As reported by Central Water Commission (CWC) under Ministry of Water Resources, Government of India, the annual average area affected by floods is 7.563 million ha. This observation was based on data for the period 1953 to 2000, with variability ranging from 1.46 million hectares in 1965 to 17.5 million hectares in 1978. On an average, floods have affected about 33 million persons between 1953–2000. There is every possibility that this figure may increase due to population growth. Flood data for 1953–2000 published by CWC (2001) shows that the Bihar is one of the worst affected states of India. The National Flood

Commission (1980) has reported that the total flood-prone area of India was 34 million hectares. It has also mentioned that an area of 10 million hectares has been protected, but the effective protection may be available to only 6 million hectares, which means that we need a sustainable approach to protect the floods and their impacts.

North Bihar: The Study Area

The state of Bihar, the ninth largest in size in the country, lies between latitudes 21°58'10" N and 27°31'15"N and longitudes 83°10'50" E and 80°17'40" E. The total reported geographical area of the State is 1, 73,877 sq km. The state comprises alluvial plains of Indo-Gangetic basin in the north and Kaimur-Chotanagpur-Santhal Pargana plateau in the south. The alluvial plains are divided into two by the river Ganga flowing from west to east. The state, therefore, can physiographically be divided into three regions: North Bihar, South Bihar and Central Bihar. North Bihar comprises the tract of alluvial plains north of Ganga, falling between the Ganga and Indo-Nepal border, having general slope from north-west to south-east and is drained by the rivers Ghaghra, Gandak, Burhi Gandak, Kosi and Mahananda, etc. (Table 1), falling into the Ganga and Bagmati-Adhwara, Kamla-Balan and other important rivers of North Bihar, which drain into the Ganga through the Kosi (Figure 1).

Figure 1

The River System of North Bihar

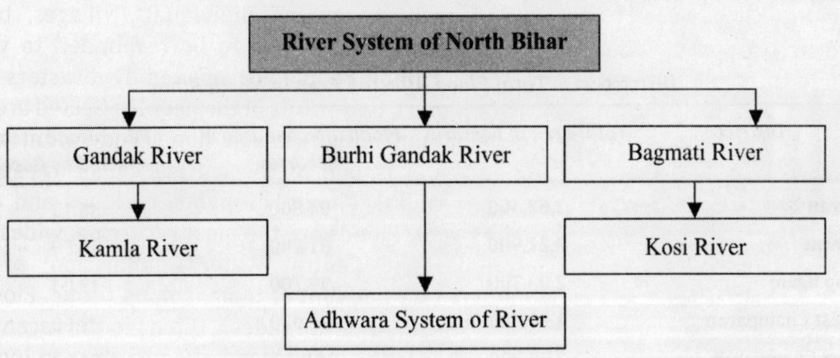

Table 1

Composite River Basin of North Bihar

Name of the basin	*Geographical area (in hectares)*
Ghaghra-Mahi-Western Gandak composite	6,48,728
Upper Eastern Gandak-Upper Burhi Gandak composite	8,82,398
Lower Eastern Gandak-Baya-Lower Burhi	6,75,666
Bagmati-Adhwara	6,49,985
Kamla-Balan	4,48,767
Kosi	11,41,019
Mahananda	6,15,006
Total	50,61,569

Table 2

Breakup of Division and Districts of North Bihar

Name of division	*Name of districts*
Saran	Saran, Siwan, Gopalganj
Tirhut	Muzaffarpur, Vaishali, East Champaran
Darbhanga	Darbhanga, Madhubani, Samastipur, Begusarai
Kosi	Saharsa, Supaul, Madhepura, Khagaria
Purnea	Purnea, Araria, Kisanganj, Kaithar

Floods in North Bihar have been its biggest problem. The region is counted among most poor (economically) regions of India (Table 2). Unemployment, illiteracy, migration and related issues have been the grief of North Bihar. Floods are a perennial problem in North Bihar. The very same water source that acts as the life-blood for the agriculture-dependent population in the state turns into an avalanche of death and misery every year. And every year, as this natural disaster strikes, it evokes temporary attention to the plight of the victims and soon to be forgotten after government commissions and helicopter visits by the bourgeois polity. But once the shock value of the images fades away, all is forgotten even if misery is compounded and the people are made to brace up for the next year's natural fury. Such is the case of floods in North Bihar districts (Table 3).

Table 3

District-wise Total Flood Affected Area in North Bihar

District	*Total area in hectares*	*Flood affected area in hectares*	*Percentage area affected by flood*
Saran	2,62,400	94,800	36.12
Siwan	2,21,900	81,200	36.59
Gopalganj	2,03,300	99,700	49.04
West Champaran	4,24,800	96,020	22.60
East Champaran	3,96,800	2,90,600	73.23
Sheohar	44,300	NA	NA
Sitamarhi	2,27,900	2,60,000	95.51
Muzzafarnagar	3,17,200	2,23,200	70.36
Vishali	2,03,600	87,100	22.77
Dharbhanga	2,58,900	2,16,000	83.77
Madhubani	3,50,100	3,29,000	93.97
Samastipur	2,59,400	1,21,600	46.87
Saharsa	1,95,500	1,05,700	54.06
Supaul	2,98,400	2,17,560	72.90
Madhepura	1,78,800	87,881	49.15
Purnia	3,22,900	2,29,800	71.16

Cont'd...

Cont'd...

Araria	2,83,000	2,30,400	81.41
Kishanganj	1,88,400	84,706	44.96
Katihar	3,05,700	2,65,300	86.78
Begusarai	1,91,800	1,03,400	53.91
Khagaria	1,48,600	96,590	65.01
Total of North Bihar	52,75,800	33,20,557	62.9

Source: Disaster Management Department, Patna, Bihar.

The basin of North Bihar catchment mostly shares the international boundaries with other countries. For example, the total catchment area of the Gandak basin up to its outfall into the Ganga is 46,300 sq km of which 7,620 sq km lie in India and rest in Nepal and same is the case with Kosi river of North Bihar. The main cause of flood problem is inadequate capacity of the river to accommodate flood discharge. The rivers have very steep slopes in the mountains but after it debauches into the plains, the slopes gradually becomes flatter, which brings enormous quantities of water and silt load during the monsoon. The silt loads carried gets dropped as the river flows though plains, resulting in a tendency to shift the course. However, in the Indian territory, the gradient being flat, various tributaries of rivers combine their flow through a single channel with inadequate capacity, resulting in widespread devastation and havoc. In some basins, due to the construction of flood embankments the rivers spill is the major problem. A large population residing there are subject to perpetual flooding (Figure 2).

Figure 2

Flood Havoc and Disastrous Situation of North Bihar

Flood disaster brings heavy damage in both the formal and the informal sectors although it is the former that receives most of the media and national attention. Every year, flood causes death, cultivated fields and irrigation systems built and managed by generations of farmers are washed away together with trails, bridges and other rural infrastructure. Table 4 summarizes the impacts and damage due to floods in North Bihar.

Table 4

Damage and Effect of Floods in North Bihar Districts in Different Time Periods

Districts	*Number of Blocks affected*			*Affected population (in lakh)*			*Houses damaged*		
	1987	*1995*	*2007*	*1987*	*1995*	*2007*	*1987*	*1995*	*2007*
West Champaran	16	4	16	4.36	0.91	7.080	6	25	6283
East Champaran	18	9	27	12.09	0.35	30.960	NA	NA	33430
Sitamarhi	16	9	17	16.83	8.63	27.860	113	124	41,128
Sheohar	NA	4	5	NA	0.86	3.860	NA	NA	12,417
Muzaffarpur	14	9	15	14.22	1.92	32.630	4	NA	30,331
Saran	14	NA	NA	8.70	NA	NA	141	NA	369
Siwan	6	NA	1	3.09	NA	0.020	NA	NA	2
Gopalganj	7	4	8	2.03	0.79	1.640	7	49	13,529
Darbhanga	12	13	18	19.71	10.25	34.410	3685	131	67,022
Samastipur	14	5	19	15.33	2.07	21.130	7625	NA	35,904
Madhubani	19	15	20	21.45	5.71	18.070	NA	NA	41,428
Saharsa	16	5	6	13.02	2.67	3.650	2259	NA	9,940
Supaul	NA	4	6	NA	1.92	2.540	NA	NA	14,435
Madhepura	7	11	3	7.28	3.21	0.700	30	NA	432
Punia	27	2	4	25.63	0.05	1.700	NA	NA	3,731
Araria	NA	NA	1	NA	NA	0.040	NA	NA	15
Kishanganj	NA	1	NA	NA	0.01	NA	NA	NA	155
Katihar	11	16	7	7.36	6.73	5.400	NA	NA	1,759
Begusarai	11	3	11	9.39	0.40	7.690	769	NA	40,983
Khagaria	6	6	7	7.37	1.70	10.10	2	15	19,288
Vaishali	11	NA	15	8.56	NA	18.750	7	NA	382

Source: Disaster Management Department, Government of Bihar, Patna.

Table 5

Details of Flood-prone Area, Flood Protection Measures and Flood Protected Area in North Bihar

Basins	*CA Within State (L.Ha)*	*Flood Prone Area (L.Ha)*	*Per-centage of CA*	*River Length (km)*	*Length of Emba-nkment Construc-ted (km)*	*Protected Area*	
						In Hectares	*In Percentage*
Ghaghra	2.995	2.530	85	833	149	0.920	86
Gandak	4.188	4.900	117	260	410	4.900	100
Burhi Gandak	9.601	6.660	69	320	751	4.390	66
Bagmati	6.500	4.440	68	394	586	3.210	72.50
Kamla-Balan	4.488	3.700	82	120	172	2.810	76
Kosi	11.410	10.150	87	260	406	7.970	78.50
Mahananda	6.150	5.150	84	376	241	1.210	23.50
Total	45.332	37.530	83	1,813	2,715	25.41	67.70

Source: The Bihar State Commission Report, 1994.

The state apart from overall planning and coordination of flood management activities has been providing central loan assistance to the State of Bihar for flood control and flood proofing measures in North Bihar, for raising and strengthening of embankments along Kamla, Bagmati, Kosi and Balan rivers in the Indian portion and for critical anti-erosion works in Ganga Basin states. With the effort of state and central government, major areas of North Bihar river basins are under the flood-protected land (Table 5).

From the above description it is very clear that flood problem in North Bihar is very serious and acute even after the management and flood protection strategies made by the state and central government. So it is very important to think beyond these constructional management activities – the answer key is 'sustainable development'. Sustainable development is the only solution for North Bihar floods. Some flood management measures have a negative impact on the quality and quantity of water, or on biodiversity-rich areas. Examples can be the building of new dams or dikes which change the river flow, by reducing water for related ecosystems in the area or which accentuate problems in dry seasons by altering the natural flow of the river. Sustainable measures which improve the storage capacities of flood water temporarily during flood events, can be effective in protecting against flooding, as well as providing other benefits deriving from ecosystem services, such as for leisure activities and nature protection.

Origin of Sustainable Development

Sustainable development was codified for the first time in the world conservation strategy (WCS), prepared by IUCN with finance provided by the UN Environment Program and the World Wildlife Fund (IUCN, 1980). Since then it has been further developed through the report of the World Commission on Environment and Development, Our Common Future (Brundtland, 1987), and the follow up to the WCS, Caring for the Earth (IUCN, 1991), before it appearance in Agenda–21 at the Rio Conference in 1992. At the heart of these documents is a vision of sustainable development strongly influenced by science, by wildlife conservation, by concerns for multilateral global economic relations, and by an emphasis on the relation management of resources to maximize human welfare.

Conceptual Framework of Sustainable Development Approach

Ever-increasing population and higher levels of human activities have made sustainable development a very complex task throughout the world. Nature provides human societies and economics with a complex life support system – air, water, food and a suitable climate for survival. It also provides the physical resources that are necessary for the sustenance of economics. Nature has supported and maintained life on earth since time immemorial and should continue to do so in the future. This is known as the sustainability of nature or ecosystems or environment. However, we have been interfering with the sustainability of the natural systems through our avaricious activities and if we continue on the same trajectory, not only the other life forms but also the very existence of mankind is threatened. There are limits to nature's capacity to absorb impacts. Once alteration of nature's initial state occurs, it cannot quickly revert back to the initial state. Nature has a limited capacity to withstand rapid change. Thus, today, the challenge before mankind is to determine the state in which we wish to live and to continue living within the limits inherent in nature's processes, within nature's carrying capacity.

The term 'sustainability' is also used to demonstrate the temporal and livelihood context of development policies. The temporal context refers to the chronological perspective in which communities maintain there cultural and economic integrity. The livelihood context of development policies is the preservation of existing values which are under threat from external economic forces leading to the collapse of a delicate natural resource balance.

The term 'development' means the social and economic improvement in a broad sense. It is needed to create opportunities, prosperity and choice for all inhabitants of the world and it must proceed in a way that leaves choices available for future generations also. It refers to a holistic growth of the human and natural environment towards autonomy and freedom. It indicates a growth pattern which makes nations more decisive in their internal and external environment.

The concept of sustainable development was envisaged to bring environmentalist ideas into the central theme of economic development policies. It sought to modify the kind of unsustainable development strategies that were being pursued. Sustainable development combine the two terms of 'sustainability' and 'development' to indicate a pattern of growth which strengthens both the national capabilities to care for their people in relation to their total relationship with the resources of the earth.

Thus, sustainable development focuses upon a relationship between humans and their environment and indicates a warning that humans cannot impose development which is against nature, as in the end it is always the nature. Sustainable development is a value based concept which appeals to the universal themes of mutual coexistence and respect for others. It is a continually evolving process bringing together cultural, social, economic, environmental and political concerns. It is a desired direction of change and provides a framework to decide development actions by nations, communities and individuals.

Sustainable flood management considers the hydrological processes across the whole catchment of a river or along a stretch to identify where measures can best be applied, with a focus on increasing water retention capacities. Examples of such measures are: Restoring natural flows by realignment of flooded areas, or reconnection of rivers with their floodplain; Restoration of wetlands which can store flood water and help "slow the flow" of flood waters; Reservoirs in agricultural areas which can store flood water during flood events, and otherwise be high nature value areas; Green Infrastructure such as green spaces, sustainable drainage and green roofs.

Sustainable flood management brings many other benefits for communities and local authorities. The approach encourages participation in decision-making processes, especially through river basin management planning. Further, it can help provide best value in community planning and is Strategic Environmental Assessment friendly. The process also greatly contributes to Local Biodiversity Action Plan duties, is a proven method for spreading pollution control and provides green space. Sustainable flood management (SFM) is an evolving way of working with rivers on a catchment scale to manage flooding. For flood management to be sustainable it must take proper account of costs and benefits to the economy, society and the environment.

Figure 3

Need for Sustainable Flood Management

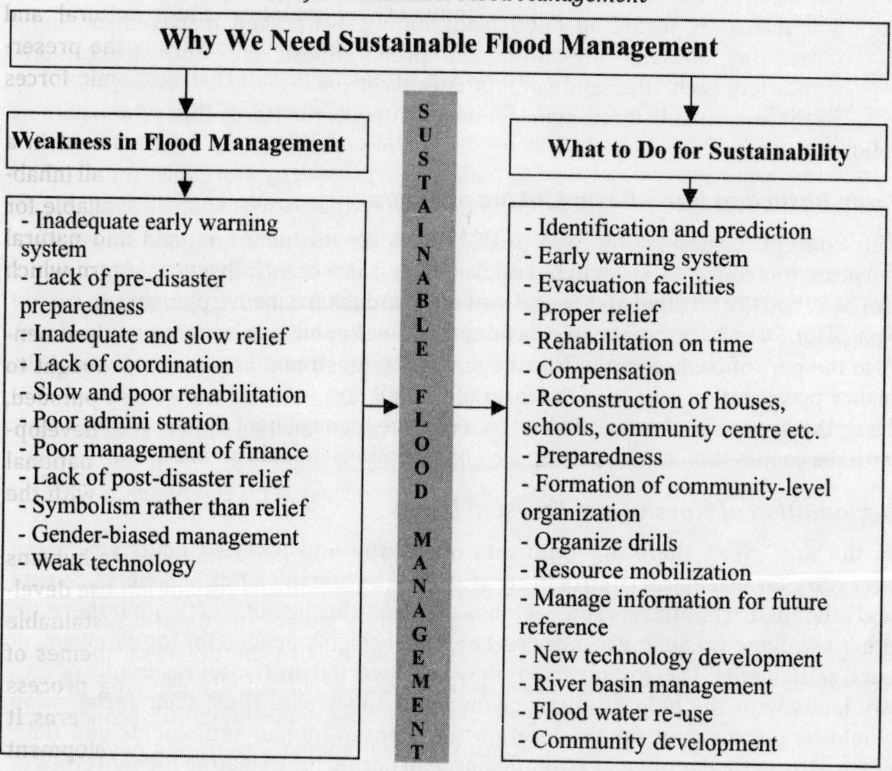

Sustainable Flood Management in North Bihar

The sustainable responses to mitigating flooding are of two types. The first response takes the form of post-event relief, which can be named as soft measures and the second is structural solutions or hard measures in the form of multi-purpose projects and embankments. On plains of North Bihar, for example, more than 3,500 km of embankments have been built in the last 40 years. The embankments have resulted in the aggradation of channel beds, and, consequently the spill over of floodwater and waterlogging. The examples of the Kosi and other embankments in the Ganga plain are cases in point (Mishra, 1997). Bihar is one of the few states in India to begin transforming its flood management practices. Data from firsthand experiences has convinced policy makers that reforms are necessary. This means hiring thousands of new staff, setting up world-class training institutes, improving the knowledge of field staff in state-of-the-art techniques of flood management and creating new quality procedures and inspection systems that can track how well an embankment is performing. It also means actively involving communities in disseminating warnings and sharing the burden of flood protection alongside its engineers. Sustainable planning for flood management does not involve absolute control of floods but implies management of flood in the most beneficial manner in the given circumstances. All the sustainable flood management measures fall broadly into two categories.

1. Hard measures involving construction of embankments, reservoirs, detention basins, inter-basin transfer of water, raising of village, etc., and
2. Soft measures including flood plain zoning, watershed management, flood forecasting, disaster mitigation and preparedness, etc. Both are complementary to each other and not mutually exclusive.

So the sustainable flood management strategies for North Bihar floods are as follows:

Inter-Basin and Intra-Basin Linking of Rivers

This concept is successfully used in USA. However, in India for flood moderation purposes this concept has yet to be realized. Inter-basin or intra-basin linking of rivers can be rationally justified and considered only through basinwise planning. In case of Kosi plain, 50 to 85 per cent of the basin of the river lies outside India, mostly in Nepal. Also the part of basin lying in Nepal is invariably upstream having steep gradients, higher precipitation – both in the form of rainfall and snowfall and erodible slopes. Thus, the approach of integrated water resource management can be adopted only with the cooperation of two principal co-basin nations, Nepal and India.

Reclamation of Marshy and Forested Lands

In the Kosi river, there are remnants of marshy and forested lands which are necessary for ecological control in rural areas. The marshy lands of Saharsa, Supaul and other districts, attracts several kinds of cranes during hot weather but there are other low-lying wastelands whose reclamation is highly needed for the extension of rural settlements. These depressions may be converted into water reservoirs or into dry lands with the help of minor channels or tubewells. Thus, their reclamation would be quite useful for the location of potential human settlements and their planned growth. Pumping of water during lean period for irrigating the rabi crops at several sites should be stopped and alternatively large flood control reservoirs should be constructed at depression sites and in the meander loops which may impound large quantities of water and thus may give substantial protection to down-river flood plains by decapitation the flood peak. Besides, the water may be used for irrigation purposes during rabi season and passage of additional water in the river during lean period will maintain regular flow and thus will be antagonistic to silting the river bed.

Control of Silt through Soil Conservation

The flood problem and incidence of land slides are concurrent factors, both having been caused by heavy precipitation. Since precipitation cannot be controlled, the flood or the run-off of a catchment and siltation has to be checked by soil conservation measures such as gully plugging, contour bunding and construction of check dams and silt ejectors across each small drainage lie in the area. A complete control of the Kosi and its tributaries by a series of these dams and ejectors is easier because the silt intensities are not very high and a proper care of soil conservation may be taken.

Land Use Management for Sustainable Development

Land use management for sustainable development refers to the use of land in all its possibilities and probabilities without adversely affecting the inherent qualities of land. It should be in accordance with the other components of environment and must not damage them. It must fulfil the needs of the local people and, above all, its must be sustainable. In this regard, the investigator suggests some measures which can be adopted by the people living in this region. For this purpose the nature of relief, the texture of soil, the drainage pattern especially the impact of flood, the presence of wetlands and *chaurs, diaralands,* etc., have been taken into accounts. The following are some of the important aspects of effective land use management:

1. Adoption and acceptance of appropriate intercropping system with suitable varieties of components crop based on the farm resources, agro-climatic conditions, farmer's needs and market acceptance will certainly enhance and sustain the farm productivity and lead to the sustainable development of this region, e.g. (i) Rice + Maize/Sugarcane in the western drier part, (ii) Rice+ Maize/Jute in the wet eastern part of the plain and, (iii) Wheat+ Maize+ Chilly as the most popular intercropping system for the Kosi basin. There is an urgent need for the production of non-traditional crops and cash crops like menthol, sugarcane, sunflower, soyabeans, etc., for supplementing agricultural income; full facilities should be given for horticulture and other occupations like poultry farming, honey bee processing, dairy farming units, piggery, etc.
2. Other aspects of land use management include planning for 'wetlands' of the plain. The wetlands comprising oxbow lakes, pond and chaurs are natural depressions formed over hundred of years and contributing to ecological stability of the region. These chaurs act as measures of flood control through valley storage. These should be preserved and used for the production of water fruits like Makhana and Singhara. This type of land is also best for aquaculture and bamboo cultivation.
3. Diaralands, also included under wastelands category have good potential for economic land use. Though they are submerged by river water during monsoon, they posses fertile land exposed after the retreat of water. They can be used for permanent pastures or as grazing lands. Highly suitable for the production of quick growing tall grasses they can provide green fodder to livestock of the region. In some of the Kosi region like Saharsa, they have been using this since long. In the Kosi embanked area, the production of Mothi, Masta, Sabai grass, Sanai and Bet can be used in the basket making, toy making and can also support paper industry on a small scale in the belt. Also, they can be used for the production of organic vegetables.
4. In this region the characteristics of the soil and climate highly favour the production of fruits. Fruit production also gives higher return to the farmers. Therefore, some agricultural land can be used under this category. Area under Shahi Lichi, Mango and Banana should be further increased and the products can be sent to national and international markets. Around 20 per cent of the area in the plains should be under forest (orchards and trees) to maintain the environmental stability, temperature and humidity. Thus, in order to increase the return among the cultivators, the state government should take an active role in the land use planning. This type of land use planning could be helpful in maximum utilization of land.

This region is rich in medicinal flora. In the absence of any sophisticated system of medicine, the indigenous village elders have been claiming the presence of numerous life-saving herbs without any side effects like modern medicines. It is common knowledge that only certain plants and certain parts like flower, leaf, bark and root are of medicinal use. Good agricultural and collection practices of herbs can also be potential sources of economic development and ecologically safer too to the region. It may also open up a new avenue in commercial cultivation for large production processing and packaging, marketing and industrial application.

Encouraging Development of Agro-based Industries

Food processing units, e.g., chips making from potato, bananas, pickels, preparation of jam, jelly, papad, masala, squash, sauce, etc., should be encouraged. Manufacturing of above products follows a simple process and thus cottage industries with low capital can come up successfully with ease. The massive extension of grass growing throughout the region could be helpful in the establishment of plywood and paper industry. Involvement of existing people will also solve the unemployment problem and ensure a fair return.

Development of Link Channels Through Rivers and Depression Sites

The linking of all the rivers and water reservoirs, especially permanent *chaurs* through large channel or underground tunnels to equalize the level of water in all seasons can greatly help in solving the problem of floods. The surplus flood waters of the Kosi river should be transferred into other channels. The 50,000 cusecs water of presently flowing in the Kosi and responsible for flooding may be transferred through a by-pass into the existing old bed of Kosi, known as Dhemradhar. Another approach to dispose the flood waters is to consider how they could be spread or arrested to recharge the groundwater reserves from where they can be extracted at convenient time and place. The idea is still in its embryonic stage but it is suggested that floods in the Kosi can be utilized to fill groundwater reserves. The storing of water in the chaurs and depression during rainy season and again utilizing and regulating it during lean months will be of great help in the agriculture and fish rearing.

1. The continuous siltation of the Kosi river bed is making it shallower and shallower almost to the ground level, in turn making the river influent. If the desiltation of the river bed is carried out in a planned way, the river channel will become deep and allow more volume of water to flow through it. Ultimately, it might change the influent condition of the river to effluent condition. Hence, it will minimize the inundation as well as waterlogging.
2. Series of fishing pond can be constructed in existing waterlogged area by excavating 100 m x 100 m×6 m size of earth material. The idea behind it is that the ponds constructed 6m in depth will create void space in the subsurface locally. In turn, the hydraulic gradient of water table will become concentric towards pond and consequently the adjoining aquifer will be de-watered. Hence the water table will be lowered to some extent and consequently waterlogging will be eradicated.

More and more bridge and culvert should be provided on the rail track and on the road so that the water can freely move through its gradient and ultimately to its channel.

New Housing Model

New housing model can act as powerful tool, technologies and efficient problem solving of flood, which in turn will be highly beneficial to the people of this region. We know that, the Government of India and various State Governments have been implementing various programmes for rural uplift. Among the various programme

"Indra Awas Yojna" (IAY) is an important one. This programme was launched on May, 1985. The ceiling of assistance for construction of new houses has been increased from ₹ 20,000 to ₹ 25,000 per unit for the plain areas and from ₹ 22,000 to ₹ 27,500 per unit for the hilly/difficult areas.

On the basis of the primary survey conducted by the investigators among a few houses functioning in the study area, it is found that houses face flood problems due to financial authorities not giving adequate subsidy to meet even the labour cost requirements; another causes are high cost of building construction, absence of quality consciousness, etc. In order to solve the various problems relating to housing of this region, the state government should give strong support for this purpose without any discrimination of cast, politics, etc. There is a need to create awareness for building and huts construction work among these people. Making a multi-purpose shelter in flood-prone villages. Double storeyed building, which is blank in the ground floor and this type of bamboo huts called 'Machan' can be also solve the problem. The panchayat should be the authority for providing double storeyed school building for tackling the flood problem.

River Morphological Studies

River morphology is concerned with the structure and form of rivers including channel configuration, channel geometry, bed form and profile caharcteristics. Various flood control structural measures such as construction of embankments, channel improvements, raising of villages, selective dredging, etc., have been implemented in the past to reduce the impact of the flood disaster on human life and property. It is essential to monitor the embankments regularly to identify the vulnerable reaches. Conventional methods of river surveys are time consuming and expensive. Most of the flood-prone rivers in India changes their course after every flood wave, eroding river banks. Satellite remote sensing based morphological studies are quite useful in following areas: In identifying the changes in river course over a time period, in identifying the erosion-prone areas along the river course, in studying the efficacy of flood management structures.

The river configuration and flood control work maps can be effectively used to identify the vulnerable river reaches and status of the flood control embankments or spurs so that necessary measures can be taken accordingly to avoid breaches. The bank erosion maps can be used for planning bank protection works. The study of river configuration will be useful to understand the behaviour of the river and can be used for laying physical models. Though the above mentioned approaches and strategies are based on extensive scientific study of flood problem. The modifications may be made as per the local need and requirement. Four essential aspects of disaster mitigations, i.e., politico-administrative, economic, social and environmental aspects are to be given due consideration while implementing these.

Flood Plain Management

Flood plain is an integral part of the river system though it is used occasionally to pass down flood flow when the river discharges are very high. Land use regulations, zoning ordinance, statutes, government purchase of property and relocation, all come under flood plain management.

It is evident that the quantum of flood plain losses depends on the land use pattern. For example, highest losses during the flood will occur on the land used for industrial and urban purposes, lower for agricultural land and the lowest on land kept for recreational purpose. There would not be practically any loss on land that is not

Figure 4

Flood Plain Management in River Basin of North Bihar

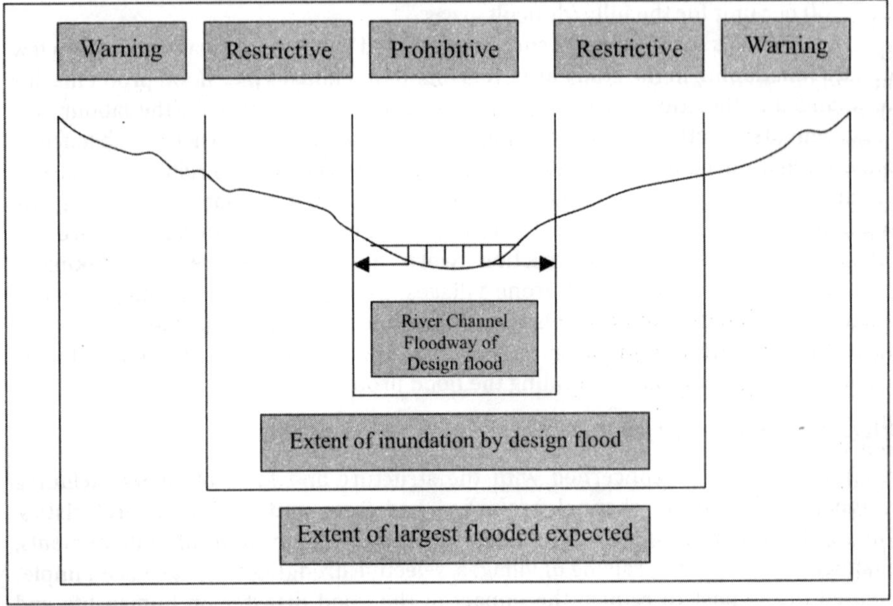

used at all. However, it will neither be sensible nor economical to keep all the development out of the flood plain. Keeping this in mind, land use pattern is to be decided and a set of land use regulations framed, as such regulations would necessarily lead to careful assessment of the costs against the benefits of flood plain occupancy. River channel and flood plains are considered as one unit in the flood zone concept. The flood plains forms a part of the river channel which transmits water only infrequently. The plains forming a part of flood plains are taken to be the boundaries of the largest estimated flood. Based on the degree of hazard, the following three zones are defined with its own regulations and set of planning devices:

Prohibitive Zone: This is the floodway of the design flood. It extends from the midpoint of the river to a designed distance on either side. It is desirable to keep it free from any encroachment and building development (Figure 4).

Restrictive Zone: In this zone flood hazard is less as this zone lies between the floodway of design flood and extent of inundation by design flood. It is known as flood fringe zone and does not contribute substantially to downstream movement and it is covered by slow moving water. Building may not be prohibited in this zone but developments need to be regulated to minimize the flood damage.

Warning Zone: This zone extends from the limits of the design flood zone to the areas covered by the largest flood in the region. Flooding in this zone will be extremely rare but not altogether improbable. Developers of this zone should be warned of the likely hazard and risk involved.

Disaster Preparedness and Response Planning

It covers advance planning of disaster mitigation, warning, emergency operation, rehabilitation and recovery. This is an important measure which directly influences the damage prevention if managed efficiently at all levels according to the prescribed procedures and guidelines. Improper management could also result directly in increased damage. The government should, therefore, ensure that all routine exercises and necessary drills are carried out systematically before every flood season and departmental instructions, manuals and rules in this regard should be widely circulated so as to make these available to all concerned. It is observed that disaster mitigation system and the preparedness programme usually get activated only just before and during the flood season and no attention is paid during the rest of the year. Experience has shown that the activity has to be maintained continuously and there is a need for increased flood awareness among the officers and staff of the concerned Department as also in the public and voluntary organizations to deal with flood emergencies.

It is essential that training programme and exercise are regularly held to improve the preparedness of officials and the public. This will develop confidence amongst all concerned to manage any emergency situation. The training programme, including education and publicity should be got arranged by the civil authorities with active participation of the officers in charge of flood management and voluntary organizations. The interception of distress codes and signals and flood waning messages being broadcast over All India Radio (Akashvani), Doordarshan and those transmitted through other channels and the effective follow up of such messages into appropriate action should be taught to all people in the flood-prone areas.

Flood Forecasting and Warning

In order to bear with the hazards of flood, attempts should be made to reduce the magnitude of damage under such situations. The other methods towards this objective are flood forecasting and flood warning. The system consists of observation and collection of hydro-meteorological data, transmitting them to the forecasting centres, assimilation of data from various sources and formulation of forecasting and then dissemination of the forecasts to the beneficiaries and users concerned. These forecasts about future flood in advance, give time for taking precautionary measures and alerting the flood fighting organizations, so that timely action is taken to advert failure of engineering structures. Flood forecasting is also used to issue flood warning, if forewarned timely action can be taken to reduce flood hazards to life and damage to properties as far as possible.

On receipt of the forecast, its dissemination to the local population in terms of likely depth of inundation and its duration in the area by the administrative authorities is very important so that affected population, cattle, movable properties, etc., are evacuated before the area gets submerged by flood waters which cause damage. For this a network of wireless stations and telephone system are necessary in the basin near vulnerable reaches of embankments and towns, etc., especially where other means of communication are not dependable or adequate. Flood warning to smaller areas like villages may be conveyed through public address system or in its absence by beat of drums; specific advice should be given to the people regarding evacuating the areas likely to be affected and also about the location which could be considered safe for the level indicated in the flood forecasts. Necessary training in this regard should be imparted to the concerned officials on a regular basis so that they are well versed in the interpretation of the forecast and for taking precautionary measures in the event of an imminent threat to life and property. This training programme should become a regular feature before the flood season every year.

Remote Sensing and GIS Application in Flood Management

Advancements in the remote sensing technology and the Geographic Information System (GIS) help in real time monitoring, early warning and quick damage assessment of flood disasters. A geographic information system is a tool that can assist flood plain managers in identifying flood-prone areas in their community. With a GIS, geographical information is stored in a database that can be queried and graphically displayed for analysis. By overlapping or intersecting different geographical layers, flood-prone areas can be identified and targeted for mitigation or stricter flood plain management.

Remote sensing and GIS techniques has successfully established its application in following areas of flood management such as flood inundation mapping, flood plain zoning and river morphological studies.

Rehabilitation of Flood Victims and Displaces

Another challenge is related with rehabilitation of flood-affected victims. Voluntary groups working in flood mitigation in Nepal suggest that the number of people getting displaced by riverbank erosion is increasing. The first rehabilitation efforts started after the incessant rainfall and landslides of 1954. Subsequent efforts were geared towards voluntary resettlement in the Tarai. Presently, government's support to landslide and flood-affected victims is limited to provision of tarpaulin and immediate relief. Some effort was made at rehabilitating the victims of 1993 flood at Sarlahi and Hetauda. There is no organization in the country with the mandate to rehabilitate displaced people and the country's capacity in this respect is limited. This limitation also impinges on the proposal to build reservoirs and raise questions about equity. The problem is not of drought or floods but of risks, which the farmers and the asset poor families face. While relief and rehabilitation are crucial from the point of view of supporting the households and families hit by floods, equally important are provisions such as risk and life insurance, and, in the case of agriculture, crop failure and livestock insurance. To overcome these challenges we need to focus on governance because making such provision needs to be part of regular governmental functioning. Responses to ameliorate the impact of flooding must be made part of the daily operation, rather than ex post facto relief. The institutional capacity to respond to floods whenever and wherever they occur must be strengthened.

People's Participation

Works of flood protection and drainage improvement affect the life of the beneficiaries and it is, therefore, necessary that such local people are involved to a reasonable extent in the formulation and execution of schemes. Some of the items of participation could be extremely useful in soil conservation, digging of drainage channels, patrolling and watch on embankments, clearance of vegetations on river banks, removal of encroachments, etc. It would be useful if the local population is made aware of the characteristics of the streams and the flood that may affect their life. They could also be trained on measures of flood fighting, survival and retrieval, as also in measures for adjustment to floods. Introducing in the subjects like ecology, soil conservation, afforestation in the educational curriculum is also likely to be of great help in this regard.

Encouraging people's participation, the programme would be implemented through Panchayati Raj Institutions (PRIs): Any sustainable development needs to do in consonance with the felt need and aspiration of the people. A predominant role for Panchayati Raj Institutions (PRIs) in their implementation so far as the people who are either direct sufferers or are potentially direct beneficiaries have been silent and passive regarding Indo-Nepal cooperation and its significance for their problems and prospects. They have to be made aware and educated about how Indo-Nepal cooperation can bring not only relief from their recurrent sufferings but also legitimate prosperity. With such awareness and education, they can motivate their governments to move positively in the matter with a sense of urgency. The issue will thus gain political expediency which governments concerned can hardly ignore specially programmes for women and children. For this it will be advisable to provide special assistance to various programmes, so that government and public participation should be in equal partnership for flood hazards' management of this region.

Indo-Nepal Cooperation

Indo-Nepal cooperation, which is imperative for integrated water resource management of the shared river basin is highly prospective for two main reasons. One, the benefits that will accrue to both is immense, without this cooperation, both will be denied these immense benefits. Two, there is tremendous mutuality and complementarity, with hardly any conflicts of interest in such cooperation. In fact, it is a classic global-win situation.

In spite of such high prospects, Indo-Nepal cooperation has not yet come about in full measures with alacrity that the situation demands and deserves, for a variety of reasons. It may be a worthwhile exercise to identify and analyse these reasons objectively and dispassionately so that misperceptions, misunderstandings and myths may not rule the roost in this matter of vital concern for large masses of people of this region suffering from poverty and miseries. While such an exercise cannot be taken up in detail in this deliberation, it may be in order to bring out some broad points.

In the matter of Indo-Nepal cooperation for development, management and multipurpose utilization of water resources of the shared river basins entailing construction of dams in Nepal, there are three concerned parties, the Government of India, the Government of Nepal and the government of concerned Indian states, primarily Bihar which has a larger and more critical stake in the matter. The Government of India should be interested in this, as it is of vital concern to large masses of its people living in its poorest region which is blessed with excellent natural resources for highly productive agriculture. It is in view of these resources that the second green revolution in India can come only from its eastern region in order to achieve a quantum jump in the stagnating national annual agricultural production. This cannot happen without necessary water resources management including flood control, for which Indo-Nepal cooperation is essential. The Government of India has constitutional responsibility and role to play in bringing about this cooperation and being by far the larger nation than Nepal, it has to take a leading role in an enlightened manner.

Unfortunately, the three parties do not seem to have moved in the matter with positive motivations as indicated above, resulting in negative perceptions and experience. The scenario regarding Indo-Nepal cooperation should improve. It has to be vibrant and optimistic. India and Nepal have a strong hydrological bond. This hydrological bond is, in fact, the most prospective of all other bonds as it can be worked to the immense benefits to the people of both countries with the aid of available technology.

Conclusion

Flood disaster in North Bihar has become a common feature, particularly because of the annual flooding in the river basin. Many attempts have been made by the government to control these floods, but with no gainful success. From 1955 to 2011 approx. 3,500 crore rupees have been spent on the flood management and control measures, but still the flood impacts and damages have increased by about 50 times. The main objective of the paper is to find out the sustainable management strategies for North Bihar's recurring and devastating floods. The paper has highlighted the situation of North Bihar with reference to floods and suitable sustainable techniques that were very fruitful in the management of floods.

References

Aggarwal, M. (2005) 'Aftermath of Disaster', in R.K. Sharma and G. Sharma (eds), *Natural Disaster: Institutional Building for Mitigating the Impact of Vulnerability Section*, New Delhi: APH Publications, 157–168.

Aggarwal, N. and B.S. Narainen (1995) 'A Supplement to Comprehensive Treaties on North Bihar Flood Problem', *Journal of Institution of Engineering*, 65: 131–133.

Ahmad, E. (1946) 'Hwangho of Bihar', *Aligarh Magazine*, Spring Issue, 47: 107–108.

—— (1965) *Bihar: A Physical, Economic and Regional Geography*, Ranchi: Ranchi University Press.

Ali, S.H. (1985) 'Tragedy of Kosi', *Economic and Political Weekly*, 20(18): 795–796.

Brundtland (1987) Our Common Future, Report of the World Commission on Environment and Development, United Nations.

Central Water Commission (2001) Report of Flood Data and Damage Assessment, Government of India, New Delhi.

Dixit, A. (2003) *Floods and Vulnerability: Need to Rethink Flood*, Kathmandu (Nepal): Nepal Water Conservation Foundation (NWCF).

International Federation of Red Cross and Red Crescent (2001) World Disaster Report: Focus on Recovery, IFRCRC, Switzerland.

IUCN (1980) World Conservation Strategy: Living Resource Conservation for Sustainable Development, United Nations: International Union for Conservation of Nature and Natural Resources.

IUCN (1991) World Conservation Strategy: Living Resource Conservation for Sustainable Development, United Nations: International Union for Conservation of Nature and Natural Resources, (Updated and Modified).

Mishra, D.K. (1997) 'The Bihar Flood Story', *Economic and Political Weekly*, 32(35): 2206–2217.

Moench, M., E. Caspari and A. Dixit (1999) *Rethinking the Mosaic: Investigation into Local Water Management*, Kathmandu (Nepal): Nepal Water Conservation Foundation.

11

Problems and Prospects of Interlinking of Rivers in Bihar

D.P. SINGH AND R.B. THAKUR

Flood and drought are common and recurrent phenomena in Bihar which has an area of 94.183 lakh ha, with a population of 8,28,00,879 (Census of India, 2001). The Ganga flowing from west to east bisects the state in two parts. The flood-affected area of Bihar was 68.80 lakh ha (73%) while it was 44.46 lakh ha (86%) in North Bihar and 24.34 lakh ha (6%) in South Bihar. Up to March 2002, about ₹ 1,087 crores were spent on flood control in the plan period. While major parts of the North Bihar were under a flood crisis, 18 districts of the State were in the grip of severe drought.

In the region of North Bihar, floods are mostly caused by rainfall in catchment areas situated outside India, mainly in Nepal. All the rivers flowing through North Bihar originate in Nepal. The State of Bihar or even the Government of India does not have any control over these rivers. Also, all the rivers of North Bihar deposit sand and silt bringing destructive floods. In South Bihar, the situation is different from that of North Bihar. The absence of rain has aggravated the problems in South Bihar. According to a rough estimate, over a 60 per cent agriculture land in the state is dependent on rains for irrigation. In Jehanabad and Arwal districts of South Bihar, the government tubewells have become non-functional.

In India, there are some states with river basins which have enough water whereas there are other states with basin areas having scarcity of water. Inter-basin water transfer link or interlinking of rivers is one of the solutions to this problem. Prominent agriculture scientist, Dr M.S. Swaminathan has said that, now, time has come when we have to see water whereas there are universal and to think over the interlinking of rivers with one another. He further said that we should construct a water grid in South India, immediately. This south water grid can create such amount of livelihood through which South India can be freed from poverty and unemployment. He further cited the example of the Yogatyaji river in China. China has planned this long run interlinking of rivers and constructed three big grids. After interlinking them, China has now a water security system. These three grids are useful in irrigation, power, flood control, drinking water, etc. The objectives of this paper are threefold, *first*, to study the historical perspective of interlinking of rivers in India, *second*, to discuss the problems of interlinking of rivers in Bihar and third, to consider the prospect of interlinking of rivers in Bihar.

Interlinking of Rivers in India: A Historical Perspective

Interlinking of rivers is not a new concept in India. Inter-basin transfer of water was possible in India even in the 19th century. The Periyar Project (1895) is a classic case. So is the Indravati dam project in Odisha, which was carried out in the 1970. The three rivers – Indravati, Kapur, Padagarh and Murg were leading to Godavari. The water was transferred from the Godavari basin to the Mahanadi basin.

The interlinking of rivers had first come for the discussion in the Ministry of Late Pandit Jawahar Lal Nehru. Dr K.L. Rao (1972) first Irrigation Minister of India and a prominent engineer, had proposed to garlanding of rivers as "Ganga-Cauvery Link". Due to financial problem, this proposal was postponed.

The Supreme Court of India asked the Union Government on October 31, 2002, to set up a high level task force to work out the modalities for interlinking of rivers within a period of ten years and to bring about consensus among the states for the completion of the project. The Supreme Court of India brushed aside the centre`s argument that the project, estimated to cost ₹ 5,60,000 crore could be completed only by 2043–45. The Supreme Court said that the project would help to tackle the twin problems of drought and floods and the apex court expects that the project taken up would be completed as expeditiously as possible but within a decade.

The interlinking of rivers was the dream project of former Prime Minister Sri Atal Bihari Vajpayee. As soon as the Congress-led government took over, one of the member of the Task Force of interlinking of rivers, Mr Deepak Das Gupta, met the Water Resources Minister, Priya Ranjan Das Munshi. Two reports of the Action Plan on interlinking of rivers have already been submitted to Supreme Court. The Task Force is headless now, since Suresh Prabhu, Head of Task Force on interlinking of rivers, has resigned.

The President of India, Dr A.P.J. Abdul Kalam, has staunchly advocated the interlinking of the rivers project. He told a joint sitting of both the Houses of Parliament on June 7, 2004, that the government will accelerate the development and use of the country's irrigation potential. He said starting with peninsular rivers, the environmental, ecological and techno-economic feasibility of linking the rivers of the country will be carefully examined. He repeated it again in the address on the eve of the 58th Independence Day on 14, August, 2004. The President also pitched for the implementation of mega programmes such as rural connectivity, regional linking of rivers, infrastructural missions, power mission and tourism so as to generate the necessary enhancement of purchasing power among the people.

The Bihar water resources Minister, Mr Jagdanand Singh said that the interlinking of rivers was the only solution for taming of the rivers. The need of the hour is not water management but flood management. "I will ask railway minister Lalooji to impress upon the centre to start the interlinking of river project in Bihar by joining the Gandak and the Kosi". Thus, the emphasis in recent years is on interlinking of rivers project in India as well as in Bihar.

Problems of Interlinking of Rivers in Bihar

The multipurpose river valley projects and other dams and canals were considered essential for meeting Bihar's critical requirements of irrigation for agriculture, electricity, for industries and flood control. Accordingly, dam construct ruction was given a high priority in the five-year plans. Plan expenditure on dams per kilometre has risen from ₹ 1.6747 the lakhs in the first plan to ₹ 578.888 lakhs in the seventh plan in Bihar. In spite of the multipurpose river valley projects in Bihar, flood control measures have failed miserably and over the years, the area affected by floods and the damage to crops, cattle and to human beings has increased sharply.

1. *Huge cost escalation and gestation period*: The first and foremost problem faced in interlinking of rivers in Bihar is that of long time period which will be between 40–45 years that would result in huge cost escalation.
2. *Natural feature of the rivers will be disturbed*: As water flows in terms of increased discharge, there is corresponding increase in the velocity. Gravity is the main force which brings excess water as well as loose shattered moveable debris helped by this velocity. The availability of mobile sediment in the flowing water is adjusted in an optimum manner down the channel. It is mainly governed by the carrying capacity of flow which is the function of volumes of water velocity and slope. If the important rivers of Bihar are interlinked, natural feature of the rivers may be disturbed.
3. *Glaciers will dry after 40 years*: Scientists say that the glacier of Gangotri will dry after 40 years. The glacier is the main source of water for the river Ganga. In fact, when glacier will not be in existence, how will the Ganges water flow regularly.
4. *Political factors*: There is also confusion among the concerned agencies involved with the project on its status in view of the political opposition to it from the left parties, which are not agreeable to the present status of the project. We are not supporting the interlinking of rivers per se. It is a project, very much in the air but the reason why we are opposed to it is because one should not talk about such a project without addressing issues that require immediate attention like the inequality in water distribution and water accessibility.
5. *Feasibility studies are going on*: As of now, pre-feasibility study has been completed and the feasibility studies are going on. The taskforce is examining the techno-economic viability on interlinking of rivers.

Prospects of Interlinking of Rivers in Bihar

1. Solve flood problems in North Bihar and drought problems in South Bihar. Many of Bihar's rivers are not perennial. However, in the case of snowfed rivers in the North Bihar, the flows are normally perennial. The characteristic of South Bihar is that the annual run-off takes place during the 4 months of monsoon rains, and the rivers are largely dry during the remaining months of the year. If interlinking of rivers in Bihar is done, it will help in solving flood problems, preventing large scale destruction of property, crops and life in North Bihar and solve the drought problems in South Bihar.
2. *Utilization of irrigation and land scientifically*: Bihar has failed hopelessly in getting the maximum benefits out of its investment in irrigation, in the sense that irrigated land has not contributed its maximum to agricultural output. The interlinking of rivers will make double cropping as well as multiple cropping possible in Bihar.
3. *Increase in the production of power and industrialization*: The most important single factor which is a constraint in economic development of Bihar, is the availability of power. The interlinking of rivers in Bihar will generate

hydroelectric power which is a renewable natural resource. It is the most economical source of power and there is no problem of atmospheric pollution.

4. *Develop fisheries*: Fisheries play an important role in the Bihar's economy, generating employment for a river's coastal population. If rivers are interlinked with one another, the dry rivers can also be helpful in raising nutritional levels, augmenting food supply and earning foreign exchange.
5. *Improve the quality of life*: 'Manage Resources and Improve Quality of Life' slogan marks the essence of present-day human agenda. The agenda of improvement of quality of life has been the guiding force to activate people to utilize resources. The interlinking of rivers may become the most natural and parallel agenda aiming at development.
6. *Develop transport, commerce and tourism*: Important river-routes were through the streams of the Ganges, the Kosi and the Gandak which formed the main artery of interstate commerce. Today, the Indian government is planning to interlink the rivers of India for permanent availability of water. If the important rivers of Bihar are interlinked, this will be historic for transport, commerce and tourism.
7. *Conserve forests and promote afforestation*: The interlinking of rivers in Bihar can conserve forests and promote afforestation. Forests have a moderating influence against floods and, thus, they protect the soil against erosion. They provide raw materials to a number of important industries, namely, furniture, paper, construction, etc.

Conclusion and Suggestions

Bihar has ample water resources. Though conditions vary from rivers of North Bihar to rivers of South Bihar, there is no doubt that there are large possibilities for the development of the Bihar`s water resources, especially in view of the interlinking of rivers. The Indian constitution provides that water is a state subject. In such a situation, central government might be impressed to bring an ordinance regarding the interlinking of rivers. Unless, an agreement on sharing of water is brought into the concurrent list, the interlinking of rivers cannot be possible. States should be taken into confidence and all of them have to agree on it. Also, there is the international aspect with neighbours like Bangladesh, Nepal, Bhutan and Pakistan who have to be taken into confidence.

References

Hindustan (2004) Aa Raha Hai Jal Swaraj: Dabi Utsab, 25 July, 1.

Iyer, R.R. (2003) 'Linking of Rivers', *Economic and Political Weekly*, March: 913–915.

Martin, C. (2003) 'Dams, Rivers and People', *Hindustan Times*, New Delhi, 10 February.

Mukherjee, S. (2003) 'Systems Approach to National River Linking Project', *Geography and You*, 3(3–4): 42–43.

Rao, K.L. (1972) *India's Water Wealth*, New Delhi: Orient Longman.

Ravinder, A. (2004)) 'Interlinking of Rivers', *Yojna*, November: 9–14.

Singh, R.B.P. (2003) 'Proposed Water-Basin, Water Transfer Links and North Bihar Resource Management and Quality of Life in North Bihar', 3rd Geographer's Conference, 16–17 May, 69.

12

Water Quality and Water-Borne Diseases in Kanpur City

KANCHAN GUPTA

With development, the urban areas are growing into bigger agglomerations with ever-increasing influx of people which in turn creates demand for support services, viz., water supply, transportation, drainage/sewerage, garbage collection and disposal, etc., that are essential but far exceeds the available supply of these services. While taking up developmental activities, the assimilative capacities of the environmental components, i.e., air, water and land to various pollutions are rarely considered. Also, lack of proper land use control is resulting in poor land use compatibility. The developmental activities being haphazard and uncontrolled are leading to over use, congestion, incompatible land use and poor living conditions. Thus, the problems of environmental pollution in urban areas are becoming complex and are creating high risk environment to the city residents in the form of deterioration of the natural and socio-economic living conditions, which specifically includes overcrowding, congestion, lack of sufficient water supply, unhygienic living conditions, air and noise pollution and consequently health.

In the process of development, the issues confronting us today are achieving the desired development for economic or social reasons on the one hand and safeguarding the environment and maintaining good quality living conditions on the other. The measures taken for pollution control in individual sectors, viz., municipal waste disposal, industry, transport, etc., are not solving the problems, due to ever-increasing gap between 'demand' and 'supply'. Such conditions pose serious health and economic stress to all residents. From health statistics, it is evident that morbidity and mortality is often predominantly related to environmental risks and are due to various factors such as air pollution from vehicular, industrial and domestic sources, noise pollution, water pollution – lack of proper stormwater drainage and sewerage system, improper and inadequate garbage collection and disposal system, haphazard siting of industries/processes, transportation, storage and handling of toxic or hazardous chemicals, and lack of adequate open spaces and green areas, etc.

Water has both the quality and quantity dimensions. Currently, the rate of urbanization, industrialization and deterioration of water quality (both surface and groundwater) is of major concern in metropolitan cities and towns in India. Kanpur city is located between the daob region of the river Ganga and Pondu. Mostly, urban domestic and industrial supply of water is only from these rivers. The rivers are highly polluted because of the sewage disposal from more than a dozen of drains from the city itself. This pollution poses a serious threat to the secured urban water supply and urban health. Thus, Kanpur city has been selected as a study area, as it is facing severe problems of water pollution and water-borne diseases because of poor water quality.

Aims and Objectives

The main objectives of this paper are: (1) to analyse the status of water quality in Kanpur city, and (2) to understand and highlight the main water-borne diseases in the study area.

Data Sources

The study is primarily based upon both secondary and as well as primary sources of data. The data is collected from various government agencies and organizations. The study includes data obtained from published and unpublished records and is supplemented by information generated through literature review. The secondary data has been collected from Kanpur Jal Nigam Department, Kanpur Jal Sansthan and Office of Central Groundwater Board, Lucknow and State Groundwater Board, Kanpur and socio-economic data from Census of India Population Totals for Uttar Pradesh, 2001, etc. Information on water resources and stream water quality and source of water pollutants have been obtained from official reports of the Directorate of Groundwater and Irrigation Department of the State and Central Pollution Control Board (CPCB). Besides, books, thesis, journals, articles, newspapers, internet websites were also consulted.

The primary data has been collected through questionnaire method on the bases of simple random sampling in different city wards to find out the impact of water on the health of the dwellers of Kanpur city and the polluted water impact on their health. The data have been tabulated and then represented through graph and maps to find out the regional variation or wards-wise variation in Kanpur city.

The Study Area

Kanpur, an industrial city of India and previously known as – Kanhaiapur or Cownpore is located about 425 km east of Delhi on the right bank of holy river Ganga and developed linearly along this river. The expansion of the city was restricted in Southern direction by the river Pandu. Kanpur city occupies a geographical area of about 278 sq km, in the central part of Uttar Pradesh, lying between 26° 20' and 26°35' North latitude and 80°10' and 80° 30' East longitude (Figure 1). Kanpur is the largest and most populous industrial city in the state of Uttar Pradesh in India.. The urban limits of Kanpur Nagar are spread over an area of 215 sq km. Kanpur was once known as the 'Manchester of Northern India' but over the years has unfortunately gained notoriety as a dirty and polluted city. All the important industries such as textiles, heavy engineering, tanneries, fertilizer and leather are situated in the heart of the city with residential areas on either side.

Figure 1

Location Map of Kanpur City

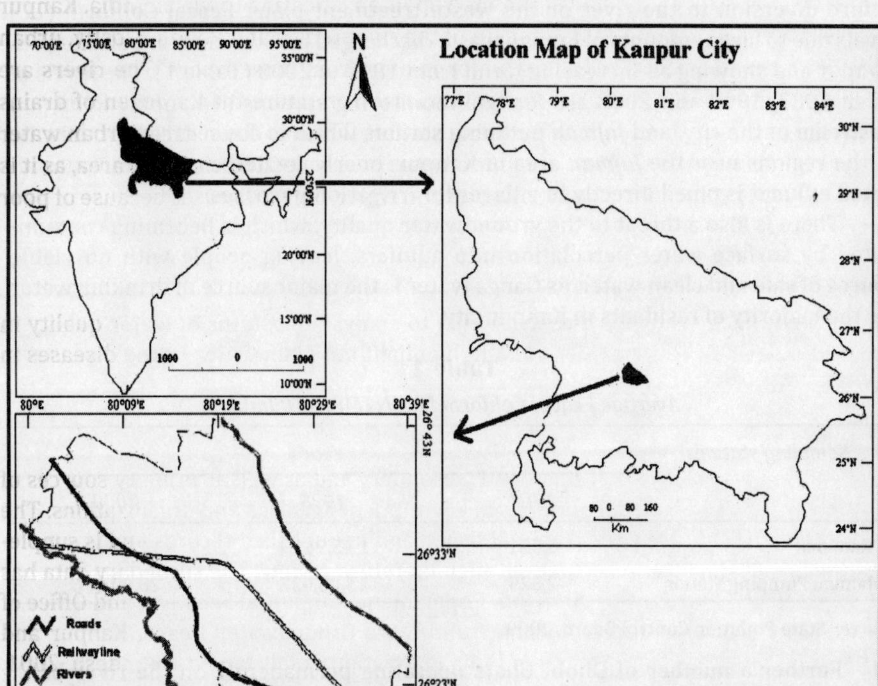

Results and Discussion

River Water Quality of Kanpur City

The Ganga River Basin is struggling with water quality problems due to pollution from untreated sewage, industrial effluent, and urban and agricultural run-off. Pollution in the Ganga includes both domestic sewage and industrial effluents, or from both point and non-point sources. There are tremendous public health consequences for the high pollution loads seen in surface water so intimately intertwined with the livelihoods of many millions of people. People in cities and towns that receive their water supplies directly from the Ganga suffer from diarrheal diseases such as cholera as well as toxic effects from unregulated industrial effluents.

Kanpur city is the home to approximately 300 leather tanneries concentrated mainly in the *Jajmau* area, most of which release their effluent directly into the Ganga. Leather industries produce a large amount of effluent concentrated with pollutants, particularly the toxic heavy metal, chromium. The total sewage generated in Kanpur is around 360 MLD (million litres per day) out of which 160 MLD was proposed to be diverted to sewage treatment plants under Phase I of the Ganga Action Plan (GAP). The remaining sewage was to be treated in the second phase of GAP.

Under the Ganga Action Plan, the larger tanneries were required to install Effluent Treatment Plants, and Combined Effluent Treatment Plants. They were slated for construction to process the effluent of tanneries that were too small to afford their own plants. These goals were laudable, but difficult to achieve, and to date many of the tanneries have still not removed the chromium from their effluent before diversion to the river or the waste treatment plant. Feacal Coliform (FC) levels due to large amounts of human waste discharged into the river are also high in Kanpur and showing an increasing trend from 1897 to 2008 (Table 1). The levels of FC in 1987, 1998 and 2008 are for two monitoring stations in Kanpur: *Ranighat,* upstream of the city, and *Jajmau* pumping station, which is downstream of the city. In the regions near the *Jajmau* area of Kanpur, poorly treated chromium contaminated effluent is piped directly to villages for irrigation purposes.

There is also a threat to the groundwater quality, which is becoming contaminated by surface water percolation into aquifers, leaving people with no viable source of safe and clean water, as Ganga water is the major source of drinking water for the majority of residents in Kanpur city.

Table 1

Average Feacal Coliform Levels (MPN/100mL)

Sampling stations	*Year*		
	1987	*1998*	*2008*
1. Ranighat	5,551	1,45,941.4	1,25,798.6
2. Jajmau Pumping Station	2,629	15,00,037	28,00,876

Source: State Pollution Control Board, 2009.

Further a number of Dhobi Ghats operating permanently on the river bank contributes substantially to water pollution. The Central Pollution Control Board (CPCB, 2004–05) periodically monitors the water quality of the city at various points studied the water quality at designated sites (Table 2). The table explains the status of different parameters during different years. Water temperature and pH in all the sampling stations were within the tolerance limit, whereas Dissolved Oxygen (DO), Biochemical Oxygen Demand (BOD) and chloride content were exceeding the standards at various sites. It is also evident that although the situation is not alarming at all sites, but it cannot be denied that the quality of water in the stretch of Ganga passing along Kanpur is not fit for local consumption and health. Degradation of water quality creates water scarcity and limits its availability for human use and ecosystem and thereby impacts the optimum management of water resources (Rao and Mamatha, 2004).

Sources of Water Pollution

There are many sources for water pollution but two general categories are important to discuss: direct and indirect contaminant sources. Direct sources include effluent outfalls from factories, refineries, and waste treatment plants, etc., that emit fluids of varying quality directly into urban water supplies. Indirect sources include contaminants that enter the water supply from soils, groundwater systems and from the atmosphere via rainwater (Kudesia, 1985).

Pollution of waterbodies is mostly from point sources such as discharge of untreated domestic sewage from the fast growing urban cities and towns located along the banks, industrial effluents, etc., and from non-point sources which comprises run-off from open defecation, agricultural fields, cattle wallowing,

Table 2

Water Qualities at Various Sampling Points

Sampling points	*Bithoor Ghat*			*Ganga Barrage (Kanpur u/s)*			*Rani Ghat (intake point)*			*Sarsia Ghat*			*Buria Ghat*		
	Years			*Years*			*Years*			*Years*			*Years*		
Parameters	07	08	09	07	08	09	07	08	09	07	08	09	07	08	09
Temperature	25.5	25.8	26.0	25.0	25.5	26.3	25.5	25.9	26.3	26.0	26.6	26.9	26.1	26.4	26.8
PH	8.4	8.0	8.5	8.2	8.2	8.3	8.2	8.0	8.4	7.8	7.6	8.0	7.8	8.3	8.0
Dissolved Oxygen	7.8	7.4	9.4	7.7	7.6	9.2	5.5	5.8	6.5	4.1	4.6	4.9	4.1	4.3	4.9
BOD (mg/l)	2.6	3.5	3.7	3.1	3.5	3.7	6.9	7.3	7.6	5.4	6.0	6.4	3.8	4.2	4.7
Total Coliform (MPN/100ml.)	7,544	13,692	5,367	7,589	4,350	3,300	9,300	13,000	15,000	46,000	53,000	55,000	21,000	22,000	18,000

Source: State Pollution Control Board, 2009.

disposal of dead bodies, etc., using the prepared inventory, pollution load run-off from different sources has been computed basin-wise. It is observed that out of the total pollution load run-off reaching the river, 95 per cent is from point sources, including 65 per cent load from municipal sewage and 28 per cent load from industries and 8 per cent from the agricultural activities in surrounding areas (Figure 2).

Figure 2

Points Sources of Water Pollution

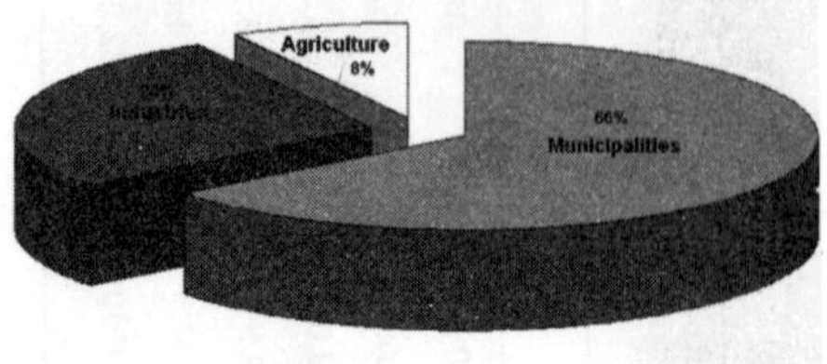

The remaining 5 per cent is contributed by non-point sources such as agricultural and forestry run-off, livestock, rural households, etc. The run-off of non-point pollution load is very small during the dry season and does not substantially affect the river water quality. However, in the wet season, the proportion of pollution load from different sources changes significantly and non-point sources also contribute a high ratio of pollutants to the river.

Water-borne Diseases in Kanpur City

Kanpur being an industrial metropolis, has a large number of industries of which leather, textile, jute and chemical industries are dominant. The unplanned disposal of domestic waste and discharge of untreated or partially treated effluents by the industries directly on land or in Ganga river are resulting in pollution of surface and sub-surface water. During the recent studies by CGWB, the contamination of groundwater by toxic constituent like hexavalent chromium (Cr+6) has been detected in the industrial pockets located at Nauriya Khera (Panki Thermal), Baburia, Rakhi Mandi, Fazalganj and Jajmau areas (Table 3). The main source of chromium concentration in groundwater being the industrial effluents from leather, textile, etc. The chromium concentration in water of phreatic aquifers in these localities are shown in Table 3.

Table 3

Chromium Concentration at Different Localities in Kanpur City

	Locality	*Range of chromium in water concentration*
1.	Baburia	0.510–7.223 mg/l
2.	Rakhi Mandi	0.007–10.00 mg/l
3.	Fazalganj	0.005–6.35 mg/l
4.	Jajmau	0.003–0.132 mg/l
5.	Nauriya Khera	0.008–8.00 mg/l

Source: Compiled from Water Quality Monitoring Reports of CPCB, 1998–2000.

Health Problems Due to Chromium

Chromium is the most toxic water pollutant. The concentration above 0.05 mg/l in drinking water may prove detrimental to human health. The higher concentration of chromium may cause cancer of lungs, nasal cavity and paranasal sinus, stomach and

Figure 3

(a) Skin Diseases from Water Contamination, (b) Water Scarcity, (c and d) Dwellers in Stagnated Polluted Water

(a) (b)

(c) (d)

larynx. Skin decolourization and peptic ulcer are common diseases in the local inhabitants of this area (Figure 3).

Health Problems by Water-Borne Diseases in Kanpur City

Water borne diseases is the general term used to denote diseases associated with poor water supply or quality. In developing world countries, four-fifths of all illness is by water-borne diseases, with diarrhoea being the leading cause of childhood death. In 2006, water-borne diseases were estimated to cause 1.8 million deaths each year while about 1.1 billion people lacked proper drinking water.

In Kanpur city, it has been observed that 75 per cent diseases are water-borne diseases while the remaining 25 per cent diseases are caused by other sources like air pollution and other pollutants in environment. The health problems related with the water-borne diseases in Kanpur city are divided into following categories:

1. *Dysentery*: Dysentery is a common water borne disease and is due to ingestion of contaminated water. It is caused by the four different species of the bacteria

Shigella. The number of bacteria required to cause an infection is small – between 10 to 100 organisms causing dysentery. Abdominal pain followed by watery diarrhea is common after the infection. About 70 per cent of surveyed population is having this type of disease. This disease is mostly pronounced in the small children and particularly those living along the Ganga and Pandu river areas.

2. *Typhoid*: Typhoid or 'enteric fever' is caused by infection with 'salmonella typhi'. Symptoms are a rapidly fluctuating temperature, drowsiness, diarrhoea, abdominal rash, delirium and coma. Immunization is effective and the disease is treatable with antibiotics. Typhoid is also highest in the zone 1, 2 and zone 4 because all the zones are all along the river Ganga area. The zones which are along the Ganga, Pandu river basins have highest concentration of typhoid patients – more than 75 per cent, whereas the zones which are away from the two river basins are having less concentration of typhoid diseases as shown in Table 4 and Figure 4.
3. *Cholera*: Cholera is defined as an acute infectious disease, which is caused by the ingestion of foods or water that has been contaminated with the bacterium Vibrio Cholerae. In severe forms it is known to be one of the most rapidly fatal illnesses known. Symptoms include very watery diarrhoea, nausea, cramps, nosebleed, rapid pulse, vomiting, and hypovolemic shock (in severe cases), at which point death can occur in 12–18 hours. Cholera is not having high intensity or high concentration but nearly 30–40 per cent of surveyed sampled people have once gone through this disease. The highest percentage are found in zone number 4 where maximum respondents reply they have had cholera disease and gone through it once.

Figure 4

Spatial Variations of Different Diseases in Different Zones of Kanpur City, 2008

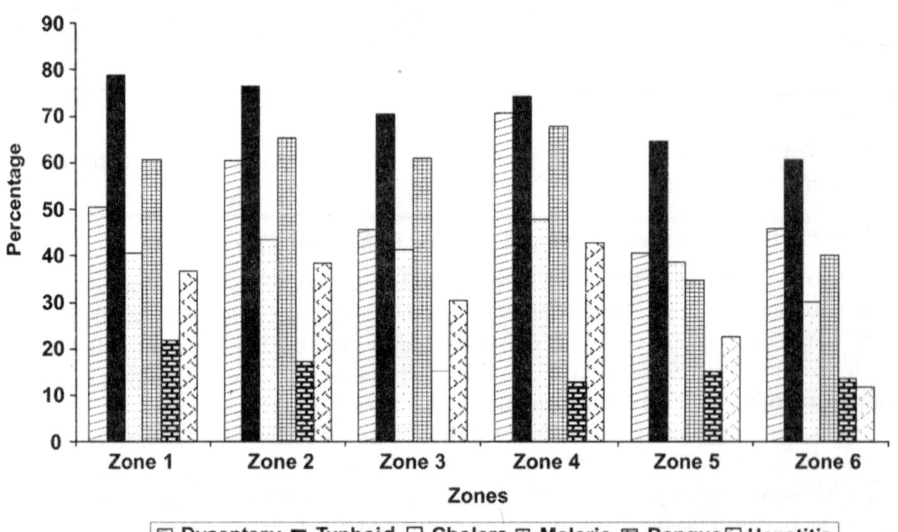

Source: Field Survey.

Table 4

Spatial Variation of Diseases in Different Zones in Kanpur City (2008) in Percentage

Type of Disease	*Zone 1*	*Zone 2*	*Zone 3*	*Zone 4*	*Zone 5*	*Zone 6*
1. Dysentery	50.6	60.4	45.6	70.6	40.6	45.8
2. Typhoid	78.80	76.6	70.4	74.4	64.6	60.8
3. Cholera	40.6	43.6	41.4	47.8	38.6	30.2
4. Malaria	60.8	65.4	61.0	67.8	34.8	40.0
5. Dengue	22.0	17.4	15.3	12.8	14.4	13.6
6. Hepatitis A	36.6	38.5	30.4	42.8	22.6	11.8

Source: Based on Field Survey.

4. Malaria is an infectious disease, which is not new to India or the tropical regions of Asia. It is a disease, which still manages to cause about 500 million infections and 2 million deaths annually worldwide. The danger of malaria is more during the monsoon season due to breeding of mosquitoes and when the water starts receding but some of it remains stagnated. The problem is worst in cities with poor drainage systems. In Kanpur city the condition of drainage system is very poor, so there is maximum risk of infectious malaria disease. In the survey and sampled zones the malaria patients are highest in zone 1, 2 and 4 where more than 60 per cent patients are found. In surveyed households 60 per cent have one or two members having had malaria during the last 5 years. Whereas the zones 3, 5 and 6 have less concentration of malaria patients because they are away from impure water bodies which are the main source regions of this disease.
5. *Dengue*: The Dengue fever is an extremely infectious virus, which is carried by the domestic mosquito and spreads from person to person through what may seem like a harmless mosquito bite. The infection with dengue viruses causes clinical illness ranging from a less dangerous non-specific viral syndrome called 'Dengue fever' to severe and fatal hemorrhagic disease of 'Dengue Hemorrhagic Fever (DHF)'. Dengue has slowly spread to more then 100 countries. In 2002 more then 2.5 billion people were at risk of infection with this virus. This would roughly work out to 40 per cent of the world population. In Kanpur city, three zones have more than 15 per cent respondents having dengue, i.e., zone 1, 2, and 4 while the remaining zones have less respondents having this disease.
6. *Hepatitis A*: Hepatitis is a general term that means inflammation of the liver. Inflammation of the liver can result from infection, from exposure to alcohol, certain medications, chemicals, or poisons, or from a disorder of the immune system. The concentration of hepatitis A in Kanpur city is also concentrated in zone 4 followed by zones 2 and 1.

Conclusions

After the above discussion regarding the health problems of dwellers of Kanpur city it may be concluded that the water quality situation is not good and is creating many water-borne diseases in the city. Therefore, it is suggested that the government must take steps to improve the quality of water and spread awareness among the local habitants about the consequences of poor water quality.

References

Caldwell, L. (1990) *Between Two Worlds: Science, the Environmental Movement and Policy Choice*, Cambridge: Cambridge University Press.

Davis, K. (1951) *The Population of India and Pakistan*, Princeton, New Jersey: Princeton University Press.

Kudesia, V.P. (1985) *Water Pollution*, Meerut: Pragati Prakashan.

National Institute of Environmental Health Sciences (NIEHS 2006–2011) *New Frontiers in Environmental Sciences and Human Health*, Strategic Plan, Research Triangle Park, NC: Environmental Health Perspectives.

Rao, S.M. and Mamatha, P. (2004) 'Water Quality in Sustainable Water Management', *Current Science*, 87(7): 942–947.

Taylor, C.E. and M.F. Hall (1967) 'Health, Population and Economic Development', *Science*, 157(789): 651–657.

World Commission on Environment and Development (1987) *Our Common Future*, Oxford: Oxford University Press.

13

Impacts of Hydropower Development on Rural Livelihood Sustainability in Sikkim Himalayas

AAKASH UPADHYAY

When the nation is going through an acute power crisis due to rapid growth in population and their increasing demands, planners and researchers came up with the initiative of developing clean and safe energy. We all know India has the best location in terms geography and natural resources. The control of environmental pollution and the development of environmentally friendly economic activities are essential features of a green economy. Adoption of green economy principles, in particular, reducing greenhouse gas emissions and instituting renewable sources of energy to mitigate climate change are strong policy drivers around the world (Rustico and Tiraboschi, 2010). Hydroelectricity is considered less polluting, clean and safe than the more common fossil fuel-based forms of electricity generation like that of coal, although hydroelectric projects require very high capital investment and have long development periods (Klimpt et al., 2002).

But they are in a way one-time investment in comparison to other kind of investments. Any kind of projects certainly has an impact on the areas nearby. Hydroelectricity projects can have a range of impacts on communities near the project sites, both beneficial and detrimental. Positive socio-economic benefits can include provision of employment (although temporary), welfare, and market accessibility (Koch, 2002). Detrimental impacts such as loss of agricultural land, reduction of production along with adverse consequences for livelihoods of affected people (Gupta and Asher, 1998: 117), altered river channels, and loss of wildlife habitat have made hydroelectricity projects the subject of strong opposition from environmental organizations. In other words, they bestow physical and, in some cases, human livelihood assets to the community at the expense of natural livelihood assets, which may not represent a balanced approach to sustaining positive livelihood outcomes.

Generally, in most of this kind of study across the world primary focus is on the major impacts like displacement and resettlement of the peoples of the affected region, as the dams are large and areas affected are huge. But in case of Sikkim, dam construction does not involve inundation of large areas , displacement and consequent resettlement because river valleys are steep and narrow. Therefore, the aim of this study was to examine community perceptions and the response of the environmental and socioeconomic impacts of hydroelectricity project on villagers and the areas nearby and consider the implications on their sustainable livelihoods.

The Study Area: Sikkim

Sikkim is one of the small hilly states of India in the north-east. It forms the part of eastern Himalayas. It shares national boundary with West Bengal and international boundary with China and Nepal. Sikkim, a state of India in the Eastern Himalayas, lying between 27°4' and 28°7'N latitude and between 88°4' and 88°55'E, longitude has an area of 7,096 km^2 and a population of 6,11,688 (2011). The population

Figure 1

The Study Area and Major Hydropower Projects in Sikkim

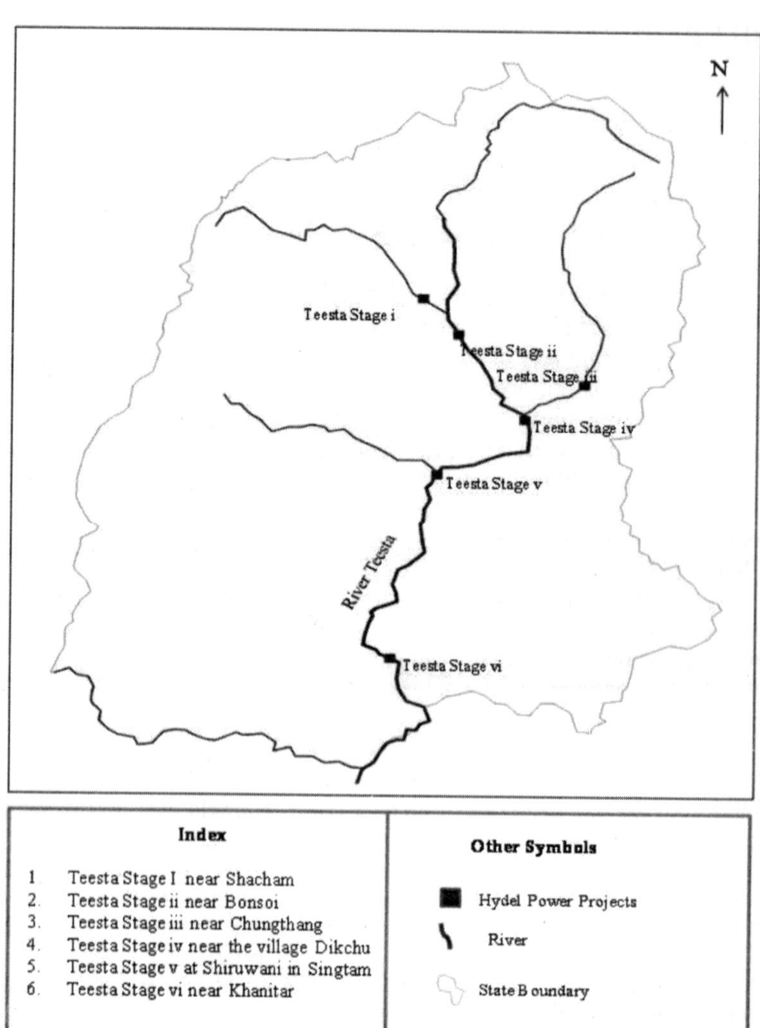

density of the state is 86 persons/sq km with the literacy rate of 81.42 per cent (2011). The sex ratio is 890 females/000 males (2011). The state has four districts with an average elevation of about 1,396 m (4,580 ft). It is well known for its biodiversity and the forests that cover 46 per cent of its land area (Forest Survey of India 2003–2007). The state has rugged terrain with unstable rocks dissected by actively eroding streams and rivers. The whole state is well drained by numerous tributaries of the river Teesta, the main one being the Rangit.

The state of Sikkim is blessed with tremendous hydroelectric power potential that has been worked out at 8,000 MW Peak and a firm base of 3,000 MW. Approximately seventy miles north-east stretch of Sikkim's territory has a land gradient that lies roughly between 500 feet to 28,000 feet above mean sea level. Due to this amazing terrain, Sikkim houses some of the most turbulent and swiftest rivulets in the world that is best suited for harnessing hydropower potential. The exploitation of water to produce electricity is considered the key to earning the large revenues required by the state for funding its welfare programmes. Private power developers are obliged to transfer 12 per cent of their profits to the Government of Sikkim initially, and 15 per cent of profits 12 years after project completion (Dahal, 2008). During the primary survey it was found that as a part of their local area development programme, hydropower companies undertake community development projects such as school repair, road and footpath construction, electrification and water supply for villages, and livelihood skill development in project-affected areas. They also organize football tournament and free football coaching to interested youths. They also promote the concept of organic farming started by the state government. Catchment management funds are utilized for maintenance of catchment values and development of communities upstream of dam locations.

Sources of Livelihood

As we know that India is an agrarian economy, so is the hilly state of Sikkim. Here, the major source of livelihood is agriculture, farming activities, animal husbandry, etc. But today the livelihood sources are changing. After the coming up of hydropower project the pressure on agriculture as a source of livelihood has been reduced since people are shifting from this sector to working in the factories. The employment structure is changing and so is the socio-economic structure. The main livelihood sources are illustrated in Table 1.

Table 1

Category-wise Division of Livelihood Source

Source of livelihood	*Percentage of people engaged (%)*
Agriculture	45
Forestry	5
Business or self-employed	10
Salaried job in NHPC/factory worker	30
Livestock and aqua culture	5
Tourism	5

Source: Primary Survey, 2013.

It can be inferred from the Table 1 that the main source of livelihood is agriculture which involves about 45 per cent of the total surveyed, while the job in the factory comprises the second main source. Recently this trend has come up in some specific places while prior to the coming of power projects the share of agriculture was more than two-thirds of the total engagement for livelihood. Also due to urbanization and developmental work these days, people are taking up different sources of livelihood as the efforts and returns in agriculture is no longer fruitful. These days, other economic activities like tourism, eco-tourism are coming up in the region. The implications of tourism to the mountain economy of Sikkim and in particular Gangtok are significant with the tourism industry providing the maximum employment opportunities next to the Government. Now eco-tourism has emerged as an important economic activity in the region which includes trekking, mountaineering, river rafting and other nature-oriented activities. As the land is degrading day by day so is the yield and the quality. People are taking up alternatives such as employment in manufacturing and tourism sector, etc., and they are effectively developing as a replacement to the traditional means of livelihood.

Database and Methodology

In order to access the problems pertaining to the hydropower plant both the method of acquiring information has been used and they are as follows:

- *Primary survey*: The base of any findings or any research work is the primary survey where you get to know the ground reality of the study area and base your interpretation accordingly. The place I visited for the primary survey was on a bylane on NH.31a towards west from Singtam market. It was 10 minutes ride from the main market. Here the village located nearby had around 100 households and 20 interviewees were taken as a model sample for the analysis of NHPC phase V project (510mw) in Dikchu, Singtam
- *Secondary data*: The secondary source of data like the NHPC website and other internet information have been used to gather the technical data or information about the project like the size, location, construction period, the estimated cost, etc.

In order to explore and discover the community response and perception of the impacts of the hydroelectricity I have tried to use moreover the qualitative aspect of research methodology like in-depth personal interviews with the local villagers, the workers and the businessmen and some students. The analysis is qualitative as the survey was based on the probable impacts and the response of the community. The study is based on the primary surveys of 40 individuals and visit to the NHPC office near the project site. The response was varied as different class like labour class, small farmers and unemployed youths were affected differently. During the survey the local guy from Sikkim University contributed immensely and helped me in the process of primary survey.

But in some cases where there is quantitative information, wherever possible quantitative techniques like table and graphs also have been used. Much emphasis was given in the qualitative aspect as there was problem pertaining to acquiring of quantitative data. Discussions were held among some interviewees, my colleagues and some knowledgeable persons on the results of my analysis and interpretations.

Results and Discussion

Impacts of Hydropower Development

Degradation of Agricultural Land

The construction of hydropower projects caused changes in land use, involving mainly conversion of agricultural land for roads, tunnels, buildings or other components of the projects. The impacts of these changes are similar in all other Hydro-power plant sites in Sikkim or any other hilly states. Although the agricultural land acquired by the project was not much, which was about 31 hectares at each site, but the impact was widespread. Agriculture land and farming activity were important rural assets for the villagers who practised farming as their main livelihood activity. Farming consisted of cultivation of cereals and vegetables on the terraced farmland and cardamom on the higher reaches of the slopes. The common cash crops like the production of ginger was affected the most. Many places with agricultural lands and cardamom fields which to a certain degree is the mainstay of the economy of the region have been adversely affected.

During the primary survey many of the respondents said that their lands were rendered useless by rolling of boulders and loosened up slopes by careless road construction work or by careless earth dumping. This is one of the biggest issues during the development of the hydropower plants which involves blasting, tunnelling and dumping. This leads to disturbing the stability of the land, some parts may be covered by the debris coming out from the construction work. The disposal of debris may be on the agricultural land which is near to the site. It is easy to dump and relatively cheaper as they do not have to go far which would cost them more. Landslides are the common features in the hill slopes of Sikkim like any other hill areas. On the installation of hydropower plant, landslides are being induced to some extent by instability caused by the vibration and the drilling. In the study area, people said that landslide was common *(pairo jharnu)*. Pairo jharnu in Nepali means landslide or a type of mudflow in hilly region which they attributed mainly to vibration caused by the drilling and blasting during construction of roads for easy access to the location by the vehicles (which would save their time and money), and also construction of tunnels to transfer water underneath. Apart from this, some of the farmlands were covered by the mudslides during the monsoon when there is heavy rainfall which initially recharges the ground and after a course of time when the saturation is reached, starts loosening up and starts flowing downstream as a mud flow or mudslide. This leads to loss of agricultural lands, crops being destroyed affecting the livelihood of some of the people. In such a case what could they do to sustain themselves, as for this is a type of *indirect loss* caused to the cropland and the farmer, no compensation is paid for such *"indirect"* damage to property. The role of agricultural land has been changing since the power plants have been installed and now they have been changed and turned into a different landscape. Some of the major and minor changes in the role of agricultural land has been highlighted in Table 2.

Table 2

Impacts of Hydropower Construction and the Changing Role of the Agricultural Land

Original land use	*Current land use*	*Direct impact*	*Indirect impact*	*Treatment/ mitigation*
Farmland	Road	Loss of farmland.	Reduction in farm production.	No effort to reclaim them.
Farmland	Road	Dust pollution	Loss of fodder, crop quantity and quality	Sprinkling to some extent but ineffective.
Farmland	Road	Dumping of debris and covering the land	Reduction in farm production	Land reclamation for agriculture by soil conservation
Cropland	Road	Landslides	Low productivity and disruption of markets	Plantation and check by engineering work
Cropland	Tunnels	Cracks of Surface Water supply Disruption	A source of impetus to seismic events and low farm product	Check dams and other soil conservation works. Other source of Irrigation
Cropland	Project infrastructure	Loss of Farmland and crops.	Reduction in crop production of farmland	No efforts
Cropland	Barren fields due to changed conditions and drying up	Increase in waste land	Reduction in farmland and production	Reclamation and revival of appropriate agricultural practices

Source: Chandy et al. (2012).

Reduction of Agricultural Productivity

The agricultural productivity may be defined as the crop yield per hectare in a given period of time. As we know Singtam is a hilly region and here, agriculture is not easy and agricultural land available is limited. Here, traditional agriculture depends on factors such as use of livestock for draught and manure production, maintenance of an adequate forest cover (for forage and fuel), availability of water for irrigation, and presence of an informal labour exchange system *adia,* which means tenancy (Chhetri and Sharma, 2006). The present condition shows that hydroelectricity development affected these factors in various ways leading to reduced agricultural productivity. The farmers and the local respondents felt the need for livestock-rearing declined due to reduced farming, and forest. Streams were adversely affected by landslides and muck disposal from tunnelling and road construction work. People and farmers in particular, also reported that they experienced poor plant growth due to dust pollution and

Figure 2

Decline in Grain Production

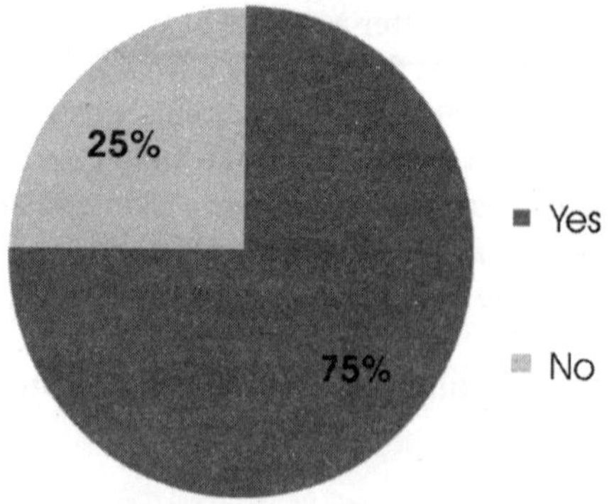

Source: Primary Survey, 2013.

dryness in the region. The plant growth has changed and plants started becoming stunted. Surface water according to most affected farmers used to be the main source of irrigation for their farms. The streams used for tapping irrigation water dried up and some had poor winter flows. Water scarcity was stated by most respondents to be the main cause of poor production of maize, paddy, millet and lentil crops. This loss of agricultural land and reduced agricultural production were the factors that drove people to change their occupation from farming to non-farming employment. During the survey it was found that out of the total sample survey, around 75 per cent of the people believe that there has been reduction in the grain production (Figure 2). They say that, may be, because of climate change or due to hydropower projects. Plus, they also said that the interest in agriculture has declined due to continuous reduction in the production. Therefore, they are migrating to other places for alternate source of livelihood.

Today, the employment scenario of the region is also in a transition due to the impact of hydropower projects. Firstly, land is being acquired for the construction of the projects which leads to the loss of agricultural land and the productivity as a whole in the long run (Figure 3). Today, these things have lead to change in the mindset of the locals who are switching on to other works. Today, the younger and the more educated people in particular, have withdrawn from agriculture and have taken up employment with private companies, because they felt this was a better livelihood option as there were no risks of low productivity and crop failure.

One of the interviewe named Milan Tamang said that he has now taken up the profession of driving the company's vehicle, as it was easy and there was a fixed and regular income from this source. Prior to this he used to work as a tenant on the

Figure 3

Relation Between Hydropower Development and Change in Occupation

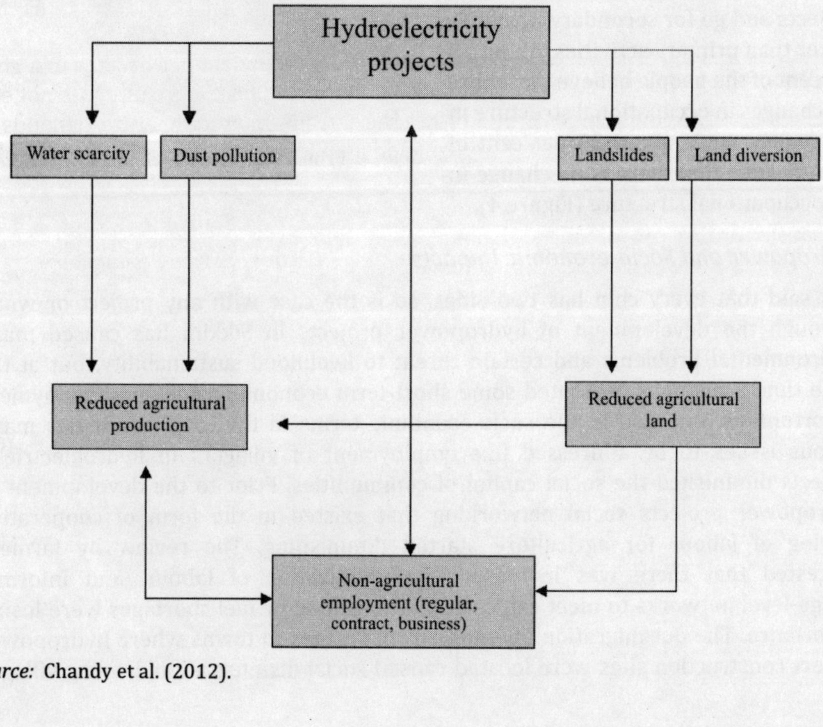

Source: Chandy et al. (2012).

farmland which his family had hired. His parents still work there but he says the yield is too little to support the family so he has taken the present profession. This attitude of the people on the preference of company job or employment over farming has resulted in loss of agricultural labour. Agricultural labour in the region is organized around two systems – a formal production-based share cropping system and an informal cooperative labour system. The schemes like Mahatma Gandhi National Rural Employment Guarantee Scheme where there is a system of high and fixed daily wages has lead to general rise in the wage rate of the local labour working in the fields. In the same way as per some of the interviewees – with this setting the traditional agricultural system is rapidly vanishing in the region. Also with the setting up of the hydroelectricity company (Lanco, Patel Engineering, Hindustan Construction Company, Bharat Heavy Electricals Limited), the general wage rate for the labour in the villages has more than doubled to match the wage rate paid by the company. This was too expensive and unaffordable to most farmers and this led to many farms being left fallow and to a reduced farm output overall. During the field survey some of the perceptions of the community was taken regarding the setting up of hydropower station and what they have experienced in the recent past, and what they think about all this with respect to their environment.

Their perception about reduction in the agricultural land and agricultural workforce was also known. They also told about the changes taking place in the occupational structure in recent times. Today, a major chunk of the youth prefers to go to work on the projects and go for secondary activities rather than primary activities. About 75 per cent of the people believe that there are changes in occupational structure in the region, while about 25 per cent of them believe that there is no change in the occupational structure (Figure 4).

Figure 4

Changes in Occupation

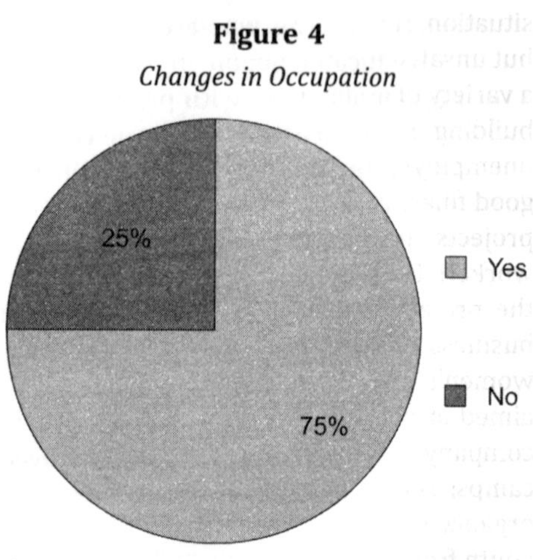

Source: Primary Survey, March 2013.

Hydropower and Socio-economic Impacts

It is said that every coin has two sides, so is the case with any project or work. Although the development of hydropower projects in Sikkim has caused many environmental problems and certain threat to livelihood sustainability, but at the same time it also has generated some short-term economic gains and employment opportunities. But also in the socio-economic terms in the long run, it has many serious issues to be addressed like employment of villagers in hydroelectricity projects diminished the social capital of communities. Prior to the development of hydropower projects social networking that existed in the form of cooperative sharing of labour for agriculture started diminishing. The review by farmers suggested that there was increased commoditization of labour, and informal village-level networks to meet exigencies such as food or fuel shortages were losing importance. The out-migration of youths from villages to towns where hydropower project construction sites were located caused social disintegration, leaving villages occupied mainly by the elderly who were unable to undertake agricultural activities and sustain informal networks. This was a big loss to the social capital of the region on all the scale of farming. The youth's knowledge and the interest on traditional agriculture which was the basis, of farmers livelihood was gone. The employment provided by hydroelectricity companies to local people helped to address some unemployment problems faced by farmers impoverished by poor agricultural production. The majority of those who benefited from employment in companies included smallholder farmers and less-educated youth who were given unskilled jobs, mostly as casual labourers or temporary watchmen at construction sites. Educated youth were employed in offices and in a variety of skilled jobs based on their level of qualification. Also, to sharpen the skills, companies imparted skills by training local people for technical jobs such as carpentry, plumbing, and electrical work, as well as some non-industrial training, such as mushroom cultivation, promotion of organic farming, etc. More affluent villagers with experience in contract work were able to obtain contracts with hydropower companies for various types of work. Most contractors said they made good profits and that this improved their financial situation. However, some contractors reported good pay rates by companies initially, but unsatisfactory rates for later work. Many villagers were also given supply jobs for a variety of items, such as sand and stones, food provision for company canteens, and building materials. One of the interviewee Krishna Bahadur Chhetri, who was unemployed before the company came up, was now a contractor and has achieved good financial gain and had accumulated much of financial capital. The hydroelectric projects, being large engineering undertakings, also resulted in immigration of workers from outside to the project townships and into residential colonies around the project sites. This provided opportunities for some local people to engage in business and trade of various kinds. The company assisted with the formation of women's self-help groups that were trained in various self-employment activities aimed at providing goods and services to company workers and their families. The company also participated in various social activities like the organization of medical camps, relief camps (during earthquake). Apart from this, from time to time, it organized many gaming events like football competition, football camps to the local youth free of cost. Recently, it also has taken initiative to encourage and promote the state initiative to develop organic farming. Company also promised to provide free electricity to the villages within the radius of 2 km.

Forestry, Environment and Sustainability

Forest and Hydropower Project

This hydropower project has been established taking up some of the agricultural land and submerging some of the forest areas nearby. When the project was planned to be set up the area had a healthy tree cover but the project was given green signal on the basis of some clauses and conditions. Even when making clauses the environmental importance was overlooked for the construction of the project which would meet the growing demand for the power in Sikkim and the areas nearby. Government of India and the state government gave the project the environment clearance without any delay. If the project was delayed they would suffer economic loss so it was cleared quickly. The project was cleared on the basis of certain conditions that NHPC is committed to comply with.

Forests are important as a source livelihood, source of manure for farming and fodder and firewood for livestock and they conserved soil and moisture. Road construction work has lead to mass deforestation in the region and damage to trees in and around the villages. The respondents gave many reasons for the loss of forest in the region, mainly after the hydropower plant was established. Some of them can be listed as follows:

1. Road cutting among the mountain slopes – Today in the entire stretch from bordering areas of west Bengal to the higher reaches of Sikkim is under construction mainly to make the places accessible by cutting through the mountains and constructing roads. It is the border road organisation (BRO) that takes care of the roads in Sikkim and today they are focusing in widening the roads and increasing the road length. This is supported by the state government, as this can connect many secondary and tertiary sectors.
2. Landslides caused by road cutting and construction – Landslides are common in hill slopes but the intensity and the frequency of landslides varies due to the impact of road cutting and tunnelling for water channel and flow. During the construction the areas are being blasted which effects the stability of the land so it becomes loose and fragile. As it is already fragile if a small trigger is imposed then landslide takes place which causes loss of property and some lives.
3. Dumping of earth material and the litter on the forest land nearby – Apart from the construction taking place in and around the region the biggest threat is of dumping of earth matter and litter. They do not dispose it off properly they just tend to dump it in the forest nearby. This not only causes problems for the trus but also may reduce the soil quality and the earth material may sometime flow down to many water sources and can pollute the water. Recently, this happened near Gangtok where mud was disposed upstream and when there was rain it got mixed up with the water and the whole water became dirty.
4. Tree mortality due to loss of water from the soil mainly because of tunnel construction – This is one of the most serious issues which is causing threat to livelihood. Tunnel construction causes many problems like the stability of the earth (the reason for the recent earthquake in Sikkim in 2011 was accredited to hydropower project and tunnel construction). The underwater streams also dry up thus causing water scarcity and problems in the future.

Many villagers said that the village forests that they used traditionally for the firewood and fodder collection were destroyed by construction work. Water scarcity due to drying of natural water flows was an impact of project development that all interviewees experienced to varying degree. While some farmers said they faced shortage of water for small amount of irrigation, what they need, some residents mentioned about the shortages of water for irrigation. Many respondents attributed water scarcity to the diversion of the surface water to lower levels of the substratum, due to tunnelling work because the shortage started after the tunnelling work started. Drying up of water was a long-term impact, because people wanted government or project company intervention to supply water by tapping new water sources. Unlike the agricultural impact, it was also found during the field survey that there was also the question of sustainability of the forest region as large amount were taken up for the construction work. When the people's perception about decline in forest land and dying of trees was known, it was found that about 80 per cent of the people said that trees are declining and dying also, while 10 per cent said no, they are not changing, while the remaining 10 per cent had no idea about the changes in the forest and tree cover.

Environment and Hydropower Project

Environment is the basis of all things in the world. Today, the people have become least concerned about the environment, as importance is given to economic prosperity than to natural prosperity. So, in this the loss that has to be sustained is sometimes more than double of the economic gain that was taken up. If an environment is affected then your overall life sustenance on the earth would be a question. The question of hydrology, natural resources and biosphere is based on the question of environment. This rapid pace of construction that is taking place is changing the natural environment and ecology that directly or indirectly has an impact on the livelihood sustainability of the region. Some of the major impacts on environment and ecology in the region may be as follows:

1. Impact on Aquatic Ecology or Hydrological Impact: This is also an important aspect of impact caused due to hydropower projects, as we know that for electricity to be generated water has to be stored in a location as reservoirs or dams. This would generate power and force for high electricity. This in turn leads to reduction in the water flow down the streams and the normal flow is disturbed. This also leads to low discharge which leads to disturbance in the water cycle. In some cases due to more extraction of water the natural source of water starts disappearing. The river ecosystem is changed or reduced into the pond or lake ecosystem. As the river is a freshwater so many species of fishes thrive here. In many places discharge of sewage, diversion of the water through tunnel and obstruction created by the dam hampered the migration of certain aquatic fauna, e.g., migratory fishes. This also has an impact on the water availability in the region like on rivers and the underground water. Issue of water availability was also asked to the community and most of them said that the problem of water availability has increased and on the long run the chances of drying of river bed is high. About 70 per cent of the people accepted the drying up of river and water problems. It can be illustrated as in Figure 5.

Figure 5

Decline in Water Availability and Drying of River Beds

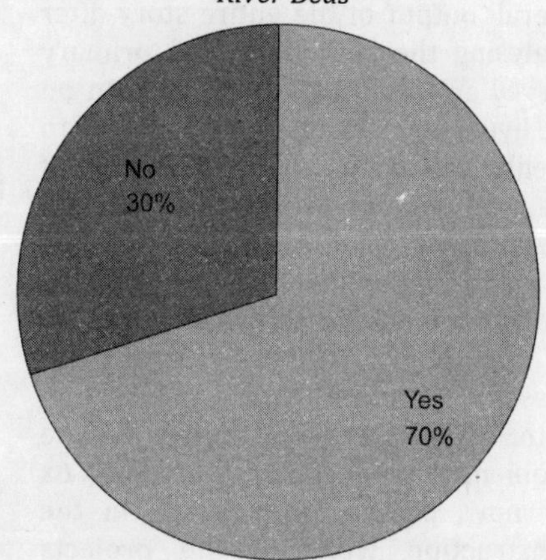

Source: Primary Survey, 2013.

2. Impact on Air Quality And Noise Environment: When construction takes place many things are crushed and used in the further process. Also, emissions due to fuel combustion in various construction equipment, crushers, drillers, trillers and other activities results in dust and may lead to deteriorations in the air quality which may in the later part lead to many health problems. Also, when the machines are being used for cutting, levelling and many other things during construction it leads to increase in the level of noise that used to be there, thus producing noise pollution. This noise may be harmful to humans but it can badly impact the small creatures like birds and insects.

3. Impact on Land Environment: The impact on land environment is the most as it is always the receptor of all things. Land is also the main source of livelihood here as land is a must for agriculture. The construction of projects is already lowering the amount of agricultural land availability, which reduces the total yield. Apart from this is a direct loss on land environment like these type of activities trigger landslides and the stability of the earth is disturbed. This also leads to the degradation in the soil quality of the region. Also during landslides, lots of agricultural land nearby is submerged under the heap of mud leading to loss of agricultural produce which is an indirect loss. Apart from there is also threat to indigenous flora and fauna and conversion of agricultural land into other use.

This was the result that was found after the primary survey of the region and how the hydropower plants are changing the socio-economic and natural landscape of the region. The overall output of the entire story after analysing the secondary and primary survey and the people's perception on the livelihood sustainability or threat to livelihood was that about 75 per cent of the total persons believe that going by the present trend there is a certain threat to livelihood in the long run. This is diagrammatically shown in Figure 6.

Figure 6

Threats to Livelihood

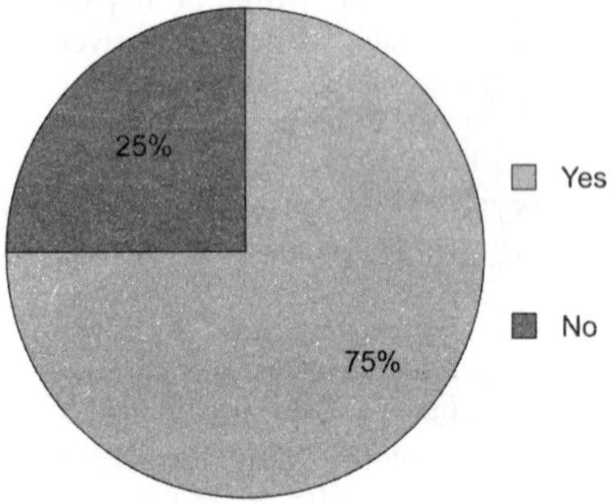

Source: Primary Survey, 2013.

It can be said that going by the present trend there will be a situation in the near future when there would be problem of livelihood sustainability. As for now, people are working in the construction work of the projects overlooking their primary base as it is lucrative; this is also causing loss of agricultural labour in the region plus reduction in the productivity. Imagine what their plight will be when all the major projects are completed and they will be left with nothing to do. So, it is time that we need to work on this aspect so as to avoid such a situation in the future. The initiatives can cover both the human and physical aspect which is not only concerned with livelihood directly but also with aspects like environment and ecology which have a role in the livelihood sustainability.

Management Plans and Initiatives

1. *Environment Management Plan*: Specific environmental issues like – management of soil heaps, ongoing waste management, and air quality. Although EIA and EMP has to be set out for the issues and management measures to be addressed by the project, so does the environmental clearance letter for the project. An Integrated Management System (IMS) is being set up and is well advanced, with procedures outlined for environmental requirements. Large quantities of earth were excavated for different project components such as dam, tunnels, power house and audits. Excavated spoil can be effectively used for land development for project colonies (residential villages), working areas, road widening and stabilization, use as aggregate (if meeting specifications), and creating level areas for other measures and some of them are underway. For example Teesta-V, the spoil disposal area has been developed into parks,

gardens, helipad, picnic area, etc. Ongoing waste management issues include solid waste generated at the colonies, bio-medical wastes from the hospital and health facilities, and hazardous wastes. Solid wastes have to be composted in a special facility using a microbial process, and the compost utilized in the gardens and planted areas. Bio-medical and hazardous wastes are also to be separated and managed as per regulatory requirements.

2. *Catchment Management*: Protection of the forest environment and the stability of the steep mountainous slopes are a high priority in this region. Although these projects tend to have an extensive catchment area treatment plans. Some of them with immediate effect where land is disturbed, tree planting especially fruits and fodder to maintain a good agro-forestry system and to improve economic condition of farmers, landslide control measures in vulnerable places, bench terracing, repair of terraces, drainage line treatment, contour hedges, and a range of soil conservation measures on agricultural land.
3. *Biodiversity and Invasive Species*: The main focus of attention has to be and has been on terrestrial biodiversity, with a particular focus on the forest environment. The power station and neighbouring land possessed some vegetation pre-project development and some timber was removed from the reservoir. Initiative should be taken up for afforestation , to replant the forest being cut and to maintain the eco balance. Compensatory aforestation has been taken up by the government on 250 ha of degraded forest land in east, north and south districts of Sikkim, with more than 0.4 million trees planted. Projects like Teesta-V also has established a herbal park at the power station to preserve endangered and rare herbal species found in Sikkim. Sikkim has a rich diversity of butterflies and moths. To conserve them, a butterfly park is being established in association with the State Forest Department. With respect to aquatic biodiversity which is also of importance, no such initiative has been taken up and has been much less an area of focus.
4. *Erosion and Sedimentation*: As we know that the Teesta river carries a naturally high sediment load due to the glacial silts plus the young mountains with lots of landslides. Reservoirs should be modified and the location and angle of the intake gates should be based with the objective to minimize sediment intake into the power station. Whereby, after water passes through the intake structures, the silt that is carried through settles out into three desilting chambers. The settled silt particles go back to the river through silt flushing tunnels. The reservoir should be routinely flushed of the remaining sediments according to the Reservoir Operating Manual.
5. *Water Quality*: Although in some projects no water quality issues need to be addressed but yes in the project near Shipgyer, Chujachen, Mabong, Lachen, Panan, Shirawni, etc., this is a problem that needs a serious concern. Water quality should be well assessed in the Environment Impact Assessment. Monitoring requirements are set out in the environmental clearance letter by the Ministry of Environment and Forests. A credible organization should be undertaking monitoring during and post-construction as per the government licence requirements.

Summary and Conclusion

After the study of the different aspects of the hydrological impacts on the local livelihood sustainability and the environmental aspects, many things have come up. Like looking at the economic base of the region prior to the development of hydropower projects and after the development of the project, the nature of economics is changing. The region was completely agrarian before the commencement of projects. So, here we can conclude saying that a closer and more important view is needed in this aspect of hydropower development and its analysis. More responsible and innovative ways should be thought of to develop sustainable means of hydropower and sustainable livelihood.

- Hydropower project construction-related depletion of arable land, forests, and water represents a loss of natural capital; a relation of employment opportunities is an improvement of villagers' human and financial capital.
- This complete dependence on temporary company work is a risk to the sustainability of the villagers' social networks (social capital) and livelihoods, so this needs to be addressed.
- The temporary nature of the employment, however, constitutes a livelihood vulnerability issue that needs to be resolved.
- People living around and those working in hydroelectricity projects need support, advice and assistance to maintain or revive land-based economic activities on abandoned agricultural lands and thus to ensure a sustainable and resilient future.
- Hydroelectricity project companies have primary responsibility for reclaiming lands degraded by their construction activities and introducing new enterprises, services, products, and production methods.
- The schemes like the livelihood diversification are considered a good strategy to augment rural incomes and to provide security from climate-related impacts.
- Also along with this the academicians and the researchers should also focus in the study related to livelihood in the small states like Sikkim.

If more research is carried out on the topic then this would make the planners and the government think of alternative new ways to tackle the situation.

References

Chandy, T. et al. (2012) 'Impacts of Hydropower Development on Rural Livelihood Sustainability in Sikkim, India: Community Perception', *Mountain Research and Development*, 32(2): 117–225.

Chhetri, N. and Sharma, E. (2006) 'Assessment of Natural Resources Use Pattern: A Case Study Along a Trekking Corridor of Sikkim Himalaya', *Resource Energy and Development*, 3(2), 21–34.

Dahal, M. (2008) 'Sikkim's Initiative in Hydropower', *Hydro Nepal Journal of Water, Energy and Environment*, 3: 38–41.

Gupta, A. and M.G. Asher (1998) *Environment and the Developing World: Principles, Policies and Management*, Chichester: John Wiley & Sons.

Klimpt, J.E., C. Rivero, H. Puranen and F. Koch (2002) 'Recommendations for Sustainable Hydroelectric Development', *Energy Policy*, 30(14): 1305–1312.

Koch, F.H. (2002) 'Hydropower: The Politics of Water and Energy', *Energy Policy*, 30(14): 1207–1213.

Rustico, L. and M. Tiraboschi (2010) 'Employment Prospects in the Green Economy: Myth and Reality', *International Journal of Comparative Labour Law and Industrial Relations*, 26(4): 369–387.

Section – 2

Regional Development

14

Globalizing India and Inter-State Disparities

Impending Dangers

GULJIT K. ARORA

The modern world has witnessed an unprecedented expansion in trade and foreign investment, internationalization of production, distribution and marketing of goods and services. Besides, the role of multinational companies (MNCs) in the world economy has become dominant, and global competition facilitated by the revolutionary changes in information and communications technologies (ICTs) and their interplay has become more intense. This globalization process and its induced competitive environment have at the same time created winners and losers by inducing a change in the entire institutional arrangements, governance frameworks and the structure of the economy including the production systems and the economic behaviour. Consequently, the economic transformation has brought out a change in the value addition, i.e., a marked decline in the share of the European Union (EU) and the significant shift towards Asia and, within Asia, away from Japan to China and India.

This change is serious and poses a challenge to the poor countries like India; and has to be understood in the context of the changes introduced by the respective countries in their macroeconomic, financial and labour market policies over the period. It has been argued by many that those policies have caused unemployment to rise and remain at high levels, and wages to lag behind productivity growth, and they have further channelled rentier incomes towards the top while leaving the backward regions to lag further behind. Ironically, the globalization backed up by technological improvements are not appropriately geared to take into account (1) the structural political-economy and social problems including the massive corruption, poor governance and weak delivery systems of the respective countries; (2) the crucial importance of the real aggregate demand and its composition rising from the requirements for capital formation, its structure and locational pattern; and (3) the distribution of the economic growth and the dynamic changes taking place in it. Consequently, the economy witnesses an adverse impact on the job creation, inequality and the lopsided economic and social transformation leading to general chaos in a number of poor countries.

The increase in the economic share of India in the world economy though less dramatic, is nevertheless significant making India as the fourth largest economy in purchasing power parity (PPP) terms. Not only India has over the years become a more open economy with the total share of imports and exports accounting close to 50 per cent of GDP, its capital inflows and outflows reached 54 per cent of GDP. It became a significant member of the global policy group of G–20 and also made a big story in the global map for having achieved a consistently high growth rate of 7–8 per cent during the last decade.

Behind these overall achievements are India's neo-liberal reforms adopted since the late 1980s to integrate with the world. India, not only reformatted its macroeconomic policies focusing on privatization, liberalization, deregulation and disinvestment but also redefined the role of the state and its regulatory spheres to give more space to the market economy. In a political economy system characterized by the federal principles, liberalized centralized economic planning and flourishing private capitalism, the government's withdrawal as a producer of commercial goods, promoter of desired activities, regulator of the social economy and the supplier of public or social goods or from areas wherein markets fail and cannot function efficiently and effectively, can have really serious implications for the socio-economic development at the regional levels in a country like India.

It is in this context, one has to examine the regional context and implications of globalization and further changes induced by it in the macroeconomic policies and their impact on states of India. Thus, it is worthwhile to have a quick look at the extent of regional variations in India.

Reviewing the Inter-State Variations and their Dynamics

India constitutes 35 administrative units including 29 states including Delhi and 6 Union Territories, viz., Chandigarh, Daman & Diu, Dadra & Nagar Haveli, Lakshadweep, Pondicherry, and Andaman & Nicobar Islands. A quick review of the burgeoning literature on regional development in India demonstrates the following:

1. The different states/administrative units exhibit glaring differences in the levels of economic development judged through the usual economic development summary parameters.
2. There are wide variations in socio-economic and political characteristics related to language, religion, caste and creed, cultures, political practices and so on.
3. The different states are endowed with different natural resources, demographic profiles, geographic areas, etc.
4. States exhibit high order of intra-state variations even including the district level and between areas and social groups within districts.
5. The different states are categorized into special and non-special states, particularly from the point of central fiscal transfers made available to them.
6. The high order of inter-state variations justify regional planning to ensure the socio-economic development of the region in an efficient and intergraded manner by functionally linking villages to the centres of growth without restricting the scope of economic development of the other regions and in the overall framework of national development planning.

These generalized inequities across the states are the end-results of the different policy measures adopted by different states from time to time and their socio-economic and historical backgrounds and the political parties in power and their vision. The first and foremost objective of all development policies is the outcome linked to human development. Thus, education, health, gender development and income, besides public spending on the services which help the people in enlarging their choices, particularly with respect to leading a healthy life, acquiring knowledge and having access to resources required for better living, assume great importance. Literacy is taken for educational achievement, sex ratio and enrolment for girls between 6 and 14 in years (I–VIII) classes for measuring gender bias and infant mortality rate (IMR) for health status.

Table 1 gives an account of human development related policy outcomes and includes infant mortality rate, sex ratio, poverty, rate of unemployment, economic growth rate. It shows that inter-state inequalities in policy outcomes are of very high order. For instance, in the case of human development index (HDI) the state of Kerala (0.79) followed by Himachal Pradesh and Punjab are at the top whereas, Chhattisgarh (0.36) followed by Bihar and Jharkhand and Uttar Pradesh are at the bottom given the all-state average of 0.47.

Table 1

Inter-State Disparities: Policy Outcomes

State/UT	*Policy outcomes*					
	HDI 2008	*IMR, ratio 2010*	*Sex ratio 2011*	*Poverty 2005, %*	*Unemployment rate (1000)*	*Growth (2004–10)*
Andhra Pradesh	0.48	46	992	29.9	46	8.73
Assam	0.45	58	954	35.4	58	5.55
Bihar	0.37	48	916	55.5	48	10.01
Chattishgarh	0.36	51	991	49.4	51	9.82
Goa			968			
Gujarat	0.53	44	918	32.8	44	10.31
Haryana	0.56	48	877	25.1	48	9.74
Himachal Pradesh	0.66	40	974	23.9	40	8.31
J&K			883			
Jharkhand	0.38	42	947	46.3	42	4.59
Karnatka	0.52	38	968	34.4	38	8.65
Kerala	0.79	13	1,084	19.7	13	8.74
Madhya Pradesh	0.38	62	930	49.6	62	7.11
Maharashtra	0.58	28	925	39.1	28	11.17
Odisha	0.37	61	978	58.2	61	9.44
Punjab	0.61	34	893	21.9	34	7.69
Rajasthan	0.44	55	926	35.4	55	6.98
Tamil Nadu	0.58	24	995	29.9	24	9.92
Uttar Pradesh	0.39	61	908	40.9	61	7.11
Uttarakhand	0.49	38	963	33.7	38	14.06

Notes: Figures are rounded off. Column 2 indicates total area of the State as percentage of total, i.e., 3276.1 thousand sq km. Column 3 is population share of the state in total, i.e., 101.2 crore. Column 4 is per capita net state domestic product of state at constant prices. Column 5 percentage of population in below poverty line as estimated by Planning Commission. Column 6 relates to population who can read/write above seven years. Column 7 is gross enrolment ratio in classes I–VIII of girls with age between 6 to 14 years. Column 8 relates to infant mortality rate measured as deaths below 6 years per thousand children. Column 9 is number of women per 1,000 men. Column 10 relates States' own tax revenues as percentage of gross State domestic product. Column 11 is outstanding debt as percentage of gross state domestic product. Sources: Economic Survey 2011–12; Report of 13th Finance Commission; Handbook of Statistics on the Indian Economy 2011–12. 10th Five Year Plan 2002–07.

IMR (measured in terms of death below 6 years per thousand children) is a sensitive indicator of health status as well as of human development. The extent of inter-state disparity in IMR is more than 4.5 times between Kerala (13) on the one hand and MP (62) and Odisha on the other with 47 being the all-state average. Gender balance as reflected in sex ratio (number of women per 1,000 man) favours men, highlighting a lower status of women in the state. By 2001, only Kerala and Pondicherry have a sex ratio in favour of females. This ratio is considerably low in states like Delhi, Haryana, Punjab and Uttar Pradesh. Gender disparities are generally found to be very high in low literacy states. In the poverty percentage, Bihar at the top exhibits about 3 times more as compared to Kerala. Poverty is said to be closely related to growth performance, as poverty is expected to decline in fast growing states. Similarly, the unemployment rate disparity is little below 5 times between Kerala (13) and MP (62). However, it is very heartening to note that a few of the traditionally BIMARU states have shown a relatively high rate of growth. States including Bihar (10%) followed by Chhattisgarh (9.8%), Odisha (9.4%) and MP (7.1%), given the all-India average of 8.6 per cent during 2004–10.

Related to the human development achievements is the available per capita income of the population of that state. In the development context, it is both a means as well as an end in itself. This is the end-result of the dynamic interconnection of a variety of factors and policy measures which enable the production to take place on the one hand and the institutional arrangements leading to the distribution of that among human beings on the other. This also explains the capacity of the state to further undertake projects leading to economic development of the state.

It is observed in Table 2 that the inter-state variations are of very high order with Bihar's Per Capita Net State Domestic Product (PCNSDP) turning out to be a little more than 1/6th of Goa. The top ranking states in per capita income are Goa (₹ 1,32,719) followed by Haryana, Maharashtra, Punjab and Gujarat. On the lowest end is Bihar (₹ 20,069) followed by UP and Odisha. In terms of growth of gross state domestic product, states like Karnataka, Gujarat, Tamil Nadu, Maharashtra, Rajasthan and West Bengal have recorded 5 to 6.4 per cent rate of growth, whereas states like Assam Delhi, J&K, UP, MP, Bihar, Odisha, Punjab have registered 1 to 3 per cent rate of growth (10 FYP Vol. III: 36, Table 3.2). It has been observed by the 10th FYP that inter-State growth in PCNSDP has increased considerably during the nineties compared to the eighties and the seventies (Vol. III: 37).

Table 2

Inter-State Disparities: Economic Base, Policy Perspective and Efforts

State/UT	*Economic size/base*				*Policy perspectives*		
	Area %	*Population (2011, %)*	*PCNSDP (₹ 2,010)*	*House const, IAY*	*Literacy 2011*	*OTX/ GSDP; 2008; %*	*DEV/ GSDP 2004–08*
Andhra Pradesh	8.40	8.47	60,458	9.57	67.7	9.2	12.2
Assam	2.39	3.12	30,413	5.88	73.2	4.8	14.4
Bihar	2.87	10.38	20,069	20.85	63.8	4.8	15.3
Chattisgarh	4.13	2.55	44,097	2.25	71.0	7.3	12.7
Goa	0.11		1,32,719		87.4	8.3	13.3

Cont'd...

Cont'd...

Gujarat	5.98	6.04	63,961	6.26	79.4	7.1	8.8
Haryana	1.35	2.54	92,327	0.66	76.7	7.9	9.3
Himachal Pradesh	1.7	0.69	58,943	0.21	83.8	6.1	17.0
J&K	6.78		33,056		68.7	8.0	28.3
Jharkhand	2.43	3.3	29,786	6.26	67.7	5.0	15.5
Karnataka	5.85	6.11	59,763	3.62	75.7	12.1	12.2
Kerala	1.19	3.34	59,179	2.12	94.0	8.4	7.6
Madhya Pradesh	9.41	7.26	27,250	2.91	70.7	8.4	14.5
Maharashtra	9.39	11.24	83,471	5.88	83.0	8.2	8.5
Odisha	4.75	4.19	36,923	6.41	73.5	6.6	9.5
Punjab	1.54	2.77	67,473	0.85	76.7	7.2	8.2
Rajasthan	10.45	6.86	39,967	2.44	68.0	8	12.0
Tamil Nadu	3.97	7.21	72,993	3.64	80.4	10.2	9.1
Uttar Pradesh	7.35	19.96	26,051	11.35	69.8	7.2	11.9
Uttarakhand	1.63	0.01	68,292	0.59	79.7	8	15.7
West Bengal	2.71	9.13	41,219	6.59	77.0	4.2	7.4
All States/India	100	120.2	54,835	100	74.0	7.8	9.1

Notes: Figures are rounded off. Column 2 indicates total area of the State as percentage of total, i.e., 3,276.1 thousand sq km. Column 3 is population share of the state in total, i.e., 101.2 crore. Column 4 is per capita net state domestic product of state at constant prices. Column 5 percentage of population in below poverty line as estimated by Planning Commission. Column 6 relates to population who can read/write above seven years. Column 7 is gross enrolment ratio in classes' I–VIII of girls with age between 6 to 14 years. Column 8 relates to infant mortality rate measured as deaths below 6 years per thousand children. Column 9 is number of women per 1,000 men. Column 10 relates States' own tax revenues as percentage of gross State domestic product. Column 11 is outstanding debt as percentage of gross state domestic product. Sources: Economic Survey 2011–12; Report of 13th Finance Commission; Handbook of Statistics on the Indian Economy 2011–12. 10th Five-Year Plan 2002–07.

Regional disparities in physical infrastructure are critical in explaining inter-state variations. For instance, the availability of productive infrastructure, like power availability and its adequate supply not only raises productivity, but also lowers cost. The other related variables including tele-density, railway route length and spread of post-offices, etc., also assume importance. How the industrial and agricultural growth takes place is another important aspect of regional development. The development of agriculture in particular, plays a crucial role. It directly influences the overall growth of the state and the income levels and well-being of the people. States like Punjab, Haryana and some parts of Uttar Pradesh (UP) have done very well due to the adoption of high yielding varieties (HYVs). In the case of food grains, UP, Punjab and West Bengal together contribute about 41 per cent of total output. In the care of wheat, UP, Punjab and Haryana contribute about 68 per cent of total output. Similarly, Rajasthan, MP and Maharashtra contribute about 55 per cent of total oilseeds output. In the case of sugarcane, about 68 per cent of total output comes from UP, Tamil Nadu and Maharashtra.

These regional variations in policy outcomes are best explained in terms of the economic size, the economic base and the economic policies pursued and their implementation by the state in the overall macroeconomic policies of the Government of India. The economic size of the state can be measured by comparing the size of population, and area of the different states. Table 2 highlights that in terms of area, Rajasthan (10.45) followed by MP and Maharashtra, UP and J&K are largest states constituting about 7–10 per cent of the all-state total geographic area. On the contrary all the north-east states, Goa and Kerala, Haryana, Himachal, Uttaranchal, Punjab, Jharkhand, West Bengal are relatively small states constituting about 3 per cent of all state areas. Similarly, Uttar Pradesh, Maharashtra, Bihar, West Bengal and AP are the most populous states, whereas Jharkhand, Assam, Punjab, Haryana, Chhattisgarh, Delhi, J&K, Uttaranchal, HP and north-eastern states are smaller states.

Fiscal base is another important determinant explaining the regional development and disparities in economic growth. This can be measured with the help of per capita net state domestic product (PCNSDP) and its growth rate. This also indicates the resource mobilization capacity of the state for undertaking the development projects. However, the debt/GSDP (Gross State Domestic Product) ratio helps us to assess the state's financial capacity to enhance its resource mobilization through mobilizing loan capital resources for development projects. As highlighted in Tenth Five-Year Plan, 2002–07, per capita plan outlay is quite high in the state like Goa (₹ 3,423) and extremely low in UP (₹ 293), and Bihar (₹ 319). The other states like Karnataka, Gujarat, Punjab and Maharashtra come in the range of ₹ 1,499 and ₹ 1,120. The plan outplay is also quite high for special category states and union territories. Similarly, in the case per capita public and private investment, Goa (₹ 56,057) tops the list and is followed by Gujarat (₹ 33,875), Tamil Nadu (₹ 26,292), Odisha (₹ 25,525) and Karnataka (₹ 24,775). On the other extreme are Bihar (₹ 2,852), UP (₹ 3,304), Jharkhand (9,106) and Haryana (₹ 9,210). The same is worse in the case of Nagaland, Meghalaya and Manipur (10th FYP 2002–07, Vol. III, Table 3.23).

The policy outcomes and policy perspectives are linked together. The kind of polices followed by different states and the political will with which those are implemented matter in explaining the growth and development of the states. For instance, it was observed that states who have cared more with respect to household construction activity under Indira Awas Yojna, employment creation under MGNREGA, literacy front, tax efforts, i.e., own taxes as percentage of SDP, devoting a higher percentage of expenditures to development and social sectors have done relatively better.

It is pertinent to mention that in every discussion of regional growth and development, the role of finance and its management cannot be ignored. The public finances assume greater importance, more so, in states trapped in a vicious circle of poverty and underdevelopment. Pressure to improve public finances will further rise with the deepening of the globalization process which require simultaneously creating more space for the private economy and reducing the role of the government, forcing the State to compete for more resources than ever before, to particularly to attract private investment. Problems get compounded given the federal polity of India in which providing socio-economic services to the people overlap in many areas and system deployed by the Union Government for devolving and supplementing financial resources to states and making the federal interventions in the structure of Centre-state fiscal arrangements as defined in the Constitution of India is lopsided and complex.

In any case, the role of financial and budgetary transfers is really critical, besides State's own efforts. Equally important are the institutional finance and banking investment, which generally get ignored. States attract these public and private capital flows both through budgetary and non-budgetary routes. These include plan transfers and outlays, the statutory devolutions, public and private investments, banking and institutional investment and externally aided projects.

As highlighted in Table 3, gross block investment in PSUs as percentage of all-states is the highest in Maharashtra (17%) followed by AP, TN, AP, UP, Gujarat,. On the other extreme are states like Goa (0.12%), Punjab, J&K, Uttarakhand. The distribution of budgetary transfers is also highly inequitable. It is heartening to note that budgetary transfers, all put together, are favourable to relatively poor states. One finds states at the highest end are UP (15.8%) followed by Bihar, AP, West Bengal, and MP. On the other hand, the share of the relatively richer states like Goa, Haryana, Punjab, and Kerala is far less.

Table 3

State-wise Budgetary Flows From Centre to States

State	*PSU gross block investment*	*Budgetary trf % all state*
	2011	*2010–11*
Andhra Pradesh	7.23	6.98
Assam	4.74	3.75
Bihar	2.65	8.78
Chattishgarh	2.65	0.00
Goa	0.12	0.27
Gujarat	5.26	2.87
Haryana	3.28	1.44
Himachal Prad	2.38	0.00
J&K	1.48	0.00
Jharkhand	2.68	0.00
Karnatka	3.71	4.56
Kerala	2.28	1.96
Madhya Prad	4.02	6.58
Maharashtra	17.00	5.97
Odisha	3.30	4.47
Punjab	1.09	1.44
Rajasthan	2.16	4.90
Tamil Nadu	7.06	4.89
Uttar Pradesh	6.62	15.87
Uttarakhand	1.74	0.00
West Bengal	5.14	6.81
All State/India	100	100

Scanning Regional Development Policies of Five-Year Plans

The subject of inter-state and regional disparities has always remained a crucial area at the policy-making level. All the five-year plans, particularly starting from the third five-year plan have discussed the issue of relatively backward areas. The third plan devoted one chapter on balanced regional development, and mentioned some measures including creation of infrastructure, spread of education, stress on the development of agriculture, small scale industry and large industrial projects; welfare for the SC/STs and other such classes. This was followed by the identification of the industrially backward regions by the National Development Council in 1968, constitution of two working groups headed by Pande and Wanchoo who worked for making recommendations on fiscal incentives for building of industries in these regions.

The Fourth plan came up with a number of specific plans and programmes for removing poverty in backward regions, whereas the Fifth plan followed a more focused approach towards developing the resource-base, target groups and incentives to be provided. The Sixth Plan (1980–85) worked on integrating area planning and sub-plan with the national development plans. It also suggested that funds should not be diverted, funds should be allotted for backward regions and the Central investment subsidy, concessional finance and industrial estate programmes should remain the motivating forces. The Seventh plan (1985–90) stressed on enhancing the agricultural productivity particularly in the eastern region, and in rain-fed and dry land areas; and strengthening the primary health care, universalization of elementary education, and achieving the minimum needs programme including rural infrastructure and so on.

The Eight plan (1992–97), which was prepared in a market-friendly environment to replace the centralized planning was not too serious about the regional planning, though it did talk about strengthening the delivery systems, development institutions and organizational capabilities in backward regions including the hill and border area, North-east and Deserts of India. The Ninth plan emphasized on planned intervention while recognizing that regional imbalances may widen under liberal policy-making environment, infrastructural investment in backward regions, agricultural development and integrating the backward regions with developed regions. The Tenth plan focused on "multi-pronged strategy", to include capital investment, states' own resources, the targeted investments, and the people's participation with an active role of NGOs. In line with this, a new scheme Rashtriya Sam Vikas Yojana (RSVY) with the provision of funding was launched to focus on areas suffering from high poverty, stagnation and poor governance, subject to the condition of undertaking reforms by the concerned States.

The Eleventh Plan specifically talked about higher level of public investment while making additional central assistance to programmes such as Backward Regions Grant Fund, the Western Ghats/Border/Hill Area Development Programmes. The Twelfth Plan intends to create a Plan within a Plan by creating a better coherence among the existing programmes such as the Backward Regions Grant Fund (BRGF), Border Area Development Programme (BADP), Hill Area Development Programme (HADP), the Kalahandi, Bolangir and Koraput (KBK) Plan, the Bihar Special Plan, the Bundelkhand Special Package, and most recently, the Integrated Action Plan (IAP) for Left Wing Extremism (LWE) affected districts.

Failure of Policies Used for Arresting Regional Diversities

The Government of India has used a comprehensive set of policies to address the problem of regional imbalances. It heavily relied on (1) industrial licensing policies to promote industrialization in industrially backward regions; (2) creating infrastructural projects like road, rail, and communication systems; (3) building up major irrigation networks, flood control and power development projects for the development of agriculture and allied activities; (4) specific development programmes, for instance to develop the north-eastern regions; and (5) special area development programmes to focus on forest areas, Western Ghats, border areas and the KBK region of Odisha; and (6) federal fiscal transfers routed through planning commission, Central Ministries and Finance commissions, etc.

In spite of these policies, the regional imbalances not only continue to grow, but also remained at a high order, and have been termed as intolerable. This may partly be explained in terms of historical backgrounds in which British capital was concentrated only in selected already developed pockets like Bombay, Calcutta, and Madras, which had the trading and manufacturing facilities and also enjoyed locational advantage. Further, given the lack of land reforms and uneven investment in irrigation systems, all regions could not develop. Maharashtra, Gujarat and Tamil Nadu being located in the western and southern parts with vast coastal areas and some others (Punjab and Haryana) having relatively high productivity of agriculture could develop faster as compared with others. However, many of the mineral-rich states (like AP, Bihar, Jharkhand, Madhya Pradesh Odisha, and West Bengal) are not developed for various reasons.

However, in post-independence period, policies followed by India also suffered on many counts. The development planning model, popularly known as Mahalnobis model adopted by India since 1956, was sector-specific and ignored regional dimension. Consequently, the significant public sector investments in Bihar, Madhya Pradesh and Odisha failed to generate backward and forward linkage for lack of comprehensive regional planning, particularly in the year when state intervention was widespread are deep. Thus, already developed areas continue to attract business and industry. A number of schemes like investment subsidy for setting up industries in backward areas, concessional finance from public sector financial institutions, location policy for putting large industrial projects, special area development progresses, etc., could not evenly spread over for lack of coordination and being bureaucratic. The planning process was faulty and could not create proper coordination and mechanism required to adjust states' plans and policies. The green-revolution induced agricultural development could not get widespread.

Some states lacked self-help effort not only in mobilizing resources, but also in good governance and development vision, and in the process could not get adequate central assistance. Even the earmarked outlays/finances could not be utilized for different reasons including for having lacked the adequate absorption capacity. The term 'BIMARU states' also emerged. On the contrary, earlier states like Maharashtra, Gujarat, Punjab, Haryana, and recently, Karnataka, Tamil Nadu, and Andhra Pradesh have come to be known as development conscious.

In view of these problems, there is a realization at the policy making level on many fronts: (1) There continues to be a feeling that inequalities across regions will get minimized overtime with planning and industrialization policies implemented to stimulate higher level of investment in relatively backward areas. However, the development of backward regions, particularly the eastern and northern parts of the country including the north-east and hilly areas is essential. (2) The balanced regional development policies including those related to Tribal Sub-Plans, etc., must be critically reviewed to make those more meaningful. (3) Infrastructure building up in areas like irrigation, road, water supply, housing, rural electrification and rural telecom connectivity can be given an important place in development perspectives.

(4) State must be encouraged to achieve the commonality of interests to maximize gains of expanding business and commerce. (5) The administrative system, particularly that of fiscal transfers must have an inbuilt system to reward the self-help efforts of the state to promote their local initiatives for development, improve governance, and further efforts undertaken to bridge intra-state disparities. However, the backward states have to design innovative policy initiatives to attract market-oriented capital flows given the experience of Andhra Pradesh and Odisha.

However, this realization requires a serious thinking on working out a systematic approach with checks and balances for the proper identification of backward areas, provisioning of additional resources, improving the delivery and governance systems to facilitate overall economic growth environment through infrastructure intervention, institution reforms, and appropriately designed incentives; implementation of the incentive system through tripartite agreements between central, State and local governments; converging all the relevant ongoing central government schemes; and more proactive role of the planning commission placed under the leadership of honest and visionary political bosses.

Conclusions: Impending Dangers

States as administrative as well as geographic units are the important constituents of the Indian Union. Their growth and development is crucial for India as a nation. However, regional inequalities over the period have continued to aggravate and have reached intolerable levels. This problem gets compounded in the federal polity in which providing socio-economic services to the people overlap and the system of devolving and supplementing financial resources meant for arresting regional inequalities are lopsided and complex. In the market-driven international economic integration, the fiscal transfers are likely to decline. This will have serious implications on the growth and development of the poorer states/regions. Given their meager resources, lack of competitiveness to attract new investments, the declining fiscal transfers for checking regional inequalities from the Centre are likely to further suffer on account of compression of expenditure on health, education and essential public services. Their inability to extend different incentives for attracting investments in the market-driven environment and with the nation state becoming relatively a less significant player, the weak regions are likely to lag far behind.

Globalization-induced pains through the consequently reduced role of the "state" is likely to further weaken the poor regions and bring a change in rules and culture that shape the system of governance. Given the high order of the economic disparities across the States, and further coupled with social differentiation and coalition politics advancing in the direction of identity nationalism, the country may get into a chaotic situation with people rising against the states. It is more so because the 73rd and 74th Amendments introduced in 1992, empowering the local people to plan from below validated by the Constitution, have not brought the intended results, neither for the poor people nor the regions. The Thirteenth Finance Commission has viewed this problem seriously.

Thus, the high order of the existing socio-economic inequalities, further induced and made complex by unchecked globalization, given our fragmented society in which people owe strong allegiances to region, religion, language, caste, culture, are likely to bring the economic disenchantment among the people living in excluded and marginalized regions. Such people are easy to become further vulnerable to the growing politicization of the society in the period of coalition politics if such regions continue to stagnate; the balanced regional development policies remain ineffective and the Central public sector investment does not make a dent in those regions. Thus, India needs a political class who could take the lead in finding a solution to the regional inequality problem, further compounded by the globalization forces, by rising above the negative politics in which peoples' feelings for development for regions and sub-regions are misused for petty political ends.

References

Arora, G.K. (1991) 'Emerging Fiscal Crisis and Centre State Fiscal Relations', *Mainstream* (Appeared in three issues, 16 February: 15–20; 23 February: 17–26; 30 February: 26–30).

— (2013) 'Demand for Smaller States in India: Impending Dangers', *Yojana*, 57(10).

— (2002) *Globalization, Federalism and Decentralization: Implications for India*, Delhi: Bookwell.

Report of the Thirteenth Finance Commission (2010–15) Vol. II and Earlier Reports also, Government of India, Planning Commission, Five Year Plan Documents.

15

Indicatorsmithy for Measuring Development

RAJESH KUMAR ABHAY

I would like to start by quoting the simple definition that has been given in the Report of the World Commission on Environment and Development (WCED): Our Common Future. It says that "The 'environment' is where we live, and 'development' is what we all do in attempting to improve our lot within abode. The two are inseparable". Though, expressed in simple words, these definitions include almost everything about both the concepts and considering the two are inseparable shows that they are complementary to each other.

Development is irreversible and implies a positive change. Once a society achieves a specific level of development, it cannot become a rural society again, therefore, it is unidirectional. Development is a process of change through time, but more often implying sustained, positive change that can be characterized as 'progress' or 'improvement'.

In general terms, development means an "event constituting a new stage in a changing situation" or the process of change per se. If not qualified, 'development' is implicitly intended as something positive or desirable. When referring to a society or to a socio-economic system, 'development' usually means improvement, either in the general situation of the system, or in some of its constituent elements. Development may occur due to some deliberate action carried out by single agents or by some authority pre-ordered to achieve improvement, to favourable circumstances in both. Development policies and private investment, in all their forms, are examples of such actions. Given this broad definition, 'development' is a multidimensional concept in its nature, because any improvement of complex systems, as indeed actual socio-economic systems are, can occur in different parts or ways, at different speeds and driven by different forces. Additionally, the development of one part of the system may be detrimental to the development of other parts, giving rise to conflicting objectives. Consequently, measuring development, i.e., determining whether and to what extent a system is developing, is an intrinsically multidimensional exercise (Brundtland, 1987).

Normally in economic textbooks, growth and development are used synonymously, and this usage is widely acceptable. However, in particular, the two terms have been distinguished by different economists as follows: To some economists, economic development refers to the process of expansion of backward economies, while economic growth relates to that of advanced economies. Development is a positive word while growth can be positive or negative. Another difference is that development is qualitative while growth is quantitative. However, the term 'economic development' is a spontaneous and discontinuous change in the stationary state which disturbs the equilibrium state previously existing. And the term 'economic growth' is used to denote a steady and gradual change in the long run which comes through a general increase in the rate of saving and population in a dynamic economy.

Basically, development is a process of societal transformation from a traditional society to a modern society, also known as modernization. Development is a process of improving the capability of a nation's institutions and value system. Development means economic growth with social change. Development may also have a political perspective that development should encompass freedom of action and expression and enabling people to have wider choices. Basic values underlying development are human dignity, equality and social justice are interrelated and interdependent. Another principle implied in social development is the emphasis on cooperation against competition and collectivity as against rugged individualism. Social development means something is more than the economic, political and environmental development. Thus, development is based on principles of human dignity, equality and social justice and can be defined as integrated, balanced and unified (social and economic) development of the society. We all need development to have sufficient food, good health, education, and the opportunity to make decisions for ourselves. Complete development of all human beings/sections of society should be the goal of any method or approach to development. The development should be measured with the help of some indicators. Based on indicators regional disparities in terms of demographic, social and economic can be measured. Therefore, the aim of this paper is to identify various indicators to measure development.

The aim of development is not to make life 'happier', because no one can guarantee happiness. But what is expected that, the process of development should, at least, create favourable conditions for people, individually and collectively, to develop their full potential and to have a reasonable chance of leading productive and creative lives in accordance with their needs and interests. The satisfaction of human needs and aspirations is the major objective of development. The UNDP has spelled out the objectives of development in terms of Millennium Development Goals (Jog, 2013).

Defining Indicators

Development can be measured with the help of indicators. The indicator has quite often been used in statistical references, but has never been defined in a precise manner. Even the dictionaries define indicator as one which shows, indicates or points out (Tewari, 1984: 16). Indicators are the quantitative expression of theoretical concepts. Indicators represent descriptive, analytical and normative aspects of any concept. Indicators combine fact with theory. Indicators are value loaded and are specific to time and space. An indicator viewed as a combination of matters of facts (data) and matters of relation (theory), which can be constructed only through a correct sequence between factual and logical order (Bell, 1974: 9). It is, therefore, through an appropriate transformation.

The indicators should essentially be of current significance, indicate current trends and be useable for current analysis, measurement of progress and determination of policies. Above all, a good indicator should have the following five properties:

1. It should be closely related to the situation and always be objective oriented.
2. It should be unique and clearly understandable.
3. It should be sensitive, such that small changes in the areal unit could be reflected in the value of the indicator.
4. As to feasibility, value of the indicator should easily be workable and information should not pose any problem, and
5. It should be stable, such that comparable values can be obtained over time and space. In other words, the data elements used in its definition should not change their meaning over time, space and agency.

Types of Indicators

The indicators are of three types:

1. Spatial (distance from which perishable commodities of daily use are obtained) and non-spatial (per capita consumption of electricity).
2. Input (percentage of irrigated area and output (production per hectare).
3. Direct (per capita income in the village) and proxy (percentage of pucca houses in the village).

   Besides, more groups of indicators can also be identified.

List of Indicators

As a matter of fact, determination of the validity of the indicators is one of the crucial problems in social sciences' research because of its selection being quite arduous. In spite of knowing very well the gravity of this major problem, efforts have been made in this paper. In the current study, the identified indicators have been classified into three categories: demographic, social and economic. Based on the these indicators and with the use of appropriate method, the level of development can be obtained in terms of demographic, social, and economic, respectively. The indicators are discussed below:

Demographic Indicators

Demographic indicators are used for the people-centred development. Here, the focus is put on the improvement of the various dimensions affecting the well-being of individuals and their relationships with the society (human resource: population, its density or growth) education (literacy), entitlements, working capabilities, empowerment, etc.) (Table 1). At the global level, human development is measured through HDI (Human Development Index). The HDI is a summary measure of human development. It measures the average achievements in a country in three basic dimensions of human development:

1. A long and healthy life, as measured by life expectancy at birth.
2. Knowledge, as measured by the adult literacy rate (with two-thirds weightage) and the combined primary, secondary and tertiary gross enrolment ratio (with one-third weightage).

3. A decent standard of living, as measured by GDP per capita in purchasing power parity (PPP) in terms of US dollars.

Table 1

Demographic Indicators

S. No.	*Demographic Indicator*	*Description*
D_1	Total Population	Absolute Population (As Human Resource)
D_2	Density of Population	Density of Population (Crude)
D_3	Population Growth	Population Growth in per cent
D_4	Sex-Ratio	No. of Females per 1,000 males
D_5	0–6 Year Age-Sex Ratio	No. of Females per 1,000 males in the 0–6 age group.
D_6	Literates	Per cent of Literates to Total Population
D_7	Urban Literates	Per cent of Urban Literates to Urban Population
D_8	Female Literates	Per cent of Female Literates to Female Population
D_9	Urban Population	Per cent of Urban Population to Total Population
D_{10}	Tribal Population	Per cent of Persons Designated as Tribal to Total Population
D_{11}	Main Working Population	Per cent of Main Working Population to Total Population
D_{12}	Secondary Workers	Per cent of Secondary Workers to Total Working Population
D_{13}	Tertiary Workers	Per cent of Tertiary Workers to Total Working Population
D_{14}	Life Expectancy	A long and healthy life, as measured by life expectancy at birth.
D_{15}	Adult Literacy Rate	Combined primary, secondary and tertiary gross enrolment ratio
D_{16}	Human Development Index	Human Development Index values

Source: Complied by the author.

The indicators from D_1 to D_5 reflect the quantity of people while from D_6 to D_9, quality of human resource. The other indicators indicate the contribution of human resource in different working sector.

Social Indicators

In the light of the role that human capital has to play in economic development, the social services (mainly education and health), which greatly assist in the process of developing human capital, automatically become of paramount importance. Even the country derives its vitality from these two sources of education and health (Tewari, 1984: 29). Accepting this as the basis for evaluation, attempt has been made here to suggest the indicators of social services in which we can assess social development in a society or region (Table 2). The indicators from S_1 to S_{10} show the inter-regional variations in education development. Health status in an area can be evaluated with the help of indicators from S_{11} to S_{17}. Besides, some indicators also hint towards the advances in modern social assets, like households owning TV, cinema talkies, mobile connections, etc. Number of post offices, banks, per capita deposits has also significant impact in the social progress of society. Therefore, some indicators also reflect this aspect in social development.

Table 2

Social Indicators

S. No.	*Social Indicator*	*Description*
S_1	Primary Schools	Primary schools per 10,000 Population
S_2	High Schools	High Schools per 10,000 Population
S_3	Colleges	All types of colleges per 10,000 Population
S_4	College Student	No. of Students in Colleges
S_5	Primary School Enrolments	Total Enrolments in Primary Schools
S_6	Middle School Enrolments	Total Enrolments in Middle Schools
S_7	High School Enrolments	Total Enrolments in High Schools
S_8	Degree Level School Enrolments	Enrolment at Degree Level and Above
S_9	Professional Enrolments	Enrolment in Professional/Technical/Vocational Institutions
S_{10}	Pupil-Teacher Ratio	No. of Pupils/Teacher
S_{11}	Adult Education Centres	Adult Education Centres per 10,000 Population
S_{12}	Hospitals	Hospitals per 10,000 Population
S_{13}	Dispensaries	Dispensaries per 10,000 Population
S_{14}	Primary Health Care Units	Primary Health Care Units per 10,000 Population
S_{15}	Family Planning Centres	Family Planning Centres per 10,000 Population
S_{16}	Hospital Beds	Hospital Beds per 1,00,000 of Population
S_{17}	Doctors Availability	No. of Doctors per 1,00,000 of Population
S_{18}	Households owning TV	Per cent of Total Households
S_{19}	Mobile Connections	No. of Mobile Connections/1,000 Persons
S_{20}	Telephones	Telephones in use per 10,000 Population
S_{21}	Households owning Motor Vehicles	Per cent of Households owning Motor Vehicles
S_{22}	Post Offices	Post Offices per 10,000 Population
S_{23}	Cinema Talkies	Cinema Talkies per 10,000 Population
S_{24}	Households having Bathroom within House	Per cent of Households having Bathroom to total Houses
S_{25}	Commercial Banks	No. of Commercial Banks per 1,00,000 Population
S_{26}	Nationalized Banks	No. of Nationalized Banks per 10,000 of population
S_{27}	Bank Deposits	Per Capita Bank Deposits in Rupees

Source: Complied by the author.

Economic Indicators

Economic development, i.e., improvement of the way endowments and goods and services are used within (or by) the system to generate new goods and services in order to provide additional consumption and/or investment possibilities to the members of the system. Therefore, one cannot ignore the importance of economic sector in the process of both social and economic development of a country or a region. Apart from providing better links to different areas through transport and communication facilities, it also assists in enhancing accessibility to countrysides. Hence, the economic development reflects the development in the primary, secondary, tertiary and quaternary sectors.

Primary sector focuses development in the agricultural sector. The indicator from E_1 to E_{16} in Table 3 represents the agricultural status and its performance in a region. The indicators like use of fertilizers, power and irrigation helps in augmenting the cropping intensity. The cropping intensity, measured through the ratio of gross to net cropped area, indicates the rate of utilization of net area under cultivation in different regions and throws light on the scope of bringing additional area under multiple cropping (Tewari, 1984: 25).

Table 3

Economic Indicators

S. No.	*Economic indicator*	*Description*
E_1	Land Holding	Per Capita Cultivate Land Holding
E_2	Net Area Sown	Net Area Sown per 100 sq km of Geographical Area
E_3	Net Irrigated Area	Net Irrigated Area per 100 sq km of Net Sown Area
E_4	Area under HYV	Area under HYV Crops per 100 sq km of Net Sown Area
E_5	Fertilizer Consumption	Consumption of Fertilizers in Kg per ha of land
E_6	Area sown more than once	Area under sown more than once 100 sq km of Net Sown Area
E_7	Workers in Agriculture	No. of Agricultural Workers in per 100 ha of Cropped Land
E_8	Cropping Intensity	Ratio of gross to net cropped area
E_9	Agricultural Credit Societies	Proportion of Agricultural Credit Societies with Rural Population
E_{10}	Electric and Oil Pumps	No. of Electric and Oil Operated Irrigation Pumps to 100 ha of Irrigated Land
E_{11}	Power Consumption	Consumption of Power per ha in Agriculture
E_{12}	Number of Tractors	No. of Tractors per 100 ha of Net Sown Area
E_{13}	Cash Crops	Percentage of Cash Crops with Net Sown Area
E_{14}	Regulated Markets	No. of Regulated Markets
E_{15}	Vegetables Yield	Production of vegetables per unit of land (yield)
E_{16}	Income from Agriculture	Percentage of Total Income from Agriculture
E_{17}	Industrial Sector and NDP	Percentage contribution of industrial sector to total net domestic product
E_{18}	Industrial Output	Value of industrial output per Kwh consumption of electricity.
E_{19}	Factories Concentration	Concentration of all factories per 1,000 sq km of area
E_{20}	Registered Industries	No. of Registered Industries per 10,000 Population
E_{21}	Workers engaged in Industrial Sector	Workers engaged in Industrial Sector per sq km of area.
E_{22}	Income from Manufacturing	Percentage of Total Income from Manufacturing
E_{23}	Roads	Length of Roads per 100 sq km of Geographical Area
E_{24}	Railways	Length of Railways per 100 sq km of Geographical Area

Cont'd...

Cont'd...

E_{25}	Distance from Road	Percentage of Villages situated within 3 km from pucca road
E_{26}	Distance from Railway Station	Percentage of Villages situated within 3 km from railway station
E_{27}	Distance from Bus Stop	Percentage of Villages situated within 3 km from bus stop
E_{28}	Vehicles	No. of Vehicles (all types) per 10,000 Population
E_{29}	Per Capita Income	In Rupees
E_{30}	Per Capita Income-Urban	In Rupees
E_{31}	Per Capita Income-Rural	In Rupees
E_{32}	Income from Services	Percentage of Total Income from Services
E_{33}	Growth in Employment	Annual Growth in Per cent
E_{34}	Employment Ratio	Per cent of Employed People
E_{35}	Permanent Houses	Percentage of Permanent Houses
E_{36}	Work Participation Rate	Percentage
E_{37}	Population Living in Slums	Percentage of Population Living in Slums
E_{38}	Credit Societies	No. of Agricultural Societies per 10,000 Population
E_{39}	Co-operative Societies	No. of Cooperative Societies per 10,000 Population
E_{40}	Electrified Villages	Percentage of Electrified Villages
E_{41}	Electricity Consumption	Per Capita Consumption of Electricity (Kwh)

Source: Complied by the author.

Besides agriculture, industrial sector also plays an important role in the economic development of different regions. Industrial units of organized sector generally provide life blood to the economic system by their leading role in transmitting growth. The suggested indicators (E_{17}-E_{22}) reflect industrial development. The selected indicator shows the degree of predominance of industrial sector in overall economy of any region.

The indicators related to road and transports are suggested for measuring the level of infrastructure development (E_{23}-E_{28}). The other indicators are related to income, employment and credit societies reflecting the economic advances of a region, should be considered while measuring the economic development.

Measuring Development through Composite Index

To derive a composite index from a set of variables, a wide variety of multivariate statistical techniques are available. Actually, the choice of the most appropriate method depends upon the type of the problem, the nature of the data and objective of the analysis. Considering these, composite index method can be applied in any study related to finding out regional disparities in any phenomena. For computing the composite development index at any level (village, district, state or country), a composite picture has been obtained through the following formula:

$$\text{Composite Index(CI)} = \frac{\text{Observed value}}{\text{Mean of the respective column (indicator)}}$$

The preservation of real variations among the different observations is the primary objective of the method for computing the composite index. Keeping this in view, the method of division by mean of the respective column is preferred as it can get rid of the extreme values in the series. As far as the determination of weightage is concerned, no special weightages can be assigned to any variable. (In other words, equal weightage can be assigned to all the selected variables to compute the development of the region). Thus, after the removal of the biasness of scale, the transformed values of the given variables can be added up linearly and the scored values of composite index can be classified into different categories of development. The categories can be high, medium and low developed regions. The process of achieving these can also be understood by an example also. Take state-wise per capita income in India as one variable. Initially, the mean of per capita income will be calculated and then each state's per capita income will be divided by the mean value of per capita income variable. Same procedure will be followed in other variables chosen for measuring the development. At the end, the values obtained by this process for each state will be added. Finally, the added values for each state can be classified into high, medium and low development categories. It will show that in terms of the selected indicators, the states are highly, moderately or less developed.

Regional Disparity in Demographic Development of Jharkhand State: An Example

Density and total population, literacy rate, urban population, scheduled tribe population, crude birth rate, age-sex ratio (0–6 years) are the important demographic indicators considered and computed by applying composite index formula. Based on seven indicators (Table 4) composite index for demographic development in the Jharkhand state for 18 districts is calculated. It is observed that it ranges between 4.51 in Chatra to 10.93 in Dhanbad and also shows the least and maximum developed district, respectively, in the state.

Table 4

Regional Variations in Demographic Indicators and Composite Index

District	*Total population, 2001*	*Population density, 2001*	*Literacy rate, 2001*	*Urban population, 2001*	*Percentage of ST population, 2001*	*Crude birth rate, 2008*	*0–6 Years age sex ratio, 2001*	*Composite index*
Bokaro	17,77,662	621	62.1	45.26	12.29705085	24.4	946	8.84
Chatra	7,91,434	213	43.2	5.31	3.839107241	32.3	984	4.51
Deoghar	11,65,390	468	50.1	13.72	12.24628665	31.5	973	6.29
Dhanbad	23,97,102	1167	67	52.37	8.457253801	23.1	953	10.93
Dumka	11,06,521	290	46.4	5.34	44.75640318	27.1	976	6.33
Garhwa	10,35,464	256	39.2	4.12	15.35147528	35.7	960	5.17
Giridih	19,04,430	382	44.5	6.43	9.68631034	33.9	961	6.08
Godda	10,47,939	496	43.1	3.53	23.62141308	29.8	996	5.95
Gumla	8,32,447	148	50.9	4.78	67.24416089	29.1	977	6.75
Hazaribagh	22,77,475	370	57.7	23.23	11.78203932	28.4	965	7.42
Koderma	4,99,403	380	52.2	17.37	0.814372361	31.4	972	5.40
Lohardaga	3,64,521	244	53.6	12.67	55.70406095	31.2	942	6.74
Pakur	7,01,664	388	30.6	5.13	44.58515757	33.2	968	6.14

Cont'd...

Cont'd...

Palamu	15,37,465	296	46.5	6.43	9.038254529	32.9	974	5.60
Pashchimi Singhbhum	12,33,945	240	46.8	15.49	65.35720798	26.8	973	7.64
PurbiSingh bhum	19,82,988	560	68.8	55.03	27.84620986	20.9	941	9.98
Ranchi	27,85,064	362	64.6	35.11	41.81677692	25	960	9.58
Sahibganj	9,27,770	580	37.6	10.58	29.14763357	33.6	972	6.66
Mean Values	13,53,815.78	414.50	50.27	17.88	26.87	29.46	966	

Source: Final Population Totals–2001, Jharkhand, Census of India.

The demographic composite index has been classified into 3 categories: high (CI value more than 7), moderate (CI value between 6–7) and low (CI value less than 6) demographic development. In high demographic development 6 district namely, Dhanbad, Purbi Singhbum, Ranchi, Bokaro, Pashchimi Singhbum, Hazaribag are included which are mainly located in the north-central and south-eastern part of the state (Table 4). These districts have higher population density, higher literacy rate and urban population which supports in their demographic development. Moderately developed category include Gumla, Lohardaga, Sahibganj, Dumka, Deoghar, Pakur and Giridih districts which are mainly located in north-eastern and south-western parts of the state. The low developed districts include Godda, Palamau, Kodarma, Garhwa, Chatra districts (Figure 1). They are found in north-western part along the border of Chattishgarh and Bihar. In this way, based on selected indicators regional disparities in the levels of development can be identified.

Figure 1

Disparities in Demographic Development in Jharkhand State

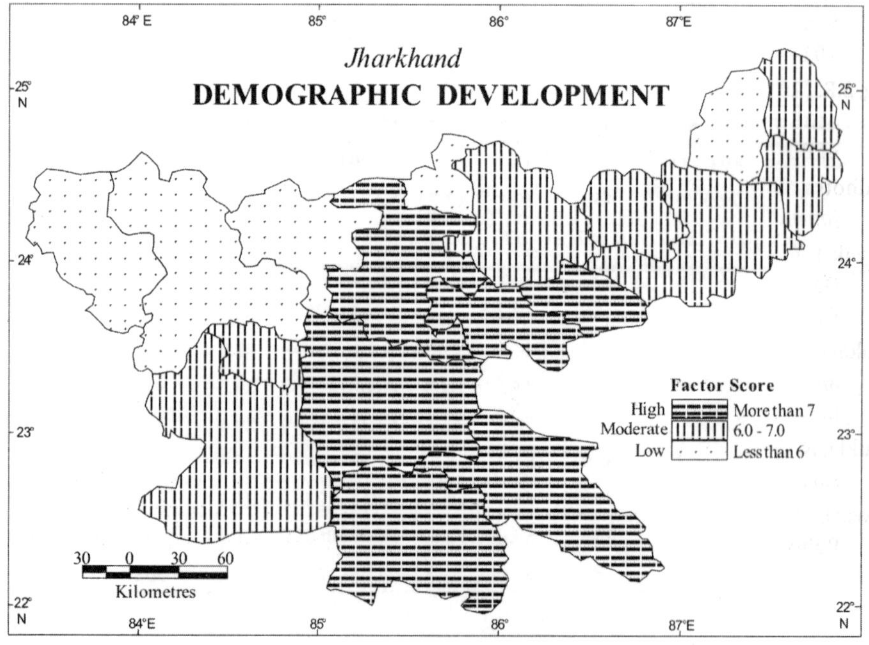

Conclusions

The above discussion provides a comprehensive list of indicators which can be considered while assessing the demographic, social or economic disparities between regions. The lists of indicators clearly explain that the development is basically an anthropogenic process. It includes all the activities carried out by humans to make life more comfortable. The selected indicators must be selected by taking the study area into consideration. While measuring the overall level of development, the adequacy, accessibility and availability of data must be ensured. The indicators must be SMART (Specific, Measurable, Attainable, Relevant and Time-bound). The unit of analysis and selected indicators should match as some of the indicators are available at the macro level only. Thus, the present study provides a comprehensive number of indicators which helps in measuring the level of development, based on indicators which will help the decision-makers to form programmes and policies.

References

Agarwal, A.K. and P.L. Hazarika (2002) 'Regional Disparities in Economic Development of Assam: A District Level Study', *Indian Journal of Regional Science*, 34(2): 121–136.

Ajagekar, B.A. and N.S. Masal (2011) 'Regional Disparities in the Levels of Agricultural Development in Kolhapur District of South Maharashtra', *Indian Streams Research Journal*, 1(2): 139–144.

Bell, D. (1974) *The Coming of Post-Industrial Society*, New Delhi: Kali for Women.

Brundtland (1987) *Our Common Future*, World Commission on Environment and Development (WCED), Oxford: Oxford University Press.

Horton, F.E., H. McConell and R. Tirtha (1970) 'Spatial Patterns of Socio-Economic Structure in India', *Tijdschrift voor Economische en Sociale Geografie*, 61(1): 101–114.

Jog, S.R. (2013) 'Environment, Development and Equity', Presidential Address Presented at 35th Indian Geographers Meet of Institute of Indian Geographers, The University of Burdwan, West Bengal.

Malhotra, N. (1999) 'Human Development in India and Inter-State Pattern', *Indian Journal of Regional Science*, 31(1): 31–45.

Nayak, L.T. and D.S. Narayankar (2009) 'Identification of Regional Disparities in Levels of Development in Bellary District, Karnataka', *Indian Journal of Regional Science*, 41(10): 37–47.

Prakasa Rao, V.L.S. and R. Ramachandran (1971) 'Some Aspects of Regional Structure and Development Policy in Andhra Pradesh: A Preliminary Study', *Analytical Geography*, 1(1): 33–47.

Shukla, N. and S. Dhagat (1999) 'Disparities of Economic Development in India: A Factor Analysis Approach', *Indian Journal of Regional Science*, 31(1): 13–18.

Tewari, R.T. (1984) *Changing Patterns of Development in India*, New Delhi: Ashish Publishing House.

16

Sex Ratio Imbalances in India

MONICA AHLAWAT

Composition of Population by Gender – World Trends

Gender composition reflects natality, mortality and migration character of a given population. Distribution pattern of male and female in a population affects relative roles and economic relationships. There are different tools to measure gender equity in a population. Sex ratio is one such widely used tool for cross-sectional analysis to measure gender balance. Sex ratio is defined in the Census of India as the number of females per 1,000 males in the population.

According to the provisional population totals of Census 2011, out of a total population of 1,21,01,93,422 persons, 62,37,24,248 are males and 58,64,69,174 females. As per this, the sex ratio of India is 940 (Table 1 and Figure 1). The sex ratio at the national level has risen by seven points since the last Census in 2001. This is the highest since 1971.

The composition of population by female sex ratio commonly known as sex ratio is the number of females per every 1,000 males in a given place. It, again, is recalculated based on the age groups like 0 years to 6 years or 6 years and above. The number of females in the age group of 0 years to 6 years is termed as child sex ratio. Sex composition is a subject of great interest to the demographers, regional planners, sociologists, economists and geographers too. Sex ratio is an index of socio-economic conditions of an area. It is an important tool of regional analysis. It has a profound effect on demographic structure of a region (Ghosh, 1987). Sex ratio influences the form and tempo of life in any country. The balance between the sexes is an important aspect of population structure. Sex ratio also has an affect on labour supply. Low sex ratio creates social problems like widowhood as well as on the fertility and population growth.

The present research work is entirely based on secondary source of data which is mainly derived from Census of India. Few information and data have been derived from the Government publications mainly from Socio-economic Review, India at a Glance, gazetteers of India, etc. For the spatial analysis of sex ratio, 2011 census year is selected. State is selected as a basic unit of study investigation. Sex ratio of the total population is calculated by using the following formula:

Sex Ratio= Total Female Population/Total Male Population X 1,000

Sex Ratio of Selected Countries

The composition of population by gender is not uniform and shows diverse patterns across different countries of the world. Table 1 presents the sex ratio in the ten most populous countries in the world during 2001 and 2011. It has been estimated that around the year 2011, the world will have 984 females against 1,000 males. As is evident from the statement, in USA, Russian Federation, Japan and Brazil females outnumber males, in the other six countries the balance is tilted towards the males. When compared to the previous decade, China, Indonesia, Nigeria and USA have shown a decline in the sex ratio in the present decade. The decline has been particularly sharp in Nigeria and Indonesia. The sex ratio in USA, Russian Federation and Japan has always remained above unity despite minor variations. The situation in the immediate neighbourhood of India reveals a mixed picture. Myanmar (1,048), Sri Lanka (1,034) and Nepal (1,014) have more females in their populations whereas in all other countries the sex ratio shows male domination.

Table 1

Trends of Sex Ratio in Ten Most Populous Countries: 2001 and 2011

S. No.	*Country*	*Sex ratio (2001)*	*Sex ratio (2011)*
1.	World	986	984
2.	China	944	926
3.	India	933	940
4.	USA	1,029	1,025
5.	Indonesia	1,004	988
6.	Brazil	1,025	1,042
7.	Pakistan	938	943
8.	Russian Fed.	1,140	1,167
9.	Bangladesh	958	978
10.	Japan	1,041	1,055
11.	Nigeria	1,016	987

Source: 2001-World Population Prospects 1998 and 2011-World Population 2008, UN.

Ever since Amartya Sen (1990) proclaimed that more than 100 million women are missing around the world, the case of "missing women" has generated considerable interest. In contrast to Europe and North America where the sex ratio (defined here as the ratio of female to male population) is around 1,050 or higher, the ratio in many Asian countries, such as in India, China, Taiwan, Hong Kong and South Korea, is as low as 940. In many of these countries, the sex ratios seem to have fallen over the second half of the twentieth century with development, declining family size and the advent of modern technologies which facilitate self-selective abortion or sex-selection (Park and Cho, 1995).

In India and probably elsewhere in Asia, however, the case of "missing women" has deep historical roots. While it is difficult to identify when the problem of "missing women" first arose in India, British officials were well aware of the problem in North India during the mid-nineteenth century. More reliable evidence from the British censuses conducted during the late nineteenth century show that the problem of "missing women" was clearly a northern rather than a southern or an

Figure 1

India: Districtwise Sex Ratio, 2011

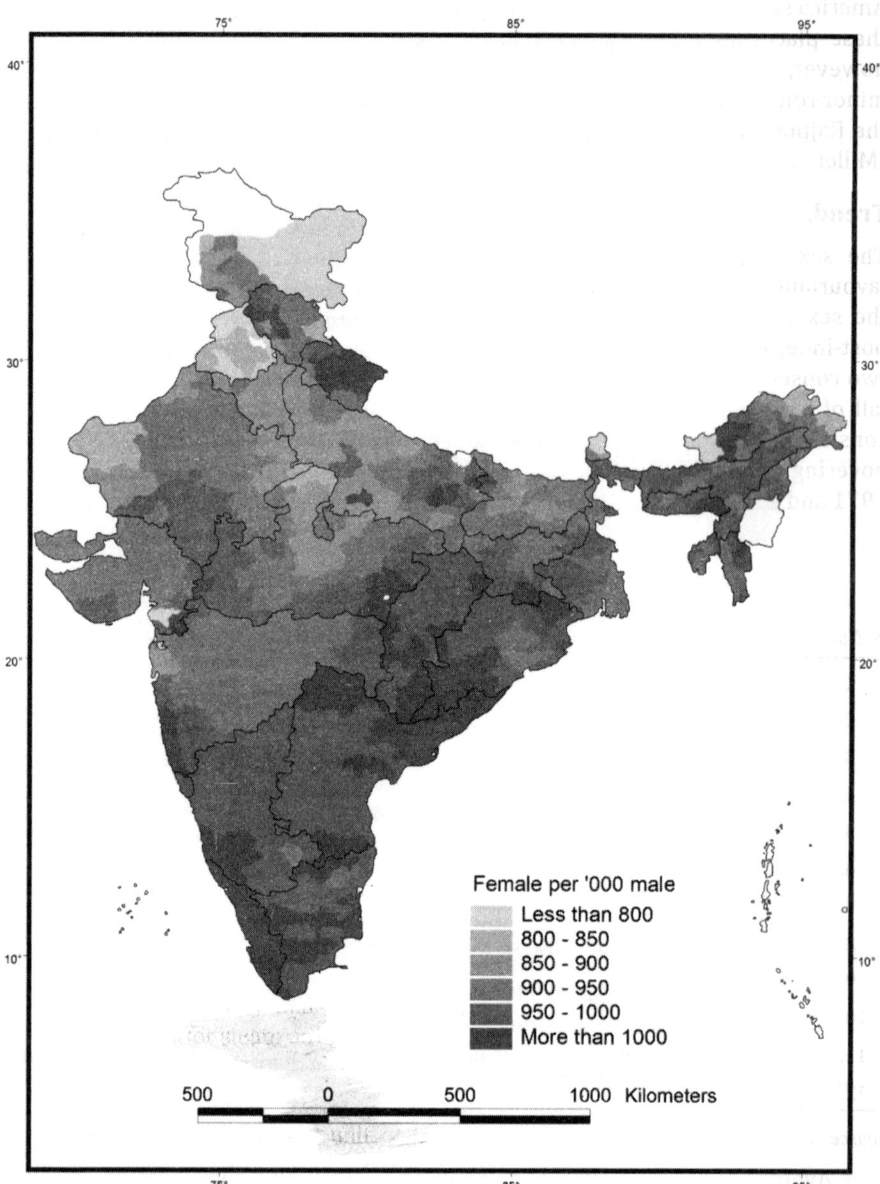

eastern problem in India. The female to male sex ratio was lowest in northern regions such as Punjab, equal in eastern regions such as Bengal, but was relatively high and favoured women in southern regions such as Chennai. Sex ratio is determined by biological as well as economic and cultural factors. From a biological perspective, scholars generally believe that biology favours the births of males, but the subject is under considerable debate. After birth, because females possess biological advantages in resisting disease, they are more likely to survive than males given equal levels of nutrition and health care. Thus, for any cohort, sex ratios at birth favour males, but favour females over time. Because Europe and North America seem to follow this pattern, scholars tend to treat the trends in sex ratios in these places as largely determined by biological factors. In many parts of Asia, however, where the male sex-bias is prevalent, biological factors are likely to play a minor role in explaining sex ratios. In North India, the British officials suspected that the Rajputs were practicing female infanticide during the mid-nineteenth century (Miller, 1981).

Trends in Sex Ratio in India

The sex ratio in India has been historically negative or in other words, not favourable to females. A look at Table 2 reveals that in the pre-independence period, the sex ratio declined consistently up to 1951 when it rose marginally. In the post-independence period, the trend continued and the sex ratio slipped down for two consecutive decades after 1951 to reach 930 in 1971. During 1961–71 a steep fall of 11 points was seen in the sex ratio. After 1971 Census, trends were not consistent, showing increase in one decade and decline in the next. However, it was hovering around 930. The sex ratio as per provisional results is the highest since 1971 and a shade below the level of 1961.

Table 2

Sex Ratio of India: 1901–2011

S. No.	*Year*	*Sex ratio (females per 1,000 males)*
1.	1901	972
2.	1911	964
3.	1921	955
4.	1931	950
5.	1941	945
6.	1951	946
7.	1961	941
8.	1971	930
9.	1981	934
10.	1991	927
11.	2001	933
12.	2011	940

Source: Census of India, 2001.

Average sex ratio of India in 2011 is 940 females per 1,000 males. The highest sex ratio (1,084 females per 1,000 males) is found in Kerala state while the lowest (877 females per 1,000 males) sex ratio is found in Haryana State (Figure 2 and 3). Sixteen states have recorded higher sex ratio than that of Indian average while remaining, i.e., twelve states have recorded lower sex ratio than that of Indian average. It is clearly seen in Figure 1 that seven States namely Manipur, Meghalaya, Orissa, Chhattisgarh, Andra Pradesh, Kerala, Tamilnadu show very high sex ratio (above 975 females per 1,000 males). Four States namely Assam, Karnataka, Himachal Pradesh and Uttaranchal shows high sex ratio (ranges between 950–975

Figure 2

Kerala: Districtwise Sex Ratio, 2011

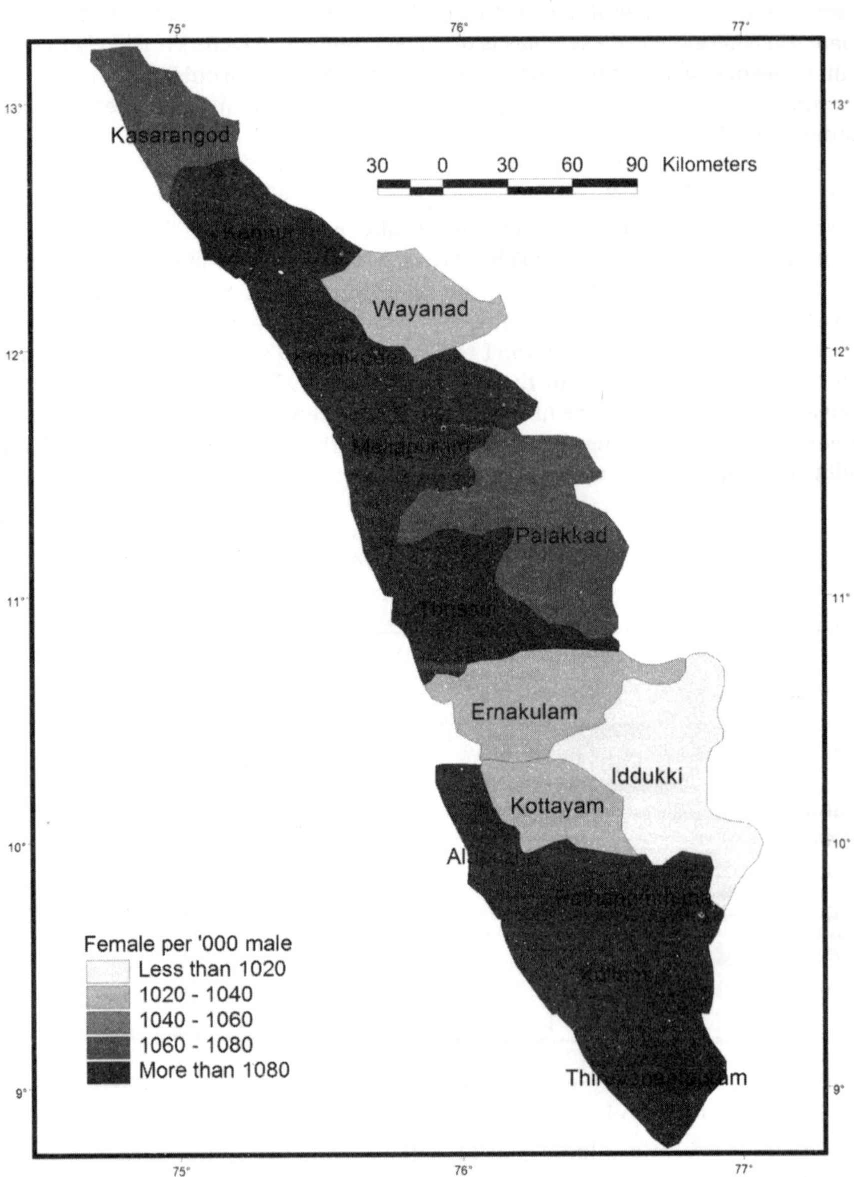

females per 1,000 males). These eleven States have recorded above the average sex ratio of the country (i.e., 940 females per 1,000 males). Unable physiographic and economic conditions, low development, heavy out-migration of male population for the sake of job opportunity, low development of industries are general causes of high sex ratio in these eleven states.

In Kerala very high sex ratio is due to the religious and economic situation. Christians give high status to females. Besides, there is more male selective out-migration in Kerala. Kerala has, therefore, recorded a very high sex ratio (1,084 females per 1,000 males). Manipur, Meghalaya, Nagaland States also have Christian population, therefore, these states also have high sex ratio as compared to that of Indian average sex ratio. Due to high male selective out-migration Tamil Nadu, Andhra Pradesh, Orissa and Chhattisgarh States have recorded a high sex ratio. Moderate sex ratio (950 females per 1,000 males) is found in 5 states, viz., Rajasthan, Nagaland, West Bengal, Jharkhand and Madhya Pradesh states. Sex ratio in West Bengal and Jharkhand States are above national average sex ratio of India. Five States, viz., Uttar Pradesh, Bihar, Gujarat, Maharashtra, Arunachal Pradesh have recorded low sex ratio (900–925 females per 1,000 males). Among them, Gujarat and Maharashtra states are highly economically developed. These two states are also industrially as well as agriculturally developed. So, male selective in-migration is high in these two states. Consequently, low sex ratio is found in Maharashtra and Gujarat states. Sex ratio is very low (below 900 females per 1,000 males) in four states namely, Jammu Kashmir, Punjab, Haryana and Sikkim. In Haryana, the females do not enjoy a high status and due to proximity to the national capital (New Delhi) is able to attract male migrants to adjoining areas for employment purpose. Besides such north-western states were largely the product of either a genetic factor (such as Sikhs) or high incidence of female feticide.

The data also show that sex ratios varied systematically by caste, language and religion. Sex ratios varied inversely by caste rank. In each region, the higher religious or landowning castes possessed the lowest sex ratios, whereas the lower artisan and menial service castes had the highest sex ratios. Sex ratios were lower among those who spoke the northern Indo-Aryan languages as compared to those who spoke the southern Dravidian language. Even when we consider this aspect by geographical regions, there seems to be systematic variations across groups who speak different languages. The data show that sex ratios varied by religion. The Hindus had significantly lower sex ratios than Muslims in Punjab and Bengal, but not in Madras where the Muslim population was extremely small. Sex ratios were significantly lower in districts with higher rainfall and greater amounts of alluvial soil. While the length of British rule is negatively correlated with sex ratios, the relationship was not statistically significant (Chakraborty and Kim, 2008). The examination of sex ratios by caste, language, religion and region generally confirm the view that kinship systems played an important role in determining sex ratios in India. Regional differences in family and kinship institutions were the most important factor. The sex ratio was lowest in the North where the kinship system provided the least autonomy of women, intermediate in the East where the northern kinship was slightly modified, and was the highest in the South where the women's autonomy was thought to have been the strongest. The inverse relationship between sex ratios and caste rank also suggest the importance of kinship. Women's autonomy was significantly lower for the higher as compared the lower caste women. The former were not allowed to work outside of the home, not allowed to initiate divorce, and their sexual and social behaviour were highly regulated by the kin-group. Finally, the variations in sex ratios by language and religion strongly suggest that northern kinship system contributed significantly to lower sex ratios in India. Table 3 gives the trends in sex ratio since 1901 for all the States and Union Territories. The table reveals that in 1951, there were as many as eleven States and

Figure 3

Haryana: Districtwise Sex Ratio, 2011

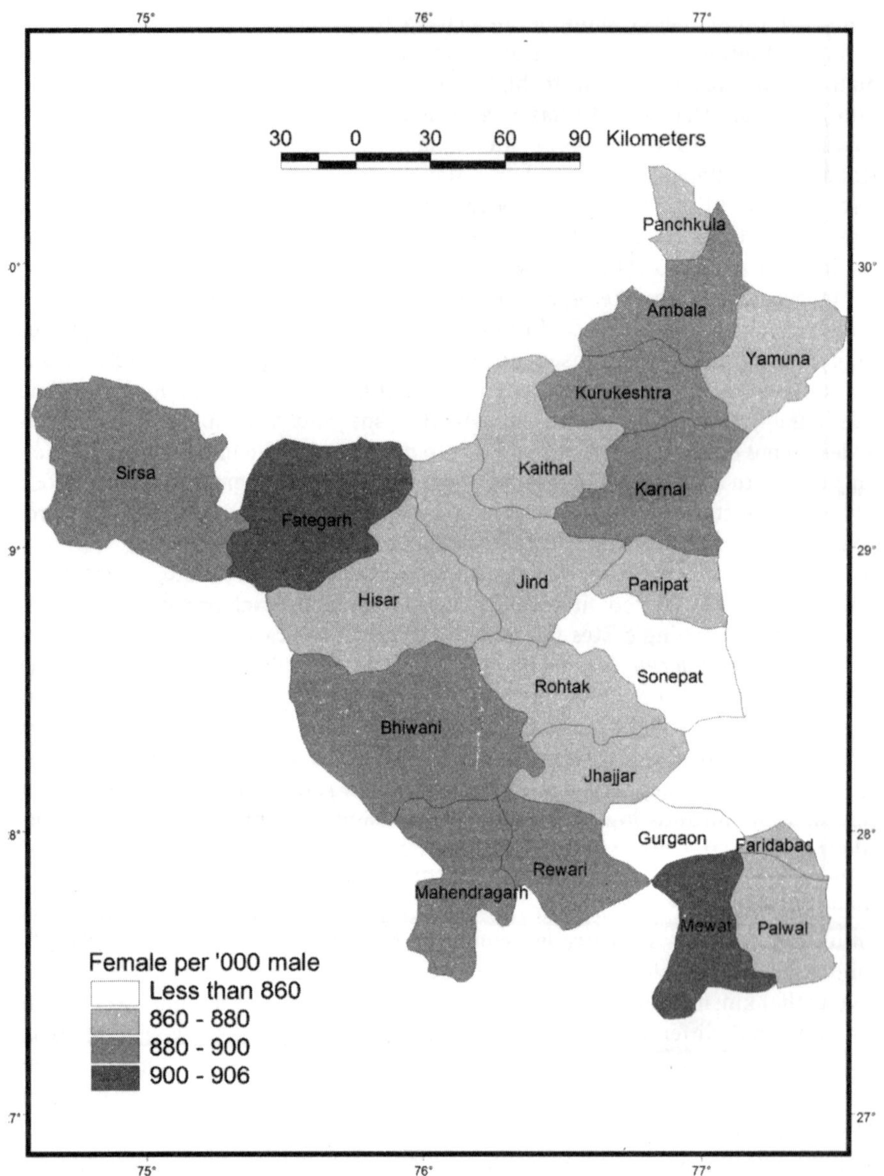

Union Territories that had sex ratio of more than unity or above 1,000. This number declined to nine in 1961, three in 1971 and two in 1981 and one in 1991. In 2001, the State of Kerala and the Union Territory of Puducherry reported above unity sex ratio. Both these States have not only retained their status but have also shown considerable increase in 2011. Besides these two, the number of States and Union Territories registering an upward trend has risen from 24 in 2001 to 29 in 2011. The

Figure 4

Delhi: Districtwise Sex Ratio, 2011

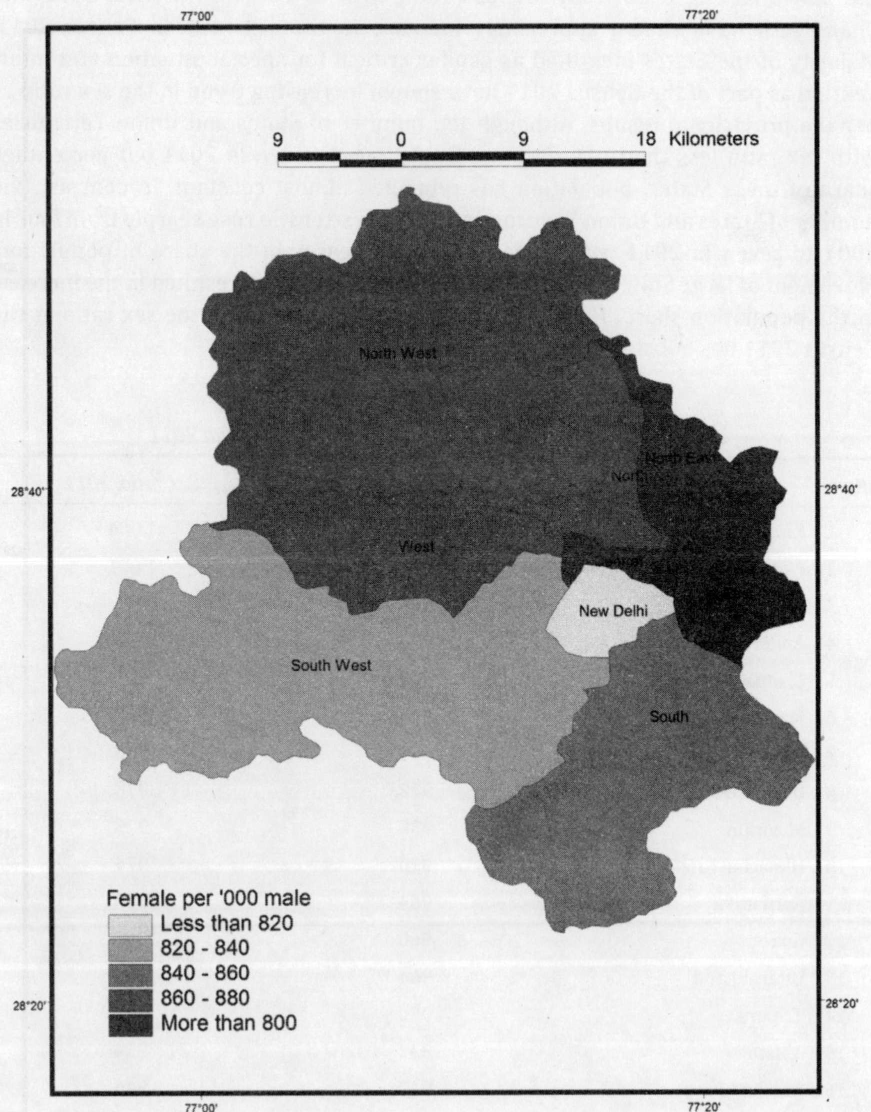

increase ranged from one point in Uttarakhand to forty-five points in the highly urbanized National Capital Territory of Delhi (Figure 4). In 18 States and Union Territories, the increase has been over ten points during 2001–2011.

Among the major States, Bihar, Jammu Kashmir and Gujarat have experienced a fall in the sex ratio. The decline ranged from 2 points in Gujarat to 9 points in Jammu & Kashmir. Other smaller Union Territories showing steep decline are Dadar & Nagar Haveli and, Daman and Diu. Perceptible increase has been observed in the major States such as Uttar Pradesh, Rajasthan, Jharkhand, Odisha, Chhattisgarh,

Madhya Pradesh, Andhra Pradesh, West Bengal, Maharashtra, Kerala, Tamil Nadu, Punjab and all the States located in the North north-east. A point to be noted is that the States having historically low sex ratio such as Punjab, Haryana, Delhi and Chandigarh have shown appreciable increase in the sex ratio in Census 2011. Majority of the States identified as gender critical for special attention and intervention as part of the Census 2011 have shown increasing trend in the sex ratio as per the provisional results. Although the number of States and Union Territories with sex ratio less than 916 declined from twelve to ten in 2011 but percentage share of these States' population has remained almost constant. In contrast, the number of States and Union Territories with high sex ratio rose sharply from four in 2001 to seven in 2011 with corresponding increases in the share of population. Movement of large States (Andhra Pradesh) in this category resulted in the increase in the population share. However, overall increasing trend in the sex ratio at the Census 2011 has boosted the sex ratio of India.

Table 3

Indian States/UTs Ranked as Per Sex Ratio: 2001 and 2011

Rank	*State/UT*	*Sex ratio, 2001*	*Sex ratio, 2011*
1	Kerala	1,058	1,084
2	Puducherry	990	1,031
3	Tamil Nadu	986	995
4	Andhra Pradesh	978	992
5	Chattisgarh	990	991
6	Manipur	978	987
7	Meghalaya	975	986
8	Orissa (Odisha)	972	978
9	Mizoram	938	975
10	Himachal Pradesh	970	974
11	Karnataka	964	968
12	Goa	960	968
13	Uttarakhand	964	963
14	Tripura	950	961
15	Assam	932	954
16	Lakshadweep	947	946
17	Jharkhand	941	947
18	West Bengal	934	947
19	Maharashtra	922	946
20	Nagaland	909	931
21	Madhya Pradesh	920	930
22	Rajasthan	922	926
23	Arunachal Pradesh	901	920

Cont'd...

Cont'd...

24	Gujarat	921	918
25	Bihar	921	916
26	Uttar Pradesh	898	908
27	Punjab	874	893
28	Sikkim	875	889
29	Jammu & Kashmir	900	883
30	Andaman & Nicobar Islands	846	878
31	Haryana	861	877
32	Delhi	821	866
33	Chandigarh	773	818
34	Dadra &Nagar Haveli	811	775
35	Daman & Diu	709	618
	INDIA	933	940

Source: Census of India, 2001 and 2011.

From the statistical data interpretation and by analysing the graphical data it can be concluded that that here has been a gradual decline, though not rapid, in the child sex ratio (0–6) years of India over the years that is from (1951–2011). Though there had been fluctuations in the overall sex ratio the 2011 census report have shown considerable improvement in the overall sex ratio since its gradual decline from 1971. The gradual decline in the child sex ratio is still an issue of concern as its condition has deteriorated over the years. The decline can be primarily attributed to the alarming figures in the North-Western States despite showing sufficient improvement in the South (Figure 5).

Figure 5

Sex Ratio Distribution Across Provinces of India, 1901–2011

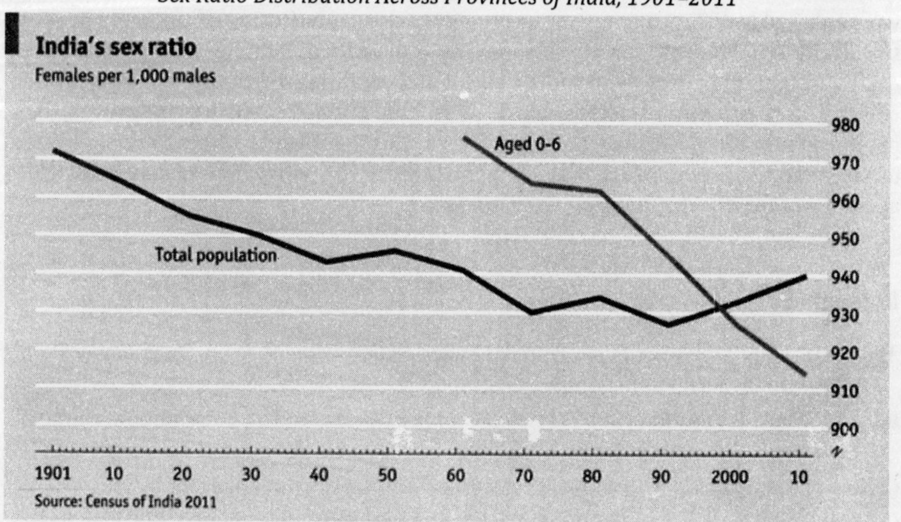

Concluding Remarks

Ever since Sen (1990) proclaimed that more than 100 million women are missing around the world, the case of "missing women" has generated considerable interest. In contrast to Europe and North America where the sex ratio (defined here as the ratio of female to male population) is around 1.05 or higher, the ratio in many Asian countries, such as in India, China, Taiwan, Hong Kong and South Korea, is as low as 0.94. In many of these countries, the sex ratios seem to have fallen over the second half of the twentieth century with development, declining family size and the advent of modern technologies which facilitate self-selective abortion or sex-selection.

In India and probably elsewhere in Asia, however, the case of "missing women" has deep historical roots. While it is difficult to identify when the problem of "missing women" first arose in India, British officials were well aware of the problem in North India during the mid-nineteenth century. More reliable evidence from the British censuses conducted during the late nineteenth century show that the problem of "missing women" was clearly a northern rather than a southern or an eastern problem in India. The female to male sex ratio was lowest in northern regions such as Punjab, equal in eastern regions such as Bengal, but was relatively high and favoured women in southern regions such as Madras.

Foregoing analysis clearly revealed that general sex ratios as well as child sex ratio differ from state to state. Present study also revealed that industrialization, urbanization, out-migration have greatly determined general sex ratio while economic development, literacy, personal attitude, modern way of life have disturbed child sex ratio in study region. For multiple reasons, India's experience is crucial to understanding the current increase in the proportion of males versus females in populations across Asia. First, rising sex ratios in India have been recorded since the early 1980s, and have since continued increasing with no sign, so far, of reversing course. The impact of this early rise is already visible among the adult population of several Indian districts. Second, even if sex-ratio values in India are still beneath those of China, its potential contribution to the overall "masculinization" of Asia (and, consequently, of the world's population) is particularly formidable in view of India's demographic weight. The prospect of further worsening of India's sex composition requires close monitoring of current sex-ratio trends in the country. Lastly, the Indian scenario of female discrimination is extremely complex in view of India's social and economic diversity: the interplay of cultural and economic factors, along with the impact of policy initiatives, has produced a heterogeneous situation; in turn, this complexity offers ways to better understand the mechanisms at work, and to inform the policy debate on the struggle against gender discrimination.

References

Agnihotri, S.B. (2000) *Sex Ratio Patterns in the Indian Population: A Fresh Exploration*, New Delhi: Sage Publications.

Bhende, A. and T. Kanitkar (2003) *Principles of Population Studies*, 16th Edition, Mumbai: Himalaya Publishing House.

Census of India (2011) Provisional Population Tables, Government of India.

Chakraborty, T. and S. Kim (2008) *Caste, Kinship and Sex Ratios in India*, Working Paper Series, Cambridge, MA: National Bureau of Economic Research.

Chandna, R.C. (2009) *Geography of Population*, New Delhi: Himalayan Publications.

Clarke, J.I. (1977) *Population Geography*, 2nd Edition, Oxford: Pergamon Press.

Croll, E. (2000) *Endangered Daughters: Discrimination and Development in Asia*, New York: Routledge.

Dyson, T. and M. Mick (1983) 'On Kinship Structure, Female Autonomy and Demographic Behaviour in India', *Population and Development Review*, 9(1): 35–60.

Gatade, D.G. and S.R. Mali (2012) 'Spatial Pattern of Sex Ratio in India: A Geographical Perspective', *Indian Streams Research Journal*, 2(4).

Ghosh, B.N. (1987) *Fundamentals of Population Geography*, 2nd Edition, New Delhi: Sterling Publishers.

Mayer, P. (1999) 'India's Falling Sex Ratios', *Population and Development Review*, 25(2): 323–343.

Miller, B. (1981) *The Endangered Sex: Neglect of Female Children in Rural North India*, Oxford: Oxford University Press.

Murthi, M., Anne-Catherine Guio and Jean Dreze (1995) 'Mortality, Fertility, and Gender Bias in India: A District-Level Analysis', *Population and Development Review*, 21(4): 745–782.

Park, C.B. and Nam-Hoon Cho (1995) 'Consequences of Son Preference in a Low-Fertility Society: Imbalance of the Sex Ratio at Birth in Korea', *Population and Development Review*, 21(1): 59–84.

Sen, A. (1990) 'More Than 100 Million Women are Missing', *New York Times*, 37(20).

17

Borrowing Trend Economy and its Impact on Education in Isolated Rural Area

A Case Study of Aurangabad District, Bihar

OM JEE RANJAN AND ANJAN SEN

Human being is not only an organic fauna but also a pure social one. Living in a society as a responsible social human being is the ultimate goal of humans. Education shapes and moulds the exhaustive deportment of human beings and nature the potentialities. It is one of the basic units of development. It is directly affected by economic activity. In the present scenario, economy casts a profound impact on the development of education. If the credit-based economy is circulating in any region, then it must be casting some impact on education. For example, education could disrupt due to unavailability of borrowing money.

In any region, the level of educational growth, approximately corresponds to the level of economic growth. Also economic growth is an important indicator of human development, and its glaring effect can be seen in many villages of Bihar, where level of economic growth and educational status, both are significantly degraded.

Overall characteristic of economic activity and education are like two wheels of development. The existence of any one without the other cannot be imagined. If it is scrutinized at micro level, then it can be seen that, the economy plays a vital role to strengthen the educational growth.

The present study area possesses excellent agricultural land and most of the people of this rural area are involved in cultivation or its related occupation. But people of isolated (without much contact with other areas) rural areas are plagued with poverty. Poverty of rural areas in Bihar is associated with limited access of land as well as poor education. Present study will be based on an isolated region of Aurangabad district of Bihar, where literacy rate is 57.50 per cent (Census, 2001). On the basis of 2001 census, the position of this district is fifth, in relation to literacy in Bihar.

Agriculture-based economy influences the standard of living of rural population. And education level is the most significant indicator of the living standard. So, education is indirectly related to agriculture in rural areas like this isolated area, where, agriculture is the mainstay of the major population and the main source of income. So, main source of income is in the harvesting period and after that they are compelled to borrow money for their domestic expenditure. Because, the period of agrarian production is fixed and it stays for few month, so until the period of next harvesting or income received from other sources, the earned money during the last harvest is floating hither and thither. During the harvest, they are capable of paying the essential cost of their own development and able to return the loan too, if they have. They even rejoice and spend money on some cultural, social activities such as – marriage, buying properties, doing pilgrimage, etc. Consequently, the maximum people of rural society, who depend on subsistence agriculture, have compulsion to borrow money for various expenditures, such as education, health, etc. This paper attempts to understand the relationship between 'income time', 'borrow money' and 'average income capability for fulfilling the demand of additional amount on education' through correlation analysis.

The trend of borrowing economy not only casts effect on farming community but also on whole society of that area because their prime source of income is agriculture. It will cast more profound effect, when the infrastructure is underdeveloped and disrupted from the link of other production areas. Thus, the borrowing trend (Bt) economy is emerging out stronger in this type of semi-close economy, because the main window of their economy opens once in a year for economic interplay, when their product go to the market. And for the remaining time, the main economic activity in this type of society is involved in "currency future trading" and "barter". Inaccessible rural areas like the present study area is directly influenced by the above situation,

Defining "borrowing trend (Bt) economy": "borrow" word is a verb, which means – to take and use (something belonging to someone else) with the intention of returning it. ? Take and use (money) from a person or bank, under agreement to pay it back later. "Borrowing trend (Bt) economy" is a type of economy system in which someone demands cash or its substitutes from the other to fulfil one's own requirement. But at the same time the receiver only promises to return that 'borrows' on a particular time and in a particular mode. There are many economic activities which happen in this system such as future trading, barter, borrow-lend, etc., borrowing trend economy is similar to following series/chains:

Figure 1

Single System of Borrowing Trend

---- *time* -----------

(Lender) A □ .... ----- *promise* ------ .... □ □ B (borrower)

[Single system]

In this, the limitation of time is almost constant. By going further than this the chain breaks, and in between the subject, the borrowing trend gets ended whereas, the promise depends on the subject. According to the above-mentioned example – in the Figure 1 the subject 'A' fulfils the economic need of the subject 'B'; in return the subject 'B' promises to pay it back to subject 'A' in a definite period of time. In the present study the last limit of the definite time, the income time of the household is the frequency. This frequency can be harvesting time, payment time, etc.

In Figure 2, 'A' is fulfilling the demand of 'B' and 'C' is fulfilling the demand of 'A'. In this example for 'C' to fulfil its promise (which is to be given to 'A'), there is its

Figure 2

Close Compound System of Borrowing Trend

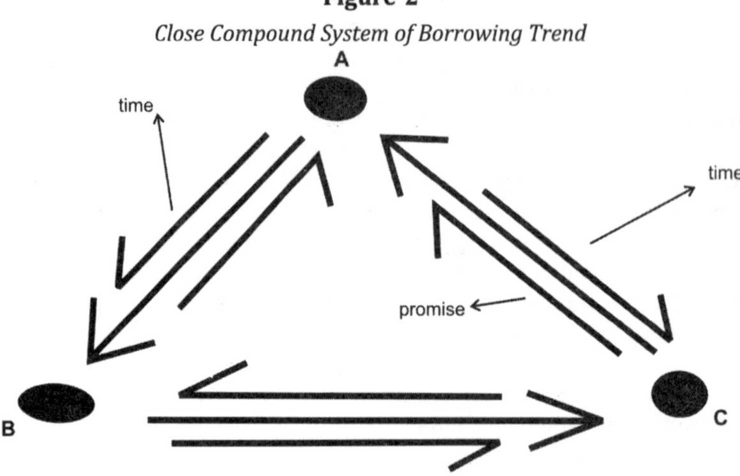

need to borrow from 'B', because of which 'B' borrows from 'A' to give it to 'C'; in this, the source of income, time and nature of each subject is different from each other. In Figure 2 the arrowhead shows the borrower.

This borrowing trend (Bt) circulates between the time intervals of getting the main income, which in certain circumstance, even crosses the limit of the main income frequency and circulate after crossing it.

Borrowing Trend (Bt) Circle and Agriculture

Actually, borrowing trend (Bt) has a circle. This circle is like a boundary line which describes the limit of an isolated area. The perimeter of this isolated area can be underlined by communicable smoothness. For example, economic activities within 15 km radius of the present study area is maximum, because there is communicational disruption from outer areas. The cities providing many commercial activities like banking are situated at a distance of at least 15 km from the centre of area. And this distance due to lack of facilities (for example – contracted/paved road, transportation, etc.) becomes inaccessible. Thus, in the gaping place of communicational network, this kind of isolated area can be situated, especially when the majority of economy of that area depends on agriculture and the basic infrastructure is in the underdevelopment stage.

In an isolated area where almost 95 per cent of population depends on subsistence agriculture the prosperity graph of people living in such areas increases only in some months of the year. Actually, in this type of places "economic warming" comes in such months only. Thereafter, there, comes a gradual declination in economic warming and 'economic coldness' (declination in flow of currency) gets increased. And with the rise of economic coldness, borrowing trend also rises side by side which gets merged with the next agrarian production.

"Borrowing Trend Effect" on Education

Every people want to increase their own prosperity. In the present age, prosperity comes through scientific and technological development. The path of development passes through education, and development of education depends on expenditure of money. So, money plays a vital role in different aspects of the human society because it determines the path of education. There are so many obstacles in educational development such as:

- Undeveloped infrastructure
- Lack of awareness
- Lack of educational facilities
- Weak education facilities
- Poverty
- Weak education policy, etc.

Beyond this, another barrier which is affecting the development of education can be named as "Borrowing trend economy".

People try to earn a valuable education to sustain themselves in the present day environment and gain further prosperity. But in rural areas, educational institutions are not sufficient or competent. However, some primary education facilities are available in these areas, but they display the growth in literacy rate only. Growth of literacy rate does not mean educational growth. Literacy as defined in Indian census operation is the ability to read and write with understanding in any one language. With this type of literacy as defined above people cannot stand strongly on stand their own feet in the present developing era. So, there is a need that they must go for potential and meaningful education, which is not available in remote rural areas of Bihar. Therefore, they compelled to go to cities for education which is far from their villages. And for that they need more money to spend on education. Nevertheless, they do not finish their education in an easy way. They have to face so many problems to continue their education. Unavailability of money is one of them. Generally, people who live in remote rural areas, do not have any regular monthly income. They have to depend on harvesting to sell their crops and earn money. So, in this period they are capable to pay for education but, there-after their cash gradually diminishes because they have to pay loan, if they have any, and secondly they invest their remaining money in various ways due to lack of banking services there. But, on the other hand, students of these areas require money on monthly basis, for their educational facilities.

In this critical situation, parents of these student are not left with any option other than to borrow money to spend on education. But it is not necessary that they will get that 'borrow' on time. So, education gets affected through this situation. It is not only the poor households but the rich households too get cursed by this borrowing trend. At this time, people do not want to keep currency in the house, so they invest money in future trading, buying properties and even give money to needy people on heavy interest. Thus, they are also trapped in the borrowing trend economy.

Why does borrowing trend play a major role in this type of area? – is not the subject of the present study but rather it would be intended here to know that how much impact the borrowing trend holds in the economy of the isolated areas. Because, the tendency of borrowing is all pervading from the beginning of economic activities. Hence, research and analysis of "Why" could be a distinct esoteric subject. Consequently, present study will be delimited and will only be trying to know the impact of borrowing trend economy on education.

So, the pithy question of the present study is: "how much impact is the tendency of borrowing in economy casting on education? Relation between economic status and educational growth in developing region has always been one of the prime concerns of researchers and administrators. Hence, various studies have been conducted on this topic. Various literatures on "impact of economic pattern on education in rural areas" such as article from journals, books and reports have been studied for understanding the conceptual framework, and methodology for the proposed study.

The Study Area

This isolated rural area is situated on the bank of Punpun River in Aurangabad of Bihar. It is bound between 24°43'43" north latitude and 84°11'13" east longitude. This isolated area is situated in inaccessible area due to lack of infrastructure. There are about 10–12 villages such as Mirzapur, Ghuja, Persa, Amba, Thumbhee, etc., situated in the concerned isolated area.

Figure 3

An Arrangement of Education in Related Isolated Rural Area

Nabinagar is a subdistrict and also the nearest town of this area which is situated 15 km away in north-western direction from present study area. Agriculture is the single largest private sector occupation in this region. It is the key to the overall development of the rural economy, but some people are involved in other economic activities out of this isolated region. But their income is limited and low. The region has attained self-sufficiency in food grain production. Adverse climate condition, like drought and floods do play a role in decreasing products. Per person farming size is about same as the district average. The region where the concerned isolated area is situated, has good climate. Predominantly, there are three seasons – hot summer (April-June), hot and humid rainy season (July–October) cool dry winter (November–March). The growing period range from 180–120 days in a year. Rice – wheat cropping system is most predominant in this region. Two crops are common but with irrigation, third crop can also be taken during summer.

The infrastructure facilities related to communication, health, banking telecommunication, etc., around this area is not available. Other kinds of basic facilities are also underdeveloped and is available at a distance of 10 to 15 km from this isolated area. According to 2001 census data, there is only one power supply facility, but that too has negligible importance in irrigation. In this area, the main source of irrigation is the tubewell, that work on without electricity.

There is no paved road connected to this area, so the people have to use mud road and footpath for going to the local market or any other nearby place. In rainy

Figure 4

Housing Patterns and its Condition in Related Isolated Rural Area

Houses of SC Category Houses of OBC Category

season, communication of this area gets disrupted because of the absence of paved road. There is no bus service facility from this isolated place. Far from here, there is only one bus service and for that people of this place walk for a distance of more than 5 km. Local passenger train service condition is the same as mentioned above. As this is an isolated area, economy is based on agriculture, therefore, people get their income seasonally. Therefore, because of fixed timing of income of people over here, this place is perfect for the study on borrowing trend economy.

Sampling Design

The core of the analysis of this paper is based on primary survey as well as secondary information. Data on socio-economic variable such as number of household, population, occupational pattern, infrastructure for targeted area will be obtained from the census of India. Therefore, secondary data will give only general information about study area for research.

Yet the authentic data of borrowing trend economy is not available. So the study is generally based on primary data collection at household level. For the calculation of 'Bt effect', data has been collected from such a household where educational activities are going on in the house (see Figures 3 and 4). In this, with the use of simple cluster sampling, the samples of 60 households are taken which are stratified based on social stratification (20 general, 20 OBC and 20 SC categories). For this study purpose, three villages namely Bishrampur, Amba and Mirzapur have been selected representing household which are engaged in economic activities. For understanding "borrowing trend (Bt) effect" the questionnaires used in the sampling is given in the (Tables 1 and 2) formed below:

Table 1

Details of Households and Their Budget

Cat.	*No. of Pers.*	*Occupation*	*Additional occupation*	*Annual income*	*Average income (monthly)*	*Expenditures in month*	*Monthly expenditure*
GEN	4	AGRI	N.A.	85,000.00	6	12	6,000.00
GEN	3	AGRI	N.A.	80,000.00	6	12	5,000.00
GEN	8	AGRI	BUSINESS	2,00,000.00	6.5	12	12,000.00

Cont'd...

Cont'd...

GEN	6	AGRI	N.A.	2,00,000.00	6	12	13,000.00
GEN	6	AGRI	BUSINESS	2,00,000.00	7	12	12,000.00
GEN	3	AGRI	N.A.	1,50,000.00	6	12	6,000.00
GEN	7	AGRI	P. JOB	3,40,000.00	9	12	20,000.00
GEN	5	AGRI	BUSINESS	2,70,000.00	6	12	16,000.00
GEN	4	AGRI	P. JOB	1,50,000.00	5.5	12	10,000.00
GEN	5	AGRI	N.A.	1,50,000.00	6	12	6,000.00
GEN	6	AGRI	P. JOB	1,74,000.00	9	12	12,000.00
GEN	7	AGRI	N.A.	1,60,000.00	6	12	11,000.00
GEN	5	AGRI	BUSINESS	3,00,000.00	9	12	20,000.00
GEN	5	AGRI	N.A.	2,00,000.00	7	12	6,000.00
GEN	5	AGRI	P. JOB	2,50,000.00	9	12	12,000.00
GEN	3	AGRI	N.A.	2,00,000.00	6	12	10,000.00
GEN	6	AGRI	N.A.	3,50,000.00	7	12	12,000.00
GEN	5	AGRI	N.A.	2,00,000.00	6	12	7,000.00
GEN	7	AGRI	BUSINESS	3,00,000.00	6	12	13,000.00
GEN	4	AGRI	N.A.	1,50,000.00	5	12	7,000.00
OBC	8	AGRI	BUSINESS	1,75,000.00	9	12	8,000.00
OBC	7	AGRI	BUSINESS	2,00,000.00	9	12	12,000.00
OBC	8	AGRI	P.JOB	1,75,000.00	9.5	12	8,000.00
OBC	6	AGRI	P.JOB	97,000.00	6	12	4,000.00
OBC	4	AGRI	BUSINESS	75,000.00	6.5	12	3,000.00
OBC	6	AGRI	P.JOB	1,13,000.00	9	12	7,000.00
OBC	11	AGRI	P.JOB	3,00,000.00	9	12	15,000.00
OBC	12	AGRI	BUSINESS	2,50,000.00	9	12	13,000.00
OBC	4	AGRI	BUSINESS	1,10,000.00	9	12	4,000.00
OBC	8	AGRI	BUSINESS	2,50,000.00	7	12	5,000.00
OBC	5	AGRI	LABOUR	76,000.00	7.5	12	5,000.00
OBC	7	AGRI	N.A.	45,000.00	8	12	3,000.00
OBC	15	AGRI	BUSINESS + JOB	1,70,000.00	8.5	12	12,000.00
OBC	8	AGRI	P.JOB	65,000.00	8.5	12	3,500.00
OBC	6	AGRI	P.JOB + GOV. JOB	3,81,000.00	8.5	12	14,000.00
OBC	9	AGRI	N.A.	1,30,000.00	6	12	7,000.00
OBC	5	AGRI	BUSINESS + JOB	90,000.00	7	12	7,000.00
OBC	6	AGRI	N.A.	60,000.00	6	12	4,500.00
OBC	5	AGRI	N.A.	1,30,000.00	6	12	5,000.00
OBC	6	AGRI	P.JOB	1,00,000.00	9	12	6,000.00
SC	6	LABOUR	N.A.	84,000.00	12	12	5,000.00

Cont'd...

Cont'd...

SC	7	LABOUR	P.JOB	1,40,000.00	11	12	10,000.00
SC	11	AGRI	P.JOB	1,55,000.00	8	12	7,000.00
SC	6	AGRI	LABOUR	50,000.00	6.5	12	3,000.00
SC	6	AGRI	LABOUR	55,000.00	6.5	12	3,000.00
SC	5	AGRI	LABOUR	65,000.00	6.5	12	4,000.00
SC	5	LABOUR	N.A.	60,000.00	9	12	3,000.00
SC	8	LABOUR	N.A.	65,000.00	9	12	5,000.00
SC	13	AGRI	BUSNESS+P.JOB	2,95,000.00	8.5	12	16,000.00
SC	11	AGRI	LABOUR	1,30,000.00	7.5	12	8,000.00
SC	3	LABOUR	N.A.	55,000.00	9	12	2,500.00
SC	5	AGRI	LABOUR	55,000.00	7	12	4,000.00
SC	9	AGRI	BUSINESS	1,43,600.00	9	12	10,000.00
SC	7	P.JOB	LABOUR	1,02,000.00	9.5	12	6,000.00
SC	7	AGRI	LABOUR+P.JOB	1,80,000.00	8.5	12	7,000.00
SC	5	AGRI	LABOUR	75,000.00	7.5	12	6,000.00
SC	5	LABOUR	N.A.	55,000.00	10	12	4,000.00
SC	8	LABOUR	N.A.	60,000.00	10	12	5,000.00
SC	5	AGRI	LABOUR+P.JOB	95,000.00	8.5	12	6,000.00
SC	6	AGRI	P.JOB	1,00,000.00	8	12	6,800.00

Source: Field Survey, 2013.

Table 2

Educational Expenditure Conditions of Households

Category	*No. of studying pers.*	*Edu. exp. in month*	*Monthly educational expenditure*	*Annual educational expenditure*	*Study place*
GEN	2	12	1,000.00	10,000.00	A = [at home]
GEN	1	12	1,000.00	3,000.00	A = [at home]
GEN	2	12	1,500.00	4,000.00	A = [at home]
GEN	3	12	3,500.00	10,000.00	A + B [B= other place]
GEN	2	12	1,500.00	4,000.00	A = [at home]
GEN	1	12	1,000.00	10,000.00	A = [at home]
GEN	2	12	2,000.00	4,000.00	A = [at home]
GEN	3	12	10,000.00	10,000.00	A + B [B= other place]
GEN	1	12	2,000.00	10,000.00	A + B [B= other place]
GEN	1	12	400.00	4,000.00	A = [at home]
GEN	2	12	1,000.00	7,000.00	A = [at home]
GEN	3	12	2,000.00	11,000.00	A = [at home]

Cont'd...

Cont'd...

GEN	3	12	5,500.00	20,000.00	B
GEN	2	12	1,500.00	7,000.00	A = [at home]
GEN	1	12	1,000.00	7,000.00	A = [at home]
GEN	1	12	6,000.00	10,000.00	B
GEN	2	12	1,500.00	5,000.00	A
GEN	2	12	2,000.00	5,000.00	A
GEN	3	12	3,000.00	7,000.00	A
GEN	2	12	2,000.00	5,000.00	A
OBC	3	12	2,000.00	10,000.00	A
OBC	5	12	5,000.00	10,000.00	A+B
OBC	4	12	4,500.00	10,000.00	A+B
OBC	2	12	500.00	2,000.00	A
OBC	2	12	500.00	3,000.00	A
OBC	1	12	400.00	2,000.00	A
OBC	4	12	3,000.00	4,000.00	A
OBC	4	12	7,000.00	40,000.00	A+B
OBC	2	12	600.00	2,000.00	A
OBC	3	12	1,000.00	10,000.00	A+B
OBC	3	12	500.00	4,000.00	A
OBC	4	12	200.00	2,000.00	A
OBC	5	12	3,000.00	12,000.00	A
OBC	5	12	400.00	5,000.00	A
OBC	2	12	4,000.00	10,000.00	A+B
OBC	4	12	4,000.00	10,000.00	A+B
OBC	1	12	300.00	3,000.00	A
OBC	4	12	800.00	3,000.00	A
OBC	3	12	2,000.00	6,000.00	A
OBC	4	12	1,000.00	3,000.00	A
SC	4	12	1,000.00	8,000.00	A
SC	4	12	5,000.00	10,000.00	A+B
SC	5	12	2,000.00	6,000.00	A
SC	2	12	500.00	2,000.00	A
SC	2	12	300.00	1,000.00	A
SC	3	12	500.00	10,000.00	A
SC	3	12	400.00	2,000.00	A
SC	5	12	500.00	1,000.00	A
SC	3	12	3,000.00	10,000.00	A+B
SC	2	12	500.00	5,000.00	A

Cont'd...

Cont'd...

SC	1	12	1,500.00	3,000.00	B
SC	2	12	3,000.00	10,000.00	A+B
SC	5	12	2,000.00	10,000.00	A
SC	2	12	500.00	1,000.00	A
SC	3	12	600.00	3,000.00	A
SC	2	12	2,000.00	5,000.00	A
SC	3	12	700.00	4,000.00	A
SC	5	12	1,500.00	1,500.00	A
SC	3	12	3,000.00	2,000.00	A+B
SC	3	12	2,500.00	5,000.00	A

Source: Field Survey, 2013.

In these tables, category, no. of people (in each household), no. of studying people, occupational condition, annual income (in time and cash), and average monthly income, consumption status and study and work place are mentioned.

Occupational Profile, Income and Consumption

Occupational profile shows that only 12 per cent of household do not have own land for agriculture. The primary occupation of 88 per cent people is agriculture. And the primary occupation of the remaining 12 per cent people in as labourer. Among these the one and only occupation of these 33 per cent people is agriculture. And 50 per cent household sustain their living on agricultural-based economic activities. Except these 50 per cent, the rest have agriculture-based income as well as medium for secondary income.

Knowingly, for general and OBC category, the primary occupation of 100 per cent household is agriculture and any household of general category is not an agricultural labourer. Looking at the occupation of each household, the collected data shows that 35 per cent have only one occupation, that undoubtedly is agriculture or agricultural labour. And almost 60 per cent of households apart from being involved in agriculture or agricultural labour, are involved in secondary occupation too. Looking further, there is only 5 per cent household involved in all three options that are – agriculture, business, and job. Thus, agricultural activities are the biggest income source for this isolated area. Mostly, the selected households of the concerned isolated area are engaged in informal sector of the economy. The informal sector include households of agriculture related activities, workers, agricultural labourer, business and private job (people who move to town out of the isolated area for work). Income of these households reveals that the annual income of only 65 per cent people is above one lakh (whose family's average no. is seven). Even then, the annual income of 35 per cent households is less than one lakh. If it is seen category-wise, then the annual income of 90 per cent households of general category is around 1.50 lakh or above. Whereas the annual income of only 40 per cent households of scheduled caste (SC) category is around one lakh or above. In OBC category, from the people taking sample, the annual income of only 65 per cent people is around one lakh or above.

For Bt effect the calculation of the number of income months in a year of any household is more important than the calculation of annual income in any household. And by calculation with this view, the collected sample shows that the no. of households having income in all the 12 months is only 1.7 per cent. The income of 93 per cent households is 9 months or even less. Therefore, it is seen that for the expenditure of the month having no income, extra arrangement has to be done. In this it is only five to seven months of income from agriculture. Even then it is one of the most important medium of income. And after that the income is obtained from private job, labour or business, etc., this secondary source of income is somewhat related to agricultural production. Both the frequency of income and its certainty are according to the nature of socio-economic system. Even the time frequency of the fast moving urban economy moves at fast rate and that is why the frequency of income time is less.

Generally, income time frequency is in days. Here, by income time frequency it means that time frequency which is there after the complete income is obtained. This interval is comparatively more in the villages than in cities. And is even more in isolated areas and remote rural areas. Income time frequency in single occupation and long time investment sector is much more than a job of any kind. If in case of economic system of the present isolated area then here the medium for basic income is agriculture, and time for agriculture production in mid-lower Ganga plain is six months at the maximum. For households depending on only agriculture, the whole annual expenditure is managed from six months of income only. A part of this, in agrarian-based economy system, the certainty of time of income also is in months. The certainty of income time should be in days in a good economy system. In the certainty of income time is generally in days in Indian cities and cities of others developing countries. 'Income time certainty' which is occurring in months, brings borrowing trend in related economy. In this behalf, analysis has been done in detail with the help of an example. Here it is just being mentioned that among the samples taken, 55 per cent have stated that their income is never on time and for the 43 per cent households, sometimes their income is received on time. There is only 2 per cent or even less households which have income from job along with the income from main source. And for 43 per cent households the income source is from business along with agriculture (whose income is sometimes on time.) Consumptions shows economic status more clearly than income. Because, the limit and nature of consumption generally extend the developing line of a society. Even the samples collected from the related isolated area shows the same.

There can be a thought that the limit of consumption of any household could be within the annual income, and if it crosses this limit then the consumption capacity of the household will degrade gradually in further years. In the taken sample the expenditure of household is noted in terms of each of month. Because, expenditure is always due to needs, it cannot be stopped, instead it should be managed. Apart from monthly expenditure, even extra educational expenditure is shown in the related table.

Analysis of Economic Component: Effect of Borrowing Trend (Bt)

Many dimensions can be possible in an economic component but here the following economic components are discussed:

Income Frequency

First of all, on specification on the income frequency of taken sample, it gives the fact that for the household in which the main and single occupation is agriculture, there are the following two dimension of income frequency – when they get their agrarian production – this almost lasts for continuous 5–7 months. The income frequency in theses months cannot be generally predicted because it is very irregular and accelerated. For example, in the month of agrarian production, the products that is sold today can also be sold immediately thereafter or even after some days, and income can be obtained from this. Contrary to this fact, after production months, the income for rest of the month has no definite source. And income obtained from the production month is the medium to be in the rest of the month until the next production time comes. And on the other side, when the additional income source is obtained apart from the income obtained from agriculture, then the income comparatively decreases but even this depends on additional income source too. If the additional income source is a permanent job or government job, then the frequency is monthly in general. And if the source is business then the frequency is generally per day. Thus, income frequency decreases or increases according to the income source. Thus, income frequency is inversely proportional to no. of income sources.

$$\textit{No. of income sources} = \frac{1}{\textit{income frequency}}$$

Income Certainty (on time)

Income certainty shows the definite time of income or the income obtained is fixed. For example, – if for a person, the chances for getting his income on the first date of a month is 100 per cent, then it can be said that this person has 100 per cent income certainty. In this way the percentage of fluctuation in his chances for getting the income also describe the percentage of income certainty. From the sample taken from this isolated area, almost 64 per cent households stated that they never have obtained their income on time. And 43 per cent households obtained their income on time not very often. And the income of the rest 3 per cent people only is on time who along with primary occupation and also involved in additional occupation like, a job. Now the question arises on the matter of fact that the maximum households are not able to get their income on time. So, for their expenditures done on determined socio-economic activities, do they have to borrow? So, for the answer of this question almost 20 per cent households told that they always have to borrow; whereas the answer of 65 per cent of households was that they have to borrow only sometimes. Now, is there any correlation between the extreme declination in income certainty and borrowing money? A correlation has been done on the basis of 'Pearson method' on SPSS which after getting examined gives the following result:

Table 3

Correlation Between Income Time and Borrowing Money

Correlation			
		Get your income on time	*borrow money(if don't get income on time)*
Get your income on time	Pearson Correlation	1	-.276*
	Sig. (2-tailed)		.033
	N	60	60
Borrow money (if don't get income on time)	Pearson Correlation	-.276*	1
	Sig. (2-tailed)	.033	
	N	60	60

* Correlation is significant at the 0.05 level (2-tailed).

In the Table 3, according to 'Pearson method' R value (–.276) representing a strong negative correlation (as one variable increases, the other variable decreases). And P value is (.033). It means the negative correlation between get your income on time and borrow money (if do not get income on time) is considered to be significant.

As the need of expenditure is controlled by the quantity of income and when the need exceeds the perimeter of income, then there comes a need to borrow money. For this the difference between 'average income' and 'capability of fulfilment of the demand of additional amount on education' , 'capability of fulfillment of the demand of additional amount on education' and 'borrow money' for education, and 'educational status' and 'borrow money' for education, when correlation calculated by 'Pearson method', following result came which are given below:

In Table 4, clearly a negative correlation between annual income and capability of fulfilment of the demand of additional amount on education can be seen with its ' R' value (-.305). And 'p' value – (.018).

Table 4

Correlation between Average Income [in months] and Capability of Fulfillment the Demand of an Additional Amount on Education

Correlation			
		Average income [in months]	*Capability of fulfilment the demand of additional amount on education*
Average income [in months]	Pearson Correlation	1	–.305*
	Sig. (2-tailed)		.018
	N	60	60
Capability of fulfilment of the demand of additional amount on education	Pearson Correlation	–.305*	1
	Sig. (2-tailed)	.018	
	N	60	60

* Correlation is significant at the 0.05 level (2-tailed).

Further the correlation between capability of fulfilment of the demand of additional amount on education and borrow money (Bm) for education, shows a strong negative correlation of 0.01 level, where 'R' value is –.631 and 'P' value is (.001) as following. Similarly, a 0.01 level of strong positive correlation can be seen between capability of fulfilment of the demand of additional amount on education and borrow money for education (Table 5).

In Table 6 the correlation between educational status and borrow money for education, shows a strong positive correlation of 0.01 level, where 'R' value is –.340 and 'P' value is (.008) as following. Similarly, a 0.01 level of strong positive correlation can be seen between education status and borrow money for education.

Even the data from the collected samples shows that almost 53 per cent households have agreed with the fact that Bt has its effect on educational development. And only 16 per cent do not agree with the fact of effect of Bt on education. Whereas, according to 30 per cent people the effect of Bt on education is only sometimes. And household opinion, now it is very clear that there is a deep impact of Bt on livelihood of people in isolated areas. Moreover, it becomes one of the important determining elements of educational status.

Table 5

Correlation Between Capabilities of Fulfilment of the Demand of an Additional Amount on Education and Borrow Money for Education

Correlation			
		Capability of fulfilment of the demand of additional amount on education	*Bm for education*
Capability of fulfilment of the demand of additional amount on education	Pearson Correlation	1	–.631**
	Sig. (2-tailed)		.000
	N	60	60
Bm for education	Pearson Correlation	-.631**	1
	Sig. (2-tailed)	.000	
	N	60	60

** Correlation is significant at the 0.01 level (2-tailed).

Table 6

Correlation Between Educational Status and Borrow Money for Education

Correlation			
		Educational status	*Bm for education*
Educational status	Pearson Correlation	1	.340**
	Sig. (2-tailed)		.008
	N	60	60
Bm for education	Pearson Correlation	.340**	1
	Sig. (2-tailed)	.008	
	N	60	60

** Correlation is significant at the 0.01 level (2-tailed).

Now the question arises that when the people belonging to the isolated areas have to borrow money to fulfil their various needs, then what is the scenario of paying it back? (Tables 7 and 8).

It is very obvious that for the people whose income frequency and income certainty is irregular, then these people are not successful in paying back their borrowed amount on promised time, even though if they wish they could. For this, when with the help of two questionnaires, their situation and opinion have been tried to be known. It was known that people borrowing money equal to or even less than their annual income, they have taken months or even years to pay that amount back. Moreover, only 13 per cent households are able to pay back the amount on time. Whereas, 28 per cent people never are able to pay back the amount on the promised time. Maximum 58 per cent people are able to pay their borrowed amount on the promise date, that too not to very regular. Hence, borrowing trend (Bt) plays an important role even in paying back the borrowed amount, so, the stronger the borrowing trend (Bt) effect, more would be it difficult to pay their borrow money back.

Table 7

Questionnaires Summary About Bt

	Options	Get income on time	BM (if don't get income on time)	Returning time (Bm)	Bm for education
Gen	Often	0	2	0	1
	Sometimes	9	15	19	11
	Never/No	11	3	1	8
OBC	Often	0	3	5	5
	Sometimes	10	13	9	6
	Never/No	10	4	6	9
SC	Often	1	8	9	1
	Sometimes	6	10	8	6
	Never/No	13	2	3	13

Total no. of households –60 (20 gen, 20 OBC, 20 SC category).

Source Field Survey, 2013.

Table 8

Questionnaires Summary About Bt Effect on Education

	Options	Capability of fulfilment of demand of additional mount on education	Educational Evelopment satisfaction	Bt role on education
Gen	Often	8	8	3
	Sometimes	11	11	10
	never/No	1	1	7
OBC	Often	4	12	12
	Sometimes	7	3	4
	never/No	9	5	4
SC	Often	1	9	16
	Sometimes	6	3	3
	never/No	13	8	1

Source: Field Survey, 2013.

Educational Status: Borrowing Trend (Bt) Effect

If there is no certainty in income, then the borrowing trend (Bt) effect will continue to increase with the increase in educational status. It can be understood with the help of graph in Figure 5.

[In this graph for, borrow money (Bm) for education and Bm –1.00 = often, 2.00= sometimes and 3.00= never. And for educational status –1.00 = till tenth, 2.00= till graduation and 3.00= till post graduation.)

There is declination in the number of people studying post graduation and, so the effect of numerical depreciation is seen in the graph with represented borrowing trend (Bt) effect.

Method of Getting Borrowing Trend (Bt) Effect

With the help of specification of the sample of the taken household, it has been established that borrowing trend (Bt) is a significant economic trend of that isolated area,

Figure 5

Situation of Borrowing Money

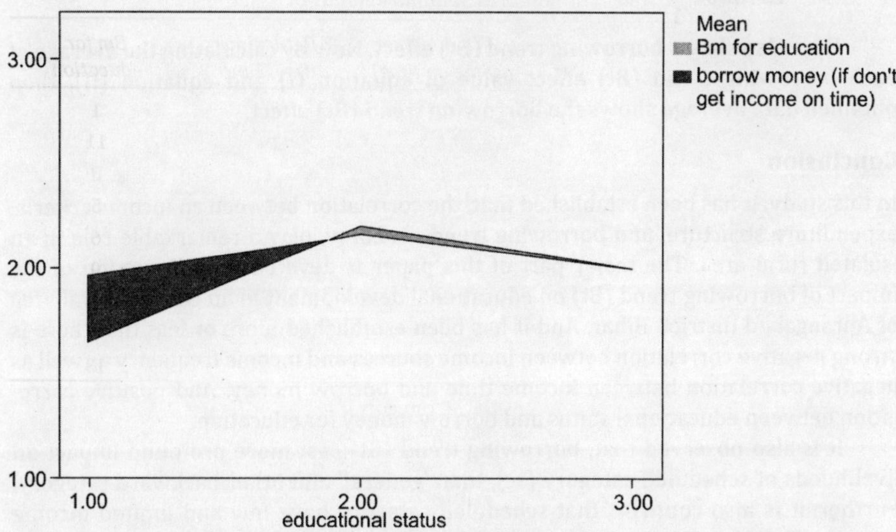

which is imbedded in the root of socio-economic activities. For calculating this borrowing trend (Bt) on the unit level, the following two formulae can be used:

➢*Bte* Borrowing trend effect

Bte) = (average time frequency of expendeture in time (Afe))/(average time frequency of income in time (Afi)) (I)

$$\succ Bte\ (on\ all\ expenditure) = \frac{(main\ income + d) \times \left(\frac{n}{n}\right)}{(expenditure) \times \left(\frac{n}{n^1}\right)} \quad \text{............(II)}$$

In the above equations: **n** = value of frequency in months, when gets main income.

$\mathbf{n^2}$ = value of expenditure frequency (in months)

d = extra income in **n**.

Bt value of above equations shows following results:

If **Bt =1**, then it means shows ± = **0**

Bt = < 1, shows borrowing trend (Bt) effect ?, the more the digit is less than 1 the more result will be stronger.

Bt = < **1**, shows opposite result of borrowing trend (Bt) ↓.

By applying equation (I) on the data from table (I), borrowing trend (Bt) effect for 1st household =1/6 = 0.166. Here Afe = 1(in month) this is generally constant because expenditure cannot be stopped, it has to be done every month. Afi = 6 the average income frequency of this household is six months. For the rest of the month, the income is almost null or very less. So, for these six months to come again, there will be a time log of six months in between (12–6=6).

So that, time frequency of income is 6, therefore, obtained result = 0.166 – it shows Bt effect. Similarly, putting the data of 27th household in equation (II), we get –

$$Bt = \frac{(3000)\times\frac{9}{9}}{184000\times\frac{9}{1}} = \frac{30\times 1}{184\times 9} = \frac{30}{1656} = 0.018$$

Here also shows borrowing trend (Bt) effect. Now by calculating the average of each borrowing trend (Bt) effect value of equation (I) and equation (II), then obtained data average shows the borrowing trend (Bt) effect.

Conclusion

In this study, it has been established that, the correlation between an income criteria, expenditure structure, and borrowing trend economy, play a remarkable role in an isolated rural area. The major part of this paper is devoted to a discussion of the impact of borrowing trend (Bt) on educational development in an isolated rural area of Aurangabad district, Bihar. And it has been established more or less that there is strong negative correlation between income sources and income frequency as well as negative correlation between income time and borrow money. And positive correlation between educational status and borrow money for education.

It is also observed that, borrowing trend (Bt) cast more profound impact on livelihoods of scheduled category (sc), than 'general' and other backward category. Further, it is also confirms that scheduled category have few and limited income sources. Therefore, generally they are not able to invest in higher education. But income sources of general category and other backward category is something more than SC category in present study area. So they invest money in higher education. Consequently, rate of borrowing money for educational expenditure is comparatively high in OBC and general category.

Further, it can be reasonably inferred that trend of borrowing economy control and rule over the agrarian-based livelihoods in an isolated rural area. And finally, it can be said that, borrowing trend (Bt) determined the human development of an isolated rural area.

References

Chorley, R.J. and P. Haggett (1967) *Socio-Economic Models in Geography*, London: Methuen.

Goodall, B. (1987) *Dictionary of Human Geography*, London: The Penguin Group Publications.

Gordon, L.C., P.F. Maryann and S.G. Meric (eds) (2000) *The Oxford Handbook of Economic Geography*, New York: Oxford Publications.

Hedge, N.G. (2001) 'Role of Non-Governmental Organizations (NGOs) in Filling Hunger and Reducing Poverty', *Indian Farming*, 51(7).

Kamle, K. and S. Adhikari (2009) 'Vertical and Horizontal Dimensions of Inequality in the Literacy Level of Bihar: A Geographical Analysis', *Geographical Review of India*, 345–357.

Mukherjee, N. (ed.) (2002) *Alternative Perspectives on Livelihoods, Agriculture and Air Pollution*, New Delhi: Concept.

Sangwan, R.S. and S. Sangwan (2010) 'Literacy in Twentieth Century and its Trends in Urban-Rural Differentials in India', *Annals of the National Association of Geographers, India*, 79–94.

18

Exclusion of the Scheduled Caste Population in Professional Occupations in Uttar Pradesh

VINOD KUMAR AND AJIT KUMAR

First of all it must be clarified that a 'job' and an 'occupation' are not the same thing. A job is a specific and sometimes a unique bundle of activities carried out by a person in the expectation of economic remuneration while an occupation is an abstract category used to group and classify similar jobs (Hauser and Warren, 1997). Economic strength of any country hinges on the pre-eminence of the professionals (Lal, 2005: 87). Persons who increase the existing stock of knowledge, apply scientific or artistic concepts and theories, teach about the foregoing in a systematic manner, or engage in any combination of these three activities are called professionals. According to NCO–2004 there are fifty-six families of occupations under the 'Professionals' division in the urban areas of Uttar Pradesh. All of the families of occupations were not found in each and every district of Uttar Pradesh. So, some prominent and commonly occurring families of occupations were identified in the districts of Uttar Pradesh. This paper investigates exclusion of the scheduled caste population in thirteen prominent families of professional occupations as classified by National Classification of Occupations (NCO–2004). The 13 families of occupations which are prominent and are found in most of the districts of the state are as follows:

I.	Civil Engineers (2,142)
II.	Electrical Engineers (2,143)
III.	Electronics and Telecommunication Engineers (2,144)
IV.	Mechanical Engineers (2,145)
V.	Chemical Engineers (2,146)
VI.	Physicians and Surgeons, Allopathic (2,221)
VII.	Physicians and Surgeons, Ayurvedic (2,222)
VIII.	Physicians and Surgeons, Homeopathic (2,223)

Cont'd...

Cont'd...

IX.	Physicians and Surgeons, Unani (2,224)
X.	College, University and Higher Education Teaching Professionals (2,310)
XI.	Lawyers (2,421)
XII.	Judges and Magistrates (2,422)
XIII.	Ordained Religious Workers (2,461)

Note: Numerals in the brackets signify families of occupations (4th Level of National Classification of Occupations–2004) under Professionals Division of NCO.

In order to facilitate the explanation, similar families of occupations were clubbed together. Civil Engineers (2,142), Electrical Engineers (2,143), Electronics and Telecommunication Engineers (2,144), and Mechanical Engineers (2,145) were clubbed together to form one family called 'Engineers'. Physicians and Surgeons, Allopathic (2,221), Physicians and Surgeons, Ayurvedic (2,222), Physicians and Surgeons, Homeopathic (2,223), and Physicians and Surgeons, Unani (2,224) were combined together to form another single family named 'Doctors'. Rest of the families were kept intact. So, six broad families of occupations were filtered out of thirteen prominent and commonly occurring families of occupations.

Further, this study also incorporates a probe into the correlates and determinants of the exclusion of SC population in professional occupations. In order to bring out a clear picture of exclusion in professional occupations, non-scheduled caste population (non-SC/ST) has also been incorporated. The study is mainly based on NCO–2004, Districtwise Development Indicators, Uttar Pradesh 2009, and the Census of India, 2001 and has been carried out in the state of Uttar Pradesh in India, focusing on the urban areas of the state. Eschewing the watertight categorization of east and west UP as usually pursued in the literature, the present study adopted a broader regional categorization based on the following seven socio-economic indicators:

1. Percentage of urban population to total population.
2. Total literacy rate.
3. Percentage of rural people below poverty line.
4. Percentage of people engaged in manufacturing.
5. Percentage of electrified villages to total inhabited villages.
6. Length of total pucca roads per thousand sq km.
7. Percentage of net irrigated area to net area sown.

After dividing all the indicators by their means, a composite index is worked out. Values of composite index are plotted on a GIS based maps using 'equal interval' class method. The following Table 1 presents the four regions of Uttar Pradesh and the districts falling under each region:

Table 1

Socio-Economic Regions of Uttar Pradesh

Regions	*Districts*
Very Highly Developed Region (VHDR)	Ghaziabad, Lucknow, Kanpur Nagar, Varanasi.
Highly Developed Region (HDR)	Meerut, Agra, Firozabad, Sant Ravidas Nagar, Bhadohi.
Medium Developed Region (MDR)	Saharanpur, Muzaffarnagar, Bijnor, Rampur, Moradabad, Jyotiba Phule Nagar, Baghpat,

Cont'd...

Cont'd...

	Gautam Buddha Nagar, Bulandshahar, Jhansi,
	Aligarh, Hathras, Mathura, Mainpuri, Bareilly,
	Shahjahanpur, Hardoi, Unnao, Rae Bareli,
	Kannauj, Etawah, Kanpur Dehat, Jalaun, Mau Kaushambi, Farrukhabad, Allahabad, Ballia,
	Jaunpur, Ghazipur, Mirzapur , Sultanpur Faizabad, Ambedkar Nagar, Chandauli.
Low Developed Region (LDR)	Etah, Budaun, Pilibhit, Mahrajganj, Bahraich,
	Mahoba, Banda, Pratapgarh, Siddharthnagar,
	Shrawasti, Balrampur, Sitapur, Kushinagar, Deoria, Basti, Hamirpur, Chitrakoot, Kheri,
	Gorakhpur, Auraiya, Azamgarh, Sonbhadra,
	Fatehpur, Gonda, Sant Kabir Nagar, Lalitpur, Barabanki.

To capture the disparities between Scheduled Caste males/females and non-SC/ST males/females in terms of professional occupations, modified David Sopher's Index has been applied. 'Overlay Analysis' method of GIS, Correlation and Regression enhance the empirical background of the study.

Presence of SC Professionals among Urban Main Workers

Professionals are classified as main workers because they work almost throughout the year. Higher levels of occupations fall under the 'Professionals' division of NCO. Every rung of the society has equal rights to achieve top slots in the 'Professionals' division of NCO–2004. But reality is diametrically opposite and this varies across the social groups. Table 2 and 3 presents the presence of urban SC population in 'Professionals' division of NCO in different context.

Table 2

Proportion of SC Professionals among Total Urban SC Main Workers in Uttar Pradesh

Regions	*SC professionals among total urban SC main workers (in%)*		
	Total	*Males*	*Females*
Very Highly Developed Region	2.69	2.35	0.340
Highly Developed Region	1.72	1.56	0.160
Medium Developed Region	2.88	2.54	0.341
Low Developed Region	3.42	3.03	0.391
Uttar Pradesh	2.73	2.41	0.319

Source: Census of India 2001, B-Series and PCA (UP).

Table 3

Proportion of SC Professionals in Total Urban Main Workers in Uttar Pradesh

Regions	*SC professionals among total urban main workers (in%)*		
	Total	*Males*	*Females*
Very Highly Developed Region	0.29	0.25	0.037
Highly Developed Region	0.29	0.26	0.027
Medium Developed Region	0.30	0.26	0.035
Low Developed Region	0.38	0.33	0.043
Uttar Pradesh	0.31	0.27	0.036

Source: Census of India 2001, B-Series and PCA (UP).

In the context of total urban SC main workers, proportion of SC professionals is very low and varies from 1.72 per cent to 3.72 per cent. In the context of total urban main workers it again plunges down to its nadir (less than 0.5%). In both the contexts 'highly developed region' registers lowest proportion of urban SC professionals. This shows that this region is absorbing SC population in some other occupations. Most probably, in the manufacturing sector as this region is predominantly a hub of secondary economic activities (Parveen, 2005: 45). Lowest percentages of SC professionals in total urban and main workers' populations indicate that a large proportion of the urban SC population is engaged in lower levels of occupations (Banerjee and Knight, 1985).

Spatial Pattern of the Incidence of SC Professionals in the Districts of Uttar Pradesh

It is assumed that professionals are concentrated in some highly developed districts such as Lucknow, Kanpur, Varanasi, etc., but the Figure 1 gives a completely different picture.

It shows the proportion of SC professionals in total urban SC population. Contrary to a common belief, SC professionals are concentrated in some less developed districts like Sonbhadra, Gonda, and, Shrawasti. Sonbhadra is an industrial area. The highest percentage of SC engineers are found in Sonbhadra. So it shows the highest proportion of SC professionals. Shrawasti has the highest percentage of doctors (0.50% of total urban SC population). That is why it shows a higher proportion of SC professionals. Gonda has high percentage of lawyers, higher education teaching professionals and exhibits a higher proportion of SC professionals. Most of the districts show lower percentages of SC professionals. Agra, Aligarh, Hathras, Firozabad, Meerut districts also show lower percentages of SC professionals even though they are highly urbanized (Parveen, 2005: 226) and have an industrial background, which shows that these districts attract workers only in some lower levels of occupations (Deshpande, 2001; Jeffrey, 2005). Many districts of the 'medium developed region' register medium percentages of SC professionals. The 'low developed' region exhibits lower proportions of SC professionals. This region lags behind all the regions as literacy rate in this region is very low (less than 50%).

Figure 1

Proportion of SC Professionals in Total Urban SC Population in Uttar Pradesh

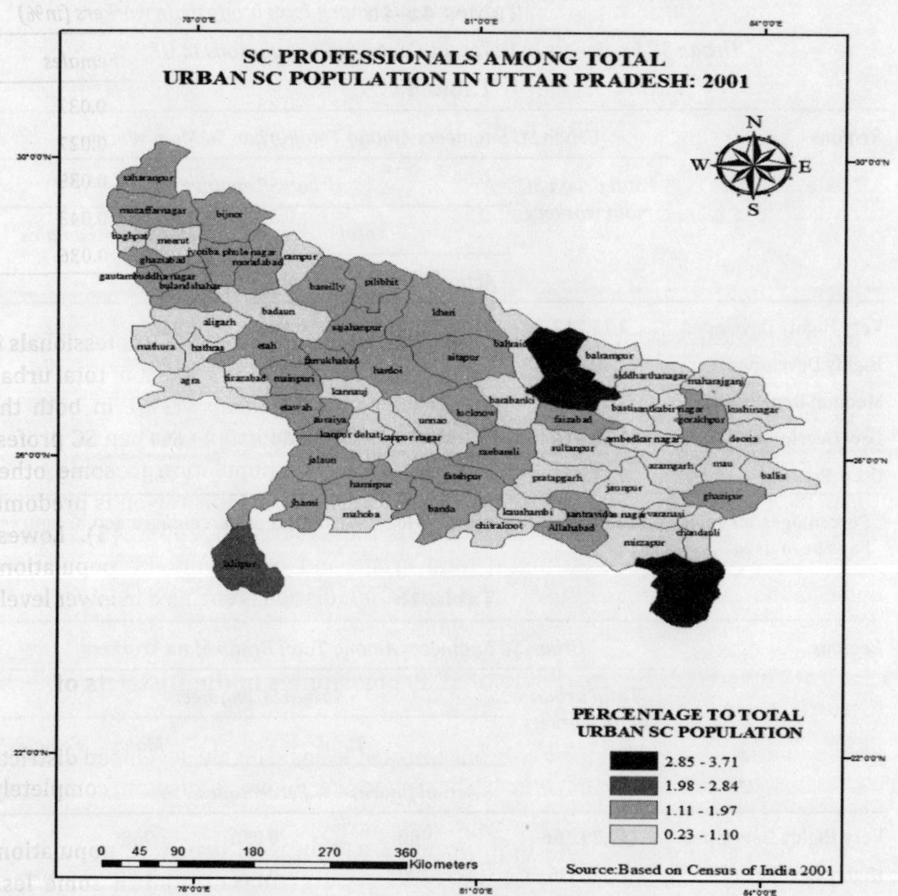

Deeper Insights

Earlier, six families of occupations have been mentioned under 'Professionals' division of National Classification of Occupations (NCO). Examining these families of occupations one by one for the urban Scheduled Caste population may give us a deeper insight. Tables 4a–4b presents the presence of SC engineers in the context of different populations. Only 0.14 per cent (2,792 SC engineers out of 20,20,528, i.e., total urban SC populations of 20–69 years of age) of total urban SC population of urban Uttar Pradesh is classified as SC engineers. When total urban population is taken into consideration, only 0.016 per cent (2,792 SC engineers out of 1,70,73,911, i.e., total urban population of age 20–69 years,) of the total urban population falls under the category of SC engineers. It is unfortunate that in spite of offering numerous educational facilities and many other incentives through reservation in higher education and in various jobs, the proportion of engineers in the total urban SC population is not impressive at all. This can be attributed to the lower attainment of technical education of SC urban population (less than 5% of the total graduates and above attained any technical degree).

Tables 4a–4b

Urban SC Engineers in Different Context of Populations in UP

Table 4a

Regions	*Urban SC Engineers Among Total Urban SC Main Workers*				
	Total urban SC main workers	*Urban SC engineers*			
		Total		*Males**	*Females**
		Actual figures	*Percentages*		
Very Highly Developed	2,13,712	980	0.46	968	12
Highly Developed	1,40,210	190	0.14	180	10
Medium Developed	3,47,932	926	0.27	916	10
Low Developed	1,28,916	696	0.54	694	2
Uttar Pradesh	8,41,722	2,792	0.33	2,758	34

* Percentages for males and females are extremely low. So, instead of percentages actual figures have been used.

Table 4b

Regions	*Urban SC Engineers Among Total Urban Main Workers*				
	Total urban main workers	*Urban SC engineers*			
		Total		*Males*	*Females*
		Actual figures	*Percentages*		
Very Highly Developed	19,79,166	980	0.050	968	12
Highly Developed	8,30,836	190	0.023	180	10
Medium Developed	33,58,512	926	0.028	916	10
Low Developed	11,66,618	696	0.060	694	2
Uttar Pradesh	74,31,522	2,792	0.038	2,758	34

Source: Census of India 2001, B-series, PCA (UP).

Both Tables 4a and 4b demonstrate the gloomy picture of SCs' presence in higher level of occupations. Not even a single urban SC main worker out of total 100 urban SC main workers is expected to turn out to be an engineer. In case of total urban main workers, percentage of SC engineers plunges to the lowest. Interestingly here also, Highly Developed Region registers the lowest figures for urban SC engineers. This fact once again strongly advocates the conclusion that most of the urban SC main workers are engaged in lower levels of occupations (Deshpande, 2001).

Next family of occupations is 'Doctors' which includes Physicians and Surgeons from Ayurvedic, Allopathic, Homeopathic, and Unani field of medical study. This family of occupations holds high regards in the society. Urban SC Population badly needs people from this family of occupations. There are 3,046 (0.15%) doctors out of total 20,20,528 urban SC persons of age 20–69 yrs. In case of total urban population this percentage stands at 0.017. Tables 5a and 5b depict the presence of SC doctors in different context of two populations.

Tables 5a–5b

Urban SC Doctors among SC and Total Urban Main Workers in UP

Regions	*Urban SC doctors among total urban SC main workers*				
	Total urban SC main workers	*Urban SC doctors*			
		Total		*Males*	*Females*
		Actual figures	*Percentages*		
Very Highly Developed	2,13,712	756	0.35	668	88
Highly Developed	1,40,210	434	0.31	406	28
Medium Developed	3,47,932	1310	0.37	1236	74
Low Developed	1,28,916	546	0.40	506	40
Uttar Pradesh	8,41,722	3,046	0.36	2,816	230

Table 5b

Urban SC Doctors Among Total Urban Main Workers

Regions	*Total urban main workers*	*Urban SC doctors*			
		Total		*Males*	*Females*
		Actual figures	*Percentages*		
Very Highly Developed	19,79,166	756	0.038	668	88
Highly Developed	8,30,836	434	0.052	406	28
Medium Developed	33,77,214	1,310	0.039	1236	74
Low Developed	12,44,306	546	0.044	506	40
Uttar Pradesh	74,31,522	3046	0.041	2816	230

Source: Census of India 2001, B-series, PCA (UP).

Once again, it is found that even the most important occupations are out of SCs' reach as in medical field also their presence is minimal. If their presence in medical field is examined in the context of total urban population, they stand nowhere.

Highly educated people direct the society towards the right path. People look up to them for proper guidance and sound decisions. Lecturers, professors, etc., are people who fall in the occupation family of 'College, University and Higher Education teaching professionals'. In Uttar Pradesh, there are only 518 college, university and higher education teaching professionals in total urban SC population of 20,20,528 between 20–69 years of age. Tables 6a and 6b present the regional distribution of college, university and higher teaching professionals among total urban SC main workers and total urban main workers.

Tables 6a–6b

Higher Education Teaching Professionals among Total Main Workers in UP

Table 6a

Regions	*Urban SC college, university and higher education teaching professionals among total urban SC main workers*				
	Total urban SC main workers	*Higher education teaching professionals*			
		Total		*Males*	*Females*
		Actual figures	*Percentages*		
Very Highly Developed	2,13,712	152	0.07	104	48
Highly Developed	1,40,210	56	0.04	48	8
Medium Developed	3,30,406	196	0.06	148	48
Low Developed	1,13,906	114	0.10	104	10
Uttar Pradesh	8,41,722	518	0.06	404	114

Table 6b

Regions	*Urban SC college, university and higher education teaching professionals among total urban main workers*				
	Total urban main workers	*Higher education teaching professionals*			
		Total		*Males*	*Females*
		Actual figures	*Percentages*		
Very Highly Developed	19,79,166	152	0.008	104	48
Highly Developed	8,30,836	56	0.006	44	8
Medium Developed	31,59,826	196	0.006	148	48
Low Developed	10,03,358	114	0.011	104	10
Uttar Pradesh	74,31,522	518	0.006	404	114

Source: Census of India 2001, B-series, PCA (UP).

As far as, this, one of the most important families of occupation is concerned; SC population is not faring better at all. All the regions exhibit the same low values as are found in case of other families of occupations.

Since atrocities and torture are not new to Scheduled Caste community and most of the time they are denied justice, they should be aware of laws and Acts meant for their protection (Thorat, 2002). Hence, legal professionals are much needed professionals for this community. In Uttar Pradesh, there are 2,442 lawyers among total urban SC population (2,02,058) of age between 20 and 69 years. Regional distribution of SC lawyers in urban areas of Uttar Pradesh is presented in Tables 7a and 7b.

After doctors, lawyer is the family of occupation which registers a little bit higher percentage in respect of total urban SC main workers. But in case of total urban main workers, there is not much improvement. Highly Developed Region registers higher values in respect of SC lawyers, otherwise it is showing low percentages for all other occupations in question.

Tables 7a–7b

SC Lawyers among Main Workers in UP

Regions	*Urban SC lawyers among total urban SC main workers*				
	Total urban SC main workers	*Urban SC lawyers*			
		Total		*Males*	*Females*
		Actual figures	*Percentages*		
Very Highly Developed	2,13,712	498	0.23	468	30
Highly Developed	1,40,210	332	0.24	316	16
Medium Developed	3,50,366	1,150	0.33	1,118	32
Low Developed	1,37,434	462	0.34	452	10
Uttar Pradesh	8,41,722	2,442	0.29	2,354	88

Table 7b

Regions	*Urban SC lawyers among total urban main workers*				
	Total urban main workers	*Urban SC lawyers*			
		Total		*Males*	*Females*
		Actual figures	*Percentages*		
Very Highly Developed	19,79,166	498	0.025	468	30
Highly Developed	8,30,836	332	0.040	316	16
Medium Developed	33,77,214	1,150	0.034	1118	32
Low Developed	12,44,306	462	0.037	452	10
Uttar Pradesh	74,31,522	2,442	0.033	2,354	88

Source: Census of India 2001, B-series, PCA (UP).

Legal professionals also include 'judges and magistrates'. They deliver justice to the society. They thoroughly understand the law of the land and can provide right explanations of the various laws and Acts and are indispensable. Only 192 SC judges and magistrates are there in the state of Uttar Pradesh. Tables 8a and 8b show regional distribution of SC judges and magistrates among SC main workers and total main workers.

Table 8a–8b

SC Judges and Magistrates among Total Main Workers in UP

Regions	*Urban SC judges and magistrates among total urban SC main workers*				
	Total urban SC main workers	*Urban SC judges and magistrates*			
		Total		*Males*	*Females*
		Actual figures	*Percentages*		
Very Highly Developed	1,90,434	30	0.016	26	4
Highly Developed	1,40,210	14	0.010	14	0
Medium Developed	2,35,776	84	0.036	80	4
Low Developed	1,00,488	64	0.064	64	0
Uttar Pradesh	8,41,722	192	0.023	184	8

Table 8b

Regions	Urban sc judges and magistrates among total urban main workers				
	Total urban main workers	Urban SC judges and magistrates			
		Total		Males	Females
		Actual figures	Percentages		
Very Highly Developed	16,71,068	30	0.002	26	4
Highly Developed	8,30,836	14	0.002	14	0
Medium Developed	22,16,990	84	0.004	80	4
Low Developed	9,19,276	64	0.064	64	0
Uttar Pradesh	74,31,522	192	0.003	184	8

Source: Census of India 2001, B-series, PCA (UP).

Once again, all the regions exhibit low percentages for SC judges and magistrates. But Highly Developed Region again registers the lowest percentages for SC judges and magistrates among all other regions. This indicates that though the Highly Developed Region has a substantial working population, the population is engaged in some lower levels of various other families of occupations (Banerjee and Knight, 1985; Deshpande, 2000).

Religion has always been a bone of contention between Scheduled Caste population and the rest of the society. From the ages past this community is denied entry into religious places and are not allowed to perform rituals and rites or head any religious ceremony (Thorat, 2008). So, in order to have an equalitarian and egalitarian society it becomes almost indispensable to have people from this community in religious places. Only 172 SC ordained religious workers are there in Uttar Pradesh. Tables 9a and 9b presents the proportion of Ordained Religious Workers in four regions of Uttar Pradesh.

Table 9a–9b

SC Ordained Religious Workers among Main Workers in UP

Regions	Urban SC ordained religious workers among total urban SC main workers				
	Total urban SC main workers	Urban SC ordained religious workers			
		Total		Males	Females
		Actual figures	Percentages		
Very Highly Developed	2,13,712	18	0.008	16	2
Highly Developed	1,05,034	16	0.015	16	0
Medium Developed	2,97,204	104	0.035	94	10
Low Developed	,103,590	32	0.031	28	4
Uttar Pradesh	8,41,722	170	0.020	154	16

Table 9b

Regions	Urban SC ordained religious workers among total urban main workers				
	Total urban main workers	*Urban SC ordained religious workers*			
		Total		*Males*	*Females*
		Actual figures	*Percentages*		
Very Highly Developed	19,79,166	18	0.001	16	2
Highly Developed	5,71,942	16	0.003	16	0
Medium Developed	28,16,716	104	0.004	94	10
Low Developed	9,49,246	32	0.003	28	4
Uttar Pradesh	74,31,522	170	0.002	154	16

Source: Census of India 2001, B-series, PCA (UP).

Both the Tables confirm that even now, this community has minimal access to the religious areas. Very Highly Developed Region exhibits the lowest percentages for SC ordained religious workers. Either religion takes a back seat or religious discrimination is prevalent in this region. Unfortunately, literature supports the latter (Galanter, 1963; Thorat, 2008).

Urban SC population does not have a healthy presence in all the six broad families of occupations. Higher occupations require higher educational qualifications. In case of SCs the root problems start at the very beginning itself. At the primary level they have very low Gross Enrolment Ratio (69) and high drop out rate from classes I-X (more than 60%) (Planning Commission, 2005). There are only 24 universities and 865 degree colleges, 9 medical colleges, 8 engineering colleges in the state and only 5.39 per cent of the total population is enrolled in higher education (*Economic Review*, UP, 2005). Poverty is rampant among SC population. Around 30 per cent of the total urban SC population is still below poverty line. All this leads the SC population to inherent socio-economic handicap which results in lowest achievements in every family of occupations.

Inequalities between SC and Non-SC/ST Populations in Respect of their Incidence in Six Broad Families of Occupations

SC population always lags behind the non-SC/ST population in each and every family of occupations. Now the question remains, what is the extent of this inequality. Figure 2 brings out the inequality in the percentages of SC and non-SC/ST professionals among the total urban professionals. It is a cruel reality that in every region the non-SC/ST professionals are leading by an incomparable margin. In all the regions their percentages are around 95 per cent of the total professionals in that region, while SC professionals stand nowhere in comparison to their counterparts. Srinivas (1966) also concludes that the "... members of the higher castes dominated the professions; the higher level posts in the government, in fact all white-collar jobs, While the lower castes provided certain essential services and goods". The reason behind this glaring inequality lies in the chronic poverty and the lower percentage of SC population in higher education (Jeffrey and Lerche, 2003).

Percentages of SC and non-SC/ST populations in the six broad families of occupation may shed some light on this glaring inequality. Table 10 presents the

Figure 2

SC and Non-SC/ST Professionals among Total Urban Professionals in UP

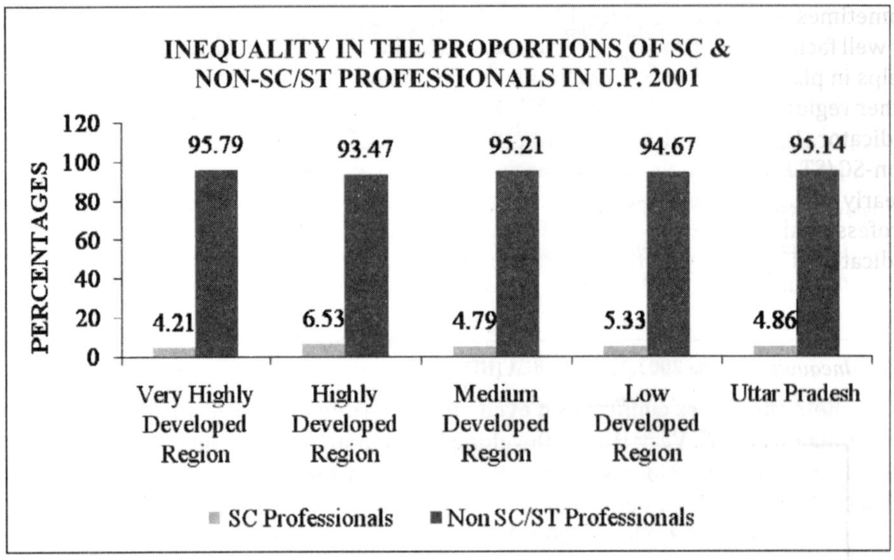

Source: Census of India 2001, B-series.

inequality in the incidence of SC and non-SC/ST populations in six broad families of occupations.

Table 10

SCs and Non-SC/STs in Main Families of Occupations among Total Professionals of UP

Six broad families of occupations	*SC (%)*	*Non SC/ST (%)*
Engineers	0.59	10.18
Doctors	0.65	12.57
College, University and Higher Education Teaching Professionals	0.11	4.72
Lawyers	0.52	13.47
Judges And Magistrates	0.04	0.39
Ordained Religious Workers	0.04	2.86

Source: Census of India 2001, B-series.

It is very clear from the Table 10 that non-SC/ST population dominates in each and every important family of occupations. Not even a single SC person is able to compete with his counterpart in any of the six main families of occupations.

So, it can be concluded that in spite of offering reserved places in public-sector employment, educational institutions, and government representative bodies, majority of SCs are concentrated in low-paid, dead-end jobs and some low-level secondary and tertiary occupations (Banerjee and Knight, 1985; Deshpande, 2000; Deshpande, 2001; Jeffrey, 2005; Mehrotra, 2006; Thorat et al. 2009). Thus, it is clear from both the present study and available literature that positive discrimination has failed to alter relationships of dominance and subordination based upon caste and class in Uttar Pradesh (Jeffrey and Lerche, 2000).

Spatial Pattern of Inequalities in the Incidence of SC and Non-SC/ST Professionals in Urban Areas of Uttar Pradesh

Sometimes, space plays a pivotal role in the development of any region. It can hinder as well facilitate the process of regional development. Spatial pattern of any variable helps in planning the development of any region. Regions which are lagging behind other regions can easily be identified through spatial pattern of any developmental indicator. District level spatial pattern of inequalities in the incidence of SC and non-SC/ST Professionals in urban areas of Uttar Pradesh is presented in Figure 3. It clearly brings out that there are higher inequalities between SC and Non-SC/ST professionals in each and every district of Uttar Pradesh. Two distinct belts are indicated. The upper northern belt starts from north-west of the state and grows

Figure 3

Inequalities Between SC and Non SC/ST Professionals in Respect of total Urban Professionals in Uttar Pradesh: 2001

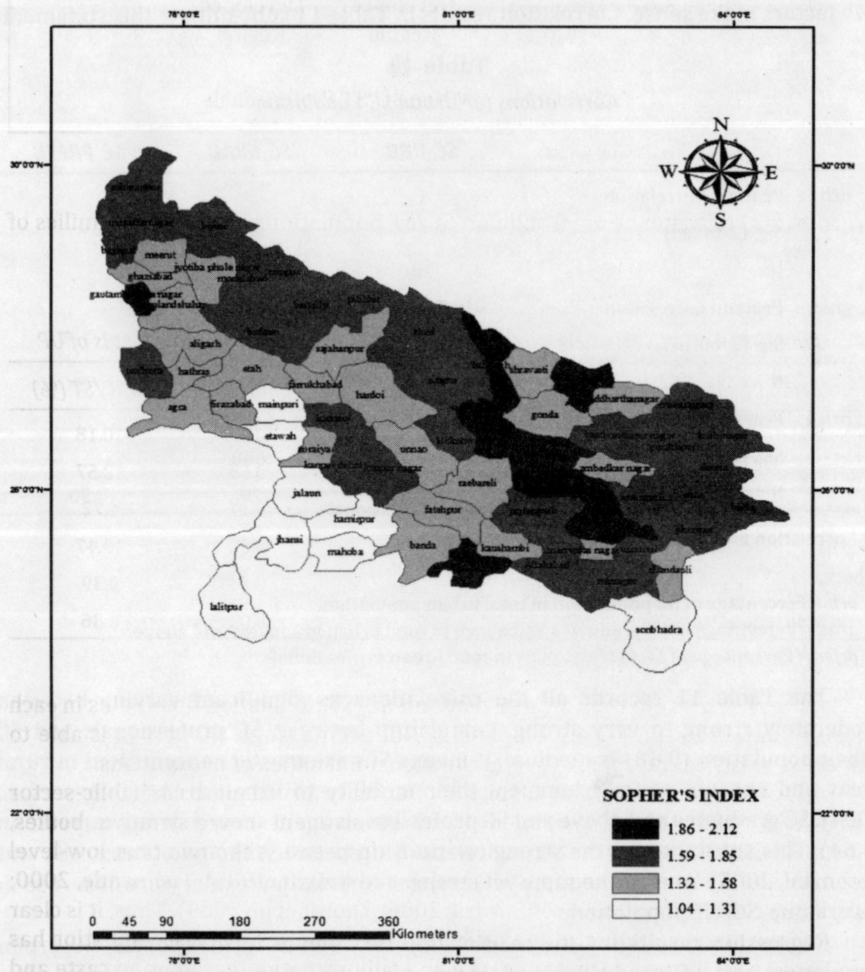

Source: Based on Census of India 2001.

thicker and thicker till it reaches the end of the Low Developed Region. It encompasses many districts of western part of Uttar Pradesh and central part of the state. It shows higher Sopher's index values which mean level of inequalities are higher in this part of the state. Gautam Budhha Nagar also shows highest levels of inequalities.

It shows that SC population is not involved in higher levels of occupations but in some lower levels of occupations. Districts commonly considered as low developed such as Jalaun, Hamirpur, Mahoba, Jhansi, Lalitpur, Mainpuri, Etawah and Sonbhadra exhibit lower levels of inequalities. These districts have low percentages of both the SC and non-SC/ST professionals. They, therefore, show a lower level of inequality.

Correlates and Determinants of the Exclusion of SC Population in Professional Occupations

Plethora of factors determines the low occurrences of SC professionals. SC urban population and SC Graduates and above are the two main factors among them. As professionals mainly work in an urban setting and they are highly educated, these two factors make sense. Correlation results in Table 11 substantiate this statement.

Table 11

Correlations for Urban SC Population

		SC_URB	*SC_GRAD*	*SC_PRFSN*
sc_urb	Pearson Correlation	1		
	Sig. (2-tailed)			
	N	70		
sc_grad	Pearson Correlation	.775**	1	
	Sig. (2-tailed)	.000		
	N	70	70	
sc_prfsn	Pearson Correlation	.481**	.647**	1
	Sig. (2-tailed)	.000	.000	
	N	70	70	70

** Correlation is significant at the 0.01 level (2-tailed).

Where,
sc_urb = Percentage of SC population in total urban population.
sc_grad = Percentage of SC graduates and above in total urban graduates and above.
sc_prfsn = Percentage of SC professionals in total urban professionals.

The Table 11 records all the correlations as significant varying between moderately strong to very strong. Correlation between SC professionals and SC urban population (0.48) is medium. It means SCs are mostly concentrated in rural areas and chronic poverty hampers their mobility to urban areas (Dubey et al. 2004). SC graduates and above and SC professionals again show a strong correlation (0.64). This substantiates the strong relationship between the two (Pascarella and Terenzini, 2005). Almost the same yet stronger correlation results were observed in case of non-SC/ST population.

Regression results for the relationship between SC professionals, SC urban population and SC graduates and above make the picture much clearer. The following Table 12 presents these results:

Table 12

Regression Results for Urban SC Graduates and above as Dependent Variable

Variables	*Coefficients*	*t-value*
Intercept	0.3951432	0.97
sc_professionals	9.103084*	4.68
sc_urban	0.2744504*	7.88
No. of observations	70	
F(2, 67)	77.56	
Prob > F	0.0000	
R-squared	0.6984	
Adj. R-squared	0.6894	

Note: Represents significance at 1 per cent level

Where,
sc_professionals = Percentage of SC professionals in total urban professionals.
sc_urban = Percentage of urban SC population in total urban population.

Table 12 shows that the model indicates a good fit model as the value of R-squared for this model is high (R^2 = 0.6984) and F-statistic [F (2, 67) = 77.56 and (Prob > F=0.0000)] is also highly significant. The value of R^2 given above indicates that 69.84 per cent variation in higher education among urban SC graduates and above is explained by two explanatory variables, i.e., percentage urban SC and percentage urban SC professionals. The F value is also significant at '0' per cent level implying that the systematic variation is considerably larger than should be explained by chance. Adj-R^2 Value (0.6894) shows that the addition of extraneous predictors would not have larger impact on the model.

The regression coefficient of the variable, percentage urban SC professionals has been found to be positive and significant at 1 per cent level. This implies that 1 unit increase in percentage urban SC professionals will foster an increase of around 9 units in percentage SC graduates and above which can be a panacea to the plethora of the problems faced by SCs. Thus, it can be concluded that higher education has got the potential to provide a real impetus to the SC population in the professional occupations.

Spatial Pattern of Relationship between Urbanization, Higher Education and Professionals Occupations

The relationship between urbanization, higher education, and occupational structure can be best shown through maps using overlay method of GIS (Geographical Information System). The nature of their influence on each other can clearly be understood from the maps. Figure 4 shows this relationship for urban Scheduled Caste population and Figure 5 shows this relationship for urban non-SC/ST population.

Figure 4 shows that urbanization and professional occupations do not have a strong and constant relationship. For example, in case of Jhansi and Jalaun where urbanization levels are high, levels of professional occupations are also high but in case of Agra and Firozabad though levels of urbanization are high, the levels of

Figure 4

Relationship between Urbanization, Higher Education and Occupational Structure for Urban SC Population in U.P. 2001

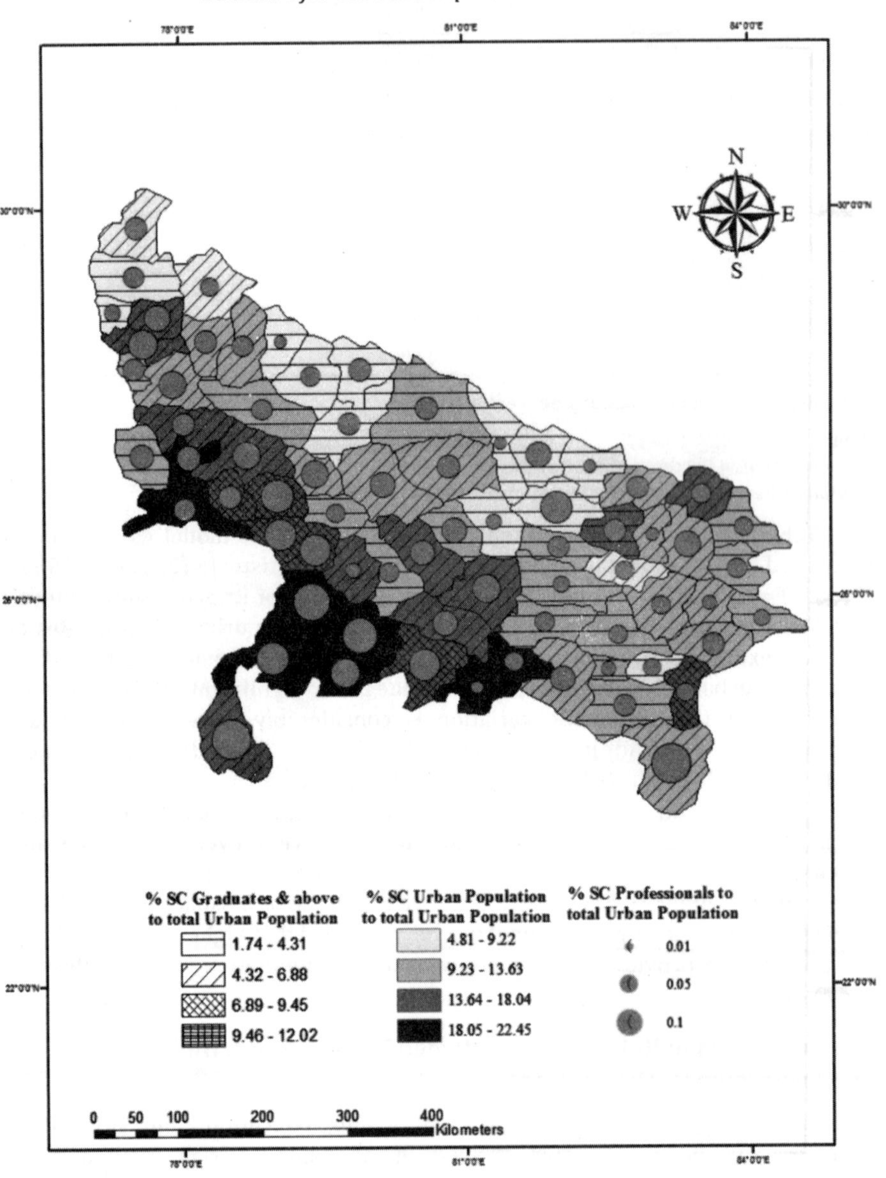

Source: Based on Census of India 2001.

professional occupations are low. So, as confirmed by correlation results, their relationship does not hold greater significance. But the relationship between higher education and urbanization holds greater significance as the map exhibits the direct proportional relationship between them. Except for a few districts, the relationship between higher education and professional occupations also holds well because as the levels of higher education rise, the levels of professional occupations soar up.

Figure 5

Relationship between Urbanization, Higher Education and Occupational Structure for Urban Non-SC/ST Population in U.P. 2001

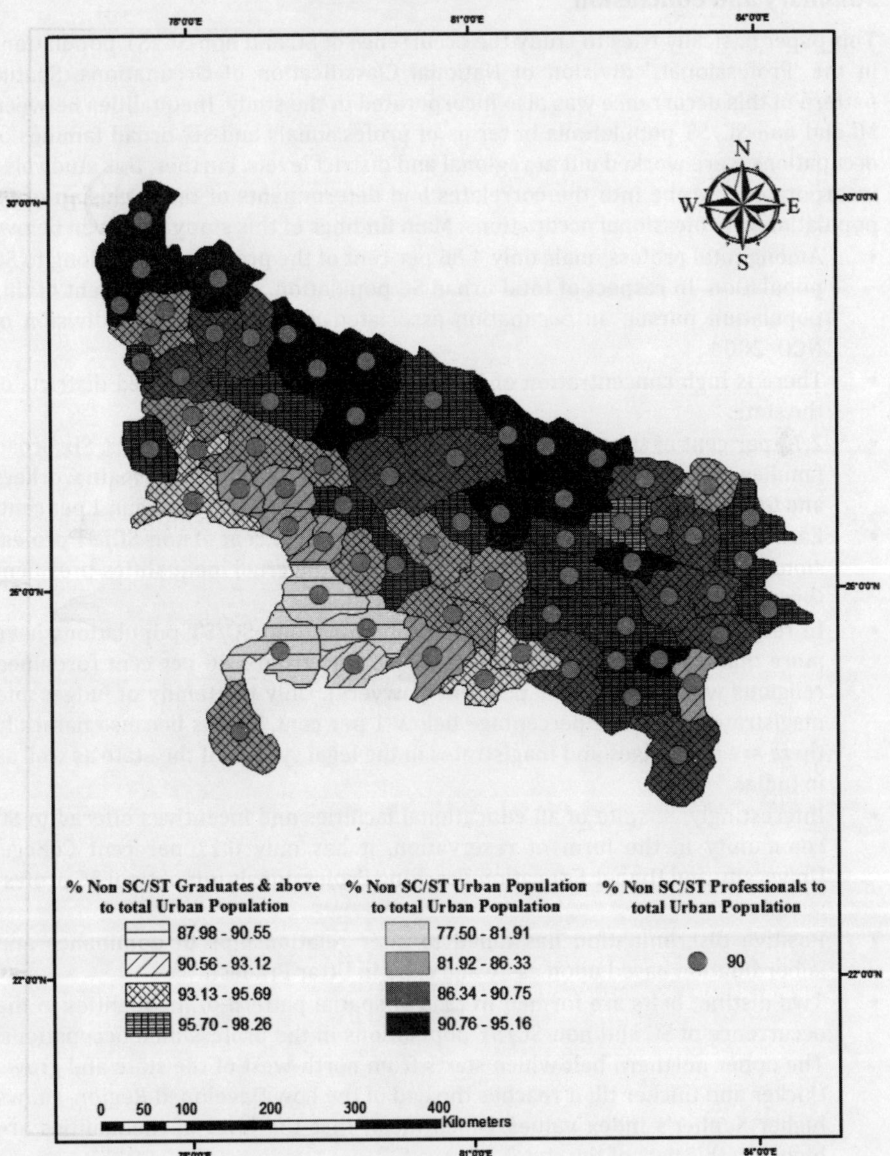

Source: Based on Census of India 2001.

Figure 5 presents the relationship between urbanization, higher education and professional occupations for non-SC/ST population. For this population also, all the relationships except the relationship between urbanization and professional occupations hold true. This relationship is not clear as in some of the districts such as Mahoba and Hamirpur where urbanization levels are low even though the levels of professional occupations are high. As the urbanization levels go up the levels of higher education also spike up.

Summary and Conclusion

This paper basically tries to study the occurrence of SC and non-SC/ST populations in the 'Professionals' division of National Classification of Occupations. Spatial pattern of this occurrence was also incorporated in the study. Inequalities between SC and non-SC/ST populations in terms of professionals and six broad families of occupations were worked out at regional and district levels. Further, this study also incorporates a probe into the correlates and determinants of the exclusion of SC population in professional occupations. Main findings of this study are given below:

- Among total professionals only 4.86 per cent of the professionals belong to SC population. In respect of total urban SC population, only 1.14 per cent of this population pursue an occupation associated with Professionals division of NCO–2004.
- There is high concentration of SC professionals in low developed districts of the state.
- 2.73 per cent of the total urban SC main workers are professionals. Six broad families of occupations were studied in context of total urban SC main workers and total urban workers, and in all of them SC population is less than 1 per cent.
- Each and every region of the state has around 95 per cent of non-SC/ST professionals among total professionals. It confirms the cruel inequalities prevalent throughout the state.
- In respect of six broad families of occupations, non-SC/ST populations have more than satisfactory percentages which vary from 2.86 per cent (ordained religious workers to 13.47 per cent (lawyers). Only the family of judges and magistrates show the percentage below 1 per cent. This is because naturally there are few judges and magistrates in the legal system of the state as well as in India.
- Interestingly, in spite of all educational facilities and incentives offered to SC community in the form of reservation, it has only 0.11 per cent College, University and Higher Education Teaching Professionals out of total SC professionals.
- Positive discrimination has failed to alter relationships of dominance and subordination based upon caste and class in Uttar Pradesh.
- Two distinct belts are formed in case of spatial pattern of inequalities in the occurrence of SC and non-SC/ST populations in the professional occupations. The upper northern belt which starts from north-west of the state and grows thicker and thicker till it reaches the end of the Low Developed Region, shows higher Sopher's index values which mean that the level of inequalities are higher in this part of the state.
- Higher education emerges as the major determinant of SC population in professional occupations.

So, it can be concluded that in terms of number of professionals, SC population stands nowhere in comparison to non-SC/ST population. The root cause of these cruel inequalities lie in poverty, caste-based discrimination, low enrolment ratio and higher drop out rates at school level which result in low percentages of SC population in higher education and this further leads to minimal presence of SC professionals in each of the regions and districts of Uttar Pradesh.

References

Banerjee, B. and J.B. Knight (1985) 'Caste Discrimination in the Indian Urban Labour Market', *Journal of Development Economics*, 17: 277–307.

Deshpande, A. (2000) 'Recasting Economic Inequality', *Review of Social Economy*, 58(3): 381–399.

— (2001) 'Caste at Birth? Redefining Disparity in India', *Review of Development Economics*, 5(1): 130–144.

Dubey, A., R. Palmer-Jones and K. Sen (2004) 'Surplus Labour, Social Structure and Rural to Urban Migration: Evidence from Indian Data', Paper Presented at the Conference on the 50th Anniversary of the Lewis Model, 6–7 July.

Galanter, M. (1963) 'Law and Caste in Modern India', *Asian Survey*, 3(11): 544–559.

Government of Uttar Pradesh (2009) *Economic Review*.

Hauser, R.M. and J.R. Warren (1997) 'Socio-Economic Indexes for Occupations: A Review of Update and Critique', *Sociological Methodology*, 27(1): 177–298.

Jeffrey, R. and J. Lerche (eds) (2003) *Social and Political Change in Uttar Pradesh: European Perspectives*, Delhi: Manohar Publications.

Jeffrey, C. (2005) 'Reproducing Difference? Schooling, Jobs and Empowerment in Uttar Pradesh, India', *World Development*, 33(12): 2085–2101.

Jeffrey, C. and J. Lerche (2000) 'Stating the Difference: State, Discourse and Class Reproduction in Uttar Pradesh, India', *Development and Change*, 31(4): 857–878.

Lal, K. (2005) 'In Quest of the Information Sector: Measuring Information Workers for India', *Malaysian Journal of Library and Information Science*, 10(2): 85–104.

Mehrotra, M. (2006) 'Well-Being and Caste in Uttar Pradesh: Why UP is Not Like Tamil Nadu', *Economic and Political Weekly*, 41(40): 4261–4271.

Parveen, S. (2005) *Changing Face and Challenges of Urbanization: A Case Study of Uttar Pradesh*, New Delhi: Concept.

Pascarella, E.T. and P.T. Terenzini (2005) *How College Affects Students*, Vol. 2, San Francisco: Jossey-Bass.

Planning Commission (2005) *Report of the Task Group on Development of Scheduled Castes and Scheduled Tribes*.

Srinivas, M.N. (1966) *Social Change in Modern India*, Berkeley: University of California Press.

Thorat, S. (2002) 'Oppression and Denial: Dalit Discrimination in the 1990s', *Economic and Political Weekly*, 37(6): 572–578.

— (2008) 'Dalit Exclusion: The Empirical Evidence', *Info Change Agenda*, 13: 22–27.

Thorat, S., P. Attewell and F.F. Rizvi (2009) 'Urban Labour Market Discrimination', Working Paper Series, Indian Institute of Dalit Studies, 1–16.

19

Growth, Morphology, Society Problems and Management of the Chandannagar City, West Bengal

MITRAJIT CHATTERJEE AND NAGESHWAR PRASAD

Chandannagar city, located on the right bank of the Hooghly River in West Bengal, is a part of the Kolkata (Calcutta) Urban Agglomeration. This small city is a former French colony having a separate entity with its own characteristics. The present paper attempts to focus on the various facets of the city, viz., the growth as a French colony in 1673 till present date, urban morphology (both structural and functional) and social structure. Chandannagar has endured the impact of progressive urbanization over the last three centuries, and its sharp rise during the last few decades. For accommodating the excess population within a limited space, drastic restructuring in residential pattern has occurred and the city has grown vertically. The old settled areas are being revamped by promoters and flats are being built after demolishing old structures. The focus will also be given on the urban society in particular. The immigration of a variety of people to this city during the long continuous process of urbanization from different economic and social backgrounds has influenced the social landscape of the city. Urbanization has led to a weaker and superficial social bond among the people. But it is not as sharp and evident like the western society or even like any metropolitan city in India. Between some units, the emotional bond is still found to exist here. This bondage surfaces annually during the time of the Jagaddhatri Puja – a major socio-cultural event in the city. The change in social fabric has been less drastic as compared to changes in the urban landscape. There has emerged two indigenous but very peculiar cottage industries of the city – well-ring manufacturing and decorative electrical lightworks employing hundreds of families for their livelihood. The lightworks is of international fame, even used in the Thames Festival and Dubai Shopping Festival. Finally, focus has been given to the problems (existing, emerging and managerial) of the city. The paper is based basically on field survey in and around Chandannagar through interviews and questionnaires of sufficient number of associated persons as well as on books, magazines and published articles.

Chandannagar, formerly known as Chandernagore or Chandernagar is a small city and former French colony located 30 kilometres north of Kolkata, in West

Bengal, India. It is the headquarters of a subdivision in Hooghly District. It is a part of the area covered by Kolkata Metropolitan Development Authority. Situated along the western banks of river Hooghly, the city has been able to maintain a separate identity different from all other cities and abides by her own characteristics. The total area is a meagre 22.14 square kilometres having a population of 162,187 (Census of India, 2001). Chandannagar is connected to Kolkata by railway, roadways and river transport and it takes about an hour to reach there by car.

Objectives

The main objectives of the study are stated below:

- To focus on the growth of the city as a French colony in 1673 till present date
- To study the urban morphology (both structural and functional) of the city
- To look into the nature of the city's urban society
- To identify the problems (existing, emerging and managerial) of the city
- To assess the functioning and nature of management by the Municipal Corporation
- To suggest suitable remedial measures.

Methodology

The preliminary knowledge about the study area has been collected from the Hooghly District Gazetteer and Census Handbook of the district of Hooghly. A map of the study area has been collected from the Urban Planning Department of the Chandannagar Municipal Corporation. For theoretical perception of this study, a number of relevant books, articles and journals have also been consulted. Due to the absence of any concrete records on the city, our total work is based on field survey in and around Chandannagar and information obtained through interviews and questionnaires of sufficient number of associated persons.

Location

The study area is a municipal corporation under Chandannagar P.S. (mostly eastern part) and Bhadreswar P.S. (western part) in the district of Hooghly, West Bengal. The Saraswati river forms its north-western and western boundary. The Hooghly river forms its entire eastern boundary. The city shares its boundary with the urban areas of Chinsurah in the north and Mankundu in the south but Nowpara and Jarua Gram Panchayet form its western boundary. At present, there are 33 wards in the Chandannagar Municipal Corporation (Figures 1 and 2).

Growth of the City

Chandannagar is a city of antiquity as well as of great historical importance. It was under French occupation for about 300 years (1688–1954). Prior to that, it was a maritime trade centre used by the traders of Europe as well as by China and other south-east Asian countries. It is only during the French rule that Chandannagar attained the status of a compact urban unit.

The growth of Chandannagar can be discussed under two broad periods – Colonial (pre-independence) period and Post-independence period.

Colonial/Pre-independence Period (1673–1954)

This period of about 300 years can further be divided into six phases.

1. *First Phase* (1673–1687): The French came to Chandannagar as also Bengal for the first time in 1673. In that year Duplessis, the French Commander, built a house after gathering a plot at Taldanga on the northern part of present Chandannagar with the permission of Ibrahim Khan, the then Nawab of Bengal. In this period either the Dutch satisfying the Nawab with gifts drove out the French or the French sensing many difficulties in their business left this place. Then, in 1687 the French Commander Deslandes started business at Bandel but coming across many inconveniences he tried to shift to another place in Hooghly and failed to receive the permission of the nawab to build a new firm at the very place obtained by Duplessis at Chandannagar.
2. *Second Phase* (1688–1700): In the year 1688, the French received the permission to carry on duty-free business in Bengal from the Mughal Emperor, Aurangzeb. From the historical point of view this was the first step to the establishment of the French rule in Chandannagar. Gradually, Chandannagar expanded with the villages of Borokrishnapur, Prosadpur, Shyampara, Sabinara and Gondalpara. The French East India Company got the legal

Figure 1

The Study Area: Chandannagar Municipal Corporation

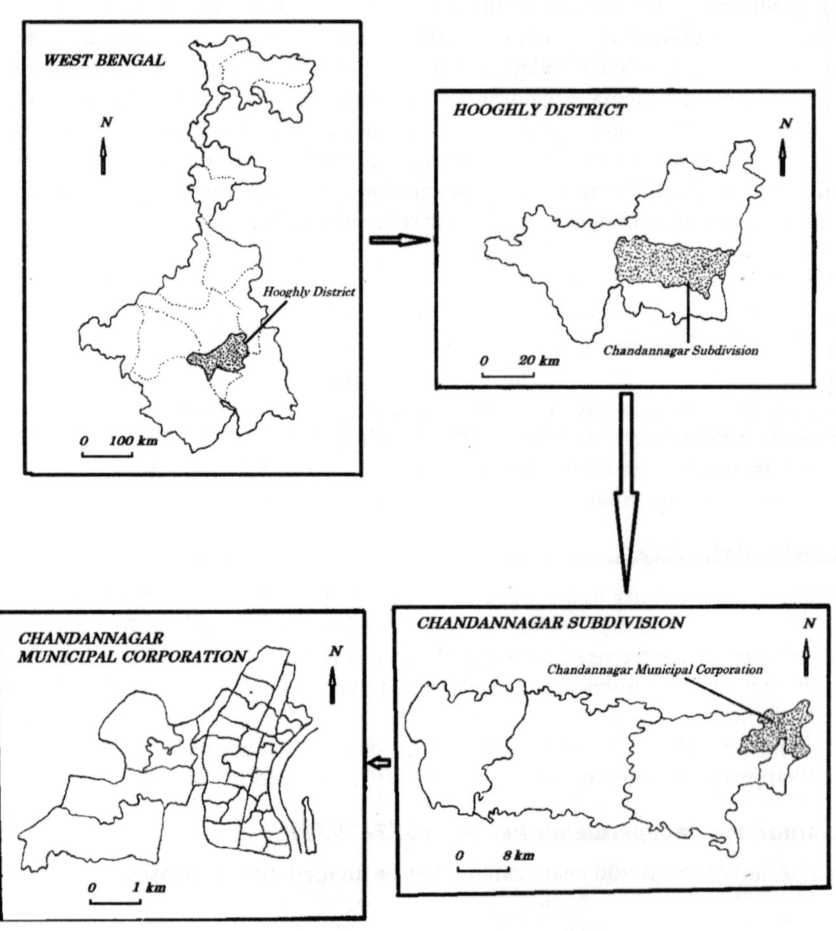

Figure 2

Ward Map of Chandannagar City

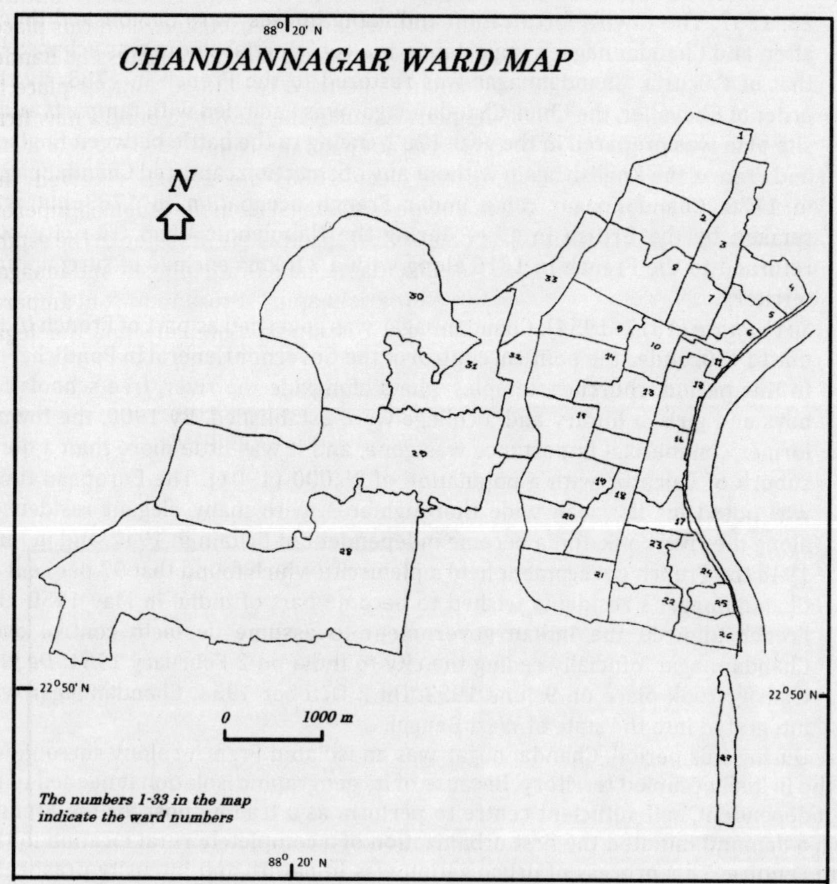

ownership of Chandannagar in the year 1693. The French built a fort at Chandannagar in 1696 for protecting their colony.

In the first two phases, the French were busy in setting up their business and protecting their colony from attack by Dutch and English and not much development in the area was noticeable.

3. *Third Phase* (1701–1730): From 1701, Chandannagar came under the rule of Pondicherry. During this period, Chandannagar came under the control of eleven Director Generals as a result of which no significant development took place.
4. *Fourth Phase* (1731–1755): Joseph Francois Dupleix was appointed the Governor of Chandannagar. During his administration, more than two thousand brick houses were erected in the town and a considerable maritime trade was carried on. Dupleix transformed the area during his stay of only ten years. Chandannagar reached the height of development in 1744. Chandannagar was far more important than Calcutta with regard to urban amenities, economic prosperity, trade and culture and evolved as the main centre for European commerce in Bengal.

5. *Fifth Phase* (1756–1816): In 1756 war broke out between France and Great Britain and Colonel Clive of the British East India Company and Admiral Watson of the British Navy bombarded and captured Chandannagar on March 23, 1757. The town's fortification and many houses were demolished thereafter, and Chandannagar's importance as a commercial centre was eclipsed by that of Calcutta. Chandannagar was restored to the French in 1763. By the order of Chevalier, the Chief, Chandannagar was encircled with ramparts and a site plan was prepared in the year 1769. Owing to the battle between England and France, the English again without any obstruction captured Chandannagar in 1778. Chandannagar came under French occupation in 1783 but was retaken by the British in 1794 during the Napoleonic Wars. The city was returned to the French in 1816 along with a 7.8 km^2 enclave of surrounding territory.
6. *Sixth Phase* (1817–1954): Chandannagar was governed as part of French India until 1950, under the political control of the Governor General in Pondicherry. In this period, churches, temples, ghats alongside the river, free schools for boys and girls, a library and a college were established. By 1900, the town's former commercial importance was gone, and it was little more than a quiet suburb of Calcutta, with a population of 25,000 (1901). The European town was noted for its clean wide thoroughfares, with many elegant residences along the riverbank. India became independent of Britain in 1947, and in June 1948 the French government held a plebiscite which found that 97 per cent of Chandannagar's residents wished to become part of India. In May 1950, the French allowed the Indian government to assume de facto control over Chandannagar, officially ceding the city to India on 2 February 1951. *De jure* transfer took place on 9 June 1952. On 2 October 1954, Chandannagar was integrated into the state of West Bengal.

During this period, Chandannagar was an isolated French colony surrounded by the British occupied territory. Because of its geographic isolation it needed to be an independent, self-sufficient centre to perform as a trading post for the French. Such a demand initiated the first urbanization of a completely rural location in the 17th century. This process of urbanization was in nature and intensity drastically different from urbanization as we understand now. Space was not yet a constraint in those times and the paddy fields were replaced by palatial administrative and residential buildings, orchards and business/trading centres. The dominantly agrarian population was replaced by clerks, serfs and different kinds of small traders required for a trading post.

Post-independence Period (1955 to present)

After the merger with the state of West Bengal in 1954, the state government declared Chandannagar as a municipal corporation on 1 September 1955. After independence, with the establishment of a different kind of government offices, new job opportunities were created. In 1957, the Howrah – Burdwan railway line was electrified and this reduced the commuting time to Calcutta. New settlements developed to accommodate the increasing local and migrant population. Residential areas of the French period were handed over, in some cases, to local affluent people or to the government for official purposes. In 1970s, most of the land surface was dominated by individual residential units. Vast spaces left unutilized were termed as open lands. There were also mango orchards or small agricultural units within town limits. Chandannnagar emerged as a Class I town with a population of 1,01,568 in

1981 Census. However, rapid change took place after 1990. Most of the people who came here after 1990 have been and are engaged in tertiary activities. Number of jobs being significant, the number of migrating population also increased significantly during this period. Chandannagar was favoured to be the hub of such activities by the prospective entrepreneurs because some basic infrastructure for such industries already existed.

There were initially 27 wards in the Chandannagar Municipal Corporation but in 1997, a significant portion of Panchayat area was added to the north-west of the main city separated by Eastern Railway main line and the *Garh* or Ditch. It covers an area of 10.5 sq km. The area was split into 6 wards and designated as 28, 29, 30, 31, 32 and 33 (Figures 2 and 3).

Thus, in the post-independence period, the scale of urbanization further intensified together with a change in its form. The country-house like mansions and orchards started being replaced by smaller residential houses and down the line by multi-storied complexes as land became costlier. The National Highway No. 2 (G.T. Road) and a Broad Gauge Railway (Howrah – Burdwan Main Line) passing through the city lent it improved connectivity to bigger trading sites like Kolkata and industrial centres like Howrah. Shrinking agricultural jobs in the rural areas located to the west maintained a steady migration of cheap unskilled labourers. This worked in favour of the growth of the city in terms of size and population.

Changing Urban Landscape of Chandannagar

Prior to the arrival of the French, majority of the settlements were located away from the river bank. Stretches along the river bank remained vacant. The French settled down along the river bank and set up residential and commercial buildings around here. People who were in service of the French government started settling in areas surrounding the French residential area. Thus, the urban landscape of the colonial period had three distinct zones:

1. The Core French area on the banks of the Hooghly river.
2. The Outermost Peripheral Zone of local people with partly agricultural occupation.
3. The Intermediate Zone housing people employed with the French government.

People of the intermediate zone came to be used by the foreign traders as intermediaries in all matters of interaction on social, financial and other important issues with the local people.

In 1954, when Chandannagar was merged with West Bengal, many government offices, courts, etc., were established in the town as it became the sub-divisional headquarters. All the official buildings, schools and college were planned during the French regime.

The G.T. Road can be considered as the main spine of the city. The railway track is another spine of the town, west of the G.T. Road (Figure 3). The eastern part within the Hooghly river and G.T. Road accomodates the commercial and institutional areas. With the passage of time there have been significant changes in land utilization pattern. The total area of land being fixed, the growing bulk of population executes a heavy pressure on the land. This has caused relative scarcity of land and this enforced escalation of land prices. Vertical growth is inevitable in such situations. The sharply increasing population density has forced the construction of high-rise buildings. The growth of schools, colleges, nursing homes, banks, shopping malls and flat complexes has transformed the cultural landscape. In the last decade, the institutional, commercial and public utilities have gained a significant place in

Figure 3

The Old and the Newly added Portion of Chandannagar City Superimposed on Toposheet No. 79 B/5

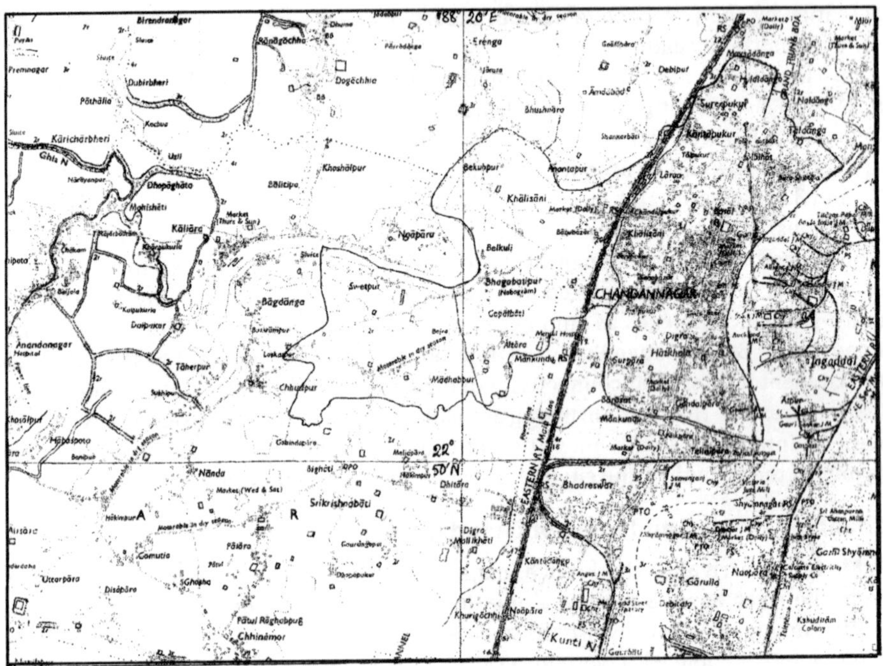

the land use structure of the town. Change in urban landscape was more visible in few particular places compared to other parts of the city. The densest residential development and rapid structural changes were seen in areas along the G.T. Road and Station road connecting the G.T. Road and Chandannagar railway station and areas surrounding the office and commercial area. These areas consist of ward nos. 9, 10, 14 and a small part of ward no. 32. With the boom in the real estate business, old residential buildings are being demolished and residential and commercial complexes are being built in their place. The restructuring that takes place has made the urban fabric of the city complex. Chandannagar Municipal Corporation has a very different type of land use in some of its added part consisting of ward nos. 28, 29, 30 and a part of 31. However, the corporation area is considered to be an urban area but these wards have a considerable amount of agricultural land and orchards. Cultivation of paddy and various seasonal vegetables are done here. A large number of orchards of mango, banana and papaya are seen here. Taken as a whole, the land use appears to be of a heterogeneously mixed character. The wardwise land use break up is given in Table 1.

Urban Morphology of Chandannagar

Considering the layout of roads, density of population, spatial distribution of houses, distribution of open spaces, water bodies and other socio-economic parameters of residents, three broad morphological zones of Chandannagar can be delineated. These broad zones may again be subdivided into several subzones (Table 2). From the morphological point of view, the city has evolved two distinct patterns, viz.

Table 1

Wardwise Land Use

Ward No.	Industrial	Commercial	Residential-cum-commercial	Govt.	Semi Govt.	Residential	Waterbody	Vacant land	Wasteland	Others	Total area	
	Area in sq m										sq m	sq km
1		8,350	18,560	0	5,430	1,20,360	1,37,843	2,75,600	15,521	2,18,675	8,00,338.62	0.8
2		4,560	15,680	0	5,240	3,91,606	68,238	56,196	7,763	16,196	5,65,479.26	0.56
3		5,690	6,760	0	4,530	4,00,969	45,196	20,070	4,595	45,170	5,32,979.97	0.53
4		6,710	5,305	0	6,759	3,66,011	30,774	50,844	23,814	10,556	5,00,773.43	0.5
5		4,560	15,680	0	3,240	2,04,108	20,070	21,412	0	23,982	2,93,052	0.29
6		9,560	35,680	0	13,780	1,00,500	3,345	16,556	0	6,556	1,85,977	0.18
7		9,560	15,680	20,500	4,240	1,35,667	50,844	56,448	592.8	46,448	3,39,979.84	0.34
8		9,786	25,680	0	15,000	2,37,671	21,804	3,75,668	2,188	1,62,668	8,50,465.45	0.85
9		15,780	15,560	5,560	5,640	3,00,589	28,098	56,289	734.3	26,289	4,54,539.3	0.45
10		16,560	10,560	13,560	3,500	1,59,400	32,112	21,744	0	76,744	3,34,180	0.33
11		3,500	7,650	0	4,500	99,130	12,760	11,241	627.3	2,241	1,41,649.28	0.14
12		3,950	12,450	86,780	4,565	37,26,021	11,373	22,676	12,253	1,92,676	40,72,744.3	0.47
13		5,690	21,412	0	6,950	2,57,290	32,781	68,225	3,478	58,225	4,54,051.04	0.45
14		17,843	15,680	3,620	3,250	3,55,221	30,105	60,205	4,263	1,52,205	6,42,392.48	0.64
15		10,680	9,560	2,625	4,650	5,94,492	32,115	62,630	18,133	72,630	8,07,514.92	0.78

Cont'd...

Cont'd...

16		12,425	5,430	4,540	21,430	3,17,837	42,816	26,760	2,827	21,760	4,55,824.54	0.45
17		9,000	5,820	1,500	3,680	1,56,400	18,732	18,356	1,156	16,356	2,30,999.67	0.23
18		18,250	5,640	16,500	10,490	2,29,921	68,238	59,235	3,371	39,235	4,50,879.65	0.45
19		5,680	9,560	1,720	4,650	2,95,958	22,746	60,140	6,015	75,140	4,81,609.24	0.48
20		5,430	12,425	3,550	6,500	2,33,446	24,084	59,235	0	63,235	4,07,905	0.41
21		30,540	29,560	0	15,500	5,00,819	74,259	32,780	5,357	62,785	7,51,600	0.76
22		10,500	15,500	19,500	10,500	2,10,403	32,789	50,650	507.7	55,650	4,05,999.67	0.4
23		5,490	45,600	0	6,500	2,00,744	16,056	36,250	699.4	36,250	3,47,589.44	0.34
24		4,560	65,450	0	9,500	1,35,245	20,070	36,125	2,124	26,435	2,99,509.44	0.31
25	43840	8,560	12,450	0	4,350	1,25,141	7,359	10,250	0	7,250	2,19,200	0.21
26	75000	5,000	10,500	0	5,000	2,00,994	12,042	10,145	568.3	8,250	3,27,499.25	0.32
27		3,000	5,000	13,000	2,500	77,000	0	0	0	0	1,00,500	0.1
28		10,000	3,000	0	4,000	7,80,859	1,18,413	8,35,364	0	12,35,364	29,87,000	3
29		10,000	4,000	0	7,500	1,44,969	36,126	50,360	0	2,00,545	4,53,500	2.36
30		12,500	5,600	0	12,500	1,95,427	21,408	46,585	0	32,66,580	35,60,600	3.62
31		15,500	10,560	5,600	5,000	1,50,000	30,774	0	0	2,50,000	4,67,434	0.4
32		5,560	0	0	0	1,65,000	0	0	0	1,50,000	3,20,560	0.6
33		4,560	0	0	0	1,07,278	0	0	1,251	16,000	1,29,089.25	0.39

Source: Chandannagar Municipal Corporation (2006) and Field Checking in 2013.

1. Areas of planned development in the eastern and central part of the city.
2. Areas of unplanned growth in the western and northern part of the city.

The various morphological zones as indicated in Table 2 have been discussed.

(i) The *historical core areas* were first occupied by the French settlers. The layout of streets and residential bungalows reveal a distinct pattern of growth, somewhat different from the rest of the town. This area bears the testimony of the colonial legacy of Chandannagar of yesteryears. Ward No. 10 bears the imprints of the historical core.

(ii) The *old residential areas* lie along the Hooghly river in the north-eastern and south-central part of the city. Characterized by congestion of buildings, lanes and by-lanes and houses with much horizontal expansion, these areas are mostly characterized by traditional architectural pattern. Ward nos. 3, 14, 15 and parts of 17, 18 and 20 fall within this sub-zone. This is the most static region of the city wherein most of the buildings are more than 100 years old. Some of these palatial residential buildings are in a dilapidated condition. New constructions are relatively few as there is less scope for further horizontal expansion. These areas have attracted the promoters who are demolishing these old buildings and constructing new buildings in their place.

(iii) The industrial area is located in the extreme south-eastern part of the city centering the only jute mill located in Ward no. 21 and 22.

(iv) The slum area is distributed in a scattered manner along northern, central and southern parts of this eastern zone (Ward nos. 18, 20 and 21).

(v) The moderately old residential areas and commercial and business areas lie along the N.H. No. 2 both along its eastern and western sides as well as on both sides of the road connecting the N.H. No. 2 and the Chandannagar railway station.

(vi) The outer or peripheral zone consists of newly developed residential areas and refugee and squatter colonies. This zone is a region of unplanned growth and is noticed in the western part of the city. Proximity of the Chandannagar railway station is the major reason of attraction for the development of this zone.

Table 2

Morphological Zones of Chandannagar City

Zone	*Name*	*Sub-zone*
I	Riverside Zone along the Hooghly river	(i) Historical Core area
		(ii) Old Residential area
		(iii) Industrial area
		(iv) Slum area
II	Inland Zone along the N.H. 2 which runs parallel to the Hooghly river in the east and the Railway line in the west	(i) Moderately old residential area
		(ii) Commercial and business area
III	Outer Zone along the western periphery of the city	(i) Newly developed residential area
		(ii) Refugee and squatter colonies

Source: Field Survey.

Functional Zones of Chandannagar

With the subsequent growth of population, the functional zones of the city have become more complex. Urban functions, therefore, reflect the complexities of urban life. It may be of interest to note that the broad functional zones of this city in many areas almost coincide with land use areas. The following functional zones have been identified:

1. *Central Business District (CBD)*: Strictly speaking, the CBD of western cities is difficult to indentify in a small city like Chandannagar. The ward nos. 9 and 10 have the resemblance of C.B.D. the greatest concentration of retail stores, offices and services are found here. Land is most expensive here and there is heavy pressure of traffic. The principal retail market and the centre of the major commercial activities of the city is Lakshmiganj Bazar (Ward No. 9 along N.H. No. 2). Offices of the government and non-government bodies, the court, banks, etc., are in Ward no. 10. About 58 per cent of the total ownership flats of Chandannagar are located here. Vacant land is negligible. The N.H. No. 2 and Urdi Bazar Road are lined by shops dealing with every conceivable varieties of merchandise. Laxmiganj Bazar was in existence even prior to the French rule. But the market then handled rice and jute, most of which were exported to other parts of the country using the Hooghly waterways. This market is now divided into a number of sectors handling specialized commodities, such as *Chaul Patty* (rice market), *Maida Patty* (flour market), *Kapar Patty* (cloth market), etc. South of the Laxmiganj Bazar, there is another wholesale market (Urdi Bazar) dealing with timber, furniture and building materials. Concentration of meat shops and slaughter houses, poultry chicken, etc., are usually handled by the Muslim community. The concentration of specialized shops like doctor's chamber, medical stores, beauty parlour, hotels and restaurants, units dealing with electronic goods are largely clustered along N.H. No. 2.
2. *Residential Zone*: With rapid increase in population the built-up areas are increasing, swallowing up the available open spaces. Residential areas continue to be the major land use of Chandannagar covering over 90 per cent of the land area. The residential areas can be categorized into five classes: *old* (located on the eastern side of N.H. No. 2 along the Hooghly river), *new* (in the outer or peripheral zone), *refugee* (in ward nos. 1, 16, 18 and 19 along the *garh* or ditch road), blights or slums (in ward nos. 4, 5, 8, 9, 10, 14, 21 and 22; Urdi Bazar, Laldighi and Gondalpara jute mill areas) and industrial-cum-residential areas (in ward nos. 25 and 26). Some posh residential areas have developed during the last 15 to 20 years in Ward No. 19 (Gopalbag, Mandal bagan, Barasat, Banerjee Para), Ward 17 (Nutanpara), and Ward 12 (Bosepara) as well as in Bidyalankar, Palpara and Barabazar areas. Thus, there is a shift in the location of high class residential areas from their original core. The ultimate result of this rapid development is vertical expansion of residential areas over their horizontal structures.
3. *Commercial Zone*: 0.46 per cent of the total area is engaged in commercial activities. The centre of commercial and business activities of the city is located around Lakshmiganj Bazar, the principal retail market of Chandannagar. From the central marketplace, the shops are found to have grown along the radiating roads. The pulse of business beats vigorously in the main artery, i.e., N.H. No. 2 from the Hospital Crossing to Sarisapara. Other linear belts of retail shopping extend along Urdibazar road, Kuthirmath road, Jhaubagan road, Maida Patty

and Nichu Patty roads, etc. Another important nucleus of commercial activity has developed at Swapna Bazar in south Chandannagar developed at the crossing of the N.H. No. 2 and Mankundu station road. Chandannagar station road (Rashbehari Avenue) is another important commercial area where ribbon-like development of wayside stalls has taken place. The junction of N.H. No. 2 and Chandannagar station road (Bagbazar area) is another zone of commercial activity. On the basis of household survey, it can be inferred that Lakshmiganj Bazar has got the credit of having the largest zone of influence followed by Swapna Bazar.

4. *Administrative Zone:* This zone is localized in ward No. 10 and part of ward No. 9. There are more than 25 government offices, court, treasury, municipal and various other offices of the State government here. The present treasury building, the women's polytechnic and some other buildings of the Barabazar area were European hotels in the colonial days. Incidentally, this was the site in the *Ville Blanche* during the French rule and as such still remains the most well-planned sector of this city.
5. *Industrial Zone:* With the exception of the south-eastern border of this city (wards nos. 21 and 22) where a jute mill is located, there is no distinct industrial function as such in Chandannagar. Small-scale and household industries do not show any distinct zone of concentration. They are rather ubiquitously distributed, viz., well-ring manufacturing units and potteries (ward nos. 11, 13, 16), printing presses and bakeries (ward no. 10), engineering units (ward nos. 1, 2, 3, 7), brickfields (along the bank of the Hooghly river in the north eastern part in ward nos. 4 and 5), illumination industry, etc.

There have emerged two indigenous but very peculiar cottage industries of the city – well-ring manufacturing and illumination industry employing hundreds of families for their livelihood.

Although well-ring manufacturing industry is not a major industry in West Bengal, it occupies an important position in Chandannagar and its immediate surroundings. With a tradition of over hundred years, it provided livelihood to more than 100 manufacturers and hundreds of families who are indirectly associated with the industry. Well-rings are manufactured as cottage industry here. This industry is heavily concentrated in Kumarpara located in the central part of the western margin of the Chandannagar city. It is reported that nearly one hundred years ago a few skilled potters invented a new technique of manufacturing well-rings made of clay. These rings are placed inside the newly excavated wells one over the other to give support to the walls of the wells. In the initial stages, the rings were used to be sold to the local consumers. But soon after, the well-rings earned a good reputation and the market extended almost all over Gangetic Bengal. Well-rings are used in those areas where the level of groundwater is not far below the surface. Previously, the well-rings were primarily used for the excavation of wells for the supply of drinking water. But during the last 50 years they are also being used for the construction of sanitary privies and soak pits, thereby increasing their demand by many folds. There are five categories of people associated with the industry directly or indirectly: (a) manufacturers, (b) labourers, (c) middlemen, (d) shop-owners and (e) well diggers. The economic condition of the labourers is the worst among all the categories. Though the number of units producing well-rings is gradually increasing in number, the industry has a number of problems associated with raw material, power, labour, marketing, transportation, finance, space, seasonal character of the industry and problem of air pollution.

Chandannagar boasts of a flourishing illumination industry that is at present vibrant and bustling. Today, this small scale industry has caused a national as well as worldwide fame. Apart from being hired by festival organizers in various parts of the country, it has received orders from erstwhile USSR, UAE, France, Malaysia, etc. The lightworks is of international fame, even used in the Thames Festival and Dubai Shopping Festival. From the early sixties, this industry gradually started taking shape. Mr Sridhar Das of S.D. Electricals of Kalupukur area in Ward No. 7 of Chandannagar is the innovator and pioneer of this famous cottage industry. The dazzling competition between the various local clubs during all festivals especially during the famous *Jagaddhatri Puja* has enabled the electrical units to produce new and better goods every year. This not only increases its demand but also paves the way for a steady income. At present, about 5,000 families depend on this industry for their sustenance. This close-knit industry and the healthy competition between the various units have also been successful in giving a fitting solution to the unemployment problem. The electricians are living examples of what can be achieved by sheer endeavour. This industry has enough potentialities to develop and provide more employment to local people. The industry being free from hazards of industrial pollution is best fit for the neat townscape of the city.

6. *Educational and Cultural Zone:* Maximum concentration is seen in ward no. 12. The Government Degree College which runs in three shifts has a riverside location. Originally known as Dupleix College, this institution was established in 1931. The reputed St. Mary's Institution of yesteryears has now changed its name to Kanailal Vidyamandir. The institutions have retained its French language section even today. St. Joseph's Convent and St. Anthony's School are English medium schools under the management of the missionaries. Women's Polytechnic is located on the Strand Road along the Hooghly river. The cultural functions are also concentrated here. The reputed cultural centres are rabindra bhavan, Chandannnagar Public Library, Kuthirmath, Mary Park, etc. Some of these have auditoriums being used for cultural functions. There are a number of dance, music and arts schools.
7. *Medical Zone*: Both the sub-divisional hospital and most of the private nursing homes are located at a distance of 0.5 to 1 km from the city core.
8. *Religious*: Chandannagar is a city of diverse religious faiths. There are about 130 temples, 2 churches and 9 mosques. The distribution pattern of religious institutions depicts a picture of segregation, viz., concentration of temples throughout the city more particularly in the riverside areas, location of Christian churches in the core area which was the abode of early French settlers and mosques in Muslim dominated areas. Religious functions in many cases have integrated with the cultural functions. In some cases, these are integrated and manifested with local fairs and festivals, wherein there is complete diffusion of religious and caste barriers. A typical example of such diffusion is *Jagaddhatri* (Goddess of the Earth) *Puja*. During the four days of the festival, the city assumes a festive look. The population of the city gets doubled, trade and commerce flourish and the municipal administration faces a lot of pressure in fulfilling the needs and requirements of the people. There are other important festivals in this city like the *Rathyatra* (pulling of the holy chariot). There is a permanent shrine of Lord Krishna at Lakshmiganj where this festival is annually held. Other festivals include *Charak* on Bengali New Year's eve at Bidyalankar and Tematha of Chandannagar. Thus, religious functions are not

clustered in a single zone but they are more diffused in the city. They help in cultural diffusion rather than religious orthodoxism.

Changing Society of Chandannagar

The immigration of a variety of people to this city during the long continuous process of urbanization from different economic and social backgrounds has influenced the social landscape of the city. The immediate result has been splitting of families. Those who migrated needed to drastically change habits, lifestyle and also the ways of interaction with neighbours. At the same time they lost the emotional support which they used to get in a joint family. Through difficult practice a new type of urbanized population was created. Their economic levels were raised by variable degrees. By that time they were relieved of the old habit of sharing assets and privileges inherent in a joint family. Tearing of the bond was not easy and caused them to suffer, from which they escaped by finally shutting out their mind from what they left in their places of origin.

Flat culture has suddenly crept into the society of Chandannagar. The old buildings are being purchased by the real estate agents at low prices and residential and commercial complexes are being built in their place. As the families are becoming nucleated and it is becoming more costly and troublesome to maintain individual houses, the residents are opting for flats. In case of flat complexes where more than one building is present, it is found that bonding between those families who are staying in the same building are better while they hardly know their neighbours living in other buildings or adjacent houses. It is also found that kinship have also been developed among people belonging to the same profession. A decrease in the participation rate of the residents in social gatherings has been noticed in recent times due to lack of interest to socialize with new people or because of conflict with organizing members.

Urbanization has led to weaker and superficial social bond among the people. But it is not as sharp and evident like the western society or even like any metropolitan city in India. Between some units, the emotional bond is still found to exist here. This bondage surfaces annually during the time of the *Jagaddhatri Puja* – a major socio-cultural event in the city. The change in social fabric has been less drastic as compared to changes in the urban landscape.

Problems and Management

Urban amenities in the city are quite satisfactory. But with the addition of newer areas, signs of degradation are noticeable.

Chandannagar is a non-industrial urbanized area. The threats of air pollution are thus due to vehicular emission and urban activity but all the values are well within the norms of Ambient Air Quality. The water quality is potable and safe except the concentration of iron is higher than the desirable limits in two locations. There is shortage of water supply in five wards (nos. 2, 5, 8, 9 and 14). Heavy rainfall during the monsoons results into flooding in some pockets within the city. The flood affected areas are ward nos. 1, 2, 5, 6, 19, 20 and 22. The main reason for waterlogging is mainly due to choked drains with household refuses and the stagnation of the moat or ditch locally known as *garh* which surrounds the city, dug by the French during the last quarter of the 18th century (1783), partly as a protection against the plunderers and partly for diverting the sewage water to the ditch. This ditch has now become derelict due to neglect. In some areas, it has been filled up illegally and encroached by unauthorized squatter colonies of the displaced persons from Bangladesh. Instead of helping in maintaining the drainage system, this stagnant ditch now creates waterlogging in several parts of the city, particularly along the western fringe during the rainy season. There is also a huge problem of solid waste disposal with the rapid increase in the population of the city.

The major ongoing environmental projects in the city are:

- Solid waste management
- Treatment of water supply
- Tree plantation
- Construction and restoration of river embankments
- Landscaping and beautification project on the river front
- Collection of flowers and other material after immersion of idols
- Awareness campaign programmes

The city generates about 36.4 MT of solid waste per day. The solid waste generated is collected from house to house and from bins and vats, partially. This covers near about 35 per cent population and is segregated at source for biodegradable and non-biodegradable matter. The authority uses 2 box type handcarts, 63 paddle tri-cycles without container, 40 paddle tri-cycles with container and 24 containers for house-to-house collection and final disposal through 7 tractors. 25.4 MT/day waste is disposed off by open dumping and 11.5 MT/day are being vermicultured. The biomedical wastes are collected separately and transported and treated as per Bio Medical Waste (M&H) Rules through Municipal Authority. The Authority has 5.2acre of land to set up a solid waste dump site and organic composting plant.

Potable and safe water is supplied from water treatment plant to the almost entire old city area. The Municipal Corporation has undertaken regular programme on tree plantation in selected wards both in old and added areas. Recent tree plantation programme in 14 selected places has been completed as a high priority environmental programme. A massive tree plantation programme (approx. 3,000 trees) has been undertaken in the vermicompost plant to improve the environment of the surrounding habitable areas.

Project work on restoration of river banks has been started from September 2006 and is still continuing on the southern part of the city with funding from the Chandannagar Municipal Corporation.

The historic Chandannagar strand which is a tourist attraction point and also a central recreational area for citizens of the city has been given top priority for beautification project. Plantation of trees, creation of landscaped area, illumination work, etc., have been undertaken to improve the environment of the mentioned area.

Chandannagar is the pioneer for taking initiative to control environment pollution due to immersion of *Jagaddhatri* and *Durga* idols. Flowers and other materials which are collected just after immersion are segregated and taken to vermicompost plant for further treatment.

Awareness campaign programme of Chandannagar Municipal Corporation for the last few years in the form of banners, hoardings and organizing fairs are carried out regularly.

Workshops and group discussions were held at all ward levels to discuss problems faced on day-to-day basis regarding environment. Solutions were chalked out for outstanding problems. The *Sadar* hospital has its morgue within the town itself. The stench contributes largely to air pollution. Similarly, smoke from brickfields and burning of chemicals in different industries are also responsible for it. Use of plastic bags is to be stopped with immediate effect as it is the common hindrance for outlet of water and smooth passage of it to the rivers. Waste management has to be handled carefully so that its contribution as an agent for polluting the environment is minimized. The wardwise environmental problems and their respective solutions are provided in Table 3.

Amidst the only few viable factors that controls the conducive viable living environment in the city, a large number of water bodies play their distinct role and are by themselves unique in the entire area; the bigger water bodies are used for a major activity of fishery and others play their role both as open spaces and landscaped areas as well as a means for receiving the surface run-off on occasions of heavy rain; a few of those smaller water bodies sporadically located here and there may be found not fulfilling the above purposes. The strategy of the physical development recommends that specific water bodies be earmarked for the development of fisheries and culture of spawns and fishlings. As a corollary to the strategy it further recommends that smaller water bodies in close proximity to one another may be unified into a larger space for open space activities; the same corollary proposes further, that few smaller ponds which may not be viable for their maintenance may be given over to other urban development, so long as they do not impede the run-off efficiency.

Table 3

Wardwise Environmental Problems and their Solutions

Ward No.	*Problems*	*Solutions*
1.	Presence of acid factory in the locality causing pollution, soil erosion along the pond side causing narrowing of roads.	Planting trees, desilting and maintenance of the garh, pond can be given to the corporation on lease and construction of embankment can be taken care of by the corporation.
2.	No such problems identified.	Not applicable.
3.	Indiscriminate cutting of trees in Choudhury Bagan Area.	Corporation to take necessary steps to stop cutting of trees.
4.	Machines of the wire factory in the residential area contribute largely to sound pollution, the smoke from generators pollutes the air, the river banks are largely used as latrines by workers of brick-fields. The cowshed in Boropanchanantala is a menace.	If possible, shifting of factories to fringe or less populated areas, construction of community latrines for brick-field workers. Proper arrangement for the production of gobar gas or manure for economical use of cow dung.
5.	The burning ghat at Boraichanditala is a major problem. For cremation, old wood is used which contributes to air pollution. At times decomposed bodies are brought and the stench makes the atmosphere vicious.	Care has to be taken to eradicate the problems of cremation.
6.	Condition of the market place is poor. Outsourcing of water of the entire town is through the drain at Rathtala which brings about health hazards and overflowing causes untoward environmental conditions during rainy season.	Use of bleaching powder in the fish market on regular basis. Alternate drainage system or construction of a high drain at Rathtala for facilitating water outlet.

Cont'd...

Cont'd...

7.	Stench from morgue and Dharapara cowshed.	Special type of phenyl to be used to reduce foul smell coming from the morgue. Cowdung produced in the cowsheds could be used as fuel or as manure instead of unscientific disposal.
8.	The waste dumping ground is causing environmental problems.	Regular and proper treatment of wastes is needed.
9.	Smoke from bakeries, disposal of wastes in ponds.	Trollies for carrying wastes to be increased.
10.	Wastes from acid factory released into ponds.	Factory owners to be warned and environmental laws should be enforced.
11.	Slaughterhouse in Kuthir Ghat area, improper drainage, lack of sanitation.	Immediate steps to be taken for improvement of slaughterhouse and drains.
12.	Disposal of flowers, leaves, plastics and other wastes in the lake.	Measures to be taken for developing the Laldighi Jhil.
13.	Excessive use of plastic.	Awareness to limit use of plastic.
14.	Presence of cowsheds.	Cowdung produced in the cowsheds could be used as fuel or as manure instead of unscientific disposal.
15.	Lack of proper sanitation.	Improvement of sanitation facilities.
16.	Excessive use of plastic packets and improper treatment.	Proper maintenance of garbage and reduction in the use of plastic packets.
17.	No significant problem reported by local people.	Not Applicable.
18.	No significant problem reported by local people.	Not Applicable.
19.	The trunk factory causes sound pollution.	Provide incentive for shifting.
20.	The plastic toys factory causes air and sound pollution.	Provide incentive for shifting.
21.	Absence of dustbins make people to throw wastes all over the place.	Awareness campaign and efficient implementation of SWM.
22.	The liquor shop at Dinemardanga is a menace.	Renewal of trade license may be conditional.
23.	No significant problem reported by local people.	Not Applicable.
24.	No significant problem reported by local people.	Not Applicable.
25.	Waste from Gondalpara Jute Mill.	Problem to be covered under SWM.
26.	Disposal of wastes on roads and drains; the entire garbage of south Chandannagar is dumped here.	Problem to be covered under SWM.
27.	Wastes from mills and biomedical wastes from ESI.	Special arrangements should be done for proper removal and disposal of chemical and biomedical wastes.

Cont'd...

Cont'd...

28.	Availability of fresh fish from nearby ponds is on decline because of chemical wastes from factory; those working in the factory are suffering from skin and other ailments.	Action to be taken by Pollution Control Board; conditional renewal of trade license.
29.	Problem of accessibility.	Steps to be taken to improve accessibility.
30.	Smoke from brick fields causes air pollution.	Action to be taken by Pollution Control Board; conditional renewal of trade license.
31.	No significant problem reported by local people.	Not Applicable.
32.	Stench from poultry, people living along the railway lines use the tracks as latrines, improper maintenance of ponds.	Setting up of community toilets.
33.	Plastic bags blocking the passage of water outlet to the Saraswati river.	Use of plastic bags to be restricted.

Source: Field Survey.

The residential developments can form a balanced development of the population and community facilities; therefore, the strategy suggests that planned programme of community facilities may be initiated before an area is phased for residential development. These community facilities may include education and health facilities as well as market facilities for daily consumption, commercial land use as well as selected government offices services and highest level institutions.

To improve the water table of the city which is essential to avoid future environmental problems, rainwater harvesting is to be taken up as an important environmental aspect to be considered in the environmental plan.

Environmental awareness campaign programme is being done intensively specially in the environmental aspects like solid waste management, plantation, cleaning of existing water bodies, etc. Emphasis is being given in the programme for general people in the form of hoardings, banners, organization of fairs, also for the school children by organizing quiz, drama, etc.

Conclusions

Chandannagar has endured the impact of progressive urbanization over the last three centuries because of French occupation and its locational advantage. However, a sharp increase in population and rapid pace of urbanization has been encountered in the Chandannagar Municipal Corporation area in the last few decades. As a municipal corporation and a sub-division town, it has attracted many people to settle down in this city. Nearness to the Kolkata metropolitan city and easy transport facility through the railway network inspired migration to this town. In order to accommodate huge mass of people, this city has experienced many restructuring in recent years. Restructuring in respect to residential pattern is most visible here. Due to lack of space, the city has grown vertically. The trend of restructuring old residential houses, open lands and orchards has started from 1990. As a result, the urban landscape of the city has changed and continues to change rapidly. The immigration of a variety of people from different economic and social backgrounds to the city has also influenced the social landscape of the town. The bonds among the residents especially the flat-dwellers are becoming weak and superficial but it is not as sharp and evident like in the western society or any metropolitan city in India. Several problems have emerged in the city with the increasing population. The Chandannagar Municipal Corporation has taken several steps to combat such problems in a very well-planned manner, so that the beautiful cityscape of Chandannagar is maintained.

References

Bose, A. (2009) 'Agricultural and Non-Agricultural Use of Soil in and Around Chandannagar Municipal Corporation', Unpublished MA Dissertation, Department of Geography, University of Burdwan.

Das, P. (1988) 'Well-Ring Manufacturing Industry of Chandernagore', *Geographical Review of India*, 50(2): 34–43.

Mukhopadhay, A.K. and K. Chakrabortty (1999) *Discover Chandernagore*, Chandannagar: Giri-Doot.

Sengupta, S. (2009) 'Changing Urban Mosaic with Special Emphasis on Restructuring and Interpersonal Relationship: A Study from Chandernagore Municipal Corporation', *Indian Journal of Landscape Systems and Ecological Studies*, 32(1): 177–188.

Ukil, A. (1996) 'Morphology of Chandannagar: An Urban Analysis', Unpublished PhD Thesis, University of Calcutta.

20

Urban Household Perception of Climate Change and Mitigation Preferences in Dehradun City, Uttarakhand

SWATI THAKUR

The Intergovernmental Panel on Climate Change (IPCC) since 1990 has issued four reports and prorogated public debate about climate change. In the recent report of 2007 the potential causes to climate change are both natural and anthropogenic. Taking into account the effects of both this is projected to increase the mean temperature on earth. It further states that anthropogenic emission grew by 70 per cent during 1970–2004. As a result, every form of life on this planet earth is likely to be subjected to the impact of climate change (Pachauri, 2007). Still, there is lack of common opinion about the scientific findings.

Until recently, mainly biological, technical and economic aspects of climate change have been illuminated; however, psychological aspects are also being widely recognized. Decision-making requires taking into account the context, including multiple value preferences for characteristics and function of natural and human systems, over short and longer time scale (Watson and Core Writing Team, 2001). Since climate change is going to seriously affect human beings, it is very necessary to explore what humans think about it. Failure to take public views into consideration will affect the acceptance of policy implementation.

Though an average citizen is typically more concerned about the weather, rather than climate in the region (NRC, 1997), still, the seriousness of the impact and emotional involvement with the problem is necessary to understand the need for actual action to resolve the problem. Understanding variations in the perception is necessary in order to achieve practical steps to address climate change. It would be useful to design the educational and policy interventions that can lead to greater convergence in belief and willingness to act (Weber, 2010).

Review of Literature

Despite its environmental, social and economic importance, climate change is a phenomenon which is not easily and accurately identified by the lay public, using their normal tools of observation and inference. Climate has a statistical expression, a term that describes average weather condition in a range of time over a region. The observations are spaced in time and memory of past events which can be faulty. Hence, climate change is not an easily detectable phenomenon by personal experience but definitely open to personal observation and evaluation. People often wrongly attribute unique weather events to climate change and also fail to detect changes in climate. The climate of a region obviously determines weather. The role of people's ability lies in expectation of stability which can frame the detection of trends in environment (Kupperman, 1982).

The way people learn about uncertain phenomena is either from personal experience or being provided with a statistical description of outcomes and then their likelihood of occurrence. This distinction of learning from experience in contrast to learning from description has received much attention in recent studies of psychological and behavioural studies to climate change (Hertwig et al., 2004).

Most of the extreme weather or climate events have a smaller probability of having occurred recently, so, they tend to have smaller impact on the decision but when and how frequently have they occurred have larger impact on related decisions. This makes learning and decision-making from experience more volatile than learning from description among people (Yechiam et al. 2005).

The processing of decision from experience is more associative and affect driven. Associative processing is a very basic human ability that does not need to be learned. They are made quickly and can turn experience into feelings of fear, dread or anxiety which then influence decision (Loewenstien, 2001). Analytical processes on other hand, works by sophisticated algorithms and are to be learned. Perception generation can attribute to learning from statistical description provided by scientists and anecdotal accounts of climate change provided by the media. Issues related to learning about climate change from external sources incorporate into the decision-making, only if it comes from a trusted source (NRC, 1999).

Hence, both learning from personal experience and from statistical description contributes to people's perception of climate change as well as variation in concerns. Accordingly, public views on climate change have been of interest to many researchers and policy makers for several years now. These have been elicited through a range of different methods, primarily quantitative social survey and more recently qualitative studies.

Public concern and knowledge of climate change have been investigated in most of the developed countries. More than a decade ago, the 1992 Gallup Health of Planet (HOP) survey indicated that more than half the respondents in 13 out of 24 countries worldwide felt climate change was a serious problem (Brechin, 2003). Out of these 13 nations, 8 were European, more than 65 per cent of the surveyed population in 23 out of 24 nations indicated climate change and global warming to be a serious issue. Opinion polls have also been investigated people's knowledge of the cause of climate change (e.g., Kempton et al.,1995; Gallup survey of lay people in Canada, USA, Mexico, Brazil and Potugal; Lorenzoni, 2003 survey of lay people in Italy and UK).

Interestingly, it was found that most developing countries response percentage was less than that of developed countries as an issue most people worry about.

A comparison of Gallup polls asking the American public how much they personally worried about the issue found that 24 per cent in 1989 and 40 per cent in 2003 categorized it 'as a great deal of worry' where as 60 per cent had a negative feeling about the images they associate with climate change. Similarily, in a study US-Americans have a moderate perception of climate change as a risk (Leiserowitz, 2006) while British people are rather concerned about the same issue (Lorenzoni 2006). In contrast, Semenza et al. (2008) found out that almost all respondents (USA) have heard about climate change or global warming, are rather concerned (women more than men) and some 50 per cent reported behavioural changes like decreased energy usage at home, reduced gasoline consumption, increased recycling and some other behaviours.

On a more localized level, a qualitative study by Bickerstaff et al. (2004) indicates that even individuals in localities are proximal to the effect of climate change, but they could draw connection where there were some immediate demonstration of impact. As supported by Eiser (2004) who argues that a lack of a directly experienced link between causes of climate change and its consequences may create false impression which leads to dangerous outcomes. For most people in the United States, judging the likelihood of climate change based on personal experience will lead to judgments that are low. Even individuals whose economic livelihood depends on weather and climate events (e.g., farmers or fishermen) and who are thus motivated to attend to them, might not receive sufficient feedback from their daily or annual personal experience to diagnose systematic changes sufficient to become alarmed. Surveys conducted in Alaska and Florida, where residents in some regions have increasingly been exposed to physical evidence of climate change show that such personal exposure greatly increases their concern and willingness to take action (Leiserowitz, 2008).

Zwick (2002) suggests that manifestation of such personal denials about direct effect and disassociation from any personal involvement depends on the subjectivity of perception of risks. In addition, human perception of climate is strongly influenced by expectations, which may have little relationship to the true nature of climate as provided by the instrumental record (Rebetez, 1996). Lay people have an ambivalent attitude towards climate change, as they attempt to balance the requisite of their daily lives with the awareness of the greater social problem that climate change represents (Lorenzoni et al. 2006).

Public opinion polls do highlight a sense of importance, urgency and negativity associated with climate change as an environmental, but not necessarily as a 'domestic', issue. However, more detailed studies on national samples serve to highlight more complex public attitudes towards climate change. Individuals characterize climate change in multiple terms, related to their everyday experiences and locality, distinguishing effects on different scales in space and time (ibid.).

Important differences in risk perceptions on a personal, compared to a societal level have been observed in relation to a range of events (Sjoberg, 2000). An individual's downplaying of a certain risk to him/herself, while recognizing its relevance to society overall, could be interpreted as a manifestation of a personal denial about direct effects and, more importantly, dissociation from any personal involvement in possible solutions. Zwick (2002) suggests that this discrepancy could be partly explained by the different ways in which individuals relate to the perceived risks of climate change and how these may be remedied. Thus, although society as a whole may be considered in danger from climate change, individuals may perceive little threat from global warming to their standards of living and health. For many, adaptation and support for the most affected (mainly in other parts of the world) would be more likely in 50 years' time with a 1.6°C rise in temperature. Such evaluations clearly relate to subjective judgments of benefits vs. risks for individuals vs. society, present vs. future generations, to developed countries vs. developing nations, rural vs. urban area raising equity and moral considerations.

Developing countries are already in the mark to face climate change threats. The question of how will individuals go to address the issue possess great interest. Moreover, according to UN report the concentration of human population is expected to double in urban centres by 2030 in developing region like Africa and Asia. Urban areas pose serious problems in regard to the impacts of climate change as they concentrate people, assets and infrastructure in ways that increase risk and vulnerability and many cities and smaller urban centres are in locations that climate change is making (or will make) particularly hazardous (Bicknell et al., 2009). A study of conceptualization of climate change was done in urban centres of Tanzania and Jakarta city (Sawio, 2008; Surbakti, 2010).

Similar attempts against the background of global concern for implications of climate change on communities and the need for sustainable adaptive measures at local levels, household perception of, and response to, causes and evidences of climate change in the peri-urban areas of an ancient African city, Ibadan, Nigeria has been evaluated by Thompson et al. (2011). Observed climatic parameters show an indication of local warming, featuring decreasing rainfall and increasing temperature. All the respondents linked deforestation, bush burning and population increase with climate change and also identified fluctuating days of rainfall, shrinking sizes of water bodies, shortage of water and loss of soil fertility as evidences of climate change. It also incorporated importance of environmental education into the school curriculum so as to achieve sustainable environmental responsibility.

One of the vulnerable nation to vagaries of climate change, Bangladesh, its urban citizens of Dhaka city felt that because of climate change the intensity of physical problem can occur with economic effects followed by psychological and environmental disorder. The study also indicated that urban people are only experiencing some changing climatic patterns, but they are not facing any serious effect due to climate changes; so there is no structured strategy solely focusing on adaptation to climate change. This may be due to the lack of working organizations, which can explain all the causes and consequences of climate change to the urban areas (Rahman et al., 2011).

Hence, urban areas have to be seen as centres having large potential advantages in building resilience to climate change impacts too. The idea behind this study was to have an understanding of mindset of the urban settlements on climate change, their level of awareness and to know their action and reactions in the changing climate scenario. Besides, the study also intervenes to understand the current adaptive and coping options of urban population.

With the release of India's first climate action plan on climate change (NAPCC), it is addressing the existing and future programmes on climate change mitigation and adaptation. It identifies eight core missions, one of which is on strategic knowledge for climate change. This mission evokes better understanding of climate science; impacts and challenges for commons. As apart of programme education to training, public awareness, public access to information, public participation and intervention to improve climate modelling is emphasized.

A study for selected urban settlements of semi-arid zone of India in major states like Tamil Nadu, Gujarat, Karnataka, Rajasthan, Maharashtra , Haryana and Uttar Pradesh was conducted (Rishi et al., 2010). Climate change perception inventory was especially designed to collect behavioural assessment at cognitive, conative and affective level. It also questioned about coping potential at individual and organizational level and possible role to address the problem of climate change. Respondents of C class or smaller cities by population, more readily and easily recognized awareness and severity regarding climate change. Acceptance of water crisis related to changing climate and need to take affirmative action to combat the impact was common for all respondents.

The Study Area

Above discussed studies should be done in all urban areas to recognize the awareness level and mapping the behavioural aspect of sensitivity for the problem. To fill the void, a similar endeavour is conducted in Dehradun city, class I capital city of Garhwal division in Uttarakhand, India. Nestled in the midst of mountain ranges of the Himalaya, blessed with a salubrious climate and urban population of less than one million, the city is also one of the three cities chosen for the programme for urban renewable mission in Uttarakhand. The city is a marked educational hub of North India with ten of the national institutes of forest, soil, wildlife, energy and remote sensing. The literacy rate amounts to 77 per cent which is higher than national average (59.7%). Hence, it became imperative to analyse the response behaviour of urban households in Dehradun city for a national and global issue.

Objectives

The main objectives for the study are: to study perception of urban households towards climate change; to study the coping strategies and to identify preferences for a public policy on climate change.

Data Sources and Methodology

The study is primarily based upon primary data. A semi-structured questionnaire survey was conducted for the households. Purposive sampling technique was used to select more than 300 households in urban area of Dehradun city. They represent various geographic locations as well as population and development dynamics. The respondent's exposure to various educational levels was also considered. The responses of 350 respondents were chosen for data computation as they attempted the survey seriously. Table 1 summarizes the statistics of respondents on the basis of socio-economic characteristics.

Table1

Summary Statistics of Respondent's Socio-Economic Characteristics

Respondents' characteristics	*Sample*	
Sex Ratio	0.78	
Age Distribution	*Age*	*% Sample*
	20–35	42
	35–50	38
	50 and above	20
Education	*Category*	*% Sample*
	Below	
	Senior Sec	30
	Graduate	41
	Above Graduate	29
Gross Average Household Income	*Category*	*% Sample*
	Upto 20,000	36
	20,000–40,000	48
	More than 40,000	16

Source: Based on Field Work.

Two sets of responses to access impact of climate change on both national and household level were documented. Questions regarding plausible causes to changing climate were open-ended and later frequency matrix were made to rank priority of aforesaid. A new set of valuation part was addéd to the questionnaire where respondents were asked WTP (willingness to pay) on behalf of the household to support any collective programme to mitigate climate change at societal or national level. Respondent who said 'Yes' were followed up with open-ended interactive response for the contribution. In addition to these questions, respondents were asked a set of socio-demographic (e.g., occupation, income, household size) and attitudinal questions (e.g., level of concern regarding climate change, relative importance of climate change mitigation policies and individual's role in the decision-making).

Probit regression analysis was done for the stated preferences about causes and impact of climate change at household level and actual behaviour to reduce carbon footprint at household level. Correlation was done to assess relation among variables with significance level.

Perception of Climate Change

Knowledge and Concern about Climate Change

Throughout this article the term 'climate change' has been used instead of a stimulus to response that of 'global warming' as the former. About 28 per cent of respondents misunderstood the description of climate change as global warming. On an average, respondents had negative feeling about the images they associate with climate change. Around 68 per cent of the respondents had heard about climate change and identified it as a 'bad thing' for the present and future generation. Commonly, myths regarding end of the world was associated with it. About 33 per cent expressed concern about lack of correct information regarding the change. Notably, the age group 20–35 years was well informed in most of the cases.

Less than a quarter (20%) of respondents indicated they were 'highly concerned' about the impact of climate change. The majority (40%) were 'concerned'. About a third of the respondents were 'somewhat concerned' while around 10 per cent were 'not so concerned'. Despite relatively high concern level detected in these surveys, the importance of climate change as a policy issue ranks low. Around 10 per cent of the respondents ranked climate change as most important. Significantly, positive correlation ($r = .425$, $p < .001$) with education level above masters and professionals were seen. About 38 per cent indicated economic development as priority issue while further law and order (28 %), health (18%) were ranked.

Regarding the question as to what is the main cause of climate change, 56 per cent respondents reported destruction of forests in nearby regions as prime factor followed by emission of greenhouse gases from sources like vehicles, house cooling system, industries as second most important factor (43%). This might be due to the fact that any extent of change and its associative degree of severity posed by that change is more easily recognized.

When asked about how far human actions are responsible, more than quarter (27%) expressed strong agreement with the statement whereas, respondents (39%) indicated a moderate level of agreement. Twenty per cent neither agreed nor disagreed and rest (14%) expressed limited understanding of human contribution of change in climate. Positive correlation was found between respondents who stated higher level of concern for climate change and also agreed that human activities induce changes. On general level, people's perception does highlight the sense of importance, urgency and negativity associated with it.

Perception of Change in Temperature and Rainfall

Following Viscusi and Zeckhauser (2006), the perceived change in average future temperature was taken as the first indicator of climate change. Respondents were first informed about the average annual temperature of the city of about 105 years (1901–2007 with data gaps). They were then presented with 5 levels of possible changes in annual average temperature ranging from decrease of 2°C from normal to increase of up to 5°C from normal. They were also asked to give their best guess of temperature change in near 30 years (2040) relative to current year. Questions were asked regarding familiarity with the issue of climate change. Respondents were also asked about the changes in rainfall over recent years and the expected change for the coming 30 years relatively to the current year.

Within the given scenario of probable degree of average temperature change in 2040 relative to the current year was 3.25°C. In comparison to official estimate of 2.6°C change projection (Rawat, 2006; Rawat and Singh, 2010) has a close match with the sample respondents. The present temperature trend stands high with 0.75°C from the respondents. Most of the guesses which were nearly exact to the official figures were also believers in human induced climate change ($r = 0.05$, $p < 0.001$). Table 2 analyses the probit regression model of scenario uncertainty for climate indicators.

Table 2

Probit Regression Model of Scenario Uncertainty

Variable name	*Variable description*	[a]*Response as dependent variable (Yes/No replies from higher education level respondents)*
Temperature	Best guess of temperature change in next 40 years (mean=4.1, SD = 3.2)	0.15** (0.07)
Discomfort	Hotter summer will cause discomfort (Yes = 1, otherwise = 0) mean=0.64, SD = 0.47)	0.24* (0.13)
Comfort	Hotter weather will be pleasant for winter (Yes = 1, otherwise = 0) mean=0.13, SD = 0.27)	0.30**(0.18)

[a] Responses to the question as acceptance or rejection as dependent variable standard error of parameter estimated between brackets.

** p<0.05, * p < 0.10 significance level.

Regarding comfort level with rising temperature in winter season, the respondents of education level above university degree did not agree with the changes and its positive impact as they were concerned about the crop loss and glaciers melt in the higher hills. The perception for changing rainfall was estimated through asking both at annual and seasonal variations. Nearly 89 per cent of them gave negative changes in regard to rainfall intensity (short duration heavy rainfall), more number of dry spells and reduced number of rainy days. The peak month of monsoon rainfall, July, was reported to decline by two-thirds of the respondents. It was well correlated by observational data studies done in this regard (Rawat, 2006; Thakur, 2009). The results show decrease in 2.73 per cent to total rainfall in 2001–08 periods compared to 1931–40 when the share of July rainfall to total annual rainfall was 31.5 per cent. Table 3 denotes the preferential causes and consequences of rainfall change by the respondents.

Table 3

Response to Changing Rainfall in Recent 30 Years (1990–2010)

	*Percentage respondents' perception**	
	Yes	*No*
Changes in rainfall pattern	82	18
Decreasing trend in rainfall	72	28
Later start of rain	78	22
Less reliable rain	92	08
Variation in normal rainfall	75	25

* N=350, surveyed in year, 2010.

** 68 per cent of the respondents could correlate the increase in average temperature and decrease in average annual rainfall.

Impacts of Unmitigated Climate Change

Expectation of the effect of the changing climate if unmitigated was also surveyed. Decreasing water supply, loss of native food crop variety, unbearable weather

Figure 1

Respondents' Perception of Climate Change Impact on Dehradun City

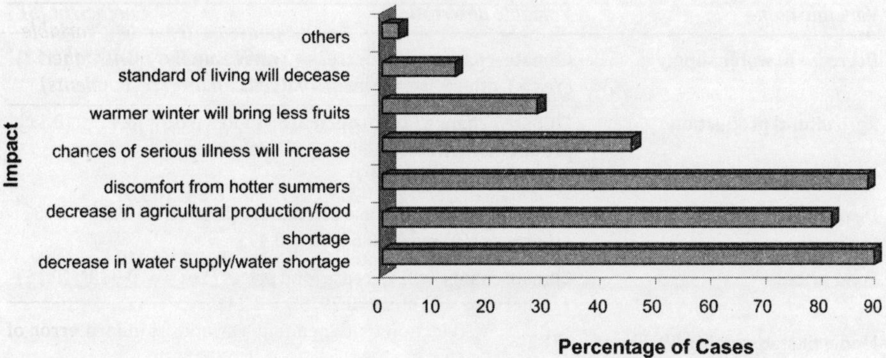

conditions were cited by the majority of the respondents as impacts. When asked to point out how they expected their households would be affected by climate, 72 per cent placed scarcity of drinking water at higher priority. Consecutively, food shortage, discomfort from hotter weather in summers, increase in chances of illness were placed next. Figure 1 summarizes the response at household level by respondents.

Contrary to this Figure 2 summarizes the response when questioned about impact on the state or nation as a whole, the priority and nature of impact changed. Fear of decreasing water supply still was in priority by majority of respondents with equal concern on loss of agricultural production, both food and cereal cropping.

The loss of traditional cropping system as "Barahnaj" (i.e., planting 12 different crops in a single season) and decreasing livelihood option in surrounding areas of Dehradun was a major concern of respondents. They linked it with occupational shift and migration towards the city, thereby, increases in pressure on available resources and infrastructure in the city was also highlighted. Table 4 presents a probit regression model of variables of impact of climate change as perceived by the respondents.

Figure 2

Respondents' Perception of Climate Change Impact on Uttarakhand

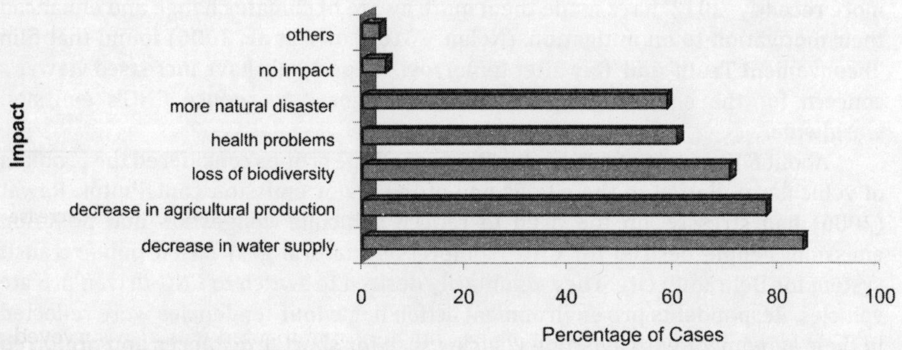

Table 4

Probit Regression Model of Perceived Impact of Climate Change

Variable name	*Variable description*	*Coefficient (SE)*
Decrease in water supply	Climate change will decrease water supply (Yes = 1, otherwise = 0) mean=0.81, SD = 0.39)	0.42*** (0.13)
Agricultural production	Climate change will decrease food crop production in Doon valley (Yes = 1, otherwise = 0) mean=0.58, SD = 0.49)	0.41***(0.12)
Discomfort	Hotter summer will cause discomfort (Yes = 1, otherwise = 0) mean=0.64, SD = 0.47)	0.24* (0.13)
Food prices	Climate change will increase food prices (Yes = 1, otherwise = 0) mean=0.79, SD = 0.34)	0.042**(0.16)
Model fit statistics log likelihood	−182	
Pseudo R squared	0.18	
N	350	

Standard error of parameter estimated between brackets

*** p< 0.01, ** p<0.05, * p < 0.10 significance level.

Household Preferences for Climate Change Mitigation

Opinions regarding efforts to mitigate climate change were an important section of this paper. Open-ended interaction with majority of the respondents revealed doubts about actions of individual to be sufficient enough to address the issue. About 79 per cent of the respondents were unaware about any stand taken by national or state governments, both in diffusing information and taking decisions about climate change. There are apparent examples from developed countries where localized motivation has enabled community and state-level mitigation initiatives involving citizens. It has become drivers of behavioural change, as the benefits become tangible to active participants (Rayner and Malone, 1997; Jones, 2004). In the absence of such personal and political will, the task of mitigation becomes surreal in India.

Nevertheless, factors which can provoke a behavioural change towards the fact about reducing the human contribution towards climate change were explored. Table 5 represent that half (48%) of the respondents indicated that watching television programme on climate change and/or reading newspaper articles and watching Hollywood fiction movies such as; 'Day after tomorrow', 'Deep Impact' and more recently '2012' have made them more aware of climate change and enhanced their motivation to on mitigation. (Nolan, 2010; Lowe et al., 2006) found that film 'Inconvenient Truth' and 'Day after tomorrow' respectively have increased viewer's concern for the environment and their willingness to reduce CNG's emission worldwide.

About 64 per cent of respondents across all age groups considered the problem of vehicular pollution in the city as one of the major emission contributor. Rawat (2006) had stressed on the need to reduce vehicular congestion and pollution emission. People desired for CNG (compressed natural gas) based public transit system for Dehradun city. They voluntarily desired to switch to CNG-driven private vehicles. Respondents pro environment action behaviour tendencies were reflected in their agreement with avoiding vehicle usage for shorter distances and preferred walking/cycling within institutional campuses and nearby market areas.

Table 5

Probit Regression Model of Actual Behaviour to Reduce Carbon Emission (Dependent Variable Reduces Car and/or Electricity Use and Switch to Greener Fuel Based Systems = 1, otherwise = 0)

Variable name	*Variable description*	*Coefficient (SE)*
Exposure to mass media TV/News (Greenathon@NDTV)	Watched television programme and/or read newspaper (Yes = 1, otherwise = 0) mean=0.87, SD = 0.32)	0.566*** (0.16)
Fiction movies on climate change	Watched (Yes = 1, otherwise = 0) mean=0.27, SD = 0.47)	0.288***(0.13)
Education	Respondents have higher university degree (Yes = 1, otherwise = 0) mean=0.53, SD = 0.50)	0.23**(0.14)
	Respondents being professional at institutions is concerned about pollution and want to switch to CNG-based public transit system (Yes = 1, otherwise = 0, mean=2.2, SD = 1.5)	0.09**(0.04)

Standard error of parameter estimated between brackets

*** p< 0.01, ** p<0.05, * p < 0.10 significance level.

The respondents positively correlated with both media exposure and willingness to reduce vehicular pollution and level of education. Both university graduates and professional at academic institutes recognize the issue with great concern. A good deal of claim by respondents is to have energy efficient homes in view of access to ample sunlight and fresh air was found so that energy consumption during daytime is minimized. The question of keeping in mind energy efficiency factor of any electric item before purchase gathered good support by 53 per cent of respondents. Around 26 per cent were unaware whereas, 21 per cent showed no interest in this regard.

Out of 350 respondents interviewed, 87 per cent rejected about any WTP (willingness to pay) for collective action or as environmental tax to the government. They strongly expressed mistrust in the government and argued upon individuals contribution for own household as a better option. Overall, it was found that regarding coping capacities to climate change, only 10.7 per cent of the respondents fully claim to have the social, economic/physical resources to cope with climate change whereas, 19.8 per cent expressed their incapability to cope with changes. A significant lot argued for incentives and private-public partnership to deal with capacity building. There was major disagreement on cities preparedness in the wake of occurring changes.

When informed about National Solar Energy Mission as part of capacity building under climate action plan, it was welcomed. The need for both national initiatives for bigger projects and household level energy transformation to convectional sources was recognized. About 43 per cent of total respondents were willing to flip into solar energy based household heating and electrification option. Table 6 enlists common discussion statements and their scale average from 1 to 4 as "strongly agree, agree, disagree, not sure".

Table 6

Respondents Pro Environment Action Behaviour Tendencies

Item No.	*Statements*	*Scale average*
1.	I am confident that individual effort will be able to slow down impacts of changing climate	3.20
2.	I generally forget to switch off lights/fan after using AC	1.96
3.	It is primarily the government to do something about climate change	2.71
4.	Policy for public transport should be compulsory for institutions/organization for their students/employees to reduce traffic	3.33
5.	I would like to initiate a campaign for car pooling and walking for shorter distances	3.35
6.	Energy efficiency of an electric item is one of the factors to make a choice before buying them	3.36
7.	I try to minimize my energy use at day time and see that the house gets sufficient sunlight and fresh air	2.89

Want of subsidy on any such green technology-based equipment came as informal discussion with 52 per cent of respondents. The coefficient of education is positively and statistically significant at 5 per cent level for having a collective plan for climate change mitigation at local and national level. About 32 per cent respondents reported a combination of individual, institutional and voluntary services as the most effective measure to mitigation action.

Conclusions

The study provided an understanding of urban Indian household's perception of climate change and preferences for mitigation strategies at individual level. Consistent with their priorities, majority of respondents showed concern about the issue which is a positive outcome of a country where citizens attempt to balance the requisites of daily life with an awareness of the threats that climate change represents. Limited understanding of cause of and solution to climate change by the respondents is reflected in the entire study. A wide range of qualitative and quantitative methodology was used to scratch out perception from the respondents about climate change. Behavioural aspects such as readiness to act, to take initiatives, to learn new ways to adjust to changing lifestyle and negotiate solutions so that climate change can be coped in a functional way was explored.

The education was found to play an important role in determining public support for problem of and solution to climate change at individual and national level. The exposure of the mass media was also a detrimental factor to broaden the associative dimension of perception building and hence, policy needfulness for effective climate change mitigation measure. It was found that the respondents were emotionally concerned about the climate stress and accepted that developed countries are more responsible due to their lifestyle, but responsibilities also lies on developing nations due to their resource dependence and population size.

However, the perceived frustration and disempowerment relating to effective individual mitigation action, contribute to retain climate change issues on priority for the vulnerable future generation. Successful action is only likely to take place if individuals feel they can and should make a difference. The findings presented in this paper also indicate that individuals alone will not voluntarily choose to alter their behaviour in the face of climate change unless they feel enabled to do so in terms of government being a facilitator for the same and also perceive the rest of the society moving in the same direction.

References

Bickerstaff, K., P. Simmons and N.F. Pidgeon (2004) 'Public Perceptions of Risk, Science and Governance: Main Findings of a Qualitative Study of Five Risk Cases', Unpublished Working Paper, Centre for Environmental Risk, University of East Anglia, Norwich, UK.

Bicknell, J., D. Dodman and D. Satterthwaite (eds) (2009) *Adapting Cities to Climate Change: Understanding and Addressing the Development Challenges*, London: Earthscan Publications.

Brechin, S.R. (2003) 'Comparative Public Opinion and Knowledge on Global Climatic Change and the Kyoto Protocol: The US Versus the Rest of World?', *International Journal of Sociology and Social Policy*, 23(10): 106–134.

Eiser, J.R. (2004) *Public Perception of Risk*, Report Prepared for Foresight Office of Science and Technology, London. Available at http://www.foresight.gov.uk/Intelligent Infrastructure Systems/Reports and Publications/Intelligent Infrastructure Futures/Public%20Perception%20of%20Risk/long paper.pdf.

Hertwig, R., G. Barron, E.U. Weber and I. Erev (2004) 'Decisions from Experience and the Effect of Rare Events', *Psychological Science*, 15: 534–539.

Intergovernmental Panel on Climate Change (IPCC) in R.K. Pachauri and A. Reisinger (eds) (2007) *Climate Change*, Synthesis Report, Geneva.

Jones, R.N. (2004) 'Incorporating Agency Into Climate Change Risk Assessments', *Climatic Change*, 67: 13–36.

Kempton, W., J.S. Boster and J.A. Hartley (1995) *Environmental Values in American Culture*, Cambridge, Massachusetts: MIT Press.

Kupperman, K.O. (1982) 'The Puzzle of the American Climate in the Early Colonial Period', *American Historical Review*, 87: 1262–1289.

Leiserowitz, A. (2006) 'Climate Change Risk Perception and Policy Preferences: The Role of Affect, Imagery and Values', *Climatic Change*, 77: 45–77.

—— (2008) 'Climate Change in the American Mind', in C. Pumphrey (ed.) *Global Climate Change: National Security Implications*, Carlisle, PA: Strategic Studies Institute, 213–226.

Loewenstein, G.F., Weber, E.U., Hsee, C.K. and Welch, E. (2001) 'Risk as Feelings', *Psychol. Bull.*, 127: 267–286.

Lorenzoni, I. (2003) 'Present Choices, Future Climates: A Cross-Cultural Study of Perceptions in Italy and in the UK', Doctoral Thesis, School of Environmental Sciences, University of East Anglia, Norwich, UK.

Lorenzoni, I., A. Leiserowitz, M. de Franca Doria, W. Poortinga and N.F. Pidgeon (2006) 'Cross-National Comparisons of Image Associations with "Global Warming" and "Climate Change" Among Laypeople in the United States of America and Great Britain', *Journal of Risk Research*, 9(3): 265–281.

Lorenzoni, I., N.F. Pidgeon and R.E. O'Connor (eds) (2005) 'Dangerous Climate Change: The Role for Risk Research', *Risk Analysis*, 25(6): 1387–1398.

Lowe, T., K. Brown, S. Dessai, M. de França Doria, K. Haynes and K. Vincent (2006) 'Does Tomorrow Ever Come? Disaster Narrative and Public Perceptions of Climate Change', *Public Understanding Science*, 15: 435–457.

National Research Council (NRC) in P. Stern, T. Dietz, V.W. Ruttan, R.H. Socolow and J. Sweeney (eds) (1997) *Environmentally Significant Consumption: Research Directions*, Washington, DC: National Academy Press.

National Research Council (NRC) in P.C. Stern and W.E. Easterling (eds) (1999) *Making Climate Forecasts Matter*, Washington, DC: National Academy Press.

Nolan, J.M. (2010) 'An Inconvenient Truth Increases Knowledge, Concern and Willingness to Reduce Greenhouse Gases', *Environmental Behaviour*, doi: 10.1177/0013916509357696

Pachauri, R.K. (2004) 'Climate and Humanity', *Global Environmental Change*, 14: 101–103.

Poortinga, W. and N.F. Pidgeon (2005) 'Trust in Risk Regulation: Cause or Consequence of the Acceptability of GM Food?', *Risk Analysis*, 25(1): 199–209.

Rahman, M.S., M. Haque and M.B.K. Khan (2011) 'Perception on Climate Change: An Exploratory Study on Urban Citizens', *European Journal of Economics, Finance and Administrative Sciences*, 31: 17–30.

Rawat, L. (1998) 'Changing Facets of Weather and Climate of Doon Valley', FRI Council of Forestry Research and Education (ICFRE), Dehradun.

—— (2006) 'Changing Trends of Climate of Doon Valley', *Indian Forester*, 132(5): 615–622.

Rawat, M.S.S and M.P. Singh (2010) 'Climatic Change and Variability in Dehradun City, Uttarakhand', *National Geographical Journal of India*, 56(1): 51–60.

Rayner, S. and Malone, E.L. (1997) 'Zen and the Art of Climate Maintenanc'e, *Nature*, 390: 332–334.

Rebetez, M. (1996) 'Public Expectation as an Element of Human Perception of Climate Change', *Climatic Change*, 32: 495–509.

Rishi, P., Omprakash, M.D. and Mudaliar, R. (2010) 'Behavioural Mapping of Indian Urban Settlements Towards Changing Climate: An Empirical Study', Available online (http://climsec.prio.no/papers/norway%20full%20paper-final.pdf), 1–16.

Sawio, C. (2008) 'Perception and Conceptualization of Urban Environmental Change: Dar es Salaam City', *The Geographical Journal*, 174(2): 164–168.

Semenza, J.C., D.E. Hall, D.J. Wilson, B.D. Bontempo, D.J. Sailor and L.A. George (2008) 'Public Perception of Climate Change, Voluntary Mitigation and Barriers to Behavior Change', *American Journal of Preventive Medicine*, 35(5): 479–487.

Sjoberg, L. (2000) 'Factors in Risk Perception', *Risk Analysis*, 20(1): 1–11.

Surbakti, I.M., C. Izhar, H.A. Simarmata and T. Firman (2010) *Jakarta City Report*, Information Related to Climate Change in Jakarta City, Paper Prepared for the Workshops of Climate Change, Vulnerability Assessment and Urban Development Planning for Asian Coastal Cities, Rose Garden, Sampran Riverside, Nakorn Pathom, Thailand, 22–28 August.

Thakur, S. (2009) 'Rainfall Variability in Doon Valley: A Statistical Analysis', *The Indian Geographical Journal*, 83(1): 35–50.

Thompson, A.A., D.O. Adejumobi and O. Kehinde (2011) 'Perception of Climate Change Issues and Household Response Patterns in Peri-Urban Areas of Ibadan, Nigeria', doi: 10.1096/C10P0212. 2011.03.004

Viscusi, W.K. and R.J. Zeckhauser (2006) 'The Perception and Valuation of the Risks of Climate Change: A Rational and Behavioral Blend', *Climatic Change*, 77: 151–177.

Watson, R.T. and Core Writing Team (eds) (2001) *Climate Change 2001: Synthesis Report*, Summary for Policymakers, Contributions of Working Groups I, II and III to the Third Assessment Report of the Intergovernmental Panel on Climate Change, Cambridge, UK: Cambridge University Press.

Weber, E.U. (2010) 'What Shapes Perception of Climate Change?', *Advanced Review*, doi: 10.1002/wcc.41

Yechiam, E., G. Barron and I. Erev (2005) 'The Role of Personal Experience in Contributing to Different Patterns of Response to Rare Terrorist Attacks', *Journal of Conflict Resolution*, 49: 430–439.

Zwick, M.M. (2002) 'Descriptive Findings of the Baden-Wurttemberg Risk Survey 2001', in M.M. Zwick and O. Renn (eds), *Perception and Evaluation of Risks: Findings of the Baden-W¨urttemberg Risk Survey 2001*, Joint Working Report by the Centre of Technology Assessment in Baden-Wurttemberg and the University of Stuttgart, Sociology of Technologies and Environment, Germany, 7–32.

Zwick, M.M. and O. Renn (eds) (2002) *Perception and Evaluation of Risks: Findings of the Baden-Wurttemberg Risk Survey 2001*, Joint Working Report by the Centre of Technology Assessment in Baden-Wurttemberg and the University of Stuttgart, Sociology of Technologies and Environment, Germany.

21

Delhi's Master Plan for 2021

A Critical Review of Evolving Approaches to City Development

PRIYANKA PURI

Master Planning is the dominant form of urban planning in India and once approved, the Master Plans become a legally binding document and a blueprint for implementation. Thus, the document provides an insight into the planning ideologies to which the plan is anchored and also opens up scope for introspection of the strategies that are adopted for city development. In the current context, Delhi was the first city to have a Master Plan in independent India and adopt master planning strategy with the process of its preparation and implementation vested in one single authority which is the Delhi Development Authority (DDA). Pertinent for Delhi, along with tremendous population pressure are the numerous urban issues. What is significant is that the magnitude of these has been increasing continuously even though planning was attempted for the city immediately after independence.

With reference to all these contexts it is of utmost importance to observe the direction to which the city is forwarded and this is best exemplified in the Master Plans which are the prime document of the city's planning. This analysis can be best conducted for the provisions of the current Master Plan which has been drawn with a perspective for 2021, which is third in the line of Master Plan documents of the city. The newer aspects of the Plan are examined here.

Data Sources and Methodology

The study involves secondary data sources. These are the ones related to literature on urban planning and master planning. Further, the three Master Plans of Delhi have been studied for the analysis of components and are cross examined for the same.

Review of Literature

Literature in the present context has been analysed with regard to the nature of master planning. This is extended to the components of the current Master Plan.

Cities are considered as the geographic concentrations where wider social processes operate (Simmie, 2001). Cities in both the ancient and medieval period were planned as their existence and location were laid consciously and a large proportion of them had formal ground plans (Hall and Jones, 2011). A metropolitan plan is defined as "a projection of growth of population and economic activities in a city and provides a framework for location in its metropolitan area of housing colonies, industrial units and institutions of higher learning, hospitals and facilities for recreation" (Nath, 2007). The purpose of town and country planning is to 'intervene' in the process of land and property development in order to achieve an outcome which is socially and environmentally preferable which the private market would not produce (Greed, 2000).

Plans have been described as a type of decision-making with which the risks of future are minimized by following a course of action (Lein, 2006). These are particularly useful when the "decisions to be made are interdependent, irreversible, and indivisible and face imperfect foresight" (Hopkins, 2001). The phenomena of the city as a catalyst could be viewed in the context of the Industrial Revolution (Blackhall, 2005) and before modern town and city planning became formalized in the period before post-War reconstruction era, the social and economic systems were more dominant in town city planning (Evans, 2001). The 1950s and early 1960s observed the emphasis on preparing a blueprint for towns which were the Master Plans or Master Planning. Master Planning became the dominant form of spatial planning after World War II (Todes et al., 2010).

The twentieth century has experienced an unprecedented increase in the number of capital cities (Gordon, 2006). A capital city is defined as "the seat of government of a nation state, province or supra national organization and have unique elements that are associated with their status as a seat of government" (ibid.) and the urban design of capital cities is special (Vale, 2006) as these cities are an important symbol for the whole country (Slack and Chattopadhyay, 2009). The literature on the above-mentioned topics can be observed as below:

Concept of Master Plan

The term Master Plan was first used in a report, 'Recent New York Legislation For The Planning Of In Built Areas: Regional Plan Of New York And Environs (1976)'. A Master Plan has been described as an 'Impermanent Constitution' by Haar (1955) in his famous article 'The Master Plan: An Impermanent Constitution'. In this article, he reiterates the view that development programmes of the 'New City' require a sound legislation and within this legal matrix the Master Plan is an established element (Haar, 1955). Four broad areas are traditionally assigned for impact by the master plan: Public works, Zoning, Subdivision and Streets (ibid.). Master Plans are also observed as a component of urban planning theory (Greed, 2000) and in this regard three components can be identified in town planning (Taylor, 1998). These include town planning as physical planning, design as central to town planning and the assumption that town planning necessarily involves the production of 'master plans' or 'blueprint plans' as the 'end state'. The Master Plan is expected to evolve planning standards from a consideration of local individualities, contemporary town planning thought and practice, recommendation of various stakeholders and study teams (Singh, 1978).

The objectives of a master plan can be specific such as removal of overcrowding, clearance of slums, planned urban expansion, reclamation of low lying areas and waste lands, segregation of industrial areas from residential areas, provision for integrated road system, provision for an integrated water supply system, provision for an integrated drainage and sewerage system, provision for metropolitan green belts, provision for open spaces in built-up areas, development of residential areas on neighbourhood principle, reservation of suitable areas for various community needs, utilization of natural amenities, stoppage of ribbon development, preservation of historical monuments, and any other proposal bearing on health, convenience and comfort of the people of the locality (ibid.).

Depending on the purpose and context, it has been connoted that 'Master Plan' has a variety of meanings. 'Comprehensive Plan', 'General Plan', 'Municipal Plan', 'City Plan', 'Long Range Plan', 'Just Plan' are also used as terminologies (Haar, 1955). The uses of a Master Plan are envisaged into six categories (ibid.) as follows:

1. Source of information.
2. A programme for correction.
3. An estimate of the future.
4. An indicator of goals.
5. A technique for coordination.
6. A device for stimulating public interest and responsibility.

Master Plan provisions are reinforced by prominence. Thus, comprehensiveness concerned with the interaction of the elements of physical development, projection and policy are its major premises in which some basic principles are explained to govern the development of a land use plan (Kelly, 2010). The concepts of zoning and subdivisions are integral to master plans.

Concept of Zoning

Zoning is defined as the practice of allocating different areas of a city for a particular use and imposing limitations on some (Relph, 1987) and is believed to have existed since as long as land and buildings in cities have been regulated, meaning thereby that zoning started with the growth of cities (Hagman, 1975). Zoning ordinances are put forth as the first widely adopted form of regulatory implementation of planning (Kelly, 2010). Regulating intensity through zoning includes four measures of intensity in zoning. These are identified as: residential intensity measured in dwelling units per acre, minimum lot sizes for single family homes which create an inverse calculation for the number of dwelling units per acre, commercial and industrial intensity measured in Floor Area Ratio (FAR) which is the maximum number allowed for the ratio of the floor area of the proposed building to the land area of the lot on which it will be built and indirect intensity regulation through maximum height restrictions (ibid.).

Zoning ordinances are generally divided into two parts (Levy, 2000): maps and text. Categories and subcategories of land uses are identified through zoning (Kelly, 2010). The zoning power has its purposes, sources, enabling acts and general and specific provisions to maintain property values, stabilize neighbourhoods, homogenize areas, traffic movement, limiting densities, minimum plot size, minimum floor space, controls, aesthetics, architectural control and preservation of cultural, historic, national and government areas (Hagman, 1975).

In its criticisms, zoning has been termed as static, serving parochial interests and a policy that cannot ensure high quality development (Porter et al., 1988; Miller and Spoolman, 2009), creation of not liked commercial development (Kelly, 2010) and in direct conflict with planning itself (Hall, 2002).

Concept of Subdivisions

Subdivisions are defined as a kind of land use control next to zoning in importance as a land use regulation (Hagman, 1975). These are defined as "Any land, or portion thereof shown on the last preceding tax rolls as a unit or as contiguous unit which is divided for purposes of sale; either immediate or future". These are considered to be an old form of land use control dating back to the early nineteenth century (Gallion and Eisner, 1984). In relation to planning, it is considered as being more close to the planning process because of nearness to policy implementation (Hagman, 1975). Subdivision is defined as the division or combination of land into parcels in accordance with local ordinances and for the purpose of sale, transfer of ownership or development (Lewis, 2007). The purposes of subdivision ordinance are defined as:

1. To encourage the orderly, efficient, and economic use of land;
2. To discourage scattered and premature subdivision of land;
3. To promote harmonious development;
4. To arrange and coordinate streets within and outside of subdivisions;
5. To ensure open and common space;
6. To ensure that adequate access, drainage and utilities are provided to the lots, and
7. To protect the health, safety and prosperity of a community (ibid.).

Subdivision regulations are believed to control the manner in which blocks of land over a certain size may be converted into building blocks. Zoning and subdivisions are identified as interrelated concepts with blurred boundaries (Cullingworth and Caves, 2009) but exhibiting the control of local governments (Wine, 2003). In the light of this text, the provisions of the current Master Plan are observed in a critical light below.

Newer Aspects Observed in the Current Master Plan of Delhi: Critical Review

About the Current Master Plan of Delhi: Master Plan With The Perspective for the Year, 2021

This plan became operational in 2007. The background studies for this plan are titled 'Sub-Group Reports for Master Plan of Delhi 2021'. These are amalgamation of reports prepared by the various 'sub-groups' formed for the Master Plan preparation. Besides members of the DDA, the members of these groups are also experts from their respective fields. There are twelve sub-groups: Sub-Group on Regional and Sub Regional Aspect, Sub-Group on Demographic Profile and Population Projection, Sub-Group on Shelter, Sub-Group on Conservation and Urban Renewal, Sub-Group on Traffic and Transportation, Sub-Group on Social Infrastructure, Sub-Group on Trade and Commerce, Sub-Group on Industrial Aspects, Sub-Group on Environment and Pollution, Sub-Group on Physical Infrastructure, Sub-Group on Mixed Landuse and Sub-Group on Development Control.

Table.1

Master Plan With The Perspective for the Year 2021: Features

Content	*Description*
Published on	7 February 2007
Preparing Agency	Delhi Development Authority
Contents	Introduction, Regional and Sub-Regional Frame, Population and Employment, Delhi Urban Area–2021, Shelter, Trade and Commerce, Wholesale Trade, Industry, Government Offices, Environment, Conservation of Built Heritage, Urban Design, Transportation, Social Infrastructure, Physical Infrastructure, Mixed Use Regulations, Land Use Plan, Development Code, Plan Review and Monitoring
Vision and Objectives of the Plan	Vision–2021 is 'to make Delhi a global metropolis and a world-class city, where all the people would be engaged in productive work with a better quality of life, living in a sustainable environment'.
Objections	7,000

A Critical Analysis of Selected Aspects

The following aspects have been introduced in the current Master Plan: The provisions discussed below are taken from the 'Master Plan of Delhi With The Perspective for the Year 2021':

Concept of World Class City and Global Metropolis

The Plan aims to make Delhi a world class city and a global metropolis. The question here is with regard to the definition of being 'world class' as cities around the world are striving to be global (Massey, 2007) and to what extent does Delhi fit in the category of being or becoming a world class city? What are the related concepts in the light of its problematic existence, continuing issues and population that outgrows every projection? Thus, a global city can be studied in the light of interrelated concepts which have gained substantial currency in urban research preceding the concept of world class city. These are – world city, global city and global city regions and the emerging concept of world class city. These can be observed as evolving in urban studies literature as below:

1. *The World City Hypothesis* (Friedmann, 1986): World cities are put forward to have existed even in the medieval times (Taylor, 2004). The term 'world cities' was coined by Patrick Geddes in his book 'Cities in Evolution' to show urban growth and conurbations in city regions outside UK (Beaverstock, Smith and Taylor, 2000). The term was reintroduced in Peter Hall's work 'The World Cities' in 1966. This discussion gained dominance with John Friedmann's seminal work 'The World City Hypothesis' building on the ideas of Cohen (1981) and Wolff (1982) (cited in Kim and Short, 2008). It is about the spatial organization of the new international division of labour and is based on seven basic assertions. The seven interrelated theses and key terms used herein are highlighted as follows:
   (i) "The form and extent of a city's integration with the world economy, and the functions assigned to the city in the new spatial division of labour, will be decisive for any structural changes occurring within it. In this context, the following is detailed.
   City – This reference is suggested for an economic purpose. A city is defined as a spatially integrated economic and social system at a given location or metropolitan region. This, for administrative purposes, can be divided into smaller units.
   (ii) Integration with the world capitalist system – Here, the reference is to the specific forms, intensity and duration of the relations that link the urban economy into the global system of markets for capital, labour and commodities.
   (iii) Functions assigned to it in the new spatial division of labour – It is within this system that different localities: national, regional and urban subsystems perform specialized roles. Metropolitan cities range on functions as singular to multiple.
   (iv) Structural changes occurring within it – Contemporary urban change is defined as a process of adaptation to changes that are externally induced. In specific terms, changes in metropolitan function, structure of metropolitan labour markets, and the physical form of cities can be explained with reference to a worldwide process that affects: the direction and volume of transnational capital flows, the spatial division of the functions

of finance, management and production and control and the employment structure of economic base activities.

(v) These economic influences are modified by certain endogenous conditions as well.

(vi) Among them, the most important one highlighted is that of 'spatial patterns of historical accumulation' followed by national policies whose aim is to protect the national economic subsystem from outside competition through partial enclosure to immigration, commodity imports, and the operation of international capital and certain social conditions such as apartheid.

(vii) Key cities throughout the world are used by global capital as 'basing points' in the spatial organization and articulation of production and markets. The resulting linkages make it possible to arrange the world cities into a complex spatial hierarchy."

World cities are points of destination for large numbers of both domestic and/or international migrants. In this regard, two kinds of migrants can be distinguished: international and inter-regional. Both contribute to the growth of primary core cities, but in the semi-periphery, world cities grow chiefly from inter-regional migration. There is also a stricter control over the entry of migrants. Delhi is not mentioned in the list of world cities drawn by Friedman in his original work (Friedmann, 1986).

In the first instance, as per the postulates of the concept, Delhi can be characterized as a city with a dominant role at the regional level. The functions are multiple as well as single in which the administrative significance is the premier one as Delhi is the seat of power for the country. But with regard to the structural changes as proposed by the concept, it can be observed that these are more in the national and particularly dominant in the regional context for the city. The main cause of this is migration from the surrounding areas. Further, as per the concept, the changes are externally induced but are not majorly the ones that integrate the city into the 'world capitalist system'.

The 'endogenous changes' can also not be identified directly in this case.

The spatial patterns of historical accumulation can be observed in certain contexts for the city such as the heritage, residential and commercial pattern; particularly the streets and layout. The existence of national policies for 'protecting' the national economic subsystem do not seem to be identifiable in Delhi's Master Plan's context with regard to the above context 'through partial enclosure to immigration, commodity imports, and the operation of international capital' although the background works of the Master Plans do identify with such issues. Paradoxically, these are totally obliterated in the practical aspect.

With reference to 'social conditions', the city stands out as the Constitution of the country proposes equality, freedom, secularism and fraternity and the observations of class and caste conflicts do not appear as issues. The concept of 'global control functions' and 'their direct reflectance in the structure and dynamics of their production sectors and employment' does not hold relevant to a large extent as these global functions are observable in a very broad context of establishing a base but not the 'basing point'. Hence, the evolving physical form of the city is not directly linked to the transnational flows. These phenomena cannot be termed as a positive or negative externality. A 'vast army' of 'low skilled' labourers is observed but this is the result of migration influx from surrounding states for employment in the city. The 'driving force' of world city growth is attributed to the global factors which in Delhi's case cannot be directly anticipated or observed as contributing to growth. Instead, a multitude of factors seem to be operational in its regional context. While the corporate headquarters are located at Gurgaon, there are no signs of a 'global transport' facility.

Further, 'ideological penetration and control' need to be clarified further. With respect to the factor of migration, the city is not a centre of international migration on a large scale but does have a large influx of population from the hinterland but this population is not concentrated in the peripheral areas as is postulated by the concept. International migration is observable in the form of 'illegal' refugees, particularly from Bangladesh. These have generated a pressure on city's infrastructure and have contributed to the city in the form of illegal encroachment of land as well as crimes. Further, no control over migration is observed while the city is facing extreme pressure arising out of increasing population.

Polarization as proposed by this concept is observed at the regional and national level. In the context of Delhi, fiscal pressure seems to be operational in the creation of infrastructure but this is more attributed to the pressure of population. Thus, the regional factors seem dominant in Delhi's context whose growth is not determined dominantly by the global factors and externalities as is put forward by the concept. Hence, the emphasis on the global context is a partial explanation. Other factors also operate in a city's geographical realm. In this, the importance of the local scale cannot be avoided (Taylor et al., 2007).

Globalization and World Cities Research Network (GaWC) analysis – The world according to GaWC (www.lboro.ac.uk) is a city-centred world of flows in contrast to the more familiar state-centred world of boundaries. Cities are assessed in terms of their advanced producer services using the interlocking network. Indirect measures of flows are derived to compute a city's network connectivity – this measures a city's integration into the world city network as follows:

"The connectivity measures are used to classify cities into levels of world city network integration. These levels are interpreted as follows:

(i) alpha++ cities – In all analyses, London and New York stand out as clearly more integrated than all other cities and constitute their own high level of integration;
(ii) alpha+ cities – Other highly integrated cities that complement London and New York, largely filling in advanced service needs for the Pacific Asia;
(iii) alpha & alpha cities – Very important world cities that link major economic regions and states into the world economy; and
(iv) beta level cities – These are important world cities that are instrumental in linking their region or state into the world economy.
(v) All gamma level cities – These can be world cities linking smaller regions or states into the world economy, or important world cities whose major global capacity is not in advanced producer services.

Cities with sufficiency of services – These are cities that are not world cities as defined here but they have sufficient services so as not to be overtly dependent on world cities. Two specialized categories of cities are common at this level of integration: smaller capital cities, and traditional centres of manufacturing regions (www.lboro.ac.uk)."

Delhi is put in the category of alpha-level cities by GaWC in 2010 (www.lboro.ac.uk). But only conducting international events or producing spatially concentrated spatial infrastructure, as has been observed during the Commonwealth Games 2010, does not necessitate the path to develop the city as the issues of the city are immense and unending, yet similar in nature ever since the inception of its planning through Master Plans. It is also mentioned that the urban question has not prominently featured in the plans that have guided urban development since independence (Ghertner, 2011). On the whole, it is very pertinent to bring out that the exclusion of the city from the category of being 'world class' or 'global' cannot be termed as a negative or positive externality.

2. The Global City Model (Sassen, 2001): The use of the global city concept is attempted to study the specificity of the global as it gets structured in the contemporary period (ibid.). The early contributions are credited to Petrella (1995) and Veltz (1996), but the concept is commonly traced back to the work of Allen Scott (2001). The difference between the world city concept and the global city concept is highlighted on the grounds that the world city concept has a 'timelessness' of some form attached to it while the global city concept 'marks a specific socio-spatial historical phase' and the 'key differentiating element' is 'the emphasis on the production of the global economic system and the production of global control capacities (Sassen, 2006). As per Sassen (2001), the concept is based on seven hypothesis as follows:
   - (i) "The geographic dispersal that marks globalization, along with the simultaneous integration of such geographically dispersed activities, is a key factor feeding the growth and importance of central corporate function;
   - (ii) These central functions become so complex that increasingly the headquarters of large firms outsource them;
   - (iii) Those specialized service firms engaged in the most complex and globalized markets are subject to agglomeration economies;
   - (iv) The more headquarters outsource their more complex, unstandardized functions particularly those subject to uncertain and changing markets and to speed, the freer they are to opt for any location because the more the work actually done in the headquarters is not subject to agglomeration economies;
   - (v) These specialized firms need to provide a global service which has meant a global network of affiliates or some other form of partnership;
   - (vi) The growing numbers of high level professionals and high profit making specialized service firms have the effect of raising the degree of spatial and socio-economic inequality evident in these cities; and
   - (vii) The dynamics prescribed in these hypothesis lead to the growing informalization of a range of economic activities which find their effective demand in these cities yet have profit rates that do not allow them to compete for various resources with the high profit making firms at the top of the system."

The functions of complexity, location of headquarters, and provision of a global service do not seem to be operational in a direct context for the city of Delhi. The location of these activities, whatsoever observed, have been initiated by the international firms located in Gurgaon, outside Delhi. The concept of socio-economic inequality as generated by these firms is to be examined in field. The city of Delhi is facing its own internal issues. Although building up equitable and inclusive cities is one of the stated tasks of the current National Urban Renewal Mission, its achievability within the overarching neoliberal framework of the mission has already provoked strong scepticism, while the recent developments observed in Delhi, boosted by the preparations for the Commonwealth Games, confirm these concerns (Dupont, 2011). Global cities are recognized on the basis of four scales –

the global world urban system, the regional interface, the placelessness of world cities and the metropolitan scale. Global and world city approaches have received a lot of criticism yet have also dominated literature (Robinson, 2006). But for Delhi, both the concepts do not seem to be operational with regard to their postulates and only some contexts in a limited way comply with the city dynamics.

3. Global City Regions (Scott et al., 2001): The concept is traced back to the 'world cities' idea of Hall, Friedmann and Wolff and that of 'global city' (Scott et al., 2001). These are conceptualized as the new key territorial units in a post-Fordist economy. The aim of this definition is to show how these city regions function as spatial nodes of the global economy and as distinct political actors on the world stage. These city regions are the drivers of the global economy and the forces shaping them have marked impacts on their internal social geography with governance issues and negative externalities as well and these regions are coming to function as territorial platforms from which concentrated groups or network of firms contest global markets (Scott et al., 2001).

City regions are also given the role of actors and act within the framework of the global economy but they also influence and shape their environment with a significant role of political factors (Segbers, 2007). Here, the metropolitan areas function as the centres and gateways of global business, culture and social relations and under the model presented by geographers and sociologists (ibid.). The forces shaping the emergence of global cities have had marked impacts on their internal social geography-patterns of social stratification.

The internal geography leads to a polycentric geographical structure comprising of the following:

(i) The traditional downtown centre, based on walking distances and radial public transport;
(ii) A newer business centre;
(iii) An 'internal edge city';
(iv) An 'external edge city';
(v) 'Outermost' edge city complexes; and
(vii) Specialized sub-centres (Scott et al., 2001).

In geographic terms, global city regions consist of dense megalopolises that are bound up in "intricate ways with an outgrowth of large metropolitan areas or contiguous sets of metropolitan areas, together with surrounding hinterlands of variable extent which may themselves be sites of scattered urban settlements" (Derruder and Witlox, 2008). In this regard, the global city regions of developing countries are highlighted to have two main observed trends.

These relate to "the tendencies for the movement of economic activities outward from metropolitan cores to fringe areas and a limited tendency in some countries for the migration of routine productive activities to smaller towns, i.e., activities that have become less dependent on the advanced services and inputs found only in large urban areas" (Gilbert, 2003). The concept of global city regions begins with the concept of a city region. In this regard, Delhi fits into the category of a city region. As a territorial unit, Delhi is dominant in the regional context. Global city regions are supposed to function as spatial nodes in the global economy but the city does not exhibit any such dominant feature and role as a 'distinct political actor' on the global stage.

4. *World Class City:* The concept has been put forward by Derudder (Derudder, 2006) in which he argues that the concept of 'world city', 'global city' and 'global city regions' are different and the emerging concept of world city is

world class city that is marked by making changes to cities in order to bring in marketing, the city to business, organizations, institutions and tourists. World class cities are termed as the 'winners' among globalizing cities and are put forward as the products of really existing globalization (Marcuse, 2008). In the current context, what however, is more important for the city is to manage its growth and resources and check the processes that tend to be issues in the current context.

The urbanization process taking place in Delhi, as is observed in other Indian cities, is termed as 'violent urbanization' (Ghertner, 2011). Delhi is termed as an 'unlikely site' for world class aspirations and the optimisms for Delhi are termed as with shaky foundations and the Master Plans are termed as the cause of this (Baviskar, 2006). This situation prevails for almost all dominant urban centres and Delhi, as observed even at the international scale, does not fare better as is highlighted by its position as observed by Johari (*The Times of India,* 8 July 2012).

Concept of Action Planning and Local Area Plans

The success of the current Plan is postulated to be dependent upon action plans and periodic reviews (DDA, 2007). Planning academics and practitioners call widely for citizen participation in planning decisions (Mohammadi, 2010). The Local Area Plan (LAP) is being drawn for Delhi's localities. These are an attempt to participatory planning. This can be categorized as action planning approach which is at first observed for the city in the current Plan.

'Urban action planning' is concerned with the 'urgent need to improve planning practice and methodology' in order to 'make urban planners more responsive to local urban problems and more effective in their capacity to guide urban development processes and improve living conditions in urban areas'. Community-based issue analysis is suggested to provide stakeholders with the opportunity to develop a detailed, shared analysis of the key issues related to their Community Vision which will give informed choices for preparing Action Plans (ICLEI, IDIRC, UNEP, 1996).

Participatory planning is sought to make sense if those in charge of urban planning process make a genuine effort to involve and engage citizens and their organizations in the debate on how the city should develop in the future (UNHSP, 2007). In this process, the stakeholders are also required to be identified. In this case, a stakeholder has been defined as "an individual, group or organization that is directly affected by one or more urban issues, has an interest in one or more urban issues, can influence urban development positively or negatively, has access to or control of resources (financial, technical or intellectual) that may be needed to support urban development" (ibid.). Today's community practitioners are advised to deal with the combined effects of global economics and escalating poverty with other challenges of wars, terrorism, massive refugee movements, rising tensions by multicultural populations and realities of racial and ethnic discrimination (Weil, 2005).

Action Plan: This is drawn for solid waste management for a period of five years and aims at the overall break down of activities for the Plan implementation and to evaluate actions required to convert strategy into practice. On this basis, the government is also drawing master plans for issues such as drainage as given by Mathur in his article (*The Times of India,* 30 July 2011) while their formulation has been in as far as 1976 and notification in 1981 as given by Pandit (*The Times of India,* 10 July 2011).

The concept of performance oriented planning with focus on implementation and monitoring is another ill-defined and unspecified concept that needs to be detailed further, and rather with efficiency and seriousness particularly in the situation where civic management is missing absolutely, as is highlighted by Pandit (*The Times of India*, 31 May 2011) and Kaul and Naqshabandi (*The Times of India*, 4 August 2011). In-situ rehabilitation of slums is again an indicator of policy failure and lack of operational control.

Unauthorized colonies are to be regularized which gives the signal that in whatsoever manner that growth takes place in the city, it has to be accommodated even while emphasizing that these are a 'serious human problem' in the Master Plan for Delhi. This is coupled with a contradictory provision of control of growth of slums by providing housing. Along with these, the growing informal sector is another cause of concern which again is encouraged indirectly as is in the case of slums and rehabilitation colonies. The provision of hawking and no hawking zones seems rather ridiculous in this regard. For a city that is not able to systematize its growth, measures of containing environmental problems such as pollution of the River seem rather impractical and out of sync provisions on which paradoxically numerous amounts have been spent.

The city might boast of the first scientific landfill site in Narela – Bawana operational now but facing issues as highlighted by TNN correspondent (*The Times of India*, 28 June 2011) or DDA's efforts to develop eco-mobility network in the city by landscaping the city drains as is given by Bhasin (*The Times of India*, 8 July 2011) but the past experiences are not indicative of any systematic planning. Although mixed land use is further encouraged, the introduction of additional Floor Area Ratio (FAR) is a new step but the need of determining FAR is still questionable. Hence, the application of this concept is limited in nature for the city in the present context as this is only in its preparatory stages.

Creation of Policy Zones

The Regional Plan 2021 has been drawn up with reference to the following four Policy Zones: (i) National Capital Territory (NCT) of Delhi, (ii) Central National Capital Region (NCR) (iii) Highway Corridor Zone, (iv) Rest of NCR. For NCT, the aim of planning is to achieve environmentally sustainable development, re-development considering the limitations of land and water with significantly improved quality of infrastructure; the execution of which is a toll taking task in the context when the city has always been under pressure of its growth which is currently also termed as unprecedented. The Central NCR (earlier the Delhi Metropolitan Area) as defined in the Regional Plan–2021, comprises of the notified/controlled development areas of the neighbouring towns of Ghaziabad-Loni, NOIDA, Gurgaon-Manesar, Faridabad-Ballabhgarh, Bahadurgarh and Sonepat-Kundli, and the extension of the ridge in Haryana, having an area of about 2,000 sq km The aim here is to maximize the opportunities to compete with the NCT of Delhi and to shift the industries here. For the highways, regulated development is proposed along with the development of Green Belts. For the rest of NCR, accelerated growth of rural and urban areas is proposed.

Preparation of a Sub-regional Plan

It is proposed to prepare a Sub-regional Plan by Government of National Capital Territory of Delhi (GNCT). As per it, it is proposed that no new Central Government and Public Sector Undertaking offices should be located in NCT of Delhi; industrial growth in Delhi should be restricted to high-tech with emphasis on units, which require skill, less manpower and energy and do not create pollution/nuisance; legal and fiscal measures should be adopted to restrict employment in industries and distributive trade, major regional transport corridor and communication network needs to be strengthened to enhance economic development within the region and decentralization of the distributive trade and the natural features such as forest, wildlife sanctuary, ridge, river Yamuna and other water bodies should be conserved and kept free from unrestricted and unplanned urban development.

Signature Projects

The introduction of signature projects is mentioned. The definition of these 'signatures' is missing and the need of its sudden commence is not specified for an already issue-ridden city. While it finds mention in shelter, the current signature construction is the 'signature bridge' modelled on the lines of the famous London Bridge. It is to be constructed on river Yamuna and is to serve as a landmark. Its exuberant cost of construction has remained controversial. Currently, the estimated cost of this breathtaking project stands at around ₹ 1,130 crore as given by Dash (*The Times of India,* 13 July 2011).

Policy for Planned and Unplanned Areas

These are divided as: Influence Zone along Mass Rapid Transit System (MRTS) and Major Transport Corridor; underutilized/low density areas; Special Area; shopping/commercial centres and Industrial Areas/clusters and settlement colonies. Re-densification of Low Density Areas and redevelopment of Other Developed Areas is proposed. The introduction of employer housing with regards to its densification is another new concept. The unplanned areas are classified as slums, JJ *(Jhuggi Jhonpri)* clusters, unauthorized colonies and villages. For the villages, the local bodies are suggested to make comprehensive plans but these are not identified. Introduction of parking in residential plots is another addition.

Provisions for Housing for Urban Poor

These have been identified as inhabitants of squatter settlements and informal service providers. Such services could `include domestic help, hawkers and vendors, low paid workers in the industrial, commercial and trade/business sectors, etc. These include both existing population and future migrants. The categorization of urban poor did not exist in the earlier plans, which is indicative of the increasing numbers of this category and yet the provisions are mentioned for accommodating them. This is indicative of the nature of planning for the city. While the Plan mentions of the land as a resource, the treatment of it is improper. Night shelter is also proposed for the shelterless.

Development of Facilities in Residential Zone

In measures for planning physical infrastructure, measures regarding the use of non-conventional energy sources are mentioned.

Changed Hierarchy of Commercial Area

The commercial areas are categorized on the basis of population with five tiers starting from the metropolitan city to a population range below 5,000. Here, the areas have been categorized as Metropolitan City Centre, District Centre, Community Centre (CC), Local Shopping Centre (LSC) and Convenience Shopping Centre (CSC). The policy for existing areas of informal sectors is to be checked with regards to its provisions and the logic of restrictions on the activities within the Use Premises also needs to be checked. The introduction of connecting the wholesale markets through the MRTS is an appreciative initiative but the restrictions on storage in these areas needs to be checked. Congestion in these markets is also mentioned as a major problem but it is to be kept in consideration that these problems have only amplified in their present context, while they were present ever since the inception of planning. New wholesale and sub-city level markets are also proposed which is a clear indicator of expansionist tendencies.

Newer Strategy for Industries

The promotion of hi-tech and low volume-high value added industries, which are not labour intensive, is encouraged along with the modernization of the existing ones. Industries are to be classified as prohibited and non-prohibited only. Redevelopment of unplanned industrial areas is also proposed but the feasibility is to be checked. While redevelopment has to be carried on by the local authorities within the time frame specified by Delhi Development Authority (DDA), the lack of a clear strategy is observable. Another important mention of Green Field Area development by relocating industries there is to be checked.

Provisions for Environmental Planning

Waste types identification is attempted which includes electronic waste also which is an indicator of the diversification and even increasing tendencies of waste generation. Groundwater finds a mention. Although water availability and supply is highlighted to be sufficient, it is the wastage that is talked of as the major culprit in terms of distribution. However, there is no mention of water supply to unauthorized constructions. Air and water pollution have given the city status of amongst the world's top most polluted cities, so what planning advocates is to be re-examined. In this regard, even the suggested measures for the rejuvenation of the River are totally futile. To make Delhi a 'Green City' is the aim of the Plan which is to be carried on further by the extension of parks and amusement parks.

Optimum Utilization of Government Land

The aspect of intensive usage of these areas is appreciative. Identification of strategy for heritage conservation and creation of heritage zones is also a newer introduction. The steps and their details have been outlined here and newer areas have been identified in the heritage zones while some are designated as archaeological parks. For such areas, each local body is entitled to draw 'Special Development Plans'. However, in this the additional planning controls are missing as is also advocated by the UNESCO (Worthing and Bond, 2008).

Proposals for Urban Design

The addition of urban corridors, city gateways and MRTS corridor in the category of significant areas for built environment is a newer concept highlighting the growth of the city. Public amenities, pedestrians, policy for tall buildings and policy on hoardings are also discussed. Public amenities do not have the analysis of the component of gender although street design mentions of provisions for the physically challenged. Urban design guidance is also required as it can set out principles on matters of importance and the processes that should be followed (Cowan, 2002).

Changes in Transport

Highlighting the phenomenal growth of traffic in Delhi from 1991–2001, it is proposed that expansion, strengthening and restructuring shall take place of the existing modes of transport with integration with the Metro. All impediments are suggested to be removed but this does not seem feasible in the light of encroachments. The identification of Influence Zone along the Delhi Metro, setting up of integrated multi-modal transport system and a renewed emphasis on the setting up of Metropolitan Transport Authority are other noteworthy aspects of analysis in the transport sector. In the hierarchy of road network, it is only in the last category of local streets that encroachments are prohibited which in policy are also violated. The introduction of underground roads in critical areas, graded separators, freeways and urban relief roads for the reduction of congestion on existing roads finds mention. The MRTS is to be further expanded. Synergy between transport and land use is advocated along with it fallout since the First Plan. The concept of 'spatial balance' is introduced as the aim is to solve to some extent the issues in transport.

The problem of parking arising out of phenomenal growth of vehicles also finds mention for which public parking including of parking fee, multi-level parking and other stringent provisions are suggested. However, the root cause is not tackled.

Provisions for Sports

Delhi is highlighted to be emerging as an important centre for national and international sports. Provision of reserving areas for international sports is also outlined.

Law and Order Concerns

These are highlighted as emerging areas of concern which is an indicator of disturbing affairs.

Disaster Management

This is a newer addition for the city. It includes steps for pre and post disaster management. Although Disaster Management Centres have been proposed to be set up, Delhi Fire Services remains the nodal agency for disaster management of the city.

Differentiated Approach for Mixed Use in Residential Areas

This is mentioned to have risen from the differentiated structure of planned and unplanned residential activity in the city and socio-economic differences. Again along with the restrictive provisions, it is mentioned that no encroachment shall be permitted on the streets or public land, but how far is this practically followed does not need to be re-emphasized.

Change in the Use Zone

The National Capital Territory of Delhi is divided into 9 land use categories (DDA, 2007). These are agriculture lands along NCR and is designated as Green Belt. Further, the definition of farm house has been altered as a dwelling on a farm (ibid.).

Mapping of Delhi Using Remote Sensing and GIS

It is proposed to have mapping of the city along with the updation of changes in land use. A Spatial Data Infrastructure Group is proposed to monitor the plan.

Plan Review and Monitoring

It mentions to check the unintended growth of the city while there neither exists any effort nor any definition as to what this implies. Further, the concept of reviewing the appropriateness of plan policies needs to be studied and identified in a practical light. The Plan period is proposed to be divided in three phases taking 2006 as the base year and if the targets are not met these are to be carried in the next plan. The targets are indicative of the expansion being promoted. Monitoring and reviewing is to be done for the physical and socio-economic change, while these are expanding in an uncontrolled manner. Management Action Groups are to be formed for it. The planning indicators are highlighted as demographic, land use, housing, social infrastructure, transport, economic aspects, environment and natural disasters.

The suggested groups for plan monitoring are – High Level Group for Sub-Regional Plan for Delhi, Environment Planning and Coordination Group, Delhi Unified Metropolitan Transport Group, Infrastructure Development Group, Enforcement and Plan Monitoring Group, Spatial Data Infrastructure Group, Local Level Participatory Planning Group, Common Platform for Building Approvals, Slum Rehabilitation and Social Housing Group and Legal Framework Review Group. The Plan has to it appendices mentioning strategies of enhancing water supply and solid waste management.

Planning Indicators

The following would be the indicators of physical and socio-economic changes to be monitored periodically – Demographic, land use, housing, social infrastructure, transport, economic aspects, environment and natural disasters (ibid.). However, the processes are uncontrolled. Henceforth, the utility of such exercises is to be checked.

Conclusion

In review of the past experiences, it has been observed that all the targets set have been underachieved and the most pertinent fact is that population growth has outnumbered all the estimates. The major challenges highlighted are that of unauthorized settlements and JJ clusters. These are suggested to be dealt in their present manifestation, future growth and proliferation. The issue which lingers from the First Plan and also, as its one of the main target has no solution to it till now and, in fact, has multiplied. The futility of strategies and lack of will is exhibited. Another 'major component' of the Plan highlighted is that of redevelopment and densification of the existing urban areas and city improvement through comprehensive development accompanied by the creation of open spaces while the Plan itself mentions that the growth of population of Delhi has had 'inevitable' implications and impact. Again the strategy seems to be missing, as for a city that is already short of meeting infrastructure needs yet aims at increasing its already high numbers. This, in turn, is followed by a phenomenal growth of automobiles which is the highest for the country. The new Plan exhibits a shift in the way of planning but the ideology of planning does not exhibit any change. The visions drawn, project the city to be made world class but this is far from reality in the current scenario of burgeoning population and related concerns of the city and the further preparation of multiple plans seems to serve no purpose.

References

Baviskar, A. (2006) 'Demolishing Delhi: World-Class City in the Making', *Mute*, 2(3): 88–95.

Beaverstock, J.V., R.G. Smith and P.J. Taylor (2005) 'World City Network: A New Metageography', in N.R. Fyfe and J.T. Kenny (eds), *The Urban Geography Reader*, London: Routledge, 63–74.

Bhasin, R. (2011) 'DDA Body Wants Drains Uncovered and Landscaped', *The Times of India*, Friday, 8 July.

Blackhall, J.C. (2005) *Planning Law and Practice*, Vol. 3, London, Portland and Oregon: Cavendish Publishing Limited.

Cowan, R. (2002) *Urban Design Guidance: Urban Design Frameworks, Development Briefs and Master Plans*, London: Thomas Telford Publishing.

Cullingworth, B. and R.W. Caves (2009) *Planning in the USA: Poilcies, Issues and Processes*, New York: Routledge.

Dash, D.K. (2012) 'Urban Growth Eats into NCR Green Cover', *The Times of India*, Thursday, 12 July.

Delhi Development Authority (2007) *Master Plan of Delhi with the Perspective for the Year 2021*.

Derudder, B. (2006) 'On Conceptual Confusion in Empirical Analysis of a Transitional Urban Network', *Urban Studies*, 43(11): 2027–2046.

Derudder, B. and F. Witlox (2008) 'What is a "World Class City"? Comparing Conceptual Specifications of Cities in the Context of a Global Urban Network', in M. Jenks, D. Kozak and P. Takkanon (eds), *World Cities and Urban Form: Fragmented, Polycentric, Sustainable?*, Oxford: Routldege, 11–24.

Dupont, V.D.N. (2011) 'The Dream of Delhi as a Global City', *International Journal of Urban and Regional Research*, 35(3): 533–554.

Evans, G. (2001) *Cultural Planning: An Urban Renaissance?*, London: Routledge.

Friedmann, J. (1986) 'The World City Hypothesis', in N. Brenner and R. Keil (eds), *The Global City Reader*, London: Routledge, 67–72.

Gallion, A.B. and S. Eisner (1984) *The Urban Pattern, City Planning and Design*, New York: Van Nostrond Reinhold.

Ghertner, A.D. (2011) 'Rule by Aesthetics: World-Class City Making in Delhi', in A. Roy and A. Ong (eds), *Worlding Cities: Asian Experiments and the Art of Being Global*, Malden, MA: Blackwell Publishing Limited, 279–306.

Gilbert, A. (2003) 'Is Urban Development in the Third World Sustainable?', in L.F. Girard, B. Forte, M. Cerreta and F. Forte (eds), *The Human Sustainable City: Challenges and Perspectives from the Habitat Agenda*, Aldershot: Ashgate, 71–88.

Gordon, D. (2006) 'Capital Cities in the Twentieth Century', in D. Gordon (ed.), *Planning Twentieth Century Capital Cities*, Abingdon, UK: Routledge, 1–7.

Greed, C. (2000) *Introducing Planning*, London: Transaction Publishers.

Haar, C.M. (1955) 'The Master Plan: An Impermanent Constitution', *Law and Contemporary Problems*, 20(3): 353–418.

Hagman, D.G. (1975) *Urban Planning and Land Development Control Law*, St Paul, MN: West.

Hall, P.S. (2002) 'Global City Regions in the Twenty-First Century', in A.J. Scott (ed.), *Global-City Regions: Trends, Theory and Policy*, Oxford: Oxford University Press, 59–77.

Hall, P. and M.T. Jones (2011) *Urban and Regional Planning*, London: Routledge.

Hopkins, L.D. (2001) *Urban Development: The Logic of Making Plans*, Washington, DC: Island Press.

ICLEI, IDRC and UNEP (1996) *The Local Agenda 21 Planning Guide: An Introduction to Sustainable Development Planning*, Vol. 1, Toronto.

Johari, A. (2012) 'India's Urban Challenge', *Hindustan Times*, Sunday, 8 July.

Kaul, R. and A. Naqshabandi (2011) 'The Cancer of Overcrowding', *Hindustan Times*, Thursday, 4 August.

Kelly, E.D. (2010) *Community Planning: An Introduction to the Comprehensive Plan*, Washington, DC: Island Press.

Kim, Y.H. and J. Short (2008) *Cities and Economics*, London: Routledge.

Lein, J.K. (2006) *Integrated Environmental Planning*, Malden, MA: Blackwell Publishing.

Levy, J.M. (2000) *Contemporary Urban Planning*, Houston: Prentice Hall.

Lewis, J.P. (2007) *Land Use Control and Property Rights: A Guide for Real Estate Professionals*, Loveland, CO: Land Use Publications.

Marcuse, P. (2008) 'Globalization and the Forms of Cities', in M. Kenks, D. Kozak and P. Takkanon (eds), *World Cities: Polycentric, Fragmented, Sustainable?*, Oxford: Routledge, 25–40.

Massey, D. (2007) *World City*, Cambridge: Polity Press.

Mathur, A. (2011) 'Inconvenience Stores All Over', *Hindustan Times*, 30 July.

Miller, G.T. and S.E. Spoolman (2009) *Living in the Environment: Principles, Connections and Solutions*, Belmont, CA: Brooks/Cole Cengage Learning.

Mohammadi, H. (2010) *Citizen Participation in Urban Planning Management: The Case of Iran, Shiraz City and Saadi Community*, Germany: Kassel University Press.

Nath, V. (2007) 'Master Plans for Metropolitan Growth Management', in S.K. Aggarwal (ed.), *Urbanisation, Urban Development and Metropolitan Cities in India*, New Delhi: Concept, 360–380.

Pandit, A. (2011) 'Drainage Plan? We Have Heard This Before', *The Times of India*, Sunday, 10 July.

Petrella, R. (1995) 'A Global Agora vs. Gated City-Regions', *New Perspectives Quarterly* (Winter): 21–22.

Porter, D.R., P.L. Phillips and T.J. Lassar (1988) *Flexible Zoning: How it Works*, Washington, DC: Urban Land Institute.

PTI (2011) 'High Speed Train, 16 Shaharon Ke Liye', *Navbharat Times*, Thursday, 30 June.

Relph, E. (1987) *The Modern Urban Landscape*, London: Croom Helm Ltd.

Robinson, J. (2006) *Ordinary Cities: Between Modernity and Development*, London and New York: Routledge.

Sassen, S. (2001) 'Global Cities and Global City Regions: A Comparison', in A.J. Scott (ed.), *Global City Regions: Trends, Theory, Policy*, Oxford: Oxford University Press, 78–95.

Sassen, S. (2006) *Territory, Authority, Rights: From Medieval to Global Assemblages*, Princeton: Princeton University Press.

Scott, A.J., J. Agnew, E.W. Soja and M. Storper (2001) 'Global City Regions', in A.J. Scott (ed.), *Global City Regions: Trends, Theories and Policy*, Oxford: Oxford University Press, 11–32.

Segbers, K. (2007) 'Introduction: Global Politics and the Making of Global City Regions', in K. Segbers (ed.), *The Making of Global City Regions, Johannesburg, Mumbai/Bombay, Sao Paulo and Shanghai*, Baltimore: The John Hopkins University Press, 1–26.

Simmie, J. (2001) 'Planning, Power and Conflict', in R. Paddison (ed.), *Handbook of Urban Studies*, London: Sage Publications, 385–401.

Singh, K.N. (1978) *Urban Development in India*, New Delhi: Abhinav Publications.

Slack, E. and R. Chattopadhyay (2009) 'Introduction', in E. Slack and R. Chattopadhyay (eds), *Thematic Issues in Federalism: Finance and Governance of Capital Cities in Federal Systems*, Montreal: Mc-Gill Queen's University Press, 3–9.

Taylor, N. (1998) *Urban Town Planning Theory Since 1945*, London: Sage Publications.

Taylor, P.J. (2004) *World City Network: A Global Urban Analysis*, London: Routledge.

Taylor, P.J., B. Derudder, P. Saey and F. Witlox (2007) 'Introduction: Cities in Globalisation', in P.J. Taylor, B. Derudder, P. Saey and F. Witlox (eds), *Cities in Globalisation: Practices, Policies and Theories*, London: Routledge, 13–18.

TNN (2011) 'Contamination to be Checked, Says DJB', *The Times of India*, Tuesday, 2 August.

Todes, A., A. Karam, N. Klug and N. Malaza (2010) 'Beyond Master Planning? New Approaches to Spatial Planning', *Habitat International*, 34: 414–420.

UNHSP (2007) *Inclusive and Sustainable Urban Planning: A Guide for Municipalities*, UN Habitat.

Vale, L.J. (2006) 'The Urban Design of Twentieth Century Capitals', in D.L. Gordon (ed.), *Planning Twentieth Century Capital Cities*, London: Routledge, 15–37.

Veltz, P. (1996) Mondialisation, villes et territoires : une économie d'archipel, Paris, PUF.

Weil, M. (2005) 'Introduction: Contexts and Challenges for 21st Century Communities', in M. Weil (ed.), *The Handbook of Community Practice*, Thousand Oaks, CA: Sage Publications, 3–33.

Wine, J.C. (2003) 'Local Legislation', in J.D. Edwards (ed.), *Iowa Legal Research Guide*, New York: William S. Hein and Co.

Worthing, D. and S. Bond (2008) *Managing Built Heritage: The Role of Cultural Significance*, Oxford: Blackwell Publishing.

22

Road Transport and Agricultural Development in Himachal Pradesh

MANJIT SINGH

Conceptual Framework

Agriculture is one of the cornerstones of rural development in developing countries. For the agricultural sector to achieve its potential, investments in both hard and soft infrastructure are necessary. Since agriculture is the backbone of rural economy, effective links need to be established between this sector through judicious investment in both hard (road, canal, bank, etc.) and soft (e-governance) rural infrastructures. It is a proven fact that improved access to all-season roads enhances a positive influence in the development of rural areas. Further, better accessibility to towns has resulted in increase of agricultural production in many parts of the world. Thus, the provision of infrastructure is of great significance to overall regional development in general, and agricultural sector in particular, in rural areas. Agriculture, though a primary activity, is the most important sector in terms of employment and dependence of people for their livelihood in India. It is only during the past few decades that the industrial and service sectors have surpassed agricultural sector in terms of their contribution to the national economy. In spite of more than half of the workforce being employed in agriculture, the level of production is low in this sector. Many reasons are put forward but one among valid reasons is lack of transport accessibility, especially in rural and physically harsh regions.

The importance of access to better equipped transport has always been stressed but the greater need is that individuals should be able to make rational economic decisions. Economic problems of developing nations related to agriculture has emphasized on improvement of transport accessibility as an essential precondition of development. A great input of investment capital and production equipment now generally accelerates development, vis-à-vis, agricultural modernization. Thus, improvement in transport efficiency has commonly been recognized as an important factor conducive to agricultural development in developing countries. An improvement in connectivity through transport infrastructure enhances the mobility factors of production, brings about reduction in cost and time, and facilitates expansion of market operations. Easier access to markets allows area expansion under the production of perishable and transport-cost-intensive products. Timely marketing of perishable products allows better price discovery. The cumulative effects of infrastructure, accentuate the process of commercialization in agriculture and rural sector. Improved connectivity facilitates better access to social necessities like healthcare centres, education institutions and access to mainland in the case of isolated villages as shown from the evidences from Thailand. Investment in roads can also bring in new areas under cultivation and increased intensity of land use, composition of employment growth of agricultural output and bank expansion.

The importance of infrastructure for the development of rural areas needs hardly any emphasis. Provision of adequate and quality infrastructure in rural areas facilitate improvement in productivity and efficiency of capital in agriculture, improving the credit absorption capacity of the area, generating employment, increasing farmer's income, etc., besides improving the quality of people in the benefited areas. The ultimate results of the commercial farming will not be realized fully without the quality supporting infrastructure. It is estimated that 15 per cent of crops are lost between the farm gate and the consumer in the world because of poor roads and storage facilities. The issue relating to the role of rural roads in economic development remains largely unsettled. However, there is an agreed view that good rural roads are a necessary condition, for rural and overall economic development. Various study from Mexico, Philippines established improvement in economic, social and human service indicators as a result of improvement in rural roads. Hirschman points out that of all the instruments and strategies, provision of social overheads (infrastructure facilities) has come to be seen as the most effective means of initiating and sustaining growth at regional levels. In meeting the requirement of regional development, the importance of transport among the infrastructure, needs no emphasis. As the country's economy is still largely agrarian in character and the settlement pattern is rural oriented, roads constitute a critical element of the transportation infrastructure. In a way the roads are the only means of communications which can remove the rural isolation and reach every village in the country. Despite the fact that an extensive road network is essential, inadequacy in this respect continues to be significant. If we are to plan for road development programme, it is imperative to assess the requirements of different regions and try to remove the existing deficiencies.

Statement of the Problem

As a mountainous state with limited rail connections, no waterways, and only three small domestic airports, this State relies exclusively on its road network for transport. The total road network of Himachal Pradesh is 28,000 km in which National Highway contributes 20,000 km, state highway 2,160 km and district road 2,240 km. In this, half of the road is unpaved, 90 per cent of national highways are single lane and fewer than half of all villages are deemed connected. The road transport shows the dominance of underdeveloped national highway and needs further expansion and quality to link with higher centres of the country. Poor development and quality of state highway and district roads highlight the problem of inaccessibility of regional and rural areas, which in turn hampers flow of goods and services in the region effecting regional and rural economy. On the other hand agricultural production is also hampered due to transport inaccessibility since the region dominates in horticulture and floriculture which need better transport accessibility due to being perishable in nature. Transport inaccessibility is further enhanced due to high vulnerable conditions of natural disasters like landslides which block roads and reduces accessibility, which ultimately delays perishable goods from reaching the market in time. All this hampers regional economy in general, and rural economy in particular.

On the other hand, Himachal Pradesh is a hilly state where most of the people are agricultural dependent. Over 93 per cent of the population depends directly on agriculture. The physical features and climatic conditions of the region are not favourable for production of food grains; hence, the only option is to cultivate cash crops (Table 1). Other problems related with agriculture are lack of irrigation facilities, transport inaccessibility, lack of credit facilities, lack of effective post-harvesting and marketing system, lack of modern ways of cultivation, no proper agricultural research system and no attention for development of cultivable fallow land. Since agriculture is directly linked with rural economy, level of income of rural people in Himachal Pradesh is low which in turn affect their standard of living. Other problems of rural people are unemployment due to low level of agricultural development which further intensifies rural-urban migration. With lack of transport accessibility, and irrigation facilities, there is need of further land reforms for inclusive growth and development in the region. Thus, a comprehensive study is needed to assess transport accessibility and agricultural development in Himachal Pradesh.

The Study Area

The state of Himachal Pradesh is spread over an area of 55,673 km^2 and is bordered by Jammu and Kashmir in the north, Punjab on the south-west, Haryana on south, Uttarakhand on the south-east and by Tibet on the east. Himachal is a mountainous region, rich in its natural resources. Elevation ranges from 450 metres to 6,500 metres above mean sea level. There is an increase notified in the elevation from west to east and from south to north. The general physiographic divisions from south to north are the outer Himalayas (Shivaliks), the lesser Himalayas (central zone) and the Great Himalayas (northern zone). Himachal Pradesh is also well known for its rich flora. Forests cover about 38 per cent of the state's total area. Thus, the complex landscape hinders in development of transport network and creates accessibility problem for flow of goods and services in the region. In total, Himachal Pradesh has 49 cities and towns. The smallest town is Naina Devi and the largest is Shimla and has a total state population of about 6,077,248. Urban population is only 7.5 per cent of the total state population. Most of the state population still resides in rural areas. The state of Himachal Pradesh consists of 12 districts, total 372 roads under new connectivity with total length of 1,466.06 km were sanctioned for construction under Pradhan Mantri Gram Sadak Yojna (PMGSY). The total expenditure of this work is ₹ 1,574.23 lakhs. Around 250 roads with length of 23,335 km and 122 roads with total length of 1,444 km are completed works and ongoing works, respectively.

Table 1

Agro-Ecological Zones of Himachal Pradesh

Zone	*Area (% of total area)*	*Elevation (M)*	*Mean annual temperature(c)*	*Soil type*	*Rainfall (mm)*	*Important crops*
Subtropical and low hills	18.47	240–1,000	15–23	Loamy sandy	>1,500	Wheat, maize, paddy, pulses, barley, sugarcane and vegetables
Subhumid or mid-hills	8.37	1,001–1,500	14.2–22.1	Clay loam	>1500	Wheat, paddy, pulses, barley, and off-season vegetables
Wet temperate or high hills	16.55	1,501–3,250	9.1–20.6	Loamy acidic	>1500	Wheat, paddy, pulses, barley, oilseed and millets
Dry temperate or high hills	56.61	3,251–4,250	9–19.7	Sandy loam	<700	Wheat, potato, barley, oilseed, vegetables, kala zeera, saffron

Source: Directorate of Agriculture, Shimla.

Objective of Study

- To analyse progress of road transport and village-level connectivity in Himachal Pradesh.
- To analyse agricultural development in Himachal Pradesh.
- To analyse relationship between road transport and agriculture development.

Data Source and Methodology

Secondary data has been used in the study. The data sources include – Himachal Road Transport Corporation, Shimla, Public Works Department and Basic Road Statistics of Himachal Pradesh. For agriculture, data has been collected from Directorate of Agriculture, Horticulture Department and Economics and Statistics Department of Himachal Pradesh.

Data has been represented with the help of Tables and Figures. Correlation, regression, factor analysis and principal component analysis has been used here as a statistical method for data analyses.

Discussion and Results

Progress of Road Transport

Most transport (private or public, passenger or freight, and motorized or non-motorized) uses the road system. The road transport is growing at an unusual rate of 10–12 per cent per annum. A recent survey showed that road transport sector turnover (freight charges) is ₹ 70,000 crore per annum with 10,00,000 trucks travelling every day on roads. Serving a land area of 3.3 million square km and a population of one billion, India's transport system is one of the largest systems in the world. Road transport accounts for 80 per cent share of land transport demand. However, despite its importance, the road system is usually managed in a fragmented and uneconomic way. Decisions on the management, expansion and maintenance of the road networks are generally taken by a gamut of agencies at different hierarchy. The scene in Himachal Pradesh is no different; there are four agencies handling roads. The National Highways are looked after by the Government of India, the State Highways by the state PWD, town roads by the municipal bodies and rural roads partly by the PWD and partly by the rural development department. There is unfortunately no agency to coordinate between these controlling organizations which often work in a compartmentalized manner. The development of roads in the state has, there fore, been very slow and selective, both in terms of total road under various categories and also districtwise. Tables 2–5 highlight the above said facts.

PMGSY: Pradhan Mantri Gramin Sadak Yojana

The tables also clearly show the slow development of road under National highway, State highway and road under PMGSY which connect the villages. On the other hand major development of roads undertaken by the PWD in urban places has left most of the villages unconnected (also see Figure 1).

Figure 1

Himachal Pradesh: Connectivity of Villages

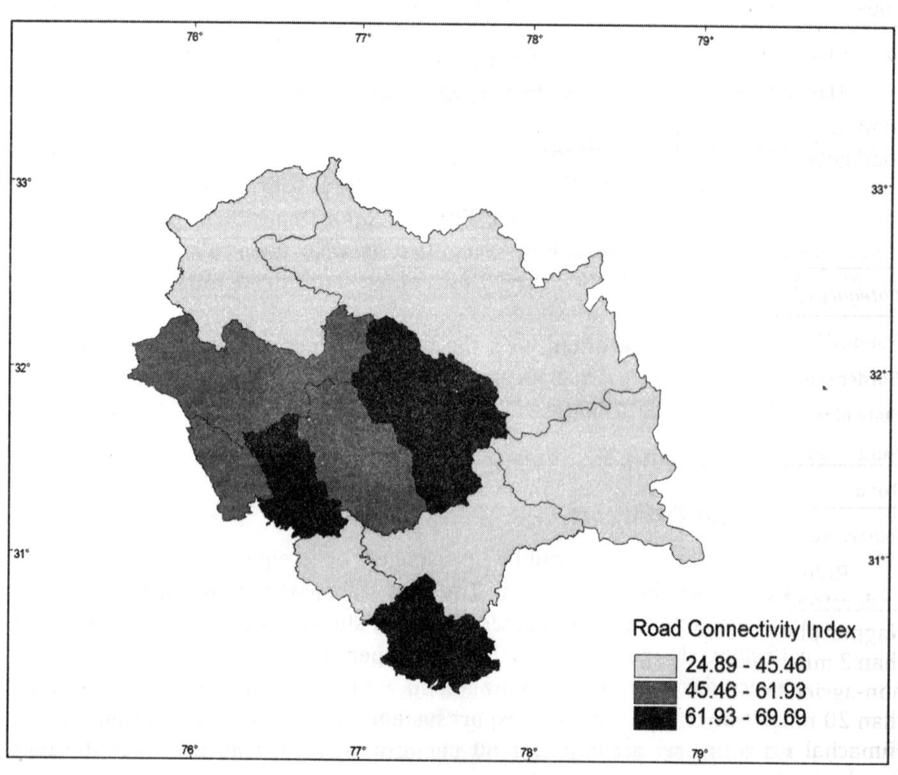

Table 2

Road Length in Himachal Pradesh

Years	Total road (TR) kms	Total national highway to TR (%)	Total state highway to TR (%)	Total PWD road to TR (%)	PMGSY to TR (%)
2004	32,582	3.70	4.65	77.75	0
2005	23,452	5.15	9.22	66.56	5.62
2006	23,614	5.11	9.16	66.10	11.34
2007	34,954	3.45	5.22	77.83	11.96
2008	36,298	3.32	5.03	78.31	15.81

Source: Public Works Department , Shimla.

Table 3

Road Quality in Himachal Pradesh

Year	National highway		State highway		PWD roads	
	Total	Surfaced	Total	Surfaced	Total	Surfaced
2004	1,208	1,208	1,518	1,365	25,331	13,487
2005	1,208	1,208	2,164	1,989	15,610	14,496
2006	1,208	1,208	2,164	1,989	15,610	14,496
2007	1,208	1,208	1,824	1,669	27,203	15,602
2008	1,208	1,208	1,824	1,669	28,428	16,390

Source: Basic road statistic of India, 2004–08.

Also, quality of road in the state demand greater attention, since most of the roads are single lane and are seasonal, especially rural roads. Over 90 per cent of the road network consists of single lane roads.

Table 4

Category of Roads in Himachal Pradesh

Category of road	Single lane	Double lane	Total
National highway	486	749	1,235
Border roads	422	269	691
State highways	901	617	1,518
Rural roads	19,291	701	19,992
Total	21,100	2,336	23,452

Source: Public Works Department, Shimla.

Role of transport accessibility in agriculture development has been very well understood by earlier planners, who define transport accessibility according to Nagpur plan "that in a highly developed agricultural area no village should be more than 2 miles away from a road or more than 5 miles from a main road. Similarly, in a non-agricultural region no village should be more than 5 miles from a road, or more than 20 miles from a main road. Going by the definition, most of the villages in the Himachal Pradesh are unconnected which posts a big problem for agricultural development (Figure 1 and Table 5).

There are various issues related with development of road transport in Himachal Pradesh. Firstly, due to hilly terrain, per kilometre expenditure on roads in the state is far higher than the plains, thus there is always inadequacy of funds. Apart from this, lack of technical capacity for construction and high cost of construction are major issues.

Table 5

Districtwise Connectivity of Villages

Name of district	*No. villages*	*No. connected village*	*No. unconnected village*
Bilaspur	962	673	289
Chamba	1,113	506	607
Hamirpur	1,634	1,101	533
Kangra	3,614	2,228	1,376
Kinnaur	233	58	175
Kullu	172	115	57
Lahaul & Spiti	284	125	159
Mandi	2,823	1,580	1,243
Shimla	2,515	992	1,523
Sirmour	966	634	332
Solan	2,378	1,072	1,306
Una	755	448	307

Source: Public Works Department, Shimla.

Agriculture Development in Himachal Pradesh

Himachal Pradesh's agriculture is a very crucial part of the state's economy as it is the chief occupation of the people. The agricultural sector of the Himachal Pradesh has more than 45 per cent contribution to its economy in terms of the state's domestic product. About 93 per cent of the state population depends directly upon agriculture. Agriculture in Himachal Pradesh provides employment to around 71 per cent of the working population in the state. The agricultural and the allied sector generate revenue of nearly 22.5 per cent of the gross State Domestic Product. The farming community of the state holds an area of 9.99 lakh hectares which is run by 8.63 lakh farmers, out of the total geographical area of 55.673 lakh hectares. Around 84.5 per cent of the total land held by the farming community of Himachal Pradesh is owned by the small and marginal farmers. Only 10.4 per cent of the area of the state is cultivated and about 80 per cent of the area experiences rainfall (see Figure 2).

The entire population of the state, more or less, depends directly upon the agriculture of Himachal Pradesh. The major portion of the revenue earning in the state's economy is carried out by the cash crops in the Himachal Pradesh agriculture. The chief food crops cultivated in Himachal Pradesh agriculture include wheat, maize, rice, barley, seed-potato, ginger, vegetables, vegetable seeds, mushrooms, chicory seeds, hops, olives, and figs. Himachal Pradesh is also known as the 'Apple State of India' for its large-scale production of fruits. Farmers have engaged themselves highly in the fruit cultivation and it is also a great blessing to the economy of the state. Some very important factors that have led to the outstanding

Figure 2

Himachal Pradesh: Cropping Intensity

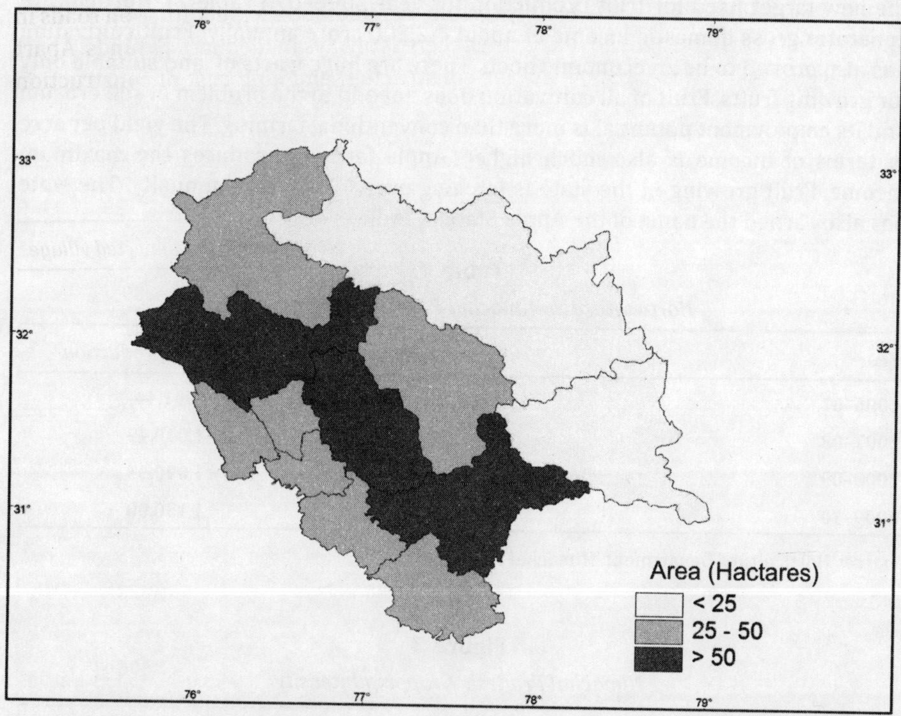

development in the agriculture of Himachal Pradesh are an efficient irrigation system, accessibility of low-cost cargo, and marketing facilities structured in an organized form. The main cereals cultivated in Himachal Pradesh agriculture are wheat, maize, rice, and barley. Kangra, Mandi district and to some extent Paonta valley of Sirmur district are the major producers of wheat, maize, and rice. Barley is cultivated largely in Shimla district of Himachal Pradesh. The main sources of irrigation in Himachal Pradesh are small water channels that are filled from the perennial and seasonal springs.

Table 6

Production of Principal Crops (,000 tonnes)

Crop	*2006–07*	*2007–08*	*2008–09*	*2009–10*
Total cereals	1,457.47	1,404.70	1,361.00	936.99
Total Pulses	19.00	35.96	38.56	19.39
Total food grain	1,476.47	1,440.66	1,399.56	956.38

Source: Directorate of Agriculture, Himachal Pradesh.

Nature has endowed Himachal Pradesh with a wide range of agro-climatic conditions, which have helped the farmers to cultivate large varieties of fruits and vegetables ranging from temperate to subtropical. The main fruits under cultivation are apple, pear, peach, plum, apricot nut and citrus fruits like mango, litchi, guava and strawberry. The total area under fruits, which was only 792 hectares in 1950, has increased to 2.23 lakh hectares now. Similarly, the fruit production has also increased from 1,200 MT in 1950 to 6.95 lakh tonnes in 2007 seven lakh tonnes is the new target fixed for fruit production for year 2006–07 (Table 7). Horticulture generates gross domestic income of about ₹ 2,200 crore annually. Fruit cultivation has also proved to be an economic boon. There are huge tracts of land suitable only for growing fruits. Fruit of all cultivation does not add to the problem of soil erosion and its employment potential is more than conventional farming. The yield per acre in terms of income is also much higher. Apple farming produces the maximum income. Fruit growing in the state is fetching over ₹ 300 crore annually. The state has also earned the name of the Apple State of India.

Table 7

Horticulture in Himachal Pradesh (,000 tonnes)

Year	*Fruits production*	*Vegetables production*
2006–07	369.10	991.44
2007–08	712.84	1,040.49
2008–09	628.08	1,090.33
2009–10	331.16	1,130.00

Source: Horticulture Department, Himachal Pradesh.

Figure 3

Himachal Pradesh: Cropping Intensity

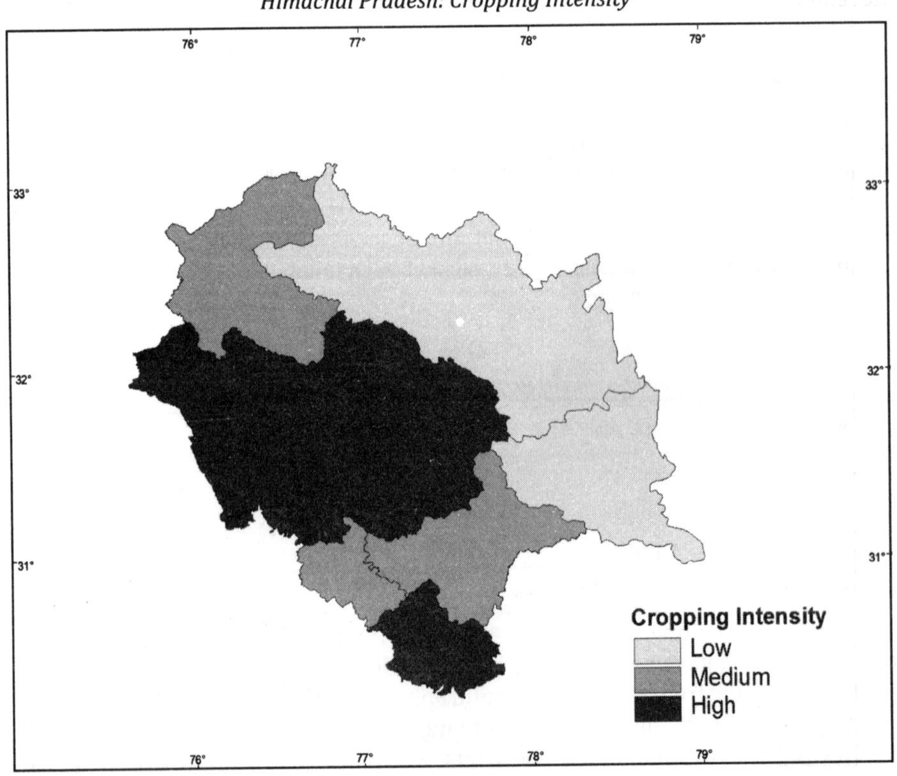

Himachal Pradesh is going through a phase of agricultural transformation. It has been noticed that agricultural land use has started changing. New crops are sown in place of traditional crops. Farmers are using more fertilizers and HYV seeds which has increased cropping intensity (Table 8). Production is directed towards market demand at various scales.

Recently, agriculture development in Himachal Pradesh has moved to next level where generic expansion has been replaced by genetic expansion. Use of fertilizers and HYV seed has increased, leading to modernization of agriculture.

Table 8

Himachal Pradesh: Agricultural Inputs

Years	*Fertilizers (MT)*	*Area under HYV seeds (Ha)*
2004	46,253	665.16
2005	47,973	671.26
2006	48,981	690.23
2007	49,958	702.86
2008	57,363	685.96

Source: Directorate of Agriculture, Himachal Pradesh.

Agriculture transformation is a holistic and comprehensive approach for agricultural development. And since majority of rural population depends upon agriculture sector, agricultural transformation can act as a milestone for rural development. Today agriculture transformation is seen as a panacea for rural development and in reduction of rural poverty. Having a large rural population and

Figure 4

Himachal Pradesh: Rural Poverty

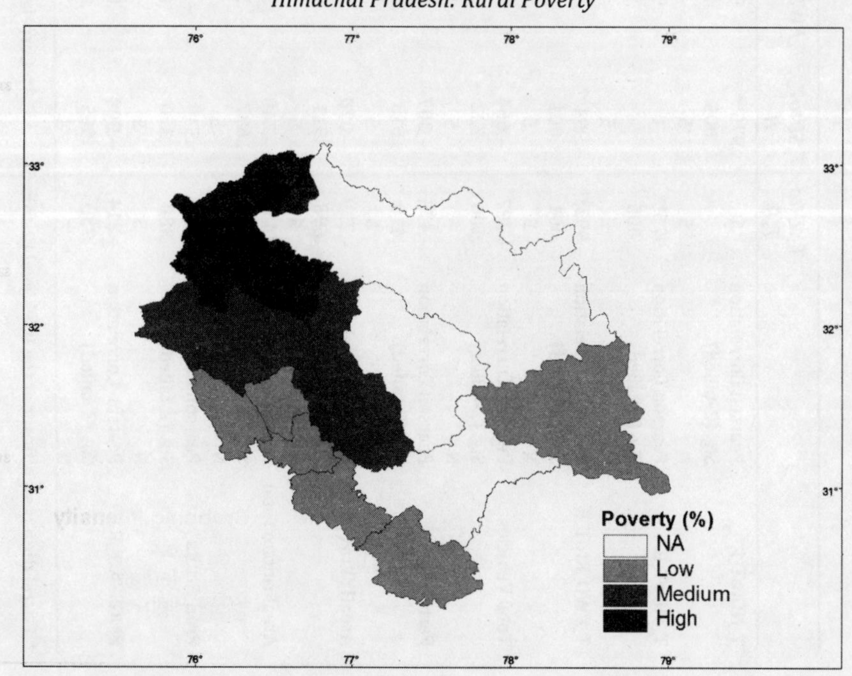

Table 9

Correlation Analysis

		T_NHto T_R	*T_SHtoT_ R*	*T_PWD_RtoT_R*	*Total vehicle*	*Fertilizers*	*AreaHYV to total*	*Area fruits to total*	*Prod_fruits*	*PMGSY to T_R*
T_NHtoT_R	Pearson Correlation	1	.975**	–.992**	–.797	–.475	–.239	–.446	.510	–.214
	Sig. (2-tailed)		.005	.001	.106	.419	.698	.452	.380	.730
	N	5	5	5	5	5	5	5	5	5
T_SHtoT_R	Pearson Correlation	.975**	1	–.994**	–.664	–.307	–.070	–.240	.519	–.004
	Sig. (2-tailed)	.005		.001	.222	.615	.911	.697	.370	.995
	N	5	5	5	5	5	5	5	5	5
T_PWD_RtoT_R	Pearson Correlation	–.992**	–.994**	1	.725	.376	.136	.326	–.528	.086
	Sig. (2-tailed)	.001	.001		.166	.533	.827	.592	.360	.891
	N	5	5	5	5	5	5	5	5	5
Total Vehicles	Pearson Correlation	–.797	–.664	.725	1	.904*	.394	.806	–.078	.668
	Sig. (2-tailed)	.106	.222	.166		.035	.512	.100	.901	.218
	N	5	5	5	5	5	5	5	5	5
Fertilizers	Pearson Correlation	–.475	–.307	.376	.904*	1	.403	.859	.282	.833
	Sig. (2-tailed)	.419	.615	.533	.035		.501	.062	.646	.080
	N	5	5	5	5	5	5	5	5	5
AreaHYVtoTotal	Pearson Correlation	–.239	–.070	.136	.394	.403	1	.808	–.446	.793
	Sig. (2-tailed)	.698	.911	.827	.512	.501		.098	.451	.109
	N	5	5	5	5	5	5	5	5	5
AreaFruitstoTotal	Pearson Correlation	–.446	–.240	.326	.806	.859	.808	1	–.095	.963**
	Sig. (2-tailed)	.452	.697	.592	.100	.062	.098		.879	.008
	N	5	5	5	5	5	5	5	5	5
Prod_Fruits	Pearson Correlation	.510	.519	–.528	–.078	.282	–.446	–.095	1	.099
	Sig. (2-tailed)	.380	.370	.360	.901	.646	.451	.879		.874
	N	5	5	5	5	5	5	5	5	5
PMGSYtoT_R	Pearson Correlation	–.214	–.004	.086	.668	.833	.793	.963**	.099	1
	Sig. (2-tailed)	.730	.995	.891	.218	.080	.109	.008	.874	
	N	5	5	5	5	5	5	5	5	5

* Correlation is significant at the 0.05 level (2-tailed). ** Correlation is significant at the 0.01 level (2-tailed).

agriculture as its main occupation, agriculture transformation can reduce rural poverty in Himachal Pradesh (Figure 4).

Relationship between Road Transport and Agriculture Development

In this case study it is assumed that road transport plays a key role in agriculture development. Here, road transport is considered as a lead sector for agriculture development. Thus, the hypothesis is "Progress in Road transport leads to Agriculture development". Certain statistical methods have been used to test the hypothesis by taking road transport as independent variable and agriculture as dependent variable.

Finding and Conclusions

From the regression analysis it is found that the value of dependent variable is completely determined by the independent variables. From the model summary it is found that model taken is fully significant. The value of correlation is perfect positive. The R square, i.e., the degree of determination is also 1 which means the value of dependent variable is completely determined by the independent variables. The t test shows that each variable has significant bearing on the value of the dependent variable. Thus, the hypothesis is accepted (see Table 9).

National highway (NH) and State highway (SH) have positive and significant relationship at 5 per cent significance level. The relationship between NH and PWD roads is found to be negative and significant. It means with the increase in the one the other decreases. Same way State highway is positively correlated with NH and fruit production, and negatively with PWD road and other variables. PWD roads have positive relationship with total fertilizers used, area under HYV seeds, fruit production and total vehicle. Total vehicle is positively correlated with PWD roads, fertilizers used, area under HYV seeds, area under fruit production and PMGSY. Use of fertilizers is directly correlated with PWD roads, total vehicle, area under fruits, fruits production and PMGSY. Area under HYV seeds is positively correlated with PWD roads, total vehicle, fertilizers used and PMGSY. And the most important finding is there is positive relationship between PMGSY and all variable except NH and SH (Table 9).

Coefficients of variation have been calculated from descriptive statistics. The formula is standard deviation divided by mean into 100. The CV shows the degree of variation in the data. The lower the variation, higher is the reliability of data.

From the factor analysis, effort is made to find the variables having impact on the level of agricultural development in the state. The initial value 1 means that each variable is contributing equally to the agricultural development. The extraction values shows which variable has more influence on agricultural development. These values are communalities which is a sum of square of Eigen vector values of each variable. The extraction value of each of the variables is very close to 1. The derivation of these values is understood by Eigen values and Eigen vector values. As there are 9 variables the number of Eigen values are 9. The Principal Component Analysis method is used in deriving factors or components. The first component accounts for 5.05 out of 9 or 56.1 per cent variance in agricultural development. The second, accounts for 28.8 per cent variance individually and together both accounts for 84.9 per cent. The third, accounts for 14.4 per cent variance in agricultural development. Together these three components explain 99.4 per cent variance. Now the question is, these components accounts for which variable. For this, we have to consider the component matrix. The component matrix explains the correlation of each variable with a factor or a component. From Table 9 it is found that factor 1 has accounted for total vehicles, area under fruits, fertilizers, PWD roads. Factor 2 comprises of SH, NH, PMGSY roads. Factor 3 includes production of fruits.

Acceptance of hypothesis proves that there is strong relationship between road transport and agriculture development. Thus, it is very clear that development of road transport is a precondition for development of agriculture in Himachal Pradesh.

References

Ahuja, A. (2006) *Agriculture and Rural Development in India*, New Delhi: New Century Publications.

Berry, B.J.L. (1966) 'Essays on Commodity Flow and Spatial Structure of Indian Economy', Research Paper No. 111, Department of Geography, University of Chicago.

Gautam, P.S. (1992) *Transport Geography of India: A Study of Chambal Division, Madhya Pradesh*, New Delhi: Mittal Publications.

Mishra, B.N. and S.N. Tripathi (1991) 'The Level of Transport Development in Basti District', *Geographical Review of India*, 53(1): 24–35.

Mohammad, N. (1981) *Perspectives in Agriculture Geography*, New Delhi: Concept.

23

Delimiting Road Transport Regions and Its Impact on Regional Development of Gaya District

KRISHNA KUMAR AND ANJAN SEN

The quality of life and socio-economic conditions of living of people may get significantly affected by the speed and ease with which they can move and carry their goods. In this sense, transport and economic development are interdependent and their relationship is both complex and dynamic. Briefly, transport promotes access to markets, materials and opportunities by facilitating movements of persons and goods and improves earning and thereby, level of living. This in turn enhances the demand for transport. This two-way interaction working through a host of inter-sectoral forward and backward linkage effects and dynamic externalities, tends to relocate industries, services and labour and thus helps to shape the economic geography of a region.

The ultimate aim of development activities, including those relating to transport infrastructure, is to promote societal welfare. However, due to the existing pattern of socio-economic structure, geopolitical and historical features, etc., the benefits of development are often not shared equitably and a variety of distributional inequalities show up at all levels – local, regional, or national. The greater part of the society often receives little or none of the benefits of development. Typically, this segment consists of the poor who mostly live in rural areas of the developing world.

Development of transport facility like road infrastructure, can, however, play a significant role in changing the socio-economic conditions of living of the people of a region through dynamic externalities that such development often generates. It can, in fact, be an important element of both direct and indirect interventions for poverty reduction and improvement of socio-economic conditions of the people. However, there has been little assessment of the socio-economic impact of an infrastructural project like construction/widening of a highway. It is, however, now being increasingly realized that the socio-economic impact analysis with a thrust on distributional issues like poverty reduction should be made to see how important the role of a transport or a ground infrastructural project may be in bringing about the distributional justice (Levy, 1996; Baker, 2000).

Recently, India has embarked upon a programme of upgrading the national highway network connecting the four metropolis and the major maritime ports of the country. This involves massive public investments. Side by side, the country also carries a crushing load of poverty, which is more pronounced in the rural areas. According to the latest estimates, more than one-fourth of the Indian rural population lives below the official poverty line (Deaton and Dreze, 2002). It would, therefore, be worthwhile to examine the socio-economic impact of such massive public investment schemes.

The Study Area

Geographically and culturally, Gaya was a part of ancient Magadha region of Bihar. Located between 84°4' to 85°5' E longitudes and 24°5' to 25°1' N latitudes, it is 100 kilometres south of Patna. It has an area of 4,856.46 sq km and a population of 3,473,428 in 2001. The district of Gaya is broadly divided into two distinct geographical units. The southern part is a hilly region with a wide belt of brushwood jungle at its base, while the northern part consists of mostly flat alluvial plain. Administratively, the district is divided into two sub-divisions and 24 Blocks. The town of Gaya is regarded as an important place of pilgrimage by the Hindus all over India. Pilgrims from far and near come to offer oblations to their deceased forefathers. Bodh Gaya is an internationally renowned place where Lord Buddha attained enlightenment more than 2,500 years ago.

Data Base and Methodology

This study is based on secondary data which has been collected from the government departments like Survey of India (Govt. of India), Road Construction Department (Govt. of Bihar), Regional Transport Office (Govt. of Bihar), Department of Education (Govt. of Bihar), Department of Health (Govt. of Bihar), Banking Statistics Handbook (Govt. of Bihar), Directorate of Statistics and Evaluation (Govt. of Bihar), Department of Water Resource (Govt. of Bihar). Statistical techniques like composite index, weightage and normalization (Z-Square) has been used to develop a regional development index. Graph theory, Buffering and Overlay method has been used with the help of various GIS and computer software like Arc GIS and Erdas to process and analyse the data for delimiting road transport region, while overlay technique has been used to analyse the relationship between road transport and regional development.

Road Transport Regions

Transport regions are the functional regions in which there is some homogeneity of attributes of transportation. Delineating a transport region is an invariable step to give a composite view of homogeneity and heterogeneity.

Road transport region has been delineated with the help of composite index method. Firstly, the four indicators: (i) percentage of registered vehicles, (ii) total road density per unit area, (iii) cyclomatic number and (iv) percentage of area accessible by surfaced roads has been selected and then they have been given weightage according to their importance with respect to transport region (Table 1–3). After giving weightage, the values of all the four indicators have been converted into a unit free value, as indicators used for delineating transport region having different units.

So in order to obtain figures which are free from units and have standardized units, normalization technique is used, which is based on the following formula:

$$x_{ij} = \frac{X_{ij} - \underset{i}{Min}\{X_{ij}\}}{\underset{i}{Max}\{X_{ij}\} - \underset{i}{Max}\{X_{ij}\}}$$

The collected data has been arranged in the form of a rectangular matrix with rows representing regions and columns representing indicators. Where *Xij* be the value of the indicator *j* corresponding to block *i*. In the second step, normalization of indicators using functional relationship has been done. It is obvious that the indicators will be in different units and scales. The methodology used in UNDP's Human Development Index (HDI) (UNDP, 2006) will be followed to normalize them. That is, in order to obtain figures which are free from the units and also to standardize their values, first they are normalized so that they all lie between 0 and 1. Normalization technique converts the value of indicators under the range from 0 to 1. Value close to 1 means high road transport region, while value closer to 0 means less road transport region. On the basis of normalized value the district has been divided into three transport regions. The three regions are as follows (Figure 1):

1. High Road Transport Region,
2. Medium Road Transport Region, and
3. Low Road Transport Region.

High-level road transport region is mainly concentrated at the centre, north-west, east and towards south direction of the district. It is because these regions mainly lie on the stretch of national highways and state highways. It is also because all the four towns of Gaya district (Gaya, Bodh Gaya, Sherghati and Tikari) lie in these directions and thus naturally have higher numbers of registered vehicles, high road density and area accessible by surfaced road. Medium level of road transport region is mainly concentrated in the extremely south-west, east and towards north direction. The reason is that it also lies on the stretch of national highways, state highways and major district roads. As most of its part lies in the rural and underdeveloped blocks of the region so it had less vehicle registration in comparison to the high transport region. However, low-level road transport region is mainly concentrated towards south-east and north-east direction which are mainly underdeveloped and rural in characteristics. It is also because the region is Naxal affected and devoid of surfaced roads due to hilly area. Besides being poor, these regions have low population concentration and low road density and thus results in low percentage of registered vehicles.

Table 1

Weightage Table

S. No.	*Indicators*	*Weight*
1.	Total road density per unit area	4
2.	Percentage of area accessible by surfaced road	3
3.	Cyclomatic Number	2
4.	Percentage of registered vehicles	1

Figure 1

Gaya: Road Transport Regions

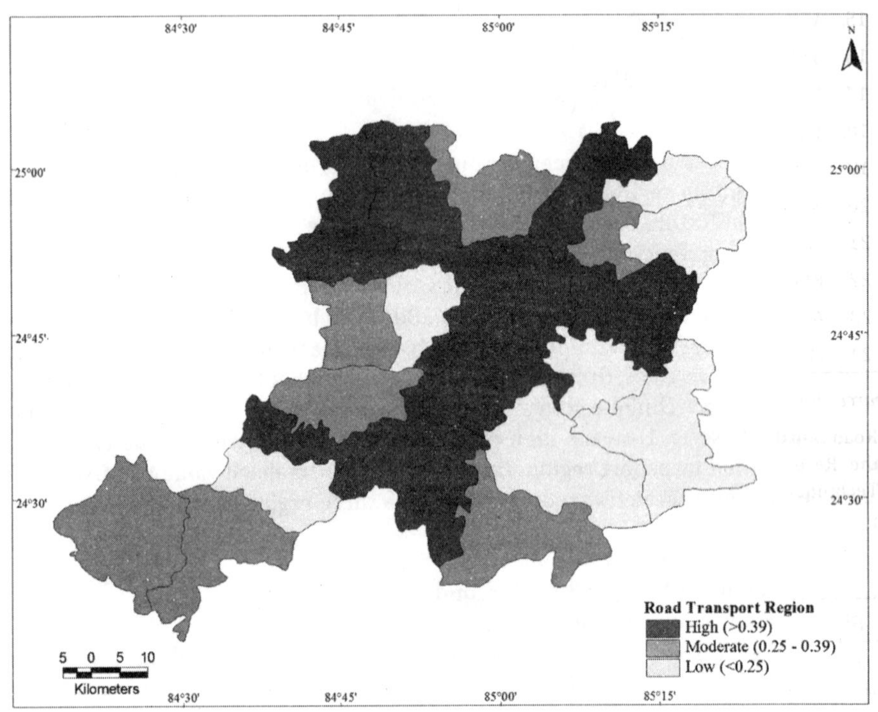

Table 2

Indicators of Road Transport Region

S. No.	*Block*	*Total road density*	*% of registered vehicle*	*Cyclomatic number*	*Area accessible by surfaced road (in %)*
1.	Dumaria	78.32	1.59	8	21.06
2.	Imamganj	66.82	1.75	14	32.31
3.	Banke Bazar	50.71	2.17	14	42.11
4.	Amas	114.61	1.74	4	83.94
5.	Gurua	89.25	1.09	4	45.15
6.	Guraru	75.97	1.91	10	58.38
7.	Konch	68.79	1.71	10	92.45
8.	Tikari	66.51	5.44	12	77.30
9.	Belaganj	51.66	2.29	7	74.10
10.	Sherghati	69.54	7.24	2	73.74
11.	Dhobi	79.72	2.29	4	71.31
12.	Barachatti	64.68	1.71	6	37.39
13.	Mohanpur	76.38	1.76	1	29.97

Cont'd...

Cont'd...

14. Fatehpur	65.51	1.99	5	44.40
15. Wazirganj	73.55	2.34	8	87.97
16. Tankuppa	69.75	2.22	1	62.02
17. Bodhgaya	61.73	16.67	9	62.08
18. Paraiya	67.71	2.75	1	77.48
19. Gaya	109.86	31.31	14	125.74
20. Neemchak Bathani	77.91	1.98	1	17.51
21. Mohra	63.73	1.33	3	57.38
22. Khizirsarai	95.85	1.88	11	84.48
23. Atri	62.56	1.31	2	93.07
24. Manpur	87.91	3.53	9	106.63

Source: Regional Transport office (Govt. of Bihar),

* Road Density, Cyclomatic Number and Area accessible by Surfaced Road have been calculated by the Researcher with the help of Digitization, Geo-refrencing, Graph Theory and Buffering Technique.

Table 3

Components of Road Transport Region Index

Block	*Vehicle index*	*Road density index*	*Cyclomatic number index*	*Surfaced area index*
Amas	0.06	1.00	0.23	0.61
Atri	0.06	0.19	0.08	0.70
Banke Bazar	0.06	0.00	1.00	0.23
Barachatti	0.04	0.22	0.38	0.18
Belaganj	0.03	0.01	0.46	0.52
Bodh Gaya	0.44	0.17	0.62	0.41
Dobhi	0.05	0.45	0.23	0.50
Dumaria	0.04	0.43	0.54	0.03
Fatehpur	0.02	0.23	0.31	0.25
Gaya	1.00	0.93	1.00	1.00
Guraru	0.04	0.40	0.69	0.38
Gurua	0.00	0.60	0.23	0.26
Imamganj	0.02	0.25	1.00	0.14
Khizirsarai	0.03	0.71	0.77	0.62
Konch	0.02	0.28	0.69	0.69
Manpur	0.11	0.58	0.62	0.82
Mohanpur	0.02	0.40	0.00	0.12
Muhra	0.04	0.20	0.15	0.37
Neemchak	0.08	0.43	0.00	0.00
Paraiya	0.11	0.27	0.00	0.55
Sherghati	0.33	0.29	0.08	0.52
Tankuppa	0.07	0.30	0.00	0.41
Tikari	0.09	0.25	0.85	0.55
Wazirganj	0.03	0.36	0.54	0.65

Indicators of Regional Development

While the Millennium Development Goals (MDGs) do not include specific references to transport, it is now widely accepted that transport infrastructure and services play a critical role in addressing the MDGs. Transport infrastructure and services provide physical access to domestic and international markets as well as jobs, thereby increasing people's potential to increase income and consumption levels. This allows them to accumulate private and social assets, which in turn can increase their productivity and reduce their vulnerability to shocks. A recent study on the impact of one section of the National Highway No. 2 in India on rural populations showed, for example, that the construction of the highway resulted in an increase in non-farm activities, higher workforce participation, an increase in school enrolment and better literacy levels, although the impact varied across different groups and areas (Asian Institute of Transport Development, 2010).

Transport infrastructure and services also facilitate access to schools, medical clinics, hospitals, cultural and religious institutions, and other facilities which contribute to their capabilities (MDGs 2, 3, 4 and 5). In some countries, such as Fiji and Nauru, free or subsidized bus and van services are provided to school children as part of the government's policies to achieve MDG Goal 2, Universal primary education. Conversely, the lack of or inadequacy of such infrastructure and services affects the ability and willingness of teachers and medical staff to access remote or isolated communities, and also increases the cost of supplying educational and medical supplies (UNICEF, 2005).

To analyse the regional development, seven socio-economic indicators have been taken into consideration. The seven indicators are as follows:

1. Total road density per unit area,
2. Irrigation facilities,
3. Drinking water facilities,
4. Banking facilities,
5. Education facilities,
6. Electrification, and
7. Medical facilities

The values of selected indicators are normalized using Z-Square technique to remove their respective units (Table 4).

Road Transport Region and Regional Development

The pattern and the degree of development of transport network in any area is a factor of crucial significance influencing political, economic and social progress and these must be considered in every stage of national and regional development planning for as Munby (1971) said "there is no escape from transport" since whether it be in western city or oriental village, the daily rhythm of life is closely geared to it. There is a general agreement that transport is vital to development, although there is no consensus with respect to its impact under differing economic and social environment. The knowledge on adequacy or otherwise of transport system is also important in enhancing or inhibiting effective realization of various regional development policies, especially those requiring decentralization of activities, involving movement of people and goods. Widespread growth of the region may be promoted or otherwise, and to some extent, regional inequalities in development can be addressed when there is adequate linkages among the regions, as good transport system may be an impetus to even development and growth. Inadequacy or absence of transport facilities may undermine the productive process. Ahmed et al. (1976), cited in Button (1993) aptly remarked that inadequacy of transport facilities is one of the bottlenecks to socio-economic development and national integration in many developing countries.

Transport infrastructure has been viewed as perhaps the prime mover in the analysis of spatial structure and functions. It has been argued, for instance, that where good quality roads exist, it allows government and private companies the access into the remote areas for the establishment of social amenities. Consequently, areas with good state of transport infrastructure tend to benefit more from the provision of social amenities than their counterparts with bad road conditions (Obot and Okpiliya, 2002). Taking these facts into consideration, transport infrastructure should be accorded priority in the catalogue of development projects by the administrative machinery of any country meant to transform the living conditions of the rural people. Transportation development is necessary due to spatial inequalities, which in turn necessitates the need for spatial interaction. Accessibility is a measure of the spatial relationship and it is therefore an essential part of the development process. Spatial connection is frequently related and reflected in the character of transportation facilities as well as in the flow of goods and services (Umoren, Atser and Ekong, 2004). In a modern society, a functional and efficient transport system has become imperative for socio-economic growth and development. The absence or inadequacy of these infrastructures will result in a retarded development.

Regional development of Gaya has been analysed with the help of the seven socio-indicators which has been mentioned earlier. A composite index map of the seven indicators has been made and overlaid on the map of road transport region. Overlaying of composite index map on the map of road transport region gives a bi-variant map of road transport region and regional development of the district. On the basis of this bi-variant map, a matrix table has been made to divide the region into nine categories. These nine categories have been further divided in the district into three categories. The three categories are as follows:

1. High,
2. Medium, and
3. Low.

From Figure 2 it is clear that road transport and development have a positive relation. In the map of road transport and regional development we can see that, generally, wherever level of transport region is high, there the development is also high. Similarly, wherever level of transport region is low, there the development is also low.

To make the matrix table (Figure 3) simple, nine categories of matrix table has been categorized into three categories. The three categories are as follows:

1. High = High (RTR) + High (D) and Moderate (RTR) + Moderate (D)
2. Moderate = Moderate (RTR) + Moderate (D), Low (RTR) + High (D) and High (RTR) + Low (D)
3. Low = Low (RTR) + Low (D), Low (RTR) + Moderate (D) and Moderate (RTR) + Low (D)

From the matrix table it has been noted that there are eleven blocks (Gaya, Bodh Gaya, Sherghati, Tikari, Manpur, Amas, Dobhi, Konch, Wazirganj, Khizirsarai and Guraru) which lies in the category of high. Similarly four blocks (Gurua, Atri, Belaganj and Paraiya) lies in the category of moderate. While, nine blocks (Dumaria, Imamganj, Barachatti, Neemchak Bathani, Fatehpur, Mohanpur, Tankuppa, Muhra and Banke Bazar) lies in the category of low.

From the matrix table it is quite clear that road transport is a prerequisite condition for development and growth. Thus, it also advocates that the development of road transport results in improvement of socio-economic infrastructural facilities and development of road transport is complementary to regional development.

Table 4

Indicators of Regional Development

Block	*Education (units per lakh)*	*Medical (units per 10,000)*	*Drinking water (sources per 10000)*	*Banking (bank per 10000*	*Irrigated area (percentage)*	*Vehicles (units per 10000)*	*Electrification (percentage of villages electrified)*
Amas	65	64	35	23	62.63	293.36	5.88
Atri	87	54	24	17	68.32	272.95	1.64
Banke Bazar	64	58	28	19	41.68	295.55	9.09
Barachatti	52	82	37	25	36.93	208.06	0.63
Belaganj	82	32	20	13	32.12	176.63	28.81
Bodh Gaya	62	56	29	17	72.28	1,466.79	82.73
Dobhi	70	68	33	21	60.74	265.70	16.15
Dumaria	87	60	35	23	21.71	217.61	4.03
Fatehpur	64	60	27	17	44.52	147.24	4.55
Gaya	62	43	20	13	62.23	3,222.53	87.36
Guraru	81	44	21	14	64.88	233.29	3.53
Gurua	92	68	38	24	74.78	98.14	11.54
Imamganj	73	79	37	24	49.39	157.57	5.13
Khizirsarai	85	37	22	14	61.51	180.38	0.00
Konch	72	52	27	16	57.38	150.48	17.52
Manpur	96	44	22	14	70.15	445.65	82.05
Mohanpur	72	96	40	26	33.32	148.75	5.63
Muhra	92	38	20	13	68.86	236.42	5.56
Neemchak	70	36	15	10	65.58	343.17	4.76
Paraiya	98	50	27	18	72.02	450.72	11.76
Sherghati	63	53	29	19	78.90	1,118.22	51.16
Tankuppa	73	81	32	21	50.50	327.45	1.98
Tikari	82	47	25	16	66.62	388.31	20.00
Wazirganj	72	52	23	16	49.42	179.86	24.49

Source: Various Departments of Government of Bihar.

Table 5

Regional Development Indices

Block	*Education index*	*Medical index*	*Water index*	*Banking index*	*Irrigation index*	*Power index*	*Composite index*
Amas	0.09	0.25	0.37	0.38	0.41	0.07	0.33
Atri	0.23	0.17	0.17	0.20	0.46	0.02	0.23
Banke Bazar	0.08	0.21	0.25	0.26	0.20	0.10	0.19
Barachatti	0.00	0.39	0.41	0.43	0.15	0.01	0.25
Belaganj	0.20	0.00	0.10	0.09	0.10	0.33	0.14
Bodh Gaya	0.06	0.19	0.27	0.21	0.50	0.95	0.44
Dobhi	0.12	0.28	0.32	0.31	0.39	0.18	0.31
Dumaria	0.23	0.22	0.36	0.36	0.00	0.05	0.24
Fatehpur	0.08	0.22	0.23	0.21	0.23	0.05	0.19
Gaya	0.07	0.09	0.09	0.09	0.40	1.00	0.51
Guraru	0.19	0.09	0.11	0.12	0.43	0.04	0.20
Gurua	0.27	0.28	0.43	0.40	0.53	0.13	0.38
Imamganj	0.14	0.37	0.41	0.40	0.28	0.06	0.18
Khizirsarai	0.22	0.04	0.13	0.13	0.40	0.00	0.20
Konch	0.13	0.16	0.23	0.17	0.35	0.20	0.23
Manpur	0.29	0.10	0.13	0.13	0.48	0.94	0.40
Mohanpur	0.14	0.50	0.47	0.46	0.12	0.06	0.17
Muhra	0.27	0.04	0.09	0.09	0.47	0.06	0.19
Neemchak	0.12	0.03	0.00	0.00	0.44	0.05	0.15
Paraiya	0.31	0.14	0.23	0.24	0.50	0.13	0.29
Sherghati	0.07	0.17	0.26	0.25	0.57	0.59	0.39
Tankuppa	0.14	0.38	0.31	0.31	0.29	0.02	0.27
Tikari	0.20	0.12	0.19	0.17	0.45	0.23	0.25
Wazirganj	0.13	0.16	0.16	0.17	0.28	0.28	0.22

Source: Computed by Author.

Figure 2

Gaya: Road Transport Region and Regional Development

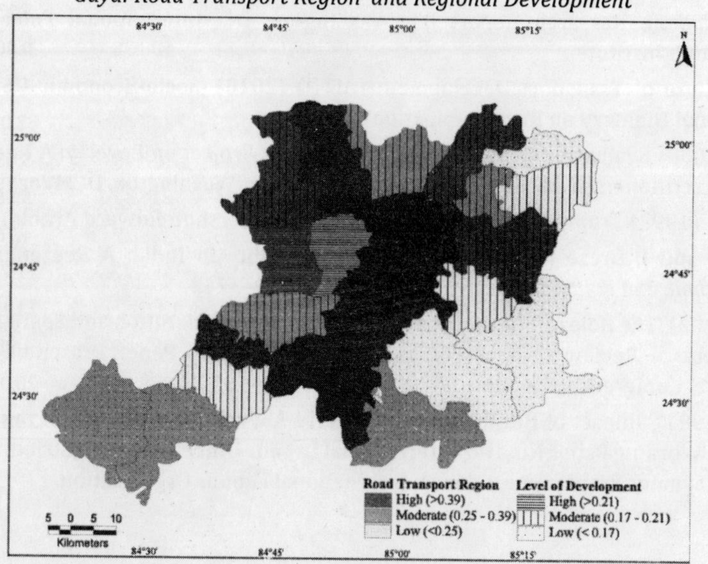

Figure 3

Road Transport Region and Regional Development Matrix

		High	*Moderate*	*Low*
Development	High	Gaya, Bodh Gaya, Sherghati, Tikari, Manpur, Amas, Dobhi	Guraru	Paraiya
	Moderate	Konch, Wazirganj, Khizirsarai	Gurua, Atri, Belaganj	Tankuppa, Banke - Bazar, Muhra
	Low		Dumaria, Imamganj, Barachatti	Neemchak Bathani, Fatehpur, Mohanpur
		High	Moderate	Low

Conclusions

There is a positive relation between road transport and regional development. Region with good road transport has high potential for development. Similarly, region with low level of transport will have low potential for development. Road transport provides number of opportunities for development as it opens development process through connectivity and opening up of the backward regions to trade and investment. The extension of transportation to rural areas helps in converting fallow land and cultivable wasteland into cultivation, marketing of agricultural products, growth in rural industries, with the expanded market network and social transformation through greater accessibility to basic amenities. Hence, development of road transport is complementary to development of a region.

References

Ahmed, R. and M. Hossain (1990) *Development Impact of Rural Infrastructure in Bangladesh*, Research Report 83, Washington, DC: International Food Policy Research Institute.

Asian Institute of Transport Development (AITD) (2010) 'Socio-Economic Impact of National Highway on Rural Population'.

Baker, J. (2000) Evaluating the Impact of Development Project on Poverty: A Handbook for Practitioners, Directions in Development Series, Washington, DC: World Bank.

Button, K.J. (1993) *Transport Economics*, 2nd Edition, Aldershot: Edward Arnold.

Deaton, A. and J. Dreze (2002) 'Poverty and Inequality in India: A Reexamination', *Economic and Political Weekly*, 7 September: 3729–3748.

Hack, J. (2002) 'The Role of Transit Investment in Urban Regeneration and Spatial Development: A Review of Research and Current Practice', Paper Presented at CIP Annual Conference, Canada.

Howe, J. (1981) 'Impact of Rural Roads on Poverty Alleviation: A Review of the Literature', Working Paper No. 106, International Labour Office, Income Distribution and Employment Programme, Geneva: International Labour Organisation.

Kansky, K.J. (1963) 'Structure of Transportation Networks: Relationship between Network Geometry and Regional Characteristics', Research Paper No. 84, Department of Geography, Chicago: University of Chicago.

Levy, H. (1996) *Socio-Economic Influence of Rural Roads Operation*, Evaluation Report, Kingdom of Morocco, Evaluation Department, Washington, DC: The World Bank.

Misra, R.P., K.V. Sundaram and V.L.S.P. Rao (1974) *Regional Development Planning in India: A New Strategy*, New Delhi: Vikas.

Mitra, A. (1965) 'Levels of Regional Development in India', Technical Paper, Census of India, New Delhi: Manager of Publications, Government of India.

Munby, D.L. (1971) *Transport*, Harmondsworth: Penguin Books.

Obot, J.U. and F.I. Okpiliya (2002) 'The Intricate Web of Relationship: The Case of Transport Infrastructure and Rural Development in Jos Environs', *Global Journal of Social Sciences*, 1(2): 87–92.

Ramachandran, H. (1981) 'Transportation and Urban Attributes: A Study of the Structural Relations', *Annals of the National Association of Geographers, India*, l: 48–68.

Raza, M. and Y. Aggarwal (1986) *Geography of India: Commodity Flows and Regional Structure of the Indian Economy*, New Delhi: Concept.

Sammer, G. (1981) 'Transport Accessibility and Regional Economic Strength', *Proceedings of the World Conference on Transport Research*, 1: 275–285.

Stutz, F.P. (1976) 'Social Aspects of Interaction and Transportation', Resource Paper No. 76–72, Association of American Geographers, Washington, DC.

Sukla, B. (1992) *Transport and Regional Development: A Case Study of West Bengal*, New Delhi: Concept.

Thomson, R.C. and D.E. Richardson (1995) 'A Graph Theory Approach to Road Network Generalisation', Proceedings of the 17th International Cartographic Conference, 1871–1880.

Tripathi, P.C. (1972) *Rural Transport and Economic Development*, New Delhi: S. Chand & Sons.

Umoren, V., J. Atser and F. Ekong (2004) 'Accessibility and Socio-Economic Development in Etinan, Nigeria', *ESUT Journal of Environmental Management*, 2(1): 1–8.

UNICEF (2005) Nauru: A Situation Analysis of Children, Women and Youth, Fiji. (Weblink: http://www.unicef.org/pacificislands/Nauru_Sitan_Report_Latest_pdf.pdf).

UNDP (2006) Human Development Report, United Nations Development Program (Weblink: Available at: http://hdr.undp.org/hdr2006/statistics/)

Wilson, G. et al. (1966) *The Impact of Highway Investment on Development*, Washington, DC: The Brookings Institution.

24

Geosheelitics

The Indian Way to Save the Earth's Future

SUDEEPTA ADHIKARI

The Darwinian tradition of *natural selection and struggle*, or *Social Darwinism* of Herbart Spencer, is still relevant in contemporary politics, in spite of the fact that the world has undergone manifold changes, following the information technological revolution. That instinct of *conflictuality* between nations still persists rather the dimension of it has widened, making the Planet as whole much vulnerable than before. Conflictuality has been revolutionized through scientific development, with the result that the traditionality of conflictuality has been replaced by Modernity and/or by post-Modernity as the case may. It has been very aptly said that: "The contemporary world is passing through complicated and confusing times, with its *spaces* being traversed by global flows, and warped by the intensity and speed of information technologies. These *changes* have ushered in a new geopolitical imagination, and a condition, which are gradually eroding or weakening the traditional and inherited human values, ontologies, territorial presence, and fixed identities, leaving behind the space by *pace*, transforming the terrestriality/territoriality into the telemetricality, resulting into networks of complex unsettled hybridity". These changes, instead of saving the earth, have pushed it on the brink of unimaginable spectrum of vulnerability. The scientific development since the mid–50s, as a process of structural change in man's material conditions, has undoubtedly caused subversive effects over the earth's surface, with its *future* being relegated to uncertainty. The traditional quest for *space, power and resource* has been renewed in a most vigorous way. Geopolitics is *re-invented*, but its substance or content, however, remains the same. Modern geopolitics or post-modern geopolitics, as the case may be, is not much different from its earlier German lineage, despite the *changes*.

Classical Geopolitics

Classical geopolitics is Eurocentric balance-of-power conception of world politics, which has dominated much of the twentieth century, and is closely bound up with the discipline of geography. From the beginning, geopolitics was intimately connected to the competitive ambitions of European states, for example, Ratzel's ideas of living space (*lebensraum*) grew out of the widespread anxiety about the position of Germany in Europe, and Halford Mackinder's heartland theory reflected similar anxieties in Britain (Parker, 1998; Heffernan, 2000; Tuathail, 1996). Geopolitics, in fact, promised a privileged *scientific perspective* on world affairs. It conceptualized politics as a territorial practice in which states and nations naturally vie for space, power and resources, quite similarly to evolutionary struggles. Geopolitics, as mentioned, was a *manifested re-incarnation* of the Darwinian lineage of continuous struggle for survival, or for that matter Social Darwinism. As such, it served to justify interstate rivalry with explicit or implicit ambition for territorial expansion throughout the twentieth century (Agnew, 1998). Geopolitics was conceived as an applied science to address problems, arising out of territorial ambitions. Human struggle, since the prehistoric days, has been pivoted around space, and acquisition of space through any means, including war, has long been recognized as the prime necessity of human being, which during the renaissance period assumed the status of the European state policy. It has been very aptly said that wars are necessarily fought for space and power. Every war, whether small or large in the twentieth century, aimed at *space* and *power*.

The German used *geopolitik* as a *means* to achieve desired territorial goal. Developments in European mainland during the inter-war period, since the Treaty of Versailles to the outbreak of the Second World War, greatly manifested the German desire to achieve that goal. In the words of de Strausz-Hupe (1942): "Much of the human crisis and misery during the Second World War simply occurred due to much adherence to techniques of *geopolitik* by Germany to further its territorial ambition. The term *holocaust* had been very much synonymous with the term *geopolitik*, which the German geographers had nourished. In the 30s and early 40s of the last century, *geopolitik* had acquired an association with the intellectual apparatus of the *Third Reich*, in part because of the works of Karl Haushofer. The Second World War had not only caused millions of human death, but also damaged the physical milieu of an unspecified dimension, particularly in areas, where deadly wars had taken place, e.g., Europe, North Africa, North Atlantic, South Asia, South-East Asia, East Asia, and the Pacific. Both, the social and physical milieu of these areas were largely damaged. German *geopolitik* was, thus, anti-human and anti-nature.

Geopolitik, being synonymous with the *Nazi* expansion became one of the most controversial terms in the history of geography (Dodds and Atkinson, 2000). Because of its negative image in the decades following the Second World War, the academic geographers around the world, including the German geographers virtually ignored *geopolitik*. Since, it was premised on (i) violent means of structuring the world map; (ii) conflict being the only way to settle the conflict; (iii) conflict being an unending process in politics; (iv) military power and the balance-of-power being the only means to achieve supremacy; and (v) exploitation of the weak by the strong. All these premises on which *geopolitik* was based, were intrinsically *immoral* and *unethical* from humane point of view, argued a number of people, who championed *peace*, as the only alternative not only to man but also to nature to remain in *co-existence*. *Geopolitik* in the 40s was, therefore, considered to be very destructive to, both, humanity and environment, or for that matter for the survival of the *earth's surface*. The prefix *geo* before *politik* lacked the proper nuance to mean the *earth's surface*, rather it meant something different.

To Maull (1936), the disciple of Karl Haushofer at the Munich Institute of Geopolitik: " *Geopolitik* concerns itself with the state not as a static concept but as living being ... and attempts to solve all problems resulting from spatial relationship ... is concerned with the spatial requirements of a state. In putting geography at the service of space-conscious politics, *geopolitik* devotes itself to questions of the future. *Geopolitik* ... is a discipline that weights and evaluates a given situation and by its conclusions seeks to guide practical politics". The words, used in the definition of *geopolitik,* few years before the outbreak of the Second World War, like *living being, spatial requirements, space-conscious politics,* and *guide to practical politics,* were all political in nature and necessarily, rather implicitly referred to the use of geography to achieve political goals *at the cost of the others.* Nowhere in the definition, one could find any reference to the earth's surface and environment in true sense of the terms as being used or applied in *pure* geography.

It was during the Second World War, Weigert (1942), quoted from the mouth-piece of the Munich Institute of Geopolitics *Zeitschrift fur Geopolitik,* said: "*Geopolitik* aims to furnish the weapons for political action, and the principles for guidance in political life ... *Geopolitik* must become the geographical conscience of the State". So, the prefix *geo* before *politik* was thoroughly misleading that corrupted the real meaning of the term *geo.*

Although, *geopolitik* was discredited from the academic usage of the discipline of geography, but its practical application in world politics got a new impetus, following the *bi-polarization* of the global system and the beginning of the cold war. The reason for this new impetus could be said to be the outcome of more and more writings, with focus on strategic analysis, which were closely bound up with foreign and security policies of the powerful states, representing rival poles. Its assumption of state-based bipolarity dovetailed neatly with the statism of the post-war social sciences more generally. However, the every day use of the term geopolitics (changed from *geopolitik*) treated geography as a *stable given-an independent* variable of sorts. To speak of geopolitics was to speak seemingly natural realities. The rhetorical power of geopolitical claims stems insignificant part from their link to such supposedly self-evident *geographical facts.*

Nevertheless, the German instinct of geopolitics survived, and during the Cold War period, it received much greater impetus than during the inter-war period, and immediately before the outbreak of the Second World War, on account of the super power rivalry, nuclearization of global politics, stock-piling of nuclear arsenals by the super powers to achieve 'mutually assured destruction' (MAD), balance of terror, and emerging 'deadly' satellite geopolitics. The words like containment, and (nuclear) deterrence became very much in use in contemporary world politics. Never in the past had the world experienced the threat of a holocaust that it witnessed during the *heyday* of the Cold War. The Cold War geopolitics had developed in an '*east-west*' spatial pattern with rivalry between the super powers for *space, resource, and power* (Taylor, 1985). The Cold War geopolitics conceptu-alized both, rivalry and dominance. In fact, ideological competition between the super powers remained and was potentially so very dangerous. To Agnew (1998) also, the Cold War geopolitical order (1945–1990/91) was premised on ideological basis that justified territorial expansion.

Scientific development in the post-War period made mankind to think of himself, being the '*master*' capable of transforming the world vis-à-vis the nature. All kinds of scientific developments on either side of the Atlantic, and the Pacific as well, were necessarily aimed at securing *dominance* over the others. Contrary to Griffith Taylor's (1951) *'stop-and-go-determinism',* humankind increasingly violated all the norms of nature to gain access to space, resource, and power through developments, discoveries and innovations. The humankind ran after *power*, forgetting his ability in the face of nature. He overestimated the sustaining capacity of the earth. But, later it was increasingly realized that humankind was capable of very little except the *destruction* of the Planet. This was the essence of the situation viewed by Johnston and Taylor (1989) as indicating '*a world in crisis*'. The super power rivalry vis-à-vis the Cold War appeared to have been the outcome of humankind's increasing realization of his mastery capable of changing the face of the earth and/or the feeling of *superiority* that humankind possessed of.

Modern Geopolitics

The end of the Cold War, which had been the containing territorial structure of the political thought for over forty years, fueled anxiety about the spatial organization of power (Agnew and Corbridge, 1995). The post-Cold War geopolitics, however, attempted to reveal its continued reliance on binary understandings of power and spatiality, on notions of East and West, security and danger, freedom and oppression (Agnew, 2003; Gregory, 2004). Geopolitics, whether pre-War, post-War, or post-Cold War has always pivoted around a *hegemon* (dominant state that can take on the world politics). There are numerous examples to substantiate this fact. The geopolitical order and geopolitical discourse, which Agnew and Corbridge (1995) referred to be the reflection of spatial practices and the representation of space, must be seen in terms of congealed and/or hardened hegemonic stance. The notion of hegemony places greater emphasis on the ensemble of rules and enmeshing and conditioning actors in world politics. *Order* refers to the routinized rules, institutions, activities and strategies through the international political economy operating in different historical periods, but *geopolitical* in that context refers to the geographical elements of the world political order. *Orders* usually have geographical characteristics. Geopolitical *discourse* is the discourse by which intellectuals of statecraft, both formal theorists and practitioners spatialize world politics. It involves the *deployment of representation of space that guide the spatial practices central to a geopolitical order* (ibid.). The organization of spatial practices becomes hegemonic geopolitical orders, while the dominant nodes of geopolitical representation become hegemonic discourse. The practical geopolitical reasoning of political elites is the link between the dominant representations of space and the geopolitical order of dominant spatial practices (ibid.).

Agnew (1998) identified three different geopolitical orders with three different geopolitical discourses under spatial practices and representations of spaces, however, based on the historical emergence of territorial states, with quest for space and power politics (Table 1).

Table 1

Identifications of Geopolitical Order and Discourse

Spatial practices	*Representations of space*
Geopolitical order	**Geopolitical discourse**
British Geopolitical Order: 1815–1875	Civilizational Geopolitics
Inter-Imperial Rivalry: 1875–1945	Naturalized Geopolitics
Cold War Geopolitical Order: 1945–1990	Ideological Geopolitics

Apart from the three specific identifications of geopolitical orders together with three geopolitical discourses, Agnew added one more geopolitical order with a geopolitical discourse, referring to the post-Cold War period, which he termed as *Transnational Liberalism* the period being the contemporary one, i.e., after the cessation of the Cold War vis-à-vis the super power rivalry, and the geopolitical discourse, he named *Enlargement Geopolitics* – a manifestation of a strategy of enlarging the community of so-called *market democracies* of the West. The legacy of the German *geopolitik* that used to conceptualize *spatial others,* treating the non-Germans, or even the non-Europeans as *backwards, racially and culturally inferior, and permanently disadvantaged,* and this feeling of *spatial others* still continues in the contemporary global geopolitics. It could be conceptualized as being the 'singular trait of modern geopolitical discourse'. It was essentially a *reflection* of geographical difference, being translated into a sequential binary schema of backward and modern that envisaged *spatialized conflictuality* in world politics.

Agnew in his *Geopolitics: Re-Visioning World Politics* (1998) sought to specify the most 'distinguishing features, or characteristics' of modern geopolitical thought, with emphasis on the 'singular trait of modern geopolitical discourse'. The *first* primary rather the most distinguishing one, according to him is the *global visualization,* without which there would have been no world politics. In fact, the development of geographical knowledge, consequent upon the discoveries of cartographic techniques since the sixteen century onwards made the global visualization possible, for it enabled the seeing of the world as a *unitary whole.* This global visualization was a particular mode of representing the global space. The Age of Exploration, followed by the territorialization of the global space by the European States, particularly those which ventured to go beyond their frontiers across the great Oceans to establish their trading posts on the *new lands,* ultimately witnessed the horizontal division of the global space into places of occupation. This trend of global visualization has not died down, rather recycled into a different mode of representation of global space. Local differences were cartographically purified and translated into all-encompassing *global danger.*

The second distinguishing characteristics of the modern geopolitics pivots around the view of *time being turned into space* that relied upon the hierarchical organization of global space into essentialist blocks, dependent on the deep logocentrism of the Western tradition: developed and backward; modern and tradition; West and East; and the Occident and the Orient. These spatial blocks, in fact, referred to hegemonic geopolitical orders, and were labelled with essential attributes of different time-periods relative to idealized historical experience of each of the blocks. The Cold War division of the globe into three worlds and Rostow's modernization theories on the stages of economic growth was merely the latest manifestations of the longstanding feature of the modern geopolitical thought and/or imagination (Tuathail, 1998).

The third characteristics of the post-Cold War modern geopolitics is its state-centric representation of the global space, which Agnew (1994) earlier referred as the *territorial trap.* This state-centric approach to world politics has evolved in both *practical* and *formal* geopolitical reasoning since the European maritime powers ventured out to monopolize overseas' possessions in the late sixteen and early seventeenth centuries that later on created a geopolitical order to be called *Inter-Imperial Rivalry* during 1875–1945. It is the *sovereign* right that gives the states an inalienable right over the territory, falling within their political jurisdiction. It is this inalienable right that sustains the state-centric approach to world politics. The applied part of the German *geopolitik* had championed this approach, and the legacy of which still can be seen in the inter-state system of the contemporary world politics.

Closely linked with the third characteristics of modern post-Cold War geopolitical imagination is the fourth characteristics, i.e., the *pursuit of primacy* by dominant states in the international system so as to create an hegemonic geopolitical order. The pursuit of primacy by the dominant powerful states, at the various spatial scales: local; regional; and global, has generated many geopolitical discourses, which have sought to explain and justify the *raison de etre* of state militarism, military action and involvement, territorial expansion, overseas imperialism and warfare as inevitable consequences of the uneven distribution of power potential over the globe and timeless *laws* of competition between states for space, power, and resources. This characteristics of the modern geopolitics is not only a reminiscent of the Darwinian heritage, or Social Darwinism, but also a scientific affirmation of Ratzel-Kjellen-Haushofer lineage of *geopolitik* that held the world engaged for nearly 6–7 years in a state of *holocaust*.

The Jewish-Arab stand off in the Middle East, The NATO-Taliban stand off in Afghanistan, India-Pakistan conflictuality in Jammu and Kashmir, the Sino-Indian conflictuality in the Himalayas, the Sino-Japanese stand off in the South China Sea, the Sino-Indian competition in the South-East Asia, the Sino-US stand off in the Pacific, besides the US-North Korea stand off in the North Pacific and the NATO-Russia stand off in East Europe, are some of the glaring examples of *competition* and *conflict* for space, power and resource, and of course hegemony. No matter what consequences would happen to the *fragile ecosystems* of the areas of conflict, as the *involved states or the coalition of the states* are least bothered. Geopolitics is geo-power, a state philosophy, a kind of a political paradigm, a weapon for guidance in political life, which is conceived and nurtured in the capitals of the *space-conscious warring* powers and/or the countries. In recent decades, the modern geopolitical project has become more precarious than before as globalization has rearranged the fast-growing interconnectivity and functional boundaries of the world's political map. It could be rightly said that: 'Geopolitics of a state or territorially-defined society means its pursuit of geographically dimensioned aims that are connected with its economic, and political power, security and military preparedness and culture, and 'space-consciousness'.

Post-Modern Geopolitics

Apart from the modern post-Cold War geopolitics, the new millennium, i.e., the 21st century has witnessed many changes, ranging from the decline of the US hegemony in the world politics, through de-territorialized or re-territorialization of the global economy and glocalization, to the rise of China to take on the USA politically, economically, strategically, and globally. These *profound* changes were accompanied by the information technological revolution that created a new geometry of power politics, initiating new types of spatial practices, and representations of space. These developments of the new millennium resulted in what has been said in the beginning: "The contemporary world is passing through complicated and confusing times, with its spaces being traversed by global flows and warped by the intensity and speed of information technologies". The prevailing contemporary condition, arising out of the global flows and the speed of information technologies seem to have problematized and unsettled the modern geopolitical map, making the inherited concept of the global visualization blurred. It is a *post-Modern condition in world geopolitics* that prompted the declaration of the 'end of modern geopolitics' (Tuathail, 1997).

Luke (1994, 1995 and 1996) identified three *geopolitical natures*, and conceptualized them into the first nature, the second nature, and the third nature, and each geopolitical nature is characterized by *distinctive* developments. The *first* nature was characterized by primordial communities with rudimentary agrarian economy, organic spatiality, terristriality, and bioscope/ecoscape/geoscape. In fact, the first geopolitical nature, according to Luke, portrayed the condition of the primordial social order that existed before the invention, and founding of cities and buildings. The *second* geopolitical order was distinguished by artificial technosphere, manufactured and built by modern industrial capitalism since the eighteenth century onward. All kinds of material developments, which we call *modern*, took place during the period. It was during this second geopolitical nature, space was mastered by states and hardware complexes like the railways, steamships, hard surface roads, canals, telephone/telegraph systems, and electric grids, etc., were invented and developed. This second nature resembled Agnew's primary feature of modern geopolitics: *global visualization*. It is often described as being the classic era of modern territorial geopolitics, of competition and conflict, bounded spatial entities for the domination of lands, oceans, and the resources of the earth. It is the period of struggle for space and power.

Luke's realm of the *third* geopolitical nature is being distinguished by the cybernetic system. This is the domain of the informational cybersphere, its electronic landscapes the cyberscapes, infoscapes, and mediascapes of *post-Modern* informational capitalism. It is in this period of third geopolitical nature that the modern *geo-graphing* is changing into post-modern *info-graphing*, with people in large number joining global webs, eroding the traditional divisions between local, national, and global, rather creating a scalar dynamic of *new world order*, composed of rearranged *glocal space*.

Using Agnew's (1998) modern geopolitical imagination and project, and Luke's (1994, 1995, 1996) geopolitical narratives of three natures, Tuathail (1998) prepared the following Table 2 to distinguish between Modern and post-Modern:

Table 2

Modern vs. Post-Modern Geopolitics

Modern geopolitics	*Post-Modern geopolitics*
Cartographic visualizations: maps	Telemetrical visualization: GIS
Perspectivist theatre	Post-perspectivist simulations
Inside/outside, Domestic/international	Global webs, glocalization
East/West	Jihad/McWorld
Territorial power	Telemetrical power
Hardware ascendant: GPR	Software ascendant: C412
Territorial enemies	Deterritorialized dangers
Fixed, rigid posture	Flexible, rapid response
Geopolitical man	Cyborg collectives
States/Leaders	Networks/cyborgs

Tuathail (1998) identified certain specific characteristics of the post-Modern geopolitics. *Firstly*, it is the growing significance of telemetrical visualization of contemporary world politics, which is the resultant effect of the advanced geographical information systems (GIS) and the visualization technologies of the world (Gray, 1997). The importance of the cartographic visualization through maps has been gradually declining, following the informationalization of the strategic techniques. The displacement of maps by the GIS techniques, of modern cartographic representations of global space by the post-modern telemetrical simulations, is symptomatic of a much broader technocultural transformation in how world politics is imagined and visually represented in the late twentieth, and the early twenty-first centuries. The world politics has, now, ceased to be the theatrical drama it was to the *geopoliticians* in the first half of the twentieth century. It is now a hyper-reality of television spectacles, and military simulations, a universe of information that encompasses and overwhelms all. Visions are now being eclipsed by vertigo (Tuathail, 1996). The speed, quantity, and intensity of information problematizes the very possibility of foreign policy as deliberative reflection and decision-making (Luke and Tuathail, 1997).

Secondly, the traditional binary conception of space as East/West, modern/backward – and the 'three worlds' of the Cold War that emerged out of them – have been replaced by post-spatial binaries like the *Jihad* and the McWorld (Barber, 1996). The Jihad represents fundamentalism and terrorism. Jihadis are considered fanatics, and religious ideologues, and have the potentials to cause harms to the mankind. In fact, they are a pervasive danger throughout the world. Nearly, two-thirds. of Asia is under the grip of the Jihadis, particularly, West Asia, the South Asia including Afghanistan, the Central Asia including China, and South-East Asia. The McWorld, however, represents the de-territorializing pace of globalization, and its different variants like MTV, FTV, McDonalds and Macintosh are diffusing across the world. The politics around the world is now being run by the Jihad versus McWorld dichotomy, which has set aside the spatial pattern of East versus West geopolitical dichotomy, with the 'end of the modern'.

Thirdly, the territorial power is being gradually replaced by the increasing significance of the telemetrical power, which has raised the relevance of technology, education, and institutional flexibility in contemporary world politics, whereas the importance of geography, population, and resource/raw materials (GPR) has declined, making the traditional geopolitical concerns of the mid-twentieth century redundant. It has happened only due to information revolution. The new information technology has made it possible to *convert hard and soft power into power plus*. Nye and Owens (1996) highlighted the strategic role of 'intelligence collection, surveillance, and reconnaissance (ISR), and command, control, communication, computer processing, and intelligence (C4I) in world politics. Gray (1997), however added inter-capability, rendering it C4I2, which provided 'dominant battlespace knowledge' in conflict situations. Information, now, is the new coin of the international realm, with its potency of hard and soft power resources through information. Cyberspace has emerged as the latest frontier, allowing proliferation of freedom of the states. The United States is well-poised in informational power, with an 'information edge' over the others.

Fourthly, after the Cold War, the meaning of security is essentially contested, and threats are increasingly represented as emanating not simply from the territorial enemies, where containment imperatives remain in force, but from a plethora of de-territorialized dangers: stateless terrorism, cybernetic sabotage and crime, narco-terrorism, global corruption, humanitarian crises, infectious diseases, environmental degradation, and the proliferation of weapons of mass destruction (Dalby, 1996; Sopko, 1996; Gray, 1997; Luke and Tuathail, 1997). These de-territorialized threats are global in nature as they do not have any fixed spatial locations. Even the powerful ones are not free from the apprehension of these types of threats. The incidents of 9/11 and 11/26 in the United States (Washington DC) and India (Mumbai) were the glaring examples of 'de-territorialized threats'. Contemporary regional instability in Asia, Europe and Africa may be said to be the outcome of the persistent nature of either de-territorialized or re-territorialized threats of stateless terrorism, narco-terrorism, and environmental degradation. The cybernetic sabotage and crime in recent days has worsened diplomatic relations between the states, which once had good relations.

Fifthly, with the collectives and cyborgs so vigorously a part of the theorization and practice of post-modern geopolitics at the end of the twentieth century and the beginning of the twenty-first century that the relevance of geopolitical men, political leaders, and states in world politics is being found to be gradually weakening. There is no Mackinder-like or Spykman-like or de Seversky-like figure and/or geopolitical man to express *anxiety* over the pervasive nature of problematized, and unsettled function of collectives of humans and non-humans in world politics. Contemporary *informationalized* geopolitics obviously provides sustenance to military collectives and their networks, therefore the networks of everyday collectives do have secret geopolitical lives. Agency in geopolitics is now with the thoroughly cyborganized networks and not with the geopoliticians. New cyborganized forms of geopolitical life are perpetually being conceived by our proliferating networks, expressing the fears and fantasies of competing and cooperative collectives (Tuathail, 1998).

Geopolitics – whether classical, modern or post-modern – has one thing very common in them that is, their intrinsic emphasis on *power potential for dominance and primacy in inter-state system, and is being increasingly conceived as a weapon to guide political practices.* Smaller nations like Israel, North Korea, Iran and Pakistan have detonated series of nuclear explosions, reasons, being regional dominance and primacy in the regional state-system. Geopolitcs has been and is being used for the purpose of the state, and particularly, justifying the processes to achieve the purposes, which inter alia is suggestive of struggle for space and power. For classical and modern geopolitics, the principal geopolitical tool was cartographic map, and for the post-modern geopolitics, it is the techniques of the geographical information system (GIS). It was the geopolitical men who used to decide the destiny of the world politics, but, now it is the cyborganized collectives and networks manoeuvring the world politics. The methodological approach of geopolitics consists in the examination of its characteristics with a view to understanding the phenomena which it reveals and the processes which have produced its morphology. Therefore, the component parts of the world politics are considered as spatial objects and their interactions as producing spatial phenomena. There is no doubt on the fact that geopolitics has caused enormous damage to environment and mankind. Most of the natural disasters seem to have stemmed from the application of principles of geopolitics for the *distinctive purposes* of the state i. e. *lebensraum.*

Of all disasters that the world has experienced on account of political-military manoeuvrings during the Cold War period were the *nuclear disasters* in former Soviet Union, Japan, the United States and Pakistan which have not only caused human loss, but also resulted in ecological damage and environmental degradation. Never before in the past had the earth's surface been as vulnerable to *destruction* as it stands today. This is simply because of the fact that man is not acting within the constraints of the environment, rather is going beyond the limits and the capabilities of the *nature*, and here lies the relevance of Taylor's (1951) philosophical explanation of *stop-and-go-determination*. Man's quest for power through *development*, ignoring nature's limitation has led Bunge (1989) to comment: "... this planet is not too small for peace but it is too small for war ...".

Cyborganized collectives, telemetricality, and complex unsettled hybridity and many more things are not only threatening the very existence of human civilization, but also raising question to the survival of the planet! All great discoveries and inventions in the field of military science and strategy are designed to sustain struggle for primacy and dominance in world politics, and which obviously point towards rivalry and conflictuality between the nations. The world, now, seems more to be disturbed than before. It is in the background of the dwindling scenario in world politics, and persistent conflicts among the nations for space and power that the traditional Indian approach to peace has been found to be the only remedy or panacea to contain war and conflictuality, and to make the world too big for peace. The Indian tradition has always been one of consensus and synthesis, which has always renounced violent spatial approach to territorial conflict, and refuted struggle for space and power, which the *Euro-centric* geopolitical approach, since the days of renaissance has pursued for dominance in world politics.

Variants of Geopolitics

Immediately before the beginning of the Cold War, the Australian geographer Griffith Taylor (1951) introduced a term *Geopacific* to contest the term *geopolitics,* rather he wanted to develop a political approach as an alternative to geopolitical approach to address the global political problems. He was convinced that conflictuality and rivalry between the nations would not end, and the world politics could not be symmetrical because *struggle* would continue in one way or other for survival – Social Darwinism. To him geopacific "is an attempt to base the teaching of freedom and humanity upon real geographical deductions: in a sense it is humanized geopolitics. It shows, for instance from a study of World Plan, where the leading nations must rise, be it understood to lead, not to conquer. It shows, how the conflicts based upon differences are usually absorbed .... It shows that we should study environmental control so as to advance in harmony with our environment". His concept of geopacifics could be said to be a *political* manifestation of his famous view of *stop-and-go-determination*. However, the concept of Taylor to provide an alternative to geopolitics could not hold on the attention of the academician and the political theorists for want of any sound theoretical basis and practicality since there was nothing *ethical* in it. Taylor himself admitted in the paper itself that it was a material concept, but not a complete one because it did not pretend to address those basic principles, which properly belonged to distinct ethical disciplines.

Demko and others (1994) introduced another term *Geopolinomics*, but not as an antithesis to geopolitics rather, it emphasized the economic components of the interstate relationship over the geostrategic structure of the world. Geopolinomics did not attempt to contest the modern geopolitical imagination of Agnew and Corbridge. To them: "... applied political geography – the geopolitics or geopolinomics – is emerging rapidly and vigorously. It is a sub-field and ambitiously attempts to explain the prevailing distribution and cultural influences, economic linkages, political power and military forces, as well as to better understand the processes that alter these distributions. International financial networks and incorporate trade together with invest pattern will to a large extent re-draw the economic map of the world on which places will have significance than telecommunication channels. Under these circumstances the nature of sovereignty of nations is being questioned, the immutability of international boundaries are being questioned by virtue of environmental catastrophe, racial minority and human right problems and the development of weapons of mass destruction". Nowhere in his geopolinomics, Demko and others used the terms like humans, non-humans collectives, cyborganized collectives and telemetrical power, etc., to address the emerging pattern as a result of geography, politics and economics combined. He mainly emphasized political economy in a spatial framework, and highlighted the economic determinism of political structure, process, and system. Economic penetration or expansion by the powerful ones, and competition and/or struggle between them to secure strong footholds in the peripheral areas of the Third World is again a reminiscent of the Euro-centric pattern of geopolitics.

All the above concepts, and approaches, however, fail to provide any remedy or panacea to the crisis-ridden world politics and ecologically-threatened biosphere. The approaches are Euro-centric, intrinsically based upon the paradigms of power potential, materialism, insensitiveness, and, of course, expansion and violence. It is in the background of *bankruptcy* of humane-based approach to address conflictuality, an Indian geographer, Sinha (1999) came out with a new approach to contest geopolitics, and the word he coined was *Geosheelitics.*

Geosheelitics

The term *geosheelitics* is a combination of three different disciplinary ideas: geography, *sheel,* and politics. Relationship between geography and politics is signified by the well-known term *geopolitics,* but the term *sheel,* put between geography and politics signifies geopolitics mediated by *sheel,* which having no equivalence in English has been put to mean jointly as *morality* and *ethics.* Thus, the term *geosheelitics* means *moralistic* and ethical *geopolitics.* The terms geography and politics are well known, and need no epistemological clarification, but the term *sheel* needs clarification. *Sheel* is a Sanskrit term, meaning righteousness, right conduct or morality and ethics, intrinsically based on the concept of *satya* (truth) and *ahimsa* (non-violence). In Buddhism, the term *sheel* comprises three stages together with eight-fold path: right speech; right action, and right livelihood. In the words of the great Indian philosopher, and former President of the Indian Republic, Sarvapalli Radhakrishnan (1927): "The Buddhism idea of sila, or good conduct – is a universal need for social discipline, cultural growth and peaceful coexistence of human beings and other biotic objects, with an aim to realize a state of mind where all diversity is synthesized and merged into oneness".

By intercalating the term *sheel,* geopolitics be designed to integrate the moral and ethical values in the behaviour of states in keeping with the Indian tradition as enshrined in the Hindu literatures and treatises, and the great epics like the *Vedas,* the *Upanishadas,* the *Ramayana,* the *Mahabharata,* and the *Buddhist texts and Jatak Kathas,* besides others religious scriptures. Kautilaya's *Arthasastra* also identifies the relevance of right conduct and right action in the inter-state relation, and strongly contradicts the use of force for unethical purposes.

According to Indian tradition (particularly Buddhist tradition) the state should not covet the territory of others to gain space and power. The aim may not be world conquest by acquiring material power in terms of space, power and resources, but to serve the world through benevolent power by doing service to humanity – the welfare of mankind and the earth. Instead of *shastra-vijaya* (conquest by arms) one should strive for *shaastra-vijaya* (conquest by wisdom), based on the tenets of *Dhamma*. The concept of *geosheelitics* is essentially the concept of *dhamma* (universal law of righteousness) within geographical specification, which is aimed at building up an attitude of mind in which social responsibility, the bahaviour of one individual and/or the state to another is considered at great relevance. It is the plea for the recognition of the dignity of man and/or the state, and for a humanistic spirit in the activities of society. The concept of *geosheelitics* is a holistic one as it seeks to bring the geographical thinking on relationship of humanity and environment to the fore. The fundamental difference between geopolitics (whether classical, modern or post-modern) and geosheelitics is that the former has no concern for the environment while the latter expresses greater concern for environment, since the philosophy is based on the Buddhist tradition of *truth* and *non-violence*, it believes that to be successful, humanity must act within the constraints of the environment and be aware both of its limitations and of its possibilities. Detonating nuclear explosions to terrorize others, and also for the sake of space and power, the powerful ones who are involved in this political process of militarization of the world politics for *dominance*, and have been consistently carrying out their mission as a part of their struggle, have caused more harms, not only to humanity but also to the environment. *Geosheeltics* treats every organism of the environment with *care* and *respect*.

The Indian tradition of *consensus* and *synthesis*, and the doctrines of *truth (satya)* and *non-violence (ahimsa)* are the basic fundamentals of *geosheelitics* that intrinsically illuminates and enriches the holistic doctrine of *basudeibokutumbakam* (treating all over the surface as relatives) strongly emphasizing *sarvabhauma/sarvodoya* (upliftment of all). The doctrine of *sarvabhauma* manifests itself in the five principles of peace, called *Panchsila*, which includes: (i) mutual respect to each other' territorial integrity and sovereignty, (ii) non-aggression, (iii) non-interference in each other's internal matter, (iv) equality and mutual benefit, and (v) peaceful coexistence. *Panchsila* or the five principles of peace is the methodology of *geosheelitics*, with its wide geographical ramifications, aiming towards a *non-conflictual* world of peace and stability – each state to remain in peace and harmony, treating each as friend not as foe in spite of differences. "If Panchsila were fully and sincerely accepted by all countries, then peace would be assumed to every one and cooperation would follow". This is the reason that *Geosheelitics* contradicts *social Darwinism*, which has long been the base of *geopolitics.* The same five principles (*Panchsila)* could be well applicable in dealing with Nature, so that *It* could survive.

Like the tradition of Ratzel – Kjellen, which had conceived state as an organism, the Indian Tradition also considered state as an organism, but the emphasis is not on expansion of its limbs (the territory), but on strengthening of its soul (ethical and moral prowess). The state is believed to behave as a human being – the same moral and ethical principles, applicable to the state as they are applicable to an individual. Here morality is concerned with self in case of individual and internal relations in case of state, while ethics is concerned with relation with others, that is, social or interpersonal relations of the individual and external or inter-state relations of the state. So far as international relations are concerned, the Gandhian model (Oceanic or Concentric Circle model) appears to be more suitable in the contemporary conditions, created by rivalries, confusions, tensions, and conflictualities than the other models. In opposition to the modern political system, which is "pyramidal with the apex being sustained by the bottom", the Gandhian model is reflective of a system in which the individuals are considered as local units and other units are ever widening but never ascending, i.e., horizontality to prevail upon verticality – the sense is equality among nations, irrespective of geographical, political and economic difference, and none will strive for moving up at the cost of the weak.

The Gandhian system envisions the entire system as an organic family, composed of the primary units of the individuals. Each circle in the system has forward and backward linkages, the larger circles getting support from the smaller circles, the smaller ones getting strength from the larger ones. This means an integrating interaction between the larger ones and smaller ones in a spirit of healthy interdependence and mutual relationship. Within the system, there will be no dominance of one over the other, rather all coexist in a spirit of belonging together. Power in the system shall not be concentrated at one level, but is decentralized in a way as each intervening unit between the individual and the world organization enjoys respect, requisite authority and resources. The economy of the unit is to be *free from exploitation in every shape and form.* The basis of success of each unit of the system is self-improvement through self-transformation aiming at self-sacrifice. The ultimate objective is the establishment of a world federation and/or international league. In this scheme, the smallest nation would feel as *tall* as the *tallest* (Gandhi, 1940). It is through this system, the world order will progressively advance towards the ultimate goal of building up of a non-violent society – *Sarvodaya* and *sarvabhauma.*

The Oceanic model of Gandhi in the present scenario appears to be geographically relevant and strategically suited for durable peace and stability in the world systems. The Oceanic model draws its strength from *Dhamma*, so that the pattern of world politics could be framed within *consensus* and *synthesis*, based on the broad foundation of *ethics* and *morality*. Holism is, therefore, expressively manifested in the Oceanic model, and that makes *geosheelitics* dynamic, meaningful and acceptable to all. War is renounced as an instrument of policy. *Geosheelitics* aims to study the events and conflicts at various spatial levels: local, regional, national, and global, in the light of the Indian tradition of consensus, tolerance, coexistence, and synthesis. It could be a sustainable political paradigm to provide workable solution to the problems – the motto of it being "May we examine each other from the view point of a friend".

Geosheelitics may be defined as the study of interrelationship between geography and politics in the light of moralistic and ethical principles. *Geosheelitics* seems to have a broad area of analysis, including in it are all the human sciences, interacting with each other in a way as to make it spatially and politically expressive. It seeks to bridge the academic disciplines of geography and international relations. Putting itself in opposition to geopolitics (whether classical, modern or post-modern) *geosheelitics* conceptualizes as a complex and problematic set of discourses, representations and practices, rather than as a coherent, neutral and objectivist science. Its main emphasis is on how to process conflict resolution between the states vying for space and power, through the application of the Buddhist and/or the Gandhian methodology, based on the finest Indian tradition of truth and non-violence. To resolve conflict, it suggests the following steps:

1. Arriving at the truth of the situation by objectively exploring the viewpoint of the contending parties;
2. Finding out the common ground and/or cause of the conflict and trying to narrow down the gaps or disagreements, so that the conflict could be lessened at the manageable level;
3. Bringing the contending parties across the negotiation table first and thereafter, if need be, with a counsellor, that is conciliation and/or pacification;
4. If the conflict is unresolved then try for arbitration, adjudication or mediation.

The ultimate objective of *geosheelitics* is to build up of a New Benevolent World Order. It is not like the geopolitical order as discussed and analysed by Agnew and Corbridge (1995), and by Agnew (1998) alone, rather it talks about an order that renounces the dominance and hegemony in world politics, but emphasizes equality regardless of uneven power distribution. *Geosheelitics* intrinsically reflects or manifests Darwin's second theme of *association and agglomeration*, but not the third theme of *natural selection and struggle* as the latter is against the spirit of ethic and morality and humanity. Association and agglomeration theme of Darwin takes into account the whole, i.e., Man and Environment together. This philosophical stance of Darwin has never been discussed at the political discourses, except for Burrow's usage of the term *human ecology*, but even that could be used to give a new dimension to world politics, not necessarily based on competition and conflictuality between the nations, regardless of their power potential.

Rooted in post-structuralism, *geosheelitics* is, at its core, intrinsically concerned with the operation, interaction and contestation of geopolitical discourses. On account of its post-structuralist orientation, *geosheeltitics* holds that realities of global political space do not simply reveal themselves to be detached, omniscient observers, rather geopolitical knowledges are seen as partial and situated, emergent from particular subject position. In this context, geopolitical practices are found to result from complex constellations of competing ideas and discourses, which they in turn modify. Plurality, rather than singularity characterizes this alternative of geopolitics.

Conclusions

Geosheelitics, based on the Indian tradition of consensus, tolerance, and synthesis, together with the doctrine of truth and non-violence, is the most holistic one to address the intricate political problems of inter-state rivalries, engagements, conflicts, and wars, besides the situations arising out of networks of complex unsettled hybridity, cyborganized collectives, de-territorialized threats and gradual loosening of inherited ontologies. *Geosheelitics* also emphasizes earth consciousness, and seeks to manifest itself both in direct environmental concerns and in the awareness of the significant role which political decision-making needs to play. The prefix *geo* in this context emphasizes the environmental consciousness in a particular discourse and as a prefix to *sheelitics* it implies the necessity for a spatial-political action to take into account the global dimension.

Geosheelitics, as a matter of fact, refers to a plural ensemble of representational practices that are spatially diffused throughout the global societies, and it seeks to disturb the objectivist perspectivism found in the history of geopolitics since the German days and in the practices of foreign policy, more generally. The objective of *geosheelitics* is to uncover the static approach of geopolitics, the one that dominated in the practices of states and is still prevailing in the contemporary world politics.

Geosheelitics offers a continued examination of suppositions which underlie specific geopolitical constructions, that is, the production and usage of geographical knowledge to different political and spatial orders, so that conflictuality could be transformed into cooperation – the geographical knowledge be used for the betterment of the society (*sarvodaya*), not as a tool for expansion, dominance, and hegemony – the world order that geopolitics has emphasized.

References

Agnew, J. and S. Corbridge (1995) *Mastering Space*, London: Routledge.

Agnew, J. (1994) 'The Territorial Trap: The Geographical Assumptions of International Relations Theory', *Review of International Political Economy*, 1(1): 53–80.

—— (1998) *Geopolitics: Revisiting World Politics*, London: Routledge.

—— (2003) *Geopolitics: Re-visioning World Politics*, 2nd Edition, London: Routledge,

Barber, B. (1996) *Jihad vs McWorld*, New York: Ballantine.

Bunge, W. (1989) 'Our Planet is Big Enough for Peace But Too Small for Peace', in R.J. Johnston and P. Taylor (eds), *A World in Crisis? Geographical Perspectives*, Oxford: Blackwell.

Dalby, S. (1996) 'The Environment as Geopolitical Threat: Reading Robert Kaplan's "Coming Anarchy"', *Ecummene*, 3: 472–496.

Demko, G.J. et al. (eds) (1994) *Reordering the World: Geopolitical Perspectives on the Twenty-First Century*, Introduction, Boulder, CO: Westview Press.

Dodds, K. and Atkinson, D. (eds) (2000) *Geopolitical Traditions: A Century of Geopolitical Thought*, London and New York: Routledge.

Gandhi, M. (1940) *My Experiments with Truth*, 2nd Edition, Ahmedabad: Navajivan Publishing House.

Gray, C.H. (1997) *Post-Modern War: The New Politics of Conflicts*, New York: Guilford.

Gregory, D. (1994) *Geographical Imaginations*, Oxford: Blackwell.

—— (2004) *The Colonial Present*, Oxford: Blackwell.

Heffernan, M. (2000) 'On the Origin of European Geopolitics', in D. Klaus and D. Atkinsons (eds), *Geopolitical Traditions: A Century of Geopolitical Thought*, London: Routledge.

Johnston, R.J. and P.A. Taylor (eds) (1989) *A World in Crisis? Geographical Perspectives*, 2nd Edition, Oxford: Blackwell.

Luke, T. (1994) 'Placing Power/Sitting Space: The Politics of Global and Local in the New World Order', *Society and Space*, 12: 613–628.

—— (1995) 'New World Order or Neo World Orders: Power, Politics and Ideology in Informationalizing Glocalities', in M. Featherstone, S. Lash and R. Robertson (eds), *Global Modernities*, London: Sage Publications.

—— (1996) 'Identity, Meaning and Globalization: Detraditionalization in Post-Modern Time-Space Compression', in P. Heelas, S. Lash and P. Morris (eds), *Detraditionalization*, Oxford: Blackwell.

Luke, T. and G.O. Tuathail (1997) 'On Videocameralistics: The Geopolitics of Failed States, the CNN International and (UN) Governmentality', *Review of International Political Economy*, 4: 709–733.

Maull, Otto (1936) *Das Wesen der Geopolitk*, Leipzig: B.G. Taubner.

Nye, J. and W. Owens (1996) 'The Information Edge', *Foreign Affairs*, 75: 20–36.

Parker, G. (1998) *Geopolitics: Past, Present and Future*, London: Printer.

Radhakrishnan, S. (1927) *Indian Philosophy*, London: George Allen and Unwin.

Sinha, R.N.P. (1999) 'Geosheelitics: An Introduction', *Geosheelitics View*, 1: 1–4.

Sopko, J. (1996) 'The Changing Proliferation Threat', *Foreign Affairs*, 105: 3–20.

Strausz-Hupe, R. (1942) *Geopolitics: The Struggle for Space and Power*, New York: Putnam.

Taylor, G. (ed.) (1951) *Geography in the Twentieth Century*, London: Methuen.

—— (1951a) 'Geopolitics and Geopacifics', in G. Taylor (ed.), *Geography in the Twentieth Century*, London: Methuen.

Taylor, P.J. (1985) *Political Geography: World-Economy, Nation-State, and Locality*, Harlow: Longman.

Tuathail, G. (1995) 'Theorizing History, Gender and World Order Amidst Crises of Global Governance', *Progress in Human Geography*, 19: 260–272.

—— (1996) *Critical Geopolitics*, London: Routledge.

—— (1997) 'At the End of Geopolitics: Reflection on a Plural Problematic at the Century's End', *Alternatives*, 22: 35–36.

—— (1998) 'Post-Modern Geopolitics: The Modern Geopolitical Imagination and Beyond', in S. Dalby and G.O. Tuathail (eds), *Re-Thinking Geopolitics*, London: Routledge.

Weigert, H.W. (1942) *Generals and Geographers*, New York: Oxford University Press.

25

Impact of Climate Change on South Asian Forests

SWARNIMA SINGH

Climate change is a long-term significant change in the expected patterns of average weather of a specific region over an appropriately significant period of time. It reflects abnormal variations to the expected climate within the earth's atmosphere and subsequent effects on other parts of the earth. United Nations Framework Convention on Climate Change (UNFCC) in its Article 1, defines climate change as a change that is attributed directly or indirectly to human activity that alters the composition of the global atmosphere and which is, in addition to natural climate variability, observed over comparable times. The cumulative effect of net greenhouse gas emissions due to human activities since the pre-industrial age (1750) has resulted in almost a 31 per cent increase in carbon dioxide by the year 1999, concentration in the atmosphere was 280ppmv to 367ppmv (part per million by volume) and of this, about 33 per cent was emitted as a result of land use change, predominantly from tropical deforestation (IPCC, 2000).

The forestry sector is unique, in that it contributes significantly to global CO_2 emissions and also provides significant opportunities to not only, reduce the current or projected emissions but also, to remove CO_2 accumulated from past emissions in the atmosphere, and sequester it in soil, vegetation and wood products. Further, forestry sector is closely linked to socio-economic systems, particularly the forest dwellers and rural communities in India. Globally, 20per cent of the carbon emission is attributed to deforestation and land use change (IPCC, 2007). Forestry or forest management is broadly included under 'land use, land use change and forestry' (LULUCF) sector in the climate convention. It includes all activities relevant to forests, pasture and rangelands, croplands and wetlands. Next to the fossil fuel sector, the focus of attention of the climate convention and scientific literature is largely on the forestry sector, for the following reasons:

- It contributes to about 20 per cent of global CO_2 emissions (ibid.).
- It provides large mitigation potential (Nabuurs et al., 2007).
- It provides low cost mitigaton opportunities in the developing countries (Sathaye and Ravindranath, 1998).

- Mitigation activities have the potential to attract industrialized countries to invest in developing countries, transfer technology and upgrade institutional capacity for forest conservation, reforestation, bio-energy and other forestry related activities.

Aims and Objectives

1. To evaluate the climate change impact studies in relation with carbon inventory in Indian land use change and forestry sector across South Asian Forests.
2. To highlight the data, modelling and research gaps relevant to the GHG inventory estimation, mitigation potential, vulnerability and impact assessments for the forest and biodiversity.

In the last three centuries, global forest area has been reduced by approximately 40 per cent, with three quarters of this loss occurring during the last two centuries. Forests have completely disappeared in 25 countries, and another 29 countries have lost more than 90 per cent of their forest cover. The *Global Forest Resources Assessment 2000* (FRA, 2000) done by the Food and Agriculture Organization of the United Nations reports that only 22 out of 137 developing countries possess a series of time-series inventories, 28 countries have no inventory, and 33 have only partial inventories. Further, 34 countries only have national forest inventories from before 1990, while only 43 have inventories completed after 1990. More than half the inventories used to compile FRA–2000 were either more than 10 years old or incomplete.

Data Base and Methodology

Given the importance of assessment of forest carbon inventory, the mitigation potential and likely impacts of climate change, a comprehensive review of the forestry studies related to climate change is needed and this paper aims to fulfil that requirement. Therefore, the following issues are addressed with reference to climate change and forests in South Asia, where the relevant published literature is reviewed on the basis of: area under forests, changes in area under forests, forest conservation and afforestation and reforestation in South Asia, greenhouse gas and CO_2 emissions inventory for South Asian forests, mitigation potential of forest sector and cost effectiveness, impact of climate change on forest ecosystems and biodiversity and adaptation , research priorities on greenhouse gas inventory, mitigation potential assessment, climate impacts and adaptation issues, relevant to climate change and forests as well as other natural ecosystems.

State of Forests in South Asia

Forest Changes in South Asia

Forest is generally described as a tract of land having plant community largely consisting of trees and other woody vegetation. However, there is no universally accepted technical definition of forest. However, with access to satellite imagery data from Forest Survey of India (FSI, 2007), improved estimates of forest area are periodically available. Food and Agriculture Organization (FAO) defines the status of forests in South Asia is 4,073('000 ha) in 2005. In the past, area under forest has been highly contested (Table 1).

Table 1

Status of Forests in South Asia

Countries	*1990*	*1995*	*2000*	*2005*
Bangladesh	6.8	..	6.8	6.7
India	21.5	..	22.7	22.8
Nepal	33.7	..	27.3	25.4
Pakistan	3.3	..	2.7	2.5
Sri Lanka	36.4	..	32.2	29.9

Source: FAO , 2007.

Figure 1

Forest Cover Trends In India

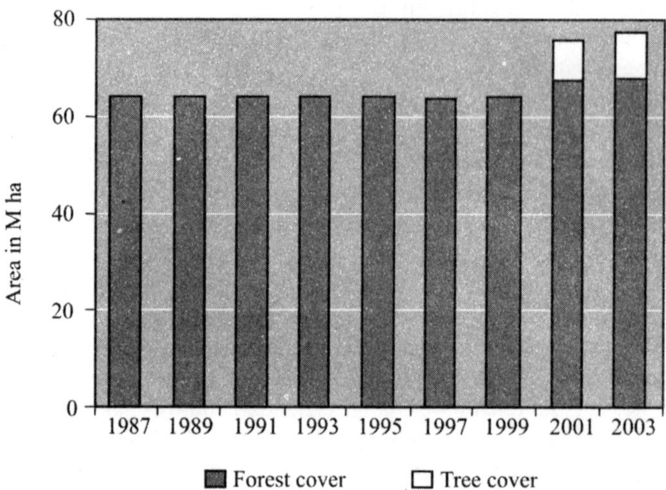

Source: FSI, 2003.

In Indian context, according to the FSI, "all lands, more than one hectare in area, with a tree canopy density of more than 10 per cent is defined as forest". The total forest cover of India according to the latest State of Forest Report, 2003 is 67.83 Mha and this constitutes 20.64 per cent of the geographic area. Dense forests dominate, by accounting for about half of the total forest cover. The tree cover (which includes forests of less than one hectare) is 9.99 Mha (3.04%). The total area under forest and tree cover is 77.82 Mha, which is 23.68 per cent of the geographic area (FSI, 2003). FSI has been periodically estimating the forest cover in India since 1987 using remote sensing techniques. The forest cover reported for the year 1987 was 64.08 Mha compared to 67.83 Mha for the year 2003 (FSI, 1987; FSI, 2003). This indicates an increase in forest cover of 3.75 Mha over a period of 15 years. It can be observed that the forest cover in India has nearly stabilized and further it is increasing marginally over the years (MOEF web) 2001 and 2003 assessments, FSI has included the tree cover, in addition to forest cover. The area under tree cover reported is also marginally increasing (Figure 1).

FAO defines forest as land having a tree canopy cover of more than 10 per cent over an area of more than 0.5 ha with forest as the principle land use. In the past, area under forest in South area has been highly contested (Table 2 and 3).

Table 2

Spatial and Temporal Change of Forests in South Asia

Country/ area	*Total area sq km*	*Total forest area (2005) sq km*	*Forest cover (2005) % of land*	*Total forest area (1990) sq km*	*Total forest area (2000) sq km*	*Annual change rate (1990–2000) sq km/yr*	*Annual change rate (2000–2005) sq km/yr*	*Primary forest (2005) % total forest*	*Annual Loss of primary forest (2000–2005) %/yr*	*Production plantation (2005) sq km*
Bangladesh	1,44,000	8,710	6.7	8,820	8,840	N/A	–20	–	N/A	1,950
India	3,287,260	6,77,010	22.8	6,39,390	6,75,540	3,620	290	–	N/A	10,530
Nepal	1,47,180	36,360	25.4	48,170	39,000	–920	–530	9.6	–2	430
Pakistan	7,96,100	19,020	2.5	25,270	21,160	–410	–430	–	N/A	3,180
Sri Lanka	65,610	19,330	29.9	23,500	20,820	–270	–300	8.6	–3.6	1,710

Source: FAO and World Bank (2007).

Table 3

Per Capita Forests Availability in South Asia

Country	*Natural forest (1,000 ha)*	*Forest plantations (1,000 ha)*	*Total forest (1,000 ha)*	*Proportion of land forested (%)*	*Forest per capita (ha/person)*
Bangladesh	769	235	1,004	8	0.01
India	51,729	13,230	64,959	22	0.08
Nepal	5,023	56	5,079	37	0.27
Pakistan	1,855	168	2,023	3	0.02
Sri Lanka	1,746	139	1,885	29	0.11
South Asia	61,122	13,828	74,950	18	0.06

Source: FAO and World Bank (2007).

Rate of Change in Forest in India: A Case Study

In India, forest cover has increased in the recent past due to the establishment of forest plantations. According to Nicholas Stern "From the Himalaya, which feed water to a billion people, to the coastal areas of Bangladesh, South Asian countries must prepare for the effects of global warming, even as they work to combat the human causes of climate change". Even though South Asia has low greenhouse gas emissions, climate change has already deeply affected the economic growth and development of South Asian countries and poses difficult challenges for the future (World Bank, web page). As South Asian economies rely mainly on agriculture, natural resources, forestry and fisheries sectors, increased risk of floods and droughts would decrease production in these sectors and pose risk to the poor people. Some of the anticipated consequences of climate change in the region include:

- Increased flooding and problems with water resource management due to melting of Himalayan glaciers.
- Added pressure on natural resources and the environment because of rapid urbanization and industrialization.
- Decrease of almost 30 per cent in crop yields by the middle of the century.
- Higher mortality rates of trees because of floods and droughts.

Biodiversity in South Asian Countries

South Asia's rich biodiversity is under stress and endowed with an exceptional array of biodiversity, Its geographical expanse include several diverse ecosystems, such as the mountains of the Himalaya-Hindu Kush, the rangelands of Bhutan, the Thar Desert, the high-altitude freshwater lakes of Nepal, the Deosai plains in Kashmir, the extended contiguous mangrove swamps of India and Bangladesh, and the coral reefs and atolls of Maldives (Table 4). Forests range from tropical, subtropical, and coastal to temperate; and the deserts from hot to cold. Bengal tigers, snow leopards, sloth bears, rhinos, elephants, red panda, wild boar, hoofed animals, birds, and reptiles dwell in these forests, savannas, and deserts. The unique topography and climate has shaped the remarkable variation within the forests, rangelands, deserts, wetlands, freshwater areas and coasts of South Asia. These ecosystems occupy about 3.6 per cent of the world's area but contain 16 per cent of floral and 12 per cent of faunal species found in the world (Sathaye et al. 2005).

Table 4

Biodiversity Profile Estimation of South Asian Countries

Categories	*Afghanistan*	*Bangladesh*	*Bhutan*	*India*	*Maldives*	*Nepal*	*Pakistan*	*Sri Lanka*
Forest Area (% of land area)	1.3	6.7	68	22.8	3.3	25.4	2.5	29.9
Deforestation (average annual %; 1990–2005)	2.7	0.1	–0.3	–0.4	0	1.9	1.9	1.3
Conservation Status								
% Threatened Animal Species	5.71	12.11	5.72	19.54	7.73	15.82	9.51	35.12
Critically Endangered (all species)	3	10	3	72	1	4	8	129
Endangered (all species)	5	28	12	161	3	18	16	127
Vulnerable (all species)	22	51	32	240	7	52	50	159
Endemic (all species)	1	1	3	276	0	2	3	361
Mammals	14	23	22	86	0	31	18	21
Birds	12	23	16	73	0	27	25	15
Reptiles	1	21	0	25	2	6	9	8
Amphibians	1	1	1	66	0	3	0	52
Fish	0	11	0	35	9	0	20	29
Invertebrates	1	0	1	22	0	0	0	52
Plants	1	10	7	166	0	7	2	238
Protected Areas								
Nationally Protected Area (% of land area)	0.3	0.5	25.6	5.3	0	18.6	9.5	27.3
Total Protected Areas (number)[a]	9	26	9	718	25	30	234	278

a Includes all IUCN category reserves (IA, IB, II, III, IV, V and VI), Ramsar Wetlands, UNESCO-MAB Reserves, World Heritage Sites and sites that are protected but do not fall in any IUCN categories.

Sources: The World Bank's The Little Green Data Book 2008; 2008 International Union for Conservation of Nature (IUCN) Red List of Threatened Species (www.iucnredlist.org), accessed on January 27, 2009; World Biodiversity Database (WBDB) 2008, joint project of BirdLife International and Conservation International; and World Database on Protected Areas (WDPA) 2007, joint project of UNEP and IUCN 2007, managed by UNEP World Conservation Monitoring Centre (UNEP-WCMC) and IUCN World Commission on Protected Areas (WCPA).

Threats of climate change upon ecosystems and biodiversity in South Asia *risks to terrestrial ecosystems vegetation shifts and loss of biodiversity in mountain and forest ecosystems threat of desertification in rangelands and semi-deserts challenges facing freshwater and marine ecosystems multiple stresses threatening freshwater, wetlands, and coastal resources;* Coral bleaching occurs when the symbiotic algae in coral tissues separate from their hosts due to sustained stress. Coral can survive this condition for a short period and even restore its symbiotic algae, but prolonged stress can cause its mortality. The impact of climate change upon ecosystems and biodiversity is a key development concern that needs to be integrated in development programmes and responses to climate change (IPCC, 2007c).

Forests contribute over two-thirds of global terrestrial net primary production (NPP). Slowing forest loss and restoring forest cover in deforested areas could thus help mitigate climate change. Forests annually provide over 3.3 billion cubic metres of wood (including 1.8 billion cubic metres of fuel wood and charcoal), as well as numerous non-wood forest products that play a significant role in the economic life of hundreds of millions of people. The rural poor are particularly dependent on forest resources. As many as 300 million people, most of them very poor, depend substantially on forest ecosystems for their subsistence and survival. The 60 million indigenous people who live in forest areas are especially dependent on forest resources and the health of forest ecosystems. World Commission on Forests and Sustainable Development (WCFSD, 1999) have voiced concern about the deepening forest crisis, and the theory and practice of making the transition to "sustainable forest management" is a topic of intensive national and international debate.

According to IPCC-WG II report on Asia: "As a result of the continued emissions of GHGs, the spatial average over the Asian region of the annual mean warming would be about 3°C in the 2050s and about 5°C in the 2080s, says the report based on GCM simulations. Under the combined influence of GHGs and sulphate aerosols, however, the warming would be restricted to about 2.5°C and about 4°C respectively. In general, according to the report, the warming is expected to be higher in the northern hemisphere (NH) during winter than summer."

South Asia and Climate Change Vulnerability

Impact of Forests on Climate Change

Climate change and forests are intrinsically linked. On the one hand, changes in global climate are already stressing forests through higher mean annual temperatures, altered precipitation patterns and more frequent and extreme weather events. At the same time, forests and the wood they produce trap and store carbon dioxide, playing a major role in mitigating climate change. And on the flip side of the coin, when destroyed or over-harvested and burned, forests can become sources of the greenhouse gas, carbon dioxide (FAO, 2007).

Forests in a Land Use Continuum

- 1.3 billion people in the tropics earn part of their subsistence from forests and trees
- Forest plays an important role in reducing vulnerability of livelihoods
- Forests (biomass and soil) stock between 430–540 Pg of carbon, maintaining these reservoirs is key
- Up to 20 per cent of the GHG come from deforestation and forest degradation in tropics/subtropics
- Forest can sequester carbon from the atmosphere helping to mitigate climate change

The impacts of climate change fall disproportionately upon developing countries, and especially their poor populations. South Asia with a population of 1.3 billion is one of the poorest regions in the world. It does not have the required capacity to respond to increased climate change and hence is highly vulnerable to its impacts. According to the United Nations Environment Programme (UNEP), it is the most disaster-prone region in the world. While floods, famine, drought and disease are not new to the region, their severity could increase if the region is not prepared to cope with the impacts of climate change. Forests are vulnerable to projected changes in climate (Maarit et al. 2001):

- The distribution of forests and forest species are expected to change in response to changes in temperature, precipitation, extreme events, pest outbreaks and fires, altering the ecosystem goods and services provided.
- Boreal systems are likely to be the most vulnerable, primarily due to changes in fire and pest outbreaks, potentially leading to forest die-back, a change in age structure and a decrease in carbon content.
- The current net global terrestrial uptake of carbon (about 1GtC year–1) will likely increase during the first half of the 21st century, and then level off or decline over time. Forest systems may even become a source of carbon by the end of the next of the 21st century.

Climate Change Prediction for South Asia

Projecting climate futures is a daunting task. Changes will depend on the unknown future path of greenhouse gas (GHG) emissions, the response of physical systems to emission levels and, non-linear feedback processes. While acknowledging the many uncertainties, a broad consensus has emerged about the likely risks and patterns of climate change under various scenarios developed by the Intergovernment Panel on Climate Change (IPCC). This section focuses on the primary climate variables – temperature; precipitation; run off and their major consequences. The more scientific details are:

Temperature

There is broad consensus that the world is warming. There is ample evidence that by mid-century, temperature increases ranging from 1°C to 2°C are likely to occur. In South Asia this warming will vary regionally, with already warm areas such as Sri Lanka and the Maldives seeing the lowest rise (about 1°C), while the higher altitude areas of Afghanistan, Bhutan, and Nepal experiencing a rise of 1.5°C to 2.5°C in the moderate scenario put forward by the IPCC.[1]

Precipitation

The wet regions will get wetter and the dry regions drier. Forecasts suggest higher but more variable and intense rainfall in South Asia, except in the relatively drier areas of Afghanistan, western India and Pakistan which could see even less rainfall. IPCC projections indicate that the number of days for which extreme events last (especially floods and droughts) would increase in duration and severity. This effect will be especially pronounced in South Asia with its reliance on the monsoons – more so than in many other parts of the world.

Run-off

Changes in precipitation and temperature are expected to interact in complex ways to change the balance between "green" water and "blue" water. Green water is the water that is used or lost in catchments before it reaches the rivers, while blue water is the run-off that reaches the rivers. The run-off is expected to change significantly in the subcontinent, with implications for agriculture. The Indus and Ganges/Brahmaputra basins are expected to experience increased run-off driven by precipitation changes and glacial melt. After the glacial melt, however, there could be significant declines in flows. By 2050, the annual run-off in the Brahmaputra is projected to decline by 14 per cent and the Indus by 27 per cent (IPCC, 2001). Afghanistan is expected to be particularly impacted by a reduction in flows with considerable implications for storage, irrigation, and the development and reliability of hydropower systems.

Why is South Asia Vulnerable to Climate Change?

Geography coupled with high levels of poverty and population density has rendered South Asia especially vulnerable to the impacts of climate change. High population levels translate into increased resource demands on an already stressed natural resource base. By 2050, the South Asia's population is likely to exceed 2.2 billion from the current level of 1.5 billion (Figure 2). With an estimated 600 million South Asians subsisting on less than US$1.25 a day, even small climate shocks can cause irreversible losses and tip a large number of people into destitution.

Through much of South Asia, poverty is still largely in the rural areas and closely intertwined with natural resource degradation. About 70 per cent of South Asians live in rural areas and account for about 75 per cent of the poor. Agriculture employs about 60 per cent of agriculture, the poor in South Asian countries are likely to be disproportionately affected by climate change but, the labour force contributes only 22 per cent of regional GDP. With their rural economies closely tied to the natural resource base and climate sensitive sectors (World Bank, 2007).

The region is already marked by climate variability and a high incidence of natural disasters compounding these risks is the region's heavy reliance on the monsoons. It carries over 70 per cent of South Asia's annual precipitation in a brief four-month period. If climate projections are indicative of future trends, the risks associated with water-related climate variability are likely to worsen.

The Himalaya has a significant influence on the climate and economy of the region. The Himalayan system shapes the critical and often unpredictable monsoon dynamics. It acts as a natural reservoir for sustaining crops and providing groundwater recharge. In fact, it is home to a unique ecosystem. With melting glaciers, flood risks would increase in the near future. In the long term, there can be no

Figure 2

Population Projections in South Asia

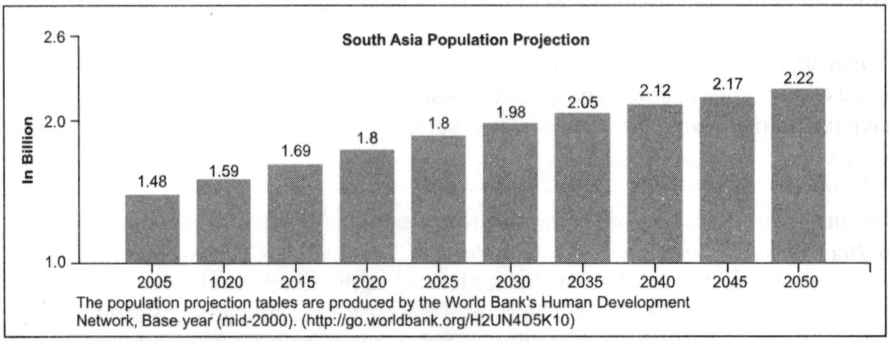

Source: World Bank's Human Development Network[2].

replacement for the water provided by glaciers, and this could result in water shortages at an unparalleled scale.

The region has a long and densely populated coastline with low-lying islands that are vulnerable to sea level rise. In sum, high population densities, a large concentration of poverty and climate variability have all combined to make South Asia highly sensitive to the consequences of climate change.

Impact on South Asia

Adverse Impact on Food Security and Farm Livelihoods

South Asian farming is characterized by fragmented lands and small landholdings by poor farmers who possess low financial and technical capacity to adapt to climate variability and change. Agricultural productivity is likely to suffer severely due to high temperature, severe drought and flood conditions, and soil degradation. As a result, food security of many countries in the region would be under threat. Temperature rise will negatively impact rice and wheat yields in tropical parts of South Asia, where these crops are already being grown close to their temperature tolerance threshold. According to an Intergovernmental Panel on Climate Change (IPCC) report on Asia, about 2.5–10 per cent decrease in crop yield is projected for parts of Asia in the 2020s and 5–30 per cent decrease in the 2050s. It is estimated that a 2–5°C increase in temperature can lower rice yields in India by 20–50 per cent and wheat yields by 35–60 per cent. Wheat yields in Pakistan are predicted to fall by 6–9 per cent.

Forests

Studies of the potential regional impacts of climate change on the forests and forestry of tropical Asia are limited. Results of research from Thailand suggest that climate change would have a profound effect on the future distribution, productivity, and health of Thailand's forests. Using climate change scenarios generated by the United Kingdom Meteorological Offices (UKMO), Boonpragob and Santisirisomboon (1996) estimated that the area of subtropical forests could decline from the current 50 per cent to either 20 per cent or 12 per cent of Thailand's total forest cover (depending on the model used), whereas the area of tropical forests could increase from 45 per cent to 80 per cent of total forest cover. Somaratne and Dhanapala (1996) used the same model for Sri Lanka and estimated a decrease in tropical rainforest of 2–11 per cent and an increase in tropical dry forest of 7–8 per cent. A northward shift of tropical wet forests into areas currently occupied by tropical dry forests also is projected.

Teak is an important wood product throughout the region; in Java, it has been shown to be sensitive to variations in climate (Whetton and Rutherford, 1994). Using climate scenarios generated by ECHAm^3, Model Achanta and Kanetkar (1996) have linked the precipitation effectiveness index (PEI) to net primary productivity of teak plantations in Kerala State, India. They estimate that a projected depletion of soil moisture would likely cause teak productivity to decline from 5.40 m^3/ha to 5.07 m^3/ha. The productivity of moist deciduous forests also could decline, from 1.8 m^3/ha to 1.5 m^3/ha.

Biodiversity

Risks to Asia's rich array of living species are climbing. As many as 1,250 of 15,000 higher plant species are threatened in India. Similar trends are evident in China, Malaysia, Myanmar, and Thailand. Many species and a large population of many other species in Asia are likely to be exterminated as a result of the synergistic effects of climate change and habitat fragmentation. In desert ecosystems, increased frequency of droughts may result in a decline in local forage around oases, causing mass mortality among local fauna and threatening their existence. With a 1-m rise in sea level, the Sundarbans (the largest mangrove ecosystems) of Bangladesh will completely disappear (IPCC WGII).

South Asia's GHG Footprint

However, increased energy consumption has been accompanied by rising GHG emissions. On an average, emissions have risen at about 3.3 per cent annually since 1990 – more rapidly than in any other region, except the Middle East. Total emissions exceed 2.5 billion tonnes of CO_2 equivalents. How South Asia meets the legitimate demands for energy and economic prosperity will have far-reaching consequences on global GHG emissions. Figure 3 confirms the growth typically spurs emissions in rough proportion to the income it generates.[3]

Figure 3

Greenhouse Gas Contributions in South Asia, 2000

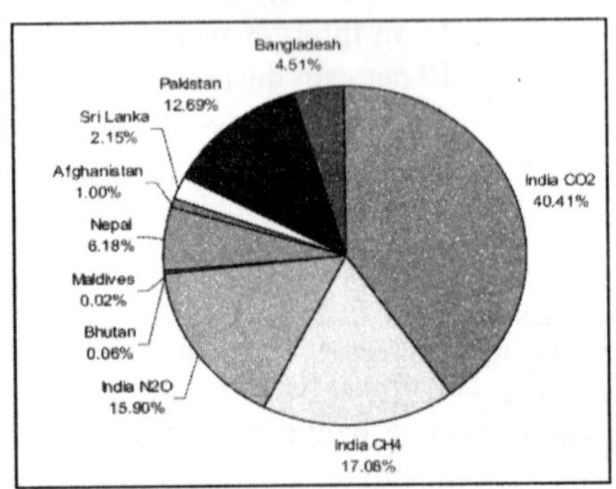

Source: World Resources Institute Climate Analysis Indicators Tool (CAIT)[4]

Impact And Vulnerability Studies

The fourth assessment report of IPCC (IPCC, 2007) concludes that recent modelling studies indicate that forest ecosystems could be seriously impacted by future climate change, even with global warming of 1–2°C. India is a mega biodiversity country where forests account for about 20per cent of the geographical area. With nearly 2 lakh villages classified as forest villages, there is large dependence of communities on forest resources (Ravindranath et al., 2007). Thus, it is important to assess the likely impacts of projected climate change on forests and develop and implement adaptation strategies for both biodiversity conservation and the livelihood of forest dependent communities (Singh, 2009).

A number of Impact assessment models (Coleman et al., 2003; Plantinga, 1999; Friend et al., 1997; Kaplan et al., 2003; Neilson, 1995; Foley et al., 1996) are available. However, the available estimates have only used BIOME3 (Haxeltine and Prentice, 1996) and BIOME4 models (Kaplan et al., 2003).

Impact Assessment Studies

Ecological systems are intrinsically dynamic and are constantly influenced by climate variations and are capable of adapting to the changes in the environment. However, climate change is expected to occur more rapidly than the rate at which ecosystems can adapt and re-establish themselves. Ravindranath et al. (2006), made

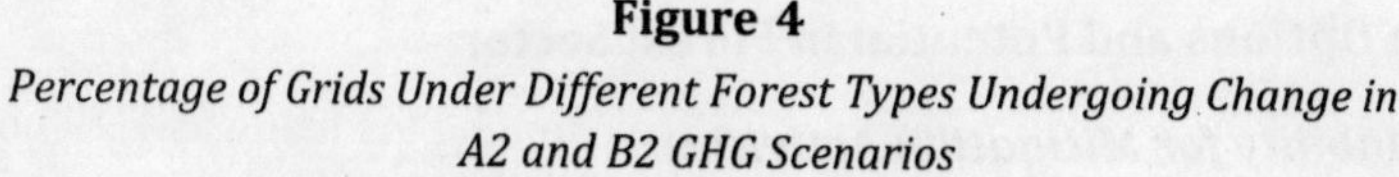

Figure 4

Percentage of Grids Under Different Forest Types Undergoing Change in A2 and B2 GHG Scenarios

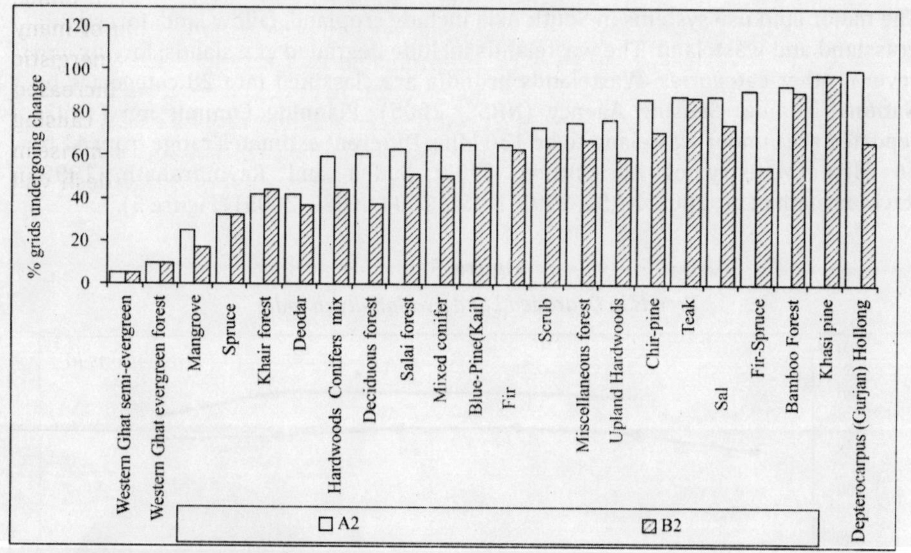

Source: Ravindranath et al., 2006.

an assessment of the impact of projected climate change on forest ecosystems in India, based on climate projections of regional climate model of Hadley Centre (HadRM3) using the A2 and B2 scenarios of Special Report on Emissions Scenario (SRES) and the BIOME 4 vegetation response model (Figure 4). The study found that under the climate projection for the year 2085, around 77 per cent and 68 per cent of the forested grids in India are likely to experience shift in forest type under A2 and B2 scenario, respectively. North-eastern region may experience a shift towards wetter forest types, whereas north-western region may experience a shift towards drier forest types in absence of human interferences.

Impact on Biodiversity

Biodiversity is likely to be impacted under the projected climate scenarios due to the changes or shifts in forest or vegetation types (in 57 to 60 per cent of forested grids), forest dieback during the transient phase, and different species responding differently to climate changes even when there is no change in forest type (Ravindranath et al., 2006).

Impact on Productivity and Biomass Production

Increasing atmospheric CO_2 concentration and climate warming could also result in doubling of net primary productivity under A2 scenario and nearly 70 per cent increase under B2 scenario. The NPP under Tropical Evergreen Forest increases by 1.5 times under the GHG scenarios. The rate of increase on NPP was lower for Cool Conifer Forest, Cold Mixed Forest and Temperate Deciduous Forest. Generally, the rate of increase is higher for warmer vegetation types (ibid.).

Mitigation Options and Potential in Forest Sector

Land Availability for Mitigation Activities

The major land use systems in South Asia include cropland, fallow land, forestland, grassland and wasteland. The wastelands include degraded grasslands, forests and several other categories. Wastelands in India are classified into 28 categories by National Remote Sensing Agency (NRSC, 2005). Planning Commission (1992) reported area under wasteland to be 130 Mha. Different estimates range from 41 to 66 Mha (Ministry of Agriculture, 1992; Sudha and Ravindranath, 1999; Ravindranath et al., 2001; NRSC, 1995; NRSC, 2004; NRSC, 2005) (Figure 5).

Figure 5

Trends in Degraded Land Availability in India

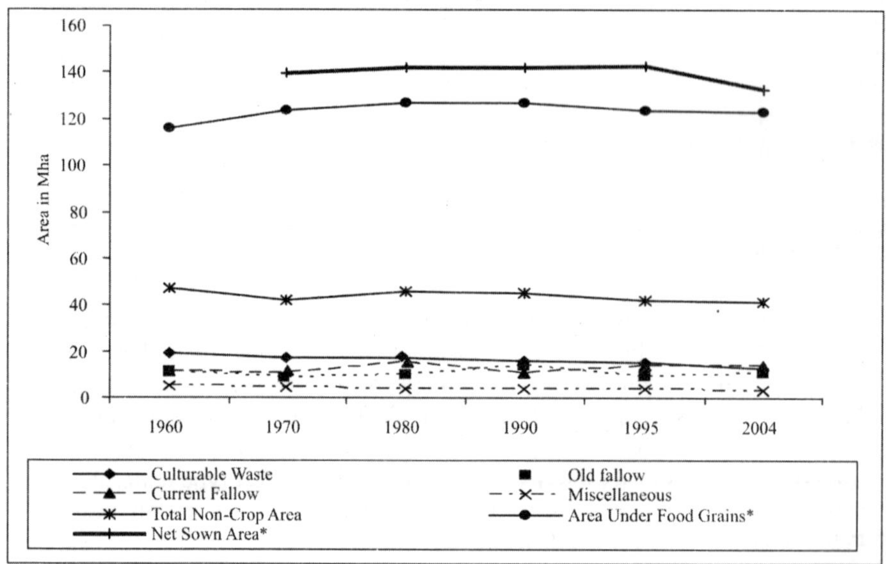

Sources: Ministry of Agriculture, 1992; Sudha and Ravindranath, 1999; Ravindranath et al. 2001; NRSC, 1995; NRSC, 2004 and NRSC, 2005.

Models Used for Mitigation Assessments

A number of models are available for the assessment of the mitigation potential, including in land use change and forestry sector (Sathaye et al., 2005; Schelhas et al., 2004; Edmonds et al., 1985; Darius et al., 1999; Plantinga et al., 1999; Sohngen et al., 2006; Maarit et al., 2004). However, only COMAP and GCOMAP models have been so far employed to estimate the mitigation potential at different levels: national and regional.

Mitigation Potential Estimates

The mitigation potential estimate depends on mitigation activity (forest conservation, afforestation, agro-forestry), species (monoculture, mixed species, short and long rotation), biomass growth rates and area. For example in India mitigation potentials are available at all the three levels (i.e., national and regional scales).

Research Gaps and Needs

Data availability for mitigation activities according to different land category of FSI at district level or micro administrative division and Agro-Ecological Zone (AEZ) level is critical. There is a need for an understanding of the barriers to land availability for mitigation activities. Most of the estimates available in the literature are technical potential without considering the barriers. Therefore, an urgent requirement for economic and market potential is needed for estimates of the mitigation potential.

Climate Change Adaptation

Adaptation is adjustment in natural or human systems in response to actual or expected climatic stimuli and their impacts on natural and socio-economic systems. Climate change could cause irreversible damage to unique forest ecosystems and biodiversity, rendering several species extinct, locally and globally. According to study by Ravindranath et al., 2006, forest ecosystems require the longest response time to adapt, say through migration and regrowth. Further, a long gestation period is involved in developing and implementing adaptation strategies in the forests. Thus, there is a need to develop and implement adaptation strategies. Currently, there is very little research on adaptation. Adaptation is not included in the modelling efforts of impact assessment. Adaptation practices may have to be developed and incorporated into afforestation and reforestation programmes. Some examples of policies and practices that need to be explored to promote adaptation are (Ravindranath et al., 2006):

- Incorporate climate concern in long-term forest policy making process and into working plans
- Conserve forests and reduce forest fragmentation
- Expand protected areas and link them wherever possible to promote migration
- Promote mixed species forestry to reduce vulnerability
- Undertake anticipatory planting and assist natural migration through transplanting plant species
- Promote *in situ* and *ex situ* gene pool conservation
- Initiate forest fire management strategies.

Mitigation and Adaptation Synergy

Working together of two things (mitigation or adaptation for example) to produce an effect greater than the sum of their individual effects is called synergy and in this case to combat climate change and forestry problem synergy establishment is a key factor. There is a realization on the need to explore and promote synergy between mitigation and adaptation while addressing climate change. A study by Ravindranath (2007c), explored the synergy between mitigation and adaptation by considering forest sector, which on the one hand is projected to be adversely impacted under the projected climate change scenarios and, on the other, provide opportunities to mitigate climate change. The study highlighted the potential and need for incorporating adaptation strategies and practices in mitigation projects. The study concluded that there is a need to ensure that mitigation programmes or projects do not increase the vulnerability of forest ecosystems and plantations. Further, several adaptation practices could be incorporated into mitigation projects to reduce vulnerability. Mitigation projects could be designed to reduce vulnerability and promote adaptation, for example; forest and biodiversity conservation, protected area management and sustainable forestry. The study on India has highlighted the need for research and field demonstration of synergy between mitigation and adaptation, so that the cost of addressing climate change impacts could be reduced and co-benefits increased. Countrywise profile for climate change and related risks in order to mitigate the problem (Table 4).

Conclusions

The implications of climate change on South Asian forest and biodiversity are very grave for reducing the vulnerability of ecosystems, developing mitigation strategies and projects, periodic inventory of the greenhouse gases, promoting sustainable management of forests, and sustainable production of timber, industrial wood, fuel wood and biomass feedstock for energy. It has been analysed through this paper that, there is a strong need for modelling the changes at regional level rather than only relying on global level output. Regional Circulation Model (RCM) is still in nascent stage though Global Circulation Models (GCM) is robust in projecting mean temperature at global level. It has been found that the region is already marked by climate variability and a high incidence of natural disasters compounding these risks is the region's heavy reliance on the monsoons; if climate projections are indicative of future trends, the risks associated with water-related climate variability are likely to worsen. The Himalaya has a significant influence on the climate and economy of the region; it shapes the critical and often unpredictable monsoon dynamics. It acts as a natural reservoir for sustaining crops and providing groundwater recharge. In fact, it is home to a unique ecosystem. With melting glaciers, flood risks would increase in the near future. In the long term, there can be no replacement for the water provided by glaciers, and this could result in water shortages at an unparalleled scale.

There is a strong uncertainty involved in projecting that precipitation changes are higher at global and particularly at regional level. Projecting rainfall is really a hard task because it involves a very high degree of uncertainty and results fluctuate from model to model. The data limitations need to be overcome by initiating studies to develop database on forest vegetation characteristics and socio-economic interaction, dependence and pressures on forest ecosystems. It is important to understand the likely impacts of climate change to ensure sustainable management of forests and flow of timber, industrial wood and non-timber products and conservation of biodiversity. Such an analysis is also required since many countries in South Asia are planning to undertake large-scale CDM (clean development mechanism) projects in the forest sector, to minimize the vulnerability of its long low-lying islands and densely populated coastline. In sum, high population densities, a large concentration of poverty and climate variability have all combined to make South Asia highly sensitive to the consequences of climate change. Therefore, it has been initiated that although development is a prerequisite, it should not proceed at the cost of environment.

Notes

1. This is one of the scenarios used by the IPCC in its climate projections. It is moderate in its assumptions about the world and the pace at which it will change. For instance, it assumes low rates of population growth and land use changes; medium availability of resources such as oil and gas; very high GDP and energy use growth; and rapid technological change, among other things (Nakicenovic and Swart, 2000).

2. Note: The input data used for the projections include a base year (mid-2000), population estimate by age and sex and base period (2000–2005), estimates of mortality, fertility and migration. The population projections tables are produced by the World Bank's Human Development Network in consultation with operational staff and country offices and provide population projections and other demographic data for nearly 200 economies. Available at http://go.worldbank.org/H4UN4D5K10.
3. Globally, 1 per cent increase in per capita income has induced – on average – 1 per cent increase in GHG emissions.
4. Note: Figure only provides contribution by gas for India in CO2 equivalents.

References

Achanta, A.N. and R. Kanetkar (1996) 'Impact of Climate Change on Forest Productivity: A Case Study of Kerala, India', Paper Presented at the Asian and Pacific Workshop on Climate Change, Vulnerability and Adaptation Assessment, Manila, Philippines, 15–19 January.

Achard, F., H. Eva, A. Glinni, P. Mayaux, T. Richards and H.J. Stibig (1998) 'Identification of Deforestation Hot Spot Areas in the Humid Tropics', Trees Series B, NE4, EUR 18079 EN, European Commission, Luxembourg, 100.

Boonpragob, K. and J. Santisirisomboon (1996) 'Modeling Potential Impacts of Climate Changes of Forest Area in Thailand Under Climate Change', in L. Erda et al. (eds), *Climate Change Variability and Adaptation in Asia and the Pacific*, Dordrecht, Netherlands: Kluwer Academic Publishers, 107–117.

Coleman, M.T., Meyer, D.W. and Scheffman, D.T. (2003) 'Climate Analyses of Mergers at the FTC: The Cruise Ships Mergers Investigation', *Review of Industrial Organization*, 23: 121–155.

Darius, F., Plantinga, A.J., Mauldin, T., Douglas, J. (1999) 'An Econometric Analysis of the Costs of Sequestering Carbon in Forests', *American Journal of Agricultural Economics*, 81(4): 812–824.

Edmunds, W.M. Guendouz, A., Mamou, A., Moulla, A., Shand, P., Zouari, K. (1985) 'Forest evolution in the Continental Intercalaria Assessment of Southern Algeria and Tunisia: Trace Element and Isotopic Indicators', *Appl. Geochem*., 18: 805–822.

Foley, J.A., I.C. Prentice, N. Ramankutty, S. Levis, D. Pollard, S. Sitch and A. Haxeltine (1996) 'An Integrated Biosphere Model of Land Surface Processes, Terrestrial Carbon Balance and Vegetation Dynamics', *Global Biogeochemical Cycles*, 10(4): 603–628.

Food and Agriculture Organization (2007) *State of the World's Forests*, Rome, Italy: FAO, 144.

FRA (2000) 'Forest Cover Mapping and Monitoring with NOAA-AVHRR and Other Coarse Spatial Resolution Sensors', 42.

Friend, A.D., A.K. Stevens, R.G. Knox and M.G.R. Cannell (1997) 'A Process-Based, Biogeochemical, Terrestrial Biosphere Model of Ecosystem Dynamics (Hybrid v3.0)', *Ecological Modelling*, 95: 249–287.

FSI (2003 and 2007) *State of Forest Report 2003–07*, Ministry of Environment and Forests, Dehradun: Forest Survey of India.

Haxeltine, A. and I.C. Prentice (1996) 'BIOME3: An Equilibrium Terrestrial Biosphere Model Based on Ecophysiological Constraints, Resource Availability and Competition Among Plant Functional Types', *Global Biogeochemical Cycles*, 10(4): 693–709.

Intergovernmental Panel on Climate Change (IPCC) (1998) *The Regional Impacts of Climate Change: An Assessment of Vulnerability*, A Special Report of the Intergovernmental Panel on Climate Change, Cambridge: Cambridge University Press.

—— (2000) *Land Use, Land-Use Change and Forestry*, Cambridge: Cambridge University Press.

—— (2001) *Synthesis Report: Climate Change 2001*, Summary for Policymakers, Wembley, UK, 24–29 September.

—— (2002) *Working Group II: Impacts, Adaptation and Vulnerability*, Geneva.

—— (2003) *Good Practice Guidance for Land Use, Land-Use Change and Forestry*, Kanagawa, Japan: Institute for Global Environmental Strategies.

—— (2007) *Synthesis Report*, Geneva: WMO and UNEP.

—— (2007a) 'Climate Change 2007: The Physical Science Basis', Contribution of Working Group I to the Fourth Assessment Report of the Intergovernmental Panel on Climate Change [S. Solomon, D. Qin, M. Manning, Z. Chen, M. Marquis, K.B. Averyt, M. Tignor and H.L. Miller (eds)], Cambridge: Cambridge University Press, 996.

—— (2007b) Synthesis Report Contribution of Working Groups I, II and III to the Fourth Assessment Report of the Intergovernmental Panel on Climate Change [Core Writing Team, R.K. Pachauri and A. Reisinger (eds)], Geneva, Switzerland, 104.

—— (2007c) 'Climate Change 2007: Impacts, Adaptation and Vulnerability', Contribution of Working Group II to the Fourth Assessment Report of the Intergovernmental Panel on Climate Change [M. L. Parry, O.F. Canziani, J.P. Palutikof, P.J. Van der Linden and C.E. Hanson (eds)], Cambridge: Cambridge University Press.

—— (2008) 'Technical Paper on Climate Change and Water', Geneva.

Kaplan, J.O. et al. (2003) 'Climate Change and Arctic Ecosystems: Modeling, Paleodata-Model Comparisons and Future Projections', *Journal of Geophysical Research: Atmospheres*, 108(8171).

Maarit, A., A.I. Kallio, Alexander Moiseyev and Birger Solberg (2004) *Technical Report 15*, European Forest Institute, Joensuu, Finland, 24.

Ministry of Agriculture (1992) 'Agricultural Statistics at a Glance', Government of India, New Delhi.

MOEF (2004) India's Initial National Communication to UNFCCC, Ministry of Environment and Forest, Government of India. Available at http://www.natcomindia.org/natcomreport.htm (Last accessed on 7 January 2009).

Nabuurs, G.J. et al. (2007) 'Forestry', in *Climate Change and Mitigation*, Cambridge: Cambridge University Press.

Nakicenovic, N. and R. Swart (eds) (2000) *IPCC Special Report on Emissions Scenarios.*

National Remote Sensing Centre (1995, 2004 and 2005) 'Integrated Mission for Sustainable Development', Technical Guidelines, NRSA, Hyderabad.

National Remote Sensing Centre (2005) http://www.nrsa.gov.in/engnrsa/products/geninformation.html, Hyderabad, India. (Last accessed: 21 December, 2005, IST. 10:55).

Neilson, R.P. (1995) 'A Model for Predicting Continental Scale Vegetation Distribution and Water Balance', *Ecol. Appl.*, 5: 362–385.

Planning Commission (1992) *Planning Review* 1980–85, New Delhi.

Plantinga, Andrew J., Thomas Mauldin and Douglas J. Miller (1999) 'An Econometric Analysis of the Costs of Sequestering Carbon in Forests', *American Journal of Agricultural Economics*, 81(4): 812–8247.

Ravindranath, N.H. et al. (2007 and 2007c) 'Impact of Climate Change on Indian Forests: A Dynamic Vegetation Modelling Approach', *Mitigation Adaptation Strategies for Global Change*, 1–24.

Ravindranath, N.H., Joshi, N.V., Sukumar, R., Saxena, A. (2006) 'Impact of Climate Change on Forest in India', *Current Science*, 90(3): 354–361.

Ravindranath, N.H., Lasco, R. and Sudha, P. (2001) 'Assessment of GHG Inventories from the LUCF Sector of Annex-I Countries', *Mitigation and Adaptation Strategies for Global Change*, 11: 233–250.

Sathaye, J. and N.H. Ravindranath (1998) 'Climate Change Mitigation in Energy and Forestry Sectors of Developing Countries', *Annual Review of Energy and the Environment*, 23: 387–437.

Sathaye, J.A. and Phadke, A. (2005) Cost and Carbon Emissions of Coal and Combined Cycle Power Plants in India: International Implications.

Sathaye, Jayant, Willy Makundi, Larry Dale and Peter Chan (2005) 'GHG Mitigation Potential, Costs and Benefits in Global Forests: A Dynamic Partial Equilibrium Approach', Ernest Orlando Lawrence Berkeley National Laboratory.

Schelhas, J., Buck, L.E. and Geisler. C.C. (2004) Introduction: The Challenge of Adaptive Collaborative Climate Management', in L.E. Buck, C.C. Geisler, J. Schelhas, and E. Wollenberg (eds) *Biological Diversity: Balancing Interests Through Adaptive Collaborative Management*, Boca Raton: CRC Press, 19–35.

Singh, S. (2009) 'GIS Application in Urban Heat Island: A Crusading Anthropogenic Driver to Climate Change', *Urban India Journal*, 30: 74–92.

Sohngen, B. and Mendelsohn, R. (2006) 'A Sensitivity Analysis of Carbon Sequestration', M. Schlesinger et al. (eds) *Human-Induced Climate Change: An Interdisciplinary Assessment*, Cambridge: Cambridge University Press.

Somaratne, S. and A.H. Dhanapala (1996) 'Potential Impact of Global Climate Change on Forest Distribution in Sri Lanka', in L. Erda et al. (eds), *Climate Change Variability and Adaptation in Asia and the Pacific*, Dordrecht, Netherlands: Kluwer Academic Publishers, 129–135.

Sudha, P. and Ravindranath, N.H. (1999) 'Land Availability and Biomass Production Potential in India', *Biomass and Bioenergy*, 16(3): 207–222.

Sudha P., D. Shubhashree, H. Khan, G.T. Hedge, I.K. Murthy, V. Shreedhara and N.H. Ravindranath (2007) 'Estimating Land Suitability and Development of Regional Baseline for a Dominant Agro-Ecological Zone of Karnataka, India', *Mitigation and Adaptation Strategies for Global Change*, 12: 1051–1075.

Whetton, P.H. and Rutherford, I. (1994) 'Historical ENSO Teleconnections in the Eastern Hemisphere', *Climate Change*, 28: 221–253.

World Bank (2007) *South Asia: Climate Change Strategy*, Washington, DC.

— (2008) *Mainstreaming Climate Change Mitigation in Cities*, Washington, DC: Environment Department.

World Commission on Forests and Sustainable Development (WCFSD) (1999) 'Our Forests Our Future', Summary Report.

World Resources Institute (WRI) (2005) *Navigating the Numbers: Greenhouse Gas Data and International Climate Policy*, Washington, DC.

26

Vulnerability in Mountain Systems to Natural and Anthropogenic Hazards

A Case of Himachal Pradesh

KRISHNANAND

It is well recognized that mountain ecosystems and their inhabitants are among the most vulnerable to climate change. Measuring the nature and scope of these vulnerabilities remains, however, a work-in-progress. Mountains provide vital goods and services for the benefit of all humankind, for supporting sustainable development at a global level, and for moving the world towards a green economy. But provision of these goods and services is at risk. Mountains cover 27 per cent of the earth's land area. About 1.2 billion people or 17 per cent of the world's population live in mountains or on their fringes. Mountains provide 60–80 per cent of the world's freshwater resources for drinking, for lowland irrigation vital to food security, for industry, and for hydropower, the most important source of green energy, contributing 20 per cent of global electricity generation. In drier areas, such as the Middle East, Central Asia, South Asia, and parts of western North America, virtually all freshwater (80–100%) comes from mountains. Mountains also supply important minerals and the genetic resources of major food crops. Around 17 of the 34 global biodiversity hotspots are in mountains. One-third of all protected areas are in mountains; many of the world's largest cities including New York, Jakarta, Tokyo, Mumbai, Nairobi, Mexico City, and Bogota rely on such areas for their water supply. In an increasingly urbanized world, mountains are major destinations for recreation and tourism. Various projections show that mountains are experiencing disproportionate warming. For instance, in the Tibetan Plateau the average temperature increase per decade over the last 50 years was in the range of 0.2 to 0.6 degrees centigrade. Similar figures exist for the Andes and other high mountain environments.

Challenges to Sustainable Mountain Development

Mountains worldwide are facing important challenges that threaten provision of these vital goods and services. Land degradation due to inappropriate farming practices and extractive industries (mining) is a major problem, exacerbated by population growth and ambiguous resource governance and tenure rights. Nearly

Figure 1

Vulnerabilities in Mountains

Source: Self Clicked.

90 per cent of the global mountain population live in transition and developing countries. Close to 30 per cent of them, or 300 million people, are vulnerable to food insecurity and many of them live in extreme poverty. Access to basic infrastructure such as health and education is often poor, increasing the marginalization of mountain communities (Figure 1). Mountains are particularly susceptible to environmental hazards, causing disasters, such as devastating floods, landslides, or avalanches leading to loss of life, property, and livelihoods. Many mountain areas are in tectonically active zones with an increased probability of earthquakes and volcanic eruptions. At a global scale, 55 per cent of mountain land is susceptible to earthquakes, as opposed to 36 per cent of non-mountainous land. Mountains are also very sensitive to climate change, as shown by the rapid melting of glaciers worldwide; the consequences reach far beyond mountain regions.

Review of the Concept of "Vulnerability"

The word 'vulnerability' is usually associated with natural hazards like flood, droughts, and social hazards like poverty, etc. Of late it is extensively used in climate change literature to denote the extent of damage a region is expected to be affected by various factors effected by climate change. In the context of climate change, there are many studies on vulnerability and its definitions vary according to the perception of the researchers (ICRISAT, 2009).

Chamber (1983) defined that vulnerability has two sides. One is an external side of risks, shocks to which an individual or household is subject to climate change and an internal side which is defenselessness, meaning a lack of means to cope without damaging loss. Blaikie et al. (1994) defined vulnerability as the characteristics of a person or group in terms of their capacity to anticipate, cope with, resist and recover from the impacts of natural hazards and states that vulnerability can be viewed along a continuum from resilience to susceptibility. According to Adger and Kelly (1999) "vulnerability is the extent to which a natural or social system is susceptible to sustaining damage from climate change. It is generally perceived to be a function of two components. The effect that an event may have on humans, referred to as capacity or social vulnerability and the risk that such an event may occur, often referred to as exposure". Watson et al. (1996) defined vulnerability as the extent to which climate change may damage or harm a system, depending not only on a system's sensitivity but also on its ability to adapt to new climatic conditions. Kasperson et al. (2000) defined vulnerability as the degree to which an exposure unit is susceptible to harm due to exposure to a perturbation or stress and the ability or lack of the exposure unit to cope, recover or fundamentally adapt to become a new system or to become extinct. O'Brien and Mileti (1992) examined the vulnerability to climate change and stated that in addition to economic well-being and stability, being important in the resilience of populations to environmental shocks, the structure and health of the population may play a key role in determining vulnerability. Age is an important consideration as the elderly and young persons tend to be inherently more susceptible to environmental risk and hazard exposure. Generally, populations with low dependency ratio and in good health are likely to have the widest coping ranges and thus be least vulnerable in the face of hazard exposure. Handmer et al. (1999) studied the coping mechanisms to environmental shock or hazard brought about by biophysical vulnerability. The factors like institutional stability and strength of public infrastructure are of crucial importance in determining the vulnerability to climate change. A well-connected population with appropriate public infrastructure will be able to deal with a hazard effectively and reduce the vulnerability. Such a society could be said to have low social vulnerability. If there is an absence of institutional capacity in terms of knowledge about the event and ability to deal with it, then such high vulnerability is likely to ensure that biophysical risk, turns into an impact on the human population. Atkins et al. (1998) studied the methodology for measurement of vulnerability and to construction of a suitable composite vulnerability index for developing countries and island states. The composite vulnerability indices were presented for a sample of 110 developing countries for which appropriate data was available. The index suggests that small states are especially prone to be vulnerable when compared to large states. Among the small states, such as Cape Verde and Trinidad and Tobago are estimated to suffer relatively low levels of vulnerability and majority of the states estimated to experience relatively high vulnerability and the states like Tonga, Antigua and Barbedas being more vulnerable to external economic and environmental factors.

Chris Easter (2000) constructed a vulnerability index for the Commonwealth countries, which is based on two principles. First, the impact of external shocks over which the country has been affected and second the resilience of a country to withstand and recover from such shocks. The analysis used a sample of 111 developing countries (37 small and 74 large) for which relevant data were available. The results indicated that among the 50 most vulnerable countries, 33 were small states within this, 27 are least developed countries and 23 are islands. In the least vulnerable 50 countries, only two were small states.

Dolan and Walker (2003) discussed the concept of vulnerability and presented a multi-scaled, integrated framework for assessing vulnerabilities and adaptive capacity. Determinants of adaptive capacity including access to and distribution of wealth, technology, and information, risk perception and awareness, social capital and critical institutional frameworks to address climate change hazards. These are identified at the individual and community level and situated within larger regional, national and international settings. Local and traditional knowledge is the key to research design and implementation and allows for locally relevant outcomes that could aid in more effective decision-making, planning and management in remote coastal regions.

Moss et al. (2001) identified ten proxies for five sectors of climate sensitivities which are settlement sensitivity, food security, human health sensitivity, ecosystem sensitivity and water availability and seven proxies for three sectors of coping and adaptive capacity, economic capacity, human resources and environmental or natural resources capacity. Proxies were aggregated into sectoral indicators, sensitivity indicators and coping or adaptive capacity indicators and finally, constructed vulnerability resilience indicators to climate change. Katharine Vincent (2004) created an index to empirically assess relative levels of social vulnerability to climate change induced variations in water availability and allow cross country comparison in Africa. An aggregated index of social vulnerability were formed through the weighted average of five composite sub-indices, which are economic well-being and stability, demographic structure, institutional stability and strength of public infrastructure, global interconnectivity and dependence on natural resources. The results indicate that using the current data, Niger, Sierra Leone, Burundi, Madagascar and Burkina Faso are the most vulnerable countries in Africa. For the purpose of our understanding, we follow the IPCC Third Assessment Report according to which vulnerability is defined as "The degree to which a system is susceptible to, or unable to cope with, adverse effects of climate change, including climate variability and extremes. Vulnerability is a function of the character, magnitude, and rate of climate variation to which a system is exposed, its sensitivity, and its adaptive capacity" (McCarthy et al., 2001). Thus as per this definition, vulnerability has three components: exposure, sensitivity and adaptive capacity. These three components are described as follows:

- Exposure can be interpreted as the direct danger (i.e., the stressor), and the nature and extent of changes to a region's climate variables (e.g., temperature, precipitation, extreme weather events).
- Sensitivity describes the human-environmental conditions that can worsen the hazard, ameliorate the hazard, or trigger an impact.
- Adaptive capacity represents the potential to implement adaptation measures that help avert potential impacts.

The first two components together represent the potential impact and adaptive capacity is the extent to which these impacts can be averted. Thus vulnerability is potential impact (*I*) minus adaptive capacity (*AC*). This leads to the following mathematical equation for vulnerability:

$$V = f(I - AC)$$

The Study Area

Himachal Pradesh is situated in the Western Himalayas between latitude 30°22′ 40″ North to 33° 12′40″ North and longitude 75° 45′ 55″ East to 79° 04′ 20″ East. It covers an area of 55,673 kilometres. It is a mountainous state with elevation ranging from about 350 metres (1,148 ft) to 6,000 metres (19,685 ft) above the sea level. The drainage system of Himachal is composed both of rivers and glaciers. Himachal Pradesh provides water to both the Indus and Ganges basins. The drainage systems of the region are the Chandra Bhaga or the Chenab, the Ravi, the Beas, the Sutlej and the Yamuna. The state has an extensive cover of natural vegetation.

Aims and Objectives

The basic aims of the study are: (i) to study the overall hazard profile of the state, and (ii) to assess the vulnerability in the state with respect to hazardous occurrences.

Data Source Methodology

The data has been collected from Himachal Pradesh State Disaster Management Authority (HPSDMA) report and other published articles. Firstly, the factoring of hazards was done to find out the most prominently occurring hazards in the state, followed by rating them on a scale of 1–5 in increasing order of occurrences. Then, weightage was given to each one of them in order of maximum to the most damaging in terms of economic losses. The overall vulnerability matrix for the state was created on the basis of these data which has been used to prepare the map of vulnerability using overlay analysis technique through the Arc View 3.2 software.

Results and Discussions

Seismically, the state lies in the great Alpine – Himalayan seismic belt running from Alps mountains through Yugoslavia, Turkey, Iran, Afghanistan, Pakistan, India, Nepal, Bhutan and Burma. The state has not only been shaken by earthquake occurring in its territory but also in the neighbouring areas of J&K in the north, Tibet in the east and UP hills in the south-east. A number of damaging earthquakes have occurred in the HP territory during the 20th century for which information is well recorded. Information about earthquake occurrence before the famous 1905 Kangra earthquake is not, however, available and is a matter of research through historical and archival records. Large earthquakes have occurred in all parts of Himachal Pradesh, the biggest being the Kangra Earthquake of 1905.There were two more big quakes, but they were not nearly as powerful as the 1905 jolt. The first was in 1906, a 6.4 on Richter scale near Kullu and the second was a 6.8 in Lahaul-Kinnaur Spiti in 1975 along the Indo-China Border. There are 250 earthquakes of Magnitude 4.0 and above including more than 60 with Magnitude 5.0 or more, which have rocked the state of HP and adjoining areas of J&K or UP in the last about 90 years (Table 1).

Table 1

Earthquake in Himachal Pradesh

Location	*Year*	*Damaged occured*
Lahul & Spiti	January, 1975	Earthquake shocks triggered the avalanche of great dimensions damaging road network.
Lahul & Spiti	March , 1978	About 30 people killed, road and property damaged.
	March, 1979	About 237 people killed, Communication disrupted.
Kinnaur	March, 1991	Tinku avalanche occurs every year, 4–5 times from Jan to March. Road was blocked for 40 days in 1991.
	September, 1995	Due to avalanche, huge chunk of debris came down which later changed into flood.

It is also seen that according to seismic zoning map of the state's five districts, namely Chamba (53.2%), Hamirpur (90.9%), Kangra (98.6%), Kullu (53.1%) and

Mandi (97.4%) have 53 to 98.6 per cent of their area liable to the severest design intensity, the remaining area of these districts being liable to the next severe intensity. Two districts, Bilaspur (25.3%) and Una (37.0%) also have substantial area in severe intensity zone. The remaining districts also are liable from low to greater intensity earthquakes.

Another form of natural hazard in the state is the occurrences of landslides. The hills and mountains of Himachal Pradesh are liable to suffer landslides during monsoons and also in high intensity earthquakes. The vulnerability of the geologically young and not so stable steep slopes in various Himalayan ranges, has been increasing at a rapid rate in the recent decade due to inappropriate human activity like deforestation, road cutting, terracing and changes in agriculture crops requiring more intense watering, etc.

The important landslides in Himachal Pradesh which caused huge damage are:

- Maling (1968): This slide damaged 1 km of NH–22 and is still active.
- Kinnaur (Dec.1982): This occurred at Sholding Nala, collapsing 3 bridges and 1.5 km of road literally vanished.
- Jhakri (March 1989): At Nathpa about 500 m of road was damaged due to this slide and is still active.
- At Luggarbhati on 12 September 1995, 65 people (39 as per official record) were buried alive during the slide.
- Prominent slides in Beas valley are at Marhi, Bhang, Chhyal, and Mandu in upper catchment of the Beas river.

Figure 2

Hazard profile of Himachal Pradesh

Hazard Profile of HP

- Hydro-Meteorological
  - Flash Floods
  - Cloudbursts
  - Forest Fires
  - Droughts
  - Hailstorms
  - Wind Storms
  - Lightening
- Geological
  - Earthquakes
  - Landslides
  - Soil erosion
  - Avalanche
- Industrial
  - Chemical
  - Industrial
- Manmade
  - Accidents
  - Building Collapse
  - Terrorism
  - Boat Capsizing
  - Stampede
  - Domestic Fires
- Biological
  - Epidemics
  - Pandemics
  - CBNR Emergencies
  - Pest Attacks

Source: HPSDMA Report, 2011.

Other hazards include cloud-burst, floods, forest fires, accidents, etc., which adds to the hazardous profile of the state (Figure 2). The hazard profile of the State can be shown through the following flow chart diagram:

Vulnerability Profile of the State

Considering the proneness of the state towards different kinds of natural hazards, a broad districtwise vulnerability status was devised for the state depending upon the vulnerability towards different hazards according to the guidelines given in Himachal Pradesh State Disaster Management Authority (HPSDMA). Vulnerability matrix (Table 2) was developed based on the qualitative weightage which was given in the scale of 0–5 for different hazards such as earthquakes, landslides, avalanches, industrial hazards, construction type and density of population. Districtwise matrix was prepared by evaluating the risk severity. The evaluation also gives weightage to the density of population likely to be affected. The matrix also includes the evaluation of hazards likely to be induced on account of development of projects such as hydel projects, roads industries, etc. In case of earthquake vulnerability, district Kangra, Hamirpur and Mandi fall in very high vulnerable category.

Districts which fall in high earthquake vulnerability are Chamba, Kullu, Kinnaur and part of Kangra and Shimla, whereas the moderate and low vulnerable districts are Una, Bilaspur, Sirmour and Solan, Shimla and Lahaul & Spiti respectively. The landslide vulnerability in case of Chamba, Kullu, Kinnaur and part of Kangra and Shimla districts is high followed by Kangra, Mandi, Bilaspur, Shimla, Sirmour and Lahaul & Spiti falling in moderate vulnerable category. The areas falling in low vulnerable category are in the districts of Una, Hamirpur and Solan. The flood hazard vulnerability map indicates that areas of Chamba, Kullu, Una and Kinnaur fall in high vulnerable districts whereas the Lahaul & Spiti, Mandi, Shimla, Kangra, Hamirpur, Bilaspur, Solan and Sirmour fall in moderate and low vulnerability areas. The overall vulnerability of the state on the basis of the matrix clearly suggests that Chamba, Kinnaur, Kullu and part of Kangra and Shimla fall in very high vulnerable risk. Similarly, district Kangra, Mandi, Una, Shimla and Lahaul and Spiti have high vulnerable risk status. District Hamirpur, Bilaspur, Solan and Sirmour fall in moderate vulnerable risk status. The disaster management strategies and infrastructure required to be evolved by taking the above factors into consideration.

Table 2

Vulnerability Profile of the Himachal Pradesh

Districts	*EQ*	*Landslide*	*Floods*	*Avalanches*	*Industry*	*Construction Type & Density*	*Overall Vulnerability*
Kangara	VH	M	L		M	VH	H
Chamba	H	H	H	M	M	H	VH
Hamirpur	VH	L	L			H	M
Madi	VH	M	M			H	M
Kullu	H	H	H	M	H	H	VH
Bilaspur	M	M	L		M	M	M
Una	M	L	H		H	M	H
Sirmour	M	M	L		H	M	M
Solan	L	L	L		H	M	M
Kinnaur	H	H	H	VH		M	VH

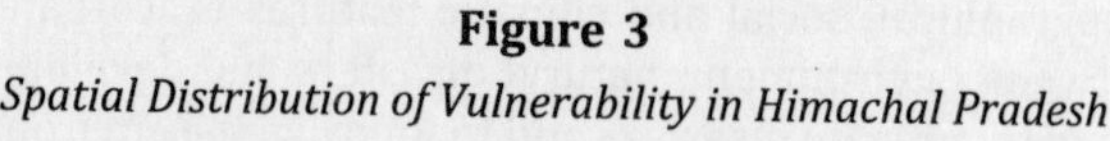

Figure 3

Spatial Distribution of Vulnerability in Himachal Pradesh

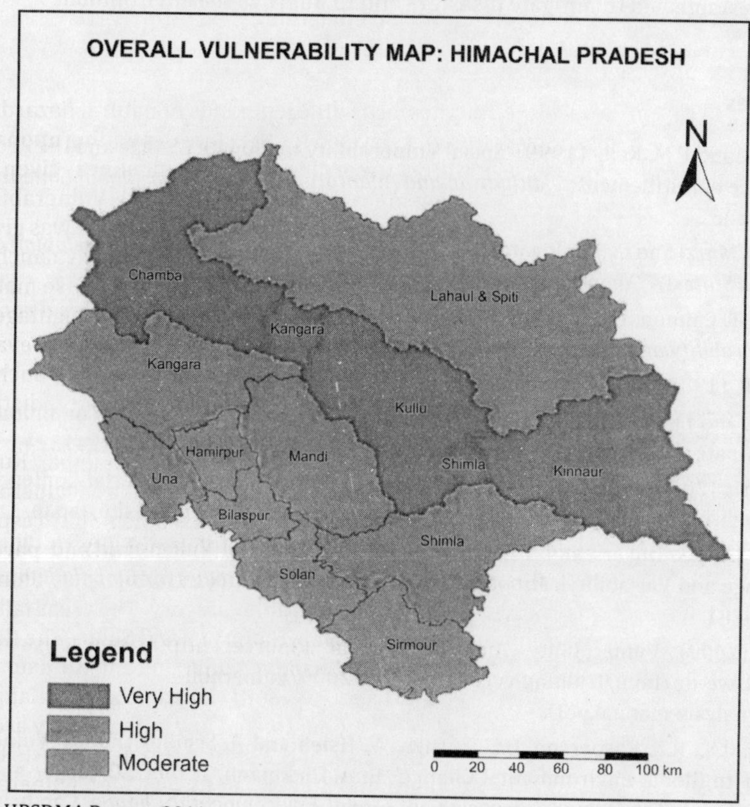

Source: HPSDMA Report, 2011.

Lahaul & Spiti	L	M	M	VH	H	M	H
Shimla	L	M	M		H	M	H

Source: HPSDMA Report, 2011

On the basis of the vulnerability matrix, the overall vulnerability mapping has been done to show the spatial distribution of the Vulnerability in the state (Figure 3).

Suggestions and Conclusions

All development projects in vulnerable areas should be formulated carefully to minimize the adverse effects of natural disasters and should be linked with disaster mitigation. The economic impact of a natural disaster should receive adequate attention, social audit and cost-benefit analysis. The policy should also incorporate the probable disaster events and mitigation programmes to undertake work in disaster prone areas.

The concept of vulnerability, therefore, leads to calculation of risk. Risk management would, therefore, mean the level of social and economic ability to cope with resulting event in order to resist major disruption or loss. This susceptibility and vulnerability to each type of threat will depend on its respective differing characteristics. It is seen that the state of Himachal Pradesh is prone to various hazards and its geographical, social and climatic features exacerbate its vulnerability. Linkages between environment, natural disasters and development need to be clearly established to mitigate disasters and to improve the environment.

References

Adger, W.N. and P.M. Kelly (1999) 'Social Vulnerability to Climate Change and the Architecture of Entitlements', *Mitigation and Adaptation Strategies for Global Change*, 4: 253–266.

Atkins, J., S. Mazzi and C. Ramlogan (1998) *A Study on the Vulnerability of Developing and Island States: A Composite Index*, UK: Commonwealth Secretariat.

Blaikie, P., T. Cannon, I. David and B. Wisner (1994) *At Risk: Natural Hazards, People's Vulnerability and Disasters*, London: Routledge.

Chamber, R. (1983) *Rural Development: Putting the Last First*, Essex: Longman.

Dolan, A.H. and I.J. Walker (2003) 'Understanding Vulnerability of Coastal Communities to Climate Change Related Risks', *Journal of Coastal Research*, 39: 1317–1324.

Easter, Chris (2000) 'The Common Wealth Vulnerability Index', Ministerial Conference on Environment and Development in Asia and the Pacific, Kitakyushu, Japan.

Handmer, J.W., S. Dovers and T.E. Downing (1999) 'Societal Vulnerability to Climate Change and Variability', *Mitigation and Adaptation Strategies for Global Change*, 4: 267–281.

ICRISAT (2009) Vulnerability Analysis Manual (Source: http://www.icrisat.org/what-we-do/impi/training-cc/october-2-3-2009/vulnerability-analysis-manual.pdf).

Kasperson, J.X., R.E. Kasperson, B.L. Turner, W. Hsieh and A. Schiller (2000) 'Vulnerability to Global Environmental Change', in A. Diekmann, T. Dietz, C. Jaeger and E. Rosa (eds), *The Human Dimensions of Global Environmental Change*, Cambridge: MIT Press.

McCarthy, J.J., O.F. Canziani, N.A. Leary, D.J. Dokken and K.S. White (eds) (2001) *Climate Change 2001: Impacts, Adaptation and Vulnerability*, Cambridge: Cambridge University Press.

Moss, R.H., A.L. Brenkert and E.L. Malone (2001) *Vulnerability to Climate Change: A Quantitative Approach*, Department of Energy, US.

O'Brien, P. and D. Mileti (1992) 'Citizen Participation in Emergency Response Following the Loma Prieta Earthquake', *International Journal of Mass Emergencies and Disasters*, 10: 71–89.

Vincent, K. (2004) 'Creating an Index of Social Vulnerability to Climate Change for Africa', Research Working Paper 56, Tyndall Centre for Climate Change.

Watson, R.T., M.C. Zinyowera and R.H. Moss (1996) *Climate Change 1995: Impacts, Adaptations and Mitigation of Climate Change: Scientific-Technical Analyses*, Cambridge: Cambridge University Press.

27

Rehabilitation Efficacy of Kutch (Bhuj) Earthquake

BARUN KUMAR

Kutch (Bhuj) Earthquake was one of the deadliest Indian earthquakes of all times, measuring 7.9 on the Richter scale killed around 30,000 people and devastated the lives of millions more (World Disaster Report, 2001, 2002). The physical, infrastructural, economic, social and psychological damage to the people of Gujarat was too intense to bear. The concern shown by the national and international agencies were overwhelming and unlasting. More than thirteen years had passed since the people of Gujarat witnessed the horrible/traumatic experience of devastating earthquake on January 26, 2001. Much water has flown in Sabarmati since then. The rescue and rehabilitation measures were adopted at an unprecedented scale; however, it did not remain free from criticism. For some, the rescue operation was started very late and precious time of evacuation and rescue were lost (48 early hours) due to lack of disaster preparedness and effective coordination (Desai, 2001). Further, the questions were raised on effective distribution of relief material to the needy persons. The general apathy of local bodies due to political reasons were also noticed and above all favouritism and mismatch in distribution of relief material was observed at a massive scale. Moreover, a lot of hue and cry was made on rehabilitation and especially in the construction of houses and resettlement colonies (Ray, 2001). This has put a permanent scare/mark on the hearts and minds on the people of Gujarat. It was felt time and again, a need to examine what had been done so far to satiate the aspirations of the strife torn people of Gujarat. It is equally important to introspect on where lies the fault and how to rectify the mistakes. In the light of aforesaid questions and available facts, a durable rescue and rehabilitation plan can be made to avoid previous mistakes and evolve a suitable strategy to optimize available resources and manpower in the best interest of the people of India.

Objectives

On the basis of the aforesaid, the following objectives of the study have been identified:

1. To carefully examine the rescue and rehabilitation measures adopted in the Kutch (Bhuj) earthquake.

2. To analyse the lessons learned through this rescue and rehabilitation exercise.
3. To come out with some key mitigation strategies to this complex disaster management issues.

Data Source and Methodology

The study is based on the secondary sources database. The essential data were generated through careful examination of various reports, surveys and topical comment by the experts and sometimes by the freelance writers and thinkers on various issues of rescue and rehabilitation in Kutch (Bhuj) earthquake. The study has made good use of the abstracts of seminars, research papers and newspaper clippings on this issue. No statistical techniques were applied. Some generalizations were made by the analysis of existing tables and available figures.

Rescue and Relief

The first immediate step of rehabilitation is to provide rescue and relief to the affected people who are waiting for some outside help. It was a formidable challenge of rescue and relief to the vast population that has been affected by this severe earthquake of our time. The main agencies/actors who took part in this operation can be grouped under following heads:

Military and Paramilitary Forces

Military and paramilitary forces were the quickest to respond and had shown their courage and character. They reached the spot within 45 minutes of the disaster from the military stations of Bhuj and Gandhinagar. They tirelessly carried the rescue and relief operations mainly to recover survivors and dead. Army also restored the arterial road communication of all the major towns and villages. Thus, in the initial few days, only the army and the police carried out all the coordinating function between various security agencies by establishing a strong communication system. The check points were established in all the affected areas of the district on 26th January itself to instil a feeling of security and to give physical protection to individual's property with the limited resources (Goel, 2001).

State Government Machinery

Gujarat State Government did not come best to the expectations of the people. The offices and official residences of the affected districts were demolished, roads and communication system was disrupted and high official bodies also lost their houses as well as their kith and kin. They did not show the commitment and heroic example which is usually expected from the governmental machinery at the time of crisis.

Immediately after the earthquake, the state government was not able to assess the requirements of the devastated towns and villages in quake affected areas. In the beginning, they were blindly sending all manpower and supplies only to Bhuj; and other affected areas like Bachau, Gandhinagar, Ropar, Anjar and Halved did not receive any relief for more than 48 hours. It resulted in a precious loss of time in extending equitable help to all the quake ravaged towns and villages. On the first day, seniormost officer, the additional chief secretary along with some officials were sent to Bhuj for supervising rescue and relief operation but failed miserably to coordinate the activities and finally he had to come back to Gandhinagar (Ray, 2001). The press and media had bitterly criticized the role of the state government, which throws light on some aspects of rescue and relief.

Gujarat government may argue that this was too severe a calamity to tame, but it cannot avoid the fact that 48 hours after nature struck the most cruel blow on the region, it simply did not know how to react, and even nine days after the tragedy there was little semblance of a government machinery on work (Desai, 2001).

When an activity is coordinated, everything works well. A coordinated activity is orderly, harmonious, efficient and successful. This was not visible in Gujarat and that is why there was a great chaos. Be it communication, handling foreign help teams and distribution of relief material including tents and blankets, on every front the government had goofed up. If the complete absence of coordination at Ahmedabad and Bhuj airports delayed the arrival of foreign teams to the collapse sites, thousands of tents and blankets remained dumped at the airports and on open grounds in Bhuj while Kutch shivered. Relief material came in plenty but 13 days after the quake, complaints continued that it is not reaching the right people, simply because the government machinery simply does not know how to handle the flow which, initially gets off-loaded on roads and grounds near highway towns. The interiors were left unattended till the NGOs themselves drove the trucks into the arteries of the desert district (ibid.). A huge chunk of relief materials was caught in red tape in Ahmedabad and Bhuj; poor and skewed distribution ensured that the food, tents and blankets did not reach to the people who needed them most. There was a mad scramble for tents and other relief materials in all the affected areas of Kutch and the adjoining areas. On February 2, in Bhuj there was a clash between the rich and the poor over distribution of tents and police had to use lathis. Initially, the District Collector issued and ordered that the distribution would be made ward-wise with the help of the local community and the councillors and the name and address of the recipients would be entered in register. But finally, tents were distributed without any lists being made. Official sources said most of the tents had gone to influential people.

International Response

International response to mitigate disaster was quick and overwhelming. More than 70 countries and 17 international organizations provided assistance to the state government to the tune of ₹ 178 crores. In addition to this, World Bank and Asian Development Bank announced to give US $ 300 million and US $ 350 million respectively. The international response can be gauged under two phases-

1. The search and rescue (SAR), and
2. The relief.

The Search and Rescue (SAR) phase began at 11 p.m. on January 27, when the Swiss SAR team arrived, closely followed by teams from the UK, Russia and Turkey. Teams continued to pour in until Feb 2 by which time 26 teams had entered Gujarat. The first team began to depart on February 1 and by February 16 almost all had departed. The remaining teams shifted their focus to more general relief tasks, some helping with body recovery; others engaged in debris clearance, relief distribution and medical support as well as providing training to local teams.

Relief phase started from January28. Initially, the relief was predominantly medical supplies or medical teams but increasingly other supplies arrived. By Feb 10, relief had arrived from 38 countries as well as United Nations agencies and many international NGOs.

Panchayat or Local Bodies

Panchayat of local bodies who often play a key part in the situation of a crisis like earthquake is considered a very important agency. It is interesting to note that gram panchayat which had a long tradition of such help in rural areas were totally absent from the scene because of the political game played by the State Government and the State politicians (Ray, 2001). After the dissolution of Panchayat, gram Panchayat election was postponed by the then Government making petty excuses. Therefore, there was no representative panchayat functioning in this region. However, those survived in the disaster engaged themselves in rescue and relief. Local doctors made themselves available in providing first aid and pre-operation care.

Non-Governmental Organizations

Voluntary organizations and NGOs took active part in rescue and relief. About 245 organizations and agencies, including at least 99 international NGOs, 55 national NGOs and 20 donor government teams, 10 UN and inter-governmental organizations and Red Cross representatives from 10 countries were involved in rescue and relief. Some public sector units like ONGC, IFFCO, KRIBHCO and others in the state were also engaged in rescue and relief work.

Some of the National NGOs has done commendable job in relief and rehabilitation like providing hot meals to the affected people, in equitable distribution of relief to the affected people living in the interior parts of Gujarat, in rescue operation and medical assistance, evacuation and removal of debris, construction of semi-permanent structures for effected residence, etc. The major national NGOs included Ramakrishna Mission, Sewa Bharti, Brahma Kumaris, Swami Narayan Sanstha, Kutch Nav Nirman Abhiyan, CARITAS India, etc. The international NGOs included UNDP, International Federation of Red Cross and Red Crescent Society and others from European Community, etc. A number of NGOs have participated under "Public Private Partnership Programme" in various stages of relief and rehabilitation.

Rehabilitation Programme

The devastating earthquake of Kutch (Bhuj) caused large scale damage to five districts of Gujarat namely, Kutch, Ahmedabad, Rajkot, Jamnagar and Surendranagar accounting for 99 per cent of the total casualties and damage. The minor damage was witnessed in rest of the districts of Gujarat. The urban and rural parts of Gujarat have equally suffered damage to variable extent. The towns totally destroyed included Ropar, Anjar, Gandhidham, Bhachau and Bhuj while towns which suffered medium losses include Mundra, Mandane, Lakhpat, Adbasa and Nakhatrana. On the other hand, all the 942 inhabited villages of Gujarat have suffered damage to variable extent. The village destroyed completely included 174 villages followed by 250 villages sustaining 70per cent damages and 518 villages suffering significantly. Almost every manmade facility or engineered structure, suffered heavily in Kutch district. A total of about 12 lakh houses, besides other community lifelines such as roads, bridges, railways, ports, hospitals, electricity, water, telephones, etc., were damaged to variable extent, broadly depending on their distance from the epicentre (Geological Survey of India, 2001). Out of about 12 lakh total affected houses about 4 lakh or so have sustained minor damages and 8 lakh houses (2.30 lakh fully damaged and rest partially collapsed houses) are the main focus of rehabilitation effort. Kutch district was the worst affected district in this regard accounting 62.3 per cent fully damaged and 28.7 per cent partially damaged houses of Gujarat. The total number of families affected were 1.87 per cent. The number of such affected families in rural and urban areas were 87,000 and 1.0 lakh, respectively. Varied claims were made regarding the human toll. According to World Disaster Report of Red Cross, the human toll was about 30,000 persons, while the claim made by the

Government of Gujarat was 13,805 persons. The total number cattle perished were 18,600. Due to huge loss of life and property in many parts of the state, fear psychosis and trauma, the economic activity, particularly in Kutch and Ahmedabad district, came to a standstill and it took months before some normalcy could be restored. The Gujarat State Disaster Management Authority (GSDMA) was conceived to give new lease of life to earthquake hit people who suffered immense physical, emotional, social, psychological and economic damage in the hands of nature. This programme undertaken by the Government of Gujarat has incorporated essential elements of rehabilitation including physical, social economic and community rehabilitation as well as technical assistance to sufferers by GSDMA. The funding of this programme was made by the World Bank, Asian Development Bank, European Commission, Netherlands Government, Prime Ministers Relief Fund (GOI), and national and international NGOs. The responsibility of this rehabilitation was offered to the project management unit (PMU) of Government of Gujarat (GOG) and donor agencies. These had evolved some suitable criteria for distribution of assistance to the best interest of the affected people in the divested area. However, this programme faced numerous problems concerning implementation of the rehabilitation programme and it was felt that there were numerous weaknesses in influencing the programme on rehabilitation.

Major Components of the Rehabilitation Programme

Housing

Housing includes the relocation and reconstruction of completely destroyed villages, in situ reconstruction of severely affected areas in Zone IV and V, assistance for destroyed/partially destroyed houses in areas away from epicentre, the construction of model houses and pilot strengthening programme. The Government of Gujarat UNDP undertook the coordination of the rehabilitation programme. Numerous aid agencies, commercial organization, NGOs and community-based organizations came forward to assist in the massive recovery programme. Assistance in shape of land, water and exemption from taxes were given to the Donor agencies to facilitate their progress.

Financial assistance was also given wherever the donor agencies faced shortage of funds. The housing reconstruction approach adopted by the government is characterized by several features including a homeowner driven process, disaster resistant criteria for all new construction and repair for damaged houses, private-public partnership nature of the recovery, and training and education, the issues related to transparency and information dissemination was also considered. The issues related to transparency and information dissemination was also considered. The government's approach involved harnessing the capacity of the public section, the private sector (NGOs, voluntary organization, private industrial houses, expert consulting assistance) and above all, the affected people themselves who are most aware of their own needs and priorities. Gujarat Government announced that they would prepare four separate packages for worst hit Bhuj, Bhachau, Anjar and Ropar.

I. Those villages where more than 70 per cent houses have collapsed or are under beyond repair category.

   Features

   1. Total number of such villages: 229.
   2. Package offers to relocate all of them at an estimated cost of ₹ 999 crores.

3. Landless and marginal farmers will be offered plots measuring up to 150 sq m with 30 as built up area.
4. Small farmers were offered 250 sq m of plot and 40 sq m as build-up area.
5. Big farmers were offered 400 sq m of plot and 50 sq m of build-up area.
6. For landless and marginal farmers it would be given all free while others would be offered a loan for 10 per cent of the amount.

II. Those villages where more than 70 per cent destructions were made and whose residents do not wish to be shifted to a new location.

Features

1. House fully destroyed of poor — ₹ 35,000
2. House fully destroyed for others — ₹ 50,000–90,000
3. Partially destroyed house which require 10–15 per cent repairs — ₹ 3,000–30,000

III. Those villages situated far away from the epicentre but where individual houses have been destroyed.

Features

1. Fully destroyed huts — ₹ 7,000
2. Fully destroyed Semi-Pucca House — ₹ 40,000
3. Fully destroyed Semi-Pucca House (50per cent destroyed) — ₹ 20,000
4. Those house which have cracks — ₹ 2,000 per house or hut

IV. For Cities:

Features

1. Houses of frame structure destroyed ₹ 350 per sq ft up to a max. of ₹ 1.75 lakh.
2. Load bearing structure ₹ 280 per sq ft with a max. of ₹1.4lakh (owners will be entitled for soft loan of ₹ 3 lakh).
3. (a) High rise building (G2) ₹ 1.0 lakh (b) Low rise building ₹ 50,000.
4. Structure with moderate damage (G3)
   (a) High Rise: ₹ 4 lakh (b) Low Rise ₹: 2 lakh.
5. Houses which suffered severe damage (G4)
   (a) High Rise: 8 lakh (b) Low Rise: 4 lakh
6. To a flat or house having:
   (i) Half an inch wide damage: — up to ₹ 2,000
   (ii) Houses with 10per cent damage : — ₹ 5,000
   (iii) Houses with 25 per cent damage: — ₹ 10,000
   (iv) Houses with 50per cent damage: — ₹ 50,000
7. Houses requiring fresh water, electricity and gutter connections would be initially given these free of charge.

V. Package for severally damaged four towns:

Features:

1. Total allocation of fund: — ₹ 1,279 crore
2. According to this package, government will provide monitoring compensation to enable people for taking up reconstruction themselves:
   (i) Completely destroyed houses (G5): — up to ₹ 1,50,000 @ ₹ 3,000per sq ft.
   (ii) Severely damaged houses (G4): — up to ₹ 45,000
   (iii) Badly damaged which can be retrofitted (G3): — up to ₹ 30,000

(iv) Slight damaged houses (G2): up to ₹ 15,000

(v) Building having no damage (G1): us 8,000 only

There are, thus, few main thrusts on the rehabilitation plan of the state:

(i) Relocation of highly affected villages

(ii) Reconstruction of houses on new or original sites

(iii) Technical and other support for construction of houses, and

(iv) Building of infrastructure

Retrofitting of Public Buildings

In the aftermath of the earthquake, a large number of public buildings have become unsafe for living and these are proposed to be strengthened by appropriate retrofitting at a cost of ₹ 84 crore. Theses public buildings included state R & B buildings, panchayat R & B buildings, primary health centre, hospitals, school buildings, etc.

Infrastructure

In a successful implementation of rehabilitation programme, infrastructural support is a must. It includes reconstruction, repair and strengthening of public buildings such as school, health centres, social service facilities, water supply system; roads and bridges; dam safety and irrigation; retrofitting; urban; moral infrastructure; power, etc., while the essential services like road, bridge, water supply were met at war footings, some other infrastructure work such as road, transit access shelters, etc., were made gradually along with housing.

With regard to restoration of infrastructure, an important issue was whether it should be restored to the pre-earthquake level or whether the rebuilt assets should conform to some well established standards, with built-in provision for seismic and cyclonic hazard resistance. For instance, while refurbishing the power transmission and distribution system, it stands to logic that the obsolete and inefficient component should be weeded out. The reconstructed irrigation dams must conform to the present-day safety norms and standard.

The total number of towns being taken up for infrastructural development are 14 in number. Area Development Authority (ADAs) have been created for four worst affected towns of Bhuj, Anjar, Hachauadrapar, all in Kutch district for which the provision of as high as ₹ 531 crore is being made for infrastructural development. For the rest of the towns, only repair work and infrastructure deficiencies would be met to the extent necessary and a provision of ₹ 135 crore is being envisaged for them. Out of these, the two worst affected towns are Gandhidham in Kutch and Morbi in Rajkot, for which a provision of ₹ 37 crore and ₹ 20 crore is made, respectively.

In the revised rehabilitation project, there is a provision of ₹ 418 crore for rural infrastructure and ₹ 604 crore for urban infrastructure. On the rural sides, the amount is almost entirely for rural water supply. On the urban side, it is proposed to undertake infrastructure development of 14 towns, out of which six are district Kutch, another six are in Surendranagar and two in Rajkot. The total cost of damage was assessed at ₹ 231.70 crores.

Area Development authority stands created for the worst affected towns of Bhuj, Anjar, Bhachauadrapar. Development plans are notified in keeping with modernized town planning norms providing wide roads and enough space for common usage and community requirements. All the projects related to infrastructural development were awarded through national competitive bidding as per the norms of the Asian Development Bank, which insists on rigorous standards and close scrutiny.

Social Rehabilitation

The social rehabilitation was a much a more challenging effort and equally important to provide emotional manifestation to those who had suffered the loss of life amongst the near and dear, living as destitute and hundreds of orphans and other individuals. They require special facilities so that their needs were prioritized, their emotional upliftment to their social rehabilitation through deliverance of facilities and essential services. The earthquake left 307 orphans, 1,192 widows, 572 aged and 931 disabled people behind without any support. Government came with a special package for the assistance and social reconstruction of affected people.

Disaster victim suffers an acute psychological trauma left within his mind which cannot react appreciably because the disaster has struck all of a sudden impairing his or her emotional stability and judgment. The person usually lacks any form of support during the time of such an event. Crisis intervention forms an essential method of managing the human sufferings after the disaster. This is affectively carried out by the professional social workers and mental health professionals. This was the missing dimension in the Gujarat earthquake rehabilitation programme; some international NGOs have pointed towards this problem and the sought the help of local doctors, students, teachers and work groups who can understand local language and their feelings (Kumar and Gopalkrishnan, 1989).

For orphaned children, the government has first of all given compensation to the children against death of parents. The foster parent scheme which was being implemented in some of the big cities have been extended to the earthquake affected areas and monthly assistance of ₹ 500 will be paid per child. A surveillance mechanism has been established to ascertain the well-being of the orphans regularly, with support from UNICEF. Three 'Bal Kutirs' have been sanctioned for orphan boys and three 'Balika Kutirs' for orphans girls at Bhuj, Anjar and Bhachau. As per the scheme, a monthly assistance of ₹ 250 is being provided for each of the inmates (Gupta et al., 2002).

A monthly pension is being provided for the widow and pension has been made for livelihood and vocational training for those women who would like to take up and learn some kind of work. Likewise, pension is being provided for the aged and three old-age home have been sanctioned for Bhuj, Anjar and Bhachau which would be managed by NGOs.

The quacke left many as disabled and the social justice department has deployed mobile vans for their assistance. A number of schemes have been sanctioned for giving assistance to the scheduled caste people and their children. An amount of ₹ 3.5 crore has been sanctioned for construction of two hospitals in Kutch. The National Scheduled Caste Finance and Development Corporation has sanctioned ₹ 15.65 crore for providing livelihood to a large number of Scheduled Caste beneficiaries who are engaged in 32 different trades.

Economic Rehabilitation

The Gujarat earthquake-affected areas are located in arid and semi-arid agro-climatic zones where water resources are limited, even scarce. These regions have faced acute droughts, two severe cyclones and floods in many urban centres of Ahmedabad and Surat prior to the earthquake disaster in Gujarat. The earthquake has, therefore, hit during the time of extreme environmental vulnerability. the economy of earthquake-affected areas was mainly guided by the industries followed by agriculture and livestock production. Tourism and services are other important economic activities in these areas. The economic impact of the earthquake falls under the following three broad heads:

1. Direct losses in the shape of losses to moveable/immoveable assets.
2. Indirect losses due to business interruption and disruption of economic activity.
3. Secondary affects in the shape of economic and fiscal costs to the public section.

The Gujarat Sate District Management Authority document places the asset losses of ₹ 15,308 crore and reconstruction cost at ₹ 11,499 crore. Economic Rehabilitation programme to the sufferers for losses to agriculturist, artisans and small industry and business communities includes provisions on grant basis. In order to revive the economy of the affected areas, Department of Agriculture, Department of Animal Husbandry and the Directorate of Industries coordinated their activities in various capacities and provided the economic support.

According to the Government of Gujarat estimates, preliminary losses of assets to the private sector in the agriculture and livestock sectors are estimated at ₹ 510 crore, nearly 80per cent of which is in the Kutch district. Major asset losses are concentrated in irrigation assets, such as bore wells, pump houses, engine rooms, submersible pumps, water storage tanks as well as storage bins, farm implements, livestock, plant protection equipment and stored output and inputs. Output losses due to the earthquake are estimated to amount to ₹ 228 crore. In addition, damage to buildings of the Agriculture Department including Gujarat Agriculture university and Animal Husbandry units were estimated at ₹ 35.3 crore. Reconstruction costs are estimated at ₹ 344 crore.

A total number of over 3,276 small and medium industrial units registered their losses with the industries department and the total loss was placed at ₹ 312 crore the severest loss of ₹ 190 crore was in Kutch district followed by ₹ 43 crore in Surendranagar. As much as 75 per cent of the damage is accounted by damage to building, 10–15 per cent on account of damage to machinery and another 7–8 per cent due to damage to raw finished materials.

The worst hit were 19,000 handicraft artisans and the salt farmers who not only lost their home but their livelihood as well. The sudden death of large number of cattle severely affected their other source of livelihood. For the rehabilitation of artisans and small business persons, an assistance package was given to restart industry/business. This programme was coordinated by the Directorate of Industries Centre (DIC), Khadi and Village Industries Board (KVIB) and District Rural Development Agency (DRDA).

Community Rehabilitation

Community rehabilitation includes the cost of works and materials to re-establish essential services in the months immediately following the earthquake. Within hours after the earthquake, masses of individuals appear to be performing seemingly random and uncoordinated work. And yet within a short time, almost a matter of hours, the tasks that need to be done are miraculously performed. Specifically, people are removed from debris, they are transported to hospitals, children are cared for, property is guarded, people become housed, and kin are informed about one another. All these, and many other tasks are done within an incredibly short time, often without the intervention of official agencies. A number of activities are usually performed in this process.

For the massive rescue and relief operations, involving clearing of the debris and removal of injured and the dead, the military and paramilitary forces were the first to respond quickly in Gujarat. Later, several international and national teams of rescue and relief came and joined the operation in a large scale.

Emergency medical aid to victims: Several local doctors came forward to provide emergency medical aid to the people in Gujarat. The NGOs took the responsibility of running the devastated government hospital on their own with high amount of success. Red Cross and other international rescue teams with the help of government adopted prophylactic measures to prevent outbreak of epidemics.

Cremation of burial of the deceased, provisional of temporary shelters and provision of food and clothing were made by the NGOs. Several charitable organizations and national and international NGOs have come out with their best in this situation of crisis. However, a general apathy of Gram Panchayat and local bodies were found in the rescue and rehabilitation of earthquake victims of Gujarat. The non-functioning of Panchayt Sabha was one of the reasons for that.

Technological Rehabilitation

Technical assistance includes design, supervision and monitoring of project components, other consultancy services and equipment, including the development of a comprehensive disaster management plan for the State of Gujarat and Seismic monitoring and research programme.

Geographical Information System (GIS) technology can facilitate urban planning and the integration of hazard and vulnerability into the urban redevelopment process. GIS database can be developed for the geographic areas of connected urban bodies, although it is not necessary that each small town be provided with this technology. In the latter case, however, it is necessary that local authorities know that the information is available and understand how to apply it during the planning process.

Deficiencies/Lacuna in Rescue and Rehabilitation

During the earthquake of Gujarat, 2001, the lack of preparedness of the State Government to tackle exigencies of this nature stands thoroughly exposed. When an activity is coordinated, everything works well. A coordinated activity is orderly, harmonious, efficient and successful. This was not visible in Gujarat and that is why there was a great chaos. The present rehabilitation strategy and disaster management plan have been prepared without giving much importance to economic development of the quake affected areas (Ray, 2001).

People are also facing several socio-cultural difficulties due to death of family members. The government has not given adequate attention to the problems and requirements of the elderly, children and orphans (ibid.). Vulnerability assessment of existing and damaged buildings has not been undertaken in a scientific manner. The present strategy of relief and rehabilitation is totally dictated by the State Government in a very centralized fashion. Activities to reduce the impact of an earthquake before it strikes again in Gujarat, like public awareness activities is not yet considered an important requirement nor the rehabilitation and redevelopment of the affected area. While in principle the decision on relocation has to be locally made, there are incentives for relocation given larger grant assistance for housing along with free plot of land, and integrated provision of infrastructure, as compared to the in-situ option. Decision to relocate had led to considerable delay and had dampened own driven relocation strategy.

There was inequality in the nature of grant assistance offered for housing in the rehabilitation plan. Rather than offering an equal grant to all affected households, with a possibility of loan assistance for those with higher demands and incomes, the policy offers higher grants, especially in urban centres. Further, compensation in zone 3 is far lower than for those in zone 4 and 5. The policy does not adequately define house type so far the nature of damage for different levels of compensation of benefits by more affluent sections of society. Lack of clarity in definition on the other hand may result in undue discretion and subjectivity at the ground level.

Lessons Learnt through Kutch (Bhuj) Earthquake

Bhuj earthquake affected more than one-third of the 18,000 villages of Gujarat, killed nearly 30,000 people, injured 1,67,000 and severely affected millions of people in Gujarat. Despite several warnings by the scientific community as well as by the experts for seismically safe structures, no particular heed was paid to it. As a result, a large number of supposedly soundly constructed structures built with conventional wisdom and in accordance with the prevailing practices collapsed. A clear lesson, which so emerges, is that all structures at least in zone V, must be built with a clear provision for seismic safety norms. This quake must be considered as a wake up call and a learning model for the entire country and should help in improving our capabilities to meet such contingencies in future (Gupta et al., 2002).

The impact of Kutch earthquake was confined not only to zone V but was also felt in zone IV and even to zone III. Even more glaring is the case of Ahmedabad city lying in zone III and situated at a distance of 230 km from the epicentre. A large number of multi-storeyed and low rise buildings (ground+3) and RCC structures either collapsed or had to be pulled down. The clear lesson which calls for attention is the multi-storeyed and other high rise and low rise buildings must adhere to seismic proofing norms even in zone III.

As clear-cut norms are prescribed for fire proofing in high-rise buildings, similarly seismic proofing should be added as another major requirement. The structural engineers must find their due place when it comes to larger buildings and strict adherence to the building norms and regulations has to be insisted upon. Gujarat faced successive drought, cyclone and earthquakes recently. In the light of these experiences, there is a comprehensive multi-hazard disaster management system for various disaster-prone districts and the state as a whole.

At the time of the earthquake disaster, the rescue equipment was very insufficient. The Ahmedabad City Fire Brigade had only one snorkel ladder and one crane of 20 tonnes capacity, which was quite inadequate. Therefore, the strengthening of the municipalities and the corporations with the required equipment to meet all type of contingencies is a must. The more important decision is to have three Emergency Response Centres to be located at Rajkot, Surat and Ahmedabad.

Key Mitigation Strategies

On the basis of threadbare analysis of rescue and rehabilitation programme in Gujarat, following observable solutions have been identified. To deal with all issues arising out of earthquake in the short-term and long-term perspectives, besides the Nodal Agency in the Government of India, the State Government should constitute a high powered committee to take quick and reliable decisions as well as review their implementation.

There is a need to give psychological counselling to the traumated families who have lost their near and dear ones. The following actions might be taken:

1. Identify such persons who are in extreme trauma and depression.
2. Provide them counselling and if need be some medicine.
3. Make them understand about the disaster and inability of human being to do anything.
4. Constant visit till they are restored to normalcy.

Harmony and goodwill among sections of the society and not party politics, communalism or regionalism should crop out in the best interest of community rehabilitation. The task of national building is very challenging; we have to work effectively in a network, extending mutual faith and goodwill and achieve excellence as a team. In a knowledge-based society of the future, success comes to those who can organize networks of multifunction and multidisciplinary systems which can deliver complex products or services, with increasing efficiency and productivity. It is keenly desired to provide assistance to develop and strengthen local NGO capabilities and activities with particular attention to local community development groups.

There is a need to study the efficiency of rehabilitation programme and assist communities in the exercise of their own role in such reviews. A greater emphasis on evaluative techniques will render all new programmes more accountable to real community needs. There should be fairness in the dealings of all types of rehabilitation programmes. This can be ensured by good governance through dedicated, honest and hardworking personnel. There is also a need to develop the culture of peace, and create confidence, will power and self-determination among the people. The agencies engaged in enforcing the rehabilitation programme should be full of compassion and dedication. They should keep themselves away from the populist design and cosmetic help.

It is equally important to ensure that the existing programmes and new initiatives promote full participation by individuals and communities in the planning, implementation and control of these programmes. Rehabilitation programme should promote private-public partnership in a big way by developing mutual trust and healthy regard for each other.

References

Desai, D. (2001) 'No Disaster Mitigation Plan Yet', *Indian Express*, 9 February.

Goel, R. (2001) 'Earthquake in Gujarat: A Case Study of Kutch', in S.L. Goel and Ram Kumar (eds), *Disaster Management*, New Delhi: Deep and Deep Publications, 129–137.

Gupta, L.C., A. Sinha and V.K. Sharma (2002) *Gujarat Earthquake: 26 January 2001*, Delhi: NIDM, IIPA.

Kumar, V.S. and S. Gopalkrishnan (1989) 'Disaster Management: A Psychological Crisis', *Social Welfare*, August: 33–34.

Pande, P. (2003) 'Kutch Earthquake: 26 January 2001', *Geological Survey of India*, Special Publication No. 76, 1–4.

Ray, C.N. (2001) 'Earthquake Relief and Rehabilitation in Gujarat: Issues in Disaster Management', *Indian Journal of Public Administration*, XLVII(1): 129–151.

World Disaster Report (2001 and 2002) International Federation of Red Cross and Ted Crescent.

Contributors

Aakash Upadhyay, Research Scholar, Department of Geography, University of Delhi, Delhi.

Abhay Shankar Prasad, Research Scholar, Department of Geography, University of Delhi, Delhi.

Ajit Kumar, Research Scholar, Centre for the Study of Regional Development, Jawaharlal Nehru University, New Delhi.

Anjan Sen, Assistant Professor of Geography, Department of Geography, University of Delhi, Delhi.

B.W. Pandey, Associate Professor, Department of Geography, University of Delhi, Delhi.

Barun Kumar, Assistant Professor of Geography, B.R. Ambedkar College, University of Delhi, Delhi.

D.P. Singh, Professor of Geography and Principal CMJ College, Madhubani, Bihar

Guljit K. Arora, Principal, B. R. Ambedkar College, University of Delhi, Delhi.

Inder Jeet, Professor, Department of Geography, M.D. University, Rohtak (Haryana).

Kanchan Gupta, Senior Research Scholar, Department of Geography, Kanpur University, Kanpur, Uttar Pradesh.

Krishna Kumar, Senior Research Scholar, Department of Geography, University of Delhi, Delhi.

Krishnanand, Research Scholar, Department of Geography, University of Delhi, Delhi

Manjit Singh, Senior Research Scholar, Department of Geography, University of Delhi, Delhi.

Mitrajit Chatterjee, Assistant Professor, Department of Geography, Dr Gour Mohan Roy College, Monteswar, Burdwan, West Bengal.

Mohammad Dilshad, Research Scholar, Department of History, Jamia Millia Islamia University, New Delhi.

Monica Ahlawat, Assistant Professor of Geography, B.R. Ambedkar College, University of Delhi, Delhi.

Nageshwar Prasad, Professor, Department of Geography, University of Burdwan, Burdwan, West Bengal.

Om Jee Ranjan, Research Scholar, Department of Geography, University of Delhi, Delhi.

Preeti Sachar, Assistant Professor of Geography, S.S.N. College, University of Delhi, Delhi.

Priyanka Puri, Assistant Professor of Geography, Miranda House, University of Delhi, Delhi.

R.B. Thakur, Professor of Economics, RB Collage, Dalsing Sarai, Bihar.

Rajeev Ranjan Kumar Sinha, Senior Deputy Collector, Gaya, Bihar.

Rajesh Kumar Abhay, Assistant Professor, Department of Geography, University of Delhi, Delhi.

Rameshwar Thakur, Associate Professor of Geography, B.R. Ambedkar College, University of Delhi, Delhi.

Shweta Rani, Senior Research Scholar, Department of Geography, University of Delhi, Delhi.

Sneh Gangwar, Assistant Professor of Geography, Aditi Mahavidyalaya, University of Delhi, Delhi.

Sudeepta Adhikari, Professor, Department of Geography, Patna University, Patna.

Surendra Singh Chawla, Associate Professor, B.R. Ambedkar College, University of Delhi, Delhi.

Swarnima Singh, Assistant Professor of Geography, Shaheed Bhagat Singh College, University of Delhi, Delhi.

Swati Thakur, Assistant Professor of Geography, Dyal Singh College, University of Delhi, Delhi.

Vinod Kumar, Assistant Professor of Geography, B.R. Ambedkar College, University of Delhi, Delhi.